COMPETITION LAW AND DEMOCRACY

Examining the normative foundations of US antitrust and EU competition law, Elias Deutscher argues that the idea of a competition–democracy nexus rests on a commitment to a republican understanding of economic liberty. The book uses this republican concept of economic liberty to analyse how US antitrust and EU competition law embodied a competition–democracy nexus and explains how the turn of competition law towards a more economic approach has led to its decline. The book offers proposals for how the nexus can be revived to allow competition law to address contemporary concerns about the concentration of corporate power.

Elias Deutscher works at the Directorate General for Competition within the European Commission. Elias is also a Visiting Fellow at the School of Law and the Centre for Competition Policy at the University of East Anglia where he was an associate professor in competition law before joining the European Commission. As a trained lawyer and political scientist, he publishes widely on the normative, conceptual, and historical foundations of competition law, and new challenges for competition policy in digital and innovation-driven markets.

GLOBAL COMPETITION LAW AND ECONOMICS POLICY

This series publishes monographs highlighting the interdisciplinary and multijurisdictional nature of competition law, economics, and policy. Global in coverage, the series should appeal to competition and antitrust specialists working as scholars, practitioners, and judges.

General Editors:

Competition Law and Democracy

MARKETS AS INSTITUTIONS OF ANTIPOWER

ELIAS DEUTSCHER

CAMBRIDGE
UNIVERSITY PRESS

CAMBRIDGE
UNIVERSITY PRESS

Shaftesbury Road, Cambridge CB2 8EA, United Kingdom

One Liberty Plaza, 20th Floor, New York, NY 10006, USA

477 Williamstown Road, Port Melbourne, VIC 3207, Australia

314–321, 3rd Floor, Plot 3, Splendor Forum, Jasola District Centre, New Delhi – 110025, India

103 Penang Road, #05–06/07, Visioncrest Commercial, Singapore 238467

Cambridge University Press is part of Cambridge University Press & Assessment, a department of the University of Cambridge.

We share the University's mission to contribute to society through the pursuit of education, learning and research at the highest international levels of excellence.

www.cambridge.org
Information on this title: www.cambridge.org/9781316513675

DOI: 10.1017/9781009075817

First published 2024

A catalogue record for this publication is available from the British Library.

A Cataloging-in-Publication data record for this book is available from the Library of Congress

ISBN 978-1-316-51367-5 Hardback

The views expressed in this book are those of the author and do not reflect the official position of the European Commission.

This book has been published with a financial subsidy from the European University Institute Department of Law and the University.

EUI EUROPEAN UNIVERSITY INSTITUTE

For Chloé, and my parents, Irmgard and Jürgen.

Contents

Preface

'Does competition law promote democracy, and if so how?' is the central question which has shaped my academic work over the last decade. This book stands at the end of this thought process. It constitutes an attempt to provide a clear, albeit certainly not conclusive, answer to this question by exploring the historiography and conceptual foundations of the idea of a competition–democracy nexus. The book builds upon the manuscript of my doctoral thesis which I defended at the Department of Law of the European University Institute in 2020. It brings together various ideas, arguments, and analytical frameworks that have been developed in previous publications of mine: notably, 'Exploring the Ordoliberal Paradigm: The Competition-Democracy Nexus' (2016) 11(2) *Competition Law Review* 181–214 (together with Stavros Makris); 'Competition and Equality – A Republican Account' in J Broulík and K Cseres (eds) *Competition Law and Economic Inequality: Global Perspectives* (Hart Publishing 2022) 15–53; and 'The Competition-Democracy Nexus Unpacked – Competition Law, Republican Liberty, and Democracy' (2022) 49 *Yearbook of European Law* 197–251. I would like to thank Hart Publishing and Oxford University Press for their permission to use some of this material in this book. The manuscript of this book has greatly benefitted from the proofreading by Dr Evans, as well as the copyediting and advice by the editorial team of Cambridge University Press.

The beauty of competition law as a legal and academic field is that it never stands still. The fast-moving and innovative nature of competition law poses, however, a number of challenges to a book project like the present one because the case law and policy making move faster than the publication process. As a result, this book presents a snapshot of the state of competition law as it presented itself towards the beginning of the calendar year 2023. Important recent case law and developments, such as the EU Digital Markets Act, the UK Digital Markets, Competition and Consumers Bill, the ongoing policy project of the Article 102 TFEU Guidelines, and the draft 2023 US Merger Guidelines are, if at all, only touched upon in passing.

The evolution of the case law and policy between the completion of the manuscript and the publication of the book stands in continuity with the final thought of the book that US antitrust law and EU competition law are at a crossroads. Recent case law seems to suggest that competition law continues to gravitate towards a 'laissez-faire antitrust' approach which this book describes as the predominant competition law paradigm during the last four decades. At the same time, recent enforcement activities by competition authorities and policy developments on both sides of the Atlantic point towards a different direction. They are suggestive of a paradigm adjustment that is consistent with a revival of the competition–democracy nexus envisaged in the last chapter of this book (Chapter 8).

The future of competition law has seldom been more open-ended than at this point in time, where the evolution of competition can go both ways. The analysis provided in this book allows for a better understanding of the preconceptions, virtues, and challenges of both possible alternative futures of competition law: the continuity of the 'laissez-faire antitrust approach' or the revival of a 'competition–democracy nexus (4.0)'. The question of how recent developments that escape the temporal scope of this book fit into the analysis provided therein will certainly be explored in greater depth in future publications.

This book is the result of wonderful years of research at the European University Institute (EUI) in Florence, the New York University (NYU) School of Law, and the University of East Anglia (UEA) Law School. I am highly indebted to all three institutions for the stimulating research and learning environment, as well as the excellent academic and professional opportunities they have offered me. I would also like to express my profound gratitude to the Deutscher Akademischer Austauschdienst, European University Institute Department of Law, and the UEA Law School for their generous financial support of my research.

In writing this book, I have greatly benefitted from the continuous support of my doctoral supervisor, Professor Giorgio Monti. His advice, inspirational way of thinking, and intellectual integrity have importantly shaped my understanding of competition law and academic work. I am sincerely grateful for his generous mentorship, patience, and kindness. I would also like to thank the three examiners of my doctoral thesis, Professors Heike Schweitzer, Spencer Weber Waller, and Hans Micklitz. Their academic work has been a source of continuous inspiration, and their comments have allowed me to transform my thesis into this book. During my research for this book, I was privileged to interact and learn from a number of scholars who importantly contributed to my understanding of the interplay between law, politics, and economics: notably Professors Rainer Bauböck, Eleonor Fox, Harry First, Michal Gal, Daniel Rubinfeld, Ioannis Lianos, and Andriani Kalintiri. I am also grateful to my colleagues, students, and PhD supervisees at the UEA and the Centre for Competition Policy which have been my academic home for the last five years. Their collegiality, friendship, support, and all the fascinating discussions and projects have allowed me to grow as an academic, teacher, and competition lawyer. My thanks go in particular to Claudina Richards, Catherine Waddams, Morten Hviid, Sebastian Peyer, Avidan Kent, Nikos Skoutaris, Nick Scharf, Andreas Stephan, Michael Harker, Sean Ennis, Bruce Lyons, Franco Mariuzzo, Farasat Bokhari, Peter Ormosi, Amelia Fletcher, and Kai-Uwe Kühn.

Writing this book would have been a lonely exercise without the company of my dear friends Juliette Rosenberger, Mehdi Abourizk, Enno Schumacher, Johannes Leininger, Fiona Marty, Alisha Molter, Augustin Gigleux, Daphné Vagogne, Antoine Droin, Romy, and Sebastian Aichner, and Matthias Hoesch and his family. This book has also benefitted from the comments I received from Matthias Hoesch and Justin Lindeboom on various parts of the manuscript. I am particularly indebted to my friend, regular co-author, and academic sparring partner Stavros Makris for the innumerable passionate discussions about everything competition and beyond, and his precious feedback throughout the various stages of this book project.

Above all, I would like to thank my brothers, Gabriel and Lukas, and my beloved parents, Irmgard and Jürgen, for their unconditional affection and support. The writing and completion of this book would not have been possible without the continuous encouragement, advice, company, and smile of Chloé Papazian. My gratitude to and admiration for her have always been and continue to be difficult to put in words.

Introduction

'Government of the people, by the people, for the people.'[1] At a time when the American nation was torn by the deep divisions of a haemorrhagic civil war, the sixteenth president of the United States of America, Abraham Lincoln, with these solemn words evoked democracy as the unifying political future for the United States. Lincoln's *Gettysburg Address* coined the triad of 'government of, by and for the people', which has since become deeply engrained in the political creed of liberal democracies.

On a chilly Saturday in October 2016, at the peak of the campaign for the US presidential elections, the then presidential candidate Donald Trump visited Gettysburg. On the same 'hallowed grounds'[2] of the battlefield of Gettysburg, 153 years after Lincoln uttered his famed definition of democracy, Donald Trump lamented that Lincoln's vision of American democracy was in tatters. He painted a dystopian picture of America as a deeply 'divided nation' whose democratic and economic 'system is totally rigged and broken'. Trump blamed a 'power structure' that was epitomised in the upsurge of industry concentration in the US economy as one of the reasons for the woes of America's political and economic system. He also lambasted several recent mergers for unifying 'far too much power in one massive entity' and 'destroy[ing] democracy'.

It is certainly not a historical coincidence that Donald Trump chose the symbolic venue of Lincoln's *Gettysburg Address* to bemoan the alleged decline of the US political and economic system. Nor is it a coincidence that he mentioned the demise of democracy in the same breath as waning market competition caused by the combination of economic power in the hands of a few. On the contrary, the view

1 The quotation is based on the reproduction of Lincoln's Gettysburg Address in RD Heffner (ed), *A Documentary History of the United States* (New York: Penguin 2013) 210.

2 All quotations in this paragraph are based on CNN, 'Trump Speaks in Pennsylvania; Examining Proposed Actions in First 100 Days of Trump Administration: Unofficial Transcript' (22 October 2016) http://transcripts.cnn.com.

that the excessive concentration of private economic power is inimical and competition conducive to democracy has over the last century become a basic tenet of the self-understanding of US democracy. This idea of a symbiotic relationship between competition and democracy – which I will call the 'competition–democracy nexus'[3] – is deeply rooted in the US antitrust law tradition.[4] It was first aired by congressmen during the legislative debates that preceded the enactment of the Sherman Act as the first federal antitrust law in the United States in 1890.[5] Today, the proposition that the concentration of economic power is detrimental and competition is conducive to democracy is widely shared across the political spectrum. Hence, it comes as little surprise that Trump's successor as US President, Joe Biden, as well as a number of high-level politicians within the Democratic Party,[6] have recently reaffirmed that competition is 'conducive to the preservation of our democratic political and social institutions'[7] and warned that 'excessive market concentration threatens basic economic liberties [and] democratic accountability'[8] to garner support for a more vigorous enforcement of US antitrust law.

The idea of a competition–democracy nexus is, however, not a uniquely American invention. In Europe, policy-makers also habitually entertain the belief that there is a positive relationship between competitive markets and democracy. For instance, references to this link permeate the speeches of Margrethe Vestager, European Commissioner for Competition. According to Vestager, 'a fair market place is part of the democracy'[9] and, consequently, European competition policy protects 'ultimately plurality and democracy'.[10] In the same vein, the General Court of the European Union and the European Commission assert that competition law can 'contribute to achieving objectives that go beyond consumer welfare, such as plurality in a democratic society.'[11] Similar to the United States, the proposition that

3 This term was first coined by E Deutscher and S Makris, 'Exploring the Ordoliberal Paradigm: The Competition-Democracy Nexus' (2016) 11(2) *Competition Law Review* 181.

4 RJ Peritz, *Competition Policy in America: History, Rhetoric, Law* (New York: Oxford University Press 2000).

5 20 Cong Rec 2455 (1890) 2458.

6 E Warren, 'Break Up Big Tech' (24 April 2020) https://2020.elizabethwarren.com; A Klobuchar, *Antitrust: Taking on Monopoly Power from the Gilded Age to the Digital Age* (New York: Alfred A. Knopf 2021).

7 Executive Order on Promoting Competition in the American Economy 9 July 2021, Executive Order 14036 s. 2; *Northern Pacific RY. Co. v United States* 356 US 1 (1958) 4.

8 Executive Order on Promoting Competition in the American Economy (n 7) s. 1.

9 M Vestager, 'Remarks by Executive Vice-President Vestager for the Political Agreement on the Digital Markets Act' (25 March 2022) SPEECH/22/2042.

10 M Vestager, 'Keynote of EVP Vestager at the European Competition Law Tuesdays: A Principles Based Approach to Competition Policy' (25 October 2022) SPEECH/22/6393.

11 European Commission, Amendments to the Communication from the Commission Guidance on the Commission's enforcement priorities in applying Article 82 of the EC Treaty to abusive exclusionary conduct by dominant undertakings. C(2023) 1923 final, para. 1. See also to this effect, Case T-604/18 *Google and Alphabet v Commission (Google Android)* ECLI:EU:T:2022:541, para. 1028.

competition and competition law play an important role for democracy also has a long tradition in Europe. As early as in the first decades of the twentieth century, in light of the rise of the German Nazi Regime and the fall of the Weimar Republic, a group of scholars at the University of Freiburg, the so-called Ordoliberals or Freiburg School, warned that the destruction of competition by industrial concentration and cartelisation ultimately undermines democracy. This Ordoliberal idea that competition contributes to the preservation of democracy has become a recurrent theme in the academic, legal, and political discourse about European competition law.[12]

Recent iterations of the claim of a competition–democracy nexus have not only shed light on its long-standing status as a fundamental predisposition – if not a foundational myth – of competition law in the United States and in Europe but also highlight its ongoing saliency. The claim that the concentration of economic power poses a threat to democracy has again moved centre stage as a result of growing societal and political concerns over the unprecedented level of industry concentration in the United States and, albeit to a lesser extent, in the European economy.[13] Soaring levels of industry concentration – epitomised by the rise of a few digital platforms, such as Google, Facebook, Amazon, or Apple – are increasingly perceived as a cause of growing economic inequalities, waning productivity, and lack of competition.[14] Not least the deeply perturbing images of the assault of the US Capitol, one of the hallmarks of liberal democracy, incited by misinformation ventilated over social media platforms raise fundamental questions about the political risks that the concentration of private economic power poses to our liberal and democratic societies. The events of Epiphany 2021 also have their own irony. The very same amalgamated power that Donald Trump singled out in his Gettysburg speech as a threat to democracy eventually acted as an amplifier of his inflammatory comments and speeches that pushed US democracy closer to the precipice.

The implications of this re-emerging debate about the adverse effects of concentrated economic power on democracy go beyond the challenges that the digital economy poses to competition law and policy. Growing economic, societal, and political concerns over excessive levels of industry concentration have triggered a

[12] See, for instance, G Amato, *Antitrust and the Bounds of Power: The Dilemma of Liberal Democracy in the History of the Market* (Oxford: Hart 1997); DJ Gerber, *Law and Competition in Twentieth Century Europe: Protecting Prometheus* (Oxford/New York: Clarendon Press/Oxford University Press 1998).

[13] See, for instance, M Bajgar et al, 'Industry Concentration in Europe and North America' (OECD Productivity Working Papers 18 2019); J de Loecker, J Eeckhout and G Unger, 'The Rise of Market Power and the Macroeconomic Implications' (2020) 135(2) *The Quarterly Journal of Economics* 561; T Philippon, *The Great Reversal: How America Gave Up on Free Markets* (Cambridge, MA: Harvard University Press 2019); Gábor Koltay, Szabolcs Lorincz, Tommaso Valletti, 'Concentration and Competition: Evidence From Europe and Implications For Policy' (2023) 19(3) *Journal of Competition Law & Economics* 466.

[14] See, for instance, J Furman and P Orszag, 'Slower Productivity and Higher Inequality: Are They Related?' (2018) Working Paper 18-4; de Loecker, Eeckhout and Unger (n 13).

fundamental reconfiguration of competition law and policy on both sides of the Atlantic. The consensus view that the sole purpose of competition law is to ensure that markets offer consumers access to products and services at the lowest possible price (the so-called consumer welfare standard) is increasingly under attack.[15] There is a growing appreciation on both sides of the Atlantic that competition law and policy have not only an economic but also a social and political function.[16] The protagonists of a new antimonopoly movement call for more rigorous enforcement of competition law, not only to protect consumers but also to impose checks on the power of corporate behemoths lest they endanger democracy.[17] The proposition that competition law constitutes a suitable tool to rein in and impose democratic checks on private economic power is no longer only shared among a marginal fringe of critical competition scholars and political activists.[18] On the contrary, the idea of a competition–democracy nexus is about to become common currency in academic conferences and the hallways of competition law agencies on both sides of the Atlantic. The resurfacing of the idea of a competition–democracy nexus has set in motion an incremental tectonic shift that is about to redefine the fundamentals of competition law.

Despite its long history and sudden renaissance, the thesis that the preservation of competitive markets through competition law is conducive to democracy is anything but well understood. To date, little effort has been made to provide a conceptually sound explanation as to why the concentration of economic power is detrimental and competition is conducive to democracy. Neither do policy-makers and academics explain how the rules prohibiting cartels, abuses of monopoly power, and anticompetitive mergers in US antitrust and EU competition law promote democracy. Instead, the idea of a competition–democracy nexus is increasingly repeated like a mantra that does not call for any further explanation. It is thus frequently treated as if it were a fundamental axiom or a prior belief of competition law that can be simply assumed to be true.

This lack of serious engagement with and patchy understanding of the idea of a competition–democracy nexus is problematic on a number of counts. Above all, the

[15] H Hovenkamp, *The Antitrust Enterprise: Principle and Execution* (Cambridge, MA: Harvard University Press 2005) 1.

[16] See, for instance, H First and S Weber Waller, 'Antitrust's Democracy Deficit' (2013) 81(5) *Fordham Law Review* 2543; S Weber Waller, 'Antitrust and Democracy' (2019) 46(4) *Florida State University Law Review* 806; EM Fox, 'Antitrust and Democracy: How Markets Protect Democracy, Democracy Protects Markets, and Illiberal Politics Threatens to Hijack Both' (2019) 46(4) *Legal Issues of Economic Integration* 317; DA Crane, 'Antitrust and Democracy: A Case Study from German Fascism' (2018) University of Michigan Law & Econ Research Paper No 18-009.

[17] L Khan, 'Amazon's Antitrust Paradox' (2017) 126(3) *Yale Law Journal* 710; T Wu, *The Curse of Bigness: Antitrust in the New Gilded Age* (New York: Columbia Global Reports 2018).

[18] BC Lynn, *Liberty from All Masters: The New American Autocracy vs. the Will of the People* (New York: St. Martin's Press 2020); M Stoller, *Goliath: The 100-Year War between Monopoly Power and Democracy* (New York: Simon & Schuster 2019).

superficial understanding of the competition–democracy nexus is unsatisfactory from an intellectual point of view. It is indeed anything but obvious that there should be a direct relationship between competitive markets, their protection through competition law, and a democratic societal or political order. Furthermore, neoclassical economic theory, as the predominant epistemological tool and normative framework of modern competition law on both sides of the Atlantic, is of very little help in elucidating the relationship between competitive markets and democracy. At the practical policy level, the insufficient grasp of the relationship between competition and democracy becomes all the more problematic as calls for reining in corporate power in the name of democracy gain political traction. Recent policy initiatives to regulate Big Tech companies and to tackle the trend towards industry concentration are informed by increasingly widespread societal and political concerns over the excessive amalgamation of economic power and its adverse effect on democracy.[19] However, without a proper comprehension of the conceptual and historical foundations of the idea of a competition–democracy nexus, neither the virtues nor the costs of a competition policy that seeks to further democracy by curtailing the concentration of economic power can be fully assessed and tested. Understanding through which channels concentrated private economic power poses a threat to democracy and how competitive markets can further democracy is also instrumental for reforming existing competition rules or designing new rules to operationalise the goal of a competition–democracy nexus.

The objective of this book is to address this knowledge gap by taking a fresh look at the often repeated but only rarely substantiated claim that there is a link between competition, competition law, and democracy. It embarks on the most comprehensive study of the relationship between competition and democracy in EU and US competition law so far undertaken. By exploring the historical, conceptual, and normative foundations of the idea of a competition–democracy nexus, this book aims to advance a clear answer to the question of how competition and competition law can promote and protect democracy.

The central claim of this book is that the idea of a competition–democracy nexus can be best explained by the republican concept of liberty as non-domination, which originated from republican thought in ancient Rome.[20] This republican

[19] See, for instance, Regulation (EU) 2022/1925 on Contestable and Fair Markets in the Digital Sector (Digital Markets Act), [2022] OJ L 265/1; H.R.3816–American Choice and Innovation Online Act ('ACIO Act') 2021, 117th Congress (2021–2022); Zehntes Gesetz zur Änderung des Gesetzes gegen Wettbewerbsbeschränkungen (die 10. GWB-Novelle), BGBl. I 2021 S. 2; Digital Markets, Competition and Consumers Bill, Bill 350 2022-23 (as amended in Public Bill Committee).

[20] See, most notably, Q Skinner, *Liberty before Liberalism* (Cambridge: Cambridge University Press 1998); Q Skinner, 'A Third Concept of Liberty: Isaiah Berlin Lecture' in The British Academy (ed), *Proceedings of the British Academy: 2001 Lectures*, Volume 117 (Oxford: Oxford University Press; British Academy 2002) 237; P Pettit, *Republicanism: A Theory of Freedom and Government* (Oxford: Oxford University Press 1997). For recent political theory scholarship that

concept of liberty differs from our predominant understanding of negative liberty, which perceives only actual or likely interference by somebody else with our choices as a source of unfreedom. In contrast, republican liberty defines unfreedom as a master–slave relationship. It considers the mere presence and defenceless subjugation to the arbitrary power and domination of another person as an obstacle to individual liberty, even if this person is benevolent and does not interfere with our choices. On a republican account, a slave or servant cannot be considered free, even if the master is benevolent and does not interfere with their choices or actions, because the benevolent master can, at any time, change their mind and interfere with the slave at will.[21] Therefore, a person cannot be said to be free as long as they are exposed to the whim and caprice of another person who has the discretionary power or capacity to interfere with them. In contrast to mainstream liberals advocating negative liberty as non-interference, proponents of republican liberty are hence not only concerned about the actual or likely interference resulting from the *exercise* of power but they also already perceive the possibility of arbitrary interference deriving from the mere *existence* of power as a source of unfreedom. This book will argue that the republican concept of economic liberty can explain the core premise underpinning the idea of a competition–democracy nexus – namely, that the mere existence of concentrated economic power is in itself incompatible with a republican democracy, even in the absence of any concrete risk of interference. The idea of a competition–democracy nexus thus revolves around the belief that by dispersing economic power, competitive markets operate as an institution of 'antipower'[22] that minimises instances of domination, and thereby promotes republican liberty and democracy.

Using the concept of republican liberty as the explanatory variable for the idea of a competition–democracy nexus, this book makes four major contributions. First, it traces the historical trajectory and conceptual foundations of the idea of a competition–democracy nexus. It shows how the belief that competitive markets enhance republican liberty as non-domination and the equal status of market participants originates in the thought of early common lawyers and political economists, such as Sir Edward Coke, the English Levellers, Montesquieu, James Steuart, and Adam Smith . These early liberal thinkers celebrated the ascent of competitive markets as a harbinger of liberty and equality, which would transform a feudal society that was characterised by hierarchical relationships of subordination and domination into a heterarchical society of free and equals. In describing how the advent of competitive markets brought about not only greater economic but also

draws a similar link between competitive markets and the ideal of republican liberty, see RS Taylor 'Market Freedom as Antipower' (2013) 107(3) *American Political Science Review* 593; O Suttle, 'The Puzzle of Competitive Fairness' (2022) 21(2) *Politics, Philosophy & Economics* 190.

[21] For this master–slave metaphor, see Pettit (n 20) 22–24.

[22] P Pettit, 'Freedom as Antipower' (1996) 106(3) *Ethics* 576, 577, 588.

political liberty, the rule of law, and a more republican or democratic form of government, these early proponents of commerce and competitive markets had already coined the proposition of a competition–democracy nexus in its rudimentary form. This book highlights that this idea of a competition–democracy nexus was reinvigorated and refined towards the end of the nineteenth and during the first decades of the twentieth century by the proponents of competition law in the United States and in Europe. By revisiting the history of US antitrust law and the Ordoliberal roots of European competition law, it also reveals how the ideal of republican liberty lies at the origins of the idea of a competition–democracy nexus in US and EU competition law.

Second, this book explores how the concern about republican liberty as the normative backbone of the competition–democracy nexus shaped the interpretation and application of US antitrust law until the 1970s and of EU competition rules until the 2000s. It analyses how US and EU antitrust policy operationalised the ideal of republican liberty as non-domination through a structuralist approach, which was geared towards the protection of competition as a polycentric market structure. Focusing on the use of rule-like presumptions of illegality, a specific conception of the standard of harm, and a particular understanding of the costs and benefits of competition law intervention, this book also identifies the principal legal mechanisms and policy levers through which US and EU competition law have translated the concern about republican liberty into concrete competition policy. On this basis, this book identifies the essential features of what one can call republican antitrust or a republican approach to competition law.

Third, this book also seeks to explain why the republican concept of liberty and with it the idea of a competition–democracy nexus became largely irrelevant for contemporary competition law. The influence of the concern about liberty as non-domination started to wane and eventually vanished with the rise of the Chicago School during the 1960s and 1970s in the United States. With the shift towards a More Economic Approach in EU competition law during the 2000s, the republican approach and the idea of a competition–democracy nexus also lost its appeal in Europe. This book sheds light on how the rise of the Chicago School in the United States and the More Economic Approach in Europe has started to displace the concern about the competition–democracy nexus and republican liberty with a negative understanding of liberty that only perceives welfare-decreasing interference as an obstacle to economic liberty. The Chicago School-inspired modernisation of US and EU competition law, and the endorsement of the consumer welfare standard have thus entailed a shift from an antitrust policy, which hinged on the concern about the adverse impact of economic concentration on republican liberty and democracy, to an approach that seeks, in the first place, to protect entrepreneurial liberty against state interference. This book identifies the main parameters through which the rise of this Chicago School-inspired laissez-faire antitrust fundamentally reconfigured the interpretation and application of the substantive US and

EU competition rules, and entrenched a competition policy that consistently leans towards the protection of negative entrepreneurial liberty of businesses against state intervention.

Finally, against the backdrop of lingering societal concerns about the concentration of economic and political power in the hands of a few industrial and digital behemoths, this book also looks ahead and asks whether a reversal towards the republican antitrust tradition is possible and desirable. It signposts the parameters that need to be recalibrated to realign modern competition law with a republican understanding of economic liberty and the ideal of a competition–democracy nexus. This book argues that this reversal towards a more republican approach would not necessarily reduce consumer welfare. At the same time, this book highlights the trade-offs and costs that such a policy reform would involve.

The argument and analysis of this book will unfold in four parts. The first part (Chapters 1 and 2) explores the historical trajectory and theoretical foundations of the competition–democracy nexus. Chapter 1 describes the object of this inquiry. It surveys the history of the idea of a competition–democracy nexus from early liberal thought on competitive markets in sixteenth-century Europe to the second half of the twentieth century. Chapter 2 introduces the conceptual claim of the book that this long-standing perception of a competition–democracy nexus turns on and can be best explained by a normative commitment to republican liberty.

The second part (Chapters 3–5) of this book analyses how the twin goal of a competition–democracy nexus and republican liberty were operationalised by various competition law paradigms, as well as US and EU antitrust jurisprudence. It thus identifies the hallmarks of what can be called a republican competition law or republican antitrust tradition. Chapter 3 canvasses the different avenues through which various schools of thought in US and European competition law envisaged the realisation of the competition–democracy nexus. Chapters 4 and 5 identify the main parameters through which courts on both sides of the Atlantic gave shape to a competition policy that is anchored in a normative commitment to republican liberty as non-domination and republican democracy.

The third part (Chapters 6 and 7) interrogates the reasons behind the decline of the idea of a competition–democracy nexus. It describes how the Chicago School-inspired modernisation of US and EU competition law has gradually replaced republican antitrust with a laissez-faire antitrust approach that turns on a commitment to negative liberty. Chapter 6 describes how the Chicago School put forward the consumer welfare standard as a versatile, principled framework to supersede the concept of republican liberty with an approach that is grounded in the concern about negative liberty and seeks, in the first place, to preserve entrepreneurial liberty against state coercion. Chapter 7 shows how this shift from republican to negative liberty as the normative bedrock of competition law has led to a recalibration of its modus operandi.

The fourth part (Chapter 8) reviews some of the potential avenues to reinvigorate the idea of a competition–democracy nexus for contemporary competition policy. Chapter 8 draws the various analytical strands of this book together and explores some of the pathways to realign competition law with the republican antitrust tradition and the idea of a competition–democracy nexus.

The overall purpose and claim of this book are, at the same time, humble and far-reaching. The humble version of its argument is that the idea of a link between competition law and democracy can be best explained by the concept of republican liberty as non-domination. The far-reaching implication of this claim is that competition law has as much to do with the aversion to the subjugation that is characteristic of a master–slave relationship that can be traced back to the ancient Roman republican thought of Cicero as with considerations about consumer welfare and efficiency. The remainder of this book will undertake the challenging task of convincing the reader of both the humble and the far-reaching version of the proposed explanation of the idea of a competition–democracy nexus and of demonstrating its relevance for contemporary competition law and policy.

PART I

The Historical and Conceptual Foundations of the Competition–Democracy Nexus

1

The Object of Inquiry

The Idea of a Competition–Democracy Nexus

1.1 INTRODUCTION

Three junctures in the history of competition law may be seen as crucial in shaping the idea of a competition–democracy nexus.

In 1598, a certain Edward Darcy, groom of Queen Elizabeth's Privy Council, obtained a patent that was granted by the Queen. This patent gave him a monopoly over the manufacture and importation of playing cards. At that time, the grant of such patents against the payment of royalties was nothing special. It constituted a recurrent practice by the English Crown to raise money or reward loyal supporters for their services.[1] Three years later, in 1601,[2] amid mounting parliamentary protests against monopolies and privileges, Darcy sued Thomas Allein, a London haberdasher, who produced and sold playing cards in violation of his patent. *Darcy v Allein*,[3] also known as *The Case of Monopolies*, marked one of the first instances where a court held that monopolies are against the common law. *Darcy v Allein* would go down in history as the birth of modern common law against monopolies. And Darcy's monopoly over the production and sale of playing cards would also be remembered as an epitome of a mercantilist system of cronyism, which was built on monarchical prerogative and the unwholly alliance between arbitrary public and private economic power.[4]

1 ST Miller, 'The Case of the Monopolies: Some of Its Results and Suggestions' (1907) 6(1) *Michigan Law Review* 1, 2–3; EF Churchill, 'Monopolies' (1925) 41(3) *Law Quarterly Review* 275, 275–78.

2 D Seaborne Davies, 'Further Light on the Case of Monopolies' (1932) 48(3) *Law Quarterly Review* 394, 404–05. Others date the start of the litigation to 1602, TB Nachbar, 'Monopoly, Mercantilism, and the Politics of Regulation' (2005) 91(5) *Virginia Law Review* 1313, 1372.

3 *Darcy v Allein ('The Case of Monopolies')* [1602] 77 ER 1260.

4 Nachbar (n 2) 1318–42; SG Calabresi and LC Leibowitz, 'Monopolies and the Constitution: A History of Crony Capitalism' (2015) 36(3) *Harvard Journal of Law & Public Policy* 983, 989–96.

Almost three centuries later, in 1879, John D. Rockefeller invented an entirely new private form of monopoly when he transformed his business empire, the Standard Oil Company, into a secret trust. The Standard Oil Trust combined some forty odd corporations and brought virtually the entire US oil and petroleum industry under Rockefeller's control.[5] This was the culmination of a decade-long campaign of consolidation and ruthless industrial warfare that had led to the absorption of rival independent producers and refiners by the Standard Oil Company and had crushed the opposition of remaining independent competitors by driving them out of business.[6] Rockefeller's Standard Oil Trust was soon emulated in other industries.[7] The term *trust* quickly became a catch-all phrase for various types of conglomerates, mergers, cartels, and monopolies that fuelled the trend towards industrial concentration that engulfed the US economy in the late nineteenth century. Growing popular discontent over the monopolistic and cartelistic behaviour of these industrial giants eventually culminated in the enactment of the first modern antitrust law, the Sherman Act, in 1890. To this day, Standard Oil is still habitually referred to as the archetype of the concentration of private economic power in the hands of an industrial behemoth that wielded its mighty influence in both the economic and political spheres.[8]

A third critical juncture in the history of the competition–democracy nexus occurred in the evening of 20 February 1933 in Berlin. Less than a month ahead of the last democratic elections of the German Reichstag in March 1933, which would pave the way for Reichskanzler Hitler's rise to absolute power, about twenty of the most important German business leaders were invited to a meeting with Hermann Göring (the then President of the German Reichstag), Hjalmar Schacht (the future Minister of the Economy), and Adolf Hitler. During this meeting, the industrialists pledged to inject new funds into the National Socialist Party's depleted campaign budget.[9] In return, Adolf Hitler promised to put an end to the instability that beset the parliamentary democracy of the Weimar Republic, protect private property, and crush the left-wing parties and trade unions.[10] This meeting was the birth of a Faustian bargain that would closely tie German conglomerates and cartels with the National Socialist regime throughout the Third Reich. In the transition towards a war economy that followed, large industrial conglomerates played an

5 *Standard Oil Co. of New Jersey v United States* 221 US 1 (1911) 34.

6 IM Tarbell, *The History of the Standard Oil Company* (New York: McClure, Phillips & Co 1904).

7 HB Thorelli, *The Federal Antitrust Policy: Origination of an American Tradition* (Baltimore: Johns Hopkins University Press 1955) 76–79; WD Collins, 'Trusts and the Origins of Antitrust' (2013) 81(5) *Fordham Law Review* 2279, 2316–17.

8 T Wu, *The Curse of Bigness: Antitrust in the New Gilded Age* (New York: Columbia Global Reports 2018).

9 A Tooze, *The Wages of Destruction: The Making & Breaking of the Nazi Economy* (London: Penguin 2007) 99–100.

10 Ibid.

essential role in propping up the destructive forces of the German military apparatus that was soon unleashed to wreak havoc over the European continent.[11]

All three events – the grant of Darcy's playing card monopoly, the creation of the Standard Oil Trust, and the Faustian pact between the German *Konzerne* and the rising National Socialist regime – throw the various dimensions of what I will call the *behemoth problem* (i.e., the problem of the concentration of private economic power) into relief. This chapter explores how the problem of concentrated economic power has historically been at the origin of the idea of a competition–democracy nexus and fashioned modern competition law. In tracing its trajectory across the history of thought about competitive markets, this chapter gives a better understanding of the predispositions and historical context that informed the idea of a competition–democracy nexus. This chapter also highlights how various iterations of the idea of a competition–democracy nexus converge in the twin-proposition that competition is conducive and the excessive concentration of economic power is detrimental to the emergence and preservation of a liberal, democratic society and polity. In tracing its genesis and historical trajectory, this chapter demonstrates that the idea of a competition–democracy nexus is firmly rooted in and has become a normative mainstay of competition law on both sides of the Atlantic.

This chapter is organised as follows. Section 1.2 describes how the idea of a competition–democracy nexus in its rudimentary form took shape in English common law and economic thought about competitive markets in early modern Europe. Section 1.3 explores how this proto-republican version of the competition–democracy nexus re-emerged with full force during the late nineteenth and early twentieth centuries when the proposition that competitive markets constitute a crucial safeguard of democracy became a central tenet of US antitrust law. Finally, Section 1.4 sheds light on the genesis of the idea of a competition–democracy nexus as a core proposition of the Ordoliberal competition law movement and traces its influence on modern competition law in Europe.

1.2 COMPETITION–DEMOCRACY NEXUS 1.0: COMPETITIVE MARKETS IN EARLY MODERN LIBERAL THOUGHT

1.2.1 *The Historical, Economic, and Political Background*

Our journey to the historical origins of the idea of a competition–democracy nexus starts in the early modern liberal thought that first emerged in England in the sixteenth to eighteenth centuries. The pronouncements about monopoly, restraints of trade, and competitive markets of early common lawyers, liberal political movements, philosophers, and economists – such as Sir Edward Coke, the English Leveller movement, Montesquieu, James Steuart, and Adam Smith – are a good

[11] Ibid.; J Diarmuid, *Hell's Cartel* (London: Bloomsbury 2008).

point of departure for our inquiry into the normative fabric and historical trajectory of the competition–democracy nexus. Marvelling at the radical economic, social, and political transformation that the ascent of competitive markets set into motion, these early proponents of free trade and competitive markets valued commerce and competition not only for their welfare-enhancing characteristics but also saw them as the harbingers of a freer and more egalitarian society and polity.

Not all of these early proponents of competitive markets were advocates of a democratic or republican government in a contemporary sense. Nevertheless, what united them was an acute awareness of the propensity of competitive markets to promote economic liberty as an important force of progress towards a freer, more egalitarian form of society and government. In the account of these early liberal thinkers, the advent of competitive markets not only meant greater economic but also greater civic and political liberty and equality. This narrative of competitive markets as catalysts for a liberal societal and political order should not come as a surprise if we consider its historical context. The beginnings of a competitive market society, documented and advocated by the early proponents of a competition–democracy nexus, coincided with an intensifying political conflict between the English Parliament and the Crown. This struggle resulted in the emergence of a republican tradition of political thought and institutions, which moved Elizabethan England closer towards a republican form of government, or what the historian Patrick Collison prominently called a 'Monarchical Republic'.[12] It is against this sociopolitical background that the seeds of the idea of a positive relationship between competitive markets and a republican form of government were sown.

1.2.2 *The Nascent Critique of Monopoly Power and the Antimonopoly Turn in English Common Law*

The beginnings of this proto-republican account of competitive markets can be traced to Thomas More's seminal and radically egalitarian narrative *Utopia*. First published in Latin in 1516 and in English in 1551,[13] *Utopia* marks the first work in

[12] P Collinson, 'The Monarchical Republic of Queen Elizabeth I' (1987) 69(2) *Bulletin of the John Rylands Library* 394.

[13] 'Quod si maxime increscat ouium numerus, precio nihil decrescit tamen; quod earum, si *monopolium* appellari non potest, quod non unus uendit, certe *oligopolium* est. Reciderunt enim fere in manus paucorum, eorundemque diuitum, quos nulla necessitas urget ante uendendi quam libet, nec ante libet quam liceat quanti libet.' T More, *The Utopia: In Latin from the Edition of March 1518, and in English from the First Edition of Ralph Robynson's Translation in 1551 with Additional Translations, Introduction and Notes by J.H. Lupton* [1516] (Oxford: Clarendon Press 1895) 54–55 (emphasis added). Barker-Smith translated this passage as 'And yet, even if the numbers of sheep should rise dramatically, the price will not fall; for although one cannot speak about a monopoly as it is not controlled by a single man, yet the wool trade is most certainly an oligopoly. It's in the hands of a small group of rich men who are under no necessity to sell before it suits them, and it only suits them when they can get their price.' T More, *Utopia: Translated, Edited and Introduced by Dominic Baker-Smith* [1516]

which the terms monopoly and oligopoly appeared in modern English. *Utopia* stands out as one of the first critiques of concentrated economic power in early modern political thought. Thomas More used the terms *monopoly* and *oligopoly* to describe and decry the accumulation of private property, wealth, and control over trade in the hands of a small group of wealthy men (*divitum*).[14] Monopoly or oligopoly in More's account are not only objectionable because they allow a small number of wealthy landowners to increase prices. *Utopia* also speaks out against concentrated economic power as a source of inequality of opportunity and wealth. More asserted that the adverse effects of monopolistic and oligopolistic power particularly hit the poorest members of society who have to bear higher food and input prices.[15] *Utopia* also advanced the proposition that the control that monopolists and oligopolists exert over their trades annihilates economic liberty and opportunities by preventing large parts of the population from taking up employment and becoming economically active.[16]

Towards the end of the sixteenth century, this proposition that monopoly power and restraints of trade by oligopolists unduly deprive tradesmen and workmen of their freedom and opportunity to exercise a legitimate economic activity and independently secure their livelihoods began to emerge as a recurrent theme in English common law. The concern about the adverse effect of concentrated economic power on economic liberty was the principal ground on which the Queen's Bench in *Darcy v Allein* established the principle that monopolies are against the common law.[17] The Queen's Bench thereby reaffirmed its prior holding in *Davenant v Hurdis*, which was decided three years before *Darcy v Allein*, that monopolies and restraints of trade which 'bring . . . all trade or traffic into the hands of one company, or one person, and . . . exclude all other, [are] illegal'.[18] *Darcy v Allein* thus marked a fundamental departure of the common law from a favourable approach towards monopoly, which throughout most of the eleventh to sixteenth centuries had treated privileges, exclusive rights, and guilds as legitimate features of a corporatist and mercantilist economic order.[19]

(London: Penguin Classics 2012) 34. See also JW Park, 'The Utopian Economics of Sir Thomas More' (1971) 30(3) *The American Journal of Economics and Sociology* 275, 277.

14 More (n 13) 55, 57.

15 Ibid. 54–55.

16 Ibid. 54–55, 57–58. See notably 'Refrenate coemptiones istas diuitum, ac uelut monopolii exercendi licentiam.' This has been translated as: 'Suffer not thies ryche men to bye vp all, to ingrosse and forstalle, and with theyr monopolye to kepe the market alone as please them.' Ibid. 57–58.

17 *Darcy v Allein ('The Case of Monopolies')* [1602] (n 3) 1262; *Ipswich Tailors' Case* [1614] 77 ER 1218, 1221. For other restraints of trade cases, see also *The Blacksmith's Case* [1587] 74 ER 643, 643; *Colgate v Bacheler* [1569] 78 ER 1097, 1097.

18 W Letwin, *Law and Economic Policy in America: The Evolution of the Sherman Antitrust Act* [1959] (Chicago: Chicago University Press 1981) 26, translating *Davenant v Hurdis* [1599] 72 ER 769, 778.

19 Letwin (n 18) 18–19; Nachbar (n 2) 1318–27.

This antimonopolistic turn of the common law went in tandem with growing parliamentarian opposition to the grant of monopolies by the English Crown.[20] Grievances against monopoly were aired in Parliament on various occasions in 1571, 1597–98, and 1601.[21] The colourful language that was used during the parliamentary debates bears testimony to the increasingly passionate public disapproval of the generous handout of patents, monopolies, and privileges by the Crown. Monopolies were decried as the 'Blood-suckers of the Common-wealth' that usurped 'the best and principallest Commodities, which the Earth ... hath given Us ... the Commodities of our own Labour, which with the Sweat of our Brows (even up to the Knees in Mire and Dirt) we have labour'd for'.[22] Members of Parliament railed against monopolies as a '[r]estraint of any thing Publick, in a City, or Common-wealth, to a Private Use',[23] a '*commune malum*' (common evil)[24] or even 'great Monster'.[25] 'There is no Act of Hers', they agitated, 'that hath been, or is more Derogatory to Her own *Majesty*, or more Odious to the Subject, or more Dangerous to the Common-Wealth, than the Granting of these *Monopolies*'.[26]

In 1601, Queen Elizabeth eventually bent to the growing parliamentary opposition and various attempts to curtail the Crown's power to grant privileges by revoking some of the least popular monopolies and recognizing the authority of common law courts to hear cases involving monopolies.[27] This 1601 Proclamation on Monopolies, for the first time, implicitly acknowledged the power of Parliament to regulate the royal prerogative to grant monopolies.[28] In clarifying that monopoly is against the common law and void, even when granted by royal decree, *Darcy v Allein* reaffirmed this first important victory for the Parliament in the constitutional contest over the ultimate authority to grant exclusive rights and patents.[29] The power struggle between the Crown and Parliament over the royal prerogative to grant monopolies and privileges culminated in the enactment of the 1623 Statute of Monopolies Act, by which the Parliament authoritatively asserted its control over

20 Letwin (n 18) 21–23.

21 DH Sacks, 'Parliament, Liberty, and the Commonweal' in JH Hexter (ed), *Parliament and Liberty from the Reign of Elizabeth to the English Civil War* (Stanford: Stanford University Press 1992) 85, 96–98; DH Sacks, 'Commonwealth Discourse and Economic Thought: The Morality of Exchange' in S Doran and N Jones (eds), *The Elizabethan World* (London: Routledge 2014) 389, 405–06.

22 H Townshend, *Historical Collections; or, An Exact Account of the Last Four Parliaments of Q. Elizabeth of Famous Memory* (London: Printed for T. Basset, W. Crooke, and W. Cademan 1680) 233–34.

23 Ibid. 230.

24 Ibid.

25 Ibid. 258.

26 Ibid. 233.

27 Prior to the Queen's 1601 Proclamation on Monopolies, cases involving monopolies granted by the Crown were heard by the Court of the Star Chamber, which was set at the royal palace and did not apply common law. Nachbar (n 2) 1331–33.

28 Calabresi and Leibowitz (n 4) 991.

29 Letwin (n 18) 27; Nachbar (n 2) 1341.

the regulation of the economy.[30] This Statute declared all monopolies to be void and against the common law,[31] while recognising a number of exemptions for monopolies and privileges granted by cities and towns,[32] as well as patents for new inventions and merchandise.[33]

The nascent antagonism in English common law against concentrated economic power and restrictive trade practices was certainly influenced by economic considerations about the exploitative effects of monopolistic rent-seeking.[34] However, the central charge against monopolies and restraints of trade was that they impair the economic liberty and opportunities of other independent tradesmen and workmen to exercise their profession. It was argued that monopolies and restraints of trade allow a minority faction (e.g., a guild) to reserve an entire trade to its members. As a result, all other independent tradesmen and workmen are shut out of the market and prevented from becoming economically active by engaging in lawful trade. As a result, they are condemned to 'idleness' and unemployment.[35] This liberty-based critique of restrictions of competition is most succinctly articulated in the *Ipswich Tailors'* case, where it was held that 'the common law abhors all monopolies, which prohibit any from working in any lawful trade'.[36] Monopolies and restraints of trade were declared to be 'against the liberty and freedom of the subject [because they] are a means . . . of oppression of young tradesmen, by the old and rich of the same trade, not permitting them to work in their trade freely; and all this is against the common law, and the commonwealth'.[37]

What stands out in this early common law critique of monopoly power and restraints of trade is that it does not refer to the individual economic liberty or freedom of market participants *tout court*. Instead, it casts monopoly and restraints of trade as being in violation of 'the liberty and freedom of the subject'.[38] Hence, monopoly power and restraints of trade were not only considered as a grievance that individuals suffered exclusively in the economic sphere but also had a profound political connotation because they deprived individuals of their liberty and status as

30 Nachbar (n 2) 1344–54.

31 1623 c. 3, s. 1.

32 Ibid. s. 9.

33 Ibid. s. 5.

34 *Davenant v Hurdis* [1599] (n 18) 772; Letwin (n 18) 25; *Darcy v Allein ('The Case of Monopolies')* [1602] (n 3) 1262–63; *Ipswich Tailors' Case* [1614] (n 17) 1220.

35 *Darcy v Allein ('The Case of Monopolies')* [1602] (n 3) 1262–63; *Ipswich Tailors' Case* [1614] (n 17) 1219–20; Letwin (n 18) 25, 28–29; *Colgate v Bacheler* [1569] (n 17) 1097; E Coke, *The Third Part of the Institutes of the Laws of England: Concerning High Treason, and Other Please of the Crown and Criminall Causes* (London: By M. Flesher for W. Lee and D. Pakeman 1644) Chapter 85, p. 180; *Davenant v Hurdis* [1599] (n 18) 770–72.

36 *Ipswich Tailors' Case* [1614] (n 17) 1219.

37 Ibid. 1221.

38 Ibid. 1220; *Darcy v Allein ('The Case of Monopolies')* [1602] (n 3) 1263. The Queen's Bench also cited in *Darcy v Allein* in support of the conclusion that monopoly is against the 'liberty of the subjects' *Davenant v Hurdis* [1599] (n 18).

'freemen'[39] that they were entitled to qua their belonging to a polity or 'body politic'.[40] This explains why monopoly and restraints of trade were not only condemned as an encroachment of liberty that violates the common law but one that goes against the 'common good'[41] or 'commonweal(th)'.[42]

Nowhere does this profoundly political dimension of economic liberty become clearer than in the writings of Sir Edward Coke, who was one of the most eminent common lawyers and vocal critics of monopoly power of his time.[43] Since there was little support for the illegality of monopolies in common law precedent, Coke ventured the – unsubstantiated and contested[44] – claim that the unlawfulness of monopolies and restraints of trade dates back to (Articles 29 and 30 of) the *Magna Carta* of 1215.[45] In suggesting that they can be directly derived from the first constitutional charter of modern history, Coke contended that economic liberty and freedom of trade are an integral part of the fundamental freedoms and rights to equal justice that individuals are bestowed with by virtue of their status as citizens of the commonwealth and which 'cannot be restrained but by Parliament'.[46]

In sum, the prohibition of monopoly in *Darcy v Allein* and the 1623 Statute of Monopolies also stood for the increasingly affirmative stance of parliamentary and republican forces in a broader constitutional conflict between the English Crown and the Parliament over the prerogative to regulate the economy. The growing opposition to restraints of trade and monopoly was an expression of a broader societal and political struggle for greater civil liberty and equality, which paved the way towards a more republican and democratic form of government and society.

1.2.3 *The English Levellers*

Even though the 1623 Statute of Monopolies broadly outlawed monopolies, it did anything but eradicate all forms of concentrated economic power and restrictions of competition. The exceptions provided in the Statute of Monopolies offered plenty of loopholes to the prohibition of monopoly and restraints of trade. Over the course of the seventeenth century, the judiciary also gradually endorsed a more forbearing

39 '[F]or being freemen, it is free for them to exercise their trade in any place.' *Colgate v Bacheler* [1569] (n 17) 1097.

40 Sacks (n 21) 86, 93–95.

41 *Davenant v Hurdis* [1599] (n 18) 772.

42 *Colgate v Bacheler* [1569] (n 17) 1097; *Darcy v Allein ('The Case of Monopolies')* [1602] (n 3) 1263; *Ipswich Tailors' Case* [1614] (n 17) 1220; Townshend (n 22) 233.

43 The early common law cases against monopoly were reported by Coke who was involved as Attorney General in *Davenant v Hurdis* and *Darcy v Allein*. Note, that Coke pleaded in *Darcy v Allein* on behalf of the Crown in defence of the monopoly right granted, although he later noted that he was not convinced by this case.

44 DO Wagner, 'Coke and the Rise of Economic Liberalism' (1935) 6(1) *The Economic History Review* 30, 32, 39–40.

45 Coke (n 35) Chapter 85, pp. 180–81; *Mitchel v Reynolds* [1711] 24 ER 347 348, 349–50.

46 Coke (n 35) Chapter 85, p. 180.

approach towards monopolies, combinations, and restrictive covenants. Instances of concentrated economic power continued to thrive. Consequently, the critique of monopoly and restraints of trade did not abate. Monopoly, privileges, and concentrated economic power continued to be a central element of the struggle between republican and monarchist forces, which culminated in the English civil wars (1642–51).

In the run up to and during the English civil wars, it was notably the radical social and political English Levellers movement that led the charge against concentrated economic power and restrictive trade practices. The Levellers were fierce opponents of the political oppression by the English Crown, and eloquent advocates of republican and democratic constitutional reforms.[47] Not only did the Levellers take issue with political despotism and privileges but they also railed against other social and economic forms of domination and subordination. The Levellers movement, therefore, also took aim at economic privileges, monopolies, patents, and other restraints of trade.[48] Echoing the common law critique of concentrated economic power, the Levellers decried monopoly and restraints of trade as private manifestations of arbitrary and unaccountable power.[49] The Levellers considered that private forms of arbitrary power or 'private government'[50] constituted, to the same extent as arbitrary public power, a source of 'oppression'[51] that was incompatible with a society of free and equals.[52]

The Levellers also heralded the propensity of competitive markets to enhance economic and civil freedoms. In their view, the advent of competitive markets bore an emancipatory and empowering promise. By securing the freedom and right of every citizen to pursue a lawful profession and trade, competitive markets unlocked broad-based economic opportunities. The expansion of competitive markets carried

47 E Anderson, 'Liberty, Equality and Private Government' in M Matheson (ed), *The Tanner Lectures on Human Values* (Cambridge: Cambridge University Press 2016) 63, 67; C Hill, *The World Turned Upside Down: Radical Ideas during the English Revolution* [1972] (London: Penguin 2020) Chapter 7.

48 Anderson (n 47) 68; W Walwyn, 'Gold Tried in the Fire [1647]' in A Sharp (ed), *The English Levellers* (Cambridge: Cambridge University Press 2004) 73, 76, 78–79; R Overton and W Walwyn, 'A Remonstrance of Many Thousand Citizens [1646]' in A Sharp (ed), *The English Levellers* (Cambridge: Cambridge University Press 2004) 33, 46; R Overton, 'An Arrow against All Tyrants [1646]' in A Sharp (ed), *The English Levellers* (Cambridge: Cambridge University Press 2004) 54, 62; J Lilburne, 'England's New Chains Discovered [1649]' in A Sharp (ed), *The English Levellers* (Cambridge: Cambridge University Press 2004) 140, 144; J Lilburne and others, 'The Petition of 11 September 1648 [1648]' in A Sharp (ed), *The English Levellers* (Cambridge: Cambridge University Press 2004) 131, 136–37.

49 Anderson (n 47) 72–73.

50 Ibid. 66.

51 Overton and Walwyn (n 48) 46. For the criticism of the 'oppressive monopoly' as a 'great abridgement of the liberties of the people', see also Walwyn (n 48) 79; Lilburne and others (n 48) 136; Lilburne (n 48) 144.

52 Anderson (n 47) 67–68.

the promising prospect of enabling an ever-growing number of individuals to secure their livelihoods, emancipate themselves, and gain personal independence from social and economic domination.[53] In enhancing economic freedom, competitive markets opened up and 'democratised' for large parts of the population so far unknown opportunities to become 'self-employed, independent, masterless men'.[54] This account of the emancipatory features of the nascent market society suggests that the Levellers were amongst the first to advocate competitive markets as 'institutional components of a free society of equals'.[55] In their view, the abolition of monopolies and restraints of trade, and the promotion of free competitive markets were important prerequisites for a transition towards a more democratic, republican form of government and society.

1.2.4 *Early Liberal Political Theorists and Economists: Montesquieu, Steuart, and Smith*

The centrality of the relationship between monopoly, competition, and economic liberty in the struggle for greater political and societal emancipation spearheaded by early liberal movements of the sixteenth and seventeenth centuries had its first systematic reception in the writings of political and economic thinkers of the eighteenth century. These political economists and theorists built on the proposition – which was coined by early liberal critics of monopoly power – that economic liberty determines the status of individuals as independent and equal citizens within a polity to postulate a systemic interdependence between the economic and political order.

One of the first prominent attempts to theorise the relationship between the economic and political order can be found in Montesquieu's *The Spirit of the Laws* (1748). In particular, Montesquieu posited that there is a direct link between the specific form of the political constitution and the type of commerce prevailing in a given economy.[56] More precisely, Montesquieu suggested that the republican form of government is closely entwined with a specific type of frugal or economic commerce. Montesquieu's concept of economic commerce already conveys a rudimentary notion of competitive markets. The distinctive feature of economic commerce lies in the fact that individual traders gain moderate profits because their competitive interaction keeps their rents in check.[57] This economic commerce is, as Howse observes, 'in its origin, the commerce of the impoverished, the powerless,

[53] Ibid. 68.

[54] Ibid. 72.

[55] Ibid. 67–68.

[56] 'Le commerce a du rapport avec la constitution.' Montesquieu, Charles-Louis de Secondat, *De l'esprit des lois* [1748] (Paris: Garnier-Flammarion 1979) Book XX, Chapter IV.

[57] Ibid. Book XX, Chapter III.

and the oppressed'.[58] Montesquieu contrasted this economic or frugal commerce with luxury commerce, which is characterized by high rents and serves, in the first place, the interests of the political elite.[59] While economic commerce is congenial with a republican form of government, luxury commerce is usually found in monarchical and despotic polities.[60]

Repeatedly referring to England as the country where economic liberty and a republican form of government are the most advanced,[61] Montesquieu asserted that nascent competitive markets and a republican form of government mutually depend on one another. This complementarity between economic commerce and a republican form of government has two dimensions. On the one hand, Montesquieu observed how the increasing involvement of the English nobility in commerce weakened and diffused the power of the English monarchy and set in motion its transition towards a more republican form of government.[62] Montesquieu thus alluded to the propensity of the centrifugal forces of competitive markets to diffuse political power and to level social hierarchies. On the other hand, Montesquieu also highlighted how the expansion of economic commerce paved the way towards a more egalitarian and republican form of government by affording all citizens with economic freedoms and opportunities to become economically active. Consequently, competitive markets bring about and maintain a certain equality of status and wealth between citizens, which characterises and is indispensable for a republican or democratic form of government.[63] *The Spirit of the Laws* also echoed some of the grievances against monopolies and restraints of trade that had previously been aired by common lawyers and the Levellers. Montesquieu associated laws that prevent citizens from choosing and freely taking up a profession with despotism.[64] Likewise, he contrasted exclusive rights and monopolies with the equality that governs the relationship between merchants[65] and likened them with monarchy, despotism, and oligarchy.[66]

Montesquieu's claim of a systematic link between the proliferation of competitive markets and the emergence of republican or democratic societies and polities resurfaced a few years later in an even more prominent form in the writings of James Steuart, who is the author of one of the earliest works in political economy

58 R Howse, 'Montesquieu on Commerce, Conquest, War and Peace' (2006) 31(3) *Brooklyn Journal of International Law* 693, 702.

59 Ibid.

60 Montesquieu (n 56) Book XX, Chapter IV; C Spector, 'Commerce' in C Volpilhac-Auger (ed), *Dictionnaire Montesquieu* (2013) § 15; Howse (n 58) 702–03.

61 Montesquieu (n 56) Book XX, Chapters XII–XIV, XXI; Spector (n 60) § 17.

62 Montesquieu (n 56) Book XX, Chapter XXI; R Douglass, 'Montesquieu and Modern Republicanism' (2012) 60(3) *Political Studies* 703, 707, 712.

63 Montesquieu (n 56) Book V, Chapter VI, see also IV and V.

64 Ibid. Book XX, Chapter XXII.

65 Ibid. Book V, Chapter VIII.

66 Ibid. Book V, Chapter VIII; Book XX, Chapters XVIII–XXI.

and was an early member of the Scottish Enlightenment.[67] Assuming that there is a direct link between the degrees of economic dependence, social subordination, and the political form of government,[68] Steuart asserted that competitive markets are more likely to lead to a republican government than feudal or mercantilist economic orders.[69] He sustained this claim by describing how nascent competitive markets tore down the patterns of economic dependence and social subordination that characterised the feudal economic and social order. By levelling these structures of economic dependence and arbitrary domination, competitive markets lead to an equal subordination of all members of society to general laws, which ensure equal freedom.[70] Competition thus ultimately paves the way toward a republican or democratic political order and society because it promotes a more equal distribution of wealth and political power.[71] On this account, Steuart postulated that the emergence of competitive markets promotes an 'extension of public liberty, by extinguishing every subordination, other than that due to established laws'.[72]

Seven years after Steuart published *An Inquiry into the Principles of Political Oeconomoy*, yet without mentioning Steuart's work, Adam Smith provided a very similar account of the levelling impact of the advent of competitive markets on social and economic hierarchies and structures of subjugation. In his seminal *Wealth of Nations* (1776), Smith celebrates the ushering in of competitive markets as a 'great revolution'[73] that dismantled the social order of feudalism. Smith thereby contrasts the liberty-enhancing and equalising dynamics of nascent competitive markets with the feudal society that was characterised by economic subordination and dependence of lower classes to a feudal elite.[74] Smith paints a bleak picture of the feudal system under which most of the population lived in 'servile dependency',[75] a 'state of war',[76] and 'subordination'[77] under the arbitrary rule and domination of the feudal lords.[78] The emergence of competitive markets gradually unravelled these structures of social subordination and domination by diminishing the economic dependence of the lower classes upon the feudal seigniors. By transforming relationships of economic dependence into more equalised forms

67 P Rosanvallon, *Le libéralisme économique: Histoire de l'idée de marché* (Paris: Seuil 1989) 48.
68 J Steuart, *An Inquiry into the Principles of Political Oeconomy: Being An Essay on the Science of Domestic Policy in Free Nations* (London: A. Millar and T. Cadell 1768) Book II, Chapter XIII, pp. 238–39; Rosanvallon (n 67) 48–49.
69 Steuart (n 68).
70 Ibid. Book II, Chapter XIII, pp. 237 and 242; Montesquieu (n 56) Book XX, Chapter xxi.
71 Steuart (n 68) Book II, Chapter XIII, p. 245.
72 Ibid. Book II, Chapter XIII, p. 248.
73 A Smith, *An Inquiry into the Nature and Causes of the Wealth of Nations* [1776] (Oxford: Oxford University Press 1976) III, iv, § 17, p. 422.
74 Steuart (n 68) Book II, Chapter XIII, pp. 240, 245; Smith (n 73) III, iii–iv.
75 Smith (n 73) III, iv, § 4, p. 412.
76 Ibid.
77 Ibid. III, iv, § 9, pp. 417–18.
78 Ibid. III, iv, §§ 4–11, pp. 412–20.

of economic exchanges, the advent of competitive markets thus promoted the emancipation and empowerment of the lower classes.[79]

These levelling dynamics of nascent competitive markets were not only felt in the realm of the economy. Smith also gives credit to the political power struggles and emancipation that went hand-in-hand with the rise of competitive markets and set in motion a gradual transition towards a more republican society. By eroding relationships of economic dependence, the emerging competitive markets also incrementally tore down structures of social and political subordination. Adam Smith colourfully described how, with the advent of competitive markets, the feudal seigniors started to lose their 'whole power and authority' over the people by trading with more productive classes.[80] With the rise of independent tradesmen, the 'great proprietors were no longer capable of interrupting the regular execution of justice, or disturbing the peace of the country'.[81] As a consequence, '[a] regular government was established in the country as well as in the city, nobody having sufficient power to disturb its operations in the one, any more than in the other'.[82] Adam Smith underscored the importance of these broader political and societal implications of the rise of competitive markets, observing that

> [c]ommerce and manufactures gradually introduced order and good government, and with them, the liberty and security of individuals, among the inhabitants of the country, who had before lived almost in a continual state of war with their neighbours, and of servile dependency upon their superiors. This, though it has been the least observed, is by far the most important of all their effects.[83]

It is against the backdrop of this political dimension of the emergence of competitive markets that Smith developed one of the most prominent critiques of concentrated economic power. In a similar way as other critics of monopoly power before him, Smith highlighted not only the adverse effects of monopoly and restraints of trade on prices and consumers[84] but also portrayed them as undue obstacles to individual economic liberty that deny the least affluent members of society the opportunity to become economically active and sustain their livelihoods.[85] Smith did not confine himself to criticise monopolies and other restraints of competition merely on account of their adverse impact on prices and unfair exploitative effects.[86] He rather condemned them more broadly as an outright attack

79 Ibid. III, iv, § 11–12, pp. 419–20. For a similar argument, see Steuart (n 68) Book II, Chapter XIII, pp. 238–40.

80 Smith (n 73) III, iv, § 10, pp. 418–19.

81 Ibid. III, iv, § 15, p. 421.

82 Ibid.

83 Ibid. III, iv, § 4, p. 412.

84 Ibid. I, viii, §§ 26–29, pp. 78–79; I, xi, b, § 5, p. 163; IV, vii, c, § 49, p. 608; IV, viii, §§ 17 and 24, pp. 647, 651; V, i, e, § 30, pp. 754–55.

85 Ibid. I, viii, § 28, p. 78; I, x, c, §§ 1–5, 12, 22, 57, pp. 135–38, 142–43, 157; IV, vii, c, § 91, p. 613.

86 Ibid. V, i, e, § 30, pp. 754–55.

against the general interest or the public at large[87] because they sacrifice the interests of consumers and other market participants for the pursuit of the self-interested goals and rents of a privileged minority.[88] From this perspective, cartels and monopolies amount to private government, as they allow producers to impose their particular, idiosyncratic interests upon other market participants and the rest of society.[89]

Smith's *Wealth of Nations* most prominently pictures and distils the recurrent theme in early liberal political, economic, and legal thought that competitive markets are conducive while monopolies are antithetical to a freer, more egalitarian republican society and form of government. Starting with Thomas More, the antimonopolistic turn of the late sixteenth- and early seventeenth-century common law, and the English Levellers movement, monopoly, oligopoly and restraints of trade were consistently characterised as undue encroachments on economic opportunities and liberty. This obstruction of economic liberty had a profoundly political dimension because it deprived individuals of their rights, liberties, and status as independent freemen to which they were entitled by virtue of their being members of the political community of the commonwealth. Montesquieu, Steuart, and Smith harnessed this idea to provide a more systematic account of the economic, societal, and political ramifications of the advent of a market society. Their accounts portray the rise of competitive markets as the driving force behind the transition from the feudal to a more liberal, republican, and democratic society and government. The idea of a competition–democracy nexus was formed against the backdrop of this 'great revolution'[90] spearheaded by More, the antimonopoly common lawyers, and the Levellers, and recounted by political and economic writers such as Montesquieu, Steuart, and Smith.

1.3 COMPETITION–DEMOCRACY NEXUS 2.0: THE MAKING OF US ANTITRUST LAW

1.3.1 *The Historical, Economic, and Political Background*

The idea coined by the early liberal thinkers that the emergence of competitive markets promotes economic and political liberties, and drives forward the transition towards a more republican or democratic form of government was the product of a pre-industrialised vision of society and economy. This vision came increasingly under stress towards the end of the nineteenth century. Technological innovation and the Industrial Revolution changed the face of Western economies and societies. Widespread progress in industrialisation and mechanisation unleashed economies

87 Ibid. I, x, c, § 27, p. 145.
88 Ibid. IV, vii, § 50, p. 661.
89 Rosanvallon (n 67) 78–79.
90 Smith (n 73) III, iv, § 17, p. 422.

of scale and network effects that enabled the organisation of production processes within ever larger economic entities.[91] The ensuing rise of large-scale corporations increasingly shook up the atomistic, pre-industrialised structure of competitive markets that was celebrated by early liberal thinkers as the catalyst for the emergence of a republican society of free and equals.

The socioeconomic challenges that were posed by the Industrial Revolution and soaring industry concentration moved centre stage in the United States towards the end of the nineteenth century. In the aftermath of the American Civil War (1861–65), the United States experienced a new wave of rampant industrialisation, mechanisation, and technological innovation, which ushered in a profound structural transformation of the US economy and society. The epitome of this transformation was the emergence and consolidation of new forms of large-scale firms. The 'centripetal attraction' of the new corporate system led to an ever-increasing aggregation of wealth and economic power in the 'hands of fewer and fewer men'.[92] The ascent of large-scale firms and industrial behemoths gradually unravelled the economic model that was built on small, locally owned businesses and small holders, which had prevailed in the United States during most of the nineteenth century.[93]

Rising levels of industry concentration and corporate power were not merely the outcome of internal organic growth but were, in many instances, accentuated by industry consolidation through vertical integration, mergers, and more or less institutionalised forms of combinations.[94] To cope with the changing economic conditions and further promote market consolidation,[95] large-scale corporations started to enter various forms of coordination and collusion, ranging from 'loose' gentlemen's agreements to 'tight' combinations, such as 'pools' and 'trusts'.[96] Soon after the creation of the Standard Oil Trust by John D. Rockefeller in 1879, the trust phenomenon began to permeate many important US industries.[97] The term *trust* was soon used as a generic shorthand to refer to all sorts of cartelistic combinations that industry members used to coordinate their business strategies and consolidate their control over an ever-growing number of industries.[98]

The disruptive effects of soaring industry consolidation, compounded by the proliferation of the new trust phenomenon, soon provoked widespread popular discontent. Popular opposition to rising levels of corporate power culminated in

[91] Thorelli (n 7) 64–65.

[92] AA Berle and GC Means, *The Modern Corporation and Private Property* (Piscataway: Transaction Publishers 1932) 18.

[93] Thorelli (n 7) 58–62; PH Brietzke, 'The Constitutionalization of Antitrust: Jefferson, Madison, Hamilton, and Thomas C. Arthur' (1987) 22(2) *Valparaiso University Law Review* 275, 282–83.

[94] Thorelli (n 7) 67–72, 83.

[95] Ibid. 72, 83.

[96] Ibid. 72; Collins (n 7) 2292–334.

[97] Thorelli (n 7) 73, 77–96.

[98] Ibid. 75.

the 1870s and 1880s.[99] Above all, small local businesses and farmers, who depended upon large corporations for both the purchase of their inputs and the sale of their produce, felt increasingly marginalised by the market power and strategies of big corporations and powerful trusts.[100] Small businesses and farmers started to organise themselves into cooperatives. For example, the well-known Granger movement brought together small holders to strengthen their bargaining power in the face of powerful trusts and corporations. The Granger movement and other grassroots antimonopoly movements soon gained traction and gave a political voice to the increasing popular apprehension about the growing industry concentration and trust phenomenon.[101]

1.3.2 *The Legislative History of the Sherman Act*

The enactment of the Sherman Act as the first federal antitrust statute in 1890 constituted a legal and political response to the growing popular discontent over concentrated corporate power.[102] This is well-documented in the legislative history of the Sherman Act. The congressional records abound with instances where the aggregation of economic power in the hands of large-scale corporations and trusts is denounced as a source of a broad range of social 'evils',[103] 'great wrongs',[104] and 'danger' to the people.[105] In the course of the congressional debates, the new industrial behemoths were vilified as 'giants',[106] 'commercial sharks',[107] 'monsters',[108] and 'enemies of the people'.[109]

The growing opposition against industrial concentration that percolates through the legislative history of the Sherman Act went clearly beyond purely economic concerns over the detrimental impact of the new trust phenomenon on consumer and total welfare.[110] On the contrary, the antitrust bill was rooted in much broader

99 EM Fox and LA Sullivan, 'Antitrust-Retrospective and Prospective: Where Are We Coming From? Where Are We Going' (1987) 62(5) *New York University Law Review* 936, 940–41.

100 Thorelli (n 7) 58–60, 67–68, 72–96; T Goebel, 'The Political Economy of American Populism from Jackson to the New Deal' (1997) 11 *Studies in American Political Development* 109, 122–24.

101 Thorelli (n 7) 58–62, 90.

102 TJ Di Lorenzo, 'The Origins of Antitrust: An Interest-Group Perspective' (1985) 5(1) *International Review of Law and Economics* 73.

103 19 Cong Rec 7512 (1890) 7513; 19 Cong Rec 8519 (1888) 8521; 20 Cong Rec 1457 (1890) 1457–58; 20 Cong Rec 2455 (1890) 2456.

104 20 Cong Rec 1765 (1890) 1768.

105 19 Cong Rec 8559 (1890) 8559.

106 20 Cong Rec 2455 (1890) (n 103) 2460.

107 20 Cong Rec 1457 (1890) (n 103) 1457.

108 Ibid.

109 19 Cong Rec 8519 (1888) (n 103) 8520.

110 Historical sources, indeed, cast doubt on Robert Bork's claim that the legislative intent of the Sherman Act was to protect welfare. RH Bork, 'Legislative Intent and the Policy of the Sherman Act' (1966) 9(1) *Journal of Law & Economics* 7; RH Bork, 'The Goals of Antitrust Policy' (1967) 57(2) *The American Economic Review* 242; RH Bork, *The Antitrust Paradox:*

considerations about the adverse economic, social, and political effects of the aggregation of economic power in the hands of a few large-scale corporations and trusts. Many of the objections against concentrated economic power that were uttered during the congressional debate closely mirrored some of the grievances against monopolies and restraints of trade aired by the early proponents of competitive markets in sixteenth- and seventeenth-century England. Like the early liberal proponents of competitive markets, the framers of the Sherman Act spoke out against increasing levels of concentration of economic power as a threat to economic liberty, distributive justice, and equality of opportunity.

The proponents of the Sherman Act pushed the critique of monopoly by early liberal thinkers to a new level. No longer were monopolies and restraints of trade merely perceived as an obstacle to a freer, more egalitarian, and republican society. Rather, concentrated economic power was now depicted as a threat to democracy itself.[111] This 'dialled-up' republican critique of concentrated economic power as a corroding force of democracy is reflective of the way in which the US founding fathers had fused republican ideals and values with the institutional innovations of modern representative democracy.[112] The notions of *republic* and *democracy* were for a long time understood as referring to different forms of government. However, after the creation of the American republic in 1787, both concepts became increasingly congruent 'as the globe's first modern republic became the world's most archetypical liberal democracy'.[113] This convergence of the concepts of *republic* and *democracy* lies at the origin of the modern version of the competition–democracy nexus 2.0, which was first coined by the framers of the Sherman Act.

This modern version of the competition–democracy nexus is habitually traced back to the famous words that Senator Sherman pronounced in support of the proposed antitrust bill:

> If the concentrated powers of this combination are intrusted to a single man, it is a kingly prerogative, inconsistent with our form of government, and should be subject to the strong resistance of the State and national authorities. If anything is wrong this is wrong. If we will not endure a king as a political power we should not endure a king over production, transportation, and sale of any of the necessaries of life.

A *Policy at War with Itself* [1978] (New York: Maxwell Macmillan 1993) 15–71. This has been notably highlighted by R Pitofsky, 'The Political Content of Antitrust' (1979) 127(4) *University of Pennsylvania Law Review* 1051.

111 G Amato, *Antitrust and the Bounds of Power: The Dilemma of Liberal Democracy in the History of the Market* (Oxford: Hart 1997) 2–4; EM Fox, 'The Symbiosis of Democracy and Markets: OECD–Directorate for Financial and Enterprise Affairs Competition Committee–Global Competition Forum–Competition and Democracy' (2017) 3 www.oecd.org; S Weber Waller, 'Antitrust and Democracy' (2019) 46(4) *Florida State University Law Review* 806, 808–09.

112 A Kalyvas and I Katznelson, *Liberal Beginnings: Making a Republic for the Moderns* (Cambridge: Cambridge University Press 2008) Chapter 4.

113 Ibid. 88.

> If we would not submit to an emperor we should not submit to an autocrat of trade, with power to prevent competition and to fix the price of any commodity.[114]

This statement encapsulates the essence of the modern rendition of the idea of a competition–democracy nexus. It asserts that the excessive concentration of economic power might easily degenerate a democratic polity into the 'tyranny' of the few.[115] Senator Sherman concluded that the excessive concentration of private economic power is incompatible with a republican democracy that rejects any form of autocracy and monarchy, be it in the political or economic sphere.

The enactment of the Sherman Act as the first federal antitrust statute was a genuinely political exercise. This political dimension and the relationship between competition and democracy become apparent in the prominence accorded to the values of liberty and equality during the congressional debates. The antitrust bill was first and foremost perceived as a tool to preserve 'free and fair competition'.[116] The idea that the preservation of liberty constitutes a central objective of the Sherman Act was perhaps most clearly articulated by Senator Sherman himself. He suggested that the Sherman Act should not be read as an ordinary piece of statutory legislation but should be interpreted in a similar way to the US Constitution as a 'remedial statute, a bill of rights, a charter of liberty'.[117] The proposed antitrust bill was thus viewed as nothing less than an attempt to 'preserve ... the rights of individuals against associated and corporate wealth and power'.[118]

This view was widely shared amongst Senator Sherman and his fellow Congressmen, who repeatedly likened the role of antitrust rules in preserving economic liberty to that of the US Constitution in protecting political liberty.[119] Just as the political constitution preserves liberty by imposing checks and balances on the power of the state, so does antitrust law safeguard economic liberty by imposing bounds on private economic power to hold it accountable.[120] The proponents of the proposed antitrust legislation thus perceived economic freedom as the corollary of constitutionally protected fundamental rights, civil liberties,[121] and pluralism.[122] To them, the

114 Senator Sherman 20 Cong Rec 2455 (1890) (n 103) 2457–58.

115 R Hofstadter, 'What Happened to the Antitrust Movement' in DA Crane and H Hovenkamp (eds), *The Making of Competition Policy: Legal and Economic Sources* (New York: Oxford University Press 2013) 223, 228.

116 Senator Sherman 20 Cong Rec 2455 (1890) (n 103) 2457; 19 Cong Rec 6041 (1888) 6041.

117 20 Cong Rec 2455 (1890) (n 103) 2461.

118 Senator Sherman Ibid. 2460.

119 T Arnold, 'Fair Fights and Foul: Chapter XIV–The Sherman Act as Charter of Economic Freedom' (1965) 10(5–6) *Antitrust Bulletin* 655, 657.

120 Brietzke (n 93) 290, 292, 299–300.

121 See Senator Sherman's reference to the Supreme Court of the State of Michigan's holding in *Richardson v Buhl* that monopoly is 'destructive of free institutions' and 'contrary to the whole scope and spirit of the Federal Constitution' 20 Cong Rec 2455 (1890) (n 103) 2458; *Richardson v Buhl et al.* 43 NW 1102,77 Mich 632.

122 LB Schwartz, 'Institutional Size and Individual Liberty: Authoritarian Aspects of Bigness' (1960) 55(1) *Northwestern University Law Review* 4, 11–12.

protection of economic liberty formed the economic counterpart to the guarantee of fundamental political freedoms and rights in a liberal republican democracy.[123]

1.3.3 *The Trustbuster Years, Progressive Antitrust Movement, and the Antitrust Revival during the Second World War*

The adoption of the Sherman Act fashioned a modern version of the idea of a competition–democracy nexus. This competition–democracy nexus 2.0 brought the idea of a symbiosis between competitive markets and a republican society that was initially envisaged by early liberal thinkers of the sixteenth to eighteenth centuries up to speed with the novel challenges of an industrialised economy. Its underlying proposition that the concentration of economic power in the hands of a few large-scale corporations undermined economic liberty and, thereby posed a danger to democracy itself became a central topos of US antitrust thought. Various iterations of the competition–democracy nexus 2.0 periodically surfaced and shaped the normative self-understanding of US antitrust law and policy until the early-1970s.

The quasi-constitutional role of antitrust law in curtailing private power became deeply ingrained in the democratic creed of the American republic. For example, President Theodore Roosevelt marshalled the notion of antitrust statutes as the 'Magna Carta of free enterprise'[124] and safeguard of 'equality of opportunity'[125] in support of his policy of 'trust-busting'. A few years later, during the 1912 presidential campaign, presidential candidate Woodrow Wilson and his economic advisor and later Supreme Court Justice Louis Brandeis put the adverse sociopolitical effects of concentrated economic power at the heart of Wilson's 'New Freedom'[126] programme. Confronted with the failure of relaxed antitrust enforcement to curb a new wave of merger-driven consolidation during the early 1900s, the progressive antitrust movement championed by Brandeis and Wilson ardently contested the widely shared position that industrial 'size is not a crime'.[127] It also challenged Roosevelt's view that antitrust policy should confine itself to addressing anticompetitive conduct and only tackle *bad* while tolerating *good* monopoly power.[128] Instead,

[123] TW Arnold, 'The Bottlenecks of Business [1940]' in DA Crane and H Hovenkamp (eds), *The Making of Competition Policy: Legal and Economic Sources* (New York: Oxford University Press 2013) 206, 209; Brietzke (n 93) 294; Fox and Sullivan (n 99) 936; Hofstadter (n 115) 233.

[124] Brietzke (n 93) 295.

[125] T Roosevelt, 'New Nationalism Speech [1910]' (15 September 2019) https://teachingamericanhistory.org; T Roosevelt, 'The Trusts, the People, and the Square Deal' in DA Crane and H Hovenkamp (eds), *The Making of Competition Policy: Legal and Economic Sources* (New York: Oxford University Press 2013) 107, 113–15.

[126] W Wilson, *The New Freedom* (Leipzig: Tauchnitz 1913).

[127] LD Brandeis, *Other People's Money and How the Bankers Use It* (New York: Frederick A. Stokes Company 1914) 163.

[128] Wilson (n 126) 182–95.

the progressive antitrust movement asserted that the very existence of concentrated economic power went against the basic principle of separation of powers that lies at the core of the US constitutional order and democracy.[129] Consequently, Wilson and Brandeis campaigned for a more vigorous antitrust enforcement that would directly take on the power of big business through separation[130] and decentralisation.[131]

Following the decline of competition policy during the New Deal era, the concern about the adverse impact of economic concentration on democracy re-emerged and instilled new momentum into antitrust enforcement in the years during and in the direct aftermath of the Second World War. This renewed hostility against bigness was fuelled by the widely shared view that the high degree of concentration and cartelisation of the European and, in particular, of the German economy had enabled the rise of fascism and totalitarianism in Europe.[132] Leading politicians[133] and antitrust enforcers, such as Assistant Attorney General Thurman Arnold,[134] perceived the shift towards centrally planned economies and the upsurge of fascist totalitarianism in Germany and other parts of Europe as the 'inevitable result of the destruction of competitive domestic markets by private combinations, cartels and trade associations'.[135] Along similar lines, President Franklin D. Roosevelt warned about the dangers of concentrated private power for liberty and democracy in the light of the success of fascism and totalitarianism in Germany and Japan. In 1938, he told Congress:

> Unhappy events abroad have retaught us two simple truths about the liberty of a democratic people. The first truth is that the liberty of a democracy is not safe if the people tolerate the growth of private power to a point where it becomes stronger than their democratic state itself. That, in its essence, is Fascism – ownership of Government by an individual, by a group, or by any other controlling private power.[136]

129 Brandeis (n 127) 6.

130 Ibid. 161.

131 Ibid. 188.

132 Arnold (n 123) 211–13; ME Stucke, 'Reconsidering Antitrust's Goals' (2012) 53(2) *Boston College Law Review* 551, 559.

133 The co-sponsor of the 1936 Robinson-Patman, Representative Wright Patman commissioned and directed a study which documented the role of big business and industry concentration in the rise of fascism in Germany and other parts of Europe. Legislative Reference Service of the Library of Congress, 'Fascism in Action: A Documented Study and Analysis of Fascism in Europe Prepared at the Instance and under the Direction of Representative Wright Patman of Texas by Legislative Reference Service of the Library of Congress under the Direction of Ernest S. Griffith' (1947) 88 onwards.

134 For the primordial role of Thurman Arnold in reviving antitrust policy after the New Deal era, see Hofstadter (n 115) 225; S Weber Waller, 'The Antitrust Legacy of Thurman Arnold' (2004) 78(3) *St. John's Law Review* 569, 569–94.

135 Arnold, 'The Bottlenecks of Business' (n 123) 211.

136 FD Roosevelt, 'Message to Congress on Curbing Monopolies [1938]' www.presidency.ucsb.edu.

Throughout the war, the involvement of cartels and big business in the rise of totalitarianism in Germany was closely followed in the United States. German emigrants such as Heinrich Kronstein,[137] who joined the US Department of Justice Antitrust Division, and Franz Neumann, who worked with various US government agencies during the war, were amongst the first to document in English the various ways in which big business and cartels contributed to the economic system and war machinery of the National Socialist regime.[138]

The growing awareness of the link between cartelisation and fascism forged a renewed political and societal consensus in support of antitrust law and gave a new impetus to antitrust enforcement.[139] During the war, the Department of Justice Antitrust Division stepped up its efforts to prosecute American enterprises that participated in international cartels. In particular, it went after US firms that had cooperated with German cartels and corporations, such as IG Farben, Krupp, AEG-Osram, or Zeiss.[140] The role of conglomerates and cartels in the rise of fascism in Germany and Japan also informed the Allies' policy to promote the decartelisation and deconcentration of the German and Japanese economies in the immediate aftermath of the Second World War. The American government saw the introduction of competition laws as an essential element of the democratisation of Germany and Japan after the fall of fascism.[141]

The perceived link between industry concentration and fascism remained a prominent theme in US antitrust law during the post-war years. Most prominently, it left its imprint on the congressional debates surrounding the reform of US merger law, § 7 of the Clayton Act, by the Celler–Kefauver amendment in 1950. The co-sponsor of the amendment, Senator Celler, argued that the role of merger policy is 'to preserve a society of small, independent, decentralised business in order to

[137] DJ Gerber, 'Heinrich Kronstein and the Development of United States Antitrust Law' in Lutter and others (eds), *Der Einfluss deutscher Emigranten auf die Rechtsentwicklung in den USA und in Deutschland* (Tübingen: Mohr Siebeck 1993) 155.

[138] WC Wells, *Antitrust and the Formation of the Postwar World* (New York: Columbia University Press 2002) 55–56; F Neumann, *Behemoth: The Structure and Practice of National Socialism, 1933–1944* [1942] (New York: Octagon 1963); RA Brady, *The Spirit and Structure of German Fascism* [1937] (New York: Citadel Press 1971).

[139] Arnold (n 119) 664–65.

[140] Wells (n 138) 17–26, 44–52.

[141] DJ Gerber, *Law and Competition in Twentieth Century Europe: Protecting Prometheus* (Oxford/New York: Clarendon Press/Oxford University Press 1998) 268–70; S Vande Walle, 'Competition and Competition Law in Japan: Between Scepticism and Embrace' in MW Dowdle, J Gillespie and Maher Imelda (eds), *Asian Capitalism and the Regulation of Competition: Towards a Regulatory Geography of Global Competition Law* (Cambridge: Cambridge University Press 2013) 123, 123–26; The Berlin Conference of the Three Heads of Government of the U.S.S.R. U.S.A. and U.K. 'Potsdam Agreement Protocol of the Proceedings, August l, 1945' (1945) Point 12. For further discussion, see Section 1.4.4.

disperse economic and political power and to assure that a Hitler could never rise to power in the United States'.[142]

1.3.4 *The Post-war Consensus*

The idea of a competition–democracy nexus continued to mould the thinking of various antitrust paradigms during the first *post-bellum* decades. The view that antitrust law had a role to play in preserving democracy against the adverse effects of concentrated private power was an important tenet of the Harvard School of thought, which shaped the economic and legal thinking of antitrust enforcers and courts during the 1950s and 1960s. While it highlighted the importance of efficiency[143] and innovation[144] as economic goals of antitrust policy, the Harvard School perceived the protection of the competitive process as the central mission of antitrust law.[145] This goal of preserving the competitive process was directly entwined with sociopolitical concerns over the excessive concentration of economic power. Harvard scholars affirmed that '[c]ompetition as an end in itself draws its justification from the desirability of limiting business power'.[146] They also linked this concern about concentrated power with democracy, pointing out that in a 'democratic, egalitarian society large areas of uncontrolled private power are not tolerated'.[147] Thus, the Harvard School considered the limitation of the power of big business and its redistribution amongst smaller firms as a distinct goal of antitrust law.[148] In recognising the role of antitrust law in preserving and furthering a 'desirable distribution of social power among business units',[149] the Harvard School remained mindful of the Jeffersonian tradition,[150] which assumes that the 'political and social power of the independent proprietor is the foundation of democracy'.[151]

[142] Quotation of Representative Celler in EM Fox, 'Modernization of Antitrust: A New Equilibrium' (1980) 66(6) *Cornell Law Review* 1140, 1151.

[143] Kaysen and Turner refer in particular to allocative efficiency as a 'distributive or relational concept, which embraces the whole economy' and productive efficiency of 'individual industries and firms'. C Kaysen and DF Turner, *Antitrust Policy: An Economic and Legal Analysis* (Cambridge, MA: Harvard University Press 1959) 12.

[144] Ibid. 12–13. On the importance of economic goals, see also The Attorney General's National Committee to Study the Antitrust Laws, 1955 *Report* (Washington: Superintendent of Documents, U.S. Government Printing Office 1955) 323.

[145] Kaysen and Turner (n 143) 14. Mason pointed out that this deontological notion of competition as an end in itself is rooted in political, as opposed to economic grounds. ES Mason, 'The Current Status of the Monopoly Problem in the United States' (1949) 62(8) *Harvard Law Review* 1265, 1266–67 and fn. 4.

[146] Kaysen and Turner (n 143) 14.

[147] Ibid. 5.

[148] Ibid. 14, 17.

[149] Ibid. 17.

[150] Ibid.

[151] Ibid. 17–18.

Unlike previous antitrust paradigms, such as the progressive antitrust movement that was championed by Wilson and Brandeis, the Harvard School accounted for the limitations of the goal of curtailing corporate power. Harvard scholars underscored that the control of concentrated economic power should be subordinate to and could most effectively be pursued under the overarching umbrella goal of preserving the competitive process.[152] Although they assumed that, most of the time, economic goals and the limitation of big business were complementary and pulled in the same direction,[153] the Harvard School acknowledged potential tensions between the various objectives they ascribed to antitrust law. Harvard scholars recognised that, under certain circumstances, the costs of curbing corporate power needed to be balanced against the goal of economic efficiency and performance.[154]

Until the 1960s, the belief that antitrust law contributed to the preservation of democracy by preventing the excessive concentration of private economic power constituted a mainstream position amongst US antitrust policy-makers and experts.[155] This becomes apparent from the 1955 Report by the Attorney General's National Committee to Study Antitrust, which brought together the leading antitrust experts and economists of the time, including future figureheads of the Chicago School, such as George Stigler. Most members of the committee were able to subscribe to the view that antitrust law was 'a distinctive American means for assuring the competitive economy on which our political and social freedom under representative government in part depend'.[156] Some of its members even went as far as maintaining that competition is 'desirable on principle and for its own sake, like political liberty and because political liberty is jeopardized if economic power drifts into relatively few hands'.[157]

Throughout most of the first half of the twentieth century, the idea that competition constitutes a fundamental component of a democratic society and polity became deeply engrained in the normative creed of US antitrust law and US democracy. This may, at least in part, explain why antitrust law was often portrayed as something 'characteristically American'.[158] However, the idea of a competition–democracy nexus was by no means a uniquely American phenomenon but also had a fundamental bearing on the making of competition law in twentieth-century Europe.

[152] Ibid. 44.

[153] Ibid. 45.

[154] Ibid.

[155] TA Freyer, *Antitrust and Global Capitalism, 1930–2004* (Cambridge: Cambridge University Press 2006) 22; Fox (n 142) 1140, 1150; Pitofsky (n 110) 1051, 1063; Arnold (n 123) 209.

[156] The Attorney General's National Committee to Study the Antitrust Laws (n 144) 2. See, however, for a member of the Committee who rejected the idea that there is a 'simple relation between the industrial structure of a society and its political and social pattern' MA Adelman, 'Effective Competition and the Antitrust Laws' (1948) 61(8) *Harvard Law Review* 1289, 1289.

[157] The Attorney General's National Committee to Study the Antitrust Laws (n 144) 2.

[158] Hofstadter (n 115) 227.

1.4 COMPETITION–DEMOCRACY NEXUS 3.0: THE ORDOLIBERAL ORIGINS OF COMPETITION LAW IN EUROPE

1.4.1 *The Historical, Economic, and Political Background*

At around the same time as the US Congress adopted the Sherman Act, European economies and, notably, the German economy also experienced a profound transformation that was propelled by a wave of technological and industrial innovation.[159] In a similar way to the United States, the emergence of large-scale corporations and the ensuing trend towards industry concentration formed the background against which a genuinely European version of a competition–democracy nexus 3.0 emerged in Germany.

The second wave of the Industrial Revolution refashioned the German industrial landscape. It led to the rise of large corporations, particularly in the heavy, electric, chemical, and automobile industries. Bayer (1863), Hoechst (1863), BASF (1865), Bosch (1883), Thyssen (1891), and Benz & Cie and Krupp (1903) are just a few examples of the new industrial powerhouses that were founded in the second half of the nineteenth and the early years of the twentieth centuries. The ensuing wave of industrial consolidation and concentration that was set in motion by the ascent of new large-scale corporations was further reinforced by a growing trend towards cartelisation that tightened its grip over ever larger parts of the German economy.[160] In the same way that large US corporations entered pools and trusts from the 1870s onwards, substantial parts of the German industry also began to form large combines and conglomerates.[161] The cartelisation of the German economy further accelerated with the worldwide economic downturn in the 1920s, when the growing financial burden of the first world-war reparations and war debt plunged the Weimar Republic into a period of deep economic and political instability and turmoil. The number of cartels skyrocketed from 385 in 1905 to 2,500 in 1925.[162] In the period 1925–28, the level of cartelisation in the mining, heavy, chemical, glass, cement and paper industries reached 65 to 90 per cent.[163]

159 Eucken also identifies 1870 as the starting point of the trend towards industry concentration of the German economy. W Eucken, *Grundsätze der Wirtschaftspolitik* (Tübingen: Mohr Siebeck 2004) 31.

160 Eucken, for instance, pointed out that cartelisation was already strong in the coal industry, ibid.

161 The high degree of cartelisation and monopolization of the German economy during the Weimar Republic is confirmed by historical research. H Knortz, *Wirtschaftsgeschichte der Weimarer Republik: Eine Einführung in Ökonomie und Gesellschaft der ersten Deutschen Republik* (Göttingen: Vandenhoeck & Ruprecht 2010) 32–35, 130–32, 193; D Abraham, *The Collapse of the Weimar Republic: Political Economy and Crisis* (New York: Holmes & Meier 1986) 23–24; Cf. T Balderston, *Economics and Politics in the Weimar Republic* (Cambridge: Cambridge University Press 2002) 65–69.

162 M Spoerer and J Steg, *Neue Deutsche Wirtschaftsgeschichte* (München 2013) 56–57; Eucken (n 159) 170, 172; Tooze (n 9) 115, 120.

163 Spoerer and Steg (n 162) 59–61.

While US Congress had enacted the Sherman Act as a firm response to the trust problem in 1890, the German judiciary and legislator failed to rein in the proliferation of cartels and monopolistic firms. Instead, they adopted a permissive attitude towards cartelisation, which took shape in two leading cases handed down in 1890 and 1897 by the German *Reichsgericht*, the highest civil court of the time. In both cases, the court declared cartel agreements permissible and upheld the legality of foreclosure practices by which the cartels disciplined deviant members with a view to maintaining their stability (*Kartellzwang*).[164] During the multiple crises of the Weimar Republic, industry groups and big businesses gained an unprecedented level of economic and political power. This allowed them to exert a growing influence on economic policy and water down measures aimed at curtailing their power.[165] As a consequence, the Cartel Act (*Kartellverordnung*) that was adopted in 1923[166] stopped short of outlawing cartels. It only established a publicity obligation, according to which certain types of cartel agreements had to be publicised. Cartels thus became potentially subject to a public interest review by the state, which could order their dissolution.[167] In the following years, this public interest review was debilitated by the judiciary. Under growing pressure from the business community,[168] the *Reichsgericht* eventually adopted a very narrow interpretation of the scope of the public interest review, thereby effectively shielding all but a few cartels from regulatory scrutiny.[169]

Towards the end of the Weimar Republic, the Brüning government started to actively support the trend towards industry concentration and cartelisation. With the gradual introduction of a centrally planned economy in response to the economic crisis of the late 1920s, consecutive governments promoted the creation and nationalisation of cartels. This policy continued under the National Socialist regime after its rise to power in 1933. Far from curbing the power of big business, the transition towards an increasingly centrally planned economy and the organisation of compulsory cartels by the state led to a further consolidation and cartelisation of already highly concentrated industries.[170] Between 1933 and 1936, 1,200 voluntary and

[164] Eucken (n 159) 306–07; F Böhm, *Freiheit und Ordnung in der Marktwirtschaft* [1971] (Baden-Baden: Nomos 1980) 242–43.

[165] Eucken (n 159) 327: Tooze (n 9) 113.

[166] Kartellverordnung, Verordnung gegen Missbrauch wirtschaftlicher Machtstellungen 3. November.1923, RGBl I, 1067.

[167] F Böhm (ed), *Wettbewerb und Monopolkampf: Eine Untersuchung zur Frage des wirtschaftlichen Kampfrechts und zur Frage der rechtlichen Struktur der geltenden Wirtschaftsordnung* [1942] (Baden-Baden: Nomos 2010) 329; Eucken (n 159) 171–72; E-J Mestmäcker (ed), *Wirtschaft und Verfassung in der Europäischen Union* (Baden-Baden: Nomos 2003) 121–24.

[168] Eucken (n 159) 172.

[169] Ibid.

[170] E-J Mestmäcker, 'The Development of German and European Competition Law with Special Reference to the EU Commission's Article 82 Guidance of 2008' in LF Pace (ed), *European Competition Law: The Impact of the Commission's Guidance on Article 102* (Cheltenham: Edward Elgar 2011) 25, 36; W Eucken, 'Das Problem der wirtschaftlichen Macht' in W Eucken

120 compulsory cartel agreements were concluded.[171] Existing cartels and conglomerates were simply transformed into private administrative bodies and transmission belts for central planning.[172]

The power of large industry leaders and their conglomerates remained largely untouched. On the contrary, their economic and financial clout was increasingly sought after by the Nazi regime to effectively implement more measures of central planning and gain important political and financial support.[173] Following the secret meeting between the representatives of the German *Konzerne* and Hitler on 20 February 1933, described in the Introduction, the German conglomerates developed close ties with the Nazi regime. This ill-fated union between private and public power shaped economic policy throughout the Third Reich.[174] The support of large cartels and conglomerates played a crucial role in the implementation of the centrally planned economic policy and the build-up of the war economy.[175] German conglomerates and cartels evolved into 'an active partner'[176] of the National Socialist regime. Not only did they gain from increased state demand for war-related production and state-funded capital, but they also greatly benefitted from the industrial exploitation and extermination of millions of forced labourers, Jews, and other minorities.[177]

1.4.2 *The Origins of the Ordoliberal Idea of a Competition–Democracy Nexus*

In the same year as the fateful 1933 reunion between the stewards of the German conglomerates and the grandees of the National Socialist Party, the economist Walter Eucken and the lawyers Franz Böhm and Hans Großmann-Doerth started to convene regularly at the University of Freiburg, a mid-sized city located in the Southwest of Germany.[178] The central theme of their discussion was the economic,

and W Oswalt (eds), *Wirtschaftsmacht und Wirtschaftsordnung: Londoner Vorträge zur Wirtschaftspolitik und zwei Beiträge zur Antimonopolpolitik* (Münster: Lit 2001) 9, 16–18.

171 Tooze (n 9) 108.

172 Ibid. 106–14.

173 Ibid. Chapter 4.

174 On the one hand, the Nazi economy relied on existing cartels and conglomerates in the sectors for steel, chemicals, and synthetic fibres. On the other hand, it promoted the massive consolidation of other sectors and implemented state-directed expansion of certain sectors, such as the aircraft industry. For a detailed analysis, see ibid.

175 W Eucken and TW Hutchison, 'On the Theory of the Centrally Administered Economy: An Analysis of the German Experiment. Part II' (1948) 15(59) *Economica* 173, 182–84; Abraham (n 161) 317–24; A Tooze, 'The German National Economy in an Era of Crisis and War, 1917–1945' in HW Smith (ed), *The Oxford Handbook of Modern German History* (Oxford: Oxford University Press 2011) 400, 411; DA Crane, 'Fascism and Monopoly' (2020) 118(7) *Michigan Law Review* 1315.

176 Tooze (n 9) 134.

177 Ibid. Chapter 4; Tooze (n 175) 411, 417; Diarmuid (n 11) 233–84.

178 Aktionskreis Freiburger Schule, 'Die Freiburger Ordoliberale Schule' www.freiburger-schule.de; R Fèvre, *A Political Economy of Power: Ordoliberalism in Context, 1932–1950* (New York: Oxford University Press 2022) 8–9.

social, and political challenges posed by the surge in industry concentration and cartelisation that had held a tight grip on the German economy since the late nineteenth century.[179] These interdisciplinary gatherings gave birth to the influential intellectual paradigm of the so-called Ordoliberal or Freiburg School, and planted the seed of the modern version of a competition–democracy nexus 3.0 in Europe.

The key tenet of Ordoliberalism was that there is a fundamental interdependence between the economic, social, and political order. Ordoliberals thus subscribed to the presupposition – which was first coined by early liberals such as Montesquieu and James Steuart – that the specific form of the economic order has direct implications for the form of the social and political system. On this premise, the Ordoliberals postulated that a capitalist market economy could only function in a way that is consistent with the ideal of a democratic society if it operates within the framework of a legal order that ensures economic freedom. However, in a modern capitalist economy, this ideal of economic liberty is constantly under threat by the excessive concentration of economic power in the hands of the state and of large-scale private corporations. Owing to its tendency to diffuse power, competition was therefore assumed to constitute the only form of economic order that is compatible with the ideal of liberty, democracy, and the rule of law.[180]

Based on this core assumption, the Ordoliberal school of thought – which was subsequently joined by the economists Leonhard Miksch, Alexander Rüstow, Wilhelm Röpke, and the lawyer Ernst-Joachim Mestmäcker[181] – developed a highly integrated[182] intellectual programme that perceived the limitation of private and public economic power as the core mission of competition law. Ordoliberal ideas also influenced the concept of the social market economy (*Soziale Marktwirtschaft*), which was coined by Ludwig Erhard and Alfred Müller-Armack.[183] The model of the social market economy emerged as the leitmotiv of (Western) Germany's economic policy after the Second World War[184]

[179] F Böhm, W Eucken and H Großmann-Doerth, 'Unsere Aufgabe (The Ordoliberal Manifesto) [1936]' in N Goldschmidt (ed), *Grundtexte zur Freiburger Tradition der Ordnungsökonomik* (Tübingen: Mohr Siebeck 2008) 27; Spoerer and Steg (n 162) 56–61.

[180] Preface by Ernst Joachim Mestmäcker in Böhm (ed) (n 167) 5.

[181] For attempts to delineate the Freiburg School, see M Foucault, *Naissance de la biopolitique: Cours au Collège de France, 1978–1979* (Paris: Gallimard; Seuil 2004) 110; F Maier-Rigaud, 'On the Normative Foundations of Competition Law: Efficiency, Political Freedom and the Freedom to Compete' in D Zimmer (ed), *The Goals of Competition Law* (Cheltenham: Edward Elgar 2012) 132.

[182] Gerber (n 141) 255.

[183] The founding father of the Social Market Economy Ludwig Erhard endorsed the Ordoliberal precept that a competitive market economy forms the economic counterpart of a democratic political order: L Erhard, *Wohlstand für alle* [1957] (Köln: Anaconda 2009) 22–23, 199, 206.

[184] Foucault (n 181) 81–133.

and also became a guiding principle of the economic order of the European Union.[185]

Historically, the Ordoliberal paradigm and its core proposition of a competition–democracy nexus emerged in the specific historical context of and in response to the role that the concentration of economic power played in the decline of the democratic institutions of the Weimar Republic and the rise of the totalitarian Nazi regime. For the Ordoliberals, the failure of the leading intellectual paradigms and political forces of the time to rein in the trend towards the concentration of economic power and cartelisation constituted one of the factors that had pushed the Weimar Republic into the abyss of totalitarianism.[186] Yet, attempts to simply reduce Ordoliberalism to a time-bound and outdated 'doomsday theory'[187] are overly simplistic and short-sighted. They ignore that the Ordoliberals developed a much more far-reaching positive vision of how competition promotes democracy that goes beyond and above a mere critique of the inadequate answer of the legal, economic, and political institutions of early twentieth-century Germany to the problem of private economic power.

1.4.3 *Economic Liberty at the Heart of the Ordoliberal Idea of a Competition–Democracy Nexus*

At the heart of the Ordoliberal idea of a competition–democracy nexus lies the conduciveness of competitive markets towards economic liberty. A central reason why the Freiburg School perceived competition as being superior to other forms of economic order was the propensity of competitive markets to bring about greater efficiency, wealth, and innovation.[188] However, the Ordoliberals identified the fact that competition outperforms other forms of economic organisation in preserving the economic freedom of individual market participants as the most important virtue of competitive markets.

[185] Article 3 (3) Treaty of the European Union describes the creation of a 'a highly competitive social market economy' as an important goal of the European Union's internal market. Consolidated version of the Treaty on European Union, [2012] OJ C 326/13.

[186] L Miksch, 'Versuch eines liberalen Programms [1949]' in N Goldschmidt (ed), *Grundtexte zur Freiburger Tradition der Ordnungsökonomik* (Tübingen: Mohr Siebeck 2008) 163, 168; L Miksch, *Wettbewerb als Aufgabe: Grundsätze einer Wettbewerbsordnung* (Godersberg: Verlag Helmut Küpper 1947) 212–17.

[187] AJ Padilla and C Ahlborn, 'From Fairness to Welfare: Implications for the Assessment of Unilateral Conduct under EC Competition Law' in C-D Ehlermann and M Marquis (eds), *European Competition Law Annual 2007: A Reformed Approach to Article 82 EC* (Oxford: Hart 2008) 55, 24.

[188] Böhm (ed) (n 167) 209, 211, 220, 223, 227, 240, 257, 260–62; W Eucken and FW Meyer, 'The Economic Situation in Germany' (1948) 260(1) *Annals of the American Academy of Political and Social Science* 53, 60–62; W Eucken and TW Hutchison, 'On the Theory of the Centrally Administered Economy: An Analysis of the German Experiment. Part I' (1948) 15(58) *Economica* 79, 88–89.

Ordoliberals viewed economic competition primarily as an order of liberty (*Freiheitsordnung*).[189] They underscored that competition ensures the harmonious self-coordination of independent and autonomous individuals through the impersonal price mechanism.[190] The functioning of competitive markets in this respect fundamentally differs from a centrally planned economy, which is based on the subordination of all individuals to a central authority. Competition instead operates as a 'coordination order' (*Koordinationsordnung*)[191] that relies on the price mechanism to coordinate the activities of independent and free individuals pursuing their respective autonomous economic plans.[192]

From an Ordoliberal standpoint, competition enhances economic liberty because it enables autonomous and independent market players to coordinate their economic activities in a way that is aligned with the public interest, yet without the need for an external authority to interfere with their individual choices.[193] To Ordoliberals, the functioning of competition simultaneously presupposes and is constitutive of economic liberty.[194] Owing to its liberty-enhancing virtues, the Ordoliberals considered competition as the central economic institution of their ideal of a society that is governed by private law – the so-called private law society (*Privatrechtsgesellschaft*).[195] In this private law society, the fundamental institutions of private law (i.e., private property, contract, and market exchanges) set the framework and provide the means for decentralised, heterarchical, and autonomous economic planning and coordination of free and equal independent market citizens through competition.[196]

The propensity of competition to promote liberty and to enable a non-hierarchical process to translate individual preferences into social choices was the basis on which the Ordoliberals construed the link between competition and democracy. The Ordoliberals apprehended the competitive process itself as some form of universal suffrage or plebiscite[197] whose outcomes – if not distorted – can be considered as the expression of the '*volonté générale*'.[198] The Ordoliberals claimed

[189] Böhm (n 164) 18, 232.
[190] F Böhm, 'Rule of Law in a Market Economy [1966]' in AT Peacock and H Willgerodt (eds), *Germany's Social Market Economy: Origins and Evolution* (Houndmills: Macmillan 1989) 46, 53–54; Eucken (n 159) 22, 246.
[191] Böhm (n 164) 25; Eucken (n 159) 22, 115.
[192] Eucken (n 159) 87, 163, 245.
[193] For the similarity between the Ordoliberal concept of competition as polycentric process and the Hayekian idea of 'spontaneous orders' see Mestmäcker (ed) (n 167) 35.
[194] Böhm (ed) (n 167) 301–02, 308; Eucken (n 159) 48, 264–79.
[195] For an account of the concept of 'private law society' in English, see Böhm (n 190); S Grundmann, 'The Concept of the Private Law Society: After 50 Years of European and European Business Law' (2008) 16(4) *European Review of Private Law* 553.
[196] Mestmäcker Preface to Böhm (ed) (n 167) 8–9; Eucken (n 159) 270–80; Böhm (n 164) 228.
[197] Miksch (n 186) 215; Böhm (n 164) 305; Eucken (n 159) 163, 244–46, 248–50.
[198] F Böhm, 'Democracy and Economic Power in Cartel and Monopoly in Modern Law [1961]' in DA Crane and H Hovenkamp (eds), *The Making of Competition Policy: Legal and Economic Sources* (New York: Oxford University Press 2013) 264, 268.

that competition could be described as 'from a technical point of view the most ideal existing manifestation of democracy'.[199] On account of these procedural similarities between competition and democracy, Ordoliberal thinkers – in a similar vein as the US proponents of a competition–democracy nexus – frequently equated economic freedom with other political rights, such as the freedom of speech or the freedom of assembly.[200] Ordoliberals went as far as likening consumer choice in a competitive market economy to the citizen's right to vote in a democracy.[201]

The Ordoliberals were adamant that competitive markets only benefit from this quasi-democratic legitimacy and contribute to a democratic society and polity for as long as the liberty of consumers and competitors is not obstructed by the excessive concentration and arbitrary exercise of private and public economic power.[202] For markets to operate in a way that ensures the economic liberty of market players, competition law needs to guarantee what Ordoliberals called performance-based competition (*Leistungswettbewerb*).[203] This concept of performance-based competition perceives competition as a rule-based process, where market participants may only outcompete each other by attracting consumer demand by offering better and more attractive products or services. In contrast, market participants are barred from engaging in hindrance competition (*Behinderungswettbewerb*),[204] where they use their market power to prevent other market participants from competing on equal terms or to foreclose them from the market.

For Ordoliberals, the central mission for competition law is to prevent hindrance competition resulting from the excessive concentration and abuse of individual or collective economic power by a single or a coalition of powerful firms. Only by keeping economic power in check could a society preserve the symbiotic relationship between competition and democracy, and guarantee competitive markets as an economic prerequisite for a democratic polity. Therefore, the need to prevent the emergence of instances of excessively concentrated economic power and its abuse constituted a central tenet of the Ordoliberal idea of a competition–democracy nexus and the social market economy.[205]

199 Böhm (n 164) 89.

200 Böhm (ed) (n 167) 298, 32; F Böhm, 'Die Bedeutung der Wirtschaftsordnung für die politische Verfassung: Kritische Betrachtungen zu dem Aufsatz von Ministerialrat Dr. Adolf ARNDT über das "Problem der Wirtschaftsdemokratie in den Verfassungsentwürfen"' (1946) 1(6) *Süddeutsche Juristen-Zeitung* 141, 141; Böhm (n 164) 256; Eucken (n 159) 48, 53, 126, 130, 176; Erhard (n 183) 22–23, 202–04; Miksch (n 186) 215–21.

201 See Mestmäcker's Preface to Böhm (ed) (n 167) 8; ibid. 209, 262, 270, 306–07; Eucken (n 159) 30; Miksch (n 186) 12, 215.

202 Eucken (n 159) 177.

203 Böhm (ed) (n 167) 206; Eucken (n 159) 42, 247–49; Miksch (n 186) 15, 54; P Behrens, 'The Ordoliberal Concept of "Abuse" of a Dominant Position and Its Impact on Article 102 TFEU' (Discussion Paper N°7/15, 2015) 11–12.

204 Böhm (ed) (n 167) 38, 240–49, 257–65, 275–76; Eucken (n 159) 43, 247–49, 267, 296, 329.

205 Erhard (n 183) 204–06; Böhm (n 198).

1.4.4 *The Competition–Democracy Nexus and the Genesis of European Competition Law*

The idea of a competition–democracy nexus 3.0 was first articulated by the Ordoliberal School in early twentieth-century Europe and lived on in German and European competition law after the Second World War. The role of the competition–democracy nexus as a central normative preconception of post-war German and European competition law is certainly not exclusively the making of Ordoliberalism alone. Indeed, the degree of influence that the Freiburg School had on the emergence and evolution of competition law in post-war Europe is contested. German and European competition laws are surely not a purist offspring of Ordoliberal thought.[206] Instead, both are the result of a compromise between various and at times antagonistic interests, national traditions, and visions of economic policy.[207] Nonetheless, Ordoliberalism certainly was one amongst a number of sources of inspiration that explain the lasting imprint of the idea of a competition–democracy nexus on the self-understanding of German and European competition law.[208] Another complementary force behind the central role of the competition–democracy nexus for the post-war economic governance in Europe was the influence of US antitrust thought (as described in Section 1.3), where the idea of a positive relationship between competitive markets and democracy had reached its apex during and after the Second World War.[209]

The conception of a competition–democracy nexus in German and European competition law is, hence, best understood as the result of the interaction and intermediation between US antitrust and Ordoliberal legal tradition in an effort to

206 A Wigger, 'Debunking the Myth of the Ordoliberal Influence on Post-war European Integration' in C Joerges and J Hien (eds), *Ordoliberalism: Law and the Rule of Economics* (Oxford: Hart 2018) 171–76; P Akman, 'Searching for the Long-Lost Soul of Article 82 EC' (CCP Working Paper, 2007).

207 For the German competition law, see P Hüttenberger, 'Wirtschaftsordnung und Interessenpolitik in der Kartellgesetzgebung der Bundesrepublik 1949–1957' (1976) 24(3) *Vierteljahrshefte für Zeitgeschichte* 287; KK Patel and H Schweitzer, 'Introduction' in KK Patel and H Schweitzer (eds), *The Historical Foundations of EU Competition Law* (Oxford: Oxford University Press 2013) 1, 10.

208 DJ Gerber, 'Constitutionalizing the Economy: German Neo-liberalism, Competition Law and the "New" Europe' (1994) 42(1) *American Journal of Comparative Law* 25; Gerber (n 141); Mestmäcker (n 170); H Schweitzer, 'The History, Interpretation and Underlying Principles of Section 2 Sherman Act and Article 82 EC' in C-D Ehlermann and M Marquis (eds), *European Competition Law Annual 2007: A Reformed Approach to Article 82 EC* (Oxford: Hart 2008) 119.

209 B Leucht, 'Expertise and the Creation of a Constitutional Order for Core Europe: Transatlantic Policy Networks in the Schuman Plan Negotiations' in W Kaiser, B Leucht and M Gehler (eds), *Transnational Networks in Regional Integration: Governing Europe 1945–83* (New York: Palgrave Macmillan 2010) 18, 22–24; B Leucht, 'Transatlantic Policy Networks in the Creation of the First European Anti-trust Law: Mediating between American Anti-trust and German Ordo-liberalism' in W Kaiser, B Leucht and M Rasmussen (eds), *The History of the European Union: Origins of a Trans- and Supranational Polity 1950–72* (New York: Routledge 2009) 56, 59.

rebuild Germany and Europe on an economic order that was anchored in the principle of free market competition.[210] Following the horrors of fascism and totalitarianism, the idea of a competition–democracy nexus developed by the Ordoliberals during the 1930s and 1940s, and shared by US antitrust paradigms, became a central element of the democratisation of Germany and Europe. At the Conference in Potsdam in 1945, the Allies agreed upon the decentralisation and decartelisation of the German economy as a prerequisite for the reconstruction of Germany on democratic principles.[211] This decentralisation and decartelisation policy was put into practice through the identical US-law 56 and British ordinance 78, which were adopted in 1947 with the aim to 'lay the groundwork for building a healthy and democratic German Economy'.[212] Both measures required that 'the German economy be reorganized and that concentration of economic power as exemplified, in particular, by cartels, syndicates, trusts, combines, and other types of monopolistic or restrictive arrangements, ... be eliminated'.[213]

The decentralisation and decartelisation of the German economy were welcomed by Ordoliberal thinkers.[214] The Ordoliberal proponents of the social market economy staunchly opposed the idea that the introduction of a competitive market economy and competition law in Germany had been imposed by the Allies, and notably the Americans.[215] Instead, Ordoliberal thinkers and the architects of the social market economy soon began to build on these deconcentration and decartelisation efforts to develop a new competition law for the post-war German economy. In his role as the Director of the Administration of the Economy (the so-called Economic Council), which was established by the three Western Allies in Frankfurt Main, the founding father of the German model of the social market economy and later Minister of the Economy and Chancellor, Ludwig Erhard, from 1948 onwards started to develop plans for a new competition law.[216] Upon his proposal, the 'Law Concerning Guiding Principles for Economic Control and Price Policy after Currency Reform' from 24 June 1948 envisaged that the post-war economic order should be grounded in the Ordoliberal principle of 'performance-based' competition. It also foresaw the elimination and public regulation of

[210] Leucht, 'Transatlantic Policy Networks' (n 209) 68; CF Ophüls, 'Das Wirtschaftsrecht des Schumanplans' (1951) 4(10) *Neue Juristische Wochenschrift* 381, 382.

[211] 'At the earliest practicable date, the German economy shall be decentralized for the purpose of eliminating the present excessive concentration of economic power as exemplified in particular by cartels, syndicates, trusts and other monopolistic arrangements.' Potsdam Agreement–Protocol of the Proceedings, August I, 1945, point 12.

[212] Mil. Gov. gaz. Germany, British Zone of Control, 412, Brit. VoBl. 1947, p. 412.

[213] Ibid.

[214] F Böhm, 'Kartellauflösung und Konzernentflechtung Spezialistenaufgabe oder Schicksalsfrage?' (1947) 2(9) *Süddeutsche Juristen-Zeitung* 495, 504–05.

[215] Erhard (n 183) 194–95.

[216] Ibid. 191.

monopolies.[217] Subsequently, the Ordoliberals took on an important role in the design of German competition law. The Ordoliberal thinker Franz Böhm, acting as an advisor to Ludwig Erhard, contributed to several drafts of the post-war competition law in Germany, notably the first so-called Josten draft from 5 July 1949. This draft provided for an outright prohibition of anticompetitive agreements. It also contemplated the breakup of monopolistic firms holding unreasonable market power, even in the absence of any anticompetitive conduct.[218]

Both the deconcentration of large German *Konzerne*, such as IG Farben, by the Allies[219] and the radical provisions envisaging the breakup of monopolistic firms in the Josten draft soon met opposition amongst German industrialists and certain parts of the government. The rules providing for the prohibition and breakup of monopolistic firms in the Josten draft did not survive their lobbying efforts.[220] Nevertheless, the final version of the first German *Gesetz gegen Wettbewerbsbeschränkungen* (Law Against Restraints of Competition; GWB), which was adopted in 1957,[221] contained important, albeit watered down, elements – most prominently, the principled prohibition of anticompetitive agreements – of various Ordoliberal proposals for a post-war competition law.[222]

The ethos of the new German GWB and the model of the social market economy was built around the Ordoliberal conception of economic liberty and its importance for a democratic society and polity. Consistent with Ordoliberal thought, the founding fathers of the social market economy viewed a competitive market economy as the most democratic form of an economic order, or even as the economic counterpart to political democracy.[223] In the eyes of the proponents of a social market economy, the reason for this link between competition and democracy lay in the crucial role of competitive markets in promoting economic liberty, both in

[217] The English version of the Law reads as follows 'In so far as the State does not control the exchange of goods and services, the principle of free competition shall be encouraged. If economic monopolies develop, these must be abolished and until this is done they shall be placed under State supervision.' The 'principle of free competition' translates 'Grundsatz des Leistungswettbewerbs' (principle of performance-based competition)' in the German version Gesetz über Leitsätze für die Bewirtschaftung und Preispolitik nach der Geldreform vom 24. Juni 1948, Ordinance No 37 Concerning Guiding Principles for Economic Control and Price Policy after Currency Reform, VfWMBl. 1948 II S. 91; Brit. VoBl. 1949, p. 77, Section III.

[218] E-J Mestmäcker, 'Competition Policy and Antitrust: Some Comparative Observations' (1980) 136(3) *Zeitschrift für die gesamte Staatswissenschaft / Journal of Institutional and Theoretical Economics* 387, 391; Schweitzer (n 208) 133–34 and fn. 70.

[219] P Müller, 'Sovereignty Trade-Offs between Politics and the Economy: The Deconcentration of IG Farben after 1945' (2022) 55(1) *Central European History* 53.

[220] Hüttenberger (n 207) 291–92.

[221] Gesetz gegen Wettbewerbsbeschränkungen, BGBl. I, 1957, 1081.

[222] Mestmäcker (n 218) 391–94; Hüttenberger (n 207) 293–307; Schweitzer (n 208) 122.

[223] Erhard (n 183) 23, 199, 206.

terms of consumer choice and the right to carry out an economic activity. Economic liberty was perceived as a fundamental, unalienable, and democratic right.[224] The founding fathers of the social market economy also subscribed to the Ordoliberal precept that firms amassing concentrated economic power posed a fundamental threat to economic liberty[225] and democracy.[226] The preservation of economic liberty through competition law was, therefore, considered to be the basic pillar[227] of the newly conceived social market economy as the model of economic governance of democratic post-war Germany.

The concern about the excessive concentration of private economic power that underpins the idea of a competition–democracy nexus in US antitrust thought and Ordoliberalism also reverberated across the early stages of the European project. The European integration process itself can, arguably at least in part, be considered to be the offspring of the fear over concentrated economic power. The creation of the European Coal and Steel Community (ECSC) in 1951 constituted an immediate response to the catastrophic impact of the Faustian pact between German conglomerates and the National Socialist regime. The Schuman Declaration[228] and Treaty of Paris establishing the ECSC,[229] which laid the foundations of the European project, embodied a radical proposition. Out of fear that the European coal and steel producers should yet again cartelise, concentrate their private corporate power, and become the driving forces of a new arms race between France and Germany,[230] the pioneers of the European integration project made the revolutionary move to create a common competitive market for two of the, at that time, strategically most important industrial sectors of the war-torn continent. A key feature of the newly created ECSC was the unprecedented idea to tame private corporate power, which controlled some of the most important industrial sectors in Europe, through supranational competition rules and the control of a supranational competition authority. In introducing competition rules regulating anticompetitive agreements (Article 65), mergers and concentrations (Article 66), as well as unfair business conduct (Articles 60, 63) and abuses of dominant position (Article 66 (7)), the ECSC treaty 'constitutionalised' the problem of concentrated economic power by subordinating private corporations to supranational legal rules.

[224] Ibid. 22–23.
[225] Ibid. 166, 193–94.
[226] Ibid. 24.
[227] Ibid. 165–66, 190; A Müller-Armack, 'The Social Market Economy as an Economic and Social Order' (1978) 36(3) *Review of Social Economy* 325, 329–30.
[228] R Schuman, 'The Schuman Declaration – 9 May 1950' https://europa.eu.
[229] Treaty Establishing the European Coal and Steel Community.
[230] For a discussion of the cooperation of European heavy industry cartels before and during the Second World War, J Gillingham, 'Zur Vorgeschichte Der Montan-Union: Westeuropas Kohle Und Stahl in Depression Und Krieg' (1986) 34(3) *Vierteljahrshefte für Zeitgeschichte* 381; Leucht, 'Transatlantic Policy Networks' (n 209) 59–60.

The competition rules in the ECSC treaty superseded prior instruments[231] that the Allies had introduced after the Second World War to control agreements, trade practices, and ownership structures in the Ruhr with a view to preventing the 'excessive concentration of economic power'.[232] A major concern during the negotiation and ratification of the ECSC treaty was to ensure that its competition rules and the High Authority of the ECSC would guarantee that the efforts to deconcentrate the German *Konzerne* are not reversed through new anticompetitive practices and mergers. Historical sources clearly show that the goal of preventing an excessive concentration of private economic and political power in the hands of large corporations was a central reason for the inclusion of competition provisions in the ECSC treaty.[233] Early policy documents of the ECSC also identified that the paramount task of the newly created competition law regime was to 'put an end to the autocratic rule of cartels, and to control the use which concentrations are making of their power'.[234]

By making national corporations subject to the control of an independent supranational authority, the ECSC also severed the unwholly alliance between national private and public power that had turned out to be disastrous during the first half of the twentieth century. Not only was the creation of a common and competitive market for coal and steel aimed at enhancing welfare, growth, and economic stability, but it also primarily served the goal of stimulating competitive interdependence between French and German industries and economies to eliminate the possibility of a new war.[235] The creation of the ECSC thus followed the assumption – which was encoded in various iterations of the competition–democracy nexus – that competitive interaction tends to secure a balance of power amongst

[231] Gesetz 75 der amerikanischen und britischen Militärregierungen zur Umgestaltung des Deutschen Kohlenbergbaues und der Deutschen Eisen- und Stahlindustrie sowie Durchführungsbestimmungen, Bundesarchiv, BArch B 109/619; Gesetz N°27 hinsichtlich der Umgestaltung des deutschen Kohlenbergbaues und der deutschen Stahl- und Eisenindustrie (16. Mai 1950); 'Agreement for an International Authority for the Ruhr (London, 28 April 1949) www.cvce.eu.

[232] Agreement for an International Authority for the Ruhr (London, 28 April 1949) (n 231) Article 18; 'Note on the relationship between the International Authority for the Ruhr and the European Coal and Steel Community (7 November 1950): Anonymous French note on the coexistence of the International Authority for the Ruhr and the High Authority of the European Coal and Steel Community (ECSC).' www.cvce.eu; 'Accord relatif à la cessation des fonctions de l'Autorité Internationale de la Ruhr (27 mai 1952)' www.cvce.eu.

[233] P Leroy-Beaulieu, 'Note de Paul Leroy-Beaulieu sur le transfert du pouvoir de déconcentration de l'Autorité internationale de la Ruhr à la Haute Autorité (11 novembre 1950)' www.cvce.eu; J Monnet, 'Lettre de Jean Monnet à Robert Schuman (Paris, 1er juillet 1952)' www.cvce.eu; J Monnet, 'Lettre de Jean Monnet à Robert Schuman (Paris, 22 janvier 1951)' www.cvce.eu; A Bureau, 'Rapport d'Albert Bureau sur la déconcentration de la sidérurgie allemande (28 juin 1951)' www.cvce.eu.

[234] European Coal and Steel Community, 'Second General Report on the Activities of the Community' (1954) 107.

[235] Schuman (n 228).

many players who keep each other in check and therefore channel their resources towards mutually beneficial rather than dominating or even openly hostile behaviour.

Concerns about the concentration of private economic power also carried over into the founding process of the European Economic Community (EEC). The Spaak report, which set the groundwork for the creation of the EEC based on an internal market with supranational competition rules, revealed the fear that cartels and monopolies might use their power to frustrate the creation of an internal market, notably by engaging in discriminatory practices. For this reason, the report called for the adoption of European competition rules as a central pillar of the future internal market to prevent 'monopoly positions and practices' and forestall the 'monopoly or partial domination of the market for a product by a single enterprise'.[236]

The historiography of European integration has established that Ordoliberal thought had a considerable influence on the negotiation process of the ECSC and the Spaak report.[237] The German delegations negotiating the ECSC treaty and the Spaak report were led by Walter Hallstein (ECSC), the later first President of the European Commission, and the diplomat Carl Friedrich Ophüls (Spaak report). Walter Hallstein (as a professor since 1941) and Ophüls (as an honorary professor since 1949) were both members of the University of Frankfurt. As colleagues of the Ordoliberal Franz Böhm, who joined the University of Frankfurt in 1946, Hallstein and Ophüls were certainly familiar with the philosophy of the Freiburg School. At the same time, Böhm, Hallstein, and other members of the German delegation negotiating the Paris Treaty and Spaak report had close ties with Heinrich Kronstein, who during the war had documented the role of cartelisation and industrial concentration in the rise of the totalitarian Nazi regime for the US government.[238] The first attempts to create European competition rules in the ECSC treaty and Spaak report also seemed to draw similar lessons from the traumatic experience of the Second World War as the Ordoliberal School did. In seeking to rein in the concentration of economic power, the ECSC competition

[236] Report by the Heads of Delegations to the Foreign Ministers 1956, SG 7 A (56) (4) 45. The French text of the report refers to '*situations ou des pratiques de monopole*' and '*l'absorption ou la domination du marché d'un produit par une seule entreprise*' P-H Spaak, 'Rapport des chefs de délégation aux Ministres des Affaires Étrangères = Report of the Heads of Delegation to the Ministers of Foreign Affairs' (21 April 1956) 55–56 http://aei.pitt.edu.

[237] Leucht, 'Transatlantic Policy Networks' (n 209) 24; B Leucht and K Seidel, 'Du Traité de Paris au règlement 17/1962: Ruptures et continuités dans la politique européenne de concurrence, 1950–1962' (2008) 27(1) *Histoire, économie & société* 35; B Leucht and M Marquis, 'American Influences on EEC Competition Law: Two Paths, How Much Dependence?' in KK Patel and H Schweitzer (eds), *The Historical Foundations of EU Competition Law* (Oxford: Oxford University Press 2013),125.

[238] On Heinrich Kronstein, see Section 1.3.3. Leucht, 'Expertise and the Creation of a Constitutional Order' (n 209) 24–25; Leucht, 'Transatlantic Policy Networks' (n 209) 66–67.

rules and the Spaak report followed the playbook of the competition–democracy nexus as it was first envisaged by the Ordoliberal School in Europe.

The influence of Ordoliberal thought and its core assumption of a competition–democracy nexus becomes even more palpable with respect to the drafting and interpretation of the competition law provisions in the EEC Treaty of Rome, which are today Articles 101 and 102 TFEU.[239] Several members of the German delegation involved in the negotiation and drafting of the competition rules of the Treaty of Rome were closely associated with the Ordoliberal School. The German delegation included the two founding fathers of the German model of the social market economy, Ludwig Erhard and Alfred Müller-Armack. Another Ordoliberal disciple, Hans von der Groeben, was involved in the drafting of the Spaak report and presided over the Common Market working group, which was tasked with the drafting of the competition rules of the Treaty of Rome.[240] Although the competition rules in the Treaty of Rome were the result of a compromise between the various Member States, the German proposals had a substantial impact on the final provisions of what is today Articles 101 and 102 TFEU.[241]

Soon after the entry into force of the Treaty of Rome, Hans von der Groeben emerged as a central figure in the interpretation and enforcement of the newly designed European competition rules. He became the first Commissioner for Competition (1958–67). At the helm of the Directorate General for Competition (DG IV) within the Commission of the EEC, Hans von der Groeben developed a vision of European competition law that was firmly anchored in the Ordoliberal conception of a competition–democracy nexus. Von der Groeben subscribed to the Ordoliberal understanding of the interdependence between the economic, social, and political order.[242] He was adamant that the newly designed system of European competition rules and the project of a common market constituted the groundwork of a new economic order that was founded on the rule of law, economic fairness, and economic liberty.[243] Just like the Ordoliberal thinkers and the proponents of a

[239] For a different position, see Akman (n 206).

[240] Schweitzer (n 208) 129, fn. 54.

[241] Ibid. 128–38. It is worth noting that after the prohibition of monopolies was removed from the drafts of the German competition law, the German delegation opposed the per se rule against monopolies envisaged in the Spaak-report to avoid conflicts between the future European and German competition rules. Ibid. 135.

[242] Der Bundesminister für Wirtschaft, 'Dokument 111: Vorschlag der Kommission zu einer ersten Durchführungsverordnung zu den Artikeln 85 und 86 des EWG-Vertrages, 31.05.1961: Protokoll einer Wirtschaftsausschußsitzung, die Fragen zum Vorschlag der Kommission zu einer 1. Durchführungsverordnung behandelt. Neben den allgemeinen Bedenken, insbesondere gegenüber einer vorgesehenen Anzeigepflicht, wird die Möglichkeit einer von deutscher Seite angestrengten Normenkontrollklage behandelt' in T Hoeren and R Schulze (eds), *Dokumente zum europäischen Recht: Band 3: Kartellrecht (bis 1957)* (Berlin: Springer 2000) 457.

[243] Commission de la Communauté Économique Européenne, 'La Communauté économique européenne et notre régime économique et social. Discours de M. Hans von der Groeben,

social market economy,[244] von der Groeben drew a direct link between economic liberty, the personal liberty of the individual, and political liberties, such as the freedom of expression.[245] Von der Groeben repeatedly stressed that this role of competition law in guaranteeing and promoting economic liberty explains its 'constitutional, social, democratic and federative significance'.[246]

Von der Groeben's understanding of competition law as a central pillar of a liberal and democratic order also went hand-in-hand with a concern over economic power. He recognised that the existence of concentrated economic power was not prohibited under the newly adopted EU competition rules. However, drawing on the Ordoliberal conception of competition, von der Groeben stressed that competition policy should seek to prevent any further increase in concentration of economic power and facilitate its erosion by preventing conduct that is not in line with the principle of performance-based competition but amounts to hindrance competition.[247] The Ordoliberal conception of competition policy was also shared by other prominent members of the DG IV who were close to the Freiburg School, such as Ernst Albrecht, von der Groeben's *chef de cabinet* and father of the current President of the European Commission Ursula von der Leyen, Hermann Schumacher, Ivo Schwartz, and Ernst-Joachim Mestmäcker, a student of Franz Böhm, who acted as an academic advisor to von der Groeben.[248]

The trend towards growing levels of industry concentration also remained a central concern of the European Commission's competition policy over the next few decades. In its ninth annual report on competition policy, the Commission, for instance, rang the alarm over the 'excessive concentration of economic, financial and commercial power' that may reach a level where 'free competition is no longer

membre de la Commission de la Communauté économique européenne. Munich, 29 novembre 1962' (1962) 3–4, 18–19; H von der Groeben, 'Competition Policy in the Common Market' (1965) 6, 8, 15; H von der Groeben, 'Competition in the Common Market. Speech by Hans von der Groeben, Member of the Commission of the European Economic Community, during the debate on the draft regulation pursuant to Articles 85 and 86 of the EEC Treaty in the European Parliament. Strasbourg, 19 October 1961. Includes French version', 8, 9, 11; H von der Groeben, 'Competition Policy as Part of Economic Policy in the Common Market' (1965) 10(5–6) *Antitrust Bulletin* 911, 912–13, 927–29.

[244] H von der Groeben, 'Policy on Competition in the EEC: Supplement to Bulletin of the European Economic Community No 7–8' (1961) 11; Commission de la Communauté Économique Européenne (n 243) 16.

[245] von der Groeben, 'Competition Policy as Part of Economic Policy in the Common Market' (n 243) 8–9; Commission de la Communauté Économique Européenne (n 243) 15.

[246] H von der Groeben, 'Competition Policy in the Common Market and in the Atlantic Partnership' (1965) 10(1) *Antitrust Bulletin* 125, 137; von der Groeben, 'Competition Policy as Part of Economic Policy in the Common Market' (n 243) 8.

[247] von der Groeben, 'Competition Policy as Part of Economic Policy in the Common Market' (n 243) 10–11; von der Groeben (n 244) 29.

[248] K Seidel, 'DG IV and the Origins of a Supranational Competition Policy: Establishing an Economic Constitution for Europe' in W Kaiser, B Leucht and M Rasmussen (eds), *The History of the European Union: Origins of a Trans- and Supranational Polity 1950–72* (New York: Routledge 2009) 131, 135–37.

able to fulfil its role as an effective regulator of economic activity'.[249] The Ordoliberal theme of a competition–democracy nexus that was prominently championed by von der Groeben during the early days of the European competition law regime continued to live on in the European competition policy discourse over most of the second half of the twentieth century. The European Commission and the European Parliament repeatedly referred to competition as a driver of the 'democratization of the markets'[250] and 'basis for a democratic society'.[251] Harnessing the Ordoliberal conception of performance competition, the Commission also characterised the 'price mechanism based on competition by performance [as the] most effective and most democratic coordinator' of individual decisions in the market place.[252] As late as in the 1980s, the European Commission appeared to perceive a direct link between the preservation of competitive markets through competition policy and liberal democracy:

> The Member States of the European Community share a common commitment to individual rights, to democratic values and to free institutions. It is those rights, values and institutions at the European and national levels that provide necessary checks and balances in our political systems. Effective competition provides a set of similar checks and balances in the market economy system. It preserves the freedom and right of initiative of the individual economic operator and it fosters the spirit of enterprise. . . . Competition policy should ensure that abusive use of market power by a few does not undermine the rights of the many.[253]

1.5 CONCLUSION

This chapter marks the first step in the intellectual journey of this book into the conceptual origins and foundations of the idea of a competition–democracy nexus. It pins down and delineates the idea of a competition–democracy nexus by tracing its historical trajectory. This chapter shows that the history of the proposition that competitive markets are conducive and concentration of economic power is detrimental to a republican or democratic society and polity spans several centuries, starting from the late sixteenth century and persisting to the second half of the twentieth century. Various renditions of the idea of a competition–democracy nexus materialised at different junctures in the history of thought about competitive markets. The first iteration of this idea (i.e., competition-democracy nexus 1.0) originated in the context of the transition from a feudal to a market society. Early

[249] European Commission, 'IXth Report on Competition Policy' (1979) 10.

[250] Resolution on the 12th Report of the Commission of the European Communities on Competition Policy 1982 rec 5.

[251] Resolution on the Eighteenth Report of the Commission of the European Communities on Competition Policy rec 2.1.5.4.

[252] European Commission, 'XVth Report on Competition Policy' (1985) 15.

[253] Ibid. 11.

proponents of commerce and competitive markets – such as English Common Lawyers, the Levellers, Montesquieu, James Steuart, and Adam Smith – celebrated the advent of competitive markets as catalysts for a freer and more egalitarian society. The second rendition (i.e., competition–democracy nexus 2.0) lay at the origins of US antitrust law in 1890 and had an important bearing on competition policy in the United States until the 1960s. The third iteration (i.e., competition–democracy nexus 3.0) was coined by the Ordoliberal School of thought in early twentieth-century Europe against the backcloth of galloping industrial concentration and cartelisation that contributed to the fall of the Weimar Republic and the rise of fascism. This Ordoliberal conception of the idea of a competition–democracy nexus left an important imprint on post-war competition law in Germany and Europe.

The synopsis of these three iterations of the idea of a competition–democracy nexus reveals some important common threads. Proponents of all three renditions of the idea of a competition–democracy nexus postulated an immediate interdependence between the way in which we organise our economic, social, and political systems. From this perspective, competitive markets are not only a welfare-maximising mechanism but are a mainstay and corollary of a social and political ordering that enhances liberty and equality. In short, competitive markets were viewed as an economic foundation and counterpart of a society of free and equals. The various versions of the idea of a competition–democracy nexus revolve around the propensity of markets to further economic, social, and political liberty and equality of opportunity. All renditions of the competition–democracy also share the view that the concentration of private and public economic power is an obstacle to economic liberty and undermines a society and polity of free and equals. Having described the idea of a competition–democracy nexus as the object of inquiry of this book in this chapter, the next chapter will explore various attempts to explain the relationship between competition, its protection through competition law, and democracy.

2

Republican Liberty as the Coupling between Competition and Democracy

2.1 INTRODUCTION

The previous chapter surveyed the historical development of the idea that competitive markets are an economic prerequisite for democracy. It showed that the claim of a competition–democracy nexus had surfaced in early modern European thought of the sixteenth to eighteenth centuries. It also described how this concept became a normative bedrock of US and European competition law and policy during the late nineteenth and early twentieth centuries. Various versions of a competition–democracy nexus that were nurtured by the proto-republican proponents of competitive markets in sixteenth- to eighteenth-century Europe (competition–democracy nexus 1.0), as well as antitrust paradigms in the United States (competition–democracy nexus 2.0) and the Ordoliberal School in Europe (competition–democracy nexus 3.0) converged in a common premise: they all shared the belief that the concentration of private economic power is incompatible with democracy and that in imposing checks on corporate power, competition law is instrumental in protecting democracy.

This long-standing proposition that competition and its protection through competition law promotes democracy is anything but obvious. For instance, empirical studies have failed to establish a clear-cut and significant correlation between democratic political regimes and the existence of competition law.[1] Moreover, the current consensus view that the paramount objective of competition law is to ensure that competitive markets benefit consumers through lower prices, greater quality, choice, and innovation prevails amongst competition experts.[2] This prevalence of

[1] N Petersen, 'Antitrust Law and the Promotion of Democracy and Economic Growth' (2013) 9 (3) *Journal of Competition Law & Economics* 593; T-C Ma, 'Antitrust and Democracy: Perspectives from Efficiency and Equity' (2016) 12(2) *Journal of Competition Law & Economics* 233.

[2] H Hovenkamp, *The Antitrust Enterprise: Principle and Execution* (Cambridge, MA: Harvard University Press 2005) 1.

the consumer welfare standard notwithstanding, competitive markets and their protection through competition law continue to be referred to as an important ingredient and safeguard of liberal democracy in the contemporary antitrust literature.[3] Yet, while the preservation of democracy has been frequently invoked as the ultimate normative justification of competition rules across the history of antitrust law, few efforts have been made so far to provide a convincing answer to the basic question underpinning the claim of a competition–democracy nexus, which asks why and how is it that competitive markets contribute to democracy?

This chapter seeks to address this question by unpacking the notion of a competition–democracy nexus that was cultivated by early liberal thinkers, proponents of US antitrust law, and Ordoliberals. To answer the question of how competition and competition law contribute to democracy, it is worth breaking down the idea of a competition–democracy nexus into its three constitutive claims. The first claim is that the concentration of private economic power has adverse consequences for society (the concentration thesis). The second claim is that at least one of these adverse societal consequences is that the concentration of private power poses a threat to democracy (the democracy thesis). The third claim is that competition law is the right tool to address the nefarious implications that the excessive concentration of private economic power entails for democracy (the competition law thesis). A convincing explanation of the competition–democracy nexus would have to explain the concentration, democracy, and competition law theses by answering three questions: First, why is concentrated economic power a problem for society? Second, how does it harm democracy? And third, why is it the role of competition law to address this problem?

This chapter starts with critically reviewing existing attempts to explain the competition–democracy nexus by assessing how they perform in addressing these three questions. It shows that existing attempts to make sense of the idea of a competition–democracy nexus remain unconvincing. Against this backdrop, this chapter puts forward a novel explanation of the competition-democracy nexus. It argues that the idea of a linkage between competition and democracy can be best explained by the republican conception of liberty as non-domination. Tracing back to republican thinking in ancient Rome, this republican understanding of liberty is the only explanatory variable that can make the proposition that competition enhances and the concentration of economic power undermines democracy understandable.

This chapter is structured as follows: Section 2.2 critically reflects on the special interest capture account as the predominant argument that antitrust scholars and policy-makers advance to claim that there is a positive relationship between

3 EM Fox, 'Antitrust and Democracy: How Markets Protect Democracy, Democracy Protects Markets, and Illiberal Politics Threatens to Hijack Both' (2019) 46(4) *Legal Issues of Economic Integration* 317; S Weber Waller, 'Antitrust and Democracy' (2019) 46(4) *Florida State University Law Review* 806; M Bernatt, *Populism and Antitrust: The Illiberal Influence of Populist Government on the Competition Law System* (Cambridge: Cambridge University Press 2022).

competition and democracy. Section 2.3 evaluates the mainstream liberal account as a second influential explanation of the competition–democracy nexus. Having identified major flaws in both accounts, Section 2.4 advances the conception of republican liberty as an alternative and, as we shall see, a superior explanation of the competition–democracy nexus. Section 2.5 describes how the republican conception of liberty allows us to explain the concentration thesis. Section 2.6 discusses how republican liberty also makes the democracy thesis intelligible. Section 2.7 highlights how republican liberty may elucidate the competition law thesis. The conclusion summarises the basic features of a republican understanding of economic liberty that underpins the idea of a competition–democracy nexus.

2.2 THE SPECIAL INTEREST CAPTURE ACCOUNT

The special interest capture account is the most recurrent and prominent explanation for the idea of a competition–democracy nexus.[4] Several attempts have been made by the contemporary proponents of the idea of a competition–democracy nexus to postulate an empirical negative relationship between concentrated corporate power and democracy. The standard explanation for this negative relationship lies in what the economist Luigi Zingales tellingly calls the 'Medici vicious cycle',[5] which assumes that large businesses can easily convert their economic power into political power through lobbying, campaign financing, and special interest capture. Greater political power, in turn, further augments corporate power. Accordingly, excessive concentration of economic power risks eroding or corrupting democratic processes and institutions, and leads to rent-seeking, oligarchy, and crony capitalism.

Recent studies lend empirical support to the special interest capture account. They show a positive relationship between industry concentration, firm size, and firms' contributions to political campaigns and lobbying expenses.[6] They also suggest that powerful corporations are more successful than smaller players and other social groups in lobbying government and capturing regulatory processes.[7]

4 L Zingales, 'Towards a Political Theory of the Firm' (2017) 31(3) *Journal of Economic Perspectives* 113, 113; T Wu, *The Curse of Bigness: Antitrust in the New Gilded Age* (New York: Columbia Global Reports 2018) 55–58; Z Teachout and L Khan, 'Market Structure and Political Law: A Taxonomy of Power' (2014) 9(2) *Duke Journal of Constitutional Law & Public Policy* 37, 41–53.

5 Zingales (n 4) 114.

6 T Philippon, *The Great Reversal: How America Gave Up on Free Markets* (Cambridge, MA: Harvard University Press 2019) 166–68; B Cowgill, A Prat and T Valletti, 'Political Power and Market Power' (2021) CEPR Press Discussion Paper No 17178.

7 See, for instance, M Gillens and BI Page, 'Testing Theories of American Politics: Elites, Interest Groups, and Average Citizens' (2014) 12(3) *Perspectives on Politics* 564; K Dellis and D Sondermann, 'Lobbying in Europe: New Firm-level Evidence' (2017) ECB Working Paper Series No 2071/June 2017; OECD, 'Market Concentration: Issues Paper by the Secretariat' (2018) DAF/COMP/WD(2018)46, 19–20.

On this basis, some antitrust scholars have recently called for a more vigorous competition law enforcement against big business with a view to disrupting this reinforcing spill-over effect[8] between economic and political power to preserve the integrity of our democratic system and institutions.[9]

Without a doubt, this concern about lobbying and special interest capture as a transmission belt between private economic and political power has had some bearing on the emergence of the idea of a competition–democracy nexus. Special interest capture and rent-seeking were arguably part of the historical origin of early competition law in the *Darcy v Allein* case.[10] Darcy's monopoly of the production and sales of playing cards granted by Queen Elizabeth I illustrates special interest capture and rent-seeking at its best.[11] Many of the privileges, monopoly rights, and restraints of trade challenged in common law cases of the sixteenth and seventeenth centuries, and decried by early liberal thinkers as undue forms of state-licensed 'private government',[12] were the ultimate outcome of regulatory capture and lobbying by powerful vested interests and guilds. The fear that powerful industrial behemoths and trusts would be able to capture democratic institutions and transform their economic power into political power was also a recurrent theme in the legislative history of the Sherman Act.[13] Against the backdrop of the political influence of large German *Konzerne* and their infamous role in the ascent of the National Socialist regime, the Ordoliberals were also alert to the risk of political institutions being seized and corroded by vested interests and powerful businesses.[14] The capture of the political institutions of the Weimar Republic by powerful companies was perceived by the Ordoliberals as one of the factors that contributed to the decline of its legitimacy and ultimate fall.[15]

Important though it is, the special interest capture account alone is insufficient to explain the relationship between competition, competition law, and democracy. First, on a conceptual level, it is far from clear why special interest capture and lobbying constitute a problem that is particularly detrimental to democracy relative

8 Zingales (n 4) 114.

9 Teachout and Khan (n 4) 70–72; Wu (n 4) 58.

10 *Darcy v Allein ('The Case of Monopolies')* [1602] 77 ER 1260.

11 SG Calabresi and LC Leibowitz, 'Monopolies and the Constitution: A History of Crony Capitalism' (2015) 36(3) *Harvard Journal of Law & Public Policy* 983.

12 E Anderson, 'Liberty, Equality and Private Government' in M Matheson (ed), *The Tanner Lectures on Human Values* (Cambridge: Cambridge University Press 2016) 63.

13 19 Cong Rec 8519 (1888) 8521–22, 8563; 20 Cong Rec 2455 (1890) 2459–60; J May, 'Antitrust in the Formative Era: Political and Economic Theory in Constitutional and Antitrust Analysis, 1880–1918' (1989) 50(2) *Ohio State Law Journal* 257, 297–98.

14 W Eucken, *Grundsätze der Wirtschaftspolitik* (Tübingen: Mohr Siebeck 2004) 53, 146, 175, 177, 294, 326–29; F Böhm, 'Democracy and Economic Power in Cartel and Monopoly in Modern Law [1961]' in DA Crane and H Hovenkamp (eds), *The Making of Competition Policy: Legal and Economic Sources* (New York: Oxford University Press 2013) 264, 273–79.

15 F Böhm, 'Kartellauflösung und Konzernentflechtung: Spezialistenaufgabe oder Schicksalsfrage?' (1947) 2(9) *Süddeutsche Juristen-Zeitung* 495, 504.

to other forms of government (democracy thesis). On the contrary, it is equally conceivable that special interest capture by big business would also undermine the integrity or impartiality of political institutions in an autocratic regime or a monarchy. While it can rightly be said that the Medici vicious cycle is likely to corrupt and undermine the impartiality of political institutions, the proponents of this account fail to explain how special interest capture actually undermines the specific democratic nature of these institutions, and is thus inimical to a democratic form of government. It also bears noting that pluralistic theories of democracy, coined by Madison's Federalist Paper No 10[16] and the work of Robert Dahl,[17] to some extent endorse lobbying, or in other words, interest group representation, as an important element and alternative channel of democratic participation.

Second, the special interest capture account also omits to explain why proponents of a competition–democracy nexus considered the protection of competitive markets through competition law as a safeguard of democracy (competition law thesis). It is indeed anything but obvious why it should actually be the role of competition law to protect democratic institutions against the corrosive effect of lobbying and rent-seeking by big business. Arguably, this problem could be addressed more effectively through the adoption of specific regulations and rules, such as stricter campaign financing and lobbying regulations, which would shield democratic processes and institutions from undue corporate influence.[18]

Third, even if one were to agree that competition law has a role to play in protecting democratic institutions against the corrosive influence of private corporate interests and excessive lobbying, the special interest capture account fails to explain why this problem necessitates a more vigorous application of competition law against big business, which seeks to reduce instances of concentration of economic power. If special interest capture and lobbying constituted the channels through which concentrated market power undermines democracy, then it would arguably be more effective and less costly to apply competition rules directly against harmful rent-seeking or lobbying activities by which firms try to obtain anticompetitive legislation than seeking to reduce the overall level of industry concentration. For instance, Robert Bork, while being firmly opposed to any attempt to address the concentration of economic power directly through the application of antitrust laws, supported the application of competition law to anticompetitive lobbying. This approach would be better targeted than a sweeping tightening of antitrust laws against big business. It would only screen out those attempts of lobbying that result

16 A Hamilton, J Madison and J Jay, *The Federalist Papers* (Oxford: Oxford University Press 2008) Federalist No 10, p. 48.

17 RA Dahl, *A Preface to Democratic Theory* (Chicago: Chicago University Press 1956); RA Dahl, *Democracy and Its Critics* (New Haven: Yale University Press 1989).

18 JB Baker, *The Antitrust Paradigm: Restoring a Competitive Economy* (Cambridge, MA: Harvard University Press 2019) 61.

in special interest capture and rent-seeking by harming competitors or consumers.[19] Nevertheless, the US Supreme Court[20] and, to some extent, the EU Courts[21] have rejected the application of competition rules to lobbying out of fear that this would chill rather than protect democracy by curtailing the right to petition and inhibiting political participation.

The argument that a stricter application of competition law against concentrated economic power is necessary to protect democracy from undue corporate influence ignores yet another solution to address special interest capture and rent-seeking that is advocated by the public choice literature. Based on George Stigler's seminal theory of regulation, many Chicago scholars argued that the easiest way to protect democracy and competition from undue special interest capture and protectionism is to cut back regulation and reduce the scope of government intervention rather than expanding it through more competition law enforcement.[22]

Even if there was a positive correlation between economic and political power, the argument that competition law should become tougher on big business to protect democracy rests on shaky ground and does not convincingly explain the idea of a competition–democracy nexus. With the democracy and competition law theses, the special interest capture account fails to explain two of the three core propositions underpinning the idea of a competition–democracy nexus; namely, that concentrated power is specifically harmful to democracy, and that competition law is the right tool to deal with it.

2.3 THE CONVENTIONAL LIBERTY ACCOUNT

Alongside attempts to explain the idea of a competition–democracy nexus by pointing to a causal relationship or correlation between economic and political power, a number of scholars have suggested that the link between competition and democracy is grounded in the fact that competition promotes economic liberty.[23] At first sight, this conventional liberty account is appealing. Several proponents of the idea of a competition–democracy nexus have highlighted the role of competitive markets in advancing economic liberty. At the same time, they also converged in their critique of

19 RH Bork, *The Antitrust Paradox: A Policy at War with Itself* [1978] (New York: Maxwell Macmillan 1993) 347–64.

20 *Eastern Railroad Presidents Conference v Noerr Motor Freight, Inc.* 365 US 127, 135 (1961); *United Mine Workers v Pennington* 381 US 657 (1965).

21 Case T-432/05 *EMC Development v Commission* ECLI:EU:T:2010:189, para 81.

22 GJ Stigler, 'The Theory of Economic Regulation' (1971) 2(1) *The Bell Journal of Economics and Management Science* 3; S Peltzman, 'Toward a More General Theory of Regulation' (1976) 19 (2) *The Journal of Law and Economics* 211.

23 R Pitofsky, 'The Political Content of Antitrust' (1979) 127(4) *University of Pennsylvania Law Review* 1051; EM Fox, 'Modernization of Antitrust: A New Equilibrium' (1980) 66(6) *Cornell Law Review* 1140; G Amato, *Antitrust and the Bounds of Power: The Dilemma of Liberal Democracy in the History of the Market* (Oxford: Hart 1997); RJ Peritz, *Competition Policy in America: History, Rhetoric, Law* (New York: Oxford University Press 2000).

concentrated economic power as an obstacle and threat to economic liberty.[24] Moreover, the conventional liberty account echoes the assertion coined by influential libertarian thinkers, such as Friedrich August von Hayek and Milton Friedman, that competitive markets and capitalism are normatively superior to other economic systems because they enhance liberty.[25] However, this liberty-based explanation of the competition–democracy nexus also leaves many questions unanswered.

2.3.1 *What Is Liberty?*

To understand the limitations of the conventional liberty account in explaining the competition–democracy nexus, it is first necessary to clarify the notion of liberty[26] itself: What do we mean when we say that someone is free? The answer to this question is anything but obvious. Indeed, people often hold different and at times contradictory views on what it takes to be free. The history of political thought abounds with these disagreements over the meaning of liberty.

The most consequential attempt to rationalise and, in part, overcome these disagreements was made by the political and legal philosopher Gerald C. MacCallum. MacCallum argued that diverging notions of liberty can always be expressed as a triadic relationship in the format: 'x is (is not) free from y to do (not do, become, not become) z'.[27] Accordingly, liberty always refers to the situation '*of* something (an agent or agents), *from* something, *to* do, not do, become, or not become something'.[28] Consequently, liberty always describes a relationship between agents (x) and preventing conditions (i.e., constraints, restrictions, interferences and barriers) (y), which affect actions (z). From this perspective, different notions of liberty represent nothing more (or less) than diverging views regarding the three key variables x, y, and z; namely:

(i) who qualifies as an agent (x),
(ii) what counts as a preventing condition (y), and
(iii) what should be included in the actions that agents might reasonably be said to be free, or not free, to perform (z).[29]

[24] See Chapter 1, Sections 1.2–1.4.

[25] FA v Hayek, *The Road to Serfdom* [1944] (London: Routledge 2001); FA v Hayek, *The Constitution of Liberty* [1960] (Chicago: University of Chicago Press 2011); M Friedman, *Capitalism and Freedom* (Chicago: University of Chicago Press 1962); JM Buchanan, 'Social Choice, Democracy, and Free Markets' (1954) 62(2) *Journal of Political Economy* 114.

[26] While 'liberty' and 'freedom' may have occasionally slightly different meanings, I use both terms interchangeably in this book. For a further discussion on the differences between 'freedom' and 'liberty', see HF Pitkin, 'Are Freedom and Liberty Twins?' (1988) 16(4) *Political Theory* 523.

[27] GC MacCallum, 'Negative and Positive Freedom' (1967) 76(3) *The Philosophical Review* 312, 314.

[28] Ibid.

[29] Ibid. 319–27, 333; I Carter, 'Liberty' in R Bellamy and A Mason (eds), *Political Concepts* (Manchester: Manchester University Press 2003) 4, 11–14.

The conventional liberty account of the competition–democracy nexus in the existing scholarly literature predominantly portrays the understanding of economic liberty celebrated by the proponents of various iterations of the competition–democracy nexus in negative terms[30] as 'freedom from something', namely, from coercion or interference.[31] This negative understanding of liberty largely dovetails with how the concept is predominantly used in our contemporary discourses. When we nowadays talk about liberty, we usually tend to describe it primarily in negative terms. Accordingly, I am free because nobody else actually or likely interferes with my otherwise unconstrained choices or actions.[32] This negative understanding of liberty was first coined by Thomas Hobbes.[33] It was subsequently endorsed by liberal thinkers such as Jeremy Bentham,[34] John Stuart Mill,[35] Benjamin Constant,[36] Isaiah Berlin,[37] Friedrich August von Hayek,[38] and Milton Friedmann.[39] Over the course of the last two centuries, the negative conception of liberty has become the predominant way of thinking about liberty.

2.3.2 *The Distinctive Features of Negative Liberty*

This negative conception of liberty defines the notion of preventing conditions (y) that can be said to inhibit freedom narrowly. Proponents of negative liberty only consider external (actual or likely) interference by human agents as a threat to liberty. On this point, negative liberty differs from the positive notion of liberty that lay at the heart of the ancient Athenian democracy and defines liberty as 'freedom to (do) something'. On a positive account of liberty, I am free when I can achieve my objectives, or my genuine inner self, and decide on my own destiny.[40] Unlike negative liberty, liberty in the positive sense also counts constraints

30 J Viner, 'Adam Smith and Laissez Faire' (1927) 35(2) *Journal of Political Economy* 198; GJ Stigler, 'Smith's Travels on the Ship of State' (1971) 3(2) *History of Political Economy* 265; AJ Meese, 'Liberty and Antitrust in the Formative Era' (1999) 79(1) *Boston University Law Review* 1, 6, 10; W Möschel, 'Competition Policy from an Ordo Point of View' in AT Peacock, H Willgerodt and D Johnson (eds), *German Neo-liberals and the Social Market Economy* (London: Macmillan 1989) 142.

31 I Berlin, 'Two Concepts of Liberty' in H Hardy (ed), *Liberty: Incorporating Four Essays on Liberty* (Oxford: Oxford University Press 2002) 166, 168–81.

32 Ibid. 168–79.

33 T Hobbes, *Leviathan: Or the Matter, Form & Power of a Common-Wealth Eclasticall and Civill* [1651] (London: Penguin Classics 1985) Part II, Chapter XXI, pp. 261–62.

34 J Bentham, 'Anarchical Fallacies' in J Bowring (ed), *The Works of Jeremy Bentham* (Edinburgh: William Tait 1843) 503; J Bentham, *Theory of Legislation* (London: Trübner 1873) 94.

35 JS Mill, *On Liberty, Utilitarianism and Other Essays* [1859] (Oxford: Oxford University Press 2015).

36 B Constant, *Political Writings* (Cambridge: Cambridge University Press 1988) 307–28.

37 Berlin (n 31).

38 Hayek (n 25); Hayek, *The Constitution of Liberty* (n 25).

39 Friedman (n 25).

40 Berlin (n 31) 168–81.

internal to the individual, such as irrational fears or desires, as obstacles to freedom when they prevent them, for instance, from realising their inner self and destiny. Negative liberty also differs from other conceptions of liberty, which recognise 'natural obstacles that limit individuals' choices or render them unable to attain their goals, such as diseases, lack of talent or resources, extreme weather events, or famines, as obstacles to liberty.[41]

The negative conception of liberty also construes the range of relevant agents (x) that can be said to be free or unfree narrowly. On a negative conception of liberty, only individuals but not collective human agents can be said to be free or unfree from interference by other agents.[42] On this point, negative liberty differs, for instance, from the positive conception of liberty, which assumed that liberty not only takes the form of individual but also collective 'self-determination'.[43]

While agreeing that only external interference can count as obstruction of liberty, the negative camp disagreed on the type of actions (z) that can be legitimately said to be restricted so that an individual qualifies as unfree. On the one hand, Hobbes asserted that an individual is free as long as they are not prevented from choosing their preferred course of action or option.[44] Suppose that an individual i has the choice between options a and b and prefers a so that aP_ib, where P_i reads as '*individual i strictly prefers*'. Hobbes would argue that the individual qualifies as free as long as they are not interfered with when choosing a. In more formalised terms, Hobbes suggests that all it takes for individual i to be free is that their individual preference aP_ib is mirrored by a social preference ordering aPb, so that $aP_ib \rightarrow aPb$, where $\rightarrow$ stands for '*if . . . then*' and P reads as '*society strictly prefers*'.[45] Hobbes posited that an individual counts as free even if they were to be exposed to interference when choosing the other option b, so that if $bP_ia \rightarrow \neg bPa$, where $\neg$ denotes '*not*'. Hobbes thus proposes a content-*de*pendent conception of freedom, where the liberty of the individual is contingent on the options that they choose. The Hobbesian version of negative liberty requires that the individual's preferences only be decisive (i.e., are respected) in the actual world where an individual chooses a but not in the nearby counterfactual world where they were to prefer b over a. In short, Hobbes understood liberty as non-frustration of actual preferences, which presupposes $aP_ib \rightarrow aPb$ but not $bP_ia \rightarrow bPa$.

The actualism of Hobbes' conception of liberty becomes even more apparent if we consider an individual i who has the choice to go through different doors and their preferred door a opens. Hobbes tells us that individual i is to be considered free, even in

41 Carter (n 29) 9–14. For such a broad notion of preventing conditions that also encompasses external, 'natural' constraints, see A Sen, *Development as Freedom* [1999] (New York: Anchor Books 2013) 15–16.

42 Carter (n 29) 10.

43 Berlin (n 31) 168–81.

44 Hobbes (n 33) Part II, Chapter XXI, pp. 261–62.

45 The formalised social choice notation of various conceptions of liberty in the following draws on C List, 'The Impossibility of a Paretian Republican?: Some Comments on Pettit and Sen' (2004) 20(1) *Economics and Philosophy* 65, Appendix.

the event where every other (non-preferred) door was locked.[46] All that is required to secure Hobbes' notion of individual liberty as non-frustration is to minimise the probability of individual i being hindered ($P(H)$) from choosing their preferred option.[47] The Hobbesian conception of liberty thus merely presupposes that $P(H \mid w_1)\, P(w_1)$ is minimised, where $P(H)$ describes the probability of individual i being hindered or harmed if they choose their preferred option, where $\mid$ stands for '*given*', $w_1, \ldots, w_k$ describe all worlds accessible from the actual world w_1 and $P(w_1), \ldots, P(w_k)$ denote the respective probabilities of occurrence of these worlds.[48] Negative liberty, in the Hobbesian sense, requires that the conditional probabilities of hindrance of an individual's choice in the given actual world w_1 ($P(H \mid w_1)$) be low. In other words, Hobbes conceived negative liberty as non-frustration or preference maximisation in the actual world.[49]

Other proponents of negative liberty, most prominently Isaiah Berlin, embraced, however, a more demanding notion of negative liberty with respect to the type of actions (z) that an individual must be able to carry out without being interfered with to count as free. Unlike Hobbes, Berlin did not believe that it suffices for an individual to be unrestrained in choosing their preferred option to enjoy liberty. Berlin objected that under Hobbes' narrow conception of negative liberty, individual i could avoid interference and become free by simply adapting their preferences.[50] Rejecting this notion of 'freedom by adaptation', Berlin instead argued that the liberty of an individual depends on the number of alternative doors through which they can pass without being interfered with, irrespective of which of the doors is currently the preferred option.[51] When choosing between options a and b, individual i can thus only be said to be free if they are unrestricted in their preferred option a but also if they were to choose the alternative option b. For Berlin, liberty of individual i presupposes that $aP_ib \rightarrow aPb$ and ($\wedge$) $bP_ia \rightarrow bPa$. Berlin thus advocated a content-*in*dependent version of liberty. To count as free, an individual's preferences must be decisive, regardless of which option is preferred,[52] so that $(aP_ib \rightarrow aPb) \wedge (bP_ia \rightarrow bPa)$.

The content-independent, Berlinian version of negative liberty requires the minimisation of the probability of hindrance $P(H)$ of individual i choosing not only

[46] VC Chappell (ed), *Hobbes and Bramhall: On Liberty and Necessity* (Cambridge: Cambridge University Press 1999) 81; P Pettit, 'Freedom and Probability: A Comment on Goodin and Jackson' (2008) 36(2) *Philosophy & Public Affairs* 206, 211.

[47] I draw here on the notation of P Pettit, *On the People's Terms: A Republican Theory and Model of Democracy* (Cambridge: Cambridge University Press 2012) 34–35.

[48] This formalisation draws on C List and L Valentini, 'Freedom as Independence' (2016) 126(4) *Ethics* 1043, 1054, fn. 23; Pettit (n 47) 34–35. $P(w_1)$ can be assumed to be 1, as w_1 refers to the actual world.

[49] P Pettit, 'The Instability of Freedom as Noninterference: The Case of Isaiah Berlin' (2011) 121(4) *Ethics* 693, 695.

[50] Ibid. 699–701.

[51] Berlin (n 31) xlviii.

[52] P Pettit, 'Capability and Freedom: A Defence of Sen' (2001) 17(1) *Economics and Philosophy* 1, 5.

their preferred option a in the actual world but also their preferred option b in a nearby counterfactual world.[53] It thus presupposes not only that the probability $P(H)$ given the actual world w_1 but also in a nearby likely counterfactual world w_2 be kept to a minimum. Accordingly, the Berlinian conception of liberty presupposes the reduction of $P(H|w_1)\,P(w_1) + P(H|w_2)\,P(w_2)$, where $P(H)$ describes the probability of individual i being hindered or harmed if they choose their preferred option, $w_1, \ldots, w_k$ describe all worlds accessible from the actual world w_1, and $P(w_1), \ldots, P(w_k)$ denote the respective probabilities of occurrence of these worlds.[54] Accordingly, an individual is only free if their preferences are not only decisive in the actual but also in a nearby likely counterfactual world. The Berlinian version of negative liberty, therefore, favoured probabilism over the purely actualist conception of liberty coined by Hobbes.[55]

2.3.3 *Shortcomings of the Conventional Liberty Account*

The previous discussion has shown that attempts to explain the competition–democracy nexus with the propensity of markets to promote economic liberty usually rely on a negative notion of liberty, which is understood as the absence of state and private interference with the sphere of autonomy and choices of (other) market agents. However, this conventional liberty account is also fraught with a number of limitations, irrespective of whether it is grounded in an actualist Hobbesian or probabilistic Berlinian notion of negative liberty.

The principal problem of attempts to explain the competition–democracy nexus by the fact that competition enhances economic liberty is that negative liberty is by no means inextricably linked with democracy. On the contrary, Berlin and Hayek have pointed out that negative liberty can be guaranteed irrespective of the specific form of the political regime in which we live, so long as there are some basic guarantees of liberty in place, such as constitutional rights and the rule of law.[56] Not least, Hayek's and Friedman's support for the free-market reforms of the authoritarian Pinochet regime in Chile provides empirical evidence showing that there is no immediate and inevitable relationship between negative economic liberty, competitive markets, and democracy.[57] Thus, the conventional liberty account of the

53 Pettit (n 47) 34–35.

54 This formalisation draws on List and Valentini (n 48) 1054, fn. 23; Pettit (n 47) 34–35.

55 Pettit (n 46) 217. For more recent proponents who share this probabilistic Berlinian conception of negative liberty, see I Carter, A *Measure of Freedom* (New York: Oxford University Press 1999) notably Chapter 8; MH Kramer, *The Quality of Freedom* (Oxford: Oxford University Press 2003) notably Chapter 2; K Dowding and M van Hees, 'The Construction of Rights' (2003) 97(2) *American Political Science Review* 281; RE Goodin and F Jackson, 'Freedom from Fear' (2007) 35(3) *Philosophy & Public Affairs* 249.

56 Berlin (n 31) 178; Hayek, *The Road to Serfdom* (n 25) 72–74.

57 J Meadowcroft and R William, 'Hayek, Friedman, and Buchanan: On Public Life, Chile, and the Relationship between Liberty and Democracy' (2014) 26(3) *Review of Political Economy*

competition–democracy nexus suffers from the major shortcoming that a negative conception of liberty cannot support any positive relationship between liberty and democracy (democracy thesis).

A second major limitation of the conventional liberty account is that it does not explain why it is precisely competition law that will promote (negative) liberty. Mainstream liberals view any form of state interference through legal rules as coercion, and hence a reduction of liberty.[58] The proposition coined by various iterations[59] of the competition–democracy nexus that competition law, which interferes with the contractual and entrepreneurial freedom of businesses, promotes liberty must therefore sound utterly counterintuitive to them. It is indeed only in carefully circumscribed and exceptional circumstances where there is 'definite damage, or definite risk of damage' to others[60] that proponents of negative liberty countenance state intervention. Hence, state intervention is only legitimate if the reduction of liberty (as non-interference) resulting from state coercion is outweighed by the harm that it prevents.[61] Without any additional qualification, calls for tougher competition law intervention to tackle concentrated economic power cannot be grounded in a normative commitment to negative liberty. All things being equal, more competition law enforcement will not result in more but rather less (negative) liberty. Instead of championing more vigorous competition law enforcement, mainstream liberals would sympathise with the Chicagoan public choice theory of regulation that considers the scaling back of state intervention as the appropriate solution to special interest capture.[62] Thus, the conventional liberty account also fails because it does not lend sufficient support to the claim that competition law furthers negative liberty (competition law thesis).

Most notably, the concept of negative economic liberty cannot explain why proponents of various versions of the idea of a competition–democracy nexus perceived the mere presence of concentrated economic power as a danger for democracy (concentration thesis). We have seen that the negative liberty of an individual is only impaired if another person or authority is actually interfering (Hobbesian version) or likely to interfere (Berlinian version) with them in such a way that they cannot carry out a course of action they would otherwise embark on in

358; B Caldwell and L Montes, 'Friedrich Hayek and His Visits to Chile' (2015) 28(3) *The Review of Austrian Economics* 261.

58 Hobbes (n 33) Part II, Chapter XXI, pp. 262–68; Bentham, 'Anarchical Fallacies' (n 34) 503; Bentham, *Theory of Legislation* (n 34) 94; P Pettit, *Republicanism: A Theory of Freedom and Government* (Oxford: Clarendon Press/Oxford University Press 1997) 37–40.

59 E Coke, *The Third Part of the Institutes of the Laws of England: Concerning High Treason, and Other Please of the Crown and Criminall Causes* (London: By M. Flesher for W. Lee and D. Pakeman 1644) Chapter 85, p. 180; 20 Cong Rec 2455 (1890) (n 13) 2457–58.

60 Mill (n 35) 80, 93.

61 P Pettit, 'Freedom as Antipower' (1996) 106(3) *Ethics* 576, 596; P Pettit, 'Freedom in the Market' (2006) 5(2) *politics, philosophy & economics* 131, 145.

62 Stigler (n 22); Peltzman (n 22).

the absence of actual or the threat of likely interference. Put simply, for the concentration of economic power, say in the hand of a giant firm, to count as obstruction of negative liberty, this power must be exercised in such a way that the giant firm interferes or is likely to interfere with the sphere of autonomy of other market participants. Absent actual or likely interference, the mere presence of concentrated economic power neither qualifies as a preventing condition (y) nor hinders an agent from performing an action (z) in such a way that it must be considered unfree.

Accounts that attribute the link between competition and democracy to the conduciveness of competitive markets to further negative economic liberty are deficient because they fall short of explaining why proponents of a competition–democracy nexus perceive the very existence and not only the exercise of concentrated economic power as being at odds with liberty and democracy. Consequently, attempts to ground the idea of a competition–democracy nexus in the role of competitive markets in enhancing economic liberty in its common negative sense are unconvincing on both a conceptual and an empirical level.

2.4 REPUBLICAN LIBERTY AS THE COUPLING BETWEEN COMPETITION AND DEMOCRACY

The previous sections show how both the special interest capture and conventional liberty accounts fail to put forth a convincing explanation as to why the mere existence of concentrated economic power constitutes a threat to democracy that should be addressed through competition law and, conversely, why the promotion of competitive markets through competition law bolsters democracy. More precisely, both accounts omit to offer a convincing explanation for the concentration, democracy, and competition law theses that underpin the idea of a competition–democracy nexus. At this point, the reader might ask what else is then the missing piece that entwines competition and democracy? The response that this book proposes is that various iterations of the idea of a competition–democracy nexus are anchored in and can be best explained by a very specific conception of liberty, namely, republican liberty as non-domination.

2.4.1 *A Distinct, Third Notion of Liberty*

While being historically much older than the concept of negative liberty, the idea of republican liberty has only recently been rediscovered by the political theorists Quentin Skinner and Philipp Pettit.[63] The origins of this republican concept of

63 See, for instance, Pettit, 'Freedom as Antipower' (n 61); Pettit (n 58); Q Skinner, *Liberty before Liberalism* (Cambridge: Cambridge University Press 1998); Q Skinner, 'A Third Concept of Liberty: Isaiah Berlin Lecture' in The British Academy (ed), *Proceedings of the British Academy: 2001 Lectures*. Volume 117 (Oxford: Oxford University Press; British Academy 2002) 237.

liberty can be traced back to the laws and political thought of the ancient Roman Republic,[64] encapsulated, for instance, in the writings of Marcus Tullius Cicero and Titus Livius, and the Justinian Code.

Roman republican thought defined liberty based on the fundamental distinction in Roman law between the free and independent citizen (*civis*) and the slave (*servus*) who is subject to the dominion and will of somebody else.[65] Accordingly, liberty was conceived as the antonym of servitude, as the capacity to act in one's own right.[66] Hence, the status of citizen in ancient Rome depended primarily on their being an independent free man[67] or, in other words, on their not being a slave. In ancient republican thought, liberty meant the absence of a situation of dependence and subjugation to the arbitrary power of someone else, which is characteristic of a master–slave relationship.[68]

Unlike negative liberty, the republican concept of liberty as non-domination considers 'dependence on the goodwill of others'[69] or 'subjugation' understood as 'defenseless susceptibility to interference, rather than actual interference'[70] as obstruction of freedom. Republican liberty as non-domination goes above and beyond the concept of negative liberty, which is merely concerned with the absence of actual or likely interference.[71] In effect, the proponents of republican liberty affirm that humans are unfree when they live in a slave-like relationship of dependence and subjugation under the dominion of a master. In this situation, a person is unfree even if the master is benevolent and, for one reason or the other, does not interfere with their choices.[72] This happens because the slave's ability to choose freely between different options is entirely contingent on the master's goodwill. Indeed, the master remains in the position of being able to interfere at will with the slave's choices on the basis of their own idiosyncratic interests, without being required to account for the interests of the slave. The subjugation to the arbitrary will of another person not only obstructs the individual's freedom as non-domination due to the permanent risk of interference but also has important psychological effects because it negatively affects their (self-)

64 Pettit (n 58) 5, 19–20; Skinner, *Liberty before Liberalism* (n 63) 38–46.

65 'Certainly, the great divide in the law of persons is this: all men are either free men or slaves.' A Watson (ed), *The Digest of Justinian: Volume I* (Philadelphia: University of Pennsylvania Press 1985) I, 5 (3); Skinner, *Liberty before Liberalism* (n 63) 38–39.

66 Skinner, 'A Third Concept of Liberty' (n 63) 248–52. Cicero and Livy for instance defined liberty in clear opposition to servitude. MT Cicero, *On the Commonwealth and on the Laws* (Cambridge: Cambridge University Press 1999) I, 47–49; II, 42–48; III, 37 b; Titus Livius (Livy), *The History of Rome: Translated from the Original with Notes and Illustrations by George Baker, A.M.* (New York: Peter A. Mesier et al. 1823) I, xxiii; III, xxxvii–xxxviii.

67 Q Skinner, 'Rethinking Political Liberty' (2006) 61(1) *History Workshop Journal* 156, 159–62.

68 Pettit (n 58) 21–28, 31–32; Skinner, 'A Third Concept of Liberty' (n 63) 248–55.

69 Skinner, 'A Third Concept of Liberty' (n 63) 247.

70 Pettit, 'Freedom as Antipower' (n 61) 577.

71 Skinner, 'A Third Concept of Liberty' (n 63) 247.

72 Pettit (n 58) 5, 22–23. See, for instance, Cicero who pointed out that liberty 'does not consist in having a just master, but in having none'. Cicero (n 66) II, 43.

awareness. From a republican vantage point, the continuous awareness of being subjugated to and dependent on another person's arbitrary will compels the individual to constrain themself and adopt cunning or ingratiating behaviour to placate the master, and thereby preempt or avoid potential interference.[73] In rejecting any notion of 'freedom by ingratiation', republican liberty seeks to secure the ability of agents to act independently without having to worry about the consequences of their conduct on the mood of the powerful.[74]

In defining unfreedom or domination as the susceptibility to *arbitrary* interference by some powerful agents, republican liberty not only differs from negative liberty in so far as it assumes that freedom can be restricted even in the absence of actual or likely interference, for instance, when a person is subjugated to a non-interfering master. A second difference is that contrary to negative liberty as non-interference, liberty as non-domination does not view every form of interference with the choices of an agent as an illegitimate restriction of individual freedom. Rather, republican liberty recognises the possibility of non-mastering or non-arbitrary interference. Such non-arbitrary interference occurs in instances where the interferer is subject to the control of the agent, with whom they interfere in such a way that they are obliged to take into account the interests or ideas of the agent. Interference is non-arbitrary or non-dominating so long as the interferer intervenes with the agent's choices, not to enhance their own interests but those of the agent.[75] From the republican vantage point, interference does not inevitably lead to a decrease or loss of someone's liberty if institutional safeguards, such as constitutional bounds of power or the rule of law, prevent the interferer from exercising arbitrary power and compel them to track the interests of the agent.[76] Therefore, republican liberty is not only opposed to an agent being subject to the arbitrary will of a non-interfering master but also accepts the possibility of a non-mastering interferer.[77]

The ways in which this twin-axiom[78] of republican liberty marks a major difference with negative liberty are summarised in Table 2.1.[79] It can be seen from this table that there is an important overlap between both forms of liberty insofar as either conception perceives the combined absence of domination and interference as synonymous with liberty (Scenario 1). Conversely, they both also view the combined presence of domination and interference as an obstacle to liberty (Scenario 2). However, differences arise in the third scenario. Domination without

73 Skinner, 'A Third Concept of Liberty' (n 63) 256–61; Pettit (n 58) 25; Pettit (n 46) 216–17.

74 Pettit (n 58) 24–25.

75 Ibid. 22–23, 65–66.

76 Ibid. 23, 26, 35. The proposition that non-arbitrary interference does not give rise to unfreedom has been criticised for proposing a moralized conception of liberty. For an insightful discussion of this criticism, see List and Valentini (n 48) 1058–65.

77 Pettit (n 58) 22–23.

78 P Pettit, 'Republican Freedom: Three Axioms, Four Theorems' in C Laborde and J Maynor (eds), *Republicanism and Political Theory* (Malden, MA: Blackwell 2008) 102, 106–10.

79 This table is largely based on the taxonomy proposed by Pettit (n 58) 23–24.

TABLE 2.1 *Difference between republican and negative liberty*

Conception of liberty	Scenario 1 No domination No interference	Scenario 2 Domination Interference	Scenario 3 Domination No interference	Scenario 4 No domination Interference
Negative	Free	Unfree	Free	Unfree
Republican	Free	Unfree	Unfree	Free

interference does not adversely affect negative liberty but is considered a source of unfreedom by the republican tradition (Scenario 3). Meanwhile, for proponents of negative liberty, non-dominating or non-arbitrary interference automatically leads to a loss of liberty, while the republican tradition views it as being in line with or even enhancing liberty as non-domination (Scenario 4).

2.4.2 A *Brief History of Republican Liberty*

Taking its roots in the Roman Republic, the distinctive understanding of liberty as non-domination and antonym of servitude survived the downfall of ancient Rome. It importantly shaped the self-understanding of the medieval and Renaissance Italian and Dutch republics as free states.[80] The republican concept of liberty had a particularly prominent place in the writings of Niccolò Machiavelli and his notion of the *vivere libero.*[81] It also lived on in the texts of common lawyers, such as Henry de Bracton, Sir Thomas Littleton, and Sir Edward Coke – the prominent critic of concentrated economic power that we encountered in the previous chapter.[82] Liberty as non-domination prominently came to the fore of modern political thought during the power struggle between the English Parliament and the crown that culminated in the English civil wars (1641–51). During this conflict, common lawyers and several political movements – amongst them most prominently the English Levellers[83] – mobilised the notion of republican liberty as non-domination to contest the prerogatives of the English Crown. They argued that living under the arbitrary rule of the monarchy made the respect of their rights subject to and dependent upon the goodwill of the monarch. The Levellers and other republican protagonists claimed that such a state of subjugation, oppression, and precarious

80 Ibid. 19, 37.

81 Like Roman republican thinkers, Machiavelli clearly perceived liberty as antonym to servitude N Machiavelli, *Discourses on Livy* (Chicago: University of Chicago Press 1998) I, 16; I, 13; II, 27; III, 7–9; Skinner, *Liberty before Liberalism* (n 63) 10–11.

82 Skinner, 'A Third Concept of Liberty' (n 63) 248; Pettit (n 58) 5, 10, 19–20.

83 D Wootton, 'Leveller Democracy and the Puritan Revolution' in JH Burns and M Goldie (eds), *The Cambridge History of Political Thought 1450–1700* (Cambridge: Cambridge University Press 2008) 412; Skinner, 'A Third Concept of Liberty' (n 63) 247, 250–55; Skinner (n 67) 160–64.

security subjected them to servitude and unfreedom, even in the absence of any actual or threat of likely interference by the Crown.[84]

The republican notion of liberty continued to have an important bearing on the late seventeenth- and eighteenth-century political thinkers, and in particular the thought of John Locke, Montesquieu, and James Harrington.[85] Through the English Settlers, the idea of republican liberty as non-domination also found its way across the Atlantic. The colonists marshalled the republican conception of liberty as non-domination to decry their subjugation to the arbitrary rule of and taxation without any form of representation by the English motherland as a state of unfreedom and to buttress their quest for independence.[86] In the attempt to draw on the lessons of the Roman Republic in designing the institutions of the nascent American polity, it was eventually the framers of the US Constitution[87] – notably Thomas Paine,[88] Thomas Jefferson,[89] and James Madison[90] – who married the ideal of republican liberty with the principles and institutions of a liberal constitutional and representative democracy. It is at this critical juncture of the birth of the American republic that the ideals of the republic and of republican liberty eventually became closely tied to our contemporary understanding of liberal democracy.[91] The ideal of republican liberty thus lay at the origin of the first republican democracy and has been the predominant way of how liberty was conceived until the late eighteenth century. It was only during the late eighteenth and nineteenth century that this republican version of liberty as non-domination was crowded out and superseded by the negative concept of liberty as non-interference, which is today the predominant conception of liberty.[92]

2.5 EXPLAINING THE CONCENTRATION THESIS: PREVENTING CONDITIONS, ACTIONS, AND AGENTS

The previous section has introduced the republican concept of liberty as non-domination as an alternative explanatory variable for the idea of a competition–democracy nexus.

84 R Overton and W Walwyn, 'A Remonstrance of Many Thousand Citizens [1646]' in A Sharp (ed), *The English Levellers* (Cambridge: Cambridge University Press 2004) 33, 34–52; J Lilburne, 'Postscript to I Freeman's Freedom Vindicated [1646]' in A Sharp (ed), *The English Levellers* (Cambridge: Cambridge University Press 2004) 31, 31; R Overton, 'An Arrow Against all Tyrants [1646]' in A Sharp (ed), *The English Levellers* (Cambridge: Cambridge University Press 2004) 54, 55–65.

85 Pettit (n 58) 10.

86 Ibid. 33–35.

87 A Kalyvas and I Katznelson, *Liberal Beginnings: Making a Republic for the Moderns* (Cambridge: Cambridge University Press 2008) Chapter 4.

88 T Paine, *Political Writings* (Cambridge: Cambridge University Press 2000).

89 T Jefferson, *Political Writings* (Cambridge: Cambridge University Press 2004).

90 Hamilton, Madison and Jay (n 16) see most notably Federalist N° 10 and 51.

91 Pettit (n 58) 19–20, 29–30; Kalyvas and Katznelson (n 87) 88–117; JGA Pocock and R Whatmore, *The Machiavellian Moment: Florentine Political Thought and the Atlantic Republican Tradition* [1975] (Princeton: Princeton University Press 2016) 506–52.

92 Pettit (n 58) 37–49.

This republican understanding of liberty as non-domination forms an inherently distinct conception of liberty that differs from negative liberty.[93] Republican liberty indeed follows a distinct logic and is characterised by its own imaginary, grammar, language,[94] and themes[95] that fashion its distinctive geometry. This and the following sections reveal that it is exactly these specific characteristics that explain why republican liberty outperforms the conventional liberty and special interest capture accounts in explaining the competition–democracy nexus. On closer inspection, various iterations of the idea of a competition–democracy nexus mobilise the imaginary and bear attributes of the distinctive geometry that typifies republican liberty as non-domination.

2.5.1 *Domination Not Interference: A Broad Notion of Preventing Conditions (Y)*

The first difference between republican and negative liberty pertains to the specific types of acts, constraints, and restrictions – that is, the preventing conditions (y) to follow MacCallum – which can legitimately be considered an abrogation of liberty. In contrast to the advocates of negative liberty, the republican tradition perceives not only actual interference or the threat of likely interference but also the mere capacity of a powerful agent to arbitrarily interfere – 'whether or not they actually chose to exercise this capacity' – as a source of unfreedom.[96]

This broad understanding of preventing conditions of the republican concept of liberty offers a first explanation of the concentration thesis, which is the proposition that the concentration of economic power constitutes a societal problem. On a negative conception of liberty as non-interference, the concentration of economic power as such cannot be said to jeopardise liberty as long as the powerful agent does not exercise its power to interfere with other market participants. However, the world looks fundamentally different through the lens of a republican conception of liberty as non-domination, which perceives the mere exposure and ensuing subordination to a powerful agent who can interfere at any time as a preventing condition of freedom. To republicans, the mere existence of concentrated economic power constitutes an obstruction of liberty because it subjugates weaker parties into a relationship of dependence upon the arbitrary will of the powerful agent. This broad notion of preventing conditions of republican liberty percolates through all iterations of the competition–democracy nexus, which converged in the assumption that concentrated economic power in itself amounts to a source of unfreedom.

93 Ibid. 3, 8; Pettit, 'Freedom as Antipower' (n 61) 578; Skinner, 'A Third Concept of Liberty' (n 63) 255, fn. 99, 262.

94 On the distinctive language of republicanism Pettit (n 58) 130–35.

95 Ibid. 31.

96 C List and P Pettit, *Group Agency: The Possibility, Design, and Status of Corporate Agents* (Oxford: Oxford University Press 2013) 135.

2.5.1.1 Competition–Democracy Nexus 1.0

The proposition that the mere existence of concentrated economic power ensuing from monopolies and restraints of trade constitutes an obstruction of liberty was already present in the writings of Thomas More. It gained traction with the anti-monopolistic turn of the English common law during the late sixteenth century and cuts across the writings of liberal thinkers of the seventeenth and eighteenth centuries. These proto-republican protagonists coined the notion that the concentration of trade and economic power within the hands of a few[97] entailed in itself an abrogation of economic liberty, regardless of whether it led to actual or likely interference with the autonomy of other market participants. Rather, they viewed the very existence of monopoly power and restraints of trade as a 'malum in se'[98] that violated the common law.[99]

Several elements hint at the distinctive republican posture of this early liberal critique of concentrated economic power. To begin with, early proto-republican opponents of concentrated economic power likened monopoly power to domination. In their account, monopoly is equated with arbitrary power and licentiousness (*licentiam*).[100] Concentrated economic power was said to enable market participants to dominate others at will, for instance, by setting prices 'as [one] pleases'[101] or reserving all trade to oneself.[102] On this count, proto-republican critics of concentrated economic power opposed monopoly and other restraints of trade not as much on grounds of actual or likely interference as for their tendency to subjugate individuals to dominion[103] and oppression.[104] To early liberals, concentrated economic power was the epitome of an illegitimate form of private government whereby the monarch and, by extension, private masters encroached on parliament's competence to legitimately regulate and, where necessary, restrict the liberty

[97] T More, *The Utopia: In Latin from the Edition of March 1518, and in English from the First Edition of Ralph Robynson's Translation in 1551 with Additional Translations, Introduction and Notes by J.H. Lupton* [1516] (Oxford: Clarendon Press 1895) 54–55, 57–58; W Letwin, *Law and Economic Policy in America: The Evolution of the Sherman Antitrust Act* [1959] (Chicago: Chicago University Press 1981) 26, translating *Davenant v Hurdis* [1599] 72 ER 769, 778.

[98] Coke (n 59) Chapter 85, p. 180.

[99] *Darcy v Allein ('The Case of Monopolies')* [1602] (n 10) 1262; *Ipswich Tailors' Case* [1614] 77 ER 1218, 1221; *Davenant v Hurdis* [1599] 72 ER 769, 778.

[100] *Darcy v Allein ('The Case of Monopolies')* [1602] (n 10) 1265; *Ipswich Tailors' Case* [1614] (n 99) 1220.

[101] *Darcy v Allein ('The Case of Monopolies')* [1602] (n 10) 1263; Coke (n 59) Chapter 85, p. 180; More (n 97) 54–55.

[102] *Darcy v Allein ('The Case of Monopolies')* [1602] (n 10) 1262–63; Coke (n 59) 180; More (n 97) 57–58.

[103] Lilburne (n 84) 31.

[104] Overton and Walwyn (n 84) 46; J Lilburne and others, 'The Petition of 11 September 1648 [1648]' in A Sharp (ed), *The English Levellers* (Cambridge: Cambridge University Press 2004) 131, 136–37; A Smith, *An Inquiry into the Nature and Causes of the Wealth of Nations* [1776] (Oxford: Oxford University Press 1976) IV, viii, § 17, pp. 647–48.

to exercise a profession.[105] Monopoly was thus associated with arbitrary monarchical and private power, which its contrasted with a non-arbitrary and more democratic regulation of the economy by parliament.

The distinctively republican understanding of economic liberty informing this early critique of monopoly also manifests itself in the republican language and imaginaries that common lawyers and early liberals mobilised to decry the dominating effects of concentrated economic power. Monopolies and restraints of trade were not only considered to be an undue interference with the individual sphere of autonomy of market participants but were also seen to be an assault on their civil liberties and status as a freeman. In *Darcy v Allein*, it was, for instance, argued that Darcy's monopoly impinged on the rights of Allein as a 'citizen and free man of the city and of that society (*civis et liber homo de civitate et societate illa*)'.[106] Along similar lines, early liberals, such as the Levellers, Smith, Steuart, and Montesquieu, construed economic liberty in opposition to the 'subordination',[107] 'dependence',[108] and 'slavery'[109] that characterised the feudal society. To early liberals, concentrated economic power was antithetical to liberty because it reversed the transition from a feudal to a market society by subjecting otherwise economically independent individuals, free men, and citizens to subordination and dependence.[110]

The anchorage of the early common law and liberal critique of monopoly in a republican, neo-Roman conception of liberty is also reflected in the fact that proto-republicans sought to derive the prohibition of monopolies and restraints of trade directly from Roman law. Given the scarce common law precedent, antimonopoly common lawyers, such as Sir Edward Coke, invoked Roman Civil Law[111] and, notably the Justinian Code, in support of their assertion that monopolies had for a long time been condemned as illegal by the law of the land.[112] These early critics of

105 *Darcy v Allein ('The Case of Monopolies')* [1602] (n 10) 1264; *Ipswich Tailors' Case* [1614] (n 99) 1220; Coke (n 59) Chapter 85, p. 180.

106 *Darcy v Allein ('The Case of Monopolies')* [1602] (n 10) 1261. See however for the argument that the grant of the monopoly in *Darcy* was 'condemned not because it was a monopoly and therefore necessarily bad, but because it was a bad monopoly'. Letwin (n 97) 28–29.

107 J Steuart, *An Inquiry into the Principles of Political Oeconomy: Being An Essay on the Science of Domestic Policy in Free Nations* (London: A. Millar and T. Cadell 1768) 238.

108 Ibid.

109 Smith (n 104) I, x, c, § 22, pp. 142–43; III, iii, § 5, p. 400; III, iv, § 15, p. 421.

110 Montesquieu, Charles-Louis de Secondat, *De l'esprit des lois* [1748] (Paris: Garnier-Flammarion 1979) Book XX, Chapter XII; Smith (n 104) I, vii, § 22, pp. 142–43; I, x, c, § 28, p. 79.

111 *Davenant v Hurdis* [1599] (n 99) 772; Coke (n 59) Chapter 85, p. 180.

112 *Darcy v Allein ('The Case of Monopolies')* [1602] (n 10) 1263. '*Apud Justinianum monopolia non esse intromittenda, quoniam non ad commodum reipublicae sed ad labem detrimentaque pertinent. Monopolia interdixerunt leges civiles, cap. De Monopoliis lege unica. Zeno imperator statuit, ut exercentes monopolia bonis omnibus spoliarentur. Adjecit Zeno, ipsa rescripta imperialia non esse audienda, si cuiquam monopolia concedant.*' The judgment refers here to Book IV, Title LIX of Justinian's Civil Code. SP Scott, 'The Enactments of Justinian – The Code – Book IV' in SP Scott (ed), *The Civil Law: Including The Twelve Tables, The Institutes of Gaius,*

concentrated economic power thus drew on the Roman legal tradition to buttress the claim that 'odious monopoly' and privileges deprive individuals of their basic civil liberties and are therefore in conflict with the 'commonweal' or 'republic' (*reipublicae*).[113] The definition of republican liberty as civil liberty – that is as not being a slave – and the hostility against monopoly power and restraints of competition thus have a common legal and intellectual pedigree in the ancient Roman legal tradition that is encapsulated in the Justinian Code.

2.5.1.2 Competition–Democracy Nexus 2.0

The idea that the very existence of monopoly power and restraints of trade amount to an obstruction of liberty, which was first coined by early modern liberal thought, resurfaced in the United States towards the end of the nineteenth century against the backdrop of the proliferation of trusts and the trend towards industry consolidation. During the congressional debates, proponents of the Sherman Act raised not only concerns about instances where powerful trusts abused their power to actually or likely interfere with other market participants, and thereby annihilate their negative liberty. Rather, Senator Sherman and his fellow Congressmen objected to the very existence of excessively concentrated economic power that subjects market participants into a state of subjugation to the 'kingly prerogative' of an 'autocrat' in trade.[114] In decrying monopoly power as a 'kingly prerogative', Senator Sherman mobilised the same anti-monarchical language with which early republican protagonists had denounced their state of subjugation to the English Crown. It is exactly this relationship of subordination and dependence that the framers of the Sherman Act deemed incompatible with the ideal of a democratic society and polity of free and equals. Instead of the actual interference with other market players' actions and choices, it is already the capacity of powerful firms to exercise arbitrary power and to interfere with other market participants at will, which the framers of the Sherman Act perceived as a source of unfreedom.

This republican concern about the mere presence of concentrated economic power also animated the critique of big business by the progressive antitrust movement spearheaded by Louis Brandeis and Woodrow Wilson.[115] Similarly to the framers of the Sherman Act, Wilson and Brandeis denounced the mere existence

The Rules of Ulpian, The Opinions of Paulus, The Enactments of Justinian, and The Constitutions of Leo: Translated from the Original Latin, Edited, and Compared with all Accessible Systems of Jurisprudence Ancient and Modern. By S. P. SCOTT, A. M. (Cincinnati: The Central Trust Company 1932) Book IV, Title LIX.

[113] *Darcy v Allein ('The Case of Monopolies')* [1602] (n 10) 1266, 1263. *'quod privilegia quae re vera sunt in praejudicium reipublicae, magis tamen speciosa habent frontispicia, et boni publici praetextum, quam bonae et legales concessiones, sed praetextu liciti non debet admitti illicitum.'*

[114] 20 Cong Rec 2455 (1890) (n 13) 2457–58.

[115] See, for instance, Wilson's notion of 'new freedom' as 'self-mastery', W Wilson, *The New Freedom* (Leipzig: Tauchnitz 1913) 36.

of concentrated economic power and firm size – or, in Brandeis' evocative terms, the 'curse of bigness'[116] – as a new form of 'tyranny'[117] or 'political despotism',[118] which are impossible to reconcile with a republican society and polity.[119]

Similar concerns about the very existence of economic power remained influential in US antitrust policy during[120] and after[121] the second world war. They informed the recurrent idea that antitrust law should promote a Jeffersonian society in which market power is deconcentrated and dispersed amongst many small and independent businesses. For instance, the dominating effects of concentrated economic power constituted a central preoccupation of the radical 'limitist' movement that advocated the limitation of all forms of economic, social, and political power held by big business irrespective of its economic costs.[122] A similar apprehension of concentrated economic power also informed, albeit in a less radical manner, the thinking of the Harvard School during the 1950s and 1960s.[123]

2.5.1.3 Competition–Democracy Nexus 3.0

The Ordoliberals also adhered to a notion of economic liberty that considered not only the exercise of economic power and the ensuing interference with other market participants but also its very existence as an obstacle to freedom. The members of the Freiburg School asserted that concentrated economic power was antithetical to the ideal of a 'domination-free economic order' (*herrschaftsfreie Wirtschaftsordnung*) that enables the mutual, decentralised coordination of autonomous economic plans.[124] Competition can only operate as a domination-free process as long as market players lack the power to impose their will on others and to steer the course

[116] LD Brandeis, *Other People's Money and How the Bankers Use It* (New York: Frederick A. Stokes Company 1914) 162.

[117] Wilson (n 115) 53.

[118] Brandeis (n 116) 6.

[119] Ibid.; KS Rahman, 'Domination, Democracy, and Constitutional Political Economy in the New Gilded Age: Towards a Fourth Wave of Legal Realism?' (2016) 94(7) *Texas Law Review* 1329, 1339–45.

[120] FD Roosevelt, 'Message to Congress on Curbing Monopolies [1938]' www.presidency.ucsb.edu.

[121] Quotation of Representative Celler in Fox (n 23) 1151; The Attorney General's National Committee to Study the Antitrust Laws, 1955 *Report* (Washington: Superintendent of Documents, U.S. Government Printing Office 1955) 2.

[122] See, for instance, FI Raymond, *The Limitist* (New York: W.W. Norton & Co 1947); TK Quinn, *Giant Business: Threat to Democracy: The Autobiography of an Insider* (New York: NY Exposition Press 1953); W Adams, 'Dissolution, Divorcement, Divestiture: The Pyrrhic Victories of Antitrust' (1951) 27(1) *Indiana Law Journal* 1; HC Simons, *Economic Policy for a Free Society* (Chicago: Chicago University Press 1948) 17, 59, 82–83.

[123] C Kaysen and DF Turner, *Antitrust Policy: An Economic and Legal Analysis* (Cambridge, MA: Harvard University Press 1959) 17–18.

[124] F Böhm (ed), *Wettbewerb und Monopolkampf: Eine Untersuchung zur Frage des wirtschaftlichen Kampfrechts und zur Frage der rechtlichen Struktur der geltenden Wirtschaftsordnung* [1933] (Baden-Baden: Nomos 2010) 303.

of economic transactions in accordance with their private interests.[125] The presence of powerful firms was therefore considered a 'denaturalisation' of a competitive market order[126] because it transforms competition as a polycentric order of coordination into an order of subordination where mighty players are in the position to exert individual or collective arbitrary power over other market participants.[127]

It is this republican understanding of economic liberty as non-domination rather than non-interference, which explains why the Ordoliberals were alarmed by the prospect that the excessive concentration of economic power would lead to a 'refeudalisation' (*Refeudalisierung*) of economic and social relationships.[128] This admonition is clearly reminiscent of the proto-republican account by Adam Smith and other early liberal thinkers, which associated the emergence of economic and civil liberties with the transition from a feudal to a market order. The Ordoliberals warned that the adverse impact of concentrated economic power on economic liberty would reverse the progress towards greater social and political liberties, which these early liberals had celebrated as the most important achievement of the transition from a feudal to a market society.[129] For the Ordoliberals, the mere existence of economic power thus injects an element of domination into the economic system, which is incompatible with the principles of the private law society (*Privatrechtsgesellschaft*)[130] as a 'domination-free social order' (*herrschaftsfreie Sozialordnung*).[131]

2.5.2 *A Robust and Non-probabilistically Weighted Concept of Liberty: A Broad Notion of Restricted Actions (Z)*

Negative and republican liberty not only differ in the type of preventing conditions (y) but also in the type of actions (z) that can be legitimately said to be restricted so that an individual counts as unfree. We have seen in the previous section that negative liberty is frustrated if there is actual interference with an individual's preferred course of action or choice (Hobbesian version) or likely interference with alternative options that the individual may choose in a nearby likely counterfactual world (Berlinian version). It follows that negative liberty requires the presence of actual interference, or at least some plausible degree of likelihood of interference,

125 F Böhm, *Freiheit und Ordnung in der Marktwirtschaft* [1971] (Baden-Baden: Nomos 1980) 225, 227.

126 Mestmäcker's Preface to Böhm (ed) (n 124) 11. See also ibid. 17.

127 Ibid. 237, 275–76; Böhm (n 125) 36, 225; Eucken (n 14) 22, 52, 137, 174, 176–77, 246, 279, 293, 334; L Miksch, *Wettbewerb als Aufgabe: Grundsätze einer Wettbewerbsordnung* (Godersberg: Verlag Helmut Küpper 1947) 54, 103.

128 Böhm (n 14) 273–79; Böhm (n 125) 258–59.

129 Böhm (n 125) 220.

130 Ibid. 225–26.

131 Ibid. 221. See also Mestmäcker's Preface to Böhm (ed) (n 124) 8–9; Böhm (ed) (n 124) 206, 300, 303, 305; Eucken (n 14) 22, 40, 52.

for an agent to be unfree. Accordingly, negative liberty is maximised if the probability of interference is minimised in the actual world or in a nearby neighbouring world.[132]

In contrast, on a republican conception, liberty is obstructed, even in the absence of any likelihood or probability of interference, as long as one party possesses the power and capacity to interfere with the choices of another party.[133] This becomes apparent in the republican imaginary of a master–slave relationship as the antonym of liberty. Suppose there are two individuals: individual 1, a slave, and individual 2, a master. Assume further that the master (individual 2) has so much power that their preferences always have priority in determining the social outcomes,[134] so that $aP_2b \rightarrow aPb$ and $bP_2a \rightarrow bPa$. Under certain circumstances, the slave (individual 1) would still be able to satisfy their preferences $aP_1b \rightarrow aPb$ and $bP_1a \rightarrow bPa$ in a content-independent manner, as long as they are congruent with the preferences (e.g., $aP_1b \rightarrow aPb$ if aP_2b) of the master or if the master remains indifferent (I) towards both options (e.g., $aP_1b \rightarrow aPb$ if aI_2b). While mainstream liberals assume that a slave is free as long as the master is not actually interfering or likely to interfere with their choices, republicans consider the slave to be unfree even in the presence of a genuinely benevolent, non-interfering master (i.e., either aP_2b *or* aI_2b).[135] For republicans, even in the absence of interference in the actual or nearby likely counterfactual world, the decisiveness of the slave's preferences remains extremely precarious. The mere capacity of the master to interfere with the slave at will imposes modal constraints on the slave's action.[136] This is because the slave remains susceptible to possible interference in a range of possible alternative worlds, following, for instance, a sudden change in the benevolent disposition of the master. This would be the case if the slave were to prefer a over b (aP_1b), whereas the master was to suddenly change their mood and instead of remaining indifferent towards both options (aI_2b) was to express a preference of b over a, so that $bP_2a \rightarrow bPa$.

Republican liberty consequently fundamentally differs from the probabilistic logic[137] of negative liberty. On a republican account, it is not sufficient for individual 1's preferences to be content-independently decisive in the actual or nearby likely world, so that $aP_1b \rightarrow aPb$ and $bP_1a \rightarrow bPa$. Therefore, ensuring a high probability of non-interference is not a sufficient basis for the modally robust conception of republican liberty to flourish. Rather, non-domination can only be achieved so long as the capacity to interfere with someone else on an arbitrary basis is, to the largest extent possible, inaccessible to other parties.[138] Republican liberty thus presupposes

132 List (n 45) 70–71; Pettit, 'Freedom as Antipower' (n 61) 600.
133 Pettit (n 58) 22.
134 List (n 45) 69.
135 Pettit (n 58) 54, 62; Pettit, 'Freedom as Antipower' (n 61) 585.
136 List and Valentini (n 48) 1049, 1052.
137 Pettit (n 58) 64; Pettit (n 47) 33–35; Pettit, 'Freedom in the Market' (n 61) 135–37, 145.
138 Skinner, 'A Third Concept of Liberty' (n 63) 255, 262; Pettit (n 58) 123.

not only the absence of but also immunity or security from interference.[139] Unlike negative liberty, it demands a 'probabilistically unweighted'[140] or modally robust[141] protection against arbitrary interference not only in the actual but across a range of all (relevant) possible worlds.[142] This robustness requirement of republican liberty indicates that the category of relevant actions (z) that an individual must be able to carry out to be legitimately considered free pertains to a range of relevant worlds in which an individual is decisive over their choice set.

Republican liberty thus goes above and beyond the more demanding Berlinian version of content-independent negative liberty that presupposes the minimisation of the probability of interference in the actual or nearby likely world.[143] Republican liberals object that even when individuals are not exposed to actual or likely interference, they are unfree if powerful agents can interfere at will with their choices should they adopt an unfriendly disposition towards them. Therefore, they postulate that individuals only qualify as free if they benefit from both a content- and context-*in*dependent form of liberty: to be free, an individual's preferences must be decisive, not only regardless of their content but also irrespective of the context in which they find themselves when making their choices.[144] This content- and context-*in*dependent preference-decisiveness presupposes that the following condition holds true: $\square((aP_1b \rightarrow aPb) \wedge (bP_1a \rightarrow bPa))$, where $\square$ reads as '*it is necessary that*'. The modal operator $\square$ indicates that it is true for all (relevant) possible worlds that if individual 1 prefers a over b (aP_1b), then society also prefers a over b (aPb), and conversely, where individual 1 prefers b over a (bP_1a), then society will give b preference over a (bPa). Republican liberty thus goes beyond the actualist or probabilistic conception of negative liberty that presupposes the minimisation of the probability of hindering interference ($P(H)$) in the actual ($P(H \mid w_1)\ P(w_1)$) or nearby likely ($P(H \mid w_1)\ P(w_1) + P(H \mid w_2)\ P(w_2)$) world. Rather, for republican liberty to come about, the probability of hindrance must be minimised across all relevant possible worlds $P(H \mid w_1)\ P(w_1) + \cdots + P(H \mid w_k)\ P(w_k)$, where $P(w_1), \ldots, P(w_k)$ denote the respective probabilities of occurrence of these worlds, and $P(H \mid w_1)$ and $P(H \mid w_{1\ldots k})$ denote the respective conditional probabilities of hindrance in a given world $w_{1\ldots k}$.[145] This context-independent dimension of republican liberty thus calls

[139] Pettit (n 58) 69.

[140] Pettit, 'Freedom in the Market' (n 61) 138.

[141] List (n 45) 83–86; C List, 'Republican Freedom and the Rule of Law' (2006) 5(2) *Politics, Philosophy & Economics* 201.

[142] List (n 45) 72–73; Pettit (n 46) 218–19.

[143] Pettit (n 47) 34–35.

[144] Pettit (n 52) 6–8; Pettit (n 49) 704–14; List (n 45) 72–73.

[145] This formalisation of rule-like presumptions draws on List and Valentini (n 48) 1054, fn. 23. Pettit (n 47) 67–68. For a critical discussion of this approach and its limitation to capture the 'non-probabilistic' concept of republican liberty, see List and Valentini (n 48) 1058 and fn. 24.

for the minimisation of the probability of hindrance in the range of worlds where powerful agents are both friendly and unfriendly.[146]

Aiming to achieve freedom in a context-independent manner, liberty as non-domination strives for a more resilient and robust protection of liberty than its negative counterpart.[147] Republican freedom is hence less sensitive to contingencies, such as the caprices of the powerful. It provides a higher degree of security than negative liberty because it ensures that individuals can enjoy their liberty without having to worry about a sudden change of mind and attitude of currently non-interfering, benevolent, but more powerful parties. The realisation of $\Box((aP_1b \rightarrow aPb) \wedge (bP_1a \rightarrow bPa))$ thus presupposes the absence of a powerful master-like individual 2 who might frustrate the preferences of individual 1 at any time when they no longer correspond with their own preferences.

Alongside the broad understanding of preventing conditions (y), the expansive notion of relevant actions (z) resulting from the modal robustness requirement of republican liberty provides a second complementary explanation for the concentration thesis. In the same way as the mere ability of a non-interfering master to arbitrarily interfere with their slave amounts to a source of unfreedom, so too does the exposure to powerful, albeit for the moment non-interfering, monopolists or combinations make market participants susceptible to arbitrary interference, and hence unfree. The hostility of various protagonists of the competition–democracy nexus to concentrated economic power indeed assumes that consumers or competitors (individual 1) cannot be considered free – in terms of content- and context-independent preference-decisiveness – as long as they are living in the shadow of a monopolist (individual 2) who has so much power that their preferences always have priority in determining the social outcomes[148] so that $aP_2b \rightarrow aPb$ and $bP_2a \rightarrow bPa$. It is conceivable that the consumers' or competitors' preferences are decisive in the actual or nearby likely world ($aP_1b \rightarrow aPb$)) as long as the monopolist is benevolent and hence not interfering (aP_2b or aI_2b). Yet, it cannot be excluded that they are interfered with whenever the monopolist changes their mood or their preferences no longer correspond with those of the monopolist (bP_2a). From a republican perspective, the presence of concentrated economic power hangs like a dark cloud over other market participants who remain susceptible to potential arbitrary interference, and are hence unfree.

2.5.2.1 Competition–Democracy Nexus 1.0

The broad notion of relevant actions (z) that typifies republican liberty was already prominent in the critique of concentrated economic power and the notion of

[146] I follow here the notation of Pettit (n 47) 67–69.
[147] Pettit (n 58) 24–25; Pettit (n 47) 67.
[148] List (n 45) 69.

economic liberty cultivated by early modern liberals. To underscore the modal constraints that concentrated market power imposes on other market participants, the proto-republicans had recourse to the republican master–slave imaginary. In several common law cases, monopolies and restraints of trade were condemned as instruments that the guild masters used to transform their apprentices into 'domestic servant[s]' by preventing them from becoming economically independent after the end of their apprenticeship.[149] Along similar lines, the English Levellers and early liberals, such as Smith and Montesquieu, decried monopolies and restraints of trade as servitude,[150] bondage,[151] and slavery.[152] In mobilising the republican imaginary of unfreedom as a master–slave relationship, early liberal thinkers reaffirmed the proposition that the mere existence of concentrated economic power itself is detrimental to economic liberty, even in the absence of interference. Regardless of whether they result in actual or likely interference, other market participants remain susceptible to arbitrary interference by powerful guilds and monopolists.

This distinctive republican, modally robust understanding of economic liberty also crystallises in the way in which Steuart and Smith defined economic liberty. Instead of perceiving liberty as the absence of interference, they associated it with the more resilient form of the 'security' of the individual[153] and 'liberty ... *actually* ... enjoyed'.[154] In equating liberty with security, their accounts suggest that the emergence of competitive markets and the concomitant transition towards a more republican and democratic society brought about a modally robust form of liberty. The advent of competitive markets freed individuals from modal constraints and structures of subordination that characterised the feudal order and empowered them by making it more difficult for the former feudal seigniors to exert domination.[155]

2.5.2.2 Competition–Democracy Nexus 2.0

The republican imaginary of a master–slave relationship is also a rhetorical device that was recurrently used by US proponents of the idea of a competition–democracy nexus to draw attention to the domination and modal constraints resulting from the mere presence of concentrated economic power. Congressmen repeatedly compared the subordination of consumers and smaller competitors to the whim of a few powerful corporations with slavery.[156] In their eyes, concentrated economic power

[149] *Ipswich Tailors' Case* [1614] (n 99) 1219; *Colgate v Bacheler* [1569] 78 ER 1097, 1097.
[150] Overton and Walwyn (n 84) 38.
[151] Smith (n 104) IV, viii, pp. 647–48; Overton and Walwyn (n 84) 34.
[152] Smith (n 104) I, vii, § 22, pp. 142–43; I, x, c, § 28, p. 79; Montesquieu (n 110) Book XX, Chapter XII.
[153] Smith (n 104) III, iv, § 4, p. 412.
[154] Steuart (n 107) Book II, Chapter XIII, p. 242.
[155] Ibid. Book II, Chapter XIII, pp. 242–45; Smith (n 104) III, iv, § 4, p. 412.
[156] 20 Cong Rec 1765 (1890) 1768.

created a state of economic dependence on and subordination to the caprice of a few powerful firms that strongly clashed with the republican understanding of liberty as self-mastery, self-ownership, and independent status that set the freemen and slaves apart. Accordingly, the framers of the Sherman Act feared that the combination and excessive concentration of economic power enabled a few players to 'regulate and control' markets 'at their will' and 'dictate' the terms of trade.[157] Even if these powerful firms were not to exercise their power and interfere with the economic liberty of other market participants, the latter remain subjugated to and dependent on their arbitrary will as these powerful players could destroy competition and competitors whenever they see fit.[158]

Reviving the ancient republican imaginary of the master–slave relationship as the epitome of unfreedom, Brandeis and Wilson identified the dependence of individuals 'upon the goodwill of large allied capitalists' as the antonym of freedom[159] and source of domination.[160] The progressive antitrust movement asserted that even if the mighty industrial behemoths were most of the time benevolent, and therefore refrained from abusing their power, the liberty of competitors and consumers will always be frustrated for as long as powerful businesses remain capable of arbitrarily interfering with them at whim.[161] Consistent with the modally robust understanding of republican liberty, Brandeis went as far as to argue that the specific interference of powerful firms with competitors 'is not so important as the fact that such power exists and that it might be so used at any time'.[162]

2.5.2.3 Competition–Democracy Nexus 3.0

In a similar vein to the early liberal critics of monopoly power and the US proponents of the competition–democracy nexus, the Ordoliberals also mobilised the traditional republican allegory of the master–slave relationship to illustrate how concentrated economic power imposes modal constraints on other market players, and thereby jeopardises liberty. The Ordoliberals underscored that the concentration of economic power renders the liberty of other market participants precarious because the extent to which they can enjoy it becomes wholly contingent upon the goodwill of powerful firms. As the concentration of market power transforms the heterarchical process of competition into a relationship of subordination, weaker market participants are turned into dependent 'vassals' (*Hintersassen*) of the mastery firms.[163]

157 20 Cong Rec 2455 (1890) (n 13) 2460.
158 Ibid. 2457, 2459.
159 Wilson (n 115) 22.
160 Brandeis (n 116) 184.
161 Wilson (n 115) 196.
162 Brandeis (n 116) 160.
163 Böhm (n 125) 221.

In consonance with the republican tradition, the Ordoliberals also emphasised that the concentration of economic power generates various forms of psychological domination (*psychologisch begründete Verfügungsgewalt*).[164] Once powerful firms possess the capacity to arbitrarily interfere with other market participants, they can use their economic power to discipline other competitors whenever they see fit. The concentration of economic power thus creates a situation of continuous uncertainty that pushes weaker market participants towards a submissive or ingratiating behaviour.[165] This observation is clearly reminiscent of the republican belief that the mere susceptibility to arbitrary interference by powerful agents will render weaker individuals unfree, and compel them to ingratiate and placate the powerful. It thus echoes the modally robust concept of republican liberty that, unlike negative liberty, rejects any notion of liberty through ingratiation.[166]

2.5.3 *The Egalitarian Dimension of Republican Liberty: A Broad Notion of Agents (X)*

The imaginary of the master–slave relationship as an allegory of unfreedom in republican thought also points to the strong egalitarian impetus of republican liberty as its third distinctive feature.[167] To republicans, liberty always means 'equal liberty'.[168] Therefore, they adhere to a broad notion of the category of agents (x) who can be said to be free or unfree. This egalitarian dimension of liberty in the republican sense also becomes manifest in the fact that it turns upon the idea of 'self-mastery' or 'self-ownership' in the sense of 'being your own man' or woman.[169] Defining freedom as non-mastery,[170] a primary concern of republican liberty is to preserve the independent status or standing of the individual as a citizen of the republic.[171] Subjugation to hierarchical relationships of dependence is consequently deemed to be incompatible with the standing of a citizen as a free-(wo)man having their independent will and self-ownership.[172]

Whereas mainstream liberals do not object to hierarchies or imbalances of power,[173] the republican tradition displayed a fervent hostility against power asymmetries. Republican liberals firmly oppose social hierarchies as being at odds with the ideal of a society and polity of free and equals. Because it aims to maximise the non-domination of all members of the society, republican liberty has an in-built

[164] Böhm (ed) (n 124) 275.
[165] Ibid. 275–76.
[166] Pettit (n 49) 704–07.
[167] Pettit (n 58) 110–11.
[168] Cicero (n 66) I, 47; Pettit (n 47) 5.
[169] Skinner (n 67) 164.
[170] Pettit (n 58) 22.
[171] Ibid. 32–33.
[172] Skinner (n 67) 160–64; Skinner, 'A Third Concept of Liberty' (n 63) 251–52, 263.
[173] Pettit (n 47) 11.

commitment towards 'structural egalitarianism'[174] that seeks to promote 'equally intense non-domination'.[175] Assuming that the intensity of non-domination that an individual enjoys is contingent on the relative power of the individual in society as a whole, republican liberals assert that the liberty of an individual depends on their own power relative to the power of others. To guard the equal liberty of all citizens, republican freedom is committed to promoting an equal structure and distribution of power amongst citizens by levelling power imbalances and hierarchies.[176]

This egalitarian understanding of liberty grounded in a broad understanding of the category of agents (x) also characterises various iterations of the competition–democracy nexus. It offers a third explanation of why proponents of a competition–democracy nexus perceived the mere existence of concentrated economic power as a source of unfreedom. Early liberal thinkers, as well as US and European proponents of a competition–democracy nexus, associated the notion of economic liberty with the equal status and equality of opportunity of independent citizens who are 'their own master'.

2.5.3.1 Competition–Democracy Nexus 1.0

This egalitarian dimension of economic liberty is discernible from the first critiques of monopoly power from the sixteenth century onwards. The central charge against monopolistic and oligopolistic market structures by More, the early common lawyers, and the English Levellers was that they were detrimental to equality of opportunity by depriving all other individuals of the possibility to become economically independent.[177] Monopolies and restraints of trade were thus deemed as a direct assault on the equality of rights and status that all citizens of the commonwealth were entitled to by virtue of their status as freemen.[178] On this account, the English Levellers lambasted restraints of competition and economic privileges as an obstacle that hinders individuals from becoming economically independent 'masterless men'.[179] Along similar lines,[180] Adam Smith denounced the negative impact of public and private restraints of trade as an obstruction of an individual's equal

[174] Pettit (n 58) 113.

[175] Ibid. 116; Pettit, 'Freedom as Antipower' (n 61) 595.

[176] Pettit, 'Freedom as Antipower' (n 61) 598.

[177] More (n 97) 54–55; 57–58; *Davenant v Hurdis* [1599] (n 99) 770–72; *Darcy v Allein ('The Case of Monopolies')* [1602] (n 10) 1262–63; *Ipswich Tailors' Case [1614]* (n 99) 1219–20; *Colgate v Bacheler* [1569] (n 149) 1097; Coke (n 59) Chapter 85, p. 180.

[178] *Darcy v Allein ('The Case of Monopolies')* [1602] (n 10) 1261; *Colgate v Bacheler* [1569] (n 149) 1097; *Ipswich Tailors' Case [1614]* (n 99) 1220; Coke (n 59) Chapter 85, p. 180.

[179] J Lilburne, 'England's New Chains Discovered [1649]' in A Sharp (ed), *The English Levellers* (Cambridge: Cambridge University Press 2004) 140, 144; Anderson (n 12) 72.

[180] S Fleischacker, 'Adam Smith on Equality' in CJ Berry, MP Paganelli and C Smith (eds), *The Oxford Handbook of Adam Smith* (Oxford: Oxford University Press 2013) 485, 489.

opportunity to engage in economic activity.[181] In the same way as the Levellers, Smith and Steuart criticised exclusive rights and other forms of privileges as undue forms of state favouritism being at odds with the principles of the rule of law and 'evidently contrary to that justice and equality of treatment which the sovereign owes to all the different orders of his subjects'.[182] Concentrated economic power was therefore seen to be a roadblock to the emergence of a society of independent and small proprietors, yeomen, and tradesmen, who were celebrated by early liberal thinkers as the epitome of the independent and virtuous republican freemen.[183]

Early liberal thinkers also drew a direct link between the adverse effect of concentrated economic power on the procedural notion of equality of opportunity and substantive equality.[184] They bemoaned that by negating large parts of the population the opportunity to become economically active masterless men, monopolies, oligopolies, and restraints of trade entrench and exacerbate substantive economic inequalities of wealth.[185] The negative distributive impact of concentrated economic power is further compounded by the fact that price increases resulting from monopoly power hit the poorer classes of society particularly hard by driving up input and consumer prices.[186] Accordingly, concentrated economic power has a double-adverse distributive effect: it undermines equality of opportunity to pursue an economic activity and, at the same time, hits the very same group of excluded individuals with exploitative prices.

To early liberal thinkers, economic liberty thus had a strong egalitarian connotation. Early proponents of competitive markets assumed that competition, by eroding instances of concentrated economic power, opening up broad-based economic opportunities, and ensuring a fair participative process, also indirectly promotes distributive equality of income and wealth because it simultaneously constrains the exercise of market power and brings about a more equal and merit-based distribution of wealth and political power.[187] They conjectured that competition,

[181] See Book I, Chapter X entitled 'Inequalities occasioned by the policy of Europe', Smith (n 104) I, x, c; see in particular §§ 1–18, pp. 135–39; E Rothschild, 'Adam Smith and Conservative Economics' (1992) 45(1) *The Economic History Review* 74, 92–93; D Boucoyannis, 'The Equalizing Hand: Why Adam Smith Thought the Market Should Produce Wealth without Steep Inequality' (2013) 11(4) *Perspectives on Politics* 1051.

[182] Smith (n 104) III, iii, § 19, pp. 423–24; IV, viii, § 30, p. 654; Steuart (n 107) Book II, Chapter XIII, pp. 244–45.

[183] Smith (n 104) III, iii, § 19, pp. 423–24; P Rosanvallon, *Le libéralisme économique: Histoire de l'idée de marché* (Paris: Seuil 1989) 77–81.

[184] Smith (n 104) I, viii, § 36, p. 96; Anderson (n 12) 67; Fleischacker (n 180) 498.

[185] More (n 97) 54–55, 57–58; Smith (n 104) I, xi, c, §§ 1 and 12, pp. 135, 138, §§ 31 and 32, p. 146; I, x, c, § 41, pp. 151–52.

[186] More (n 97) 54–55; *Davenant v Hurdis* [1599] (n 99) 772; *Darcy v Allein ('The Case of Monopolies')* [1602] (n 10) 1262–63; *Ipswich Tailors' Case* [1614] (n 99) 1220. See, for instance, Smith's description of the wealth transfer from consumers to monopolists as unfair 'taxation' Smith (n 104) V, I, e, § 30, pp. 754–55.

[187] Steuart (n 107) Book II, Chapter XIII, p. 245.

by dispersing and bringing about a more equalised distribution of wealth and property, will promote equality of opportunity and allow individuals to emancipate themselves by becoming independent economic agents.[188] By equalising economic exchanges, the emergence of competitive markets thus creates the framework of 'social relations between free and equal persons'[189] and ensures rough equality of power and wealth that is considered a precondition of a democratic polity.[190]

If there is an allegory that fully captures the equalising tendency of competitive markets and their propensity to secure equality of opportunity, then it is Smith's 'impartial spectator' [191] in the *Theory of Moral Sentiments*. Smith, here, has recourse to the competitive process to illustrate the notion of procedural fairness:

> In the race for wealth, and honours, and preferments, he may run as hard as he can, and strain every nerve and every muscle, in order to outstrip all his competitors. But if he should jostle, or throw down any of them, the indulgence of the spectators is entirely at an end. It is a violation of fair play, which they cannot admit.[192]

Smith's allegory of the impartial spectator portrays competition as an institution that ensures a level playing field and equal opportunities for all market participants. By contrasting fair competitive ('may run as hard as he can, and strain every nerve and every muscle, in order to outstrip all his competitor') with unfair, anticompetitive conduct ('should jostle, or throw down any of them'), the allegory already encapsulates a distinction between what we would call today *competition on the merits* and *unfair competition*. Early liberal thinkers thus understood competitive markets as catalysts for and safeguards of an egalitarian form of economic liberty as equal opportunity and status. Their understanding of economic liberty thus fundamentally differed from our contemporary negative concept of liberty as non-interference, which is largely indifferent towards the concentration and imbalances of economic power, and ensuing inequalities in terms of opportunities or wealth.[193]

2.5.3.2 Competition–Democracy Nexus 2.0

This egalitarian dimension of the republican concept of liberty that so prominently transpires from early liberal thought also shaped the very beginnings of US antitrust law. The framers of the Sherman Act conceptualised liberty as equal liberty and status, claiming that 'industrial liberty . . . lies at the foundation of the equality of all rights and privileges'.[194] Echoing the accounts of the emerging market society by

[188] Anderson (n 12) 76–77.
[189] Ibid. 65; Rosanvallon (n 183) 71.
[190] Montesquieu (n 110) Book V, VI; J-J Rousseau, *Du contrat social* [1767] (Paris: Flammarion 2001) I, ix, p. 64 and III, iv, p. 106.
[191] Fleischacker (n 180) 487.
[192] A Smith, *The Theory of Moral Sentiments* [1759] (New York: Penguin 2009) II, ii, p. 101.
[193] Pettit (n 47) 11.
[194] 20 Cong Rec 2455 (1890) (n 13) 2457.

early liberals, the framers of the Sherman Act portrayed economic concentration as a relic of the social hierarchies and relationships of subjugation that shaped the feudal and absolutist order.[195] The concentration of economic power in the hands of a few large-scale corporations and the ensuing forms of dependence and subjugation were considered to be at odds with the Jeffersonian ideal of an egalitarian yeomen society in which power and wealth are atomised amongst a multitude of independent and equal masterless men.[196]

The framers of the Sherman Act articulated this egalitarian understanding of economic liberty by depicting the proposed antitrust rules as a safeguard of the equality of opportunity of small and independent businessmen.[197] They thereby responded to the widespread popular discontent about practices by big businesses that stifled smaller competitors' ability and opportunity to compete,[198] and 'crush [ed] out the little men and little enterprises'.[199] This egalitarian concern was most clearly expressed by Senator Sherman, who repeatedly warned against the adverse effect of economic concentration on equality and its destabilising repercussions on the social and political order:

> Society is now disturbed by forces never felt before. The popular mind is agitated with problems that may disturb social order, and among them all none is more threatening than the inequality of condition, of wealth and opportunity that has grown within a single generation out of the concentration of capital into vast combinations to control production and trade and to break down competition.[200]

Senator Sherman's statement, linking the detrimental impact of industry concentration on equality of opportunity with 'inequality of condition [and] wealth', mimics the presupposition first coined by proto-republicans that the inequality of opportunities resulting from concentrated economic power also feeds through into substantive inequality of wealth. Along similar lines, proponents of the Sherman Act repeatedly stressed the unfair distributive effects of monopoly and cartelisation, in

195 See T Roosevelt, 'The Trusts, the People, and the Square Deal' in DA Crane and H Hovenkamp (eds), *The Making of Competition Policy: Legal and Economic Sources* (New York: Oxford University Press 2013) 107, 113; TW Arnold, 'The Bottlenecks of Business [1940]' in DA Crane and H Hovenkamp (eds), *The Making of Competition Policy: Legal and Economic Sources* (New York: Oxford University Press 2013) 206, 209.

196 R Hofstadter, 'What Happened to the Antitrust Movement?' in DA Crane and H Hovenkamp (eds), *The Making of Competition Policy: Legal and Economic Sources* (New York: Oxford University Press 2013) 223, 227; PH Brietzke, 'The Constitutionalization of Antitrust: Jefferson, Madison, Hamilton, and Thomas C. Arthur' (1987) 22 (2) *Valparaiso University Law Review* 275, 276; Pitofsky (n 23) 1058–59.

197 20 Cong Rec 2455 (1890) (n 13) 2457, 2460.

198 19 Cong Rec 8559 (1890) 8561; 20 Cong Rec 2455 (1890) (n 13) 2457.

199 19 Cong Rec 8559 (1890) (n 198) 8561; 20 Cong Rec 2455 (1890) (n 13) 2457; Fox (n 23) 1151–52; JJ Flynn, 'Antitrust Policy and the Concept of a Competitive Process' (1990) 35(4) *New York Law School Law Review* 893, 910.

200 20 Cong Rec 2455 (1890) (n 13) 2460.

particular on poorer classes.[201] By vilifying trusts as 'robber barons' and 'plunderers',[202] the framers of the Sherman Act condemned the wealth transfer from consumers and competitors to monopolies and cartels as an unfair, coercive form of enrichment,[203] which is incompatible with the idea of distributive justice and equal freedom.[204] Echoing the egalitarian understanding of republican liberty as self-ownership, the proponents of the Sherman Act affirmed that '[i]f the proceeds of the labour of our men and women are not to be their own we have no liberty and our Government is a farce and a fraud'.[205]

This egalitarian understanding of economic liberty continued to reverberate through the progressive antitrust movement. In a similar vein to the framers of the Sherman Act, Brandeis and Wilson put on guard against the adverse effects of economic concentration on the equality of opportunity and the equal status of small and independent businesses.[206] They warned that large businesses disposed of and regularly made use of the power to 'crush the little man'.[207] Underscoring the role of antitrust laws to 'keep open the path of opportunity'[208] and 'look after the men who are on the make rather than the men who are already made',[209] Wilson and Brandeis revived the Jeffersonian ideal of a yeomen republic and resonated the proto-republican praise of the virtues of small and independent businessmen as promoters of social and economic progress.[210]

Similar considerations about fairness and the preservation of a Jeffersonian society of free and equals in which power and wealth are dispersed amongst the many remained influential during the 1950s and 1960s.[211] For instance, egalitarian concerns about the concentration of economic power informed calls by the limitist movement for the deconcentration of large-scale firms and consolidated industries. In line with this understanding of republican liberty as structural equality, the Harvard School also emphasised the role of the competitive process in guaranteeing

201 19 Cong Rec 6041 (1888) 6041; 20 Cong Rec 1457 (1890) 1457–58; 20 Cong Rec 2455 (1890) (n 13) 2458, 2460.

202 20 Cong Rec 1457 (1890) (n 201) 1458.

203 20 Cong Rec 1765 (1890) (n 156) 1768.

204 20 Cong Rec 1457 (1890) (n 201) 1458. According to some scholars, the prevention of wealth transfer even constitutes the primary goal of US antitrust. RH Lande, 'Wealth Transfers as the Original and Primary Concern of Antitrust: The Efficiency Interpretation Challenged' (1982) 34(1) *Hastings Law Journal* 65.

205 20 Cong Rec 1457 (1890) (n 201) 1457.

206 Brandeis (n 116) 152; Wilson (n 115) 23.

207 Wilson (n 115) 190.

208 L Brandeis, 'Shall We Abandon the Policy of Competition?: Reprinted from The Curse of Bigness [1934]' in DA Crane and H Hovenkamp (eds), *The Making of Competition Policy: Legal and Economic Sources* (New York: Oxford University Press 2013) 185, 189.

209 Wilson (n 115) 23–24.

210 Brandeis (n 116) 135, 150, 163.

211 Fox (n 23) 1153; EM Fox and LA Sullivan, 'Antitrust-Retrospective and Prospective: Where Are We Coming From – Where Are We Going?' (1987) 62(5) *New York University Law Review* 936, 1180.

equality of opportunity and procedural fairness[212] and recognised that 'fairness' or 'fair conduct' might constitute a distinct goal of antitrust law.[213]

2.5.3.3 Competition–Democracy Nexus 3.0

A similar egalitarian conception of economic liberty, which was shared by early liberal thinkers and various US antitrust paradigms, also percolated through Ordoliberal thought. Consistent with the republican tradition, the members of the Ordoliberal School understood economic liberty as equal freedom of all market participants.[214] In continuity with early liberal thinkers, the Ordoliberals drew a direct analogy between economic independence and the equal status, the *status civilis*, of citizens in a society of free and equals.[215] The Ordoliberals conceived competitive markets as 'open markets',[216] which operate as an inclusive process that guarantees equal opportunities to carry out an economic activity.[217] In securing broad-based economic opportunities, competition acts as a catalyst for equal freedom.[218] This egalitarian understanding of economic liberty also underpinned the Ordoliberal warning that the excessive concentration of private economic power would reconvert the heterarchical market society into a hierarchical neo-feudal order.[219]

By putting the principle of equal opportunity at the heart of their conception of competition, the Ordoliberals echoed Adam Smith's understanding of equality of opportunity and fairness as central virtues of the competitive process.[220] The Ordoliberals reverted to Smith's famous allegory of the 'impartial spectator'[221] to

212 Kaysen and Turner (n 123) 14–15, 17; The Attorney General's National Committee to Study the Antitrust Laws (n 121) 2.

213 Kaysen and Turner (n 123) 17.

214 F Böhm, 'Rule of Law in a Market Economy [1966]' in AT Peacock and H Willgerodt (eds), *Germany's Social Market Economy: Origins and Evolution* (Houndmills: Macmillan 1989) 46, 51.

215 Böhm (n 125) 12, 18, 106–09, 226; Eucken (n 14) 52, 336; E-J Mestmäcker (ed), *Wirtschaft und Verfassung in der Europäischen Union* (Baden-Baden: Nomos 2003) 36–37.

216 Eucken (n 14) 42, 264–69; Miksch (n 127) 38.

217 Böhm (ed) (n 124) 272; F Böhm, 'Freiheit und Ordnung in der Marktwirtschaft [1971]' in N Goldschmidt (ed), *Grundtexte zur Freiburger Tradition der Ordnungsökonomik* (Tübingen: Mohr Siebeck 2008) 299, 306; DJ Gerber, 'Constitutionalizing the Economy: German Neo-liberalism, Competition Law and the "New" Europe' (1994) 42(1) *American Journal of Comparative Law* 25, 38.

218 Böhm (n 125) 12; W Röpke, *Jenseits von Angebot und Nachfrage* [1958] (Düsseldorf: Verl.-Anst. Handwerk 2009) 17–19.

219 Böhm (n 14) 273–79; Böhm (n 125) 258–59.

220 For a discussion of the impact of Adam Smith's ideal of justice on the Ordoliberal thought, see Mestmäcker's Preface to Böhm (ed) (n 124) 7–11.

221 Böhm directly refers to a German translation of Smith's famous passage in the *Theory of Moral Sentiments* to illustrate the notion of equality of opportunity underpinning the competitive process ibid. 239. Smith (n 192) II. Ii, 101.

illustrate how competition ensures fairness and equality of opportunity.[222] Indeed, the Smithian notion of the impartial spectator informs the Ordoliberal distinction between performance-based and hindrance competition. When competing for the goodwill of consumers as an 'impartial spectator',[223] market players are free to do everything to enhance their economic performance as long as they do not hinder other competitors from doing the same. In contrast, any form of conduct whereby a player tries to take advantage over their competitor by reducing the latter's opportunity to compete is considered to be an illegitimate form of hindrance competition at odds with the rules of fair play.[224]

In stressing the propensity of competitive markets to ensure broad-based economic opportunity, the Ordoliberal notion of economic liberty primarily turned on a procedural understanding of equality and fairness. Unlike various US antitrust movements, the Ordoliberals did not necessarily perceive the role of competition (law) as promoting an egalitarian society in which power and wealth are equally spread amongst a multitude of small businesses. This, however, does not mean that substantive or distributive fairness and equality considerations were totally alien to Ordoliberal thought.[225] On the contrary, they objected to concentrated economic power because it unsettles the fairness of exchange that characterises economic transactions in competitive markets and leads to unfair wealth transfers from consumers to monopolists or cartelists. Moreover, the Ordoliberals highlighted the importance of the rules of the game in determining the opportunities of economic agents to participate in the competitive process, which, in turn, influence the distribution of income and wealth.[226] By ensuring equality before the law and equal opportunities, the private law society and competitive process play a vital role in ensuring that economic inequalities are only the result of differences in the economic performance of the individual market participants rather than the outcome of power imbalances.[227]

The members of the Freiburg School thus recognised that the design of the institutional rules underpinning competition and private law has far-reaching distributive consequences.[228] The extent to which the outcomes of the economic process can be considered fair crucially depends on the specific design of the rules of the game. The particular way and pattern in which competition law and other

[222] Mestmäcker's Preface to Böhm (ed) (n 124) 9.
[223] Mestmäcker's Preface to ibid.
[224] Ibid. 227, 239, 240.
[225] Mestmäcker (ed) (n 215) 36.
[226] Böhm (ed) (n 124) 257, 300–01.
[227] F Böhm, 'Die Bedeutung der Wirtschaftsordnung für die politische Verfassung: Kritische Betrachtungen zu dem Aufsatz von Ministerialrat Dr. Adolf ARNDT über das "Problem der Wirtschaftsdemokratie in den Verfassungsentwürfen"' (1946) 1(6) *Süddeutsche Juristen-Zeitung* 141, 147; Miksch (n 127) 54; Böhm (ed) (n 124) 257–62, 271–72.
[228] Böhm (ed) (n 124) 256.

fields of private law configure and allocate the rights of market agents to participate in the competitive process importantly (pre)determine distributive outcomes. Instead of perceiving competition law as a tool for redistribution, the Ordoliberals underscored its role in securing a fair pre-distribution of market access rights, and hence opportunities for market participants to take part in the competitive race. At the same time, various thinkers close to the Ordoliberal School also highlighted the importance of redistributive taxation and social policies as pillars of the social market economy in correcting the inequalities of wealth that result from undistorted market processes.[229]

The various iterations of the idea of a competition–democracy nexus thus cultivated a conception of economic liberty that is characterised by a distinctly republican posture, which fundamentally differs from a negative conception of liberty as non-interference. These differences, with respect to agents (x), preventing conditions (y), and relevant actions (z), explain why the republican conception of liberty as non-domination outperforms the special interest capture and conventional liberty accounts in unpacking the competition–democracy nexus. The thick notion of republican liberty provides a better conceptual explanation of the concentration thesis (i.e., the proposition that concentration of power as such has adverse societal consequences) that is often implied by the idea of a competition–democracy nexus. Unlike the probabilistic notion of negative liberty that underpins the conventional liberty account, the modally robust republican concept of liberty allows us to explain why proponents of a competition–democracy nexus perceived the existence of concentrated power in *itself*, and not only its exercise as a 'kingly prerogative' incompatible with 'our form of government'.[230]

From the perspective of negative liberty, concentrated economic power can only represent a source of unfreedom when it gives rise to actual or likely interference. In contrast, the republican tradition is not only alert to the actual or likely interference resulting from the *exercise* of power but also perceives the potential of arbitrary interference deriving from the mere *existence* of power as a source of unfreedom. From this vantage point, it is the mere existence of concentrated power and the concomitant subjugation of market participants to powerful firms which are capable of arbitrarily interfering with them whenever they see fit that constitutes an obstacle to economic liberty. Whereas negative liberty is indifferent towards asymmetries of economic power, the context-independent, modal robustness, and egalitarian dimension of republican liberty elucidate the reasons why the concentration of economic power is often perceived as being at odds with a society of free and equals. From a republican perspective, living in the

[229] Eucken (n 14) 300–01; L Erhard, *Wohlstand für alle* [1957] (Köln: Anaconda 2009).
[230] 20 Cong Rec 2455 (1890) (n 13) 2458.

presence of concentrated economic power is like living under the domination of a benevolent, non-interfering master.

2.6 EXPLAINING THE DEMOCRACY THESIS: A STRONG COMMITMENT TO REPUBLICAN DEMOCRACY

A fourth feature in which negative and republican liberty diverge is their attitude towards the role of institutions and the form of government in securing liberty. The republican tradition acknowledged that liberty in its modally robust form as non-domination could not simply be brought about through spontaneous balances of power that are achieved through individual self-help and self-defence. Since the ancient Roman Republic, the proponents of republican freedom instead devised protective institutions to preserve liberty as non-domination by creating and sustaining institutional balances of reciprocal power.[231] Therefore, the republican tradition is based on the belief that liberty as non-domination presupposes a specific political regime and institutional safeguards that counter-balance power structures.[232]

Republican liberals highlight the importance of protective institutions – Philip Pettit calls them institutions of 'antipower'[233] – that actively contribute to the reduction or elimination of power imbalances without, however, creating new forms of domination.[234] Instead of merely shielding individuals from any form of actual or likely coercion, institutions of antipower also secure liberty in a modally robust sense by actively equalising power relationships and enhancing individual empowerment and emancipation.[235] Institutions of antipower promote modally robust liberty through the redistribution of power and equalisation of patterns of hierarchical dependence within and outside the political sphere.[236]

This instrumental role of institutions of antipower in maximising non-domination explains why republican liberty, unlike its negative counterpart, is firmly committed to democracy.[237] The republican tradition argues that citizens could only be said to be free, independent, and not subject to a state of servitude if they do not live under the authority of somebody else. Consequently, enjoying republican liberty presupposes that one lives under a free form of government, which ensures that the citizens

[231] JP McCormick, 'Machiavellian Democracy: Controlling Elites with Ferocious Populism' (2001) 95(2) *American Political Science Review* 297.
[232] Pettit, 'Freedom as Antipower' (n 61) 601.
[233] Ibid. 588.
[234] Ibid.
[235] Ibid. 591, 595.
[236] Ibid. 602.
[237] Skinner, *Liberty before Liberalism* (n 63) 23–28.

can decide upon their own laws.[238] Republican liberals indeed assert that liberty can only be secured under a specific form of government or polity that provides for specific public, institutional safeguards against arbitrary power and interference.[239] Republican liberty is, therefore, closely associated with a specific form of republican polity in which the end of all government is to guarantee civil liberty as non-domination. Unlike negative liberty, republican liberty cannot exist under any form of government. It can only thrive under a specific, republican form of government – in short, a republican democracy.[240]

It is this crucial link between the perception of concentrated power as an obstruction of republican liberty and the close kinship between republican liberty and republican democracy that underpin and allow us to make sense of the democracy thesis (i.e., the proposition that concentrated economic power poses a distinctive threat to democracy as opposed to other forms of government). While it may sound absurd to proponents of negative liberty, the proposition of interdependence between the economic and political order shared by early liberal proponents of competitive markets, American antitrust paradigms, and Ordoliberals alike can make perfect sense from the perspective of a republican conception of liberty. For republicans, a republican form of democratic government derives its ultimate legitimacy from promoting or maximising republican liberty as non-domination by guaranteeing electoral and non-electoral institutions of antipower that enable the contestability both of public and private power.[241] As concentrated economic power is considered to be a source of domination, and hence unfreedom, both the mere existence and abuse of economic power give rise to a reduction of liberty that constitutes an assault on a republican democracy itself and undermines its legitimacy. Keeping economic power in check and thereby averting domination in the economic sphere thus becomes a core task and source of legitimacy of a republican form of democracy. This explains why early liberals, proponents of antitrust laws in the United States, and Ordoliberals alike not only perceive concentrated economic power and its abuse as an obstruction to welfare or individual liberty but also as an assault on the polity – the commonwealth, *res publica*, or democracy – itself.[242]

[238] See, for instance, Skinner, *Liberty before Liberalism* (n 63) 23–28. While positive and republican liberty overlap in this point, unlike proponents of positive liberty, republican thinkers generally advocated representative rather than direct democracy.

[239] Pettit (n 58) 27.

[240] For tensions between republicanism and (popular) democracy, see JP McCormick, 'Republicanism and Democracy' in A Niederberger and P Schink (eds), *Republican Democracy: Liberty, Law and Politics* (Edinburgh: Edinburgh University Press 2014) 89, 89.

[241] Pettit (n 58) ix, 180–205; Pettit (n 47) 22, 179–84, 302.

[242] 19 Cong Rec 8519 (1888) (n 13) 8521; 20 Cong Rec 2455 (1890) (n 13) 2460, 2469; Darcy v Allein ('The Case of Monopolies') [1602] (n 10) 1266.

2.7 EXPLAINING THE COMPETITION LAW THESIS: ARBITRARY AND NON-ARBITRARY INTERFERENCE

A fifth differentiating factor between negative and republican liberty is their respective attitudes towards legal rules. For mainstream liberals, any kind of state intervention and law that interferes with private choices reduces liberty.[243] On this account, mainstream liberals posit that legitimate state interference must be subject to a delicate balancing exercise. The state may only intervene when the entailing loss in freedom of the individual with whose choices it interferes is compensated by an at least commensurate increase in freedom for other individuals, for instance, as the result of reduced danger.[244] For state intervention to be legitimate, the entailing loss in freedom of the individual with whose choices it interferes needs to be compensated or outweighed by an at least commensurate increase in freedom for other individuals.[245] Legitimate state intervention thus presupposes some form of balancing of rights or a cost–benefit analysis, which shows that state interference maximises the overall level of negative liberty in society. This is the case if the gains in liberty achieved by preventing an agent from unduly interfering with the choices of other individuals compensate for the reduction in liberty of the agent caused by the state intervention to prevent this interference.[246] Conversely, this means that the state may only step in to prevent one private party from interfering with the liberty of another party if the private interference is unreasonable; that is, if the loss in liberty for the other party is so disproportionately high that it outweighs the cost in terms of loss of liberty on the part of the interfering party as a consequence of state intervention.

In contrast, because it recognises the possibility of non-mastering or non-arbitrary interference,[247] republican liberty as non-domination does not classify every form of, but only arbitrary, interference with the choices of an agent as an illegitimate restriction of their freedom.[248] The republican belief that non-arbitrary interference does not inevitably reduce liberty reshapes the calculus of the balancing of rights to decide when state intervention is justified to prevent or remedy an undue restriction of liberty. Unlike mainstream liberals, the proponents of republican liberty do not assume that every form of state interference with private autonomy through legislation also automatically obstructs individual freedom.[249] Laws and regulations adopted in a democratic republic through processes that ensure their non-arbitrary

[243] Pettit (n 58) 23–24, 36–40; Pettit, 'Freedom in the Market' (n 61) 147.
[244] Pettit, 'Freedom as Antipower' (n 61) 596; Pettit, 'Freedom in the Market' (n 61) 145; Pettit (n 58) 35; Mill (n 35) 80, 93.
[245] Pettit (n 58) 35; Pettit, 'Freedom in the Market' (n 61) 145.
[246] Pettit (n 58) 35; Pettit, 'Freedom as Antipower' (n 61) 596.
[247] Pettit, 'Freedom as Antipower' (n 61) 595–97.
[248] Pettit (n 58) 22–23, 65–66.
[249] Ibid. 23–24, 36–40.

character by tracking citizens' interests and complying with the rule of law and constitutional safeguards do not inevitably reduce the citizens' freedom because they do not subjugate them to arbitrary interference or domination.[250] Therefore, republican liberals assert that non-arbitrary state interference, unlike private interference,[251] does not necessarily undermine liberty, even if it restricts the individual's sphere of autonomy.[252]

To republicans, non-arbitrary state interference does not inevitably compromise freedom, and hence creates much less or no costs (in terms of reduction of freedom) at all. At the same time, in the eyes of proponents of republican liberty, state intervention in the form of legal rules or laws may also generate higher benefits than those recognised by mainstream liberals. Republican liberals are acutely aware of the fact that legal rules are constitutive[253] of a resilient, modally robust form of liberty. This is because legal rules do not only prevent isolated occurrences of arbitrary interference at a given point in time; but, by making certain forms of arbitrary interference inaccessible, or at least prohibitively costly, to private parties, laws may also reduce the capacity and ability of powerful agents to indulge in arbitrary interference in the future. Legal rules are, therefore, capable of decreasing the 'level of domination overall' in a society.[254]

The republican tradition thus conceives legal rules as authoritative propositions that prescribe how the world should work, and thereby define classes of permissible worlds.[255] From this point of view, legal rules constitute moral desiderata that have a modal character because they propose facts that are true across all permissible worlds.[256] This modal character of legal rules is nicely captured by the difference between the necessity operator OA, which is to be read that '*it is obligatory that* A' and the possibility operator PA, which is to be read as '*it is permissible that* A'. Legal rules ensure $O((aP_ib \rightarrow aPb) \wedge (bP_ia \rightarrow bPa))$, so that the preference-decisiveness of individual i $(aP_ib \rightarrow aPb) \wedge (bP_ia \rightarrow bPa)$ is true across all permissible worlds in a relevant class relative to the actual world. Legal rules thus play a crucial role in securing the modally robust form of republican liberty because they guarantee that society is organised in such a way that whenever there is a moral desideratum $O((aP_ib \rightarrow aPb) \wedge (bP_ia \rightarrow bPa))$, the modal fact $\Box((aP_ib \rightarrow aPb) \wedge (bP_ia \rightarrow bPa))$ also holds. In contrast, less stringent legal commands, such as legal standards ensuring a balancing of rights consistent with a negative conception of liberty, take the form $P((aP_ib \rightarrow aPb) \wedge (bP_ia \rightarrow bPa))$. Legal standards thus indicate that it is possible ($\Diamond$),

[250] Pettit, 'Freedom as Antipower' (n 61) 586–87.
[251] Pettit, 'Freedom in the Market' (n 61) 146.
[252] Ibid. 135; E Gill-Pedro, 'Freedom to Conduct Business in EU Law: Freedom from Interference or Freedom from Domination?' (2017) 9(2) *European Journal of Legal Studies* 103, 105–09.
[253] Pettit (n 58) 35.
[254] Pettit, 'Freedom in the Market' (n 61) 146.
[255] List (n 141) 205–06.
[256] Ibid. 206–07.

and hence true in some but not all permissible worlds that individual *i*'s preferences are decisive: that is, $\Diamond((aP_ib \rightarrow aPb) \wedge (bP_ia \rightarrow bPa))$. Conversely, $P((aP_ib \rightarrow aPb) \wedge (bP_ia \rightarrow bPa))$ also implies the possibility that in some relevant worlds, individual *i*'s preferences are not decisive: $\Diamond((aP_ib \rightarrow \neg aPb) \vee (bP_ia \rightarrow \neg bPa))$, where $\Diamond$ reads as '*it is possible*', $\wedge$ as '*and*', $\vee$ as '*or*' and $\neg$ as '*not*'. This might be the case where the balancing of rights indicates that the costs of state intervention ensuring preference-decisiveness of individual *i* against interference would outweigh its benefits because it would reduce the liberty of the interferer more than it would enhance the liberty of individual *i*.

Understood in the republican sense as modal moral desiderata, legal rules can thus define right sets of individuals that are guaranteed across all relevant possible worlds. This is the reason why legal rules form a crucial tool to ensure the modally robust, context-independent, and non-probabilistic conception of liberty as non-domination.[257] Republican liberty, therefore, has 'a built-in rule of law requirement',[258] which secures its non-probabilistic and modally robust nature. Both the belief that non-arbitrary state interference may be legitimate and the recognition that legal rules play a primordial role in guaranteeing republican liberty explain why it is much easier for republicans than for mainstream liberals to justify state interference.

For republican liberals, there is hence no immediate tension between calls for more vigorous competition law enforcement against concentrated economic power and economic liberty. All to the contrary, republican liberals posit that economic liberty cannot exist absent protective legal rules. This constitutive role of legal rules in ensuring liberty as non-domination explains why early liberals, proponents of US antitrust law, and Ordoliberals advocated legal rules against monopoly power and restrictions of competition as a safeguard of – rather than an obstacle to – liberty. This republican 'law-liberty' theme[259] had already taken shape in Sir Edward Coke's attempt to root economic liberty and the protection of competition in the Magna Carta.[260] In arguing that economic liberty has been recognised in the 'ancient and fundamentall laws of the kingdom', which are enshrined in the quasi-constitutional Magna Carta, Coke made for the first time the argumentative move to elevate economic liberty to a quasi-constitutional right that ought to be guaranteed in a modally robust manner to all traders *qua* their status as citizens of the common-wealth.[261] Along similar lines, Montesquieu and Smith stressed the importance of legal rules in securing economic liberty, observing that economic liberty does not

[257] Ibid. 210–11.
[258] Ibid. 211.
[259] Pettit identifies the 'law-liberty' theme as a distinctive feature of the Republican tradition. Pettit (n 58) 35.
[260] Coke (n 59) Chapter 85, p. 180.
[261] Ibid.

presuppose the absence of laws but that such lawlessness would entail 'servitude' instead of freedom.[262]

This law-liberty theme also reverberates across the US and Ordoliberal competition law tradition. In direct continuity of Sir Edward Coke's attempt to derive the right to economic liberty from the Magna Carta, the framers of the Sherman Act habitually referred to the newly adopted antitrust laws as a 'remedial statute, a bill of rights, a charter of liberty'[263] that empowers the weaker parties, and ensures the non-contingent guarantee of their economic freedom through some form of quasi-constitutional rights and bounds of power. The Ordoliberals also harnessed the imaginary of a constitutional charter to underscore the importance of legal rules in securing economic freedom. The constitutive role of legal rules for economic liberty is embodied in the Ordoliberal concept of an 'Economic Constitution' (*Wirtschaftsverfassung*).[264] The Economic Constitution preserves economic liberty by guaranteeing the preconditions of competition as the organising principle of the economic order through a broad set of legal rights and rules,[265] amongst which competition law rules play a primordial role.

The paramount importance of institutions and legal rules in safeguarding republican liberty also elucidates the reason why proponents of the competition–democracy nexus assert that it is for competition law to promote democracy, even though there is, at first sight, no straightforward link between competition in the economic and democracy in the political sphere. For republican liberals, the remit of various institutions of antipower to operate as an antidote to domination is not confined to the realm of politics. Instead, their role is to guarantee the status of citizens as free and equals, not only in the vertical relationship between private individuals and the state but also in the horizontal relationship between the private individuals to one another.[266] The proponents of the competition–democracy nexus were wary of the ability of powerful firms to convert their economic into political power, and thereby capture democratic institutions. Nevertheless, for various proponents of the competition–democracy nexus, the primary channel through which concentrated economic power harms democracy is by creating instances of

262 Rosanvallon (n 183) 86; Smith (n 104) IV, ix, § 51, p. 687; Montesquieu (n 110) Book XX, Chapter XXII.

263 20 Cong Rec 2455 (1890) (n 13) 2461; *Northern Pacific RY. Co. v United States* 356 US 1 (1958) 4; *United States v Topco Assocs. Inc.* 405 US 596 (1972) 610.

264 Eucken (n 14) 55, 245, 257–59, 270–72; L Miksch, 'Versuch eines liberalen Programms [1949]' in N Goldschmidt (ed), *Grundtexte zur Freiburger Tradition der Ordnungsökonomik* (Tübingen: Mohr Siebeck 2008) 163, 167; E-J Mestmäcker, 'Wirtschaftsordnung und Staatsverfassung' in F Böhm, E-J Mestmäcker and H Sauermann (eds), *Wirtschaftsordnung und Staatsverfassung: Festschrift f. Franz Böhm z. 80. Geburtstag* (Tübingen: Mohr Siebeck 1975) 383, 383.

265 Mestmäcker's Preface to Böhm (ed) (n 124) 9, 12; Böhm (ed) (n 124) 17; Mestmäcker (ed) (n 215) 117.

266 Pettit (n 47) 136, 181.

economic domination and frustrating the republican liberty as non-domination of market participants.

The concept of republican liberty thus explains why the proponents of the idea of a competition–democracy nexus affirmed that the answer to the danger that concentrated economic power poses to democracy lies primarily in competition laws and not in, for instance, stricter rules on lobbying or campaign financing. To them, the immediate solution to the dominating and liberty-reducing effect of concentrated economic power is to promote and preserve by means of competition law polycentric[267] competitive markets whose centrifugal forces prevent the emergence of and disperse existing instances of concentrated individual and collective economic power. Early liberal thinkers, proponents of US antitrust law, and Ordoliberals alike perceived the propensity of competitive markets to disperse concentrated economic power as a central solution to the behemoth problem. For instance, Smith highlighted how deconcentrated markets in which economic capital and power are distributed amongst many players prevent the emergence of dominating coalitions.[268] The proponents of US antitrust law also held the belief that by diffusing economic power, competitive markets would make the exercise of individual and collective arbitrary power or domination more difficult.[269] The Ordoliberals also emphasised the dispersion of power as a central virtue of competition by celebrating polycentric competitive markets as the 'most remarkable and ingenious instrument for reducing power known in history'.[270]

Various proponents of the competition–democracy nexus thus perceived competitive markets as legal constructs that operate as institutions of antipower. By dispersing economic power, competition maximises republican liberty in the socioeconomic sphere by making dominating conduct more difficult or impossible. In so doing, competitive markets secure the economic prerequisites of a republican society and polity of free and equals, in short a republican democracy. The various iterations of the idea of a competition–democracy nexus hinged on the insight that republican liberty can only emerge and flourish in a republican democracy and presupposes the existence of republican laws and institutions of antipower that ensure the contestability of power in the political and non-political sphere alike.

267 For the notion of polycentricity, see M Polanyi, *The Logic of Liberty* (London: Routledge 1951) Chapters 2–6; V Ostrom, 'Polycentricity: The Structural Basis of Self-Governing Systems' in F Sabetti and P Dragos Aligica (eds), *Choice, Rules and Collective Action: The Ostroms on the Study of Institutions and Governance* (Colchester: ECPR Press 2014) 45.

268 Smith (n 104) II, v, § 7, pp. 361–62; see also I, x, c, § 23, p. 143; IV, viii, § 34, pp. 654–55; II, v, § 7, pp. 361–62.

269 20 Cong Rec 2455 (1890) (n 13) 2457–60; T Arnold, 'Fair Fights and Foul: Chapter XIV–The Sherman Act as Charter of Economic Freedom' (1965) 10(5–6) *Antitrust Bulletin* 655, 661–62, 666.

270 Böhm (n 14) 279; Eucken (n 14) 50, 237.

2.8 CONCLUSION

All of the distinctive attributes of republican liberty, discussed in the previous sections and summarised in Table 2.2, explain why republican liberty outperforms the special interest capture and conventional liberty accounts in unpacking the idea of a competition–democracy nexus. First, on a republican conception of liberty, not only interference but also the mere susceptibility to arbitrary interference and hence the exposure or subordination to a powerful agent capable of interfering with someone's choices at will already constitute an obstacle to liberty. Republican liberty thus views a larger set of preventing conditions (y) as obstructions to freedom than its negative counterpart.

Second, republican liberty also differs from the probabilistic logic of negative liberty in the robustness of protection of the individual's sphere of liberty that it requires for that individual to be considered free. Owing to its modally robust character, republican liberty is not only wary of interference with actual or likely preferred courses of action of an individual but also seeks to protect the individual's choice set across a whole range of relevant possible worlds. Hence, republican liberty also recognises a broader range of actions (z) whose restriction can be said to frustrate individual liberty. The broader scope of the republican concept of liberty suggests that republican liberty as non-domination offers a thicker and more resilient concept of liberty than the more recent negative version of liberty as non-interference.[271] This broad notion of preventing conditions (y) and range of actions (z) allows us to understand the proposition by various iterations of the competition–democracy nexus that concentrated power as such constitutes a source of unfreedom, and hence predicament for society, irrespective of the presence of actual or likely interference.

The conceptual thickness of republican liberty also manifests itself in its profoundly egalitarian dimension. Republican liberty has an in-built egalitarian commitment because it recognises a broad range of agents (x) as being bestowed with liberty as equal status. This strong egalitarian dimension explains why proponents of the competition–democracy nexus – unlike mainstream liberals – were firmly opposed to economic power imbalances that lead to patterns of hierarchy, subordination, and dependence and undermine equality of opportunity and wealth.

The thickness of republican liberty also entails that its realisation presupposes more demanding institutional safeguards than its negative counterpart. While negative liberty is even compatible with an authoritarian system of government as long as interference is kept to a minimum, republican liberty can only emerge and flourish in a republican democracy and is predicated on the existence of republican laws and institutions of antipower that ensure the contestability of power in the political and non-political sphere. This strong commitment of republican liberty to a republican

[271] Pettit (n 47) Chapter I, pp. 26–77.

TABLE 2.2 *Republican liberty as an explanatory variable for the competition–democracy nexus*

	Negative liberty	Republican liberty	Republican liberty explains
Type of agents (x)	No in-built commitment towards egalitarianism	In-built commitment towards egalitarianism	Concentration thesis
Type of preventing conditions (y)	Interference	Domination (arbitrary interference)	
Range of restricted actions (z)	Preference-decisiveness in the actual world $(aP_ib \rightarrow aPb)$ (minimisation of $P(H \mid w_1)\ P(w_1)$) or nearby likely world $(aP_ib \rightarrow aPb) \wedge (bP_ia \rightarrow bPa)$ (minimisation of $P(H \mid w_1)\ P(w_1) + P(H \mid w_2)\ P(w_2)$)	Preference-decisiveness across all (relevant) possible friendly and unfriendly worlds $\Box((aP_ib \rightarrow aPb) \wedge (bP_ia \rightarrow bPa))$ (minimisation of $P(H \mid w_1)\ P(w_1) + \cdots + P(H \mid w_k)\ P(w_k)$)	
Form of polity	Any form of government with constitutional safeguards and rule of law	Republican democracy	Democracy thesis
State interference	Reduction of liberty	No reduction of liberty if non-arbitrary	Competition law thesis
Attitude to legal rules	Balancing of rights (legal standards) $P((aP_ib \rightarrow aPb) \wedge (bP_ia \rightarrow bPa))$	Legal rules as modally robust normative desiderata $O((aP_ib \rightarrow aPb) \wedge (bP_ia \rightarrow bPa))$	
Institutions	Constitutional rights; rule of law	Constitutional rights; rule of law; political and non-political institutions of antipower	

form of government and institutions of antipower explains why proponents of a competition–democracy nexus consider the adverse effects of economic power on economic liberty to be incompatible with democracy and perceive the need for competition law to be used to prevent excessive concentration of economic power in the private sphere.

This chapter has shown that various conceptions of liberty vary in how narrowly or broadly they define the three variables of agents (x), preventing conditions (y), and range of actions (z), which shape the thickness of liberty in terms of its scope and robustness. Negative and republican liberty position each other differently with respect to each of these variables, and hence follow a distinct logic. This chapter has uncovered that it is precisely this distinctive logic, grammar, and geometry of republican liberty which underlie various renditions of the competition–democracy nexus.

This chapter thus has set out and illustrated the core thesis of this book, which is that republican liberty constitutes the connecting piece between competition and democracy and offers a powerful explanatory variable that can make the idea of a competition–democracy nexus intelligible. The model of republican liberty constructed in this chapter sheds light on how various iterations of the competition–democracy nexus revolve around the institutional proposition that republican liberty can only be protected through institutions of antipower. From this perspective, competition (and competition law protecting it) promotes republican liberty and indirectly republican democracy by operating as an institution of antipower.[272] Competition, as a rivalrous and polycentric market structure, and its preservation through legal rules, can thus be understood as an institution that guarantees a robust form of economic liberty as non-domination, which in turn is a prerequisite for a republican society and democracy. By ensuring the capacity of competitive markets to operate as institutions of antipower that secure the continuous dispersal and contestation of economic power, competition law is able to maximise republican liberty and contributes to a society of domination-free, heterarchical interaction: in short, a republican society of free and equals. The next chapter will take a closer look at how various iterations of the competition–democracy nexus perceived the role that markets and competition law play in securing competition as an institution of antipower that prevents the concentration and abuse of economic power by dispersing it amongst many players who, through their rivalrous interaction, keep one another in check and constantly contest existing instances of power.

[272] Pettit, 'Freedom as Antipower' (n 61) 577, 588.

PART II

The Operationalisation of the Competition–Democracy Nexus

3

The Building Blocks of a Republican Competition Law Approach

3.1 INTRODUCTION

The previous chapter has explored how the republican conception of liberty as non-domination constitutes a central explanatory variable for the idea of a competition–democracy nexus. It has shown that various iterations of the competition–democracy nexus – coined by early liberal thinkers, US antitrust advocates, and the Ordoliberals – can be explained by their shared normative commitment to a republican concept of economic liberty. In stark contrast to our contemporary concept of liberty as non-interference, various protagonists of the idea of a competition–democracy nexus perceived the very existence of economic power as an obstruction of liberty that is incompatible with a republican society and polity of free and equals.

This chapter will further trace the trajectory of republican liberty as an explanatory variable and unifying theme of the competition–democracy nexus across the intellectual history of competition law. It interrogates the republican notion of competition as an institution of antipower by exploring some of the solutions that the proponents of the idea of a competition–democracy nexus have put forth to address the dominating effect of concentrated economic power, or what we have called the behemoth problem in previous chapters. In particular, it enquires into the various institutional and legal designs that the protagonists of the republican competition tradition contemplated to operationalise and realise the ideal of a competition–democracy nexus by designing markets in such a way that they operate as institutions of antipower.

This chapter shows that all iterations of the competition–democracy nexus converged in the assumption that the behemoth problem and its adverse effect on liberty and democracy are best remedied by promoting competition as a polycentric market structure that prevents the emergence of economic concentration in the first place and erodes existing instances of concentrated power. Accordingly, competition operates as an institution of antipower that maximises liberty as non-domination and promotes republican democracy as long as it diffuses economic power polycentrically amongst a multitude of independent economic agents. Based on this assumption, all iterations of the competition–democracy nexus saw the role of legal rules and, most notably, competition law as securing a polycentric and deconcentrated market structure. Various republican antitrust paradigms also envisaged different ways through which competition law can guarantee and preserve polycentric competitive markets. These design approaches can be largely divided into two categories: situational and conduct-based structuralism. The objective of preserving deconcentrated markets as institutions of antipower and each of these two forms of structuralist rule design formed the building blocks of a republican antitrust approach, which will be further explored in the following chapters.

This chapter first analyses how the various proponents of the competition–democracy nexus conceived the role of competitive markets as institutions of antipower (Section 3.2). It then focuses on situational structuralism (Section 3.3) and conduct-based structuralism (Section 3.4) as two approaches to designing competition rules that are geared towards maintaining polycentric markets as institutions of antipower. It also highlights the complementarities and common predispositions of both approaches (Section 3.5).

3.2 POLYCENTRIC COMPETITION AS AN INSTITUTION OF ANTIPOWER

The many different strands of the competition–democracy nexus in modern thought about competitive markets started from the same observation: concentrated economic power is a source of unfreedom that jeopardises the liberty as non-domination of citizens in the economic sphere. This dominating effect of concentrated economic power corrodes the societal and economic prerequisites of a republican society and government of free and equals. However, the protagonists of this republican competition paradigm not only agreed in their diagnosis of the problem but also contemplated a similar solution to minimise the domination emanating from instances of concentrated economic power. They advocated for the promotion of competition as a deconcentrated and polycentric market structure whose centrifugal forces diffuse power amongst many players who keep each other in check, and thereby make domination more difficult, if not impossible. Hence, competition, understood as a polycentric and deconcentrated market structure, was perceived as an institution of antipower that operates as an antidote to domination by making power contestable and distributing it equally.

3.2.1 *Competition–Democracy Nexus 1.0*

The idea of competition as an institution of antipower first appeared in the writings of early liberal political and economic thinkers, whose works celebrated the propensity of competitive markets to dissipate power as the main driver of the transition from the hierarchical feudal system to a heterarchical market society. Adam Smith most prominently underscored how the advent of polycentric competitive markets gradually dispersed the economic power of the feudal elite amongst a multitude of emerging independent tradesmen. Whereas under the feudal order, seigniors could simply exploit their serfs at will to finance their extravagant lifestyle, in a market society they can no longer have recourse to arbitrary coercion to satisfy their needs. On the contrary, they suddenly have to enter into economic exchanges that account for the interests of both parties. The advent of competitive markets hence compels the feudal seigniors to engage in economic transactions with independent traders to satisfy their fancy lifestyle and passion for the 'most childish vanity'.[1] The feudal lords, in Smith's account, gradually barter away their power to more productive tradesmen who pursue 'their own interest'.[2]

By dispersing the economic power of the feudal elite through the proliferation of polycentric, heterarchical economic relationships, the advent of competitive markets incrementally augments the independence and liberty of market agents. In feudal society, Smith observed, the lower classes of serfs were dependent upon a single feudal seignior to ensure their economic subsistence. This situation changes dramatically when the former serfs become tradesmen in a market society. In a competitive economy, their subsistence no longer depends on 'one, but of a hundred or a thousand different customers.'[3] Being no more dependent upon one but a multitude of economic parties, the former serfs cease to be subject to the whims and passions of a single man. Instead, they become trading partners of equal and independent standing to the feudal seignior. To Smith, this new form of economic independence and the gain of liberty of market agents are the immediate consequence of the multiplication and diversification of economic relationships brought about by the emergence of competitive markets. Smith hence portrayed the diffusion of economic power of the feudal elite and the concomitant increase in economic independence and liberty of ordinary tradesmen and workmen as nothing more than the spontaneous outcome of polycentric self-interested interaction between individual market players.

This account, Albert Hirschman points out,[4] echoes the idea that the interplay and pitting against each other of conflicting passions and interests will restrict the human lust for power.[5] The rivalrous, polycentric interaction of self-interested players will thus bring about a balance of interests and power that ensures peaceful

1 A Smith, *An Inquiry into the Nature and Causes of the Wealth of Nations* [1776] (Oxford: Oxford University Press 1976) III, iv, § 17, p. 422.

2 Ibid.

3 Ibid. III, iv, § 11–12, pp. 419–20.

4 AO Hirschman, *The Passions and the Interests: Political Arguments for Capitalism before Its Triumph* (Princeton: Princeton University Press 1977) 103, 110–12.

5 Smith, *Wealth of Nations* (n 1) III, iv, § 10, pp. 418–19.

coexistence within a society of free and equals.[6] This pre-industrial, Smithian model of competition, which is most prominently encapsulated in Smith's allegory of the 'invisible hand',[7] posits that polycentric competitive markets channel the individual's self-interest in a way that compels each player to integrate the needs and self-interest of other players into their maximisation calculus.[8] Each economic bargain takes the form of 'Give me that which I want and you shall have this which you want'.[9] This polycentric coordination of economic exchanges eventually brings about a balance or equilibrium of countervailing interests[10] and reciprocal power[11] that requires and enables individuals to engage in a continuous interaction of mutual adjustment and re-adjustment.[12] The Smithian model of competition pictures polycentric interaction and rivalry between independent, self-interested players as an institutional arrangement that ensures liberty as non-domination. In stimulating polycentric rivalrous interaction, competition operates as an accountability mechanism that reduces the capacity of economic agents to exert domination. Instead, it obliges market participants to mutually adapt themselves to the choices made by consumers and other competitors without having recourse to domination.[13]

This discussion shows that Smith and other early liberal thinkers understood the new phenomenon of competitive markets primarily in structural terms. In their account, competition is characterised by a market structure where the centres of independent economic decision-making and power are spread polycentrically and evenly amongst multiple agents. By diffusing power amongst roughly equally sized atomistic market agents, competition brings about a balance of power amongst heterarchical players whose strategic interaction keeps each other in check. This Smithian model of competition forged a direct link between polycentric market structure, firm behaviour, and domination. It assumed that the absence or elimination of polycentric market structures would automatically put economic agents into a situation of conflict of interest where they have the ability and incentive to impose their self-interests on others. This structure–conduct assumption is most clearly

[6] Hirschman (n 4) 9–48. In this respect, the Smithian account follows a similar logic as the argument that free trade or commerce will lead to peace between nations. Montesquieu, Charles-Louis de Secondat, *De l'esprit des lois* [1748] (Paris: Garnier-Flammarion 1979) Book XX, Chapters 2–3; P Rosanvallon, *Le libéralisme économique: Histoire de l'idée de marché* (Paris: Seuil 1989) 28–29, 43–44.

[7] Smith, *Wealth of Nations* (n 1) IV, ii, § 9, pp. 455–56.

[8] Ibid. I, ii, § 2, pp. 25–27; E Anderson, 'Liberty, Equality and Private Government' in M Matheson (ed), *The Tanner Lectures on Human Values* (Cambridge: Cambridge University Press 2016) 63, 63–66.

[9] Smith, *Wealth of Nations* (n 1) I, ii, § 2, pp. 25–27.

[10] Rosanvallon (n 6) 60, 76.

[11] P Pettit, *Republicanism: A Theory of Freedom and Government* (Oxford: Clarendon Press; Oxford University Press 1997) 67.

[12] M Polanyi, *The Logic of Liberty* (London: Routledge 1951) 114–22.

[13] Smith, *Wealth of Nations* (n 1) I, x, c, § 31, p. 146; I, xi, b, § 5, p. 163; V, i, e. § 30, pp. 754–55.

encapsulated in Adam Smith's famous adage that '[p]eople of the same trade seldom meet together, even for merriment and diversion, but the conversation ends in a conspiracy against the publick, or in some contrivance to raise prices.'[14]

The Smithian model of competition stipulates that market agents are more likely to exert domination, for instance, in the form of restraints of trade and collusion in concentrated than in polycentric competitive markets.[15] This structure–conduct assumption encapsulated in the Smithian model of competition presages Mancur Olson's theory of collective action.[16] It assumes that in a concentrated market composed of a small group of players having a narrow set of minoritarian interests and low organisation costs[17] those players are more capable of exercising domination through anticompetitive coordination. By reducing organisation and coordination costs, industry concentration enables minoritarian interest groups to exercise disproportionate power because they fare much better than the large, unorganised majority groups of consumers or other competitors with diffused costs and interests in furthering their goals.[18]

This structure–conduct assumption that underpins the Smithian model of competition also explains why early economic thinkers perceived polycentric competition as an institutional solution through which domination by minoritarian interests can be averted. The promotion of polycentric markets, in which economic power is dispersed amongst a multitude of small, independent players, reduces or even eliminates the structural factors that vest economic agents with the capacity to exercise dominating economic power. Smith asserted that deconcentrated market structures, where economic agents are 'dispersed in distant places', ensure that they 'cannot easily combine together'.[19] On this account, Smith advocated the preservation of a society of small, independent proprietors not only to promote equal economic opportunity but also to counteract market structures that facilitate coordination and collusion by minoritarian vested interests.[20] The Smithian model thus posits that polycentric markets, in which economic activity is decentralised amongst many small and independent players,[21] preserve liberty as non-domination by raising the costs of coordination and domination through the multiplication of players.[22] Accordingly, Smith observed,

> If this capital is divided between two different grocers, their competition will end to make both of them sell cheaper, than if it were in the hands of one only; and if it

14 Ibid. I, x, c, § 27, p. 145; see also I, x, c, § 5, pp. 135–36.
15 Ibid. I, x, c, § 22, pp. 142–43; IV, viii, § 34, pp. 654–55.
16 M Olson, *The Logic of Collective Action: Public Goods and the Theory of Groups* [1965] (Harvard: Harvard University Press 1971).
17 Ibid. 46–47.
18 Ibid. 52, 128.
19 Smith, *Wealth of Nations* (n 1) I, x, c. § 23, p. 143.
20 Ibid. IV, viii, § 34, pp. 654–55.
21 Ibid. I, x, c. § 23, p. 143.
22 Olson (n 16) 48.

> were divided among twenty, their competition would be just so much the greater, and the chance of their combining together, in order to raise price, just so much the less.[23]

Unlike contemporary economic theories of competition, the pre-industrialist understanding of competition testifies to a more holistic perspective on the socioeconomic and political implications of competitive markets. The Smithian model of competition does not confine itself to the economic sphere in the strict sense but rather proposes a political economy of power that identifies polycentric competition as a central element of a society of free and equals, and as an institutional solution to the behemoth problem of concentrated private economic power.[24]

The close ties between the political economy of power that is encapsulated in the Smithian model of competition and the political ideal of republican liberty become even more apparent if one considers its influence on the political thought of the American founding fathers.[25] For instance, this influence crystallises in Thomas Jefferson's ideal of a 'yeoman republic'.[26] Like the English Levellers and Smith, Jefferson praised the virtue of small proprietors and perceived an agrarian society that is fragmented into a multitude of independent masterless men as a central societal pillar of the nascent American republican democracy.[27]

The Smithian model of competition also had an important bearing on how the framers of the US Constitution envisaged the design of political and social institutions to preserve liberty as non-domination within the nascent American democratic republic. This influence most clearly emerges in James Madison's essays Federalist No 10 and 51. Just as Adam Smith warned against the domination by colluding producers who try to impose their minoritarian interests on the rest of the economy, so did Madison identify the combined power of interest groups and factions as the most important vice in a democratic society.[28] Madison feared that under the guise of liberty of expression and faith, social factions might cast the seed of chaos and civil war by annihilating the liberty of all other citizens and imposing their self-interest upon the rest of the society.[29] In the same way as the early political economists, Madison envisaged polycentric competition as the institutional solution

[23] Smith, *Wealth of Nations* (n 1) II, v, § 7, pp. 361–62.

[24] Ibid. III, iv, § 4, p. 412.

[25] S Fleischacker, 'Adam Smith's Reception among the American Founders, 1776–1790' (2002) 59 (4) *The William and Mary Quarterly* 897.

[26] S Elkins and E McKitrick, *The Age of Federalism* (Oxford: Oxford University Press 1993) 200; R Hofstadter, *The American Political Tradition and the Men Who Made It* (New York: Vintage Books 1948) 37.

[27] T Jefferson, *Political Writings* (Cambridge: Cambridge University Press 1999) xxii, 188–89, 197, 206–09, 221, 385–86; PH Brietzke, 'The Constitutionalization of Antitrust: Jefferson, Madison, Hamilton, and Thomas C. Arthur' (1987) 22(2) *Valparaiso University Law Review* 275.

[28] A Hamilton, J Madison, and J Jay, *The Federalist Papers* (Oxford: Oxford University Press 2008) Federalist No 10, p. 49.

[29] Ibid. Federalist No 10, pp. 49, 52.

to the problem of potential domination by factions.[30] To safeguard liberty, he, therefore, recommended that

> society itself will be broken into so many parts, interests and classes of citizens, that the rights of individuals, or of the minority, will be in little danger from interested combinations of the majority.[31]

Madison assumed that the centrifugal forces of competition between factions will disperse the power of each societal group and generate a situation where each faction imposes checks on the other's power. Competition between factions ensures that none of these groups becomes dominant or majoritarian. Consequently, polycentric competition creates a balance of reciprocal powers that prevents domination by making coordination and collusion more difficult.[32] Observing that this 'policy of supplying, by opposite and rival interests, the defect of better motives, might be traced through the whole system of human affairs, private as well as public',[33] Madison pointed out that polycentricity is not only an organising principle of political but also of social and economic institutions of antipower.

The examples of the Jeffersonian ideal of a yeoman republic and Madison's competitive pluralism illustrate the feedback loops and cross-fertilisation between economic and political thought that the early liberal idea of polycentric competition as a safeguard of republican liberty has generated. In continuity with the republican tradition, early liberal economic and political thinkers viewed the polycentric structuring of power as an essential institutional safeguard of equality and liberty.[34] They advocated polycentric competition as an economic and social institution of antipower that ensures a society of free and equals by virtue of its tendency to diffuse economic power amongst many players, and thereby increase the costs of domination. Already these early liberal proponents of competitive markets recognised what Philip Pettit has identified as a common feature of social and economic institutions of antipower: they preserve liberty as non-domination 'by ensuring competition between those who are powerful'.[35]

3.2.2 *Competition–Democracy Nexus 2.0*

The proposition by early liberal thinkers that competition as a polycentric market structure may operate as an institution of antipower came under immense strain when the behemoth problem of concentrated economic power moved centre stage in the American political discourse of the late-nineteenth century. Over the course

30 Ibid. Federalist No 51, p. 257.
31 Ibid. Federalist No 51, pp. 258–59.
32 Ibid. Federalist No 10, pp. 52, 54.
33 Ibid. Federalist No 51, p. 257.
34 I Shapiro, *The State of Democratic Theory* (Oxford: Oxford University Press 2004) 51.
35 P Pettit, 'Freedom as Antipower' (1996) 106(3) *Ethics* 576, 591.

of the eighteenth and nineteenth centuries, rampant industrialisation and the rise of large-scale corporations had gradually obliterated the Smithian model of competition as a polycentric market structure and its societal counterpart of a Jeffersonian society in which economic power is atomised and diffused amongst a multitude of small independent local tradesmen, yeomen, and businesses. The transition from a pre-industrialised to an industrialised economy built on mass production and mass employment fundamentally called into question the ideal of the self-employed free man and of the 'universal self-government in the realm of production'[36] that was championed by the Smithian model of competition. In other words, '[e]conomies of scale overwhelmed the economy of small proprietors'.[37]

The Industrial Revolution and the rise of large-scale corporations also fundamentally altered how legal and economic theory approached concentrated economic power. Monopoly power, industrial size, and industry concentration could no longer solely be explained as the mere outcome of illegitimate special interest capture and privileges that were granted through mercantilist policies and state favouritism.[38] Rather, they were at least in part the result of superior efficiency, and the creature of private property rights and contractual freedom. This insight had an important bearing on the English and American common law that over the course of the eighteenth and nineteenth centuries adopted a more welcoming approach towards restraints of trade and monopolies.[39] This change in attitude coincided with the triumph of the negative concept of liberty as non-interference, which became the predominant understanding of liberty during the eighteenth and nineteenth centuries.[40] Consistent with this negative concept of liberty, common law increasingly followed a laissez-faire doctrine that primarily sought to protect contractual freedom and property rights against state interference. As it increasingly perceived restraints of trade and monopolistic practices as the result of contractual freedom, nineteenth-century common law only tackled contracts or agreements that interfered with other market participants' economic liberty to an unreasonable degree, for instance, by imposing excessive restraints on the parties' contractual freedom or leaving third parties without any commercial alternatives.[41] Other restraints of trade that directly restricted competition or prevented market access

36 Anderson (n 8) 85.

37 Ibid. 85, 77.

38 T Goebel, 'The Political Economy of American Populism from Jackson to the New Deal' (1997) 11(1) *Studies in American Political Development* 109, 111; 19 Cong Rec 8519 (1888) 8521; 20 Cong Rec 2455 (1890) 2457.

39 W Letwin, *Law and Economic Policy in America: The Evolution of the Sherman Antitrust Act* [1959] (Chicago: Chicago University Press 1981) 41–46, 48–52; J May, 'Antitrust in the Formative Era: Political and Economic Theory in Constitutional and Antitrust Analysis, 1880–1918' (1989) 50(2) *Ohio State Law Journal* 257, 270–83; *Mogul Steamship Co Ltd v McGregor, Gow & Co* [1892] AC 25.

40 Pettit, *Republicanism* (n 11) 45–50.

41 RJ Peritz, *Competition Policy in America: History, Rhetoric, Law* (New York: Oxford University Press 2000) 11–12.

were upheld as a reasonable, and hence a legitimate and legally enforceable, emanation of contractual freedom.[42]

This laissez-faire attitude of nineteenth-century common law towards restraints of trade and monopoly also found support in influential economic thought about competition and industry concentration of the time. Many business leaders and economists expressed their firm opposition against any sort of federal regulation of monopolies and restraints of competition. Inspired by the tenets of the theory of Social Darwinism, which was developed by Herbert Spencer and William Graham Sumner, these business leaders portrayed industry concentration and monopoly as the natural outcome of competition understood as a rivalrous fight for the survival of the fittest.[43] These organic theories of industry concentration primarily perceived competition as a process of natural selection or rationalisation[44] that would eliminate all but a few very efficient and fit players.[45] From this perspective, industry concentration and the rise of powerful companies were not so much illegitimate manifestations of economic power as the natural consequence of a merciless process of natural selection and technological innovation.[46] Consequently, monopoly and firm size were celebrated as the essence of competition, and the natural outcome of superior economies of scale and efficiency.[47]

The Smithian model of polycentric competition came under further strain with the rise of new economic theories of imperfect and monopolistic competition during the first half of the twentieth century. The pioneering studies by Edward Chamberlin[48] and Joan Robinson[49] on imperfect oligopolistic and monopolistic competition highlighted the shortcomings of the model of perfect competition, which was developed by the economists Léon Walras[50] and Alfred Marshall[51] to translate the Smithian conception of competition into the formalised language of neoclassical economics. The new theories of imperfect competition pointed out that the conditions of perfect competition are only exceptionally present in real-world markets, which are often characterised by fierce competitive rivalry between a limited number of players. On this basis, they suggested that a limited number of existing competitors is not necessarily indicative of market power and the absence of

42 For a detailed analysis, see HB Thorelli, *The Federal Antitrust Policy: Origination of an American Tradition* (Baltimore: Johns Hopkins Press 1955) 9–50.

43 Ibid. 71, 109–32.

44 Ibid. 114–15.

45 Ibid. 71.

46 Ibid. 116, 125.

47 Ibid. 71, 113, 116–17, 123, 130. See also H Hovenkamp, 'Antitrust Policy after Chicago' (1985) 84 (2) *Michigan Law Review* 213, 220–21; Brietzke (n 27) 277–78.

48 E Chamberlin, *Theory of Monopolistic Competition* (Cambridge, MA: Harvard University Press 1933).

49 J Robinson, *The Economics of Imperfect Competition* (London: Macmillan 1933).

50 L Walras, *Elements of Pure Economics: Or, the Theory of Social Wealth* (Fairfield: A.M. Kelley 1977, 1954).

51 A Marshall, *Principles of Economics: An Introductory Volume* (London: Macmillan 1920).

competition.[52] The theories of dynamic competition coined by Joseph Alois Schumpeter added further momentum to the objection that the focus of the Smithian model of competition on market structure was unwarranted. Instead, Schumpeter affirmed that potential competition might constrain powerful firms, even in the absence of rivalry in the market.[53] Far from constituting a sign of insufficient competition, Schumpeter suggested that temporary market power and industry concentration are only a transient state that allows firms to recoup their investments in innovation before they are dislodged by dynamic competition. Consequently, Schumpeter forcefully discredited the traditional hostility of antitrust law against big business as a misguided ideology.[54] These emerging theories of imperfect and dynamic competition shook up the economic foundations of the hostility against industry concentration that underpinned the Smithian vision of polycentric competition. On the contrary, they instead suggested that concentrated markets may often yield outcomes that are similar or even superior to that of perfect competition.[55]

Although the Smithian vision of polycentric competition as an institution of antipower was increasingly challenged by industrialisation and changing ideological and economic theories, it experienced a sudden revival with the adoption of the Sherman Act. The framers of the Sherman Act acknowledged that large-scale production and corporations have a great potential to enhance economic efficiency and welfare.[56] Nevertheless, in light of the surge in industry consolidation and the proliferation of the trust problem, the proponents of the Sherman Act viewed the laissez-faire approach of nineteenth-century common law towards monopoly and restraints of trade as insufficient to cope with the new economic, social, and political challenges that were posed by the concentration and abuse of economic power.[57] Instead of embracing trusts and industrial size as a superior and more efficient form of organising the economy, or as the legitimate outcome of contractual freedom, they turned their attention to the pre-industrialised vision of competition as an institution of antipower that was fashioned by early liberal thinkers as the solution

52 MA Adelman, 'Effective Competition and the Antitrust Laws' (1948) 61(8) *Harvard Law Review* 1289, 1299.

53 JA Schumpeter, *Capitalism, Socialism and Democracy* [1942] (New York: Harper & Row 1962) 82–88; ES Mason, 'Monopoly in Law and Economics' (1937) 47(1) *The Yale Law Journal* 34, 47–48.

54 Schumpeter (n 53) 85; ES Mason, 'Schumpeter on Monopoly and the Large Firm' (1951) 33(2) *The Review of Economics and Statistics* 139, 139, 141; ES Mason, 'The Current Status of the Monopoly Problem in the United States' (1949) 62(8) *Harvard Law Review* 1265, 1271.

55 For the impact of these theories on the curtailment of the antitrust policy during the new deal era, see Hovenkamp (n 47) 214, 221, 224.

56 Senator Sherman, for instance, referred to the 'corporation' as 'most useful agencies of modern civilization' and underlined the 'good results of corporate power' which he saw realised in the 'enormous increase in business and production'. 20 Cong Rec 2455 (1890) (n 38) 2457; 19th Cong Rec 6041 (1888) 6041.

57 May (n 39) 261–88.

to the trust problem. Echoing Adam Smith, Senator Sherman observed that economic power cannot give rise to instances of domination as long as it is more or less equally dispersed amongst a sufficient number of competing corporations.[58]

The arguments that were advanced during the legislative debates in support of the protection of competition as a polycentric market structure clearly followed a strategy that was directly taken from the playbook of the Smithian political economy of power coined by early liberal thinkers. In line with the Smithian understanding of polycentric competition as an institution of antipower, the framers of the Sherman Act cast competition as an accountability mechanism.[59] Accordingly, competition imposes constraints on the self-interest of corporations and pushes them to account for the interests of consumers. The preservation of a polycentric market structure was thus conceived as an institutional mechanism of checks-and-balances. Early proponents of antitrust law highlighted how competitive markets decentralise power and pit the antagonistic interests of market players against each other. In bringing about a balance of reciprocal powers, polycentric competition was assumed to make the exercise of individual and collective arbitrary power or domination more difficult, if not impossible.[60]

The idea that the preservation of competition as a polycentric market structure would eliminate instances of domination radiated far beyond the legislative history of the Sherman Act.[61] The Smithian ideal of a polycentric market structure, and its political counterpart of a Jeffersonian society of small and independent businessmen also animated the anti-bigness movement championed by Wilson and Brandeis. To tackle the dominating effects of concentrated economic power, the progressive antitrust movement forcefully advocated the breakup of powerful firms with a view to restoring a Jeffersonian society in which economic power and wealth are dispersed amongst many small market participants.[62]

The last and most sophisticated attempt in US antitrust thought to translate the early liberal idea of polycentric competition as an institution of antipower into a coherent economic and policy framework was made by the Harvard School. In light of the critique of the model of perfect competition by the novel theories of imperfect and monopolistic competition, the Harvard School gradually endorsed the concept

58 20 Cong Rec 2455 (1890) (n 38) 2457.

59 R Pitofsky, 'The Political Content of Antitrust' (1979) 127(4) *University of Pennsylvania Law Review* 1051, 1057–58; EM Fox, 'Modernization of Antitrust: A New Equilibrium' (1980) 66(6) *Cornell Law Review* 1140, 1140, 1051, 1182.

60 20 Cong Rec 2455 (1890) (n 38) 2457–60; T Arnold, 'Fair Fights and Foul: Chapter XIV – The Sherman Act as Charter of Economic Freedom' (1965) 10(5–6) *Antitrust Bulletin* 655, 661–62, 666.

61 Brietzke (n 27) 280–88.

62 W Wilson, 'The Tariff and the Trusts' in DA Crane and H Hovenkamp (eds), *The Making of Competition Policy: Legal and Economic Sources* (New York: Oxford University Press 2013) 119, 124, 208–09; LD Brandeis, *Other People's Money and How the Bankers Use It* (New York: Frederick A. Stokes Company 1914) 135, 150, 163.

of 'workable competition',[63] or 'effective competition'. Harvard scholars perceived workable or effective competition as a second-best solution to perfect competition. Effective competition sits somewhere between the two extremes of perfect competition on the one end and monopolistic markets on the other end of the spectrum.[64] While acknowledging that some limited market power is inevitable in an industrialised economy, the Harvard School considered workable competition as a market structure that is characterised by the absence of unreasonable market power.[65] In some way, the concept of effective or workable competition constituted an attempt to update the Smithian understanding of polycentric competition as an institution of antipower to a modern economy that is built on large-scale economic production: while competition could no longer be expected to curb domination by eliminating economic power in its entirety, its role continues to be to minimise domination by preventing the emergence of or eroding instances of unreasonable market power.

The concept of workable competition lay at the core of the Harvard School's attempt to translate the structural understanding of competition as an institution of antipower into a comprehensive economic and analytical framework, the so-called Structure–Conduct–Performance (S–C–P) paradigm. The core assumption of the S–C–P paradigm bears striking similarities with the structure–conduct assumption of early liberal economic thinkers. Like Smith, the Harvard School posited that the market structure decisively shapes the conduct of firms, and thereby influences their performance.[66] Drawing on empirical studies which indicated that high market concentration (i.e., 75–80 per cent market share held by four or less market players[67]) is correlated with higher profit margins than moderate or low seller concentration,[68] the S–C–P scholars concluded that high degrees of industry

[63] Clark defined 'workable competition' as 'rivalry in selling goods in which each selling unit normally seeks maximum net revenue, under conditions such that the price or prices each seller can charge are effectively limited by the free option of the buyer to buy from a rival seller or sellers of what they think of as "the same" product, necessitating an effort by each seller to equal or exceed the attractiveness of the others' offerings to a sufficient number of buyers to accomplish the end in view.' JM Clark, 'Toward a Concept of Workable Competition' (1940) 30(2) *The American Economic Review* 241, 143.

[64] See, for instance, JS Bain, 'Workable Competition in Oligopoly: Theoretical Considerations and Some Empirical Evidence' (1950) 40(2) *American Economic Review* 35.

[65] C Kaysen and DF Turner, *Antitrust Policy: An Economic and Legal Analysis* (Cambridge, MA: Harvard University Press 1959) 81.

[66] JS Bain, *Barriers to New Competition* (Cambridge, MA: Harvard University Press 1956) 81; Kaysen and Turner, *Antitrust Policy* (n 65) 59–71, 80; DA Crane, 'Structuralism: Introduction' in DA Crane and H Hovenkamp (eds), *The Making of Competition Policy: Legal and Economic Sources* (New York: Oxford University Press 2013) 318, 318.

[67] JS Bain, 'Industrial Organization: Chapter 10 – The Relation of Market Structure to Market Performance' in DA Crane and H Hovenkamp (eds), *The Making of Competition Policy: Legal and Economic Sources* (New York: Oxford University Press 2013) 320, 333–35.

[68] Ibid. 325.

concentration generally result in lower economic performance.[69] Proponents of the S–C–P paradigm argued that high levels of industry concentration and profit margins were a clear indicator of the absence of workable or effective competition and were not the result of efficiencies. On this basis, the Harvard School concluded that the analysis of market structure would allow antitrust authorities and courts to determine whether a certain market is conducive to compelling firms to act competitively, and thus to maximise the market's overall economic performance, or whether it is characterised by unreasonable market power.[70] By extension, the Harvard scholars also assumed that competition policy would need to act on the market structure to preserve workable competition and increase economic performance.

While highlighting the link between market structure and economic performance, the structural approach of the Harvard School dismissed attempts to define workable competition exclusively based on outcome-oriented benchmarks that focus only on market performance in terms of efficiency and innovation.[71] Instead, Harvard scholars emphasised the importance of the procedural dimension of competition,[72] which imposes a check upon economic power. In line with this structural Smithian understanding of competition, Kaysen and Turner asserted that 'competition requires the existence of competitors, in the plural'.[73] Therefore, the Harvard School considered economic performance and efficiency only as one amongst several goals of competition policy. The outcome-oriented goal of economic efficiency remained subordinate to the overarching objective of preserving a competitive process which was understood as a workably competitive market structure that operates as an institution of antipower.

3.2.3 *Competition–Democracy Nexus 3.0*

The Ordoliberals, in a similar vein as competition paradigms and notably the Harvard School in the United States, made an attempt to revive the structural understanding of competition as an institution of antipower against the backdrop of rising levels of industry concentration and cartelisation of the German economy during the first half of the twentieth century. The members of the Freiburg School departed from the growing consensus coined by laissez-faire liberalism[74] and

[69] Ibid. 327; Kaysen and Turner, *Antitrust Policy* (n 65) 62–64.

[70] Kaysen and Turner, *Antitrust Policy* (n 65) 71.

[71] Ibid. 82.

[72] Mason, 'The Current Status of the Monopoly Problem in the United States' (n 54) 1266.

[73] Kaysen and Turner, *Antitrust Policy* (n 65) 7. In a similar vein, see The Attorney General's National Committee to Study the Antitrust Laws, 1955 *Report* (Washington, DC: Superintendent of Documents, U.S. Government Printing Office 1955) 322.

[74] W Eucken, 'Das Problem der wirtschaftlichen Macht' in W Eucken and W Oswalt (eds), *Wirtschaftsmacht und Wirtschaftsordnung: Londoner Vorträge zur Wirtschaftspolitik und zwei Beiträge zur Antimonopolpolitik* (Münster: Lit 2001) 9, 12–13; F Böhm, 'Das Problem der

corporatist[75] paradigms that the Industrial Revolution and technological innovation had made the Smithian model of competition as a polycentric market structure obsolete.[76] In particular, the Ordoliberals contested the claim that there is a clear positive correlation between greater firm size or higher levels of industry concentration and efficiency or technological progress.[77] Above all, they levelled their criticism against the widespread view, which was nourished by laissez-faire liberals and proponents of corporatism alike, that cartels and monopolies constitute the ultimate outcome of contractual liberty or a 'higher form' of economic organisation.[78] Several Ordoliberals also explicitly rejected Schumpeter's account of dynamic competition that casts innovation and technological progress as a major source of industrial concentration.[79] While acknowledging that high levels of industry concentration can, under certain circumstances, be explained by superior efficiencies and innovation,[80] the Ordoliberals underscored that the failure of the German legal system to rein in the trend towards cartelisation was at least of equal importance in explaining the increase in industry concentration.[81]

Instead of tolerating economic concentration as the natural outcome of competitive markets, the Ordoliberals also reverted to the Smithian[82] model of competition as a polycentric market structure to devise a solution to the behemoth problem of concentrated economic power. The Ordoliberals echoed Smith's account of the advent of competitive markets, which ascribed the transition from a hierarchical, feudal to a heterarchical, republican society to the polycentric dispersal of economic power previously held by the feudal elites through increasingly equalised and competitive economic relationships.[83] In line with the early liberal proponents of

privaten Macht. Ein Beitrag zur Monopolfrage [1928]' in N Goldschmidt (ed), *Grundtexte zur Freiburger Tradition der Ordnungsökonomik* (Tübingen: Mohr Siebeck 2008) 49, 53–55, 65–66; M Foucault, *Naissance de la biopolitique: Cours au Collège de France, 1978–1979* (Paris: Gallimard; Seuil 2004) 105.

75 W Eucken, *Grundsätze der Wirtschaftspolitik* (Tübingen: Mohr Siebeck 2004) 53–55, 145, 148, 200–12, 225–27, 235–37, 239; F Böhm, W Eucken, and H Großmann-Doerth, 'Unsere Aufgabe (The Ordoliberal Manifesto) [1936]' in N Goldschmidt (ed), *Grundtexte zur Freiburger Tradition der Ordnungsökonomik* (Tübingen: Mohr Siebeck 2008) 27.

76 Eucken, *Grundsätze der Wirtschaftspolitik* (n 75) 226.

77 Ibid. 225–26.

78 F Böhm (ed), *Wettbewerb und Monopolkampf: Eine Untersuchung zur Frage des wirtschaftlichen Kampfrechts und zur Frage der rechtlichen Struktur der geltenden Wirtschaftsordnung* [1933] (Baden-Baden: Nomos 2010) 234; Eucken, *Grundsätze der Wirtschaftspolitik* (n 75) 226–27, 237–39.

79 Böhm (ed), *Wettbewerb und Monopolkampf* (n 78) 67, 231; Eucken, *Grundsätze der Wirtschaftspolitik* (n 75) 225–33, 239; L Miksch, *Wettbewerb als Aufgabe: Grundsätze einer Wettbewerbsordnung* (Godersberg: Verlag Helmut Küpper 1947) 76.

80 F Böhm, *Freiheit und Ordnung in der Marktwirtschaft* [1971] (Baden-Baden: Nomos 1980) 214–15.

81 Eucken, *Grundsätze der Wirtschaftspolitik* (n 75) 235.

82 Mestmäcker's preface in Böhm (ed), *Wettbewerb und Monopolkampf* (n 78) 7; Böhm (ed), *Wettbewerb und Monopolkampf* (n 78) 239; Miksch (n 79) 11.

83 Böhm, *Freiheit und Ordnung in der Marktwirtschaft* (n 80) 226, 237–55.

competitive markets, the Freiburg scholars argued that a market structure in which power is dispersed amongst many players is the only form of competition that enables a mode of social and economic coordination that is compatible with a society of free and equals.[84] Only for as a long as they operate as a polycentric process, can competitive markets enable the non-hierarchical organisation of economic activities through decentralised coordination of the independent and autonomous economic plans of a multitude of players based on continuous self-adaptation and learning.[85]

In a similar way to the Harvard School, the Ordoliberals thus subscribed to the structural assumption that underpins the Smithian understanding of competition. Accordingly, they assumed that a competitive market composed of a high number of players automatically reduces their capacity to wield unilateral and collective power as it disperses economic power amongst many players.[86] By diffusing economic power, polycentric competition operates as a checks-and-balances or accountability mechanism,[87] which ensures that each market player's capacity to exert arbitrary power is constrained by the aggregate autonomous and independent decisions of all competitors and the choices of consumers.[88] Accordingly, competition minimises the instances where private players can exert individual or collective arbitrary power.[89] To the Ordoliberals, diffusing and keeping power contestable constitutes an essential role of competitive markets.[90]

This notion of polycentric competition as an institution of antipower also shaped the Ordoliberal understanding of competition law and its role in ensuring performance-based competition – *Leistungswettbewerb*, a term which can be best translated into English as 'competition on the merits'.[91] The concept of performance-based competition understands competition as a process in which all market participants enter into a rivalrous rule-based[92] contest for consumer demand.[93] Accordingly, market participants may only try to obtain the favour of

[84] F Böhm, 'Democracy and Economic Power in Cartel and Monopoly in Modern Law [1961]' in DA Crane and H Hovenkamp (eds), *The Making of Competition Policy: Legal and Economic Sources* (New York: Oxford University Press 2013) 264, 269; Eucken, *Grundsätze der Wirtschaftspolitik* (n 75) 249.

[85] Böhm, *Freiheit und Ordnung in der Marktwirtschaft* (n 80) 120, 164.

[86] Miksch (n 79) 41, 66, 247; Eucken, *Grundsätze der Wirtschaftspolitik* (n 75) 163, 244, 279, 291.

[87] Böhm (ed), *Wettbewerb und Monopolkampf* (n 78) 229, 309, 326; Eucken, *Grundsätze der Wirtschaftspolitik* (n 75) 41, 50, 237, 245–49, 291; Miksch (n 79) 40–41.

[88] Böhm, *Freiheit und Ordnung in der Marktwirtschaft* (n 80) 36.

[89] F Böhm, 'Rule of Law in a Market Economy [1966]' in AT Peacock and H Willgerodt (eds), *Germany's Social Market Economy: Origins and Evolution* (Houndmill: Macmillan 1989) 46, 36, 54; Eucken, *Grundsätze der Wirtschaftspolitik* (n 75) 41–42, 237.

[90] Böhm, 'Democracy and Economic Power' (n 84) 279; Eucken, *Grundsätze der Wirtschaftspolitik* (n 75) 50, 237.

[91] Böhm (ed), *Wettbewerb und Monopolkampf* (n 78) 206; Eucken, *Grundsätze der Wirtschaftspolitik* (n 75) 42, 247–49; Miksch (n 79) 15, 54.

[92] Böhm (ed), *Wettbewerb und Monopolkampf* (n 78) 206.

[93] Ibid. 207–09, 240, 257; Eucken, *Grundsätze der Wirtschaftspolitik* (n 75) 244–49.

consumers through their own performance, without making attempts to win the race by using their power to hinder their rivals' ability to compete.[94] Consequently, as a rule-based rivalry, performance-based competition ensures a domination-free process of economic coordination by reducing the range of means or arms that each rival may legitimately use to win the contest.[95]

The Freiburg School contrasted performance-based competition with hindrance competition (*Behinderungswettbewerb*). Whereas market players who engage in performance-based competition strive to attract consumer demand by only improving their own economic performance, hindrance competition refers to any attempt to win the competitive race by deteriorating or preventing their rivals' ability to compete.[96] Hence, performance-based competition always has to take the form of what Böhm called a 'parallel fight' (*Parallelkampf*),[97] in which rivals enter into a head-to-head competition by running on parallel racetracks without hindering the other competitor from winning by putting a spoke in their wheel.[98] In contrast, hindrance competition takes the form of a duel (*Zweikampf*), such as a boxing fight, in which one player wins by beating his rival to the ground.[99]

The Ordoliberals assumed that competition law would keep the concentration and abuse of economic power in check by promoting performance-based and outlawing hindrance competition. To achieve performance-based competition, the Ordoliberals advocated the structural policy standard of 'complete competition' (*vollständiger Wettbewerb*). Following the complete competition standard, competition policy should ensure a market structure where all market participants act as price-takers,[100] without the possibility of exercising market power by influencing the coordination function of the impersonal price mechanism through their market strategies.[101]

While highlighting its theoretical value, the Ordoliberals were acutely aware of the limitations of the perfect competition model for real-life competition policy.[102] The Ordoliberals thus understood complete competition in a similar way to the

[94] Böhm (ed), *Wettbewerb und Monopolkampf* (n 78) 208; Eucken, *Grundsätze der Wirtschaftspolitik* (n 75) 42, 247–49.

[95] Böhm (ed), *Wettbewerb und Monopolkampf* (n 78) 254.

[96] Ibid. 38, 240–49, 257–65, 275–76; Eucken, *Grundsätze der Wirtschaftspolitik* (n 75) 43, 247–49, 267, 296, 329.

[97] Böhm (ed), *Wettbewerb und Monopolkampf* (n 78) 209; Eucken, *Grundsätze der Wirtschaftspolitik* (n 75) 42.

[98] Böhm (ed), *Wettbewerb und Monopolkampf* (n 78) 209, 219.

[99] Ibid. 208; Eucken, *Grundsätze der Wirtschaftspolitik* (n 75) 247.

[100] Eucken, *Grundsätze der Wirtschaftspolitik* (n 75) 237, 248–49, 279, 291.

[101] Miksch (n 79) 40–41, 80; Eucken, *Grundsätze der Wirtschaftspolitik* (n 75) 40–43, 60, 80, 120, 244–49.

[102] Eucken, *Grundsätze der Wirtschaftspolitik* (n 75) 244–45; F Böhm, 'Kartellauflösung und Konzernentflechtung: Spezialistenaufgabe oder Schicksalsfrage?' (1947) 2(9) *Süddeutsche Juristen-Zeitung* 495, 500.

Harvard scholars as 'workable' or 'effective competition'.[103] Instead of seeking to realise all conditions of perfect competition, they envisaged complete competition as a market structure that ensures the absence of instances of power by preventing collusion and excessive oligopoly or monopoly power.[104] Under the complete competition standard, the Ordoliberals contemplated a competition policy that would prevent oligopolistic market structures that facilitate collusion and the exclusion of residual or potential competitors, which would otherwise erode the market power of oligopolistic and dominant firms.[105]

The core mission of competition law was to bring about markets that are characterised by the presence of a sufficient number of market participants and relative ease of market entry to keep the power of the incumbents in check.[106] By preventing firms from collectively or unilaterally engaging in conduct that entrenches or abuses market power, competition law secures the openness and contestability of markets. Through the preservation of a market structure in which economic power remains reasonably deconcentrated and evenly dispersed amongst competitors, competition law ensures that remaining instances of economic power can – at least in the medium term – be eroded by residual competition. In a similar vein as the proponents of the competition–democracy in the United States, the Ordoliberals endorsed a structural understanding of competition. They therefore subscribed to the proposition – first coined by early liberal thinkers – that competition as a polycentric market structure operates as an institution of antipower, which minimises the dangers that excessive concentration of economic power poses to a republican polity and society.

Early liberal, US, and European iterations of the idea of a competition–democracy nexus shared a commitment to a structural notion of competition as an institution of antipower that guarantees economic liberty as non-domination by diffusing economic power amongst many market participants. This understanding of polycentric competitive markets as an institution of antipower informed the various ways in which the different strands of the republican antitrust tradition sought to operationalise the competition–democracy nexus through the design of competition law. Several protagonists of the competition–democracy nexus took the view that competition law should follow a structural approach, whose principal goal

[103] Böhm (ed), *Wettbewerb und Monopolkampf* (n 78) 25; Miksch (n 79) 32–40, 66; Eucken, *Grundsätze der Wirtschaftspolitik* (n 75) 245; DJ Gerber, *Law and Competition in Twentieth Century Europe: Protecting Prometheus* (Oxford, New York: Clarendon Press; Oxford University Press 1998) 245 fn. 52.

[104] Miksch (n 79) 28–36, 65–67, 82–93, 106–14, 116; Eucken, *Grundsätze der Wirtschaftspolitik* (n 75) 22, 208; Böhm (ed), *Wettbewerb und Monopolkampf* (n 78) 35.

[105] Eucken, *Grundsätze der Wirtschaftspolitik* (n 75) 116–17; Böhm (ed), *Wettbewerb und Monopolkampf* (n 78) 35.

[106] Miksch (n 79) 16, 33–34, 38, 66–67, 80; Eucken, *Grundsätze der Wirtschaftspolitik* (n 75) 248–49.

consists of protecting competition as a polycentric market structure by keeping the concentration of economic power to a sustainable level. However, they envisaged different strategies to translate this structuralist operationalisation of the competition–democracy nexus into legal rules and tests. These strategies to maintain competition as an institution of antipower and keep industry concentration to a sustainable level can be classified into two categories: situational and conduct-based structuralism. Situational structuralism will be explored in the next section, and conduct-based structuralism will be discussed in following section.

3.3 SITUATIONAL STRUCTURALISM

As a first strategy to realise the structural notion of competition as an institution of antipower, the protagonists of the republican antitrust tradition advocated a situational approach to market power. This situational structuralism assumes that competition law can and should tackle instances of economic power directly, regardless of whether firms actually abuse or are likely to abuse their market power in an anticompetitive way. In this point, situational structuralism markedly departs from a pure conduct-based test. Unlike conduct-based approaches, situational structuralism does not limit competition law intervention and liability to specific types of unlawful conduct that amount to an undue exercise of market power. Instead, situational structuralism revolves around a situational test, whereby antitrust intervention is triggered by the mere finding of excessive or unreasonable concentration of economic power within the hands of a single or a few firms. This means that situational structuralism relies on a non-fault approach. The mere presence of concentrated economic power is a necessary and sufficient condition to entail antitrust intervention and liability; no wrongful conduct is required in addition.

3.3.1 *Early Manifestations of Situational Structuralism*

In its most rudimentary form, situational structuralism already characterised the early common law approach towards monopoly and restraints of trade in the sixteenth and early-seventeenth centuries. Early common law cases articulated a strict situational approach that held the very existence of monopoly to be against the common law.[107] This situational approach was also subsequently codified in the 1623 Statute of Monopolies, which broadly outlawed the very existence of monopoly

[107] *Davenant v Hurdis* [1599] 72 E.R. 769 778; *Darcy v Allein ('The Case of Monopolies')* [1602] 77 E.R. 1260 1262; *Ipswich Tailors' Case* [1614] 77 E.R. 1218 1221. See also E Coke, *The Third Part of the Institutes of the Laws of England: Concerning High Treason, and other Please of the Crown and Criminall Causes* (London: By M. Flesher for W. Lee and D. Pakeman 1644) Chapter 85, 180.

power.[108] However, the Statute carved out a number of exemptions for legitimate monopolies[109], and its enforcement remained feeble.

A similar situational approach was also envisaged by Adam Smith. His adage that '[p]eople of the same trade seldom meet together, even for merriment and diversion, but the conversation ends in a conspiracy against the publick, or in some contrivance to raise prices'[110] is often cited as the ultimate justification for competition rules.[111] Nonetheless, opponents of strict antitrust law enforcement habitually observe that Smith thought that legal rules against collusion would be ineffective.[112] This reading, however, ignores that Smith contemplated a much more radical, structural solution to address the problem of collusion and concentration of economic power than outlawing them. Smith indeed consistently advocated policies that would enhance a polycentric, deconcentrated market structure and prevent the amalgamation of capital and wealth.[113] To this end, Smith called for changes to tax[114] or inheritance law, such as the abolition of primogeniture, to promote a more equalised distribution of property, and the emergence of a polycentric societal and market structure of small and independent proprietors and tradesmen.[115] He further rejected any policy that tends to restrict the number of market players, notably privileges and other restraints of trade.[116] Most importantly, Smith opposed corporations and incorporation, and hence the creation of large-scale firms itself.[117] Though he did not advocate specific competition rules, Smith supported a legal framework that did prevent the emergence of concentrated economic power.

3.3.2 *Situational Structuralism in the US Antitrust Tradition*

Iterations of this situational structuralism, first envisaged by common lawyers and early liberals, were taken up by various protagonists of the republican antitrust tradition in the United States. The most radical version of this situational structuralism was proposed by the so-called limitist movement after the Second World War. The limitists called for the limitation of all forms of economic, social, and political

[108] 1623 c. 3 s. 1.

[109] Ibid. ss. 6 and 9.

[110] Smith, *Wealth of Nations* (n 1) I, x, c, § 27, p. 145; see also I, x, c, § 5, pp. 135–36.

[111] F Smith, 'Why Not Abolish Antitrust?' (1983) 7(1) *Regulation* 23, 23–24.

[112] 'It is impossible indeed to prevent such meetings, by any law which either could be executed, or would be consistent with liberty and justice. But though the law cannot hinder people of the same trade from sometimes assembling together, it ought to do nothing to facilitate such assemblies, much less to render them necessary.' Smith, *Wealth of Nations* (n 1) I, x, c, § 27, p. 145.

[113] Ibid. II, v, § 7, pp. 361–62.

[114] Ibid. I, x, c, § 29, p. 145.

[115] Ibid. III, iv, § 19, pp. 423–24.

[116] Ibid. Smith (n 1) I, x, c, §§ 30–32, pp. 145–46.

[117] Ibid. Smith (n 1) I, x, c, §§ 30–31, pp. 145–46; Anderson (n 8) 77.

power held by big business, irrespective of its economic costs.[118] The limitist movement primarily rooted antitrust policy in the republican concern about bigness and the Jeffersonian ideal of a society of free and equals. It, therefore, elevated the limitation of big business and the redistribution of social power between large and small enterprises to a primary goal of antitrust policy. To this end, the limitist movement proposed to subject powerful firms to intrusive direct government regulation. It also envisaged the radical reorganisation of firm size and the limitation of firm growth[119] through the dissolution of large companies and the enforcement of a one-plant-one-firm rule, irrespective of the concomitant welfare costs.[120]

The Harvard School also embraced situational structuralism, albeit in a less radical form, as a strategy to secure a workable competitive market structure. Assuming that unilateral conduct by monopolistic firms and tacit collusion in oligopolistic markets constitute a primarily structural problem,[121] the Harvard School contemplated direct antitrust intervention in concentrated markets, even in the absence of unlawful conduct. For this purpose, the prominent Harvard scholars, Donald F. Turner and Carl Kaysen, proposed a situational test[122] that prohibits the possession of 'unreasonable market power' by an individual firm or a group of firms. The rationale of this situational approach was to enable the enforcers of competition law to directly address the problem of excessive concentration of economic power in the hands of a single company and to tackle oligopolistic market structures that facilitate tacit collusion.[123]

The situational test championed by Kaysen and Turner operated on a rebuttable presumption of unreasonable market power. This presumption is activated 'where, for five years or more, one company has accounted for 50 per cent or more of annual sales in the market, or four or fewer companies, have accounted for 80 per cent of such sales.'[124] When a competition authority established that a firm or group of firms had such unreasonable market power, it could impose structural remedies in the

[118] See, for instance, W Adams, 'Dissolution, Divorcement, Divestiture: The Pyrrhic Victories of Antitrust' (1951) 27(1) *Indiana Law Journal* 1; W Adams, 'The Aluminium Case: Legal Victory–Economic Defeat' (1951) 41(5) *The American Economic Review* 915; W Adams, 'The Rule of Reason: Workable Competition or Workable Monopoly' (1954) 63(3) *Yale Law Journal* 348; FI Raymond, *The Limitist* (New York: W.W. Norton & Co 1947); Kaysen and Turner, *Antitrust Policy* (n 65) 50, fn. 4.

[119] Kaysen and Turner, *Antitrust Policy* (n 65) 49.

[120] For criticism, see Ibid. 51–52.

[121] DF Turner, 'The Definition of Agreement under the Sherman Act: Conscious Parallelism and Refusals to Deal' (1962) 75(4) *Harvard Law Review* 655, 661, 665–66, 671; DF Turner, 'The Scope of Antitrust and Other Economic Regulatory Policies' (1969) 82(6) *Harvard Law Review* 1207, 1212–31.

[122] Kaysen and Turner, *Antitrust Policy* (n 65) 46–49, 111–12.

[123] Ibid. 44, 76; Turner, 'The Scope of Antitrust and Other Economic Regulatory Policies' (n 121) 1212–31.

[124] Kaysen and Turner, *Antitrust Policy* (n 65) 98.

form of divestiture and corporate breakup.[125] However, the Harvard School conceded that firms should be given the possibility to put forth an efficiency defence to rebut the finding of unreasonable market power. Accordingly, firms whose market shares exceed the critical market share threshold should still be able to defeat the finding of unreasonable market power by proffering evidence that their market power is the outcome of (i) economies of scale, (ii) the lawful use of patents, or (iii) innovation in terms of new processes, products, or marketing techniques.[126] Moreover, Kaysen and Turner also formulated limiting principles for the use of structural remedies. In their view, structural remedies could only be imposed as long as they do not lead to losses in economic performance.[127]

The recognition of this efficiency defence and limiting principle for structural remedies highlight the Harvard School's awareness of the difficult trade-off between efficiencies and the goal of curbing excessive industry concentration. Harvard scholars clearly acknowledged that the elimination of unreasonable market power through deconcentration might sometimes come at high costs. This would be the case where the breakup of a powerful firm entails that its production is taken over by a multitude of less efficient, smaller firms.[128] The goal of limiting and decentralising market power should, therefore, only be pursued as long as it does not give rise to substantial costs in terms of lost efficiency and innovation.[129] Yet, Kaysen and Turner posited that most of the time, a policy of limiting and decentralising market power tends to be conducive to economic efficiency or performance rather than undermining it.[130] This assumption also shaped the design and allocation of the evidentiary burden under the situational unreasonable market power test. The combined effect of the low evidentiary threshold for finding unreasonable market power and the high threshold for rebutting the ensuing presumption of illegality by means of an efficiency defence entails that, in situations of doubt, concerns about the limitation of market power take precedence over performance considerations. Hence, Kaysen and Turner were willing to tolerate some short-term efficiency losses if they were necessary to achieve a long-term reduction in market power.[131]

Similar situational approaches were also advocated by other antitrust scholars of the time. Building on the Harvard School's S–C–P paradigm and the Kaysen–Turner proposal,[132] in 1969, a White House Taskforce on Antitrust Policy appointed

[125] Ibid. 80.
[126] Ibid. 78–79, 81.
[127] Ibid. 80.
[128] Ibid. 79.
[129] Ibid. 82.
[130] Ibid. 81, 100–19.
[131] Ibid. xx ii.
[132] PC Neal and others, 'Report of the White House Task Force on Antitrust Policy' (1968–1969) 2 (2) *Antitrust Law & Economics Review* 11, 21–24, 30. For further analysis Crane (n 66); H Hovenkamp, 'The Neal Report and the Crisis in Antitrust' (2009). Penn Law Faculty Scholarship 1794.

by President Lyndon B. Johnson and presided by Phil C. Neal issued a report (the so-called Neal Report) that envisaged major structural antitrust interventions in concentrated industries. As a flagship proposal, the report advocated the adoption of a Concentrated Industries Act. Under this act, the Attorney General would be tasked with ordering divestiture remedies in oligopolistic markets characterised by the presence of four firms with a collective market share (four-firm concentration ratio) in excess of 75 per cent. The stated objective of the proposal was to reduce the four-firm concentration ratio across all industries below 50 per cent and individual market shares of each industry player below 12 per cent.[133] Although the Concentrated Industries Act was not turned into concrete legislation, situational structuralism remained influential until the mid-1970s. For instance, the Industrial Reorganization Act,[134] which was introduced by Senator Hart in 1972, provided for a rebuttable presumption of unlawful monopoly power for any market with four-firm concentration ratios of 50 per cent or more. The various policy proposals show that until the 1970s, situational structuralism remained a credible policy option firmly anchored in the S–C–P antitrust orthodoxy of the time.

3.3.3 *Situational Structuralism and the Ordoliberal School*

Situational structuralism also found support on the other side of the Atlantic. Some Ordoliberals, notably the economists Walter Eucken and Leonhard Miksch but also the early Franz Böhm,[135] envisaged a situational approach to address the dominating impact of excessive industry concentration. The type of situational structuralism advocated by the Ordoliberals turned on a differentiated application of competition rules that is adjusted to, and escalates in accordance with, the market structure at hand.[136]

For completely competitive markets,[137] the Ordoliberals assumed that it would be sufficient to apply what they called 'general competition law' (*allgemeines Wettbewerbsrecht*) that merely comprises a prohibition of anticompetitive agreements.[138] In contrast, for more concentrated oligopolistic or monopolistic markets, Böhm, Eucken, and Miksch contemplated a proactive competition policy that would directly tackle instances of excessive industry concentration. These markets should become subject to a set of specific competition-enhancing regulations (*spezielles Wettbewerbsrecht*)[139] that are geared towards converting them as quickly

[133] Neal and others (n 132) 12, 14–15, 30–33.

[134] S.1167–Industrial Reorganization Act 1973, 93rd Congress (1973–1974); Editors, 'The Industrial Reorganization Act: An Antitrust Proposal to Restructure the American Economy' (1973) 73(3) *Columbia Law Review* 635.

[135] Böhm, 'Kartellauflösung und Konzernentflechtung' (n 102).

[136] Miksch (n 79) 16, 34.

[137] Ibid. 56.

[138] Ibid. 16, 55–56.

[139] Ibid. 16, 108–21.

as possible into completely competitive markets.[140] Under this specific competition law, oligopolistic and monopolistic firms would be placed under a bespoke and continuous regulatory oversight by the competition authority. In addition, powerful market players would be subject to the obligation to act in line with the principle of a so-called 'bound competition'[141] (*gebundene Konkurrenz*) or 'as-if competition' (*Als-ob-Wettbewerb*).[142] Oligopolistic firms or firms with significant market power would thus be required to comply with competition rules and, if need be, specifically tailored behavioural remedies.[143] The as-if competition principle, backed up with behavioural remedies, constrains the conduct of powerful firms in a way that leaves them no other possibility than to act as if they were subject to complete competition.[144] Accordingly, the as-if competition approach aimed to minimise domination by putting firms with significant market power into a corset of legal rules that would be enforced under the direct supervision of the competition authority. These rules replicate the constraints powerful firms would otherwise be subject to in a polycentric market structure characterised by complete competition.[145]

For cases of persistent substantial market power in which the as-if approach and behavioural remedies proved insufficient to restore complete competition, the Ordoliberals envisaged that competition authorities could have recourse to structural remedies. In a similar way to the Harvard School, Böhm, Eucken, and Miksch called for the breakup of powerful firms, even in the absence of any specific anticompetitive conduct.[146] Instead, they deemed the mere presence of unassailable market power and ensuing persistent levels of excessive industry concentration as a legitimate basis for competition law intervention to actively pursue the deconcentration of markets.[147] While in the early years all Ordoliberals supported the breakup of monopolistic firms as *ultima ratio*, Miksch went a step further.

He advocated the nationalisation and state control (*Lenkung*)[148] of monopolistic firms whose deconcentration is unworkable or likely to cause excessive welfare losses, for instance, because they are natural monopolies.[149] As a solution of last resort,[150] Miksch thus called for a public utility regulation for markets in which the

[140] Ibid. 35.
[141] Ibid. 123–29.
[142] Ibid. 16, 137, 144; Eucken, *Grundsätze der Wirtschaftspolitik* (n 75) 290, 294; Böhm, 'Kartellauflösung und Konzernentflechtung' (n 102) 502.
[143] Miksch (n 79) 223.
[144] Ibid. 137, 222–23; Eucken, *Grundsätze der Wirtschaftspolitik* (n 75) 293, 295–96.
[145] Miksch (n 79) 62–63.
[146] Ibid. 119; Eucken, *Grundsätze der Wirtschaftspolitik* (n 75) 292.
[147] Eucken, *Grundsätze der Wirtschaftspolitik* (n 75) 290, 294, 375–76.
[148] Miksch (n 79) 17, 34, 98.
[149] Unlike Miksch, Eucken remained highly sceptical about subjecting monopolies to state control, let alone solving the problem of monopolisation through nationalisation. Eucken, *Grundsätze der Wirtschaftspolitik* (n 75) 211, 293, 298.
[150] Miksch (n 79) 99–100.

presence of natural monopolies would prevent the emergence of a polycentric market structure.[151]

Various protagonists of the republican competition tradition thus embraced situational structuralism as one way to give effect to the republican goal of liberty as non-domination. Situational structuralism does not condition competition law intervention on the finding of any concrete instance of abusive firm conduct. Instead, it seeks to proactively minimise the domination arising from concentrated market power through direct intervention. Its goal is to bring about a more deconcentrated market structure, even in the absence of any anticompetitive conduct.

3.4 CONDUCT-BASED STRUCTURALISM

Aside from situational structuralism, the protagonists of the republican antitrust tradition also advocated a conduct-based structural approach as a second strategy to operationalise the twin goals of republican liberty and the competition–democracy nexus. Whereas situational structuralism seeks to preserve the role of competitive markets as an institution of antipower directly by intervening against the very existence of economic power, conduct-based structuralism aims to tackle excessive concentration of economic power indirectly by preventing conduct that undermines the deconcentrated functioning and structure of markets.

3.4.1 *Conduct-Based Structuralism in the English Common Law Tradition*

Elements of conduct-based structuralism can already be found in the early English common law on monopoly and restraints of trade. Early common law doctrines singled out specific types of conduct as an undue exercise of monopoly power and prohibited them as monopolistic offences. This conduct-based approach informed the common law on forestalling, engrossing, and regrating.[152] The offences of forestalling, engrossing, and regrating were directed at various strategies whereby sellers purchased large quantities of products before they could reach the market. Early proponents of competitive markets, such as Sir Edward Coke, assumed that forestalling, engrossing, and regrating led to an excessive concentration of the supply of products in the hands of one or a few sellers, while preventing other economic agents from accessing and selling the product on the market.[153] All three types of conduct were thought to enable economic agents to concentrate the supply of products, gain monopoly power, and artificially raise prices by circumventing or preempting the constraining forces of competitive markets. From today's perspective, there is little economic support for the prohibition of forestalling, engrossing,

[151] Miksch (n 79) 101, 103; Eucken, *Grundsätze der Wirtschaftspolitik* (n 75) 296, 298–99.
[152] Coke (n 107) Chapter 89, 195–97.
[153] Thorelli (n 42) 15–17; Letwin (n 39) 32–39; Coke (n 107) 196.

and regrating. In many instances, these offences were also used by the owners of markets themselves to protect their own economic privileges and monopoly rents.[154] Nevertheless, until the nineteenth century, all three forms of conduct remained closely associated with monopoly power and were often used as synonyms for monopoly itself.[155]

The conduct-based approach also underpinned the early common law doctrine against contracts in restraint of trade. As early as the fifteenth century onwards,[156] common law prohibited stipulations in contracts whereby economic agents agreed not to exercise a profession or practice trade in competition with other local traders. Until the early-eighteenth century, the common law operated on a strong presumption[157] that contracts in restraint of trade amount to unlawful restrictions of competition and are not enforceable. A central charge against these restraints of trade was that they were oppressive and deprived economic agents of their economic liberty and opportunities.[158] Early common law also gradually extended the presumptions against restraints of trade to various agreements, combinations, and conspiracies amongst economic agents to jointly raise prices, exclude other competitors, or restrict competition otherwise.[159] Agreements whose primary or sole purpose was to restrict competition were conclusively held to be unlawful.[160]

Early proponents of competitive markets not only cultivated a situational approach considering monopoly power itself to be against the common law but they also developed a rudimentary form of conduct-based structuralism that outlawed specific types of conduct for their presumptive anticompetitive effects. This conduct-based approach relied on the assumption that specific types of conduct, such as forestalling, engrossing, regrating, as well as contracts and combinations in restraint of trade, undermine a competitive market structure, and thereby enable the creation and abuse of concentrated economic power.

3.4.2 *Conduct-Based Structuralism in the US Antitrust Tradition*

Conduct-based structuralism also constituted a second avenue for the republican antitrust tradition in the United States to operationalise the idea of a competition–democracy nexus. For instance, the Harvard School supported a conduct-based test for competition law intervention next to the situational test.[161] This conduct-based test aimed to protect the competitive process by limiting market power through the

[154] Letwin (n 39) 35–36, 38.
[155] Ibid. 33.
[156] *Dyer's case* (1414) 2 Hen. V, fol. 5, pl. 26.
[157] Thorelli (n 42) 17; Letwin (n 39) 39–40.
[158] *Darcy v Allein ('The Case of Monopolies')* [1602] (n 107) 1262, 1264; *Colgate v Bacheler* [1569] 78 E.R. 1097 1097.
[159] Thorelli (n 42) 27; *Gloucester Grammar School's Case* (1410) YB 11 Hen IV, fo. pl. 201, 23.
[160] Thorelli (n 42) 27–28.
[161] Kaysen and Turner, *Antitrust Policy* (n 65) 59.

prohibition of conduct that either creates positions of market power or strengthens the market position of powerful incumbents.[162] The proposed conduct test was structured along three categories.

For the first category, the Harvard School considered the use of per se rules, which establish an irrebuttable presumption against conduct 'whose sole and major aim is restraint of competition' and whose effects on competition do not depend on the specific market context.[163] Harvard scholars highlighted the virtues of such hard-and-fast per se rules in ensuring legal certainty, enhancing administrability, reducing enforcement costs, and making conduct resulting in large-scale harm effectively unavailable.[164] On this count, the members of the Harvard School expressed their support for a broad application of per se rules to price fixing agreements,[165] certain forms of price-related information exchange (e.g., trade association reporting),[166] market sharing agreements,[167] collective refusals to deal (group boycotts),[168] and tying arrangements.[169]

Aside from hard-and-fast per se rules, the Harvard School also advocated the use of rebuttable presumptions against a second category of conduct that has the potential to substantially harm competition but might have under certain circumstances pro-competitive justifications. Harvard scholars deemed the application of rebuttable presumptions of anticompetitiveness to be appropriate to deal with exclusive dealing and requirement agreements foreclosing a substantial market share,[170] predatory price discrimination employed by firms with substantial market power,[171] and other forms of non-linear pricing, such as loyalty discounts or English clauses.[172] In addition, the Harvard School also supported the creation of rebuttable presumptions against horizontal and vertical mergers creating market power.[173]

In addition to irrebuttable (per se rules) and rebuttable rule-like presumptions of anticompetitiveness, the Harvard School also envisaged the use of more open-textured rule of reason standards as a third analytical category for the conduct test. By requiring a more searching rule of reason analysis, these standards would be reserved to conduct for which there might exist an important business justification and the distortive effect of which is contingent upon the market context.[174] Given the Harvard School's support for the application of the per se rule and rule-like

[162] Ibid. 89.
[163] Ibid. 90.
[164] Ibid. 142–43.
[165] Ibid. 151, 154–55.
[166] Ibid. 154–55.
[167] Ibid. 144.
[168] Ibid. 144, 156.
[169] Ibid. 157–59.
[170] Ibid. 159–60.
[171] Ibid. 180, 185–86.
[172] Ibid. 186.
[173] Ibid. 130–35.
[174] Ibid. 89.

rebuttable presumptions to a broad category of conduct, the rule of reason standard was thought to apply to a relatively narrow, residual subset of conduct.

It is noteworthy that the primary focus of this trifurcated conduct test advocated by the Harvard School lay on the impact of specific conduct on market power or market structure rather than its welfare effects. Harvard scholars were indeed sceptical about calls for a performance-based test[175] that would determine the legality of business conduct merely on the basis of its specific effects on economic welfare.[176] For this reason, the relevant criterion for ascertaining the anticompetitive character of a given conduct under the Harvard School's conduct test was not whether it harmed welfare, efficiency, or innovation but whether it undermined the competitive process, understood as a polycentric market structure, by increasing or contributing to the maintenance of market power.[177]

3.4.3 *Conduct-Based Structuralism and Ordoliberalism*

Conduct-based structuralism also features prominently in the Ordoliberal conception of competition law. While the Ordoliberals envisaged that competition law could tackle the problem of concentrated economic power directly through a situational test and the application of as-if competition rules, they also supported a conduct-based approach.[178] Instead of prohibiting economic power as such,[179] the conduct-based approach prohibits conduct that undermines the capacity of the competitive process to limit, disperse, and hold market power accountable.[180] By prohibiting specific types of anticompetitive conduct, the conduct-based approach seeks to ensure that positions of market power remain contestable and can be eroded by residual competition or new market entry in the medium to long

[175] Such a test was proposed by various authors and business groups. See, for instance, Business Advisory Council, 'Effective Competition: Report to the Secretary of Commerce by His Business Advisory Council with a Letter of Comment from the Secretary of Commerce' (1952); CS Oppenheim, 'Federal Antitrust Legislation: Guideposts to a Revised National Antitrust Policy' (1952) 50(8) *Michigan Law Review* 1139.

[176] Kaysen and Turner, *Antitrust Policy* (n 65) 53–56.

[177] Ibid. 89–90.

[178] The importance of conduct-based structuralism is often ignored by the existing literature. See to that effect E-J Mestmäcker, 'The Development of German and European Competition Law with Special Reference to the EU Commission's Article 82 Guidance of 2008' in LF Pace (ed), *European Competition Law: The Impact of the Commission's Guidance on Article 102* (Cheltenham: Edward Elgar 2011) 25, 42. For some of the misleading accounts, see AJ Padilla and C Ahlborn, 'From Fairness to Welfare: Implications for the Assessment of Unilateral Conduct under EC Competition Law' in C-D Ehlermann and M Marquis (eds), *European Competition Law Annual 2007: A Reformed Approach to Article 82 EC* (Oxford: Hart 2008) 55, 56, 61, 62–66; P Akman, 'Searching for the Long-Lost Soul of Article 82 EC' (CCP Working Paper, 2007) 7.

[179] Böhm (ed), *Wettbewerb und Monopolkampf* (n 78) 65.

[180] Böhm, 'Democracy and Economic Power' (n 84) 279.

term.[181] Following a conduct-based approach, competition law aims to preserve the remaining competitive structure and residual rivalry in the market to keep the economic power of the incumbents in check[182] and to restrain the scope of arbitrary action (*Verhaltensspielräume*) of individually or collectively powerful players.[183] Accordingly, the central task of competition law and policy is to ensure the structural preconditions of workable competition, which guarantee that all market players act freely and independently.[184]

The conduct standard advocated notably by Mestmäcker, as well as Eucken and Böhm – who initially supported a combination of situational and conduct-based structuralism – revolved around the distinction between legitimate performance-based (*Leistungswettbewerb*) and illegitimate hindrance (*Behinderungswettbewerb*) competition.[185] In a similar vein to the Harvard School, the members of the Freiburg School envisaged a combination of rule-like presumptions and legal standards to put the conduct-based approach into practice.

For the most egregious forms of hindrance competition, which can be presumed to be by their very nature in breach of the principle of performance-based competition on the merits, the Ordoliberals supported the application of rule-like presumptions of unlawfulness. These rule-like presumptions of anticompetitiveness cover types of business conduct that experience has shown to harm competition[186] because they undermine the polycentric functioning and openness of markets.[187] These practices not only have a clear restrictive effect on competition but also exhibit an overt anticompetitive objective.[188] Horizontal cartels – in particular, horizontal price fixing agreements, group boycotts, and market sharing agreements – fall within the scope of rule-like presumptions of anticompetitiveness because they have no purpose other than the elimination of competition.[189] Similar rule-like presumptions also apply to specific unilateral conduct of dominant firms, which is perfectly legal in the absence of market power.[190] The list of unilateral conduct by powerful firms that is presumed to be anticompetitive and, hence, prima facie illegal includes exclusivity contracts, fidelity rebates,[191] refusals to deal,[192] margin squeeze,[193] and (secondary-line) price discrimination that distorts competition on

[181] Böhm (ed), *Wettbewerb und Monopolkampf* (n 78) 259.
[182] Ibid. 259–60; Böhm, 'Democracy and Economic Power' (n 84) 279.
[183] E-J Mestmäcker (ed), *Wirtschaft und Verfassung in der Europäischen Union* (Baden-Baden: Nomos 2003) 466, 477.
[184] Ibid. 477.
[185] Böhm (ed), *Wettbewerb und Monopolkampf* (n 78) 206–10, 213, 240–42.
[186] Ibid. 268.
[187] Ibid. 265–67.
[188] Ibid.
[189] Ibid. 234–35, 261, 266–68.
[190] Ibid. 249, 265–67.
[191] Ibid. 267, 295–96.
[192] Ibid. 64–65, 259, 265, 268, 293; Eucken, *Grundsätze der Wirtschaftspolitik* (n 75) 267, 295–96.
[193] Böhm (ed), *Wettbewerb und Monopolkampf* (n 78) 259.

downstream or upstream markets.[194] The Ordoliberals complemented the use of rule-like presumptions with a second category of legal standards that require a more searching analysis. This second category would apply to conduct that can only be classified as hindrance competition upon a more thorough economic analysis. For instance, it encompasses predatory pricing[195] and excessive pricing.[196] This second category thus accounts for the difficulties in drawing a clear line between performance-based and hindrance competition.[197]

Early liberal thinkers, various US antitrust paradigms, and the Ordoliberal School alike considered conduct-based structuralism as an alternative to situational antitrust to operationalise the ideal of competition as a polycentric institution of antipower. Situational structuralism seeks to secure economic liberty as non-domination and realise the competition–democracy nexus by bestowing market participants with an extremely broad right to be economically active without being exposed to any firms with unreasonable market power. In contrast, conduct-based structuralism guarantees a more tailored right set that shields market participants against specific types of conduct that frustrate economic liberty by undermining a competitive market structure and/or facilitating the exercise of arbitrary power.

3.5 THE COMPLEMENTARITY BETWEEN SITUATIONAL AND CONDUCT-BASED STRUCTURALISM

The proponents of republican antitrust envisaged situational and conduct-based structuralism as complementary designs for competition law to operationalise the concern about republican liberty and the related ideal of a competition–democracy nexus. Situational and conduct-based structuralism rely on two different, albeit complementary, strategies to enhance republican liberty.

3.5.1 *Structural Egalitarianism as a Common Denominator*

Under situational structuralism, competition law is used to secure republican liberty by directly addressing the problem of concentrated private economic power. Situational structuralism thus constitutes the most far-reaching approach to operationalise the republican idea of a competition–democracy nexus. By levelling imbalances of power and promoting a polycentric market structure, situational structuralism seeks to engineer structural egalitarianism that presupposes a roughly equal distribution of economic power.[198] This structural approach maximises the market participants' intensity of non-domination by equalising their

[194] Ibid. 259, 265; Eucken, *Grundsätze der Wirtschaftspolitik* (n 75) 267, 295–96.
[195] Böhm (ed), *Wettbewerb und Monopolkampf* (n 78) 221, 267, 275, 284.
[196] Eucken, *Grundsätze der Wirtschaftspolitik* (n 75) 296–97.
[197] Böhm (ed), *Wettbewerb und Monopolkampf* (n 78) 289.
[198] Pettit *Republicanism* (n 11) 113–17.

relative powers or power ratios, for instance in terms of concentration ratios or market shares. In bringing about a more dispersed and equalised distribution of relative economic power, situational structuralism actively constructs a polycentric market structure. It thus seeks to (re)set the structural conditions for competition as an institution of antipower in which the interaction of market players keeps their power in check and secures their equal status. If successful, situational structuralism would make domination structurally impossible because the market players simply lack the structural capacity collectively or unilaterally to exert power. Situational structuralism maximises republican liberty by eliminating the structural sources of domination.

Under conduct-based structuralism, competition law seeks to preserve liberty as non-domination by addressing the problem of excessive concentration of power indirectly. Instead of reducing domination by eliminating its structural sources, conduct-based structuralism constrains the ability of powerful firms to exert domination. While situational structuralism seeks to make the exercise of domination structurally impossible by dispersing economic power polycentrically, conduct-based structuralism acts on the incentives of powerful firms by making dominating conduct unavailable or prohibitively costly.[199] In ensuring the openness of markets, the rule-like presumptions of conduct-based structuralism also seek to guarantee that residual competitors constrain and in the long run assail and erode positions of concentrated economic power. Ultimately, conduct-based structuralism pursues the same objective as situational structuralism of bringing about a polycentric market structure in which structural egalitarianism makes domination structurally impossible.

3.5.2 *The Blending of Situational and Conduct-based Structuralism*

The complementarity of situational- and conduct-based structuralism also becomes apparent from the fact that both approaches do not operate in isolation but are often blended. This blending may arise from the cross-fertilisation of situational and conduct-based structuralism. For instance, the conduct-based approaches envisaged by the Harvard School and Ordoliberalism relied on some situational elements. With respect to unilateral conduct, both paradigms used structural factors that trigger a presumption against specific forms of unilateral conduct once a firm holds a dominant position[200] or substantial market power.[201] Defendant firms can only rebut the presumption of anticompetitiveness if they proffer an objective justification which shows that their conduct was nonetheless a genuine attempt to

[199] Ibid. 93; P Pettit, 'Freedom in the Market' (2006) 5(2) *Politics, Philosophy & Economics* 131, 146.
[200] Böhm (ed), *Wettbewerb und Monopolkampf* (n 78) 295.
[201] Kaysen and Turner, *Antitrust Policy* (n 65) 184–86.

enhance their own performance or to meet competition.[202] In this respect, market power plays a crucial role as it may give rise to a presumption of illegality against certain unilateral conduct that is normally considered to be in line with performance-based competition. To rebut the presumption, it is for the dominant firm to show that a certain practice does not amount to hindrance competition.[203]

Situational and conduct-based structuralism are consequently not binary alternatives. The Harvard School and Ordoliberals, such as Böhm, Eucken, and Miksch, indeed assumed that both approaches could be employed in parallel. In fact, conduct-based and situational structuralism can be fine-tuned, blended, and escalated depending on the market structure at hand.[204] An example of this blended approach can be found in the Ordoliberal proposals for the design of a new competition law for post-war Germany. The first draft of a post-war German competition law by an expert group led by Paul Josten and Franz Böhm – the so-called Josten draft – followed a situational approach that provided for the prohibition and the breakup of monopolistic firms when other interventions by the competition authority proved insufficient to deconcentrate existing monopolies (s. 15 of the draft). This prohibition could, however, be rebutted if firms showed that they had obtained their monopolistic position by means of competition on the merits.[205] At the same time, the Josten draft also employed a conduct-based approach. Alongside establishing a per se prohibition against cartels, it also addressed certain forms of anticompetitive collective and unilateral discrimination, refusals to deal, and predatory pricing.[206] While the conduct-based approach towards unilateral conduct and notably the per se prohibition against cartels were retained,[207] the situational approach against monopolistic firms was dropped in later drafts[208] and did not appear in the final version of the German Law Against Restraints of Competition.[209] After the removal of situational structuralism from the drafts for the national competition law, the German delegation negotiating the Treaty of Rome also opposed a similar per se rule against monopoly power,

[202] Böhm (ed), *Wettbewerb und Monopolkampf* (n 78) 288–89, 293; Kaysen and Turner, *Antitrust Policy* (n 65) 185.

[203] Böhm (ed), *Wettbewerb und Monopolkampf* (n 78) 64–65, 249, 288–89, 292–93, 296; Mestmäcker (ed), *Wirtschaft und Verfassung in der Europäischen Union* (n 183) 125–26.

[204] Miksch (n 79) 17, 34, 98.

[205] E-J Mestmäcker, 'Competition Policy and Antitrust: Some Comparative Observations' (1980) 136(3) *Zeitschrift für die gesamte Staatswissenschaft/Journal of Institutional and Theoretical Economics* 387, 391; H Schweitzer, 'The History, Interpretation and Underlying Principles of Section 2 Sherman Act and Article 82 EC' in C-D Ehlermann and M Marquis (eds), *European Competition Law Annual 2007: A Reformed Approach to Article 82 EC* (Oxford: Hart 2008) 119, 133–34, and fn. 70.

[206] Mestmäcker, 'Competition Policy and Antitrust' (n 205) 391.

[207] Ibid. 391–94; P Hüttenberger, 'Wirtschaftsordnung und Interessenpolitik in der Kartellgesetzgebung der Bundesrepublik 1949–1957' (1976) 24(3) *Vierteljahrshefte für Zeitgeschichte* 287, 293–307.

[208] Hüttenberger (n 207) 291–92.

[209] Gesetz gegen Wettbewerbsbeschränkungen, BGBl. I, 1957, 1081.

which was initially envisaged in the Spaak report, at the European level to avoid conflicting approaches under German and European competition law.[210] In the following decades, the Ordoliberals moved away from situational structuralism and instead championed conduct-based structuralism as a default approach for national and European competition law.[211]

3.5.3 *An Intervention-Friendly Error–Cost Framework*

Situational and conduct-based structuralism also converged in their approach towards the costs of (erroneous) antitrust intervention. The design of situational and conduct-based structuralism alike followed an intervention-friendly rationale that assumes that the benefits of antitrust intervention outweigh its costs. By relying on rule-like presumptions against either the excessive concentration of economic power or specific forms of conduct, which shift the evidentiary burden towards the defending parties, situational and conduct-based structuralism both gave effect to an enforcement approach that leans in the case of doubt towards state intervention. In reverting to presumptions of illegality, situational and conduct-based structuralism designed a burden-shifting mechanism, which ensures that, in the case of doubt, the risk and costs of errors are borne by the powerful firms rather than by the rest of society.[212] This bias in favour of antitrust intervention was, in the case of the Ordoliberals, further compounded by the fact that they did not recognise a fully-fledged efficiency defence. Unlike the Harvard scholars, the Ordoliberals asserted that hindrance competition should not be justifiable by any increase of efficiency or welfare. Rather than balancing the welfare effects of a specific conduct, Mestmäcker, for instance, suggested that competition law should balance the competing rights and interests of market participants in light of the paramount goal of protecting free competition.[213]

The various protagonists of the republican antitrust tradition thus adhered to a similar intervention-friendly calculus of the costs and benefits of antitrust intervention. This calculus, which can be understood as an error–cost framework, tips the scales in the case of doubt in favour of antitrust intervention, and therefore displays some tolerance towards type I errors (false positives).[214] This intervention-friendly design of the error–cost framework can be explained by the underpinning economic assumptions. Republican antitrust paradigms, such as the Harvard and Ordoliberal Schools, all harboured doubts about the ability of markets to self-correct distortions

[210] Schweitzer (n 205) 134–35.
[211] Mestmäcker, 'The Development of German and European Competition Law' (n 178).
[212] Böhm (ed), *Wettbewerb und Monopolkampf* (n 78) 288–89, 293.
[213] Mestmäcker, 'The Development of German and European Competition Law' (n 178) 48; Böhm (ed), *Wettbewerb und Monopolkampf* (n 78), 14, 267, 303.
[214] Kaysen and Turner, *Antitrust Policy* (n 65) 5–6, 10–11; Böhm(ed), *Wettbewerb und Monopolkampf* (n 78) 220; P Larouche and MP Schinkel, 'Continental Drift in the Treatment of Dominant Firms: Article 102 TFEU in Contrast to § 2 Sherman Act' (TILEC Discussion Paper No 2013-02, Tilburg 2013) 13.

of competition and excessive levels of economic concentration.[215] Conversely, they were also doubtful about any positive correlation between firm size, economies of scale, and efficiency.[216] On the contrary, they assumed that in most cases, the prevention and elimination of industry concentration would not only protect economic liberty but also enhance efficiency.[217]

The intervention-friendly error–cost framework that was embraced by Harvard and Ordoliberal scholars alike is also informed by their political understanding of competition. Both republican antitrust paradigms not only focused on the adverse effects of potential domination in the economic sphere but also accounted for its repercussions in the political sphere on democracy.[218] From this perspective, the magnitude of harm resulting from the existence and arbitrary exercise of market power is high because it goes beyond mere economic welfare losses. By assuming that the harm flowing from excessive economic concentration is not only confined to interference with the negative economic liberty of other market participants that gives rise to welfare losses but also calls into doubt the very basis of a democratic society and polity, the Harvard and Ordoliberal Schools attributed less weight to the potential welfare losses ensuing from state intervention. Accordingly, they took the view that economic concentration, which distorts the competitive process, poses a problem for competition and a democratic society alike, even if it enhances efficiency.[219] This political dimension of the error–cost calculus has most lucidly been articulated by Böhm:

> If it should prove that serious dangers to freedom and justice will ensue, we must resolve to place any conceivable obstacle in the way of the establishment of economic power, and must not allow ourselves to be deterred from this resolution by a regard for the possible useful effects of this power any more than we would waver in our resolution to defend our democratic system, should anybody try to show us how many wonderful projects could be realized if only we decided to replace our democracy by a totalitarian dictatorship. Nothing in this world can be had without paying for it, including freedom. If we want freedom we have no option but to sacrifice some advantage which we could obtain only by employing concentrated power.[220]

3.6 CONCLUSION

The republican conception of liberty having been identified in the previous chapter as the normative backbone of the idea of a competition–democracy nexus, this

[215] Crane (n 66) 319.

[216] Böhm (ed), *Wettbewerb und Monopolkampf* (n 78) 218, 231; Eucken, *Grundsätze der Wirtschaftspolitik* (n 75) 226–36; Kaysen and Turner (n 65) 5, 81, 83–85, 110–19.

[217] Kaysen and Turner, *Antitrust Policy* (n 65) 59.

[218] Böhm, *Freiheit und Ordnung in der Marktwirtschaft* (n 80) 215; Kaysen and Turner, *Antitrust Policy* (n 65) 5.

[219] Böhm (ed), *Wettbewerb und Monopolkampf* (n 78) 214.

[220] Böhm, 'Democracy and Economic Power' (n 84) 271.

chapter has examined some of the ways in which various schools of thought envisaged its operationalisation through concrete competition policy.

This chapter makes three important contributions to our understanding of the competition-democracy nexus. First, it shows that various iterations of the competition–democracy nexus supported a competition policy that gives effect to the idea of a competition–democracy nexus by securing a polycentric competitive market structure. Thus, various proponents of the idea of a positive link between competition and democracy adhered to a structural understanding of competition as an institution of antipower that reduces overall domination in the economy and society by diffusing economic power amongst many players.

Second, this chapter has identified two principal strategies through which the proponents of a competition–democracy nexus contemplated translating this structuralist understanding of competition into a concrete design of competition laws. Situational structuralism seeks to directly tackle the problem of concentrated economic power by outlawing unreasonable market power and providing for structural interventions that bring about a more polycentric market structure. Conduct-based structuralism indirectly addresses the problem of concentrated economic power by creating presumptions of illegality against specific forms of conduct that undermine a polycentric market structure and prevent residual competitors from challenging instances of concentrated power.

Third, this chapter has demonstrated that both approaches are complementary in so far as they pursue the same goal of maintaining polycentric competitive markets as an institution of antipower. Elements of situational and conduct-based structuralism can also be easily blended and applied in parallel. Moreover, both approaches give effect to an intervention-friendly error–cost framework that condones efficiency losses as an inevitable sacrifice for the preservation of polycentric markets as institutions of antipower, on both economic and political grounds.

With the structural understanding of competition, situational and conduct-based structuralism, as well as an intervention-friendly error–cost framework, this chapter has identified the elementary building blocks of the republican competition law tradition. The next chapter will continue this analysis of the operationalisation of the idea of a competition–democracy nexus by focusing on how this republican competition law tradition influenced the judicial interpretation of competition law on both sides of the Atlantic.

4

The Competition–Democracy Nexus in US Antitrust and EU Competition Law Jurisprudence

4.1 INTRODUCTION

In the previous chapters, we discussed the intellectual pedigree and basic conceptual presuppositions of the idea of a competition–democracy nexus and its relationship with the concept of republican liberty. This account of the crucial link between competition, republican liberty, and a democratic form of government shows that competitive markets have never been solely perceived as a mechanism that optimises the allocation of resources, generates growth, and ensures economic welfare. Rather, at different points in time, proponents of a competition–democracy nexus have emphasised the role of competition in enhancing liberty as non-domination by dissipating power and emancipating individuals from relationships of subjugation. Various iterations of the idea of a competition–democracy nexus viewed the centrifugal forces of competition between roughly equally sized players as a system of antipower that preserves the republican liberty of all market participants against domination and thereby tackles the behemoth problem of concentrated private economic power.

The previous chapter explored various approaches envisaged by different schools of thought to put into effect the idea of a competition–democracy nexus by preserving competitive markets as institutions of antipower. This and the following chapters will break down this discussion of the operationalisation of the idea of a competition–democracy nexus from a theoretical to a practical level. They will assess how the competition–democracy nexus and the concern about republican liberty have been translated into a concrete antitrust policy. To this end, they focus on the bearing of the idea of a competition–democracy nexus and its conceptualisation by various schools of thought on the concrete design, application, and judicial interpretation of competition law by courts and competition authorities on both sides of the Atlantic. In particular, they will inquire into how the idea of a competition–democracy nexus fashioned the judicial interpretation of the three pillars of substantive competition law in the United States and the European

Union: namely, (i) the prohibition of collusive conduct (§ 1 of the US Sherman Act[1] in the United States and Article 101 TFEU[2] in the European Union), (ii) the regulation of dominant firm conduct (§ 2 of the US Sherman Act and §§ 2 and 3 of the US Clayton Act,[3] as subsequently amended by the Robinson–Patman Act (1936)[4] in the United States and Article 102 TFEU in the European Union), and (iii) the prohibition of mergers that substantially lessen competition (SLC) (§ 7 of the US Clayton Act[5] in the United States) or lead to a significant impediment to effective competition (SIEC) (Regulation 139/2004 EC[6] in the European Union).

This chapter sets out how all three sets of rules were, at different points in time, linked with the ideals of republican liberty and democracy. It describes how all three substantive pillars of competition law were interpreted in accordance with a republican conception of economic liberty as non-domination that perceived the very existence of concentrated economic power as an obstacle to economic freedom and democracy until the 1970s in the United States and the late 1990s in the European Union. US antitrust law and EU competition law were, on various occasions, viewed as safeguards of the ideal of republican liberty that avert and tame the power of industrial behemoths. This republican concern about liberty as non-domination as the central element of the competition–democracy nexus primarily manifested itself in the overarching policy goal of preserving a polycentric market structure. The republican antitrust tradition in the United States and in Europe built upon the structuralist approaches envisaged by various antitrust paradigms to operationalise the idea of a competition–democracy nexus that we discussed in the previous chapter.

The remainder of this chapter is organised as follows. Section 2 shows how the concern over the excessive concentration of economic power featured prominently as a central preoccupation in the formative case law of US and European courts and competition authorities. Section 3 describes the specific republican posture of this apprehension of concentrated economic power. Finally, Section 4 analyses how competition authorities and courts in the United States and European Union used various elements of situational and conduct-based structuralism to give effect to the twin goal of republican liberty and a competition–democracy nexus.

4.2 THE CONCENTRATION OF ECONOMIC POWER AS A MAJOR CONCERN OF US ANTITRUST AND EU COMPETITION LAW

Historically, the apprehension about the concentration of economic power constituted an essential consideration of various antitrust paradigms in the United States

1 15 U.S. Code Chapter 1 §§ 1–11.
2 Consolidated version of the Treaty on the Functioning of the European Union, [2012] OJ C 326/47.
3 15 U.S. Code Chapter 1 § 12–14.
4 15 U.S. Code Chapter 1 § 13.
5 15 U.S. Code Chapter 1 § 18.
6 Council Regulation (EC) No 139/2004 on the Control of Concentrations between Undertakings, [2004] OJ L 24/1.

and Europe. Over the course of the late nineteenth and the twentieth centuries, it also importantly shaped the judicial interpretation of all three branches of US and EU competition law.

4.2.1 *Concern about Economic Concentration in US Antitrust Law*

Until the 1970s, US antitrust jurisprudence abounds with examples where enforcers and courts perceived the prevention of excessive concentration of economic power by means of collusive coalitions, single-firm conduct, and mergers as the central mission of antitrust law. The concern that economic concentration constitutes a source of domination that annihilates economic liberty cuts across all three branches of US antitrust law.

For a long time, the case law under § 1 of the Sherman Act revolved around the apprehension that otherwise independent firms might be able to coordinate their actions and enter coalitions to combine their power and impose their interests upon other market participants.[7] Justice Harlan, for instance, warned that

> when several combine and direct their united energies to the accomplishment of a bad purpose, the combination is formidable. ... Its power for evil increases as its numbers increase. [...] The combination becomes dangerous and subversive of the rights of others, and the law wisely says it is a crime.[8]

Concerns over the dominating effect of collusive coalitions on the economic liberty[9] of other market participants had a long-standing impact on the interpretation of § 1 of the Sherman Act. The Supreme Court habitually grounded its strict approach towards horizontal and vertical price fixing agreements,[10] market division agreements,[11] and collective refusals to deal (group boycotts)[12] in the fear that they would bring about instances of collective power that would allow otherwise independent market players to impose their interests on the rest of society.

[7] *United States v E. C. Knight Co.* 156 U.S. 1 (1895) Justice Harlan dissenting, 35; *National Cotton Oil Co. v Texas* 197 U.S. 115 (1905) 129; *Chicago Board of Trade v United States* 246 US 231 (1918) 238; *United States v Trenton Potteries Co.* 273 U.S. 392 (1927) 397; *United States v Socony-Vacuum Oil Co.* 310 U.S. 150 (1940) 221, 224, 226 fn. 59; *United States v Topco Assocs. Inc.* 405 U.S. 596 (1972) 610.

[8] Ibid. Justice Harlan dissenting, 35.

[9] *Eastern States Lumber Ass'n v United States* 234 U.S. 600 (1914) 611; *United States v Socony-Vacuum Oil Co.* (n 7) 221; *Silver v New York Stock Exchange*, 373 U.S. 341 (1963) 359; *United States v Topco Assocs. Inc.* (n 7) 610.

[10] *United States v Trenton Potteries Co.* (n 7) 397; *United States v Socony-Vacuum Oil Co.* (n 7) 221; *Dr. Miles Medical Co. v John D. Park & Sons Co.* 220 U.S. 373 (1911) 399–409.

[11] *Addyston Pipe & Steel Co. v United States* 175 U.S. 211 (1899); *Timken Roller Bearing Co. v United States* 341 U.S. 593 (1951) 598; *United States v Sealy, Inc.* 388 U.S. 350 (1967) 355–57.

[12] *Montague & Co. v Lowry* 193 U.S. 38 (1904) 48; *Eastern States Lumber Ass'n v United States* (n 9) 608–09, 612, 614; *Fashion Originators' Guild, Inc. v FTC* 312 U.S. 457 (1941) 463–65, 468.

The early US case law on single-firm conduct and monopoly power under § 2 of the Sherman Act, § 3 and § 2 (a) of the 1914 Clayton Act[13] and their amendment by the 1936 Robinson–Patman Act[14] displayed a similar concern about concentrated economic power. From the formative case law onwards, monopoly was repeatedly scorned as

> odious to our form of government [. . .] destructive of free institutions and repugnant to the instincts of a free people, and contrary to the whole scope and spirit of the Federal Constitution.[15]

This hostility against concentrated monopoly power under § 2 of the Sherman Act reached its pinnacle in the second half of the 1940s. In a line of cases, the US judiciary went as far as holding that

> monopoly power, whether lawfully or unlawfully acquired, may itself constitute an evil and stand condemned under § 2 even it remains unexercised. For § 2 of the Act is aimed, inter alia, at the acquisition or retention of effective market control.[16]

Along similar lines, US merger control, which was introduced by the prohibition of mergers leading to a substantial lessening of competition in § 7 of the 1914 Clayton Act and strengthened by the 1950 Celler–Kefauver amendment, displayed concerns about the excessive concentration of economic power.[17] This fear reached its apex in the early 1950s. Against the backdrop of the recent totalitarian experience in Europe, which had revealed the close ties between big business and the totalitarian state in Nazi Germany,[18] it was argued that the Clayton Act sought 'to preserve a society of small, independent, decentralized business in order to disperse economic and political power and to assure that a Hitler could never rise to power in the United States'.[19] Under the mandate of Chief Justice Warren, the US Supreme Court identified the 'concentration of economic power in the hands of a few' as the major evil against which the Clayton Act was enacted[20] and posited that § 7 of the Clayton Act hinged on the 'premise that mergers are a major cause of domination'.[21]

[13] 15 U.S. Code Chapter 1 (n 2).

[14] 15 U.S. Code § 13. Discrimination in price, services, or facilities (n 3).

[15] *United States v E. C. Knight Co.* (n 7) Justice Harlan dissenting, 31.

[16] *United States v Griffith* 334 U.S. 100 (1948) 107; *United States v Paramount Pictures* 334 U.S. 131 (1948) 137; *Schine Theatres v United States* 334 U.S. 110 (1948) 129–30.

[17] For a comprehensive discussion of the legislative history of the Celler–Kefauver amendment, see *Brown Shoe Co. Inc. v United States* 370 U.S. 294 (1962) 311–23.

[18] TA Freyer, *Antitrust and Global Capitalism, 1930–2004* (Cambridge, New York: Cambridge University Press 2006) 55–58; LB Schwartz, '"Justice" and Other Non-economic Goals of Antitrust' (1979) 127(4) *University of Pennsylvania Law Review* 1076, 1078.

[19] Quotation of Representative Celler in EM Fox, 'Modernization of Antitrust: A New Equilibrium' (1980) 66(6) *Cornell Law Review* 1140, 1151.

[20] *United States v Von's Grocery Co.* 384 U.S. 270 (1966) 274.

[21] *United States v Pabst Brewing Co.* 384 U.S. 546 (1966) 552.

4.2.2 *Concern about Economic Concentration in EU Competition Law*

EU competition law never exhibited the type of antibigness fervour that characterised republican antitrust in the United States, notably during the Warren Court era. Nevertheless, the formative era of EU competition law revealed similar concerns about the concentration of economic power. Although the EU Commission and Courts articulated this fear less prominently than their US counterparts, the apprehension that market agents could exert domination through coalitions, the consolidation of monopoly power, or mergers for a long time constituted a common thread that bound together the three pillars of EU competition law.

The concern that otherwise independent firms might combine their economic power and exert domination by entering coalitions has been a recurrent theme in the formative interpretation of the prohibition of anticompetitive coordinated conduct under Article 101 TFEU. Instead of exclusively focusing on their negative consequences on prices or output, the European Courts and the European Commission frequently struck down agreements or other forms of coordination that would enable otherwise independent operators to join forces and adopt a collective policy.[22] The EU judiciary repeatedly observed that collusive arrangements creating a position of collective power would allow market operators to control and change the functioning and structure of competition,[23] thereby arbitrarily interfering with the economic liberty of other market participants.[24] The concept of restriction of competition was, therefore, equated with the limitation of 'commercial freedom' or 'economic freedom' of both the parties to the agreement and the competitors or consumers, who may suffer harm as a result of the agreement.[25]

Fears about the excessive concentration of economic power also animated the judicial interpretation of Article 102 TFEU. Though it did not articulate the same degree of hostility against monopoly power as the US case law, notably during the Warren Court era, the apprehension of excessive economic concentration had an important bearing on the early interpretation of Article 102 TFEU. This becomes apparent in the *Continental Can* case, which settled one of the first interpretative struggles in the history of EU competition law about the proper interpretation of the prohibition of abuse of a dominant position.[26] On the one hand, Professor

[22] Case C-7/95 P *Deere v Commission* ECLI:EU:C:1998:256 paras. 86–88; Case C-209/07 *Beef Industry Development and Barry Brothers (BIDS)* ECLI:EU:C:2008:643 paras. 34–40.

[23] Case C-209/07 *Beef Industry Development and Barry Brothers (BIDS)* (n 22) paras. 31–33, 38.

[24] Ibid. paras. 38–39. See also, for instance, Case 96/82 *IAZ v Commission* ECLI:EU:C:1983:310 paras. 25, 38.

[25] Case 56/64 *Consten and Grundig v Commission of the EEC* ECLI:EU:C:1966:41 343; Case 86/82 *Hasselblad v Commission* ECLI:EU:C:1984:65 para. 46; Case C-238/99 P *Limburgse Vinyl Maatschappij and Others v Commission* ECLI:EU:C:2002:582 para. 494.

[26] H Schweitzer, 'The History, Interpretation and Underlying Principles of Section 2 Sherman Act and Article 82 EC' in C-D Ehlermann and M Marquis (eds), *European Competition Law Annual 2007: A Reformed Approach to Article 82 EC* (Oxford: Hart 2008) 119, 138–39.

Joliet – who would later become Judge at the Court of Justice – prominently contended that the express reference in Article 102 TFEU to specific abuses of a dominant position was a clear sign that the provision was not directed against the mere existence of a dominant position as such. Judge Joliet affirmed that the

> approach taken by [Article 102] is based upon an attitude of neutrality toward the existence of dominant positions. It does not try to break up monopolistic positions, but instead, is confined to supervising the conduct and performance of dominant firms.[27]

On this count, Judge Joliet claimed that Article 102 only outlawed exploitative abuses of market power that harm consumers. Therefore, unlike § 2 of the Sherman Act, Article 102 TFEU could not be used to tackle monopoly power as such or take action against exclusionary abuses whereby the dominant firm drives other competitors from the market.[28]

On the other hand, Professor Ernst-Joachim Mestmäcker, who was at the time a special adviser to the Directorate General for Competition within the European Commission,[29] took a diametrically opposed view. As a disciple of Franz Böhm, Mestmäcker was closely associated with the Ordoliberal School, which perceived the concentration of economic power in itself as a source of domination and unfreedom. While conceding that Article 102 does not prohibit the existence of concentrated economic power or the possession of a dominant position as such, Mestmäcker insisted that it nonetheless sought to prevent an excessive concentration of economic power by preserving an effectively competitive market structure.[30] On this account, he repudiated Joliet's claim that Article 102 TFEU was only concerned about exploitative abuses that harmed consumer welfare directly. Instead, Mestmäcker asserted that Article 102 TFEU is primarily directed against exclusionary conduct whereby dominant firms eliminate the remaining residual competition in the market.[31] On this basis, Mestmäcker advanced the view that the existence of an abuse of dominance could not be determined based on the immediate effect of single-firm conduct on third parties; that is, consumers and competitors.[32] What matters is rather the extent to which certain conduct allows the dominant firm to control the market and insulate or strengthen its dominant

[27] R Joliet, *Monopolization and Abuse of Dominant Position: A Comparative Study of the American and European Approaches to the Control of Economic Power* (La Haye/Liège: Martinus Nijhoff 1970) 127–28.

[28] Ibid. 131.

[29] Schweitzer, 'The History, Interpretation and Underlying Principles' (n 26) 139.

[30] E-J Mestmäcker, 'Die Beurteilung von Unternehmenszusammenschlüssen nach Artikel 86 des Vertrages über die Europäische Wirtschaftsgemeinschaft [1965]' in E-J Mestmäcker (ed), *Wirtschaft und Verfassung in der Europäischen Union* (Baden-Baden: Nomos 2003) 597, 604; Schweitzer, 'The History, Interpretation and Underlying Principles' (n 26) 139–40.

[31] Schweitzer, 'The History, Interpretation and Underlying Principles' (n 26) 139–40.

[32] Ibid. 140.

position by eliminating actual or potential competitors that might otherwise constrain or diffuse its market power.[33]

In *Continental Can*, the Court of Justice settled the interpretative struggle between Judge Joliet and Professor Mestmäcker by siding with the latter. It held that the provision of Article 102 TFEU must be read as pursuing, in the same way as Article 101 TFEU, the goal of protecting 'effective competition' in the market.[34] Accordingly, Article 102 TFEU 'is not only aimed at practices which may cause damage to consumers directly, but also at those which are detrimental to them through their impact on an effective competition structure'.[35] The Court warned that the goal of preserving an effectively competitive market structure would be seriously jeopardised, were Article 102 TFEU to permit firms to 'reach such a dominant position that any serious chance of competition is practically rendered impossible'.[36] On this basis, the Court held that an

> [a]buse may therefore occur if an undertaking in a dominant position strengthens such position in such a way that the degree of dominance reached substantially fetters competition, i.e. that only undertakings remain in the market whose behaviour depends on the dominant one.[37]

The perceived need to prevent the excessive concentration of economic power also shaped EU merger policy until the early-2000s. After the failure to roll over existing merger rules from the Treaty of Paris[38] to the Treaty of Rome,[39] the Commission made several attempts to convince the Member States to confer it the power to review mergers. To this end, it highlighted the pressing need to preserve effective competition in the internal market against the backdrop of the growing trend towards merger-induced industrial concentration.[40] It repeatedly warned that the rise in concentration levels undermined the maintenance of a

33 Mestmäcker, 'Die Beurteilung von Unternehmenszusammenschlüssen' (n 30) 606, 608.

34 Case 6/72 *Europemballage Corporation and Continental Can Company v Commission* ECLI:EU:C:1973:22 para. 25.

35 Ibid. para. 26. See also Case C-95/04 P *British Airways plc v Commission of the European Communities* ECLI:EU:C:2007:166 para. 106.

36 Case 6/72 *Europemballage Corporation and Continental Can Company v Commission* (n 34) para. 25.

37 Ibid. para. 26. See also Case C-395/96 P *Compagnie Maritime Belge Transports and Others v Commission* ECLI:EU:C:2000:132 para. 113; Opinion of Advocate General Fennelly in Case C-395/96 P *Compagnie Maritime Belge Transports and Others v Commission* ECLI:EU:C:1998:518 para. 131.

38 Treaty Establishing the European Coal and Steel Community Article 66.

39 Treaty Establishing the European Economic Community. For a detailed discussion, see E Schwartz, 'Politics as Usual: The History of European Community Merger Control' (1993) 18(2) *Yale Journal of International Law* 607, 610–14.

40 European Commission, 'Le problème de la concentration dans le marché commun: The problem of concentration in the Common Market' (1966) Information Memo P-1/66 9–11.

decentralised market structure and led to a substantial increase in economic power in the hands of a few firms.[41]

This concern about the excessive concentration of economic power was also embodied in the legal test of the first EC Merger Regulation (EEC) 4064/89 (ECMR), which was adopted in 1989.[42] Instead of referring to adverse effects on output or prices, the ECMR identified the structural question of whether a merger created or strengthened a dominant position as the requisite test to determine whether it was detrimental to competition, and should therefore be prohibited or challenged. Accordingly, 'any concentration which creates or strengthens a dominant position as a result of which effective competition would be significantly impeded in the common market or in a substantial part of it' was to be prohibited under the ECMR.[43]

Early merger decisions by the EU Commission bear testimony to this concern about the excessive concentration of economic power. In its first prohibition decision enjoining the *Aerospatiale-Alenia/de Havilland* merger, the Commission based its finding of a SIEC primarily on the fact that the merger would lead to a significant increase in concentration because it would strengthen the dominant position of the merged entity in a number of relevant markets.[44] In other decisions, the Commission also inferred anticompetitive effects from the 'sheer size'[45] of the merged entity and its concomitant ability to act to an appreciable extent independently from the constraints that competitors and consumers would have imposed on it in the absence of the merger.

Along similar lines, the early case law of the Court of Justice identified the prevention of all mergers which 'because of their effect on the structure of competition [. . .] prove incompatible with the system of undistorted competition envisaged by the Treaty'[46] as the central goal of EU merger control. Accordingly, the mission of EU merger policy was to 'prevent anticompetitive market structures from arising or being strengthened'.[47] EU merger policy was hence clearly driven by the goal of averting the excessive concentration[48] of economic power. Until the 2000s, EU

[41] Ibid. 9, 11; Proposal for a Regulation (EEC) of the Council on the Control of Concentrations between Undertakings 1973, COM (73) 1210 final 6, 8; European Commission, 'Vth Report on competition policy' (1975) 13–14; European Commission, 'VIIth Report on Competition Policy' (1977) 10, 17; European Commission, 'IXth Report on Competition Policy' (1979) 10.

[42] Council Regulation (EEC) No 4064/89 on the Control of Concentrations between Undertakings, [1989] OJ L 395/1.

[43] Ibid. Article 2 (3).

[44] Case No IV/M.053 *Aerospatiale-Alenia/de Havilland*, [1991] OJ L 334/42 para. 27.

[45] Case No COMP/M.1741 *MCI WorldCom/Sprint*, [2003] OJ L 300/1 para. 145. Annulled on procedural grounds in Case T-310/00 *MCI, Inc. v Commission* ECLI:EU:T:2004:275.

[46] Case C-68/94 *France and Société commerciale des potasses et de l'azote and Entreprise minière et chimique v Commission* ECLI:EU:C:1998:148 para. 170; Case T-102/96 *Gencor v Commission* ECLI:EU:T:1999:65 para. 150.

[47] Case T-102/96 *Gencor v Commission* (n 46) para. 277.

[48] For the proposition that EU merger control under the 'old' dominance test focused on the adverse effects of concentration on competition, see G Monti, *EC Competition Law* (Cambridge: Cambridge University Press 2007) 249.

merger policy 'revealed a generalized concern about too much economic power in too few hands, but did not explain what danger emanated from such a position or what harm it expected a powerful undertaking to inflict on society'.[49]

4.3 THREE REPUBLICAN ATTRIBUTES

The fear of economic concentration featured prominently in US antitrust law until the 1970s and, albeit to a lesser extent, in EU competition law until the early-2000s. On both sides of the Atlantic, this concern was characterised by the three core features that we identified in the previous chapters as characteristic attributes of a republican conception of economic liberty.

4.3.1 *The Concentration of Economic Power as a Source of Unfreedom*

The first common thread that shaped the interpretation of US antitrust and EU competition rules on collusion, monopoly power, and mergers is that the US and EU judiciary identified not only the exercise of concentrated power but also its very existence as a threat to society. On this count, the early US and EU case law clearly followed a republican understanding of liberty that, unlike its negative counterpart, opposes instances of power regardless of whether it was actually or likely to be used to interfere with the liberty of market participants.

The early interpretation of § 1 of the Sherman Act, for instance, viewed the potential domination flowing from the 'mere existence of [...] a combination and the power acquired'[50] as a source of unfreedom. Similarly, the hostility against monopoly power of the early § 2 case law was primarily animated by concerns over 'effective control' and 'domination'[51] that emanate from the 'concentrations of power'[52] rather than any actual or likely interference resulting from its exercise. This republican reading of § 2 of the Sherman Act assumed that the Sherman Act 'is founded on a theory of hostility to the concentration in private hands of power so great that only a government of the people should have it'.[53] In other words, the republican interpretation of § 2 of the Sherman Act turned on the proposition that '[p]ower that controls the economy should be in the hands of elected representatives of the people, not in the hands of an industrial oligarchy'.[54] Along similar lines, the

49 A Witt, *The More Economic Approach to EU Antitrust Law* (Oxford: Hart 2016) 132.

50 *Northern Securities Co. v United States* 193 U.S. 197 (1904) 339, 343, 357; *United States v Trans-Missouri Freight Asso.* 166 U.S. 290 (1897) 319; *United States v E. C. Knight Co.* (n 7) Justice Harlan dissenting, 43.

51 *United States v Columbia Steel Co.* 334 U.S. 495 (1948) Justice Douglas, Black, Murphy, Rutledge dissenting 540; *United States v Paramount Pictures* (n 16) 165.

52 *United States v United Shoe Machinery Corp.* 110 F. Supp. 295 (D. Mass. 1953) 347.

53 *United States v Columbia Steel Co.* (n 51) Justice Douglas, Black, Murphy, Rutledge dissenting, 536.

54 Ibid. Justice Douglas, Black, Murphy, Rutledge dissenting 536, 539–40.

Supreme Court's interpretation of § 7 of the Clayton Act was informed by the Congressional intent to rein in the trend towards industry concentration, lest it be 'developed to the point that a market was left in the grip of a few big companies'.[55]

In a similar way to the republican tradition in US antitrust case law, the formative EU case law perceived the very concentration of economic power by means of concertation, monopoly power, and merger as an obstruction of economic freedom. Under Article 101 TFEU, the EU judiciary found it sufficient for market participants to have departed from the principle of 'decision-making autonomy'[56] to combine their forces and adopt a common policy that deviates from competition to find their cooperation to be a threat to other market participants' economic liberty and hence unlawful. Accordingly, the EU judiciary did not require any proof of actual or likely interference, for instance in the form of consumer harm, as a prerequisite for finding a violation of Article 101 TFEU.[57] Rather, consistent with the republican notion of economic liberty, the mere existence of such instances of collective economic power and the ensuing ability of firms to arbitrarily interfere with other market agents were perceived as a source of unfreedom.

A similar distinctively republican notion of economic liberty also manifests itself in the formative Article 102 TFEU case law. In *Continental Can*, the Court refrained from associating the concept of abuse of dominance with any specific conduct whereby the dominant firm interferes with the liberty of other market participants. It therefore resisted Judge Joliet's reading of Article 102, which, consistent with a negative conception of liberty, did not view the existence of concentrated market power but only its abuse in the form of conduct that actually or likely interferes with the liberty of, and harms, consumers as an abuse of dominance.[58] Instead, the Court embraced Professor Mestmäcker's interpretation of Article 102 TFEU, which was, above all, concerned about the consolidation of market power[59] and the potential abuse of power by dominant firms following the weakening of a competitive market structure.[60] The Court, accordingly, defined the notion of abuse of dominance as a situation where economic power is concentrated in such a way that it gives rise to a substantial reduction in competition and places the remaining market participants in a relationship of dependence[61] on the dominant firm. Moreover, the Court took the

[55] *United States v Von's Grocery Co.* 384 U.S. 270 (1966) 277; *United States v Pabst Brewing Co.* 384 U.S. 546 (1966) 551–52.

[56] Case C-7/95 P *Deere v Commission* (n 22) para. 88; Case C-8/08 *T-Mobile Netherlands BV and Others* ECLI:EU:C:2009:343 paras. 32–34..

[57] Case C-8/08 *T-Mobile Netherlands BV and Others* (n 56) paras. 38–39.

[58] Joliet (n 27) 127–28.

[59] Case 40/73 *Suiker Unie and Others v Commission* ECLI:EU:C:1975:174 para. 505; Case 85/76 *Hoffmann-La Roche v Commission* ECLI:EU:C:1979:36 paras. 90–91.

[60] Case 6/72 *Europemballage Corporation and Continental Can Company v Commission* (n 34) para. 26.

[61] Ibid.; Case C-395/96 P *Compagnie Maritime Belge Transports and Others v Commission* (n 37) para. 113; Opinion of Advocate General Fennelly in Case C-395/96 P *Compagnie Maritime Belge Transports and Others v Commission* (n 37) para. 131.

view that the concept of abuse of dominance did not presuppose a link of causality between the dominant position and the abuse,[62] and clarified that Article 102 TFEU applies to conduct by dominant firms 'irrespective of any fault'.[63] Such a non-fault abuse of dominance may occur if an 'undertaking holds a position so dominant that the objectives of the Treaty are circumvented by an alteration to the supply structure which seriously endangers the consumer's freedom of action in the market'.[64] This is the case if competition is eliminated to the extent that 'remaining competitors could no more provide a sufficient counterweight'.[65]

EU merger policy also displayed features that were consistent with a republican notion of liberty. Far from focusing exclusively on actual or likely interference in the form of higher prices or exclusionary conduct, it identified the creation of a single or collective situation of a dominant position as such as a SIEC.[66] As a result, the ECMR mandated competition law intervention on the mere basis that a merger leads to an excessive concentration of economic power. Showing that the merger would result in actual or likely interference with other market participants was not required.

In perceiving the concentration of economic power as a source of societal harm and unfreedom, US antitrust law until the 1970s and EU competition law until the 2000s shared a broad notion of preventing conditions (y) that typifies the republican conception of liberty. US antitrust law and EU competition law went beyond an approach grounded in negative liberty, which perceives only actual or likely interference as an obstacle to liberty. Instead, they operated in a way that is consistent with a republican conception of liberty, as championed by various proponents of a competition–democracy nexus surveyed in the previous three chapters, which considers domination and the mere potential of arbitrary interference resulting from the existence of concentrated power as an obstruction of liberty.

4.3.2 *The Master–Slave and Law–Liberty Topoi*

Competition law jurisprudence in the United States and in Europe also highlighted the modal constraints that concentrated economic power imposes on other market participants. To this end, the judiciary habitually mobilised, in a similar vein to various proponents of a competition–democracy nexus, the republican imaginary of the relationship between a slave and their arbitrary master. Justice Harlan, for instance, asserted that anticompetitive agreements and combinations would put market participants 'entirely at the mercy of combinations which arbitrarily control'

62 Case 6/72 *Europemballage Corporation and Continental Can Company v Commission* (n 34) para. 27.
63 Ibid. para. 29.
64 Ibid.
65 Ibid.
66 Case No IV/M.053 *Aerospatiale-Alenia/de Havilland* (n 44) paras. 27, 34, 43, 51–52.

markets.[67] Even if the combining firms were to refrain from actually exercising their power, all other market participants would nonetheless be unfree because they are subjected to the 'oppression'[68] and 'human slavery' resulting from the concentration of economic power.[69] Consistent with a modally robust republican understanding of economic liberty, the early case law was not only concerned about actual or likely interference but also expressed strong apprehension about the tendency of combined corporate power to create situations of hierarchical subjugation and dependency.[70]

Along similar lines, § 2 of the Sherman Act was considered to be directed against the concentration of economic power to ensure 'that the fortunes of the people will not be dependent on the whim or caprice, the political prejudices, the emotional stability of a few self-appointed men'.[71] The judicial interpretation of § 7 of the Clayton Act also exhibited awareness of the modal constraints that concentrated economic power imposes on other market participants. Indeed, the Court took the view that mergers pose a 'continuous, pervasive threat to small businesses'.[72] Consequently, merger policy was considered to be of crucial importance in preventing the economic liberty of small businesses from being frustrated as they are 'being made dependent upon monster concentration'.[73]

The EU judiciary, albeit in a less explicit way than their US counterpart, also had recourse to the republican imaginary of a master–slave relationship to underscore the modal constraints that the presence of concentrated economic power or relationships of economic subordination impose on other market participants. For instance, in *Continental Can* the Court located the source of unfreedom of other market participants in the mere existence of a situation of dependency on the dominant firm.[74] Along similar lines, the formative case law found dominant firm conduct – for instance, exclusive dealing, tying arrangements, and rebates – that reinforces the dependence of customers and competitors on the dominant firm to be in breach of Article 102 TFEU.[75] The Court thus clarified that the prohibition of

67 *United States v E. C. Knight Co.* (n 7) Justice Harlan dissenting, 43.

68 *Standard Oil Co. of New Jersey v United States* 221 U.S. 1 (1911) Justice Harlan dissenting, 84.

69 Ibid. Justice Harlan dissenting, 83.

70 *United States v E. C. Knight Co.* (n 7) Justice Harlan dissenting, 26. *United States v Trans-Missouri Freight Asso.* (n 50) 323–24.

71 *United States v Columbia Steel Co.* (n 51) Justice Douglas, Black, Murphy, Rutledge dissenting, 536.

72 *United States v Von's Grocery Co.* (n 55) 275.

73 Ibid. 275–76 fn. 10 quoting remarks by Representative Celler.

74 Case 6/72 *Europemballage Corporation and Continental Can Company v Commission* (n 34) para. 26; Case C-395/96 P *Compagnie Maritime Belge Transports and Others v Commission* (n 37) para. 113; Opinion of Advocate General Fennelly in Case C-395/96 P *Compagnie Maritime Belge Transports and Others v Commission* (n 37) para. 131.

75 Case 85/76 *Hoffmann-La Roche v Commission* (n 59) paras. 89–90; Case 322/81 *Michelin v Commission (Michelin I)* ECLI:EU:C:1983:313 para. 85; Case T-83/91 *Tetra Pak v Commission (Tetra Pak II)* ECLI:EU:T:1994:246 paras. 135, 137, 140.

abuse of dominance has not only a behavioural but also a situational element. By prohibiting abusive conduct, it also seeks to address the situation of domination, subordination, and dependence market participants are subject to in the presence of the excessive concentration of economic power within the hands of a dominant firm.

The master–slave theme also percolates the Article 101 TFEU case law. The Court, for instance, repeatedly held that vertical restraints may restrict the economic liberty of retailers and distort competition regardless of whether they are consistently enforced by manufacturers. Even if manufacturers were to refrain from strictly enforcing vertical restrictions, 'their very existence may create a "visual and psychological" background' that compels retailers to comply with the restraints and adapt their behaviour in a way that restricts competition.[76] This case law thus echoes the insight of republican liberty that the mere awareness of the ability of a powerful master to interfere with their slave may compel the slave to engage in ingratiating behaviour.[77]

The distinctive republican pedigree of economic liberty underpinning antitrust law until the 1970s also becomes apparent in the recurrent use of the *law–liberty* theme as a characteristic feature of the republican tradition. Echoing Sir Edward Coke and the framers of the US Sherman Act, the US Supreme Court repeatedly celebrated the antitrust statutes as a 'charter of freedom',[78] 'comprehensive charter of economic liberty',[79] and 'magna Carta of free enterprise'.[80] In contrast to a negative understanding of liberty, the US courts perceived legal rules not as obstacles to but as being constitutive of economic liberty. The role of antitrust laws in securing economic liberty was consistently viewed to be the connecting piece between competition and a democratic society and polity. This becomes most apparent in *Northern Pacific Railroads Company* where the Court famously held:

> The Sherman Act was designed to be a comprehensive charter of economic liberty aimed at preserving free and unfettered competition as the rule of trade. It rests on the premise that the unrestrained interaction of competitive forces will yield the best allocation of our economic resources, the lowest prices, the highest quality and the greatest material progress, while at the same time providing an environment conducive to the preservation of our democratic political and social institutions.[81]

Along similar lines, the EU judiciary and Commission also repeatedly stressed the role of EU competition law in safeguarding the rights of market participants. The

[76] Case 19/77 *Miller v Commission* ECLI:EU:C:1978:19 para. 7; Case 86/82 *Hasselblad v Commission* (n 25) para. 46.

[77] P Pettit, *Republicanism: A Theory of Freedom and Government* (Oxford: Oxford University Press 1997) 23–25.

[78] *United States v Socony-Vacuum Oil Co.* (n 7) 221.

[79] *Northern Pac. Ry. Co. v United States* 356 U.S. 1 (1958) 4.

[80] *United States v Topco Assocs. Inc.* (n 7) 610.

[81] *Northern Pac. Ry. Co. v United States* (n 79)4.

EU Courts habitually emphasised that the mandate of competition law is to protect the interests of consumers and competitors.[82] The Court also highlighted the importance of competition law within the broader EU legal order in protecting a system in which competition is not distorted and promoting an open-market economy.[83] The European Commission even went as far as to compare the role of competition law with constitutional bounds of power to highlight the role of competition rules in preserving individual economic freedom.[84] Consistent with the Ordoliberal perception of competition law, the EU judiciary and Commission viewed legal rules not as an obstacle to but as being a prerequisite for an open and free market economy.

The prominent role of the master–slave and law–liberty topoi shows how US antitrust and EU competition law also mirrored the broad conception of the range of actions (z) that characterises the republican conception of liberty. US antitrust and EU competition law thus gave expression to the distinctively robust and thick republican understanding of liberty that is cognisant of the modal constraints that concentrated power imposes on other individuals not only in the actual or nearby likely but also across a range of relevant possible worlds.

4.3.3 *The Egalitarian Dimension of Republican Liberty*

A third distinctive feature of US antitrust law until the 1970s and EU competition law until the 2000s is that they revealed a strong egalitarian impetus that typifies the republican notion of liberty.[85]

4.3.3.1 The Egalitarian Understanding of Economic Liberty in US Antitrust Law

In the United States, this egalitarian understanding of economic liberty was closely associated with the ideal of a Jeffersonian society in which economic power, wealth, and opportunities are spread equally amongst a multitude of small and independent businesses. From its formative case law onwards, the US Supreme Court habitually referred to competition law as an essential instrument to safeguard the ideal of a Jeffersonian society composed of independent businessmen as free and equals. The judiciary repeatedly highlighted that a core mission of antitrust law was to prevent

82 Case 6/72 *Europemballage Corporation and Continental Can Company v Commission* (n 34) para. 26; Case C-95/04 P *British Airways plc v Commission of the European Communities* (n 35) para. 106; Case C-501/06 P *GlaxoSmithKline Services and Others v Commission and Others* ECLI:EU:C:2009:610 paras. 63–64.

83 Case C-9/99 *Échirolles Distribution* ECLI:EU:C:2000:532 para. 25; Opinion of Advocate General Alber in Case C-9/99 *Échirolles Distribution* ECLI:EU:C:2000:299 para. 27.

84 European Commission, 'XVth Report on Competition Policy' (1985) 11.

85 Pettit (n 77) 110–20.

powerful firms from 'driving out of business the small dealers and worthy men whose lives have been spent therein'.[86] The formative antitrust jurisprudence was pervaded by the fear that combinations of economic power would transform the 'independent business man ... into a mere servant or agent of a corporation ... bound to obey orders issued by others'[87] and subject to 'the sole power and ... the sole will of one powerful combination of capital'.[88] Concentration of power was objected to because it enabled mighty firms at any time to 'crush their feebler rivals' and wage a 'war of extermination' on them.[89] The antitrust laws were therefore seen as a safeguard of the economic opportunities and independent status of market participants, and in particular of 'small, local enterprises'.[90] Preserving a market structure that secures broad-based economic opportunities for small independent businesses was a central objective of the formative antitrust law. On numerous occasions, the Court indeed emphasised the importance of protecting the competitive process as a safeguard of procedural fairness by ensuring that 'every business, no matter how small' can take part in the competitive race.[91]

One area in which the egalitarian objective of preserving the economic opportunity and independent status of small dealers played a particularly prominent role was the application of § 1 of the Sherman Act to vertical agreements. For a long time, vertical restraints were perceived by the Supreme Court as an illegitimate form of subordination and domination, which subjugates retailers to the arbitrary will of manufacturers.[92] In *Dr Miles*, the Supreme Court grounded this strict approach towards vertical restraints in the ancient common law doctrine of restraints upon alienation. This doctrine, originally coined by Sir Edward Coke,[93] dates back to the antimonopoly movement of sixteenth century common law. It postulates that a seller of an article or product cannot rely on their right to property and contractual freedom to impose restraints on the future sales of that product once it has been sold on the market against remuneration.[94] By approaching them as a restraint of alienation, the early case law cast vertical restraints as an undue expansion of the producer's control

86 *United States v Trans-Missouri Freight Asso.* (n 50) 323; *Fashion Originators' Guild, Inc. v FTC* (n 12) 467.

87 *United States v Trans-Missouri Freight Asso.* (n 50) 323–24.

88 *Fashion Originators' Guild, Inc. v FTC* (n 12) 467.

89 *United States v Swift & Co.* 286 U.S. 106 (1932) 116, 118. A similar concern also informed the adoption of the Clayton Act in 1914. Senate Report No 698, to accompany H.R. 15,657, 63rd Cong. 2nd sess. (1914) 13–14.

90 *United States v Columbia Steel Co.* (n 51) Justice Douglas, Black, Murphy, Rutledge dissenting, 538; *United States v Paramount Pictures* (n 16) 159, 162, 164–65.

91 *United States v Topco Assocs. Inc.* (n 7) 610. See also *Klor's, Inc. v Broadway-Hale Stores, Inc.* 359 U.S. 207 (1959) 212–13; *Radiant Burners, Inc. v Peoples Gas Light & Coke Co.* 364 U.S. 656 (1960) 660.

92 *Dr. Miles Medical Co. v John D. Park & Sons Co.* (n 10) 408.

93 E Coke, *Institutes of the Laws of England* [1628].

94 *Dr. Miles Medical Co. v John D. Park & Sons Co.* (n 10) 403, for a full discussion 403–06. See also *White Motor Co. v United States* 372 U.S. 253 (1963) Justice Brennan concurring, 264.

and dominion over their retailers.[95] This strict approach towards vertical restraints aimed to prevent manufacturers from subjecting retailers to a hierarchical relationship of control and subordination, which goes beyond the perimeters of their property rights or of their firm.[96] Despite attempts to significantly curtail the implications of *Dr Miles*,[97] the Court relied on the doctrine of restraints upon alienation to find minimum and maximum resale price maintenance,[98] and vertical territorial restraints[99] in breach of § 1 of the Sherman Act. The republican antitrust tradition thus perceived vertical restraints imposed by manufacturers once they have parted with their dominion over a product as a form of undue domination that undermines the freedom, equal status, and economic opportunities of independent retailers.[100]

The ideal of a Jeffersonian society of free and equals also informed the application of US antitrust rules to monopoly power and single-firm conduct. This egalitarian dimension of economic liberty in its republican sense was on full display in *Alcoa*. In this case, Judge Learned Hand advanced the view that the Sherman Act embodied a clear preference for 'a system of small producers, each dependent for his success upon his own skill and character, to one which the great mass of those engaged must accept the direction of a few'.[101] Invoking the independent status of the small producer as the ideal type of the republican free man or citizen, Learned Hand affirmed that one of the purposes of antitrust law 'was to perpetuate and preserve, for its own sake and in spite of possible cost, an organization of industry in small units which can effectively compete with each other'.[102]

The egalitarian concern of preserving a Jeffersonian society composed of small and independent businesses was also a key driver of the enactment of the 1936 Robinson–Patman Act, which amended and tightened the prohibition of price discrimination under § 2 (a) of the Clayton Act. In the first place, the adoption of the Robinson–Patman Act was a reaction to the rise of large chain-stores and their ability to adopt aggressive pricing strategies, which increasingly threatened the competitive opportunities and livelihood of small dealers.[103] The fear that the rise of large-scale retail stores would crowd out small independent dealers also carried over into the Supreme Court's interpretation of § 2 (a) of the Clayton Act, as amended by the Robinson–Patman Act. Primary-line price discrimination and

95 *Dr. Miles Medical Co. v John D. Park & Sons Co.* (n 10) 408.
96 Ibid. 405. See also *Cont'l T.V. v GTE Sylvania* 433 U.S. 36 (1978) Justice White dissenting, 67.
97 *United States v Colgate & Co.* 250 U.S. 300 (1919).
98 *Kiefer-Stewart Co. v Seagram & Sons* 340 U.S. 211 (1951) 213; *Albrecht v Globe-Democrat Publishing Co.* 390 U.S. 145 (1968) 152–53.
99 *United States v Arnold, Schwinn & Co.* 388 U.S. 365 (1967) 377–81. See, however, *White Motor Co. v United States* (n 94) 261–62, Justice Brennan concurring, 264–65.
100 *United States v Arnold, Schwinn & Co.* (n 99) 380.
101 *United States v Alcoa* 148 F.2d 416 (2d Cir. 1945) 427.
102 Ibid. 429; *United States v United Shoe Machinery Corp.* (n 52) 342.
103 HC Hansen, 'Robinson-Patman Law: A Review and Analysis' (1983) 51(6) *Fordham Law Review* 1113, 1117, 1121–22.

predatory pricing cases, such as *Moore v Mead's Fine Bread* and *Utah Pie*, are prime examples of this egalitarian concern of the republican antitrust tradition, notably during the Warren Court era. These cases turned upon the concern that geographic price discrimination and under-cutting by large-scale corporations would undermine the competitive opportunities of smaller local competitors, and this would lead to a deterioration of the market structure to the benefit of large companies.[104] The US courts translated this concern into a relatively loose test, which set the bar to condemn discriminatory price-cutting by powerful firms very low.[105]

Merger policy was also guided by the aspiration to preserve a Jeffersonian society of small and independent dealers, notably during the Warren Court era. The Warren Court pushed the egalitarian dimension of republican antitrust to an extreme. It no longer only sought to protect a competitive market structure, but it also aimed at 'keeping a large number of small competitors in business', regardless of their efficiencies.[106] On this account, it took the view that efficiencies benefiting larger firms may offend § 7 of the Clayton Act when they entrench economic concentration and drive smaller, less efficient competitors out of the market. In *Brown Shoe*, the Supreme Court candidly endorsed an 'efficiency offense'.[107] It made it clear that efficiencies of economic integration would only be accounted for as a pro-competitive justification for mergers if they strengthen the competitive force and opportunities of small businesses by enabling them to more effectively challenge larger industry players.[108] The Warren Court case law no longer only sought to secure a procedural form of equality of opportunity by guaranteeing a level playing field, but it also tried to enhance greater distributive equality. Consequently, antitrust law was used to bring about a society in which economic opportunity and ownership are distributed amongst the many rather than the few.[109]

4.3.3.2 The Egalitarian Understanding of Economic Liberty in EU Competition Law

This egalitarian understanding of economic liberty was not alien to EU competition law either. In a similar way as in the United States, this egalitarian dimension of

[104] *Moore v Mead's Fine Bread Co.* 348 U.S. 115 (1954) 119; *Utah Pie Co. v Continental Baking Co.* 386 U.S. 685 (1967) 689; RJ Peritz, *Competition Policy in America: History, Rhetoric, Law* (New York: Oxford University Press 2000) 225–28.

[105] *Moore v Mead's Fine Bread Co.* (n 104) 118–19; *Utah Pie Co. v Continental Baking Co.* (n 104) 694, 696–97; *FTC v Anheuser-Busch, Inc.* 363 U.S. 536 (1960) 550, 553; JD Hurwitz and WE Kovacic, 'Judicial Analysis of Predation: The Emerging Trends' (1982) 35(1) *Vanderbilt Law Review* 63, 86–92.

[106] *United States v Von's Grocery Co.* (n 55) 275–77.

[107] *United States v Continental Can Co.* 378 U.S. 441 (1964) 463–64.

[108] *Brown Shoe Co. Inc. v United States* (n 17) 319, 346; Antitrust Division of the US Department of Justice, 1968 Merger Guidelines paras. 9–10.

[109] *United States v Von's Grocery Co.* (n 55) 274–78.

republican liberty found its expression in a profound hostility against hierarchical relationships of subordination. Like in the United States, the concern about preserving the independent status and competitive opportunities of small traders gave effect to a hostile approach of the formative EU competition law towards vertical restraints. As early as in *Consten and Grundig*, the Court held that vertical territorial restraints, which led to the creation of a de facto ban on parallel imports by independent distributors, amounted to a serious by-object restriction of competition in breach of Article 101 (1) TFEU.[110] This approach closely replicated the doctrine of restraints upon alienation that had guided the US Supreme Court's republican approach towards vertical restraints.[111] In analogy with the doctrine of restraints upon alienation, the EU Commission's and the Court's analysis of vertical restraints was based on the implicit assumption that as soon as manufacturers have sold their products at market price to an independent retailer, then they part with their title over the product and therefore no longer have a legitimate reason for exercising control over its resale.[112]

Vertical restraints were consequently considered as instances of illegitimate domination, whereby the manufacturers subject otherwise independent distributors to a relationship of subordination and project their power beyond the perimeters of their property rights and the boundaries of their firm. On this basis, the Commission and the Court consistently treated vertical territorial[113] and price restraints[114] through which manufacturers reduce the freedom of action of retailers as restrictions of competition that were in breach of Article 101 TFEU,[115] even in cases where the retailers themselves asked the manufacturer to adopt the restraints.[116]

This concern about preserving the independent status and equality of opportunity of traders played a particularly prominent role in cases involving vertical restraints that hindered distributors from engaging in parallel trade between Member States. Following *Consten and Grundig*, the Commission and the EU Courts consistently condemned vertical restraints, which entailed a de facto ban on parallel imports by

[110] Case 56/64 *Consten and Grundig v Commission of the EEC* (n 25) 344.

[111] Ibid. 309, 340; Notice on exclusive dealing contracts with commercial agents, OJ [1962] 139/2921, 2921–22; Case C-266/93 *Bundeskartellamt v Volkswagen and VAG Leasing* ECLI:EU:C:1995:345 paras. 19, 24.

[112] Notice on exclusive dealing contracts with commercial agents (n 111) 2921–22; Case 56/64 *Consten and Grundig v Commission of the EEC* (n 25) 338, 340; Case 40/73 *Suiker Unie and Others v Commission* (n 59) paras. 539–41.

[113] Case 19/77 *Miller v Commission* (n 76) see, for instance, the Commission submissions on p. 143 and para. 7; Case 32/78 *BMW Belgium v Commission* ECLI:EU:C:1979:191 para. 36; Case 86/82 *Hasselblad v Commission* (n 25) para. 46.

[114] Case 107/82 *AEG v Commission* ECLI:EU:C:1983:293 paras. 43, 60, 107–35; Case 311/85 *VVR v Sociale Dienst van de Plaatselijke en Gewestelijke Overheidsdiensten* ECLI:EU:C:1987:418 para. 17; Case 27/87 *Erauw-Jacquery v La Hesbignonne* ECLI:EU:C:1988:183 para. 15.

[115] See, for instance, Case C-306/96 *Javico v Yves Saint Laurent Parfums* ECLI:EU:C:1998:173 paras. 14–15 and case law cited therein.

[116] Case 19/77 *Miller v Commission* (n 76) para. 7.

independent distributors as a restriction of competition by object.[117] This hostile approach against vertical restrictions of parallel trade reflects the fundamental role of small and independent traders as 'heroes'[118] and drivers of the European economic integration process. In the same way as the Jeffersonian goal of preserving the opportunities of small and independent entrepreneurs importantly influenced the interpretation of § 1 of the Sherman Act, the protection of the opportunities and independent status of traders, parallel importers, and foreign competitors also lay at the heart of the interpretation of Article 101 TFEU. While the Supreme Court idealised the small and independent entrepreneur as the prototype citizen in a Jeffersonian republic, the independent parallel importer became the epitome of the republican free man or 'market citizen'[119] of a nascent European polity. By making use of their free movement rights and by interpenetrating national markets, independent dealers and parallel traders were perceived as key players in the achievement of a genuine European internal market and the political project of a nascent European polity.[120]

The egalitarian dimension of republican liberty and its realisation through a market structure that ensures the equality of competitive opportunities and the independent status of market participants also had an important bearing on Article 102 TFEU. Unlike their US counterparts, the EU judicature and European Commission never explicitly endorsed the protection of small and medium-sized businesses as an independent goal of Article 102 TFEU.[121] Nonetheless, the Court perceived Article 102 as an important tool to preserve the equality of opportunity between dominant firms and smaller competitors. This concern about equality of opportunity is apparent in the Court's interpretation of the principle of special responsibility. In *Michelin I*, the Court insisted that dominant firms are subject to 'a special responsibility not to allow [their] conduct to impair genuine undistorted competition on the common market'.[122] This principle of special responsibility accounts for the asymmetry in power and inequality of arms that exists between dominant firms and their non-dominant rivals. It assumes that certain forms of conduct in the hands of dominant firms may have an exclusionary effect on other

[117] Case 56/64 *Consten and Grundig v Commission of the EEC* (n 25) 344; Case C-501/06 *P GlaxoSmithKline Services and Others v Commission and Others* (n 82) paras. 59–61; Case C-439/09 *Pierre Fabre Dermo-Cosmétique* ECLI:EU:C:2011:649 paras. 47, 53–54. For a similarly strict approach against horizontal agreements restricting parallel trade, see Case 96/82 *IAZ v Commission* (n 24) para. 25.

[118] L Gyselen, 'Vertical Restraints in the Distribution Process: Strength and Weakness of the Free-Rider Rationale under EEC Competition Law' (1984) 21(4) *Common Market Law Review* 647.

[119] For a critical discussion of the prominent role of the concept of market citizenship for the construction of EU citizenship, see N Nic Shuibhne, 'The Resilience of EU Market Citizenship' (2010) 47(6) *Common Market Law Review, Issue* 1597.

[120] Gyselen (n 118) 649.

[121] H Schweitzer, 'Das Wettbewerbsrecht und das Problem privater Macht' in F Möslein (ed), *Private Macht* (Tübingen: Mohr Siebeck 2016) 447, 456–57.

[122] Case 322/81 *Michelin v Commission (Michelin I)* (n 75) para. 57.

market participants, while this is not the case if non-dominant firms adopt the same conduct.[123] The principle of special responsibility recognises that certain conduct bestows dominant firms with a competitive advantage, which non-dominant firms can impossibly replicate. This inequality of arms is not necessarily the result of different degrees of efficiency but might be the result of the mere difference in size, scale, and financial resources between dominant firms and smaller competitors.

This concern about the inequality of arms between dominant and non-dominant firms crystallised most prominently in the Court's approach towards predatory pricing and selective price cuts. The Court held that, under certain circumstances, Article 102 TFEU also prevents dominant firms from charging prices that exceed their Average Variable Costs (AVC) but do not cover their Average Total Costs (ATC).[124] In some instances, the EU Courts and Commission even went as far as applying Article 102 TFEU to above-cost (ATC) price cuts[125] The Court justified this strict approach towards aggressive pricing by dominant firms by the fact that pricing in excess of AVC 'can drive from the market undertakings which are perhaps as efficient as the dominant undertaking but which, because of their smaller financial resources, are incapable of withstanding the competition waged against them'.[126]

The classical case law attributed little consideration to the question of whether the competitors foreclosed by the above-AVC pricing were equally or less efficient than the dominant firm.[127] It thus expressed a strong egalitarian concern for the preservation of the independent status of market participants and the openness of markets as a level playing field.[128] In some cases, the Court of Justice made the importance of equality of opportunity of smaller rivals even more explicit. The Court repeatedly stressed 'that a system of undistorted competition [...] can be guaranteed only if equality of opportunity is secured as between the various economic operators'.[129] Given that it did not necessarily make the equality of opportunity and right of smaller competitors to compete conditional upon equal efficiency, the classical abuse of dominance case law endorsed an inclusive notion of the competitive process.

[123] Case 27/76 *United Brands v Commission* ECLI:EU:C:1978:22 para. 189; Case C-333/94 P *Tetra Pak v Commission* ECLI:EU:C:1996:436 paras. 32, 37; Case C-62/86 *AKZO v Commission* ECLI:EU:C:1991:286 paras. 69–70; Case C-202/07 P *France Télécom v Commission* ECLI:EU:C:2009:214 paras. 106–07.

[124] Case C-62/86 *AKZO v Commission* (n 123) para. 72.

[125] Case C-395/96 P *Compagnie Maritime Belge Transports and Others v Commission* (n 37) paras. 116–17; Case T-30/89 *Hilti v Commission* ECLI:EU:T:1991:70 para. 100; Case T-228/97 *Irish Sugar v Commission* ECLI:EU:T:1999:246 paras. 117–24; 215–25.

[126] Case C-62/86 *AKZO v Commission* (n 123) para. 72.

[127] Case C-395/96 P *Compagnie Maritime Belge Transports and Others v Commission* (n 37) paras. 116–17.

[128] Case 40/73 *Suiker Unie and Others v Commission* (n 59) para. 505.

[129] Case C-202/88 *France v Commission* ECLI:EU:C:1991:120 para. 51; Case C-18/88 *RTT v GB-Inno-BM* ECLI:EU:C:1991:474 para. 25; Case C-49/07 *MOTOE* ECLI:EU:C:2008:376 para. 51; Case C-327/03 *ISIS Multimedia and Firma 02* ECLI:EU:C:2005:622 para. 39.

The preservation of broad-based economic opportunities for smaller competitors also played an important role in EU merger policy. Unlike the US Supreme Court, the EU Commission and Courts never explicitly endorsed the preservation of the competitive opportunities and livelihood of small dealers as a distinct goal of merger policy. However, this does not mean that the concern about small and medium-sized businesses played no role in EU merger control. Quite the contrary. In calling for the adoption of a European regime of merger control, the Commission expressed the fear that the creation of powerful players through mergers would jeopardise the competitive opportunities of small and medium-sized enterprises. The Commission also insisted on the 'specific role' of small and medium-sized businesses in the maintenance of effective competition within the internal market.[130] The Commission thus viewed the preservation of a polycentric market structure not only as a bulwark against the domination of industrial behemoths created by merger but also as a tool to promote the competitive opportunities of independent SMEs.[131]

The goal of preserving the competitive opportunities of SMEs also had an important bearing on concrete merger decisions under the EC Merger Regulation. For example, in *Aerospatiale-Alenia/de Havilland*, the Commission enjoined the merger between the two leading producers of regional aircraft not only because it would lead to the creation of a dominant position but also because it feared that it would adversely affect the competitive opportunities of smaller competitors and customers.[132] Notably, the Commission saw an unfair competitive advantage in the increased ability of the merged entity to leverage its broad range of product lines through rebates or bundling (so-called portfolio effects)[133] that would hamper the competitive opportunities of smaller competitors.[134] The similarities with the Warren Court's approach in *Brown Shoe* are striking. The Commission did not account for the broadening of the product portfolio, and the ensuing decrease in transaction costs and prices for airline customers as pro-competitive efficiencies that would alleviate competition concerns raised by the merger.[135] To the contrary, it perceived efficiencies as an offence and threat to the competitive opportunities of less efficient small and medium-sized customers, namely regional European airlines.[136]

[130] European Commission, 'Le problème de la concentration dans le marché commun' (n 40) 9–10; European Commission, 'VIIth Report on Competition Policy' (n 41) 10–11; Witt (n 49) 96.

[131] European Commission, ''VIIth Report on Competition Policy' (n 41) 10–11; European Commission, 'XIIth Report on Competition Policy' (1982) 13.

[132] Case No IV/M.053 *Aerospatiale-Alenia/de Havilland* (n 44) paras. 31–33.

[133] Ibid. para. 30.

[134] Ibid. paras. 30, 69–70.

[135] Ibid. para. 69.

[136] Ibid. paras. 46, 70. See also Case No COMP/M.2220 *General Electric/Honeywell*, C(2001) 1746 final paras. 344–427.

The republican ideals of economic liberty and equality of opportunity thus fundamentally shaped the interpretation of all three substantive areas of EU competition law. This prominent role of equality of opportunity in the case law calls into doubt the misguided attempts to associate EU competition law with a 'big is good tradition'.[137] On the contrary, until the late-1990s, concerns about the negative impact of excessive economic concentration and imbalances of power on the equality of opportunity of small and independent competitors played a prominent role in EU competition law.

The importance of equality of opportunity in the judicial interpretation of competition law on both sides of the Atlantic highlights that US antitrust and EU competition law also operated on an egalitarian understanding of economic liberty that is one of the hallmarks of the republican tradition. In seeking to secure broad-based economic opportunities and equality of status for economic agents, in many instances regardless of their efficiency, US antitrust and EU competition law also shared the broad understanding of agents (x) that was advocated by various republican proponents of a competition–democracy nexus.

4.4 STRUCTURALISM AS AN OPERATIONALISATION OF THE COMPETITION–DEMOCRACY NEXUS IN US ANTITRUST AND EU COMPETITION LAW JURISPRUDENCE

US antitrust law until the 1970s and EU competition law until the 2000s not only perceived the concentration of economic power as a source of unfreedom, but they also followed the structuralist playbook of various republican competition paradigms to tackle the behemoth problem. The formative case law of both competition law regimes was characterised by a structuralist competition policy standard that aimed to preserve competition in the form of a polycentric market structure. This structural approach rendered competition law on both sides of the Atlantic hospitable towards the republican antitrust tradition that perceives polycentric markets in which power is dispersed amongst many players as an institution of antipower.

4.4.1 *Structuralism in US Antitrust Law*

Judicial pronouncements on this structuralist approach can be traced back to *US v Knight*, which was the first antitrust case decided under the Sherman Act. In his dissenting opinion, Justice Harlan observed that '[s]o long as competition was free',

137 See for such an attempt N Petit, 'Competition Cases Involving Platforms – Lessons from Europe: Comment on Federal Trade Commission ("FTC") Hearing #3 on Competition and Consumer Protection in the 21st Century' (2018) 3.

the 'interest of the public' is safe.[138] He went on to explain that the liberties of market participants and the general interest are safeguarded in the presence of polycentric competition because 'any one man, or any one of several men acting independently, is powerless'.[139] Harlan posited that polycentric competition operates as an accountability mechanism, which ensures that the 'individual error or folly will generally find a correction in the conduct of others'.[140] On this account, he likened the role of polycentric competition in constraining power with the constitutional safeguards of separation of powers and checks-and-balances.[141] Accordingly, polycentric competition minimises domination by preserving an equilibrium of power between antagonising equally sized players.

This structural approach notably fashioned the interpretation of antitrust rules against monopoly power. Throughout the first half of the twentieth century, US antitrust case law oscillated between a conduct-based and situational structuralist approach.[142] The case law centred on the question of whether the possession of monopoly power, and hence the excessive concentration of economic power, is in and of itself prohibited[143] under antitrust laws or whether some exclusionary conduct must be demonstrated in addition.[144] In the *US Steel* case, the Supreme Court held that § 2 of the Sherman Act does not 'make mere size [...] or the existence of unexerted power an offence'.[145] However, it qualified this position in subsequent cases, insisting that 'mere size [...] is not an offense against the Sherman Act unless magnified to the point at which it amounts to a monopoly [...] but size carries with it an opportunity for abuse that is not to be ignored when the opportunity is proved to have been utilised in the past'.[146]

The structuralist approach reached its pinnacle in the second half of the 1940s. In a line of cases, the US judiciary reaffirmed the republican notion that size and monopoly power in themselves – regardless of the legality of their acquisition and absent any specific exclusionary conduct[147] – were sufficient to find unlawful

[138] *United States v E. C. Knight Co.* (n 7) Justice Harlan dissenting, 28–29; *Northern Securities Co. v United States* (n 50) 340.

[139] *United States v E. C. Knight Co.* (n 7) Justice Harlan dissenting, 35.

[140] Ibid. Justice Harlan, dissenting, 26; *Northern Securities Co. v United States* (n 50) 339.

[141] *United States v E. C. Knight Co.* (n 7) Justice Harlan, dissenting, 35.

[142] See in this regard also Judge Wyzanski's account of the evolution of the § 2 case law in *United States v United Shoe Machinery Corp.* (n 52) 341.

[143] *Northern Securities Co. v United States* (n 50) 351–52, see also 335, 337–38, 340; LA Sullivan, *Antitrust* (St. Paul: West Publishing 1977) 34–35.

[144] *Standard Oil Co. of New Jersey v United States* (n 68) 62; EH Levi, 'The Antitrust Laws and Monopoly' (1947) 14(2) *University of Chicago Law Review* 153, 157.

[145] *United States v U.S. Steel Corp.* 251 U.S. 417 (1920) 451. See also *United States v Int. Harvester Co.* 274 U.S. 693 (1927) 708.

[146] *United States v Swift & Co.* (n 89) 116.

[147] *United States v Alcoa* (n 101) 429, 432; *American Tobacco Co. v United States* 328 U.S. 781 (1946) 813–14.

monopolization in breach of § 2 of the Sherman Act.[148] At least temporarily, the US courts thus came down on the side of situational structuralism. Pursuant to this situational approach, a finding of illegal monopolization in breach of § 2 of the Sherman Act could be sustained by the mere showing that a firm held a monopoly position combined with 'the intent and purpose to exercise such power'.[149] Once the holding of monopoly power was established, the onus fell on the defendant to demonstrate that it had not abused its monopoly position[150] or that it was the outcome of superior efficiency.[151]

US merger policy also followed the structuralist playbook. During the Warren Court era, the Supreme Court acknowledged that the Celler–Kefauver amendment was informed by the 'fear of [...] a rising tide of economic concentration in the American Economy'.[152] On this count, the Court reaffirmed the so-called 'incipiency theory'.[153] It observed that Congress gave the government and courts the mandate to arrest mergers 'when the trend to a lessening of competition in a line of commerce was still in its incipiency' to bring a halt to the tendency towards economic concentration 'before it gathered momentum'.[154] Accordingly, the Supreme Court took the view that § 7 of the Clayton Act was directed against all mergers that lead to a significant increase in concentration.[155] In *Brown Shoe*, the Court noted that although the Clayton Act sought to protect 'competition, not competitors',[156] it could not

> fail to recognise Congress' desire to promote competition through the protection of viable, small, locally owned businesses. Congress appreciated that occasional higher costs and prices might result from the maintenance of fragmented industries and markets. It resolved these competing considerations in favor of decentralization.[157]

The Department of Justice's 1968 Merger Guidelines also identified 'the primary role of Section 7 enforcement to preserve and promote market structures conducive to competition'.[158] To this end, the primary task of merger policy was to 'prevent

[148] *United States v Alcoa* (n 101) 429–32; *American Tobacco Co. v United States* (n 147) 809–11; *United States v Griffith* (n 16) 107; *United States v Paramount Pictures* (n 16) 137; *Schine Theatres v United States* (n 16) 129–30; *United States v Columbia Steel Co.* (n 51) 524–25.

[149] *American Tobacco Co. v United States* (n 147) 809, 814–15.

[150] *United States v Alcoa* (n 101) 427.

[151] Ibid. 429–31.

[152] *Brown Shoe Co. Inc. v United States* (n 17) 315–17; *United States v Philadelphia National Bank* 374 U.S. 321 (1963) 362–63.

[153] The 'incipiency doctrine' has guided the interpretation of the Clayton Act since *Standard Fashion Company v Magrane-Houston Company* 346 U.S. 258 (1921) 356.

[154] *Brown Shoe Co. Inc. v United States* (n 17) 317–18.

[155] *United States v Philadelphia National Bank* (n 152) 363.

[156] *Brown Shoe Co. Inc. v United States* (n 17) 320, 344.

[157] Ibid. 344.

[158] 1968 Merger Guidelines (n 108) para. 2.

significant increases in concentration in a market' and maintain 'significant possibilities for eventual deconcentration in a concentrated market'.[159] During the Warren Court era, US courts and enforcers pushed the pursuit of a deconcentrated market structure to the extreme. They set the critical threshold above which industry concentration would raise concerns about domination at an extremely low level, suggesting that even mergers with a combined market share of as low as 5 per cent could give rise to a lessening of competition that would be substantial enough to warrant intervention.[160]

This structuralist understanding of competition, which experienced its apex in the Warren Court era, tallied with the prevailing economic Structure–Conduct–Performance (S–C–P) paradigm of the time, which assumed that 'competition is greatest where there are many sellers'.[161] Republican antitrust was anchored in the notion of a perfect consonance between the political and economic goals of competition law. The republican ideal of preserving a polycentric market structure in which power is diffused amongst many decentralised players accorded well with the prevailing economic view of the time – supported not only by the members of the Harvard School but also by early Chicago School economists[162] – that the preservation of competition and the protection of a deconcentrated economy were one and the same thing. Hence, republican antitrust revolved around the assumption that 'concentration [is] inimical to the free play of competition'.[163] The US courts, therefore, treated increases in industry concentration and the lessening of competition as synonyms.[164]

Until the 1970s, this structural approach was the main parameter through which the republican approach towards US antitrust gave effect to the ideal of economic liberty and democracy. The preservation of a polycentric competitive market structure was considered to be a central safeguard of economic liberty and democracy because it operates as an institution of antipower that reduces overall domination in society by dispersing power amongst many players whose competitive interaction keeps various market players in check.[165]

159 Ibid. para. 4.

160 *United States v Pabst Brewing Co.* (n 55) 550–52; *United States v Von's Grocery Co.* (n 55) 272–73.

161 *United States v Philadelphia National Bank* (n 152) 363 and fn. 38 and 39. Citing, for instance, JS Bain, *Barriers to New Competition* (Harvard: Harvard University Press 1956) 27.

162 C Kaysen and DF Turner, *Antitrust Policy: An Economic and Legal Analysis* (Cambridge, MA: Harvard University Press 1959) 133; DC Bok, 'Section 7 of the Clayton Act and the Merging of Law and Economics' (1960) 74(2) *Harvard Law Review* 226, 308–16, 328; GJ Stigler, 'Mergers and Preventive Antitrust Policy: Reprinted from University of Pennsylvania Law Review, Vol. 104, No 2 (1955)' in GJ Stigler (ed), *The Organization of Industry* (Chicago: University of Chicago Press 1968) 296.

163 *United States v Philadelphia National Bank* (n 152) 369.

164 *United States v Von's Grocery Co.* (n 55) 278.

165 *United States v Trenton Potteries Co.* (n 7) 397; *Silver v New York Stock Exchange* (n 9) 359–60.

4.4.2 *Structuralism in EU Competition Law*

The formative EU competition law not only adhered in a similar vein as US antitrust law until the 1970s to a republican conception of economic liberty but it also relied on a similar structuralist strategy to operationalise the twin goal of liberty as non-domination and republican democracy. Throughout the formative era, the EU Commission and Court clearly rejected a purely welfarist and consequentialist interpretation of EU competition law according to which consumer welfare constitutes the ultimate goal of competition law. This reading found support amongst prominent scholars, such as Judge Joliet who argued that the prevention of welfare-reducing conduct was the sole mission of EU competition law.[166] Instead, the Court consistently held that EU competition law is ultimately concerned with conduct that undermines 'an effective competition structure'.[167] In a similar way to the republican antitrust tradition in the United States, the formative EU case law thus championed the preservation of a deconcentrated and polycentric market structure as the ultimate goal of EU competition law.

This structural interpretation of EU competition law was closely aligned with the idea of polycentric markets as an institution of antipower and safeguard of liberty supported by the Ordoliberal School. Ordoliberal authors, such as Böhm, had referred to competition as an institution[168] or game[169] which is based on and protected by specific rules and principles that require independent economic decision-making on the part of the players. As we have seen in Chapter 3, the Ordoliberals stressed that competition by diffusing market power amongst several players ensures a process whereby the players constrain each other's power through their independent decision-making.[170]

It was eventually Ernst-Joachim Mestmäcker, the second-generation Ordoliberal, who prominently transposed this idea of competition as an institution of antipower into the context of EU competition law. Mestmäcker suggested that EU competition law does not only seek to protect the individual rights and economic freedom of consumers and competitors against anticompetitive practices (*Individualschutz*) but in protecting economic liberty and requiring independent decision-making of

[166] Joliet (n 27) 127–31; Schweitzer, 'The History, Interpretation and Underlying Principles' (n 26) 138–40.

[167] Case 6/72 *Europemballage Corporation and Continental Can Company v Commission* (n 34) para. 26. See also Case 85/76 *Hoffmann-La Roche v Commission* (n 59) para. 126; Case C-95/04 P *British Airways plc v Commission of the European Communities* (n 35) para. 106.

[168] F Böhm (ed), *Wettbewerb und Monopolkampf: Eine Untersuchung zur Frage des wirtschaftlichen Kampfrechts und zur Frage der rechtlichen Struktur der geltenden Wirtschaftsordnung* [1933] (Baden-Baden: Nomos 2010) 220, 232, 260, 270, 327.

[169] Ibid. 206, 227, 254, 303.

[170] F Böhm, 'Democracy and Economic Power in Cartel and Monopoly in Modern Law [1961]' in DA Crane and H Hovenkamp (eds), *The Making of Competition Policy: Legal and Economic Sources* (New York: Oxford University Press 2013) 264, 279.

market participants competition law also ensures the protection of competition as an institution (*Institutionenschutz*).[171] In line with the Ordoliberal tradition, Mestmäcker thus highlighted the role of polycentric competition as an institutional safeguard of a domination-free economic and societal order, which enhances liberty as non-domination.[172] When it coined the principle that EU competition law does not only preserve the immediate interests of consumers and competitors but seeks to preserve a competitive market structure in its own right, the Court of Justice espoused the Ordoliberal proposition that competition law has a twin-mission of protecting individual rights (*Individualschutz*) and protecting a competitive market structure as an institution (*Institutionenschutz*).[173]

This structural understanding of polycentric competition as an institution of antipower also had an important bearing on the concrete application of all three pillars of EU competition law. The interpretation of Articles 101, 102, and merger control was guided by a structural approach that seeks to promote polycentric markets as a checks-and-balances system, which prevents the exercise of unilateral and collective economic power.

Throughout the formative era, the Court of Justice of the European Union identified the preservation of a polycentric market structure as the basic rationale of Article 101 TFEU. According to this interpretation, Article 101 (1) TFEU was directed against those forms of coordination that allowed competitors to escape the constrictions that their independent and decentralised interaction imposed on each other. The Court consistently held that Article 101 (1) TFEU prohibits agreements that are not in line

> with the concept inherent in the [EU] Treaty provisions relating to competition, according to which each economic operator must determine independently the policy which it intends to adopt on the common market. Article [101 (1) TFEU] is intended to prohibit any form of coordination which deliberately substitutes practical cooperation between undertakings for the risks of competition.[174]

The Court routinely emphasised that Article 101 (1) TFEU creates a 'requirement of independence'[175] for market participants that obliges them to act as independent decision-makers. This is most clearly articulated by Advocated General Kokott, who

[171] Mestmäcker, 'Die Beurteilung von Unternehmenszusammenschlüssen' (n 30) 608.

[172] Böhm, 'Democracy and Economic Power' (n 170) 279; W Eucken, *Grundsätze der Wirtschaftspolitik* (Tübingen: Mohr Siebeck 2004) 50, 237.

[173] It was notably the German Advocate General Kokott who highlighted the role of the competitive process as an 'institution' which has an intrinsic value. Opinion of Advocate General Kokott in Case C-8/08 *T-Mobile Netherlands BV and Others* ECLI:EU:C:2009:110 para. 58.

[174] Case C-209/07 *Beef Industry Development and Barry Brothers (BIDS)* (n 22) para. 34; Case 40/73 *Suiker Unie and Others v Commission* (n 59) para. 173; Case 172/80 *Züchner v Bayerische Vereinsbank* ECLI:EU:C:1981:178 para. 13.

[175] Case 40/73 *Suiker Unie and Others v Commission* (n 59) para. 174; Case C-199/92 P *Hüls v Commission* ECLI:EU:C:1999:358 para. 160; Case C-8/08 *T-Mobile Netherlands BV and Others* (n 56) para. 33.

identified polycentricity in the form of 'independence of economic participants [as] one of the basic requirements for competition to function'.[176] Accordingly, the purpose of Article 101 TFEU was to prohibit coordinated strategies whereby market participants manage to escape the constraints of polycentric competition and are in a position to exert control over and impose their interest upon other market participants. Against the backdrop of this apprehension, Advocate General Kokott argued that the existence of polycentric competition itself is the best safeguard of the interests of consumers and competitors[177] because competition prevents market players from forming coalitions to impose their idiosyncratic interests on the rest of the society.

The early Article 102 case law also strikingly echoed the republican imaginary of polycentric competition as an accountability mechanism or system of checks-and-balances that builds a counterweight to the power of mighty firms, and thereby prevents them from exercising domination. In *Continental Can*, the Court pointed out that an abuse of a dominant position may arise when a market is controlled by a dominant entity to the extent that 'remaining competitors could no more provide a sufficient counterweight'.[178]

This understanding of a deconcentrated market structure as a checks-and-balances mechanism of antipower also resonates in the definition of the concept of dominant position. The Court consistently held that the notion of dominant position under Article 102 TFEU

> relates to a position of economic strength enjoyed by an undertaking which enables it to prevent effective competition being maintained on the relevant market by giving it the power to behave to an appreciable extent independently of its competitors, customers and ultimately of its consumers.[179]

This definition of dominant position goes beyond a purely economic understanding of dominance as significant market power, which is understood as the ability to profitably raise prices or restrict output.[180] Rather, it proposes a relational definition of dominance as a situation where the market structure and degree of polycentric rivalry are weakened to the extent that rival competitors or consumers are no longer able to impose countervailing constraints on the discretion of the dominant firm.

176 Opinion of Advocate General Kokott in Case C-8/08 *T-Mobile Netherlands BV and Others* (n 173) para. 52.
177 Ibid. para. 58.
178 Case 6/72 *Europemballage Corporation and Continental Can Company v Commission* (n 34) para. 29.
179 Case 27/76 *United Brands v Commission* (n 123) para. 65; Case 85/76 *Hoffmann-La Roche v Commission* (n 59) para. 38.
180 G Monti, 'The Concept of Dominance in Article 82' (2006) 2 (sup1) *European Competition Journal* 31, 39–40.

The definition of abuse of dominance, which was coined in *Hoffmann-La Roche*, also turns on this structural understanding of competition as an institution of anti-power. The Court consistently defined the notion of abuse of dominance as

> an objective concept relating to the behaviour of an undertaking in a dominant position which is such as to influence the structure of a market where, as a result of the very presence of the undertaking in question, the degree of competition is weakened and which, through recourse to methods different from those which condition normal competition in products or services on the basis of the transactions of commercial operators, has the effect of hindering the maintenance of the degree of competition still existing in the market or the growth of that competition.[181]

Unlike US courts during the heydays of the republican approach, the EU judiciary never went as far as prohibiting the mere possession of monopoly power. Instead, *Hoffmann-La Roche* and its progeny fashioned a conduct-based test for the application of Article 102 TFEU to dominant firms. Accordingly, Article 102 TFEU only prohibits dominant firm conduct that adversely affects the competitive market structure through methods other than 'normal competition'[182] or 'competition on the merits'.[183]

The EU Courts thus pursued a less maximalist approach to combat domination flowing from the excessive concentration of economic power than their US counterparts in the mid-twentieth century. Although situational approaches against monopoly power were briefly contemplated in Europe,[184] the EU judiciary eventually grounded the interpretation of the concept of abuse of dominance in conduct-based structuralism. Instead of outlawing the concentration of economic power as such, it pursued the less extreme strategy of preserving residual competition, and hence the remaining polycentric market structure, which was favoured by some Ordoliberals, such as the late Böhm and Mestmäcker. Having as its objective the protection of residual competition, the Court's interpretation of the concept of abuse of dominance resonated the Ordoliberal assumption that the remaining rivals should be able to hold the dominant firm in check, and in the long term to assail and erode its economic power.[185] Instead of tackling economic concentration directly, Article 102 TFEU addressed it indirectly by averting conduct whereby the dominant firm lessens the constraints that the remaining degree of polycentric competition would otherwise impose on its power. In other words, Article

[181] Case 85/76 *Hoffmann-La Roche v Commission* (n 59) para. 91; Case C-62/86 *AKZO v Commission* (n 123) paras. 69–70.

[182] Case 85/76 *Hoffmann-La Roche v Commission* (n 59) para. 90.

[183] Case T-228/97 *Irish Sugar v Commission* (n 125) para. 111; Case T-203/01 *Michelin v Commission (Michelin II)* ECLI:EU:T:2003:250 para. 97.

[184] Schweitzer, 'The History, Interpretation and Underlying Principles' (n 26) 123, 129–31, 139–40.

[185] Böhm, 'Democracy and Economic Power' (n 170) 279; Mestmäcker, 'Die Beurteilung von Unternehmenszusammenschlüssen' (n 30) 605–08; Schweitzer, 'The History, Interpretation and Underlying Principles' (n 26) 138–40.

102 TFEU seeks to prevent dominant firms from adopting conduct that maintains or furthers the concentration of economic power in their hands, and thereby increases the degree of dependence of the remaining market players.[186]

The goal of protecting residual competition also informs the principle of special responsibility that dominant firms are bound by under Article 102 TFEU. This principle of special responsibility applies 'irrespective of the reasons for which it has such a dominant position'.[187] In *Michelin I*, the Court made it plain that even if the concept of Article 102 TFEU does not prohibit the existence of a dominant position and hence size as such,[188] it nonetheless imposes additional obligations on the dominant firm. This is the case even if the dominant firm has obtained its position of economic power due to superior efficiency. Under the principle of special responsibility, the dominant firm is required to refrain from conduct that has the potential to adversely affect the market structure by hampering or foreclosing residual competition, although the very same conduct does not give rise to any concerns if it is adopted by non-dominant firms.[189]

In creating an additional cage of rules to tame dominant behemoths, the principle of special responsibility seeks to replicate the constraints that polycentric competition would otherwise impose on small and roughly equally sized firms. It accounts for the fact that residual competition may no longer be capable of holding the dominant firm fully accountable in the presence of concentrated market power. The concept of special responsibility obliges the dominant firm to act as if it was constrained by effective competition. It thus echoes the Ordoliberal idea of as-if competition.[190] However, the concept of as-if competition that was encoded in the concept of special responsibility differs from how this notion was framed by the Ordoliberals. Members of the Freiburg School, such as Eucken and Miksch, conceived the concept of as-if competition as a guiding principle for some form of public utility-style regulation that imposes on dominant firms the positive obligation to act as if they were constrained by effective competition.[191] In contrast, the concept of special responsibility operationalises the idea of as-if competition in a less intrusive fashion.[192] It merely imposes a limited number of negative obligations

186 Mestmäcker, 'Die Beurteilung von Unternehmenszusammenschlüssen' (n 30) 606.

187 Case 322/81 *Michelin v Commission (Michelin I)* (n 75) para. 57.

188 Ibid.

189 Schweitzer, 'Das Wettbewerbsrecht und das Problem privater Macht' (n 121) 463–64.

190 AJ Padilla and C Ahlborn, 'From Fairness to Welfare: Implications for the Assessment of Unilateral Conduct under EC Competition Law' in C-D Ehlermann and M Marquis (eds), *European Competition Law Annual 2007: A Reformed Approach to Article 82 EC* (Oxford: Hart 2008) 55, 72.

191 W Eucken (n 172) 293; L Miksch, *Wettbewerb als Aufgabe: Grundsätze einer Wettbewerbsordnung* (Godersberg: Verlag Helmut Küpper 1947) 147–49, 211–12; L Miksch, 'Die Wirtschaftspolitik des Als-Ob' (1948) 105(2) *Zeitschrift für die gesamte Staatswissenschaft* 310, 310.

192 E-J Mestmäcker, 'The Development of German and European Competition Law with Special Reference to the EU Commission's Article 82 Guidance of 2008' in LF Pace (ed), *European*

on the dominant firm to refrain from conduct that undermines an effectively competitive market structure. While the EU Courts never went as far as their US counterparts during the Warren Court era in protecting smaller, often less efficient, competitors in their own right, its structural approach was animated by the insight that the protection of competition will inescapably require the protection of competitors, even if they happen to be less efficient.[193]

EU merger policy was also anchored in a structuralist approach that was geared towards the preservation of polycentric competition as an institution of antipower. The first Merger Control Regulation clearly was in the mould of this structural understanding of competition. It identified as the overarching purpose of EU merger policy to vet mergers with respect to their 'effect on the structure of competition'.[194] Accordingly, the ECMR was directed against mergers that bring about 'significant structural changes' in the market.[195] In keeping with the structuralist approach, the Commission and EU Courts focused primarily on how a merger affects market structure to determine their legality. However, the dominance test under the ECMR meant that EU merger policy never went as far as US antitrust law during the Warren Court era in blocking mergers with a combined market share of less than 5–10 per cent whose impact on industry concentration was marginal. Instead, EU merger control applied a higher threshold, above which merger-induced market concentration would raise concerns about domination. Yet, the dominance criterion did not limit the scope of EU merger control to mergers to monopoly. Instead, the EU Commission[196] and judiciary[197] recognised that mergers which create a collective dominant position in the form of a tightly concentrated oligopolistic market structure may also run afoul of the EU merger rules. Consistent with this structural approach, the Commission and the Courts used EU merger policy as a tool to avert mergers that would undermine a polycentric market structure which keeps power in check by creating excessively concentrated monopolistic or oligopolistic markets.

4.5 CONCLUSION

This chapter forms the first step into our inquiry of how the republican ideal of liberty as non-domination and the related concept of a competition–democracy

Competition Law: The Impact of the Commission's Guidance on Article 102 (Cheltenham: Edward Elgar 2011) 25, 42.

193 E-J Mestmäcker and H Schweitzer, *Europäisches Wettbewerbsrecht* (München: Beck 2014) § 15, Rn. 31–34, 386–87.

194 Council Regulation (EEC) No 4064/89 on the Control of Concentrations between Undertakings (n 42) rec. 7.

195 Ibid. rec. 9.

196 Case No IV/M.190 *Nestlé/Perrier*, [1992] OJ L 356/1 paras. 62–63, 108–16; Case No IV/M.619 *Gencor/Lonrho*, [1997] OJ L 11/30 paras. 138–59, 179–92.

197 Case C-68/94 *France and Société commerciale des potasses et de l'azote and Entreprise minière et chimique v Commission* (n 46) paras. 159–69, 176–77; Case T-102/96 *Gencor v Commission* (n 46) paras. 125–29, 134–36, 149.

TABLE 4.1 *Triangulating the attributes of republican liberty and the structuralist competition law jurisprudence*

	Attributes of republican liberty	The link between the structuralist competition law jurisprudence and the attributes of republican liberty
Type of agents (x)	In-built commitment towards egalitarianism	• Hostility against power imbalances • Equality of opportunity and status • Inclusive notion of the competitive process
Type of preventing conditions (y)	Domination (arbitrary interference)	Domination resulting from the mere existence of concentrated economic power (rather than actual or likely interference) as a source of societal harm and unfreedom
Range of restricted actions (z)	Preference-decisiveness across all (relevant) possible friendly and unfriendly worlds	Modal constraints resulting from the presence of concentrated economic power (master–slave and law–liberty topoi)

nexus have been operationalised through the interpretation of competition law by US and EU courts and competition authorities until the 1970s (US) and 2000s (EU). It identifies the structural policy objective of preserving a polycentric, competitive market structure as a central channel through which the republican ideal of liberty as non-domination has been implemented by all three pillars of competition law on both sides of the Atlantic. This structural policy goal was grounded in a common apprehension of concentrated economic power that transpires from both US antitrust and EU competition law jurisprudence.

This concern over concentrated economic power was informed by considerations that closely matched the specific topography of the republican conception of liberty that was discussed in the previous chapters. Table 4.1 summarises how the concern about economic concentration in US antitrust and EU competition law jurisprudence was grounded in a broad understanding of the preventing conditions (y) of economic liberty. US antitrust and EU competition law jurisprudence considered domination ensuing from the very existence of concentrated economic power as an obstacle to liberty, regardless of any concrete threat of actual or likely interference. US antitrust and EU competition law jurisprudence also reverted to the master–slave and law–liberty topoi as two distinctively republican themes to articulate the modal constraints that market participants are exposed to in the presence of concentrated economic power. They thus adhered to the broad notion of the relevant range of actions (z) that typifies republican liberty. In expressing concerns over power imbalances, vertical hierarchies, and dependencies, as well as promoting equality of opportunity and status, US antitrust and EU competition law jurisprudence also mirrored the egalitarian impetus of republican liberty. By seeking

TABLE 4.2 *Commonalities and differences in the structuralist approaches by US antitrust law and EU competition law*

	US antitrust law	EU competition law
Coordinated conduct	• Independence: prevention of coalitions • Strict approach towards vertical restraints	• Independence: prevention of coalitions • Strict approach towards vertical restraints, notably those preventing parallel trade
Monopoly power and dominant firm conduct	• Oscillation between conduct-based and situational (monopoly power as such) standard • Protection of less efficient competitors to preserve the livelihood of small local businesses	• Conduct-based standard and principle of special responsibility to preserve residual competition • Protection of less efficient competitors to preserve equality of opportunity and residual competition
Merger policy	• Incipiency doctrine • Efficiency offence to protect less efficient competitors and preserve the livelihood of small local businesses	• Collective and single-firm dominance • Sporadic efficiency offence to protect less efficient competitors and preserve equality of opportunity and residual competition

to preserve an inclusive competitive process that guarantees broad-based economic opportunities regardless of the efficiency of the market participants, competition law jurisprudence on both sides of the Atlantic also subscribed to a broad notion of agents (x) that characterises republican liberty.

Although the structural approach constitutes a common feature of the republican antitrust traditions in both the United States and in the European Union, there are some important differences between the implementation of the goal of a polycentric market structure in both systems, which are summarised in Table 4.2. Marked dissimilarities come to the fore in the regulation of monopoly power and mergers, while the republican approach of US antitrust and EU competition law towards coordinated conduct was largely aligned.[198] Republican antitrust in the United States took a more maximalist approach in seeking to reduce domination flowing from concentrated economic power than the European blend of republican antitrust. While EU competition law never went as far as outlawing the mere possession of monopoly power, US courts, at least, in some instances, adopted a situational approach that seemed to be directed against size as such. Under the incipiency

[198] For important differences regarding the structure of § 1 of the US Sherman Act and Article 101 TFEU, see the following chapter and R Whish and B Sufrin, 'Article 85 and the Rule of Reason' (1987) 7(1) *Yearbook of European Law* 1.

doctrine, US merger policy also set the bar much lower for industry concentration to raise competition law issues than EU competition law. While EU merger policy only intervened against mergers that would create an oligopolistic (collective dominance) or monopolistic market (single dominance) structure, US merger control during the Warren Court era impugned mergers with a combined market share of as low as 5 per cent. Even though EU competition law was also alert to the preservation of equality of opportunity of smaller competitors, it showed itself to be less willing to protect less efficient competitors than US antitrust law during the Warren Court era.

Despite these differences, the structuralist approaches on both sides of the Atlantic converged in the objective of securing a polycentric market structure. They were thus anchored in the Smithian understanding of competition as a system of antipower, which was endorsed by various schools of thought as an institutional safeguard of republican liberty and a pathway to operationalise the idea of a competition–democracy nexus. On the one hand, this structural approach put into practice the negative dimension of republican liberty. In averting the concentration of economic power through coordinated conduct, dominant firm conduct, or mergers, all three pillars sought to prevent markets from degenerating into a state of domination. Accordingly, republican antitrust harnessed all three pillars of competition law to promote competition as a checks-and-balances system, whereby the independent decision-making of each player imposes impersonal checks on each other's capacity to exert domination. By preserving a polycentric market structure, all three pillars of competition law thus enhanced republican liberty by inhibiting and shackling the economic power of behemoths.

On the other hand, the structuralist approach also gave effect to the positive, egalitarian dimension of republican liberty. By promoting polycentric competition, the interpretation of all three pillars of antitrust on both sides of the Atlantic placed themselves in the egalitarian tradition of early, republican proponents of competitive markets, such as the English Levellers and Adam Smith, who perceived competition as an institution that enables small businesspeople to emancipate themselves from a feudal economic order based on subordination. Through the guarantee of broad-based economic opportunities, US antitrust and EU competition law sought to allow businesspeople to gain the independent status of free and equal republican citizens, which republican antitrust on both sides celebrated as pillars of a Jeffersonian or nascent European republic.

This chapter identified a structuralist competition policy as the overarching policy objective through which courts and competition authorities on both sides of the Atlantic operationalised the twin goal of republican liberty and the competition–democracy nexus. The next chapter takes a closer look at the various legal commands, standards, and mechanisms through which US and EU courts and enforcers designed a competition policy that was hospitable to a republican notion of economic liberty and the ideal of a competition–democracy nexus.

5

The Policy Parameters of Republican Antitrust

Presumptions, Standard of Harm, and the Error–Cost Framework

5.1 INTRODUCTION

This chapter goes one step further in our analysis of how the ideal of republican liberty and the concept of a competition–democracy nexus have been translated into concrete competition policy. The previous chapter has identified the structuralist goal of preserving a polycentric market structure as what one can call the overarching 'target' or 'target variable'[1] of republican antitrust in the United States and in Europe. This chapter will examine the specific features that made US antitrust and EU competition law particularly conducive to a republican understanding of economic liberty. It will shed light on how the ideal of republican liberty was given shape through a specific legal modus operandi, in terms of the structure of legal commands,[2] standards of assessment and institutional principles. These legal filters can be considered to be the main parameters[3] or policy levers of a distinctive republican approach towards antitrust policy.

Three are the main policy levers of republican antitrust. The first policy lever of republican antitrust was the extensive use of broadly construed rule-like presumptions of illegality. Under all three pillars of competition law, the US and the EU courts implemented the concern about protecting republican liberty through broadly designed structural presumptions of anticompetitiveness. These presumptions inferred the legality of impugned business conduct from its form

1 This chapter follows the terminology coined by the seminal work of the economist Jan Tinbergen, *On the Theory of Economic Policy* (Amsterdam: North-Holland Publishing Company 1952) 1, 4, 6. Note, that I do not assume here that the antitrust policy must follow the so-called Tinbergen rule which postulates that the number of policy instruments must equal the number of policy targets.

2 For the notion of legal commands, see L Kaplow, 'Rules versus Standards: An Economic Analysis' (1992) 42(3) *Duke Law Journal* 557, 559–60.

3 Tinbergen (n 1) 7.

and impact on a polycentric market structure rather than inquiring into their actual or likely effects on competitors and consumers.

A second central policy lever of the republican approach guiding the application of all three pillars of US and EU competition law at different points in time was a specific possibilist 'capability standard'[4] of harm. In keeping with the republican premise that liberty is frustrated by the mere possibility of arbitrary interference – rather than actual or likely interference – on numerous occasions the US and EU Courts merely required it to be shown that the impugned conduct led to potential – rather than actual or likely – anticompetitive effects to establish a violation of competition law rules. Accordingly, for antitrust intervention to be warranted under the republican approach, it was sufficient to demonstrate that a particular business conduct or market constellation was capable of adversely tampering with the polycentric market structure and of harming competitors or consumers.

The third policy parameter of republican competition policy governing the application of all three pillars of antitrust was a specific precautionary understanding of the costs and benefits – in modern antitrust lingo, this is often referred to as the error–cost framework – of antitrust intervention. This precautionary posture towards competition law enforcement followed a balance of rights, which in the case of doubt tilted in favour of prophylactic antitrust intervention. The goal of preventing domination resulting from excessive economic concentration, as well as a standard of harm which counselled for antitrust intervention in the light of potential harm, impelled a pro-active application of antitrust rules. This arithmetic of rights was clearly in line with the republican understanding of liberty, which does not perceive republican laws and state interference as an antonym of liberty as long as they are adopted and enforced in a non-arbitrary way.

Together with the discussion of the structural policy target detailed in the previous chapter, this chapter complements our understanding of how the ideal of republican liberty has been translated into concrete competition policy on both sides of the Atlantic. By identifying the common features and central parameters of a republican interpretation of competition law in the United States and in the European Union, this chapter provides further elements for a clear framework to understand the main variables of what one can call republican antitrust. It shows how the interplay of all four parameters enabled the republican antitrust tradition in the United States and European Union to ensure a modally robust, 'probabilistically unweighted'[5] protection of economic liberty as non-domination.

The remainder of this chapter is organised as follows. Section 5.2 sheds light on the role of presumptions of illegality in the republican antitrust tradition on both

[4] PI Colomo and A Lamadrid de Pablo, 'On the Notion of Restriction of Competition: What We Know and What We Do Not Know We Know' in D Gerard, M Merola, and B Meyring (eds), *The Notion of Restriction of Competition: Revisiting the Foundations of Antitrust Enforcement in Europe* (Brussles: Bruylant 2017) 333, 361–63.

[5] P Pettit, 'Freedom in the Market' (2006) 5(2) *Politics, Philosophy & Economics* 131, 137–38.

sides of the Atlantic. Section 5.3 interrogates the non-probabilistic standard of harm that typifies republican antitrust approaches in US and EU competition law. Section 5.4 takes a closer look at how the structural approach (as discussed in the previous chapter), the considerable weight of presumptions of illegality, as well as the possibilist standard of harm gave shape to an error–cost framework that, in the case of doubt, errs on the side of antitrust intervention.

5.2 THE OPERATIONALISATION OF REPUBLICAN LIBERTY THROUGH PRESUMPTIONS OF ILLEGALITY

The first parameter that meant that US antitrust law and EU competition law were, for a long time, conducive to a republican ideal of liberty as non-domination was their extensive reliance on structural presumptions of illegality. Legal or so-called substantive presumptions are 'analytical shortcuts'.[6] Presumptions allow a decision-maker to infer a certain legal conclusion, such as the anticompetitive nature or illegality of a particular conduct, from a limited set of specific facts without the need to engage in a full-fledged analysis of case-specific facts and evidence.[7] Substantive presumptions are the primary vehicle of a deductive mode of competition law analysis. Instead of establishing probability estimates about the anticompetitive effects of specific conduct on the basis of an inductive and careful analysis of case-specific evidence, legal presumptions enable the factfinder to deduce the legality of the impugned conduct from prior beliefs about their anticompetitive nature. The reliance on broadly construed legal presumptions was indeed a common thread throughout the formative era of US and EU competition policy which facilitated the implementation of a competition policy hospitable towards republican liberty.

5.2.1 *Presumptions in US Antitrust Law*

Presumptions of illegality played a central role in the interpretation and enforcement of US antitrust law until the 1970s. All three pillars of US antitrust law routinely had recourse to presumptions of anticompetitiveness against specific types of market constellations or conduct. These presumptions were given a broad interpretation. Consequently, US courts heavily relied on deductive reasoning

6 A Kalintiri, 'Analytical Shortcuts in EU Competition Enforcement: Proxies, Premises, and Presumptions' (2020) 16(3) *Journal of Competition Law & Economics* 392, 393.

7 For recent discussions of different types of presumptions and their role in US antitrust and EU competition law SC Salop, 'An Enquiry Meet for the Case: Decision Theory, Presumptions, and Evidentiary Burdens in Formulating Antitrust Legal Standards' (2017) 2–6 https://scholarship.law.georgetown.edu; A Kalintiri, *Evidence Standards in EU Competition Enforcement: The EU Approach* (Oxford: Hart 2019) 146–47, 165–68; F La Castillo de Torre and E Gippini Fournier, *Evidence, Proof and Judicial Review in EU Competition Law* (Cheltenham: Edward Elgar 2017) 61–66; C Ritter, 'Presumptions in EU Competition Law' (2018) 6(2) *Journal of Antitrust Enforcement* 189, 189–200.

rather than inductive analysis of case-specific evidence to make legal determinations about coordinated conduct, dominant firm conduct, and mergers.

5.2.1.1 Coordinated Conduct

The archetype of presumptions in competition law is the so-called per se rule. At least in its 'embryonic'[8] form, the per se rule was introduced for the first time in the 1911 *Standard Oil*[9] and *American Tobacco*[10] cases. In both watershed rulings, the US Supreme Court departed from its previous literalist reading that assumed that § 1 of the Sherman Act prohibits all restraints of trade.[11] Instead, the Court asserted that the Sherman Act would need to be interpreted in keeping with the flexible common law tradition[12] 'in the light of reason'.[13] Consistent with this rule of reason standard, a factfinder could no longer merely rely on the fact that a contract or agreement amounted to a restraint of trade but had to establish that it was an 'unreasonable' one.[14] To this end, the factfinder would need to determine whether 'in a given case a particular act had or had not brought about the wrong against which the statue provided'.[15]

Under this rule of reason standard, the Court recognised in *Standard Oil* and *American Tobacco* two complementary[16] analytical routes that a factfinder can embark on to determine the reasonableness of a restraint of trade under § 1 of the Sherman Act.[17] On the one hand, the anticompetitive nature of a restraint could be ascertained through an inductive rule of reason analysis, whereby the factfinder analyses the actual or likely 'direct or indirect effect'[18] of an agreement on competition on the basis of the assessment of case-specific evidence[19] and 'surrounding circumstances'.[20] On the other hand, the reasonableness of a restraint of trade could

8 LA Sullivan, *Antitrust* (St. Paul: West Publishing 1977) 174, 182.
9 *Standard Oil Co. of New Jersey v United States* 221 U.S. 1 (1911).
10 *United States v American Tobacco* 221 U.S. 106 (1911).
11 *United States v E. C. Knight Co.* 156 U.S. 1 (1895) Justice Harlan dissenting, 26, 28; *United States v Trans-Missouri Freight Asso.* 166 U.S. 290 (1897) 324, 327, 336; *United States v Joint Traffic Ass'n* 171 U.S. 505 (1898) 561–62; *Northern Securities Co. v United States* 193 U.S. 197 (1904) 332.
12 *Standard Oil Co. of New Jersey v United States* (n 9) 51, 55–56, 59, 69.
13 Ibid. 63–64, 67–68; *United States v American Tobacco* (n 10) 178–83.
14 See, for instance, *Chicago Board of Trade v United States* 246 US 231 (1918) 238.
15 *Standard Oil Co. of New Jersey v United States* (n 9) 60, 62–63, 66, 75–76. See also *United States v American Tobacco* (n 10) 177, 179–82.
16 *Standard Oil Co. of New Jersey v United States* (n 9) 60–64; H Hovenkamp, 'The Rule of Reason' (2018) 70(1) *Florida Law Review* 81, 86.
17 *Standard Oil Co. of New Jersey v United States* (n 9) 63, 65; *United States v American Tobacco* (n 10) 179.
18 *Standard Oil Co. of New Jersey v United States* (n 9) 66; *United States v American Tobacco* (n 10) 180.
19 *Appalachian Coals, Inc. v United States* 288 U.S. 344 (1933) 377.
20 *Standard Oil Co. of New Jersey v United States* (n 9) 58.

also be established via a deductive, per se rule approach that prohibits certain types of restraints based on the legal presumption that they are by their very 'nature or character'[21] restrictive of competition due to their inherent 'monopolistic tendency'.[22]

In subsequent cases, the Court forged the per se rule as an irrebuttable presumption of illegality for certain types of agreements that could not be reversed by any countervailing evidence. Under this presumption, the Court considered the existence of certain types of agreements itself as evidence for a restriction of competition, and thus a violation of the Sherman Act.[23] The Court repeatedly held that § 1 conclusively outlaws

> certain agreements or practices which because of their pernicious effect on competition and lack of any redeeming virtue are conclusively presumed to be unreasonable and therefore illegal without elaborate inquiry as to the precise harm they have caused or the business excuse for their use.[24]

Until the 1970s, the Court gave a broad reading to the per se rule, especially against horizontal and vertical price fixing agreements,[25] horizontal and vertical market division agreements,[26] group boycotts,[27] and information exchange on prices (in oligopolistic markets).[28] At the same time, the inductive rule of reason analysis had a considerably narrower application.[29] This meant that *Standard Oil* did not conclusively discard the literalist interpretation that had shaped the early case law. Rather, the literalist approach continued to operate in a more focused and tempered form under the per se rule. Unlike under the literalist approach, the presumption of illegality under the per se rule no longer applied to all forms of coordinated elimination of polycentric competition. Instead, the Court limited this presumption to specific categories of agreements whose negative impact on competition and

[21] Ibid.; *United States v Trenton Potteries Co.* 273 U.S. 392 (1927) 397–99; *United States v Arnold, Schwinn & Co.* 388 U.S. 365 (1967) 379.

[22] *Standard Oil Co. of New Jersey v United States* (n 9) 62, 64.

[23] ES Mason, 'Monopoly in Law and Economics' (1937) 47(1) *The Yale Law Journal* 34, 41.

[24] *Northern Pac. Ry. Co. v United States* 356 U.S. 1 (1958) 5; *White Motor Co. v United States* 372 U.S. 253 (1963) 262.

[25] *United States v Trenton Potteries Co.* (n 21) 392; *United States v Socony-Vacuum Oil Co.* 310 U.S. 150 (1940) 218; *Dr. Miles Medical Co. v John D. Park & Sons Co.* 220 U.S. 373 (1911).

[26] *United States v Sealy, Inc.* 388 U.S. 350 (1967) 358; *United States v Arnold, Schwinn & Co.* (n 21) 390; *United States v Topco Assocs. Inc.* 405 U.S. 596 (1972) 608–10.

[27] *Eastern States Lumber Ass'n v United States* 234 U.S. 600 (1914) 609–11; *Klor's, Inc. v Broadway-Hale Stores, Inc.* 359 U.S. 207 (1959) 210; *Fashion Originators' Guild, Inc. v FTC* 312 U.S. 457 (1941) 465–67.

[28] *United States v Container Corp.* 393 U.S. 333 (1969) 337–38; RA Posner, 'Information and Antitrust: Reflections on the Gypsum and Engineers Decisions' (1979) 67(5) *Georgetown Law Journal* 1187, 1196.

[29] Mason, 'Monopoly in Law and Economics' (n 23) 42. See, for instance, *Chicago Board of Trade v United States* (n 14); *Appalachian Coals, Inc. v United States* (n 19).

competitors had been established by long-standing judicial experience, and could therefore be generalised.[30]

5.2.1.2 Monopoly Power and Dominant Firm Conduct

With the recognition of the rule of reason in *Standard Oil* and *American Tobacco*,[31] the Court also took its distance from its previous situational interpretation of the Sherman Act as being directed against the possession of monopoly power in itself, without there being any need to demonstrate unreasonable conduct.[32] It instead insisted that the Sherman Act had not established any 'direct provision against monopoly in the concrete'.[33] Monopoly power would only be subject to § 2 liability if it was accompanied by conduct that was not in line with competition on the merits because it excluded competitors.

The *Standard Oil* and *American Tobacco* cases, however, failed to conclusively dispel the notion that monopoly power as such may trigger a presumption of unlawfulness under § 2 of the Sherman Act. On the contrary, until the mid-twentieth century, the interpretation of § 2 of the Sherman Act continued to vacillate between a situational approach, which would outlaw the existence of monopoly power as such, and a conduct-based approach, which only prohibits dominant firms from indulging in conduct that harmed competition by foreclosing competitors.[34] The situational approach towards monopoly reached its zenith with *Alcoa* and subsequent case law.[35] These cases created a presumption of illegality against the possession of monopoly power as such, irrespective of any abusive conduct.[36] However, unlike the per se rule under § 1 of the Sherman Act, this presumption of illegality of monopoly power remained rebuttable. A defendant monopolist thus remained free to defeat the presumption by showing that they had 'not [...] achieved monopoly' but that 'monopoly [had] been thrust upon it'[37] by reason of 'his superior skill, foresight and industry.'[38] Yet, this efficiency defence

[30] *United States v Socony-Vacuum Oil Co.* (n 25) 218; *United States v Topco Assocs. Inc.* (n 26) 608.

[31] In both cases, the Court seemed to suggest that the rule of reason applied to § 1 and §2 of the Sherman Act alike *Standard Oil Co. of New Jersey v United States* (n 9) 62; *United States v American Tobacco* (n 10) 177, 179.

[32] *Northern Securities Co. v United States* (n 11) 351–52; Sullivan, *Antitrust* (n 8) 34–35.

[33] *Standard Oil Co. of New Jersey v United States* (n 9) 62.

[34] Ibid. 75–76; *United States v American Tobacco* (n 10) 179, 181–82; Mason, 'Monopoly in Law and Economics' (n 23) 43.

[35] ES Mason, *Economic Concentration and the Monopoly Problem* (Cambridge, MA: Harvard University Press 1959) 361.

[36] For an insightful summary of the evolution of the § 2 case law by Judge Wyzanski, see *United States v United Shoe Machinery Corp.* 110 F. Supp. 295 (D. Mass. 1953) 341.

[37] *United States v Alcoa* 148 F.2d 416 (2d Cir. 1945) 429; *American Tobacco Co. v United States* 328 U.S. 781 (1946) 786, 800–04.

[38] *United States v Alcoa* (n 37) 430–31. See also *United States v United Shoe Machinery Corp.* (n 36) 341.

was interpreted very narrowly.[39] Some cases, such as *Alcoa*, went as far as suggesting that the superior efficiency of a monopolist may constitute an offence rather than a defence under § 2 of the Sherman Act.[40]

The judicial attempt to cut back on the anti-monopoly thrust of the early years of the Sherman Act through the recognition of the rule of reason in *Standard Oil* was also curtailed three years later by the enactment of the Clayton Act. With the adoption of the Clayton Act in 1914, Congress responded to growing fears that following the recognition of the rule of reason, too many restraints of trade would go unchallenged.[41] The central element of this legislative attempt to limit, if not partially reverse, the rule of reason[42] was § 3 of the Clayton Act. This provision established a conditional[43] per se[44] prohibition for exclusive dealing, tying, and discounting whose 'effect [...] may be to substantially lessen competition or tend to create a monopoly'.[45] The Supreme Court subsequently interpreted the use of the formulation 'effect may be' as an indication of the Congressional intent to establish under the 'substantial lessening of competition' (SLC) test of the Clayton Act a stricter standard than that governing the application of § 1 and 2 of the Sherman Act under the newly adopted rule of reason, and thereby to prevent monopoly in its incipiency.[46] Similarly, § 2 (a) of the Clayton Act, which was further amended by the 1936 Robinson–Patman Act, also introduced a prohibition against certain forms of geographic price discrimination to prevent large businesses from leveraging their financial strength and engaging in localised price-cutting to destroy local dealers.[47]

The Supreme Court read the prohibition of specific unilateral conduct under the Clayton Act as creating a presumption of illegality against exclusive dealing[48] and tying[49] agreements when adopted by firms with market power. The Court condemned these forms of conduct on the basis of their mere tendency

39 *American Tobacco Co. v United States* (n 37) 796; *United States v Swift & Co.* 286 U.S. 106 (1932) 116.

40 *United States v Alcoa* (n 37) 431.

41 These concerns were further fuelled by the *Dick* case in which the Court upheld a tying agreement. *Henry v Dick Co.* 224 U.S. 1 (1911) 11–12, 51–53, 70; Stevens, WHS 'The Clayton Act' (1915) 5(1) *The American Economic Review* 38, 41.

42 Sullivan, *Antitrust* (n 8) 432.

43 Ibid.

44 Stevens, W. H. S. (n 41), 42.

45 15 U.S. Code Chapter 1 § 12–14.

46 *Standard Fashion Company v Magrane-Houston Company* 346 U.S. 258 (1921) 356; Editors, 'Section 3 of the Clayton Act – "Law Unto Itself"' (22) 1954(1) *University of Chicago Law Review* 233, 236.

47 *Moore v Mead's Fine Bread Co.* 348 U.S. 115 (1954) 119; *FTC v Anheuser-Busch, Inc.* 363 U.S. 536 (1960) 539–40, 543; Sullivan, *Antitrust* (n 8) 677, 679–84.

48 *Standard Fashion Company v Magrane-Houston Company* (n 46) 357; *Standard Oil Co. v United States* 337 U.S. 293 (1949) 302–03; *Tampa Electric Co. v Nashville Coal Co.* 365 U.S. 320 (1961) 326.

49 *Standard Fashion Company v Magrane-Houston Company* (n 46) 357; *United Shoe Mach. Co. v United States* 258 U.S. 451 (1922) 457–58.

to restrict competition and enhance the concentration of economic power,[50] thereby bestowing firms with the 'potential power for evil over an industry'.[51] In *International Salt* and subsequent case law,[52] the Supreme Court also added tying agreements to the list of per se violations of § 1 Sherman Act. While gradually adopting a more relaxed approach towards exclusive dealing, the Court maintained a presumption of illegality against exclusive dealing agreements that foreclosed a substantial share of the market.[53] During the Warren Court era, the Supreme Court also seemed to rely on a presumption against discriminatory forms of localised price-cutting by powerful firms. Although the wording of § 2 (a) of the Clayton Act, as amended by the Robinson–Patman Act, required the showing of competitive injury in addition to price discrimination, the Court routinely inferred predatory intent to exclude competitors from the discriminatory form of price-cutting rather than focusing on whether it amounted to below-cost pricing.[54] This presumption against discriminatory price cuts was rebuttable because it remained open to the defendant firms to show that the low prices charged covered their costs, or could be explained by cost savings or their attempt to meet competition by aggressive rivals.[55] At different points in time, the enforcement of antitrust laws against powerful firms thus also turned on structural presumptions that inferred the anticompetitive harm from the mere existence of concentrated economic power (situational presumption) or specific forms of unilateral conduct (conduct-based presumptions).

5.2.1.3 Mergers

Structural presumptions also fashioned the application of US antitrust rules to mergers. In *Philadelphia National Bank*, the Court affirmed that the Congressional intent to prevent the trend towards industry concentration in its incipiency would be frustrated, and legal certainty of businesses would be undermined by a legal test that requires a 'too broad economic investigation' into the competitive impact of mergers.[56] Therefore, the pursuit of the ultimate purpose of the Clayton Act to tackle economic concentration in its incipiency would demand to dispense 'in certain cases, with elaborate proof of market structure, market behaviour or probable

50 *United Shoe Mach. Co. v United States* (n 49) 457; *Int'l Salt Co. v United States* 332 U.S. 392 (1947) 396.

51 *Motion Picture Co. v Universal Film Co.* 243 U.S. 502 (1917) 519.

52 *Int'l Salt Co. v United States* (n 50) 396; *Times-Picayune Pub. Co. v United States* 345 U.S. 594 (1953) 605; *Northern Pac. Ry. Co. v United States* (n 24) 6–8; *Fortner Enterprises v U.S. Steel (Fortner I)* 394 U.S. 495 (1969) 593–94.

53 *Standard Oil Co. v United States* (n 48) 314; *Tampa Electric Co. v Nashville Coal Co.* (n 48) 326.

54 *Utah Pie Co. v Continental Baking Co.* 386 U.S. 685 (1967) 694, 696–97 fn. 12; *Moore v Mead's Fine Bread Co.* (n 47) 119–20; *FTC v Anheuser-Busch, Inc.* (n 47) 550, 552–53. See also HC Hansen, 'Robinson-Patman Law: A Review and Analysis' (1983) 51(6) *Fordham Law Review* 1113, 1137.

55 *FTC v Anheuser-Busch, Inc.* (n 47) 541, 553.

56 *United States v Philadelphia National Bank* 374 U.S. 321 (1963) 362.

anticompetitive effects.'[57] On this account, *Philadelphia National Bank* fashioned a rebuttable structural presumption of illegality[58] according to which

> a merger which produces a firm controlling an undue percentage share of the relevant market, and results in a significant increase in the concentration of firms in that market, is so inherently likely to lessen competition substantially that it must be enjoined in the absence of evidence clearly showing that the merger is not likely to have such anticompetitive effects.[59]

The *Philadelphia National Bank* (PNB) presumption thus established a presumption of illegality against mergers whose market share or impact on concentration indicate their 'inherently anticompetitive tendency'.[60] It expressly alleviated 'the burden of proving illegality' for mergers 'whose size makes them inherently suspect in light of Congress' design in § 7 to prevent undue concentration'.[61] In *Philadelphia National Bank*, the Court intimated that any merger leading to a post-merger market share in excess of 20[62] to 30 per cent[63] or an increase in market concentration of 7 to 8 per cent[64] could be presumed to substantially lessen competition.[65] In other cases, however, the Warren Court made extensive use of the incipiency doctrine[66] to expand the PNB presumption to mergers with a combined market share of 7.5 per cent,[67] 5 per cent[68] or even less,[69] although the merged firms continued to face a multitude of competitors[70] and the actual increase in concentration resulting from the merger was marginal.[71] The 1968 Merger Guidelines also codified this low market share threshold for the structural PNB presumption to become effective. The Guidelines clarified that in highly

[57] Ibid. 363; *United States v Continental Can Co.* 378 U.S. 441 (1964) 458.

[58] For further discussion SC Salop, 'The Evolution and Vitality of Merger Presumptions: A Decision-Theoretic Approach' (2015) 80(2) *Antitrust Law Journal* 269, 269–74; SP Sullivan, 'What Structural Presumption: Reuniting Evidence and Economics on the Role of Market Concentration in Horizontal Merger Analysis' (2016) 42(2) *Journal of Corporation Law* 403, 410–11.

[59] *United States v Philadelphia National Bank* (n 56) 363.

[60] Ibid. 366.

[61] Ibid. 363.

[62] This threshold was proposed by C Kaysen and DF Turner, *Antitrust Policy: An Economic and Legal Analysis* (Cambridge, MA: Harvard University Press 1959) 133.

[63] This threshold was proposed by GJ Stigler, 'Mergers and Preventive Antitrust Policy: Reprinted from University of Pennsylvania Law Review, Vol. 104, No 2 (1955)' in GJ Stigler (ed), *The Organization of Industry* (Chicago: University of Chicago Press 1968) 296, 300–03.

[64] This threshold was proposed by DC Bok, 'Section 7 of the Clayton Act and the Merging of Law and Economics' (1960) 74(2) *Harvard Law Review* 226, 316.

[65] *United States v Philadelphia National Bank* (n 56) 364 fn. 41, 365.

[66] *Brown Shoe Co. Inc. v United States* 370 U.S. 294 (1962) 328, 331–34, 343–44.

[67] *United States v Von's Grocery Co.* 384 U.S. 270 (1966) 272–73.

[68] *Brown Shoe Co. Inc. v United States* (n 66) 328, 331–34, 343–44.

[69] *United States v Pabst Brewing Co.* 384 U.S. 546 (1966) 550–52.

[70] *United States v Von's Grocery Co.* (n 67) 272–73.

[71] *United States v Pabst Brewing Co.* (n 69) 552.

concentrated markets in which the four largest firms hold more than 75 per cent (which roughly corresponds to an HHI in excess of 1400), the government would block any merger combining two firms with a market share of 4 per cent or any merger whereby one firm with a market share of 15 per cent or more acquires a firm with a market share of 1 per cent or more.[72]

Even though *Philadelphia National Bank* explicitly recognised the possibility for the merging parties to rebut the structural presumption, with the term 'clearly showing' it imposed a very demanding (akin to the clear and convincing evidence)[73] standard of proof on the merging parties. Moreover, the Supreme Court displayed considerable scepticism against any efficiency defences for mergers. Instead, it affirmed that by amending the Clayton Act with a view to preventing economic concentration in its incipiency, Congress had encoded an implicit balance in the SLC test that would, in case of doubt, always tip towards the protection of a deconcentrated market structure and against growth by merger.[74] Along similar lines, the 1968 Guidelines stated that the Department of Justice would only accept efficiency defences under 'exceptional circumstances'.[75] This left the merging parties with only two possibilities to rebut the PNB presumption: they could either show that the merger was necessary to keep a failing firm in the market[76] or that it allowed small competitors to gain the necessary efficiencies to challenge the market leaders.[77] Consequently, the Supreme Court and the 1968 Merger Guidelines structured the PNB presumption in a way that struck a balance in favour of preventing concentration and preserving a polycentric market structure to the detriment of efficiency considerations.

Presumptions of illegality thus constituted a central feature of the enforcement of competition law throughout the first seven decades of US antitrust law. Presumptions under all three pillars of US antitrust had in common that they were primarily grounded in structural considerations. The rebuttable and irrebuttable presumptions gave effect to the overarching policy objective[78] of preserving a deconcentrated market structure as an institution of antipower that safeguards economic liberty. At the same time, the presumptions of anticompetitiveness were also informed by the prevailing economic theory of the time. The broad per se approach against various types of coordination that most directly undermined the polycentric structure and functioning of competition was supported by the Harvard School's S–C–P paradigm, which treated collusion as a primarily structural

72 Antitrust Division of the US Department of Justice, 1968 Merger Guidelines para. 5.

73 Salop, 'The Evolution and Vitality of Merger Presumptions' (n 58) 282, 294–96.

74 *Brown Shoe Co. Inc. v United States* (n 66) 344, 346.

75 1968 Merger Guidelines (n 72) para. 10.

76 Ibid. para. 9.

77 Ibid. para. 10.

78 For the role of overarching policy goals as sources of presumptions, see Salop, 'An Enquiry Meet for the Case' (n 7) 23.

problem.[79] The situational presumption against monopoly power and certain types of leveraging[80] conduct also drew support from the limitist[81] antitrust movement and the Harvard School.[82] For instance, the legal presumptions against tying, certain forms of exclusive dealing agreements, and non-linear pricing turned on the so-called leverage theory,[83] which was supported by the leading antitrust scholars of the time. This theory encapsulated the assumption that tying and exclusive dealing agreements have a detrimental effect on a competitive market structure because they allow dominant firms to expand or leverage their market power from markets (or portions of the market) where they are shielded from competition to neighbouring markets where they face competition.[84] Along similar lines, the presumption against non-linear pricing by dominant firms similarly hinged upon a leverage theory,[85] which assumed that non-linear pricing enables powerful firms to leverage their size advantage, superior financial resources, or multi-market presence to wage havoc on smaller competitors and deter entry.[86] Similarly, the PNB presumption accorded with the economic assumption of the predominant S–C–P paradigm that the market

79 DF Turner, 'The Definition of Agreement under the Sherman Act: Conscious Parallelism and Refusals to Deal' (1962) 75(4) *Harvard Law Review* 655, 665–66.

80 DF Turner, 'The Validity of Tying Arrangements under the Antitrust Laws' (1958) 72(1) *Harvard Law Review* 50.

81 FI Raymond, *The Limitist* (New York: W.W. Norton & Co 1947); W Adams, 'Dissolution, Divorcement, Divestiture: The Pyrrhic Victories of Antitrust' (1951) 27(1) *Indiana Law Journal* 1; W Adams, 'The Aluminium Case: Legal Victory – Economic Defeat' (1951) 41(5) *The American Economic Review* 915; W Adams, 'The Rule of Reason: Workable Competition or Workable Monopoly' (1954) 63(1) *Yale Law Journal* 348; W Adams, *The Structure of American Industry* (London: Macmillan 1971); CD Ewards, 'An Appraisal of the Antitrust Laws' (1946) 36 (2) *The American Economic Review* 172; CD Ewards, 'Can the Antitrust Laws Preserve Competition?' (1940) 30(1) *The American Economic Review* 164; EV Rostow, 'The New Sherman Act: A Positive Instrument of Progress' (1947) 14(4) *The University of Chicago Law Review* 567; EV Rostow, 'Monopoly under the Sherman Act: Power or Purpose' (1949) 43(6) *Illinois Law Review* 745.

82 Kaysen and Turner, *Antitrust Policy* (n 62) 76, 79.

83 *Northern Pac. Ry. Co. v United States* (n 24) 6; *United States v Griffith* 334 U.S. 100 (1948) 100, 102–09.

84 Kaysen and Turner, *Antitrust Policy* (n 62) 157; Turner, 'The Validity of Tying Arrangements' (n 80) 60–61; The Attorney General's National Committee to Study the Antitrust Laws, 1955 *Report* (Washington, DC: Superintendent of Documents, U.S. Government Printing Office 1955) 137–40, 144–45, 149, 238.

85 This leverage theory was even shared by antitrust experts who were critical of the Robinson Patman Act. Kaysen and Turner, *Antitrust Policy* (n 62) 180. Kaysen and Turner advocated a reform of the Robinson Patman Act which created a statutory rule prohibiting certain forms of discriminatory price cutting. Ibid. 184–86. This approach fundamentally differed from the Areeda-Turner test advocated less than two decades later to address predatory pricing. P Areeda and DF Turner, 'Predatory Pricing and Related Practices under Section 2 of the Sherman Act' (1975) 88(4) *Harvard Law Review* 697.

86 *Utah Pie Co. v Continental Baking Co.* (n 54) 690, 693–94, 698, 701; JF Brodley and GA Hay, 'Predatory Pricing: Competing Economic Theories and the Evolution of Legal Standards' (1980–1981) 66(4) *Cornell Law Review* 738, 766.

structure fundamentally shapes firm conduct and performance.[87] The structural presumptions hence embodied the marriage between the political republican ideal of competition as a deconcentrated market structure and the economic understanding of competition of the time.[88]

5.2.2 *Presumptions in EU Competition Law*

A broad application of presumptions also characterised EU competition law until the early-2000s. All three pillars of EU competition law followed what is often labelled a 'form-based approach'.[89] Instead of carrying out an inductive assessment of their actual or likely effects on competition based on case-specific evidence, the Commission and the EU judiciary frequently inferred the legality of a large category of coordinated and unilateral conduct, as well as mergers, from their specific legal and economic form and presumed impact on market structure.

5.2.2.1 Coordinated Conduct

The most prominent example of a presumption of illegality under EU competition law is the concept of restrictions of competition by-object, which structures the determination of the legality of coordinated conduct under Article 101 (1) TFEU. Starting with *Société Technique Minière*, the Court consistently held that when confronted with an allegedly anticompetitive agreement,[90] the factfinder would first have to ascertain whether it has as its object the restriction of competition. To this end, the factfinder needs to analyse the 'precise purpose' of the agreement within its economic and legal context.[91] If the clauses or the agreement in its entirety indicate that it is 'sufficiently deleterious'[92] or 'injurious'[93] to competition, then the agreement can be presumed to be restrictive of competition, and hence prima facie unlawful under Article 101 (1) TFEU[94] without the need to assess its 'concrete effects'.[95] Only if the agreement does not qualify as a by-object restriction of competition would a more searching analysis of its actual or likely consequences

[87] See footnotes 60–64 above and *United States v Philadelphia National Bank* (n 56) 363, fn. 38–39.

[88] H Hovenkamp and C Shapiro, 'Horizontal Mergers, Market Structure, and Burdens of Proof' (2018) 127(7) *The Yale Law Journal* 1996, 2001–02.

[89] For a critical discussion of the concept of a 'form-based' approach, J Lindeboom, 'Formalism in Competition Law' (2022) 18(4) *Journal of Competition Law and Economics* 832.

[90] In the following, I use 'agreement' as a shortcut for all types of coordinated conduct caught by Article 101 (1) TFEU.

[91] Case 56/65 *Société Technique Minière v Maschinenbau Ulm* ECLI:EU:C:1966:38 249.

[92] Ibid; Case C-8/08 *T-Mobile Netherlands BV and Others* ECLI:EU:C:2009:343 para. 28.

[93] Case C-8/08 *T-Mobile Netherlands BV and Others* (n 92) para. 29; Case C-209/07 *Beef Industry Development and Barry Brothers (BIDS)* ECLI:EU:C:2008:643 para. 17.

[94] Case 56/65 *Société Technique Minière v Maschinenbau Ulm* (n 91) 249.

[95] Case 56/64 *Consten and Grundig v Commission of the EEC* ECLI:EU:C:1966:41 342, 344.

become necessary to determine whether it has as its effect the restriction of competition, and thus runs afoul of Article 101 (1) TFEU.[96]

While the view has been widely held that the by-object category should neither be given an overly wide nor 'an unduly strict' interpretation,[97] until 2014 the EU judicature adopted a rather broad,[98] if not expansive,[99] reading of the types of agreements that qualify as a restriction of competition by-object. Up to the 2000s, the by-object restriction was applied to price fixing,[100] output restricting[101] and market sharing agreements,[102] information exchange on prices,[103] as well as resale price maintenance[104] and territorial restrictions[105] bringing about absolute territorial protection.

By devising the category of by-object restrictions, the Court created a presumption of illegality for certain forms of agreements. Agreements falling into the by-object category can be deemed to restrict competition and infringe Article 101 (1) TFEU without much further case-specific analysis.[106] Similarly to the per se rule under § 1 of the Sherman Act, the presumption of illegality encoded in the by-object category is directed against the most egregious forms of anticompetitive agreements that can be regarded 'by their very nature as being injurious [or harmful] to the proper functioning of normal competition.'[107] In a similar vein as the US Supreme Court, the EU judicature thus forged a presumption of illegality against coordinated conduct that substantially tampered with the polycentric structure and operation of markets. The Court also repeatedly held that for an agreement to be deemed a by-object restriction of competition, it is irrelevant whether it leads to actual or likely harm and interference with other market participants.[108] Rather, in a similar vein to the per se rule under § 1 of the Sherman Act, the concept of the restriction by-object was directed against coordinated conduct that leads to potential harm to competition.[109]

96 Case 56/65 *Société Technique Minière v Maschinenbau Ulm* (n 91) 249–50.
97 Opinion of Advocate General Kokott in Case C-8/08 *T-Mobile Netherlands BV and Others* ECLI:EU:C:2009:110 para. 43.
98 Case C-209/07 *Beef Industry Development and Barry Brothers (BIDS)* (n 93) para. 23; Opinion of Advocate General Kokott in Case C-226/11 *Expedia* ECLI:EU:C:2012:544 para. 51.
99 See, for instance, Case C-32/11 *Allianz Hungária Biztosító and Others* ECLI:EU:C:2013:160.
100 Case 123/83 *BNIC v Clair* ECLI:EU:C:1985:33 para. 22.
101 Case 136/86 *BNIC v Aubert* ECLI:EU:C:1987:524 para. 17.
102 Case 41/69 *Chemiefarma v Commission* ECLI:EU:C:1970:71 paras. 116, 128.
103 Case C-8/08 *T-Mobile Netherlands BV and Others* (n 92) paras. 35–36.
104 Case 243/83 *Binon v AMP* ECLI:EU:C:1985:284.
105 Case 56/64 *Consten and Grundig v Commission of the EEC* (n 95); Case C-501/06 P *GlaxoSmithKline Services and Others v Commission and Others* ECLI:EU:C:2009:610.
106 D Bailey, 'Presumptions in EU Competition Law' (2010) 31(9) *European Competition Law Review* 362, 364–65; Ritter (n 7) 192, 198.
107 Case C-8/08 *T-Mobile Netherlands BV and Others* (n 92) para. 43.
108 Case C-226/11 *Expedia* ECLI:EU:C:2012:795 para. 37, see also paras. 21–29.
109 Opinion of Advocate General Kokott in Case C-8/08 *T-Mobile Netherlands BV and Others* (n 97) paras. 43, 47; Case C-226/11 *Expedia* (n 108) para. 50.

The fundamental difference[110] between the by-object category under Article 101 (1) TFEU and the per se rule under § 1 of the Sherman Act lies in the extent to which they can be rebutted. While the per se rule under § 1 Sherman Act creates a conclusive, irrebuttable presumption, the finding of a restriction of competition by-object remains rebuttable. Until recently, parties had two pathways to rebut the presumption of illegality triggered by the finding of a by-object restriction of competition: either they advanced undermining evidence to show that the form-based inference of the anticompetitive nature of the agreement did not hold true in the case at hand; or they proffered offsetting evidence to demonstrate that the anticompetitive harm caused by the impugned agreement was outweighed by economic benefits or efficiencies.[111]

The range of admissible undermining evidence was, however, extremely narrow. The defendants could not simply rely on the fact that the agreement did not bring about the hoped-for anticompetitive effects to overturn a form-based presumption.[112] The sole type of undermining evidence whereby defendants could show that the presumption of anticompetitiveness did not hold true in the case at hand was to demonstrate that the impugned conduct was not arbitrary but ancillary to the pursuit of a legitimate objective.[113]

The possibility for defendants to rebut the presumption of illegality attached to by-object restrictions by proffering offsetting evidence under Article 101 (3) TFEU was also limited. While by-object restrictions could still qualify for an exemption under Article 101 (3) TFEU,[114] the European judicature and the European Commission consistently held that by-object restrictions of competition were unlikely to fulfil the four cumulative conditions of that provision.[115] Moreover, until the reform of the

[110] Case T-691/14 *Servier and Others v Commission* ECLI:EU:T:2018:922 para. 294; R Whish and B Sufrin, 'Article 85 and the Rule of Reason' (1987) 7(1) *Yearbook of European Law* 1. The EU Courts however routinely referred to the by-object category as per se rule and the by-effects analysis as rule of reason analysis. See, for instance, Case T-14/89 *Montedipe v Commission* ECLI:EU:T:1992:36 para. 265.

[111] For the distinction between undermining and offsetting evidence, see Salop, 'An Enquiry Meet for the Case' (n 7) 10.

[112] See, for instance, Case C-235/92 P *Montecatini v Commission* ECLI:EU:C:1999:362 paras. 121–28; Case C-8/08 *T-Mobile Netherlands BV and Others* (n 92) paras. 29–31; Opinion of Advocate General Kokott in Case C-8/08 *T-Mobile Netherlands BV and Others* (n 97) para. 45; Kalintiri, 'Analytical Shortcuts in EU Competition Enforcement' (n 6) 407.

[113] See, for instance, Case 42/84 *Remia v Commission* ECLI:EU:C:1985:327 para. 20; Case C-399/93 *Oude Luttikhuis and Others v Verenigde Coöperatieve Melkindustrie Coberco* ECLI:EU:C:1995:434 para. 14.

[114] Case 56/64 *Consten and Grundig v Commission of the EEC* (n 95) 347–49; Case T-17/93 *Matra Hachette v Commission* ECLI:EU:T:1994:89 para. 46.

[115] EU Commission, Guidelines on the Application of Article 81(3) of the Treaty, [2004] OJ C 101/97 para. 46. See also A Jones and WE Kovacic, 'Identifying Anticompetitive Agreements in the United States and the European Union: Developing a Coherent Antitrust Analytical Framework' (2017) 62(2) *The Antitrust Bulletin* 254, 281.

application of Article 101 (3) TFEU by Regulation 1/2003 EC,[116] defendants seeking to rebut the presumption of illegality triggered by the finding of a by-object restriction by advancing offsetting evidence had first to notify their agreement to the European Commission to benefit from the exemption of Article 101 (3) TFEU. The Commission then possessed the sole competence to decide whether the agreement could benefit from an exemption under Article 101 (3) TFEU. Owing to this institutional design for the implementation of the exemption of Article 101 (3) TFEU under Regulation 17/62 EEC,[117] a rebuttal of the by-object restriction based on offsetting evidence required the intervention of a public authority. Until the early-2000s, the by-object category therefore operated in most cases as a quasi-per se rule because the defendants were seriously constrained in their ability to rebut the presumption of illegality of by-object restrictions and the finding of a by-object restriction inevitably entailed intervention by the European Commission.[118]

5.2.2.2 Dominant Firm Conduct

Presumptions of illegality also fashioned the formative case law under Article 102 TFEU. Unlike the US courts, the Court of Justice has never had recourse to situational presumptions against the possession of monopoly power as such. Rather, the application of Article 102 TFEU hinged on presumptions of illegality against certain forms of conduct by a dominant firm.

The blueprint for this form-based approach has been set out in *Hofmann-La Roche* and subsequent cases. In *Hofmann-La Roche*, the Court drew a distinction between two categories of dominant firm conduct – it juxtaposed 'normal competition' based on 'economic performance'[119] to conduct that has the 'effect of hindering'[120] competition. This dichotomy evoked the Ordoliberal distinction between performance-based (*Leistungswettbewerb*) and hindrance (*Behinderungswettbewerb*) competition.[121]

[116] Council Regulation (EC) No 1/2003 on the implementation of the rules on competition laid down in Articles 81 and 82 of the Treaty, [2003] OJ L 1/1.

[117] EEC Council Regulation 17/62 implementing Articles 85 and 86 of the Treaty, [1962] OJ L 13/204.

[118] For a rare rebuttal of the presumption of illegality attached to a by-object restriction (price fixing agreement) under Article 101 (3) TFEU, see Case No IV/36.748 *Reims II*, [1999] OJ L 275/17.

[119] Case 322/81 *Michelin v Commission (Michelin I)* ECLI:EU:C:1983:313 para. 70. In this sense also Case C-62/86 *AKZO v Commission* ECLI:EU:C:1991:286 para. 70.

[120] Case 85/76 *Hoffmann-La Roche v Commission* ECLI:EU:C:1979:36 para. 91; Case 322/81 *Michelin v Commission (Michelin I)* (n 119) para. 70; Case C-95/04 P *British Airways plc v Commission of the European Communities* ECLI:EU:C:2007:166 para. 66.

[121] See, for instance, F Böhm (ed), *Wettbewerb und Monopolkampf: Eine Untersuchung zur Frage des wirtschaftlichen Kampfrechts und zur Frage der rechtlichen Struktur der geltenden Wirtschaftsordnung* [1933] (Baden-Baden: Nomos 2010) 242, 275–76; W Eucken, *Grundsätze der Wirtschaftspolitik* (Tübingen: Mohr Siebeck 2004) 247. See also to this effect, J Kallaugher and B Sher, 'Rebates Revisited: Anti-competitive Effects and Exclusionary Abuse under Article 82' (2004) 25(5) *European Competition Law Review* 263, 268–72.

While dominant firms should remain free to compete based on superior economic performance, the Ordoliberals suggested that competition law ought to outlaw certain types of conduct that amount to hindrance competition because they are capable of inhibiting competition, in particular by foreclosing competitors.

This performance-based and hindrance competition divide, as well as the concept of special responsibility,[122] constituted the fundamental building blocks of legal presumptions under Article 102 TFEU. Indeed, the Court of Justice devised several presumptions of illegality by labelling exclusive dealing agreements,[123] loyalty rebates,[124] tying arrangements,[125] and below-average cost price cuts[126] as forms of hindrance competition based on the assumption that they adversely affect the competitive market structure by hampering or foreclosing residual competition. In contrast, the legality of other types of conduct, such as loyalty-enhancing rebates[127] and refusals to deal,[128] could only be determined through the analysis of more case-specific evidence.

In creating these presumptions of illegality, the EU Courts established, in a similar way as under Article 101 (1) TFEU, a category of unilateral dominant firm conduct that has as its 'object'[129] the restriction of competition.[130] These presumptions of illegality were not based on the assumption that anticompetitive foreclosure of competitors and consumer harm had actually occurred or were likely to result from a particular form of dominant firm conduct. Rather, the presumptions of illegality turned on the premise that they constitute clear forms of hindrance competition because they are incompatible with 'normal competition'[131] or 'competition on the merits',[132] which is exclusively driven by the performance[133] of the economic operators.[134] Exclusivity agreements rebates, tying arrangements, and

[122] Case 322/81 *Michelin v Commission (Michelin I)* (n 119) para. 57.

[123] Case 40/73 *Suiker Unie and Others v Commission* ECLI:EU:C:1975:174 paras. 502–05; Case 85/76 *Hoffmann-La Roche v Commission* (n 119) paras. 89–90.

[124] Case 40/73 *Suiker Unie and Others v Commission* (n 123) paras. 502–05; Case 85/76 *Hoffmann-La Roche v Commission* (n 120) paras. 89–90, 121.

[125] Case T-30/89 *Hilti v Commission* ECLI:EU:T:1991:70 paras. 64–78, 89–94; Case T-83/91 *Tetra Pak v Commission (Tetra Pak II)* ECLI:EU:T:1994:246 paras. 135, 137; Case C-333/94 P *Tetra Pak v Commission* ECLI:EU:C:1996:436 para. 37.

[126] Case C-62/86 *AKZO v Commission* (n 119) para. 71; Ritter (n 7) 209.

[127] Case 322/81 *Michelin v Commission (Michelin I)* (n 119) paras. 71–86; Case T-203/01 *Michelin v Commission (Michelin II)* ECLI:EU:T:2003:250 para. 59.

[128] Case C-7/97 *Bronner v Mediaprint* ECLI:EU:C:1998:569 paras. 37–47.

[129] Case T-203/01 *Michelin v Commission (Michelin II)* (n 119) para. 241.

[130] See to this effect Colomo and Lamadrid de Pablo (n 4) 346.

[131] Case 85/76 *Hoffmann-La Roche v Commission* (n 119) para. 91; Case 322/81 *Michelin v Commission (Michelin I)* (n 119) para. 70; Case T-203/01 *Michelin v Commission (Michelin II)* (n 119) paras. 98, 238.

[132] Case T-203/01 *Michelin v Commission (Michelin II)* (n 119) para. 97; Case T-228/97 *Irish Sugar v Commission* ECLI:EU:T:1999:246 para. 111.

[133] Case 322/81 *Michelin v Commission (Michelin I)* (n 119) para. 70.

[134] Kallaugher and Sher (n 121) 270–71.

predatory price cuts were considered to be strategies that a dominant firm could use to leverage its size – in the form of a broader customer base, broader range of product lines, multi-market presence, and ability to absorb losses – to annihilate the economic liberty of smaller, independent competitors, and reduce the freedom of choice of their customers.[135] In a similar way to conduct-based presumptions against unilateral conduct under US antitrust law, the presumptions of illegality under Article 102 were predicated on a leverage theory of harm that was coined by the S–C–P paradigm in the United States.

The legal presumptions under Article 102 TFEU also remained rebuttable. Article 102 TFEU does not provide for a similar exemption as exists under Article 101 (3) TFEU.[136] Nevertheless, the Court consistently held that dominant firms have the possibility to rebut the presumption of illegality against prima facie abusive conduct by proffering an objective economic justification.[137] This objective justification was not primarily conceived as an efficiency defence whereby the dominant firm could justify its behaviour by showing that its anticompetitive effects are outweighed by its pro-competitive efficiencies.[138] Instead, the objective justification was supposed to offer the dominant firms the possibility to overturn the presumption of abuse against specific conduct by showing that it was actually motivated by other grounds than an exclusionary purpose[139] and can be explained by the legitimate commercial interests of the dominant firm[140] or other legitimate reasons.[141] However, the EU Courts gave the objective justification a narrow interpretation and imposed a high evidentiary threshold on dominant firms to rebut presumptions of illegality.[142]

[135] Case 40/73 *Suiker Unie and Others v Commission* (n 123) para. 503; Case 85/76 *Hoffmann-La Roche v Commission* (n 119) paras. 89–90; Case C-62/86 *AKZO v Commission* (n 119) para. 149; Case T-83/91 *Tetra Pak v Commission (Tetra Pak II)* (n 125) paras. 135, 137, 140; L Gyselen, 'Rebates: Competition on the Merits or Exclusionary Practice?' in C-D Ehlermann and I Atanasiu (eds), *European Competition Law Annual 2003: What Is an Abuse of a Dominant Position?* (Oxford: Hart 2003) 287, 320.

[136] Case 66/86 *Ahmed Saeed Flugreisen and Others v Zentrale zur Bekämpfung unlauteren Wettbewerbs* ECLI:EU:C:1989:140 para. 31.

[137] Case 40/70 *Sirena v Eda* ECLI:EU:C:1971:18 paras. 16–17; Case 27/76 *United Brands v Commission* ECLI:EU:C:1978:22 paras. 158, 184, 188–91, 228; Case T-83/91 *Tetra Pak v Commission (Tetra Pak II)* (n 125) para. 138.

[138] Efficiency considerations appear for the first time as elements of the objective justification in the Court of First Instance's ruling in Case T-228/97 *Irish Sugar v Commission* (n 132) para. 189; A Llorens Albors, 'The Role of Objective Justification and Efficiencies in the Application of Article 82 EC' (2007) 44(6) *Common Market Law Review* 1727, 1727–35, 1746.

[139] Case C-62/86 *AKZO v Commission* (n 119) paras. 140, 146.

[140] Case 27/76 *United Brands v Commission* (n 137) paras. 189; Case 322/81 *Michelin v Commission (Michelin I)* (n 119) para. 90.

[141] Case 77/77 *B.P. v Commission* ECLI:EU:C:1978:141 para. 33.

[142] Case 27/76 *United Brands v Commission* (n 137) paras. 158, 190–91; Case T-65/89 *BPB Industries and British Gypsum v Commission* ECLI:EU:T:1993:31 paras. 117–18; Case T-30/89 *Hilti v Commission* (n 125) para. 118.

5.2.2.3 Mergers

Presumptions of illegality also had an important bearing on the formative era of EU merger control. The 1989 EC Merger Regulation (ECMR) established a two-pronged test to determine when a merger must be considered incompatible with the internal market, and therefore unlawful. Such is the case if the merger leads to (i) the creation or strengthening of a dominant position, and thereby gives rise to (ii) a significant impediment to effective competition (SIEC). In subsequent cases, however, the Commission and the EU Courts inferred the finding of a SIEC from the fact that the merger entails the strengthening or creation of a dominant position.[143]

The EU Commission and Courts thus relied on a structural presumption that deduced the existence of a SIEC from the finding that the merger led to a strengthening or creation of a dominant position. Accordingly, the Court and the Commission were able to prohibit mergers for the mere reason that they fostered the concentration of market power within the hands of a single firm without there being the need to show that the merger would lead to likely interference with other market participants and entail adverse welfare effects.[144] While the ECMR did not set out a threshold for a structural presumption of illegality, the EU Commission and the Court of First Instance transposed the so-called *Akzo* presumption of dominance, pursuant to which a market share of 50 per cent or more is in itself considered evidence for the existence of a dominant position, from Article 102 TFEU to EU merger policy.[145] In some instances, the Commission found that mergers leading to a combined market share of between 40 and 50 per cent[146] or even below 40 per cent[147] may entail the creation or strengthening of a dominant position.

Although the EU Courts never adopted as low a concentration threshold triggering a presumption of illegality as the US courts during the Warren Court era, they nonetheless expanded the presumption of illegality to oligopolistic markets. *Kali und Salz* and *Gencor* clarified that mergers giving rise to a collective dominant position in oligopolistic markets may activate the presumption of illegality attached

[143] G Monti, *EC Competition Law* (Cambridge: Cambridge University Press 2007) 249–50. See, for instance, Case T-2/93 *Air France v Commission* ECLI:EU:T:1994:55 paras. 79–80; Case T-290/94 *Kaysersberg v Commission* ECLI:EU:T:1997:186 paras. 179, 185. Cf. L-H Röller and M De la Mano, 'The Impact of the New Substantive Test in European Merger Control' (2006) 2(1) *European Competition Journal* 9, 10–13.

[144] AC Witt, 'From Airtours to Ryanair: Is the More Economic Approach to EU Merger Law Really about More Economics?' (2012) 49(1) *Common Market Law Review* 217, 225.

[145] Case C-62/86 *AKZO v Commission* (n 119) para. 60; Case No IV/M.784 *Kesko/Tuko*, [1997] OJ L 110/53 para. 106; Case T-221/95 *Endemol v Commission* ECLI:EU:T:1999:85 para. 134; Case T-102/96 *Gencor v Commission* ECLI:EU:T:1999:65 para. 205; Monti (n 143) 251.

[146] Case No COMP/M.2337 *Nestlé/Ralston Purina*, Document No 301 M2337 paras. 48–50.

[147] Case No IV/M.1221 *Rewe/Meinl*, [1999] OJ L 274/1 paras. 98–114; Case No COMP/M.2337 *Nestlé/Ralston Purina* (n 146) paras. 44–47.

to the finding of dominance, even if they do not lead to a combined market share in excess of 25 per cent.[148] However, the presumption affixed to the finding of collective dominance was more differentiated than the presumption that was triggered by the finding of single dominance. The Commission had to ascertain more case-specific information to establish a collective dominance position than in single dominance cases.[149]

In a similar vein to the Warren Court case law and the 1968 Guidelines, the EU merger policy under the ECMR only recognised very limited possibilities for merging parties to rebut the structural presumption under the dominance test. In particular, the ECMR did not provide for an explicit efficiency or failing firm defence.[150] Instead, Article 2 (1) (b) foresaw that the European Commission would have to assess efficiencies as part of its appraisal of whether the merger gives rise to a SIEC.[151] However, in cases such as the *Aerospatial-Alenia/deHavilland* merger, the Commission gave little weight to efficiency considerations. Instead, it construed the possibilities for merging parties to rebut the structural presumption very narrowly. The Commission even appeared to perceive efficiency as a potential offence, as it raised the concern that the merger-generated efficiencies might have a detrimental impact on competitors.[152]

Similarly to US antitrust law until the 1970s, presumptions of illegality were a hallmark of the form-based approach under EU competition law. However, presumptions under EU competition law were less far-reaching than those in US antitrust law. Unlike the per se rule under § 1 of the Sherman Act, all presumptions in EU competition law remained rebuttable. Moreover, EU competition law did not have recourse to any situational presumption against the very existence of a dominant firm, while such a situational presumption against unreasonable monopoly power existed for a short period during the apex of the republican antitrust approach in the United States. Instead, the abuse of dominance case law relied exclusively on conduct-based presumptions. Situational presumptions against single and collective dominance in EU merger policy were less strict than the interpretation of the PNB presumption during the Warren Court era in the United States.

[148] Case C-68/94 *France and Société commerciale des potasses et de l'azote and Entreprise minière et chimique v Commission* ECLI:EU:C:1998:148 paras. 176–77; Case T-102/96 *Gencor v Commission* (n 145) paras. 134–36.

[149] See, for instance, Case C-68/94 *France and Société commerciale des potasses et de l'azote and Entreprise minière et chimique v Commission* (n 148) para. 226; Case T-102/96 *Gencor v Commission* (n 145) para. 206.

[150] Case No IV/M.308 *Kali-Salz/MdK/Treuhand*, [1994] OJ L 186/38 paras. 70–90; Case C-68/94 *France and Société commerciale des potasses et de l'azote and Entreprise minière et chimique v Commission* (n 148) paras. 112–16.

[151] Council Regulation (EEC) No 4064/89 on the Control of Concentrations between Undertakings, [1989] OJ L 395/1 Article 2 (1) (b).

[152] Case No IV/M.053 *Aerospatiale-Alenia/de Havilland*, [1991] OJ L 334/42 paras. 30, 69.

5.2.3 *Presumptions and the Resilience of Republican Liberty*

For quite some time, all three pillars of EU and US competition law thus extensively relied on presumptions of illegality. Conventional antitrust scholarship explains the use of presumptions by their role in securing procedural economy, administrability, and legal certainty in competition law enforcement.[153] Legal presumptions allow competition authorities and courts to condemn particular forms of firm conduct, while dispensing with the resource-intensive, time-consuming, and costly inquiry into case-specific evidence to determine their actual or likely economic consequences. At the same time, rule-like presumptions enhance legal certainty for businesses that receive clear guidance as to which conduct is incompatible with competition rules.[154] Antitrust scholars, however, tend to ignore that rule-like presumptions constitute a specific form of legal commands, which played a crucial role in rendering competition law on both sides of the Atlantic conducive to a republican understanding of economic liberty.

5.2.3.1 The Structural Rationale of Presumptions

The first way in which presumptions made US antitrust and EU competition law hospitable to republican liberty was their structural rationale. Legal presumptions were the primary channel through which US antitrust and EU competition law gave shape to the structuralist policy objective of preserving polycentric markets as an institution of antipower that safeguards republican liberty. Republican antitrust on both sides of the Atlantic reverted to legal presumptions as predilect instruments to translate the concern about market structure into legal rules. Indeed, legal presumptions offered republican antitrust an effective instrument to regulate the level of concentration of economic power.

On the one hand, conduct-based presumptions address market concentration indirectly by attaching a prima facie or per se illegality to those types of coordinated or unilateral conduct that experience shows to have the most detrimental impact on the polycentric structure and functioning of markets. On the other hand, situational legal presumptions also allow competition policy to regulate the level of concentration directly by establishing structural thresholds above which industry concentration through monopoly or merger is deemed to be excessive. From a republican vantage point, the ability of firms to exert domination is negatively correlated to the degree to which they are constrained by polycentric competition. In directly (situational) or indirectly (conduct-based) capping the level of market concentration,

[153] CF Beckner and SC Salop, 'Decision Theory and Antitrust Rules' (1999) 67(1) *Antitrust Law Journal* 41, 43–61; Ritter (n 7) 211.

[154] See, for instance, *Northern Pac. Ry. Co. v United States* (n 24) 5; *United States v Topco Assocs. Inc.* (n 26) 607; Opinion of Advocate General Kokott in Case C-8/08 *T-Mobile Netherlands BV and Others* (n 97) paras. 42–43.

legal presumptions immediately tackle the level of domination prevailing in the market.

Presumptions of illegality were hence directed against specific forms of conduct and market constellations that were regarded as a source of domination due to their capacity or potential to adversely affect the polycentric functioning and structure of markets and to confer the parties the power to control the market.[155] They therefore encapsulated a prophylactic approach that sought to prevent conduct leading to a situation where parties 'have it in their power to destroy or drastically impair the competitive system'.[156]

5.2.3.2 Rule-Like Presumptions and Private Government

The second way in which legal presumptions enhance republican liberty is that rebuttable and irrebuttable presumptions of illegality – by creating either a conditional or unconditional (per se) rule against certain forms of anticompetitive agreements, dominant firm conduct, and mergers – reduce the ability of private actors to impose their interests upon other market participants and engage in private government. The republican antitrust tradition in the United States and in the European Union rested on the assumption that legal presumptions are more effective than legal standards in protecting market participants against the arbitrary exercise of power and private government by other firms.[157]

The courts in the United States until the early-1970s and in the European Union until the early-2000s adopted a broad interpretation of presumptions of illegality. At the same time, they exhibited considerable reluctance to engage in a sweeping and unstructured rule of reason analysis, which presupposes a detailed economic analysis and balancing of anticompetitive effects and pro-competitive virtues of business conduct.[158] In support of this broad application of presumptions under the per se rule, the Supreme Court repeatedly highlighted that, due to their rule-like character, legal presumptions considerably limit the discretion of private parties to decide when the pro-competitive virtues of a particular conduct are sufficiently important to justify a restriction of competition. For instance, the US Supreme Court cautioned that too broad an application of a rule of reason analysis might lead to

[155] Mason, 'Monopoly in Law and Economics' (n 23) 41.

[156] *United States v Socony-Vacuum Oil Co.* (n 25) 221. In a similar sense Opinion of Advocate General Kokott in Case C-8/08 *T-Mobile Netherlands BV and Others* (n 97) para. 43.

[157] For the propensity of rules to limit discretion A Christiansen and W Kerber, 'Competition Policy with Optimally Differentiated Rules Instead of per se Rules vs. Rule of Reason' (2006) 2 (2) *Journal of Competition Law and Economics* 215, 219–20; JB Baker, *The Antitrust Paradigm: Restoring a Competitive Economy* (Cambridge, MA: Harvard University Press 2019) 66–69; Kaplow, 'Rules versus Standards' (n 2) 609. Cf. DA Crane, 'Rules versus Standards in Antitrust Adjudication' (2007) 64(1) *Washington and Lee Law Review* 49, 97–98.

[158] *United States v Trenton Potteries Co.* (n 21) 397; *United States v Socony-Vacuum Oil Co.* (n 25) 221; *Northern Pac. Ry. Co. v United States* (n 24) 5.

situations of arbitrary domination because '[p]rivate forces are too keenly aware of their own interests in making such decisions.'[159] Therefore, the Supreme Court repeatedly refused to weigh anticompetitive and pro-competitive effects of per se offences. It instead insisted that 'a decision [...] to sacrifice competition in one portion of the economy for greater competition in another portion [...] must be made by Congress and not by private forces or by courts.'[160] The extensive use of legal presumptions in US antitrust law until the 1970s was thus driven by the concern that the rule of reason standard gives private firms more possibilities to impose their interests and value judgments upon other market participants, and hence to exercise private government.[161]

Similar concerns about private government and domination also prompted the EU Courts and the Commission to rely on a broad interpretation of presumptions. These were even applied against conduct that did not exclusively pursue the goal of restricting competition. For example, the Courts and the Commission encountered claims that anticompetitive agreements containing by-object restrictions were necessary to address market failures or to ensure compliance with existing regulations with scepticism. They held that any redeeming virtues of these agreements could only be taken into account under Article 101 (3) TFEU.[162] The EU Courts and the Commission also made it clear that private parties cannot rely on the need to ensure the compliance of other market participants with existing regulations to justify their anticompetitive agreements or exclusionary conduct. Instead, they took the view that it is not the role of private, self-interested players but the exclusive competence of public authorities to ensure the compliance of market participants with the law.[163] This strict approach sought to prevent private actors from imposing their own idiosyncratic views on other market participants and to minimise their ability to subject other economic operators to their private rule-making and government.

5.2.3.3 The Modal Scope of Presumptions in Republican Antitrust

The third common feature that made rule-like presumptions particularly conducive to the realisation of a republican conception of liberty was their modal character. Rule-like presumptions were used to outlaw certain types of conduct on the basis of their

[159] *United States v Topco Assocs. Inc.* (n 26) 611.

[160] Ibid. 611; *Timken Roller Bearing Co. v United States* 341 U.S. 593 (1951) 597; *United States v Sealy, Inc.* (n 26) 357; *United States v Philadelphia National Bank* (n 56) 370–72.

[161] *United States v Socony-Vacuum Oil Co.* (n 25) 212, 221–22, 225; *United States v Topco Assocs. Inc.* (n 26) 611; *Fashion Originators' Guild, Inc. v FTC* (n 27) 461, 468.

[162] Case 136/86 *BNIC v Aubert* (n 101) para. 22; Case C-209/07 *Beef Industry Development and Barry Brothers (BIDS)* (n 93) para. 21.

[163] Case T-30/89 *Hilti v Commission* (n 125) para. 118; Case T-83/91 *Tetra Pak v Commission (Tetra Pak II)* (n 125) para. 138; Case C-68/12 *Slovenská sporiteľňa* ECLI:EU:C:2013:71 para. 20.

'capacity'[164] or 'tendency'[165] – not likelihood – to harm competition and allow the defendants to 'effectively dominat[e] the market'.[166] To activate these presumptions, factfinders or plaintiffs were not required to show any actual or likely interference with other market participants. Rather, the rule-like presumptions of republican antitrust inferred the tendency of conduct to result in harmful consequences from its impact on market structure. The adverse impact of certain market constellations or conduct on a decentralised market structure served as a proxy for the potential harm and degree of domination that the situation or conduct may cause. Rule-like presumptions thus enabled competition law to protect the liberty of market participants against a broad range of preventing conditions (y) that counts not only actual or likely interference but also the mere ability to interfere as an obstruction of liberty. As many of these presumptions applied without any assessment of the efficiency of the harmed market participants, legal presumptions also enabled US and EU competition law to protect the economic liberty of a broad range of economic agents (x), and thereby guarantee the inclusivity of the competitive process.

This use of presumptions diverges from an approach that, in line with the probabilistic logic of negative liberty, would only countenance antitrust intervention if the impugned conduct or merger gives rise to actual or likely interference with the economic liberty of competitors and consumers. The relevant criterion to determine whether a specific conduct or market constellation was caught by the presumption of anticompetitiveness was not primarily the likelihood[167] of specific conduct resulting in harm in the actual or nearby likely world. Presumptions in the republican approach thus differed from the way in which modern evidence theory expresses presumptions as a prior Bayesian odds ratio $\frac{P(H)}{P(B)}$, where $P(H)$ describes the probability of conduct resulting in hindrance or harm and $P(B)$ describes the probability of conduct resulting in benefits or being competitively neutral in the actual or nearby likely world.[168] Instead, rule-like presumptions incorporated a prior belief about the scale, gravity, or significance of the potential harm to competition that might result from the impugned conduct across various relevant possible worlds, $w_1, \ldots, w_k$. Presumptions in republican antitrust thus took the form $\frac{P(H|w_1)\,P(w_1) + \cdots + P(H|w_k)\,P(w_k)}{P(B|w_1)\,P(w_1) + \cdots + P(B|w_k)\,P(w_k)}$, where $|$ reads as 'given', $w_1, \ldots, w_k$ describe all

[164] Opinion of Advocate General Kokott in Case C-8/08 *T-Mobile Netherlands BV and Others* (n 97) paras. 43, 47; Case C-226/11 *Expedia* (n 108) para. 50.

[165] *Fashion Originators' Guild, Inc. v FTC* (n 27) 468; *Int'l Salt Co. v United States* (n 50) 396; *Klor's, Inc. v Broadway-Hale Stores, Inc.* (n 27) 211.

[166] *United States v Socony-Vacuum Oil Co.* (n 25) 221. See also for § 2 Sherman Act, *United States v Alcoa* (n 37) 427, 429, 432; *American Tobacco Co. v United States* (n 37) 809, 810–11. For § 3 Clayton Act *United Shoe Mach. Co. v United States* (n 49) 457. For § 7 of the Clayton Act, *United States v Philadelphia National Bank* (n 56) 366.

[167] Salop, 'An Enquiry Meet for the Case' (n 7) 2.

[168] AW Martin and DA Schum, 'Quantifying Burdens of Proof: A Likelihood Ratio Approach' (1987) 27(4) *Jurimetrics* 383; L Kaplow, 'Likelihood Ratio Tests and Legal Decision Rules' (2014) 16(1) *American Law and Economics Review* 1.

worlds accessible from the actual world, $P(w_1)$, …, $P(w_k)$ denote the respective probabilities of occurrence of these worlds, and $P(H|w_{1\ldots k})$ and $P(B|w_{1\ldots k})$ stand for the respective conditional probabilities of conduct being harmful or beneficial in a given world $w \ldots k$.[169]

The expansive use and weight of legal presumptions in republican antitrust can thus be formalised by means of a modified Bayesian decision-making model. The modus operandi of republican antitrust decision-making on both sides of the Atlantic took the following form: $\alpha \frac{P(H|w_1)\,P(w_1) + \cdots + P(H|w_k)\,P(w_k)}{P(B|w_1)\,P(w_1) + \cdots + P(B|w_k)\,P(w_k)} \times \beta \frac{P(e|H)}{P(e|B)} = \frac{P(H|e)}{P(B|e)}$. Factfinders extensively relied on a prior belief that took into account the tendency of conduct to result in harm (H) and benefits (B) across various possible worlds. This prior was attributed considerable weight α. Depending on the circumstances, this presumption was subsequently revised and updated in the light of additional case-specific evidence e about the probable impact of the impugned conduct on competition in the specific case $\frac{P(e|H)}{P(e|B)}$. The odds ratio of additional evidence $\frac{P(e|H)}{P(e|B)}$ denotes the conditional probability of finding case-specific evidence e given that the impugned conduct is truly harmful $P(e|H)$ relative to the conditional probability of the evidence at hand being associated with truly innocuous or beneficial conduct $P(e|B)$. Given the strength α of the presumption, republican antitrust attributed only very limited weight to the assessment of additional evidence. In the case of the irrebuttable presumption of the per se rule under § 1 of the Sherman Act, the assessment of additional evidence carried no weight at all (i.e., $\beta = 0$).

By combining the prior $\alpha \frac{P(H|w_1)\,P(w1) + \cdots + P(H|w_k)\,P(w_k)}{P(B|w_1)\,P(w1) + \cdots + P(B|w_k)\,P(w_k)}$ and the odds ratio of additional evidence $\beta \frac{P(e|H)}{P(e|B)}$, the fact finders then established a revised estimate of the (posterior) probabilities $\frac{P(H|e)}{P(B|e)}$. This odds ratio $\frac{P(H|e)}{P(B|e)}$ gauges the probability of conduct causing anticompetitive harm compared to the probability of it being beneficial. At the end of the competition law proceedings, the fact finders thus made a determination about the competitive nature of the impugned conduct based on this posterior probability that the conduct is harmful (relative to that it is not harmful) given the additional evidence e. The key feature of the modus operandi of republican antitrust decision-making was its genuinely deductive mode of analysis, under which rule-like presumptions carried considerably more weight than case-specific evidence, so that $\alpha > \beta$. As a result of this deductive mode of analysis, the revised posterior odds

[169] This formalisation of republican presumptions draws on C List and L Valentini, 'Freedom as Independence' (2016) 126(4) *Ethics* 1043, 1054, fn. 23; P Pettit, *On the People's Terms: A Republican Theory and Model of Democracy* (Cambridge: Cambridge University Press 2012) 67–68. For a critical discussion of this approach and its limitation to capture the 'non-probabilistic' concept of republican liberty, see List and Valentini (n 169) 1058 and fn. 24.

ratio of a factfinder in republican antitrust attributed more weight to the potential of conduct to generate harm across various relevant possible worlds than to the likelihood of conduct to cause harm in the actual or nearby likely world.

5.2.3.4 The Modal Robustness of Rule-Like Presumptions

The fourth way in which legal presumptions under US and EU competition law made the value of republican liberty operative also relates to their rule-like character. The various presumptions under US and EU competition law were not entirely identical in the amount of case-specific information that they required the factfinder to consider to determine the illegality of specific conduct. In other words, the presumptions differed in the degree of differentiation in which they laid down legal commands or rules.[170] Some of the presumptions were not differentiated at all (e.g., the per se rule against price fixing agreements). They simply encoded a straightforward prohibition of specific conduct. In contrast, others only became operative after the consideration of additional assessment criteria (e.g., the presumption against exclusive dealing agreements in the United States, the by-object restriction under Article 101 TFEU, or the presumption against loyalty rebates or collective dominance in the European Union). However, despite their higher degree of differentiation, none of them required a fully-fledged analysis of the case-specific effects of the impugned conduct. Rather, they established clear bright-line rules against certain forms of coordinated and unilateral conduct, as well as mergers on the basis of their tendency or potential to give rise to harm and domination. Therefore, the presumptions of illegality shared a rule-like character, which was further accentuated by their limited rebuttability. In reality, even formally rebuttable presumptions were extremely difficult to overturn.

Owing to their rule-like character, these legal presumptions provided for a broader protective scope of economic liberty than legal standards because they guard economic players against domination rather than merely actual or likely interference, and hence secure their liberty against a larger set of preventing conditions (y). Simultaneously, rule-like presumptions also ensured a greater intensity or level of protection by protecting a wider range of relevant actions (z) than legal standards that governed the rule of reason or by-effects analysis. Unlike the rule of reason and by-effects standards, rule-like presumptions not only address and prevent a specific incidence of arbitrary interference but also make access to such interference unavailable or, at least, very costly.[171] Consequently, they prevent certain forms of interference not just in the actual world but in a range of possible worlds where contingencies are different.[172] As a result, the protection of market participants against the potential harm of certain agreements, monopolistic conduct,

[170] Christiansen and Kerber (n 157).

[171] Pettit, 'Freedom in the Market' (n 5) 145–46.

[172] P Pettit, *Republicanism: A Theory of Freedom and Government* (Oxford: Oxford University Press 1997) 25–26; Pettit, *On the People's Terms* (n 169) 67.

or mergers is not contingent upon whether the factfinder establishes in the concrete case that they unduly interfere with their choices or forecloses competitors. Rather, by categorically preventing firms from engaging in certain conduct that is tainted by a tendency to entail arbitrary interference, rule-like presumptions made certain forms of conduct inadmissible. They thereby reduced firms' access to what one could consider as 'resources for domination'.[173] Simultaneously, legal presumptions enhanced legal certainty for weaker market operators because they not only protect them against actual or likely interference but also limit a firm's overall capacity to interfere in an arbitrary way with other market participants by having recourse to certain forms of unilateral or coordinated conduct.[174]

Republican antitrust thus enhanced liberty as non-domination by relying on rule-like presumptions that operated as normative desiderata outlawing certain conduct, not only in the actual but across all (relevant) possible worlds. This modal character of rule-like presumptions and their difference with legal standards can again be illustrated by the distinction between the necessity operator OA which is to be read as '*it is obligatory that* A', and the possibility operator PA, which is to be read as '*it is permissible that* A'. While OA suggests that A is true across *all permissible* worlds, PA merely indicates that A is true in *some permissible* worlds but not necessarily in others.[175] Rule-like presumptions can be thought of as a legal command that affixes the necessity operator O to a specific prohibition. Accordingly, rule-like presumptions indicate that the prohibition of specific forms of conduct holds true in all, or at least almost all, (relevant) *permissible* worlds. By way of example, consider a presumption *O¬{price fixing cartels, loyalty rebates, tying, mergers in concentrated markets}*, where ¬ stands for '*not*'. This rule-like presumption creates modally robust prohibitions that outlaw certain types of conduct (here price fixing cartels, loyalty rebates, tying, and mergers in concentrated markets) in all (relevant) permissible worlds. In contrast, legal standards only indicate that certain conduct may be prohibited and that this prohibition holds true in some (relevant) permissible worlds, depending on the specific circumstances. A legal standard can be conceived of as a legal command assigning the possibility operator P to a specific prohibition. Take, for instance, the legal standard *P¬{price fixing cartels, loyalty rebates, tying, mergers in concentrated markets}*. This standard merely signals that '*it is permissible that*' specific types of conduct (here price fixing cartels, loyalty rebates, tying, mergers in concentrated markets) do not materialise (¬ stands for '*not*') in some relevant permissible worlds. Consequently, the choice between rule-like presumptions and legal standards crucially affects the modal robustness of the prohibitions and rights established by legal commands.

In formulating moral desiderata that hold true in all (relevant) possible worlds, rule-like legal presumptions are able to distinguish in a modally robust manner the

173 P Pettit, 'Freedom as Antipower' (1996) 106(3) *Ethics* 576, 590.

174 Pettit, *Republicanism: A Theory of Freedom and Government* (n 172) 26.

175 C List, 'Republican Freedom and the Rule of Law' (2006) 5(2) *Politics, Philosophy & Economics* 201, 206.

admissible and inadmissible business strategies for market players. As they rule out certain types of conduct as inadmissible dominating strategies, rule-like legal presumptions also specify clear-cut and non-contingent sets of individual rights for all market participants.[176] By delineating some concrete market freedoms that shield market participants from dominating conduct (e.g., anticompetitive cartels, tying, or loyalty rebates), legal presumptions carve out spheres of autonomy or right sets for consumers and competitors within which they are able to act as their own masters because their preferences remain content- and context-independently decisive.[177] If there is a presumption of the form presumption *O¬{price fixing cartels, loyalty rebates, tying, mergers in concentrated markets}*, these sets of market freedoms take the form of negative rights □¬*{price fixing cartels, loyalty rebates, tying, mergers in concentrated markets}*, where □ reads as '*it is necessary that*'. Accordingly, it holds true across all relevant possible worlds that market players are shielded against the outlawed conduct (e.g., here price fixing cartels, loyalty rebates, tying, and mergers in concentrated markets). The protection conferred against arbitrarily interfering conduct through rule-like presumptions is modally more robust than a similar right set that is established by legal standards. A legal standard *P¬{price fixing cartels, loyalty rebates, tying, mergers in concentrated markets}* would translate into a right set taking the form ◇¬*{price fixing cartels, loyalty rebates, tying, mergers in concentrated markets}*, where ◇ reads as '*it is possible that*'. In relying on rule-like presumptions of anticompetitiveness against broad categories of conduct, US antitrust and EU competition law have guaranteed broad right sets against dominating conduct across all (relevant) possible worlds.

The modally robust and resilient protection of the right sets guaranteed by these presumptions was further compounded by the fact that they carried considerable weight because the defendants had only limited possibilities to rebut them. Rule-like presumptions thus laid down modally robust rules of the game for market participants. They gave shape to a framework or 'outcome function'[178] that specifies the set of legally and socially permissible and impermissible strategies across all relevant possible worlds. In making dominating conduct unavailable or prohibitively costly across all permissible worlds, rule-like legal presumptions reduced the overall level of domination within a given market and society at large.

The reliance of the formative case law on rule-like presumptions thus replicated the modally robust, context-independent feature of republican liberty,[179] which harnesses legal rules to secure a relevant range of unrestrained actions (z) across

[176] For this game-theoretic modelling of individual rights, see W Gaertner, PK Pattanaik, and K Suzumura, 'Individual Rights Revisited' (1992) 59(234) *Economica* 161, 173–75.

[177] C List, 'The Impossibility of a Paretian Republican?: Some Comments on Pettit and Sen' (2004) 20(1) *Economics and Philosophy* 65, 73; List, 'Republican Freedom and the Rule of Law' (n 175) 211.

[178] Gaertner and others (n 176) 174.

[179] List, 'Republican Freedom and the Rule of Law' (n 175) 203–11.

all relevant possible worlds. In enhancing legal certainty that specific dominating conduct is outlawed in all permissible worlds, these presumptions not only ensure that the probability of harmful interference ($P(H)$) is minimised in the actual world ($P(H|w_1)\ P(w_1)$) or in a nearby neighbouring world ($P(H|w_1)\ P(w_1) + P(H|w_2)\ P(w_2)$)[180] but across all relevant possible worlds ($P(H|w_1)\ P(w_1) + \cdots + P(H|w_k)\ P(w_k)$) irrespective of the friendly or unfriendly disposition of powerful market participants.[181] Rule-like legal presumptions indeed bring about a situation where the market participants' preferences become content- and context-independently decisive. Under these circumstances, the following condition holds true: $\Box((aP_ib \rightarrow aPb) \wedge (bP_ia \rightarrow bPa))$ where $\Box$ reads as *'it is necessary that'*, $\rightarrow$ as *'if … then'* and $\wedge$ as *'and'*. Accordingly, rule-like presumptions ensure for all (relevant) possible worlds ($\Box$) that if individual i prefers a over b (aP_ib), then society also prefers a over b (aPb); and, conversely, where individual i prefers b over a (bP_ia), then society will give b preference over a (bPa). The protection of right sets through rule-like presumptions consequently goes beyond context-dependent forms of negative liberty which merely presuppose that $\Diamond((aP_ib \rightarrow aPb) \wedge (bP_ia \rightarrow bPa))$ because the individual's preferences are decisive in the actual ($aP_ib \rightarrow aPb$) (Hobbesian conception of negative liberty) or actual and nearby likely world ($aP_ib \rightarrow aPb) \wedge (bP_ia \rightarrow bPa$) (Berlinian conception of negative liberty).

The broadly construed rule-like presumptions thus guarantee a resilient protection of the republican liberty of other weaker market players as they vest them with legally enforceable guarantees that their liberty is protected, irrespective of the actual contingencies of the situation they find themselves in. At the same time, they also empower market participants against power imbalances by providing them with legal defence mechanisms to contest potentially dominating conduct by dominant firms.[182] In removing strategies whereby powerful players can impose their interests on the other market players from the set of admissible strategies, legal presumptions minimise situations of domination where it is possible ($\Diamond$) across various relevant worlds that individual i's preferences (aP_ib and bP_ia) are not satisfied by social choices ($\neg\, aPb$ or $\neg\, bPa$): $\Diamond((aP_ib \wedge \neg\, aPb) \vee (bP_ia \wedge \neg\, bPa))$, where $\Diamond$ reads as *'it is possible'*, $\wedge$ as *'and'*, $\vee$ as *'or'* and $\neg$ as *'not'*.[183]

This commonality of the design of legal commands notwithstanding, there still remain a few subtle differences in the way in which the republican antitrust approaches in the United States and the European Union secured the modally robust form of republican liberty through rule-like presumptions. Under situational structuralism, US antitrust law, for a limited period of time, outlawed the very

180 List, 'The Impossibility of a Paretian Republican?' (n 177) 70–71; Pettit, 'Freedom as Antipower' (n 173) 600.

181 Pettit, *On the People's Terms* (n 169) 67–69.

182 Pettit, *Republicanism: A Theory of Freedom and Government* (n 172) 64, 67–69, 92–95.

183 Pettit, *Republicanism: A Theory of Freedom and Government* (n 172) 64, 73–75, 95, 106–109; Pettit *On the People's Terms* (n 169) 67–69.

existence of excessive concentration as such by creating presumptions against unreasonable monopoly power and mergers bringing about a limited increase in concentration. This situational structuralism secured economic liberty as non-domination by bestowing market participants with an extremely broad right to be economically active without being exposed to any firms with unreasonable market power. Situational presumptions thus eliminate the possibility of domination by seeking to prevent across all permissible worlds the very existence of market players who are powerful enough to impose their individual preferences on other market participants. However, in the United States, situational structuralism against monopoly power remained short-lived and never gained the support of the EU judiciary. Yet, situational structuralism continued to inform presumptions in US and EU merger control that prohibited, albeit to different degrees, the creation of market players with the power to arbitrarily interfere with the preferences of other market participants.

Aside from merger control, US and EU competition law relied primarily on conduct-based presumptions, which endowed market players with more tailored right sets. Instead of giving market players the right not to be exposed to market agents who hold the power to impose their preferences through arbitrary interference, conduct-based presumptions secure their content- and context-independent preference-decisiveness against specific types of dominating conduct that are known to allow powerful individual or coalition of players to arbitrarily impose their interests on others by undermining the polycentric functioning of markets. Only the per se rule under § 1 of the Sherman Act, which was an irrebuttable presumption, outlawed conduct across all relevant possible worlds. The remaining rebuttable presumptions in US and EU competition law provided a slightly less far-reaching modal protection against dominating conduct. They shielded the market participants' content- and context-independent preference-decisiveness across most relevant possible worlds. However, they left open the possibility that they are rebutted in a narrow set of worlds, such as where certain conduct proved non-arbitrary or the protection of context- and content-independent preference-decisiveness turned out to be too costly.

On the whole, for republican antitrust on both sides of the Atlantic, legal presumptions played a fundamental role in preserving a thick republican conception of economic liberty of market participants, which is modally robust and hence less contingent than negative liberty. Rule-like presumptions empowered competitors and consumers much more effectively against arbitrary interference by other firms than rule of reason-like standards. By diminishing the 'precarious contingency' of arbitrary interference,[184] the extensive use of legal presumptions in US and EU competition law ensured a more 'resilient absence of interference'[185] than would have been possible under a broad application of a rule of reason-like standard.

[184] Ibid. 24.
[185] Ibid. 26.

5.3 THE STANDARD OF HARM

A second parameter, alongside presumptions, that rendered US antitrust and EU competition law conducive to the goal of republican liberty as non-domination was the substantive 'standard of harm'.[186] This substantive standard of harm determines the requisite threshold of the plausibility of anticompetitive effects that must be met for a competition authority or court to be able to conclude that certain conduct violates competition law and warrants state intervention.

Republican antitrust law on both sides of the Atlantic relied on a standard of harm that was closely aligned with the republican concern about domination. This standard of harm dovetailed the non-probabilistic logic of republican liberty that is, unlike negative liberty, not merely concerned about actual or the threat of likely interference. Rather, republican liberty perceives the mere capacity of other individuals to engage in arbitrary interference, and hence the sheer possibility of potential harm emanating from the existence of instances of concentrated economic power as a source of unfreedom. Instead of adopting a probabilistic standard of harm in line with negative liberty, the US Supreme Court until the 1970s and the EU judicature until the 2000s relied on a possibilist standard of harm that is consistent with republican liberty because it requires the showing of potential, rather than actual or likely harm, for antitrust intervention to be warranted.[187]

5.3.1 *The Possibilist Standard of Harm in US Antitrust Law*

This possibilist standard of harm, which merely requires the showing of potential anticompetitive effects, for a long time shaped the enforcement of all three branches of US antitrust.

[186] The 'standard of harm' is often also referred to as the (substantive) 'standard of proof' by commentators and, occasionally, also by the EU Courts. See, for instance, D Bailey, 'Standard of Proof in EC Merger Proceedings: A Common Law Perspective' (2003) 40(4) *Common Market Law Review* 845; Beckner and Salop, 'Decision Theory and Antitrust Rules' (n 153) 61–62; Case T-399/16 *CK Telecoms UK Investments v Commission* ECLI:EU:T:2020:217 para. 118; Case C-376/20 P *Commission v CK Telecoms UK Investments* ECLI:EU:C:2023:561 paras. 69–88. However, Andriani Kalintiri contends that the question of the requisite probability of anticompetitive harm pertains to the substantive test rather than the standard of proof. Kalintiri, *Evidence Standards in EU Competition Enforcement* (n 7) 78–81. I use here the notion of 'standard of harm' to ensure conceptual clarity and avoid falling into the pitfall of conflating the standard of proof with the substantive test. For a more detailed discussion of the concept of standard of harm, see E Deutscher, 'Causation and Counterfactual Analysis in Abuse of Dominance Cases: Lessons from the General Court's Qualcomm ruling' *European Competition Journal* (2023) 19(3) 481, 503–06.

[187] For this distinction between possibilist and probabilistic conceptions of republican and negative liberty, see RE Goodin and F Jackson, 'Freedom from Fear' (2007) 35(3) *Philosophy & Public Affairs* 249; P Pettit, 'Freedom and Probability: A Comment on Goodin and Jackson' (2008) 36(2) *Philosophy & Public Affairs* 206.

The US Supreme Court, for instance, repeatedly held that for an agreement to be prohibited by the per se rule under § 1 of the Sherman Act, it does not have to entail any actual or likely interference. Instead, the per se rule was directed against agreements that 'create […] potential power'[188] to adversely affect competition without there being the need to show that it has been exercised in an unreasonable manner.[189] Hence, the per se rule gave effect to a prophylactic approach that prohibits certain agreements irrespective of the likelihood of anticompetitive effects. Indeed, it was deemed sufficient that agreements have a 'tendency'[190] to restrict competition for them to be caught by the prohibition of § 1 of the Sherman Act.

Likewise, the US courts did not require proof of actual or likely anticompetitive effects under § 2 of the Sherman Act. In the *American Tobacco* case, the US Supreme Court observed that no 'proof of exertion of the power to exclude nor proof of actual exclusion of existing or potential competitors' was necessary to sustain a finding of unlawful monopolization.[191] Instead, the Court relied on a standard of harm that merely required the showing of potential harm resulting from the possession and abuse of monopoly power.[192] Based on the incipiency doctrine,[193] the Supreme Court also interpreted the prohibition of exclusive dealing and tying under § 3 of the Clayton Act in line with a possibilist standard of harm that obligated plaintiffs to demonstrate potential rather than actual or likely harm. Consistent with this possibilist standard, it condemned tying and exclusive dealing agreements by dominant firms because they bestowed them with the 'potential power for evil over an industry'.[194] The incipiency doctrine also prompted the Court to apply a similarly unexacting standard to predatory pricing cases. Instead of requiring likely or actual harm to competitors or consumers to be shown, the Supreme Court deemed it sufficient for the price cuts to carry a 'reasonable possibility' to harm competition to run afoul of antitrust rules.[195]

US merger policy also endorsed a similarly unexacting standard of harm that empowered the government to intervene against mergers on the basis of potential – rather than actual or likely – adverse effects arising from the concentration of economic power. The Supreme Court took the view that the use of the words 'may be to substantially lessen competition' in § 7 of the Clayton Act precluded the

[188] *United States v Socony-Vacuum Oil Co.* (n 25) 218; *Fashion Originators' Guild, Inc. v FTC* (n 27) 468.

[189] *United States v Trenton Potteries Co.* (n 21) 397–98.

[190] *Fashion Originators' Guild, Inc. v FTC* (n 27) 468; *Int'l Salt Co. v United States* (n 50) 396; *Klor's, Inc. v Broadway-Hale Stores, Inc.* (n 27) 211.

[191] *American Tobacco Co. v United States* (n 37) 809–10.

[192] *United States v Columbia Steel Co.* 334 U.S. 495 (1948) Justice Douglas, Black, Murphy, Rutledge dissenting, 535–36.

[193] *Standard Fashion Company v Magrane-Houston Company* (n 46) 356; Sullivan, *Antitrust* (n 8) 432.

[194] *Motion Picture Co. v Universal Film Co.* (n 51) 519.

[195] *Utah Pie Co. v Continental Baking Co.* (n 54) 696 fn. 12, 698–702.

challenging of mergers on the basis of merely 'ephemeral possibilities' of anticompetitive harm. At the same time, it made it clear that the wording of § 7 of the Clayton Act did not go as far as requiring the government to demonstrate that a merger resulted in actual or likely anticompetitive effects. Rather, to find a violation of the Act, the merger would have to be shown with reasonable 'probabilities, not certainties' to engender anticompetitive effects.[196]

The Warren Court clearly resisted a purely probabilistic standard of harm that would have required the showing of actual or likely anticompetitive effects. Instead, it emphasised the need to inhibit excessive economic power in its incipiency. On this basis, it noted that § 7 of the Clayton Act was directed against mergers 'that may tend to lessen competition'[197] or create a '*tendency* towards monopoly'.[198] The Court also highlighted the importance of ascertaining the plausibility of anticompetitive effects, not only with respect to the 'probable effects of the merger on the economics of the particular markets affected but also [...] its probable effects upon the economic way of life sought to be preserved by Congress.'[199] Under this standard, government intervention was also warranted against mergers that would frustrate the Congressional intent of preserving a polycentric industry structure and society 'composed of many independent units',[200] irrespective of their actual or likely effects on prices or output.

This broad interpretation of the incipiency doctrine arguably led the Warren Court to support government intervention in mergers with a remote possibility of causing anticompetitive effects. Consequently, the Court extrapolated an overall trend towards concentration, even in mergers that brought about a marginal increase in concentration. It indeed assumed that the clearance of a small merger could trigger a cumulative series of similar small acquisitions. Under a consistent merger policy, these mergers of similar small size would have to be equally approved. Eventually, the cumulative effects of such a wave of multiple small acquisitions would increase industry concentration and would frustrate the Congressional intent to inhibit economic concentration in its incipiency.[201] The prophylactic impetus of the incipiency doctrine prompted the Warren Court to infer potential harm to competition and domination, even in mergers creating merged entities with tiny market shares of about 5 per cent.[202]

[196] *Brown Shoe Co. Inc. v United States* (n 66) 323 and fn. 39; Kaysen and Turner (n 62) 130.
[197] *Brown Shoe Co. Inc. v United States* (n 66) 317, 320, 335, 346, fn. 69. See also *United States v Philadelphia National Bank* (n 56) 367.
[198] Ibid. 367 (emphasis in the original); *FTC v Procter & Gamble* 386 U.S. 568 (1967) Justice Harlan concurring, 589.
[199] *Brown Shoe Co. Inc. v United States* (n 66) 333.
[200] Ibid. 333; *United States v Pabst Brewing Co.* (n 69).
[201] *Brown Shoe Co. Inc. v United States* (n 66) 334, 345–46.
[202] Ibid.

The line drawn by the Court between merely 'possible', 'reasonably probable', and 'certain' anticompetitive effects hence remained a blurry one.[203] Though the Court phrased the requisite standard of harm in probabilistic terms as requiring 'probable' anticompetitive effects,[204] it resisted making the determination of a violation of § 7 Clayton Act subject to a finding that anticompetitive effects were on a 'balance of probabilities' or the 'preponderance of evidence' more likely than not.[205] Instead, the government remained free to enjoin a merger on the basis of a distinct (in contrast to ephemeral) possibility of anticompetitive harm. Until the 1970s, the standard of harm under US merger laws thus resembled what is known as the realistic prospect standard of proof in phase I of the current UK merger control regime. Under this standard, the competition authority has to show that the likelihood of a merger to result in a SLC is greater than fanciful but may fall short of the 'balance of probabilities' standard of 50 per cent.[206] The Warren Court thus adhered to an extremely broad notion of what amounts to a reasonable probability of anticompetitive effects. On several occasions, it blocked mergers based on the mere possibility, rather than probability, that a particular market may 'slowly but inevitably gravitate from a market of small competitors to one dominated by one or a few giants, and competition would thereby destroyed'.[207]

5.3.2 *The Possibilist Standard of Harm in EU Competition Law*

Until the early 2000s, EU Courts also relied on a similarly possibilist standard of harm, whereby antitrust plaintiffs only had to demonstrate potential – rather than actual or likely – anticompetitive harm to support the prima facie finding of a violation of EU competition law.

Under Article 101 (1) TFEU, the Court of Justice repeatedly held that for an agreement to qualify as a by-object restriction, it is sufficient that it 'has the potential to have a negative impact on competition' or 'in other words [is] capable in an individual case [...] of resulting' in a restriction of competition.[208] This 'capability

[203] Ibid. 323 and fn. 39; *FTC v Procter & Gamble* (n 198) Justice Harlan concurring, 584, 586.

[204] *Brown Shoe Co. Inc. v United States* (n 66) 323, 325.

[205] For the difficulties to reconcile the incipiency doctrine with a standard of harm requiring probabilities, rather than mere possibilities, see Kaysen and Turner (n 62) 129–30. Bok also argued that 'reasonable probability' cannot be understood in a statistical sense as requiring the showing that the merger on a balance of probabilities is more likely than not to lead to anticompetitive effects. Bok (n 64) 255–56.

[206] UK Competition and Markets Authority, Merger Assessment Guidelines 2021, CMA 129 para. 2.33; see also 2.31–34.

[207] *United States v Von's Grocery Co.* (n 67) 278.

[208] Case C-8/08 *T-Mobile Netherlands BV and Others* (n 92) para. 31; Opinion of Advocate General Kokott in Case C-226/11 *Expedia* (n 98) para. 49; Case C-32/11 *Allianz Hungária Biztosító and Others* (n 99) para. 38. See in this sense also Case C-189/02 P *Dansk Rørindustri and Others v Commission* ECLI:EU:C:2005:408 para. 143.

standard'[209] of harm establishes a relatively low threshold for an agreement to be caught as a by-object restriction. The Court repeatedly held that the Commission was under no obligation to prove the actual effects of an anticompetitive (by-object) agreement on competition to engage the parties' liability under Article 101 (1) TFEU.[210] Nor was it relevant that those anticompetitive effects were unlikely to materialise, for instance, because the defendant was incapable of implementing the agreement.[211] Accordingly, no analysis of the actual or likely effects of the agreement, for instance, on consumer welfare,[212] was necessary to establish a violation of Article 101 TFEU.

Along similar lines, the classical form-based interpretation of Article 102 TFEU by the EU judicature and Commission condemned certain forms of dominant firm conduct because of their mere capacity to bring about anticompetitive harm. Accordingly, intervention under Article 102 TFEU was justified before unilateral conduct reached the stage where it constituted an actual or a concrete threat of likely interference with the actions and choices of competitors and consumers.[213] Under this 'minimalist'[214] standard of harm, the EU Courts consistently held that for dominant firm conduct to violate Article 102 TFEU, it is sufficient that it has the tendency ('tends to')[215] or capacity ('is capable of')[216] to foreclose competitors. Like under Article 101 TFEU, this capability standard of harm focuses on the potential[217] rather than actual or likely effects of the impugned conduct. The finding of an abuse of dominance was not predicated on any proof of actual anticompetitive effects, for instance in terms of price increases.[218] By way of example, in *Michelin II*, evidence that prices and the market share of the dominant firm fell during the alleged period of abuse did not prevent the Commission and the Court of First Instance from

[209] Colomo and Lamadrid de Pablo (n 4) 361–63.

[210] Case C-189/02 P *Dansk Rørindustri and Others v Commission* (n 208) para. 145.

[211] Ibid. paras. 144–46; Case C-238/99 P *Limburgse Vinyl Maatschappij and Others v Commission* ECLI:EU:C:2002:582 paras. 508–10.

[212] Case C-8/08 *T-Mobile Netherlands BV and Others* (n 92) paras. 29–30, 38; Opinion of Advocate General Kokott in Case C-8/08 *T-Mobile Netherlands BV and Others* (n 97) paras. 58, 60; Case C-501/06 P *GlaxoSmithKline Services and Others v Commission and Others* (n 105) para. 63.

[213] For this standard of harm requiring potential harm in tying cases, see Case No IV/31043 *Tetra Pak II*, [1992] OJ L 72/1 paras. 105, 117, 120; Case T-201/04 *Microsoft Corp v Commission* ECLI:EU:T:2007:289 857, 867. For a similar standard of harm in exclusive dealing and loyalty rebates cases, see Case 85/76 *Hoffmann-La Roche v Commission* (n 119) paras. 90, 127. For a similar standard of harm in predatory pricing cases, see Case C-62/86 *AKZO v Commission* (n 119) para. 72.

[214] Kallaugher and Sher (n 121) 263.

[215] See, for instance, Case 85/76 *Hoffmann-La Roche v Commission* (n 119) para. 90; Case 322/81 *Michelin v Commission (Michelin I)* (n 119) paras. 73, 81.

[216] Case 85/76 *Hoffmann-La Roche v Commission* (n 119) para. 127; Case C-62/86 *AKZO v Commission* (n 119) para. 72; Case C-95/04 P *British Airways plc v Commission of the European Communities* (n 119) paras. 68, 77.

[217] Gyselen (n 135) 293–94; Kallaugher and Sher (n 121) 264.

[218] Case C-95/04 P *British Airways plc v Commission of the European Communities* (n 120) para. 106.

concluding that Michelin's loyalty-enhancing rebates amounted to an abuse of a dominant position. On the contrary, they observed that the fact the result sought by the rebate scheme had not been achieved is irrelevant to their assessment under Article 102 TFEU.[219]

Under the form-based dominance test, EU merger policy was equally anchored in a possibilist standard of harm that required the showing of potential instead of actual or likely effects on competition. The early merger case law by the EU Courts identified the finding of dominance as the essential legal benchmark to determine the legality of a merger. Once the definition of the relevant market and the analysis of the market shares indicated the creation or absence of dominance, the Commission was under an obligation to prohibit or clear the merger without any further inquiry into its actual effects on competition.[220] The standard of harm adopted by the EU Courts and the Commission thus clearly fell short of requiring the showing that the merger was likely to lead to anticompetitive effects (e.g., in the form of higher prices or lower output). The prohibition of a merger could instead be sustained by the finding of potential harm that might ensue from the creation of a dominant position.

Yet, the EU Courts adopted a much narrower understanding of when a merger is capable of harming competition than did the Warren Court under the incipiency doctrine. As it further expanded the situations where a merger is capable of harming competition from single firm dominance to situations of collective dominance, the EU judicature also incrementally tightened the standard of harm. The Court held in *Kali und Salz* that the Commission has to support the finding of collective dominance by 'a sufficiently cogent and consistent body of evidence',[221] which demonstrates 'to a sufficient degree of probability'[222] that the merger will lead to anticompetitive effects. It even went a step further by referring to the likelihood of anticompetitive effects.[223]

By adopting a more demanding standard for the finding of collective dominance, the Court clarified that a finding of collective dominance could not be based on the analysis of market shares alone.[224] However, despite this apparent tightening of the standard of harm in collective dominance cases, the analysis of collective dominance in the early case law remained largely confined to an assessment of structural market characteristics to determine the extent to which the merger will lead to an

[219] Case T-203/01 *Michelin v Commission (Michelin II)* (n 119) para. 245.

[220] Case T-2/93 *Air France v Commission* (n 143) paras. 79–80; Case T-290/94 *Kaysersberg v Commission* (n 143) paras. 170–84.

[221] Case C-68/94 *France and Société commerciale des potasses et de l'azote and Entreprise minière et chimique v Commission* (n 148) para. 228.

[222] Ibid. para. 246.

[223] Ibid. paras. 170, 219; Case T-102/96 *Gencor v Commission* (n 145) para. 222.

[224] Case C-68/94 *France and Société commerciale des potasses and de l'azote and Entreprise minière et chimique v Commission* (n 148) para. 226; Case T-102/96 *Gencor v Commission* (n 145) para. 206.

oligopolistic market structure that is conducive to tacit collusion or conscious parallelism.[225] In contrast, the Commission and Courts attributed little weight to the assessment of behavioural factors and incentives, which would suggest that the collectively dominant firms were likely to abuse their collective market power and tacitly collude post-merger.[226] Accordingly, although the Courts referred to the likelihood of anticompetitive effects as a precondition for the finding of collective dominance, in effect, mergers could be blocked on the basis of the potential harm ensuing from the creation of a collective dominant position, without any further analysis of whether the merging and non-merging parties were likely to exert their collective market power by raising prices or decreasing output in parallel. In no instance, however, did the EU Courts or Commission go as far as their US counterparts during the Warren Court era in condemning mergers that had only a remote probability of harming competition based on the conjecture that the clearance of a number of small mergers would cumulatively undermine an effectively competitive market structure.

5.3.3 *The Possibilist Standard of Harm and Republican Liberty*

The possibilist standard of harm that mandates antitrust intervention based on the proof of potential or reasonably probable rather than actual or likely harm was a hallmark of US antitrust policy until the 1970s and EU competition policy until the 2000s. This possibilist standard of harm constituted a second policy variable that rendered US and EU competition law conducive towards the realisation of a republican understanding of liberty. Unlike an approach grounded in negative liberty, this possibilist standard of harm did not exclusively focus on the probability of interference of impugned conduct but also took into consideration the magnitude of potential harm that certain forms of collusion, unilateral conduct, and mergers may entail. It thus encoded a balance-of-harm approach that justified the prohibition of certain types of conduct on the basis of their potentially substantial harm to competition, regardless of the concrete likelihood of this harm to eventuate.

This balance-of-harm standard can also be formalised. Unlike an approach grounded in negative liberty, this possibilist balance-of-harm standard did not require it to be shown that the impugned conduct is, on a balance of probabilities, more likely to give rise to anticompetitive conduct than not. This would be the case if the posterior probability of H given evidence e slightly exceeds 50 per cent so that

[225] Case T-102/96 *Gencor v Commission* (n 145) para. 276. See also G Monti, 'The Scope of Collective Dominance under Articles 82 EC' (2001) 38(1) *Common Market Law Review* 131, 134–35.

[226] For the relevant factors, see Case C-68/94 *France and Société commerciale des potasses et de l'azote and Entreprise minière et chimique v Commission* (n 148) paras. 221–50; Case T-102/96 *Gencor v Commission* (n 145) paras. 206–96.

$P(H|e) > 0.5$ or the odds ratio of posterior probabilities $\frac{P(H|e)}{P(B|e)} > 1$. Rather, the republican approach took into account the magnitude of the benefits (gains G) and costs (losses *L*) of preventing or not preventing potential harm that certain forms of collusion, unilateral conduct, and mergers may entail. Under this balance-of-harm approach, antitrust intervention was warranted as soon as the posterior probability of conduct resulting in harm multiplied by the costs (i.e., gains G of intervention) of not preventing that harm $(P(H|e) \times G)$ exceeded the posterior probability of the conduct being benign multiplied by the costs (i.e., losses L of intervention) resulting from its erroneous prohibition $(P(B|e) \times L)$, that is, $P(H|e) \times G > P(B|e) \times L$. If expressed as an odds ratio, then republican antitrust mandated antitrust intervention whenever the odds ratio of posterior probabilities exceeded the cost-benefit ratio $\left(\frac{L}{G}\right)$ of antitrust intervention $\frac{P(H|e)}{P(B|e)} > \frac{L}{G}$.

While the modern probabilistic balance of probabilities standard of harm $\frac{P(H|e)}{P(B|e)} > 1$ focuses exclusively on the probabilities of conduct resulting in anticompetitive effects, the possibilist balance-of-harm standard $\left(\frac{P(H|e)}{P(B|e)} > \frac{L}{G}\right)$ is primarily concerned with the relative magnitude of harm that might result from specific conduct. This possibilist standard of harm attributed more weight to the magnitude of potential harm that specific types of conduct might cause across various possible worlds than to the actual probability of that harm to materialise in the actual case. It thus also enabled the application of competition law in cases where anticompetitive harm can be considered to be a low-probability-but-high-impact event. Like the extensive reliance on rule-like presumptions, this standard of harm was essential for republican antitrust to ensure a 'probabilistically unweighted'[227] or at least a probabilistically de-weighted protection of market participants against arbitrary interference, which is in keeping with the thick and resilient understanding of republican liberty.

The possibilist standard of harm thus also contributed to a modally robust protection of a broad range of an individual market agent's relevant actions (z), by minimising the probability of harm $(P(H))$ not only in the actual $(P(H|w_1)\ P(w_1))$ or nearby likely $(P(H|w_1)\ P(w_1) + P(H|w_2)\ P(w_2))$ but across all relevant possible worlds $(P(H|w_1)\ P(w_1) + \cdots + P(H|w_k)\ P(w_k))$. It guarantees the modally robust content- and context-independent decisiveness of individual market players' preferences by enabling antitrust law to intervene not only in situations where $\Diamond((aP_ib \wedge \neg\, aPb) \vee (bP_ia \wedge \neg\, bPa))$ may materialise with a probability of more than 50 per cent because another player actually or likely interferes with their choices. Rather, the possibilist standard of harm mandates antitrust intervention against anticompetitive conduct

[227] Pettit, 'Freedom in the Market' (n 5) 137.

that may lead to interference in a counterfactual world other than the nearby likely world, where $\Diamond((aP_ib \wedge \neg aPb) \vee (bP_ia \wedge \neg bPa))$ may materialise, without that possibility reaching a probability of 50 per cent, so that it is more likely than another outcome. The possibilist standard of harm thus crucially ensures that $\Box((aP_ib \rightarrow aPb) \wedge (bP_ia \rightarrow bPa))$ holds true across all relevant possible worlds.

5.4 THE PRECAUTIONARY ERROR–COST FRAMEWORK

The third policy variable that made US and EU antitrust law more amenable towards a republican ideal of economic liberty was a specific understanding of the costs and benefits of antitrust intervention. This error–cost framework expressed a clear preference for false positives (i.e., type I errors). It hence erred in the case of doubt on the side of over-enforcement and condoned the sacrifice of efficiencies to prevent anticompetitive harm. This precautionary logic, which slanted the error–cost framework in favour of preventive state intervention, was informed by economic and political considerations which shaped a balance of rights that is firmly in line with the logic of republican liberty.

5.4.1 A *Taxonomy of Error–Cost Frameworks*

To illustrate this point, let us start by considering the potential costs and benefits that may arise from antitrust enforcement. In the abstract language of decision theory, factfinders in competition proceedings are confronted with the basic task of testing the plausibility of two hypotheses: either the hypothesis ($H1$) that the impugned conduct is harmful or the null hypothesis ($H0$) that the conduct is innocuous (i.e., pro-competitive or competitively neutral) is true. If $H1$ is correct, then antitrust intervention generates benefits (gains G) in terms of averted or remedied anticompetitive harm. If $H0$ is true, then antitrust intervention creates costs (losses L) in terms of mistakenly prohibited and deterred pro-competitive conduct. As competition authorities and courts decide antitrust cases under imperfect information, errors are inevitable.[228] These errors can take the form of false positives (type I errors) when the factfinder mistakenly accepts $H1$, while $H0$ is true. The type I error rate α describes the share of decisions in which $H1$ is accepted, while $H0$ is true. Conversely, $(1 - \alpha)$ determines the specificity of the factfinder's testing; that is, the frequency at which the factfinder correctly accepts $H0$ and finds true negatives. Errors can also take the form of false negatives (type II errors) if the factfinder mistakenly accepts $H0$, although $H1$ is true. The type II error rate β describes the share of decisions in which such false negatives arise. Meanwhile, $(1 - \beta)$ determines the

[228] Beckner and Salop, 'Decision Theory and Antitrust Rules' (n 153) 43.

TABLE 5.1 *Outcomes of antitrust intervention and stylised pay-offs*

	$H1$ is true	$H0$ is true
Intervention	True positives $(1 - \beta)G$	False positives αL
Non-intervention	False negatives βG	True negatives $(1 - \alpha)L$

sensitivity of the factfinder's testing, that is the frequency at which the factfinder correctly accepts $H1$ and finds true positives.[229]

Table 5.1 provides an overview of these four potential outcomes of antitrust investigations and their stylised pay-offs. In the case of false positives, antitrust intervention generates losses (αL). At the same time, in producing true positives, antitrust intervention also brings about accuracy benefits ($(1 - \beta)$ G).[230] Similarly, non-intervention will entail losses resulting from false negatives (βG) and accuracy benefits in the form of true negatives ($(1 - \alpha)L$).

This discussion of error-costs provides us with a taxonomy of three different types of error–cost frameworks that shape how competition law regimes strike a balance between the benefits and costs of competition law enforcement. An antitrust regime based on a neutral error–cost framework operates on the assumption that the costs and benefits of intervention equal each other ($G = L$). In contrast, a regime that grounds in a laissez-faire error–cost framework rests on the assumption that the losses of state intervention outweigh its benefits ($L > G$). Finally, a precautionary error–cost framework is predicated on the assumption that the benefits of competition law intervention outweigh its costs ($G > L$).

The importance that the republican antitrust tradition on both sides of the Atlantic placed on broadly construed legal presumptions and a relatively unexacting possibilist standard of harm meant that it clearly fell into the latter category of being built on an interventionist precautionary error–cost framework. The US and European iterations of republican antitrust were grounded in the assumption that the benefits (G) of broadly prohibiting certain forms of agreements, unilateral conduct, or mergers exceed the costs (L) caused by the application of inherently over-inclusive legal presumptions that might give rise to false positives (type I errors) by catching

229 This discussion draws on Christiansen and Kerber (n 157) 225–29; MM Burtis, JB Gelbach, and BH Kobayashi, 'Error Costs, Legal Standards of Proof, and Statistical Significance' (2017) 25(1) *Supreme Court Economic Review* 1, 10–11.

230 For sake of linguistic clarity, the following discussion uses the terms 'accuracy benefits of intervention' to refer to the benefits of true positives and 'accuracy benefits of non-intervention' to describe the benefits of true negatives. For the notion of 'accuracy benefits', see H First and S Weber Waller, 'Antitrust's Democracy Deficit' (2013) 81(5) *Fordham Law Review* 2543, 2570–72.

innocuous conduct.[231] In increasing the sensitivity of antitrust policy and facilitating intervention, the broadly construed presumptions and unexacting possibilist standard of harm of republican antitrust reduced the frequency of false negatives (β) relative to a more differentiated and searching antitrust analysis. At the same time, owing to their over-inclusive nature, the broad application of presumptions and the unexacting standard of harm reduce the specificity of antitrust policy, and hence increase the frequency of false positives (α). In condoning a more frequent occurrence of false positives ($\alpha > \beta$), US antitrust and EU competition law during the republican era reflected the implicit value judgment that the benefits ($(1 - \beta)G$) of categorically outlawing certain forms of conduct exceed the costs of potential over-enforcement, and hence false positives (αL). In other words, the accuracy benefits flowing from the true positives generated through the deterrence or remedying of anticompetitive conduct secured by broadly construed presumptions and a low standard of harm were thought to dominate the accuracy benefits ($(1 - \alpha)L$) deriving from the true negatives of non-intervention secured by a more differentiated and careful rule of reason-type analysis, which would reduce those type I errors by screening out and insulating pro-competitive conduct from antitrust liability based on a case-by-case analysis; that is, $(1 - \beta)G > (1 - \alpha)L$.

Overall, the way in which the republican approach conceived legal presumptions and designed the requisite standard of harm reflected an implied preference for over-enforcement (type I errors) over under-enforcement (type II errors). This skewed precautionary error–cost framework of the republican antitrust approach gave expression to the assumption that '[i]t would be more in keeping with the spirit of the Sherman Act to give the benefits of any doubts to the struggling competitors.'[232] The republican antitrust tradition thus relied on an error–cost framework that, in the case of doubt, tipped the balance of rights towards state interference to protect the rights of competitors and consumers.

5.4.2 *The Economic Assumptions Underpinning the Republican Error–Cost Framework*

There are several economic and political reasons that can explain this precautionary error–cost framework that characterised US antitrust law until the 1970s and EU competition law until the early-2000s. In terms of economic assumptions, the broad application of legal presumptions was informed by economic theory that broadly associated economic concentration with reduced economic performance and classified a wide population of business conduct as potentially anticompetitive. Republican antitrust on both sides of the Atlantic was also confident in the ability of administrative and judicial institutions to accurately identify anticompetitive

[231] *Northern Pac. Ry. Co. v United States* (n 24) 5; *United States v Topco Assocs. Inc.* (n 26) 607.
[232] *United States v Columbia Steel Co.* (n 192) 539.

conduct. The prevailing economic theory of the time thus assumed the likelihood of erroneous intervention (α) to be low, while lending support to an approach that reduces the likelihood of erroneous non-intervention (β). The proposition that the benefits of robust antitrust enforcement outweigh its costs was further corroborated by the belief that markets were unlikely to self-correct false negatives. Accordingly, the foregone accuracy benefits (G) of antitrust enforcement – in the form of deterred or remedied antitrust harm – that result from erroneous non-intervention were largely assumed to be lost forever, while antitrust harm was assumed to stay for a long time, if not forever, uncorrected. For this reason, the prevailing economic and legal theory of the time assumed that for a broadly construed category of anticompetitive conduct, state interference is more beneficial than leaving the remediation of (undetected) anticompetitive effects to self-correcting market forces. The precautionary error–cost framework clearly accounted for the fragility of markets and harboured doubts about their capacity to remedy anticompetitive behaviour that has gone undetected by antitrust enforcement (under a more differentiated rule of reason analysis).[233]

This preference for type I errors tallied nicely with the views about the costs and benefits of antitrust intervention that were held by the Harvard and Ordoliberal Schools. Both schools of thought suggested that the benefits of robust antitrust intervention exceeded its costs because it normally does not chill efficient business conduct.[234] In other words, both paradigms assumed that the costs of false positives (L) are low because lost gains from efficient mergers, unilateral, or coordinated conduct could easily be replicated by independent behaviour, smaller firms, or organic growth. This assumption about the low costs of false positives hinged on the belief that economic concentration and monopoly are a source of economic inefficiencies rather than the breeding ground of superior economic performance, progress, and innovation,[235] while small and inventive businesses were viewed as drivers of efficiency, innovation, and progress.[236] This view explains why for quite some time both the US and the EU enforcers and courts approached efficiency claims in merger proceedings with scepticism and were prepared to accept the sacrifice of merger-induced efficiencies as a price for the preservation of a deconcentrated market structure.[237]

233 P Larouche and MP Schinkel, 'Continental Drift in the Treatment of Dominant Firms: Article 102 TFEU in Contrast to § 2 Sherman Act' (TILEC Discussion Paper No 2013-02, Tilburg 2013) 11.

234 Kaysen and Turner, *Antitrust Policy* (n 62) 6, 10–11. See also Larouche and Schinkel (n 233) 11.

235 *United States v Columbia Steel Co.* (n 192) Justice Douglas, Black, Murphy, Rutledge dissenting, 534–35 fn. 1.

236 See, for instance, Temporary National Economic Committee, 'Relative Efficiency of Large, Medium-Sized, and Small Business' (1941). TNEC Monograph 13.

237 *Brown Shoe Co. Inc. v United States* (n 66) 344–45 and fn. 72; Case No IV/M.053 *Aerospatiale-Alenia/de Havilland* (n 152) paras. 69–71. See also Kaysen and Turner, *Antitrust Policy* (n 62)

5.4.3 *The Republican Balancing of Rights Underpinning the Precautionary Error–Cost Framework*

Apart from economic considerations, the precautionary error–cost framework was also clearly animated by the republican attitude towards state interference and the underlying calculus of the balancing of rights. The value of republican liberty shaped this error–cost framework in a number of ways. First, the precautionary error–cost framework encoded the assumption that the costs in terms of losses in liberty (understood as non-domination) due to erroneous non-intervention of antitrust law, and hence the accuracy benefits of antitrust enforcement (G), are high. This assumption was the immediate consequence of the thick understanding of republican liberty. What distinguishes republican liberty from negative liberty is the belief that liberty is not only jeopardised if an anticompetitive agreement, unilateral conduct, or merger brings about an actual or likely interference with the economic choices and actions of other market participants. Rather, from the perspective of republican liberty, the potential interference resulting from the mere existence of individual or collective monopoly power is sufficient to undermine the liberty of all market participants. On a republican account, the evil of domination is much bigger than the evil of interference because it is not confined to an isolated incidence of interference but continues to undermine liberty as long as the option to arbitrarily interfere remains available for powerful firms.[238] As a consequence, the magnitude of the potential harm of business conduct that tampers with a polycentric market structure and increases economic concentration is far greater from a republican vantage point than it is from the perspective of the thin, negative conception of liberty, which only perceives conduct that leads to actual or likely interference as an obstruction of liberty. It follows from this that for proponents of republican liberty as non-domination the costs of type II errors are much higher than for proponents of a negative concept of liberty.

From the vantage point of republican liberty, the costs of type II errors and accuracy benefits (G) of antitrust enforcement are further amplified by the fact that the multifaceted harm flowing from domination caused by an increased concentration of economic power is not strictly confined to the realm of the market or limited to welfare losses. Rather, increased concentration of economic power raises the spectre of a decrease in the ability of polycentric competition to impose constraints on the ability of powerful firms to exert domination. A higher level of industry concentration may also lead to a reduction in consumer choice[239] and the elimination of small business people as pillars of a republican society. Most

82–85; FM Scherer and D Ross, *Industrial Market Structure and Economic Performance* (Boston: Houghton Mifflin 1990) 159–74.

[238] See in this respect Pettit, 'Freedom in the Market' (n 5) 145.

[239] *United States v Philadelphia National Bank* (n 56) 367.

importantly, given the close link between economic liberty as non-domination and a republican society and polity, the harm of erroneous non-intervention may even eventually undermine democracy itself. The republican error–cost framework therefore gives considerable weight to type II errors. This also explains the limited role of efficiency considerations for republican antitrust. As the potential harm of type II errors (G) goes beyond welfare losses, it is rather unlikely to be outweighed by any efficiency gains that are achieved through the reduction of the costs of over-enforcement (*L*) (e.g., through a rule of reason analysis or a relatively low threshold for rebutting a presumption of illegality). Under the republican approach, the expected magnitude of harm and potential costs of erroneous non-intervention clearly tipped the scales in favour of the illegality of certain forms of agreements, dominant firm conduct, or forms of economic concentration.[240]

On a republican account, not only the losses of non-intervention but also the gains of state intervention are considerably higher than from the perspective of a thin, negative understanding of liberty as non-interference.[241] Republicans assume that state intervention not only advances liberty by preventing or remedying the isolated incidence of interference (e.g., by cartelists or a monopolist) with the negative liberty of other market participants but also enhances liberty in reducing the overall level of domination prevailing in the market. Through an extensive use of rule-like presumptions and a possibilist standard of harm, republican antitrust law makes firms' access to certain forms of dominating conduct unavailable or very costly. It also diminishes the concentration of economic power, for instance, by ensuring that residual competition in the middle to long run erodes the economic power of the dominant firm. Both channels enable republican antitrust to reduce the access of powerful firms to resources of domination and enhance the protective function of polycentric competition as an institution of antipower that shields market participants also against future domination. Consequently, state intervention averts harm of a much higher magnitude than from the perspective of negative liberty.[242] These benefits of antitrust intervention (G) are further amplified because the positive effects of guarding economic liberty against domination are not limited to the economic sphere. Given the importance of republican liberty for a republican and democratic society and polity, antitrust intervention generates positive externalities in the societal and political sphere. In contrast, on a mainstream liberal account, the gains of state intervention are limited to the prevention of a (isolated instance of) loss of liberty that would otherwise be caused by actual or expected interference. For this reason, from the perspective of republican liberty, the gains of antitrust intervention clearly exceed the benefits proponents of negative liberty associate with state interference.

240 RH Bork, *The Antitrust Paradox: A Policy at War with Itself* [1978] (New York: Maxwell Macmillan 1993) 210.

241 This argument draws on Pettit, 'Freedom in the Market' (n 5) 145–46.

242 Ibid. 146; *United States v Joint Traffic Ass'n* (n 11) 572.

Not only do republican liberals assume the costs of non-intervention and the benefits from state intervention to be higher than mainstream liberals but they also argue that the costs (L) of state intervention are much lower than mainstream liberals like to claim.[243] Unlike proponents of negative liberty,[244] the republican tradition did not automatically consider laws and state interference as an invasion of liberty. Instead, we have seen that the republican tradition assumes that non-arbitrary state interference, unlike private interference,[245] does not necessarily undermine liberty, even if it restricts individuals' economic autonomy.[246] This explains why the republican approach conceived antitrust intervention not as an antonym but rather as a safeguard of liberty as non-domination, although it interferes with the contractual freedom and right to property of businesses.[247] In reducing or even defining away losses of liberty resulting from state intervention, this understanding of non-arbitrary state interference further pulls the scales of the precautionary error–cost framework towards type I errors. It also assumes that the occurrence of harmful erroneous state intervention is low because public institutions are less likely than self-interested private players to engage in arbitrary interference. Therefore, from a republican perspective, the benefits (G) of state interference are not only much higher than mainstream liberals tend to assume but the losses (L) of liberty due to a broad application of competition law and state interference are also much lower and less likely (α) than from the perspective of negative liberty.[248]

This republican balance of rights approach underpinning the precautionary error–cost framework thus clearly differed from the balancing of rights cultivated by proponents of negative liberty. For proponents of negative liberty, any kind of state intervention leads to a reduction of the economic liberty of the members of a cartel, a dominant firm, or merging parties. Therefore, state intervention is only permissible if this reduction of liberty is outweighed by the gains of liberty of other market players resulting from the prevention of interference through state intervention.[249] State intervention thus requires a balancing of rights which shows that the anticompetitive conduct interferes with the liberty of other market participants in an unreasonable way that exceeds a certain proportionality threshold. The limitation of liberty on the part of parties of an agreement, a dominant firm, or merging parties by means of antitrust intervention can only be justified if this is the case. Under this balancing of rights calculus, state intervention is only permissible if the harm ensuing from the reduction of liberty of other market participants as a consequence of the restraint of competition at issue outweighs the reduction of liberty caused by

[243] Pettit, *Republicanism: A Theory of Freedom and Government* (n 172) 35–41.
[244] Ibid. 37–39.
[245] Pettit, 'Freedom in the Market' (n 5) 146.
[246] Pettit, 'Freedom as Antipower' (n 173) 586, 597; Pettit, 'Freedom in the Market' (n 5) 135.
[247] *Northern Securities Co. v United States* (n 11) 331.
[248] Pettit, 'Freedom in the Market' (n 5) 146.
[249] Ibid. 145.

the state interference with the defendants' economic liberty. Consequently, it requires some form of utilitarian balancing of the costs and benefits of government and private interference. Antitrust intervention is only justified when the costs of private interference are unreasonably high because they harm social welfare.

The ideal of republican liberty as non-domination of republican antitrust on both sides of the Atlantic shaped an error–cost framework and balancing of rights that expressed a clear preference in favour of preventative state intervention, which primarily aims at reducing anticompetitive harm and hence reducing the occurrence (β) and costs (G) of under-enforcement (type II errors). Republican antitrust law operated on the assumption that the costs of type II errors ((β)G) by far exceed those of type I errors ((α)L). Conversely, they were confident that the accuracy benefits of preventative antitrust enforcement outweighed the benefits of a less robust and light-touch approach ($(1-\beta)G > (1-\alpha)L$).

The balancing of rights underpinning this error–cost framework was, on the one hand, informed by the economic assumption that competitive markets are not always self-correcting and that industry concentration and firm size are often a source of low economic performance rather than of efficiencies. On the other hand, this bias in the error–cost framework is testament to an (implicit) normative commitment to a thick concept of republican liberty as non-domination. From the republican perspective, non-arbitrary state interference does not automatically lead to a reduction of liberty, and therefore the costs of state intervention are relatively low. In contrast, because the adverse effects of domination resulting from concentrated economic power go beyond economic welfare losses but may even have adverse repercussions on a republican or democratic polity, the costs of non-intervention are much higher than potential efficiency savings. This explains why the republican approach likened potential losses of productive and dynamic efficiency caused by robust antitrust intervention and the deconcentration of economic power to the inefficiencies and 'wastes' of democracy, whose benefits nonetheless outweigh the efficiencies of absolutism.[250]

5.5 CONCLUSION

This chapter has further described how the ideal of republican liberty has been operationalised through concrete competition policy. By analysing the application of US antitrust and EU competition law rules to coordinated conduct, dominant firm conduct, and mergers, it has been able to identify the three principal policy levers that made antitrust on both sides of the Atlantic particularly receptive to the value of republican liberty and facilitated its operationalisation through the

[250] *United States v Columbia Steel Co.* (n 192) Justice Douglas, Black, Murphy, Rutledge dissenting, 534–35 fn. 1; Böhm, 'Democracy and Economic Power in Cartel and Monopoly in Modern Law [1961]' in DA Crane and H Hovenkamp (eds), The Making of Competition Policy: Legal and Economic Sources (New York: Oxford University Press 2013) 264, 271.

protection of a polycentric market structure (as discussed in the previous chapter). In implementing the overarching policy goal of structuralism as the target variable, rule-like structural presumptions of anticompetitiveness, a possibilist standard of harm, as well as an error–cost framework that was consistently slanted in favour of state intervention constituted the key policy levers of the republican antitrust tradition in the United States and the European Union. All four parameters played a crucial role in giving shape to the key marks of a republican notion of economic liberty. Table 5.2 summarises how these four parameters concretised the specific attributes of republican liberty through competition policy.

Rule-like structural presumptions gave effect to a broad notion of preventing conditions (y) that perceives not only interference but also domination as an obstacle to liberty. Moreover, because they were not conditioned on the efficiency of the protected economic agents, rule-like presumptions were also able to secure an egalitarian understanding of economic liberty comprising a broad range of agents (x). The modal character of rule-like presumptions, the possibilist standard of harm, and the intervention-friendly precautionary error–cost framework also gave shape to a modal understanding of restricted actions (z) that covers not only the actual or nearby likely but all relevant possible worlds. The precautionary error–cost framework was also an expression of the republican assumption that the harm resulting from anticompetitive market outcomes is not confined to the economic but may also adversely affect the political sphere by undermining the economic prerequisites of republican democracy. At the same time, this intervention-friendly error–cost framework also reflected the republican view that non-arbitrary state intervention does not automatically entail a reduction in liberty. The precautionary error–cost framework and the rule-like presumptions thus also concretised the rule of law commitment of republican liberty, which understands rules as being constitutive of, rather than antithetical to, liberty. In giving shape to the overarching policy goal of structuralism, the rule-like structural presumptions played a crucial role in securing polycentric competition as an institution of antipower.

The overarching policy goal of structuralism and the specific design of all three policy levers thus enabled republican antitrust on both sides of the Atlantic to preserve a robust and resilient form of economic liberty as non-domination that protects market participants against not only actual or likely but also potential arbitrary interference. The combined effect of the structuralist policy goal and all three levers gave shape to a modus operandi of antitrust decision-making which ensured that competition law, in the case of doubt, tended to err in favour of reducing instances of economic concentration, and eventually protecting democracy, even if this involved efficiency costs and state interference with the negative entrepreneurial liberty.

All four parameters (i.e., the structural approach, the reliance on legal presumptions, a possibilist standard of harm, and a precautionary error–cost framework) constitute the four main components of a distinctive republican

TABLE 5.2 *The attributes of republican liberty and its operationalisation by republican antitrust*

	Attributes of republican liberty	Variables operationalising the republican conception of liberty
Type of agents (x)	In-built commitment towards egalitarianism	• Structuralism • Rule-like presumptions as trump cards for weaker market participants
Type of preventing conditions (y)	Domination (arbitrary interference)	• Structuralism • Modal character of rule-like presumptions • Possibilist standard of harm $\frac{P(H\|e)}{P(B\|e)} > \frac{L}{G}$ • Precautionary error–cost framework $((1-\beta)G) > \alpha L)$
Range of restricted actions (z)	Preference-decisiveness across all (relevant) possible friendly and unfriendly worlds $\Box((aP_ib \rightarrow aPb) \wedge (bP_ia \rightarrow bPa))$ (minimisation of $P(H\|w_1)\ P(w_1) + \cdots + P(H\|w_k)\ P(w_k)$)	• Rule-like presumptions guaranteeing modally robust right sets $O((aP_ib \rightarrow aPb) \wedge (bP_ia \rightarrow bPa)$ so that $\Box((aP_ib \rightarrow aPb) \wedge (bP_ia \rightarrow bPa))$ • Possibilist standard of harm $\frac{P(H\|e)}{P(B\|e)} > \frac{L}{G}$ • Precautionary error–cost framework $((1-\beta)\ G) > \alpha L)$
Form of polity	Republican democracy	• Precautionary error–cost framework $((1-\beta)G) > \alpha L)$
State interference	No reduction of liberty if non-arbitrary	• Precautionary error–cost framework $((1-\beta)G) > \alpha L)$
Attitude towards legal rules	Legal rules as modally robust normative desiderata $O((aP_ib \rightarrow aPb) \wedge (bP_ia \rightarrow bPa)$	• Rule-like presumptions guaranteeing modally robust right sets $O((aP_ib \rightarrow aPb) \wedge (bP_ia \rightarrow bPa)$ so that $\Box((aP_ib \rightarrow aPb) \wedge (bP_ia \rightarrow bPa))$ • Precautionary error–cost framework $((1-\beta)G) > \alpha L)$
Institutions	Constitutional rights; rule of law; political and non-political institutions of antipower	• Structuralism • Rule-like structural presumptions

antitrust approach. They also built the foundations of the tight cage that republican antitrust built around the industrial behemoths to preserve republican liberty against domination and private government. By shackling the industrial behemoths, the republican antitrust tradition sought to uphold the promise encoded in Adam Smith's allegory of the invisible hand that the interaction between self-interested individuals will contribute to a stable society and a moderate, republican form of government. The foundations of this cage started to crumble from the 1970s onwards. The next chapter will explore how, with the ascent of the Chicago School, the industrial behemoths were unleashed from what was increasingly perceived as a straightjacket of competition law under the banner of welfare, growth, and entrepreneurial liberty.

PART III

The Decline of the Competition–Democracy Nexus

6

The Making of Laissez-Faire Antitrust

6.1 INTRODUCTION

Until very recently the value of republican liberty, and the idea of a link between competition and democracy had almost entirely disappeared from the normative landscape of modern antitrust law. Antitrust textbooks barely refer to economic liberty and democracy as goals of competition law and policy. And if they do so, then they portray both ideals as dusty relics of long-gone times. Mainstream antitrust scholarship suggests not only that considerations about liberty and democracy have lost their relevance for modern antitrust but it also cautions against any attempt to reinvigorate their influence on the interpretation of contemporary competition law.

This chapter explains why and how the edifice of republican antitrust has collapsed. It seeks to answer a simple question: How is it that the values of republican liberty and the idea of a competition–democracy nexus, which for more than half a century had played such a central role for antitrust movements and the interpretation of competition law in the United States and in Europe, suddenly disappeared? The answer to this question lies primarily in what is often referred to as the Chicago School 'antitrust revolution'.[1] From the late-1950s onwards, a group of legal scholars led by Aaron Director, Robert Bork, and Richard Posner and inspired by emblematic Chicago economists such as George Stigler, Milton Friedman, Harold Demsetz, Lester Telser, and Ronald Coase succeeded in fundamentally reshaping how we think about competition and competition law. The Chicago School swept away more than three centuries of republican antitrust tradition, which was rooted in the idea that it is the role of competition law to promote, alongside economic welfare and efficiency, the non-welfarist values of liberty, equality, and democracy through the preservation of a deconcentrated market

[1] H Hovenkamp, 'Antitrust Policy after Chicago' (1985) 84(2) *Michigan Law Review* 213, 217.

structure. Instead, the Chicago School entrenched the nowadays hegemonic view that competition law should, as its exclusive goal, promote welfare and efficiency. From the early-2000s onwards, this single-edged focus on welfare and the economic effects of business conduct on prices and output has also been increasingly emulated by the so-called More Economic Approach in Europe.

Conventional antitrust literature explains the rise of the Chicagoan More Economic Approach and the displacement of socioeconomic and political goals of competition law primarily by the successful attempt of Chicago scholars to bring antitrust law in line with neoclassical price theory and welfare economics. On this account, the eradication of the idea of a competition–democracy nexus from antitrust textbooks is the ultimate outcome of the triumph of economics over politics.[2] This chapter puts forward a different explanation for the decline of the republican antitrust tradition and the competition–democracy nexus. It argues that the Chicago School toppled republican antitrust through two lines of attack. The first line of attack was economics. The Chicago School dealt the ideal of republican liberty and its operationalisation through a structuralist interpretation of antitrust laws an important blow by revealing the methodological flaws of the Harvard School's Structure–Conduct–Performance (S–C–P) paradigm and laying bare the economic welfare costs of republican antitrust. Thus, the Chicago School stripped republican antitrust of its economic foundations. The second line of attack, which is rarely discussed in the antitrust literature, was through politics and ideology. This chapter shows that the Chicago School developed the consumer welfare standard as a powerful and versatile framework to ground antitrust law on a narrow concept of negative liberty as non-interference.[3] By putting forth an alternative conception of economic liberty and a workable framework to implement it through antitrust policy, the Chicago School coined a novel laissez-faire approach to antitrust law that superseded the republican understanding of economic liberty and the concept of a competition–democracy nexus. This laissez-faire approach, which was shaped by the Chicago School, became predominant on both sides of the Atlantic, as it was gradually endorsed by post-Chicago scholars in the United States and by proponents of the More Economic Approach in Europe alike.

The adoption of the consumer welfare standard in the United States and in the European Union laid down the blueprint for an interpretation of competition law that is only concerned about business conduct resulting in welfare-decreasing

[2] See, for instance, RA Posner, 'The Chicago School of Antitrust Analysis' (1979) 127(4) *University of Pennsylvania Law Review* 925, 933–34; R Pitofsky, 'The Political Content of Antitrust' (1979) 127(4) *University of Pennsylvania Law Review* 1051, 1051; EM Fox, 'Modernization of Antitrust: A New Equilibrium' (1980) 66(6) *Cornell Law Review* 1140, 1140, 1145, 1155.

[3] For a similar argument, see EM Fox, 'Consumer Beware Chicago' (1986) 84(8) *Michigan Law Review* 1714, 1715; EM Fox, 'The Politics of Law and Economics in Judicial Decision Making: Antitrust as a Window' (1986) 61(4) *New York University Law Review* 554, 558 fn. 14, 588.

interference and shields the exercise of negative entrepreneurial liberty to the largest extent possible from state intervention. It is exactly this displacement of the republican ideal of liberty as non-domination by the thinner concept of negative liberty encapsulated in the consumer welfare standard that eventually severed the link between the anti-cartel, anti-monopoly, and anti-merger pillars of competition law and democracy.

The remainder of this chapter unfolds as follows. Section 6.2 provides an overview of the fundamental priors of the Chicago School antitrust movement. Section 6.3 describes how the Chicago School successfully unpicked the economic predispositions of the republican antitrust tradition. Section 6.4 sheds light on how the Chicago School devised the consumer welfare standard and the analysis of judicial errors as a normative framework to promote a laissez-faire interpretation of antitrust law whose ultimate purpose is the preservation of a negative conception of liberty. Section 6.5 summarises how the Chicago School revolution altered the basic geometry of economic liberty protected by contemporary competition law.

6.2 THE BASIC PRECEPTS OF THE CHICAGO REVOLUTION

The republican antitrust tradition has never been unchallenged. Quite to the contrary. Throughout its history, republican antitrust has been constantly contested and has received several important blows. Over the course of the eighteenth and nineteenth centuries, the common law increasingly moved away from the anti-monopoly fervour that had fashioned the early case law on monopoly and restraints of trade. Towards the end of the nineteenth century, the common law had embraced a negative and laissez-faire understanding of economic liberty to the extent that it condoned conspicuous restraints of trade and collusion as a legitimate manifestation of entrepreneurial and contractual freedom that ought to be protected against state interference.[4]

The republican approach of the literalist era during the first years after the adoption of the Sherman Act was also fervently opposed by proponents of a negative conception of economic liberty. They feared that an overly inclusive interpretation of the prohibition of contracts in restraint of trade would destroy property rights, as well as contractual and entrepreneurial freedom.[5] The creation of the rule of reason in *Standard Oil*[6] constitutes an immediate answer to this concern. It marked the first recognition in modern antitrust law that an interpretation of competition law grounded in a republican ideal of economic liberty may

4 See for instance *Mogul Steamship Co Ltd v McGregor, Gow & Co* [1892] AC 25.

5 *United States v Trans-Missouri Freight Assoc.* 166 U.S. 290 (1897) Justice White dissenting, 344, 346–51, 354–55; *United States v Joint Traffic Ass'n* 171 U.S. 505 (1898) 559, 571–72; *Addyston Pipe & Steel Co. v United States* 175 U.S. 211 (1899) 277; *Northern Securities Co. v United States* 193 U.S. 197 (1904) Justice Holmes, Chief Justice White, Justice Peckham dissenting, 411.

6 *Standard Oil Co. of New Jersey v United States* 221 U.S. 1 (1911).

frustrate the negative contractual and entrepreneurial liberties of businesses.[7] Similar interpretative struggles between proponents of an antitrust policy grounded in a republican and negative understanding of economic liberty continued to simmer below the surface of and flare up in the antitrust jurisprudence of the first half of the twentieth century.[8] Likewise, from the early case law onwards, proponents of a competition policy grounded in a negative conception of economic liberty also called for a rule of reason approach towards anticompetitive agreements and dominant firm conduct in Europe.[9] However, none of these numerous critiques of the republican antitrust tradition has been as consequential as the one levelled by the Chicago School. Unlike previous attempts to align competition law with a negative conception of economic liberty, the Chicago School managed to topple the republican antitrust tradition for good.

6.2.1 *The Crisis in Antitrust*

The Chicago School's challenge to republican antitrust took shape around the year 1956 when Aaron Director and Edward H. Levi published a short article cryptically entitled 'Law and the Future: Trade Regulation'.[10] This article would become one of the most influential papers in the history of antitrust law. Its central message was that the way in which US courts applied antitrust law was fundamentally at odds with the basic insights of modern welfare economics. The paper also set out a stark choice for the near future of antitrust law: either antitrust law sticks to its multi-value approach of pursuing, amongst other things, political goals, such as republican liberty – in this case, competition law would be anything but economic law – or antitrust law would undergo a radical reform and align itself with the basic tenets of modern welfare economics.[11]

The year of 1956 thus marked the birth of modern antitrust law as we know it today. The Director/Levi paper laid the intellectual foundations of our contemporary understanding of competition law. It set in motion what would become known as the most profound transformation of antitrust law – the Chicago School antitrust revolution. In their paper, Director and Levi framed a clear research and policy agenda, which was henceforth ardently pursued by economists and lawyers associated with the University of Chicago. The starting point of the Chicago School

[7] Ibid. 78.

[8] This interpretative struggle becomes obvious in the contrasting holdings of *United States v U. S. Steel Corp.* 251 U.S. 417 (1920) 451; *United States v Swift & Co.* 286 U.S. 106 (1932) 116.

[9] Opinion of Advocate General Roemer in Case 56/64 *Consten and Grundig v Commission of the EEC* ECLI:EU:C:1966:19; R Joliet, *Monopolization and Abuse of Dominant Position: A Comparative Study of the American and European Approaches to the Control of Economic Power* (La Haye/Liège: Martinus Nijhoff 1970).

[10] A Director and EH Levi, 'Law and the Future: Trade Regulation' (1956) 51(2) *Northwestern University Law Review* 281.

[11] Ibid. 282, 296.

analysis was the diagnosis that the 'crisis in antitrust'[12] originates from the fact that republican antitrust law was hitherto an inherently political enterprise. Alongside the goal of consumer welfare, republican antitrust also recognised non-welfarist goals, such as the preservation of republican freedom through the limitation of concentration and abuses of economic power or the protection of small and local businesses.[13] This attempt to pursue and reconcile a 'randomized mix'[14] of often conflicting economic and non-economic goals produced in the eyes of the Chicago scholars 'bad policy and bad law', which ignored the genuine interests of consumers and undermined legal certainty for businesses.[15]

6.2.2 *The Chicagoan Consumer Welfare Framework*

Starting from this diagnosis, the Chicago School developed the blueprint for the reform of antitrust policy. This reform would soon revolutionise antitrust analysis and set the foundations of what became, under the banner of the so-called More Economic Approach, the predominant competition law paradigm on both sides of the Atlantic. Within a few years, the Chicago School succeeded in rewriting the history and altering the face of US antitrust law by putting forward a parsimonious and coherent framework for antitrust policy.

The starting point of the Chicago School's attempt to reform antitrust law was the observation that a coherent antitrust policy is only possible once we settle the question of its policy goals for good.[16] Therefore, Chicago scholars advocated that antitrust law should be grounded in the sole objective of ensuring consumer welfare.[17] Offering a selective reading of the legislative debates of the Sherman Act and the formative case law, some Chicagoans even went as far as claiming that welfare considerations constituted the major, if not only, concern that inspired the enactment of US antitrust statutes by Congress and their subsequent interpretation by the Supreme Court.[18]

Alongside legislative history, the Chicago School also put forth forceful methodological claims about why welfare maximisation should constitute the unique goal of competition law. In the eyes of many Chicagoans, the perceived inconsistencies and

[12] RH Bork and WS Bowman Jr., 'The Crisis in Antitrust' (1965) 65(3) *Columbia Law Journal* 363.

[13] RA Posner, *Antitrust Law* (Chicago: University of Chicago Press 2001) 24–28.

[14] TE Kauper, 'The Influence of Conservative Economic Analysis on the Development of the Law of Antitrust' in R Pitofsky (ed), *How the Chicago School Overshot the Mark: The Effect of Conservative Economic Analysis on U.S. Antitrust* (Oxford: Oxford University Press 2008) 40, 43.

[15] RH Bork, 'The Goals of Antitrust Policy' (1967) 57(2) *The American Economic Review* 242, 242.

[16] See, for instance, Director and Levi (n 10) 296; RH Bork, *The Antitrust Paradox: A Policy at War with Itself* [1978] (New York: Maxwell Macmillan 1993) 5, 7.

[17] Bork, *The Antitrust Paradox* (n 16) 80–115; Posner, *Antitrust Law* (n 13) 2, 21–29.

[18] RH Bork, 'Legislative Intent and the Policy of the Sherman Act' (1966) 9(1) *Journal of Law & Economics* 7; Bork, *The Antitrust Paradox* (n 16) Chapters 1 to 3, and in particular 15–71.

woes of antitrust law during the Warren Court era were primarily the result of a profound confusion that was caused by the hodgepodge of various social, economic, and political goals promoted by the Harvard School and other antitrust movements of the time. Only a radical cure of purging antitrust policy from these various, often contradictory, objectives and their substitution with a clear, precise, and unique goal of consumer welfare could restore the consistency of antitrust enforcement and jurisprudence.[19] Chicago scholars asserted that the goal of consumer welfare was directly derived from what they portrayed as the objective and scientific truth of economic neoclassical price theory. Based on this claim of scientific objectivity, they posited that the goal of consumer welfare could offer a reliable normative focal point for a workable and sound antitrust policy.[20] Adopting consumer welfare as a policy goal thus had the appeal of firmly grounding competition policy in the discipline of modern economics as the 'theory of antitrust'.[21]

In enthroning consumer welfare as the sole legitimate aim of antitrust law, the Chicago School discarded any other policy goal, such as the protection of economic freedom, a deconcentrated market structure, or the competitive process.[22] The Chicago School justified the removal of these values from the normative landscape of antitrust law, arguing that concerns about market structure and economic liberty would inevitably transform antitrust law into a 'protectionist'[23] tool to protect competitors rather than competition. Instead of focusing on the effect of impugned conduct on the competitive process, the market structure, or competitors, antitrust policy should exclusively be concerned with the 'effects of business behaviour on consumers'.[24]

The Chicago School thus posited that competition should exclusively be considered as an outcome in terms of efficiency or consumer welfare. Both outcome parameters of efficiency or welfare were increasingly viewed as the only performance indicators that could enable competition policy-makers and judges to measure the effectiveness of competition. Consumer welfare was touted as a clear normative benchmark for antitrust policy to single out specific harm to competition that warrants antitrust intervention, namely business conduct that adversely affects prices and output.[25] In contrast, the process dimension of competition as rivalrous interaction or a polycentric market structure played, at best, only a subsidiary role to these outcome considerations. From the Chicagoan perspective, the competitive process or a deconcentrated market structure merited protection only as long as they maximise consumer welfare.

[19] Bork, 'The Goals of Antitrust Policy' (n 15) 244–46; Bork, *The Antitrust Paradox* (n 16) 90–129.
[20] Bork, *The Antitrust Paradox* (n 16) 8, 91.
[21] Ibid. 5, 116–29.
[22] Bork, 'The Goals of Antitrust Policy' (n 15) 252–53.
[23] Bork and Bowman, 'The Crisis in Antitrust' (n 12) 364.
[24] Bork, *The Antitrust Paradox* (n 16) 90.
[25] Ibid. 123.

6.2.3 *The Many Meanings of Consumer Welfare*

Though the Chicago School advocated consumer welfare as a clear-cut and easily administrable policy objective, the very meaning of the concept of consumer welfare remained unsettled. Even though Robert Bork coined the terminology of 'consumer welfare', he and other Chicago scholars remained largely unconcerned about business conduct that reduced consumer surplus, by transforming the consumer into producer surplus and entailing a wealth transfer from consumers to producers.[26] They argued that antitrust law should abstain from taking into consideration the distributive consequences of monopoly power and anticompetitive conduct.[27] The way Bork and fellow Chicagoans used the term 'consumer welfare' in reality comes closer to a 'total welfare' standard,[28] as they likened consumer welfare with allocative efficiency.[29] From this perspective, the only evil of monopoly or firm conduct that antitrust law should be concerned about is deadweight loss.[30] This deadweight loss results from the fact that some consumers will no longer be able to afford the monopolised product and will have to deflect their demand to a second-best option, which they prefer less and whose production costs society more than the production of the monopolised good.

The Chicagoans also pointed out that the finding that conduct restricts output and entails a reduction in allocative efficiency is not sufficient to support the conclusion that it has net adverse effects on consumer or total welfare. Rather than merely inquiring into whether business conduct reduces allocative efficiency by lowering output and increasing prices, antitrust law should also take into account the extent to which these losses are potentially offset by gains in productive efficiency. Drawing upon the seminal work of the economist Oliver E. Williamson,[31] Bork argued that antitrust law should only prohibit those business practices that bring about a reduction in allocative efficiency which outweighs any increase in productive efficiency.[32] The essential challenge for antitrust analysis is hence to draw the right balance in this welfare trade-off between reductions in allocative and potential increases in productive efficiency brought about by specific business conduct. Accordingly, the whole 'task of antitrust can be summed up as an

26 BY Orbach, 'The Antitrust Consumer Welfare Paradox' (2011) 7(1) *Journal of Competition Law and Economics* 133, 138–49.

27 Posner, *Antitrust Law* (n 13) 21–24, 28–29, 202–03; Bork, *The Antitrust Paradox* (n 16) 110–13.

28 EM Fox and LA Sullivan, 'Antitrust-Retrospective and Prospective: Where Are We Coming From? Where Are We Going?' (1987) 62(5) *New York University Law Review* 936, 957–59; ME Stucke, 'Reconsidering Antitrust's Goals' (2012) 53(2) *Boston College Law Review* 551, 566.

29 Bork, *The Antitrust Paradox* (n 16) 90.

30 Posner, *Antitrust Law* (n 13) 26.

31 OE Williamson, 'Economies as an Antitrust Defense: The Welfare Tradeoffs' (1968) 58(1) *The American Economic Review* 18.

32 Bork, *The Antitrust Paradox* (n 16) 107–10.

effort to improve allocative efficiency without impairing productive efficiency so greatly as to produce either no gain or net loss in consumer welfare'.[33]

The disruptive character and far-reaching implications of the Chicagoan critique of the economic and methodological shortcomings of the republican antitrust tradition and its attempt to rebuild antitrust policy around the sole objective of consumer welfare can hardly be overstated. The Chicagoan antitrust revolution dealt the ideal of republican liberty, and thus the idea of a competition–democracy nexus, a deadly blow. By elevating welfare maximisation to the unique normative goal of antitrust policy and benchmark for the assessment of the legality of business practices, the Chicago School delegitimised the hitherto prevailing concern about the adverse, dominating impact of concentrated economic power on republican liberty as non-domination and the egalitarian, Jeffersonian ideal of a society that ensures broad-based economic opportunities to independent and small business-people.[34] The Chicago School vilified republican antitrust as being inherently biased in favour of a privileged and inefficient class of small producers and shop keepers. It claimed that in pursuing the goal of preserving a decentralised market structure and reining in the excessive concentration of economic power, the pre-dominant republican antitrust policy of the time did nothing else than ensure the survival of a small, yet inefficient, middle-class at the expense of the silent majority of consumers.[35]

6.3 THE ECONOMIC CRITIQUE OF REPUBLICAN ANTITRUST

The brisk displacement of the republican antitrust tradition by the Chicago School antitrust paradigm raises questions about the reasons behind the rapid ascent of the Chicago School and the overwhelming success of the consumer welfare standard. How exactly did the Chicago School succeed in toppling republican antitrust? The answer is that Chicago School waged its attack on the republican antitrust tradition along two lines: the first, discussed in this section, was economic; the second, discussed in the following section, was ideological.

6.3.1 *The Chicago School Critique of the S–C–P Paradigm*

This first line of attack was directed against the economic presuppositions that underpinned the republican antitrust tradition. The Chicago critique particularly targeted the teachings of the Harvard School and the S–C–P paradigm that provided economic arguments in support of the republican hostility against industry

[33] Ibid. 91.
[34] Ibid. 110–13; Posner, *Antitrust Law* (n 13) 18–22, 24.
[35] Bork and Bowman, 'The Crisis in Antitrust' (n 12) 375–76; RJ Peritz, 'A Counter-History of Antitrust Law' (1990) 39(2) *Duke Law Journal* 263, 299–303.

concentration and bigness.[36] Based on empirical studies suggesting a strong correlation between concentrated market structures and high profitability, the Harvard School argued that high levels of industry concentration were indicative of a lack of competition and economic performance. This finding rested on the assumption that markups were primarily caused by high levels of industry concentration, which facilitate oligopolistic or monopolistic firm conduct.[37] On this basis, the S–C–P paradigm posited that there is a deterministic relationship where market structure as an independent variable shapes firm conduct and economic performance as dependent variables.

The members of the Chicago School perceived this assumption of a deterministic link between market structure and performance as a major force behind the hostile stance of republican antitrust against industry concentration. To them, the S–C–P paradigm and its structural understanding of competition offered an intellectual breeding ground for an excessively interventionist antitrust policy. The Chicago School therefore spared no pains in unpicking the methodological and theoretical premises of the S–C–P paradigm. It laid bare what it perceived as the economic flaws of the republican antitrust tradition. The Chicago critique thus conclusively severed the notion of competitive markets from a structural understanding of competition as a polycentric market structure.[38]

At the crosshairs of the Chicago School critique lay the core tenet of the S–C–P paradigm that high levels of industry concentration are indicative of a lack of competition.[39] The Chicago scholars objected that the S–C–P paradigm all too easily assumed that high profitability was caused by a market structure that facilitated anticompetitive oligopolistic or monopolistic conduct. The relationship between structure and performance could well be the other way around if it is greater efficiency (e.g., due to economies of scale) that causes market shares of the leading firms to grow. The Chicagoans argued that the S–C–P paradigm was beset by a classic endogeneity problem: it ignored that industry concentration (S) may well be the outcome of greater performance (P) or efficient competitive strategies (C), and is hence endogenous to the competitive process rather than being a sign of the lack of competition.[40]

36 For a more detailed analysis of the S–C–P paradigm, see the discussion in Chapter 3. Bork, 'The Goals of Antitrust Policy' (n 15) 251–53.

37 JS Bain, 'Relation of Profit Rate to Industry Concentration: American Manufacturing, 1936–1940' (1951) 65(3) *The Quarterly Journal of Economics* 292; JS Bain, *Industrial Organization* (New York: John Wiley & Sons 1959).

38 In this sense, GJ Stigler, 'Imperfections in the Capital Market' Reprinted from *Journal of Political Economy*, Vol. LXXV, No. 3, June 1967' in GJ Stigler (ed), *The Organization of Industry* (Chicago: University of Chicago Press 1968) 113, 117.

39 Director and Levi (n 10) 282, 285–86; Bork, *The Antitrust Paradox* (n 16) 163–97; H Demsetz, 'Two Systems of Belief about Monopoly' in Goldschmid, Mann, and Weston (eds), *Industrial Concentration: The New Learning* (Boston: Little Brown 1974) 164.

40 See, in this sense, W Evans, LM Froeb and GJ Werden, 'Endogeneity in the Concentration–Price Relationship: Causes, Consequences, and Cures' (1993) XLI(4) *The Journal of Industrial Economics* 432, 432–34.

Consequently, the S–C–P paradigm unduly overlooked alternative, pro-competitive explanations for firm size, high levels of industry concentration, and profitability, which may equally be the result of superior productive or even dynamic efficiency.

Chicago scholars argued that this disregard for the endogeneity of industry concentration and the more efficient leader problem explains why republican antitrust paid so little attention to efficiency considerations or even perceived efficiency as a competition problem.[41] By turning a blind eye to how industry concentration and monopoly power come about in the first place,[42] the republican antitrust policy and its hostility against industry concentration and size ignored their welfare implications. Therefore, an antitrust policy that was guided by the goal of indiscriminately preventing industry concentration was inescapably condemned to harm consumer welfare by depriving consumers of the benefits of industrial growth and large-scale production.[43]

The proposition that entry barriers are in general low provided the Chicago School with further ammunition to challenge structural assumptions against concentrated markets.[44] Asserting that market entry is much easier than assumed by the Harvard School, the Chicago School argued that even concentrated oligopolistic or monopolistic markets remain competitive and that market power in these markets is ephemeral.[45] Any attempt by an incumbent to raise prices and the ensuing prospect of supra-competitive profits would, at some point, automatically lure new entrants. The threat of entry and potential competition ensured that even incumbents in a highly concentrated industry remained constrained by potential competition. Conversely, based on the assumption that entry barriers are rare, Chicago scholars posited that high levels of industry concentration could only be explained by the superior efficiency of the incumbents.[46]

6.3.2 A *Narrow Definition of Anticompetitive Harm*

The Chicagoan critique of the economic assumptions of the S–C–P paradigm not only asserted that republican antitrust was built upon fallacious economic premises but also highlighted how the concern over industry concentration resulted in imprecise, inconsistent, and over-inclusive legal definitions of the concepts of 'restriction of competition' and 'anticompetitive harm'. The Chicago School

41 Director and Levi (n 10) 282–88; Posner, *Antitrust Law* (n 13) 101–17.

42 Bork, *The Antitrust Paradox* (n 16) 164–65, 192–97; Posner, *Antitrust Law* (n 13) 113–16.

43 Director and Levi (n 10) 283–85.

44 Posner, 'The Chicago School of Antitrust Analysis' (n 2) 929–33; GJ Stigler, 'Barriers to Entry, Economies of Scale, and Firm Size' in GJ Stigler (ed), *The Organization of Industry* (Chicago: University of Chicago Press 1968) 67.

45 DL Rubinfeld, 'On the Foundations of Antitrust Law and Economics' in R Pitofsky (ed), *How the Chicago School Overshot the Mark: The Effect of Conservative Economic Analysis on U.S. Antitrust* (Oxford: Oxford University Press 2008) 51, 54.

46 Bork, *The Antitrust Paradox* (n 16) 195–96; Posner, *Antitrust Law* (n 13) 114–15.

contended that the Harvard School[47] and the republican approach had coined an overly broad notion of exclusionary monopoly conduct. Chicago scholars strikingly argued that any kind of business activity excludes and harms competitors in one way or another because even superior efficiency will eventually drive competitors out of the market.[48] Starting from the premise that monopoly power is, in most circumstances, contestable and constrained by market forces and entry,[49] the Chicago scholars posited that powerful firms could only on rare occasions leverage their market power to unfairly foreclose competitors from the market and expand their monopoly position.[50] On the contrary, smaller competitors should be expected to be able to compete on equal terms with the dominant firm. Most proponents of the Chicago[51] and later also post-Chicago Schools[52] therefore argued that antitrust laws should only outlaw unilateral conduct that leads to an actual or likely foreclosure of competitors by means other than efficiency, thereby causing price increases or restrictions in output to the detriment of consumer welfare.[53]

The Chicagoan critique of the S–C–P paradigm also disputed the broad definition of anticompetitive collusion that informed the republican antitrust tradition. In particular, the Chicagoans challenged the structuralist analysis of coordinated conduct of the S–C–P paradigm which assumed that collusion and oligopolistic pricing are the inevitable outcomes of a concentrated market structure.[54] Instead, the Chicago School considered collusion as a primarily behavioural problem. It observed that even in highly concentrated, oligopolistic markets, collusion between firms is inherently unstable. Accordingly, collusion could only be maintained if industry members were able to credibly detect and punish cheating, and thereby preserve the incentives of the firms involved not to defect from the terms of coordination to maximise their profits.[55] Assuming that collusive arrangements are inherently instable, the Chicago scholars claimed that anticompetitive collusion was

47 See, for instance, DF Turner, 'The Validity of Tying Arrangements under the Antitrust Laws' (1958) 72(1) *Harvard Law Review* 50.

48 Bork, *The Antitrust Paradox* (n 16) 137.

49 Ibid. 179, 195, Chapters 4 and 6; Posner, 'The Chicago School of Antitrust Analysis' (n 2) 931–32, 945–48.

50 Director and Levi (n 10) 289–91; WS Bowman Jr., 'Tying Arrangements and the Leverage Problem' (1957) 67(1) *Yale Law Journal* 19.

51 Bork even went as far as to argue that exclusionary conduct should be normally subject to a presumption of per se legality, see Bork, *The Antitrust Paradox* (n 16) 157. Other Chicago scholars, such as Posner, rejected this extreme position and instead advocated an intervention against single-firm conduct that forecloses equally efficient competitors, see Posner, 'The Chicago School of Antitrust Analysis' (n 2) 928–29, 933; Posner, *Antitrust Law* (n 13) 4, 194.

52 See, for instance, TG Krattenmaker and SC Salop, 'Anticompetitive Exclusion: Raising Rivals' Costs to Achieve Power over Price' (1986) 96(3) *The Yale Law Journal* 209.

53 Director and Levi (n 10) 287, 293; Posner, *Antitrust Law* (n 13) 194–95.

54 RA Posner, 'Oligopoly and the Antitrust Laws: A Suggested Approach' (1968–1969) 21 *Stanford Law Review* 1562, 1571.

55 GJ Stigler, 'A Theory of Oligopoly: Reprinted from Journal of Political Economy Vol. LXXII, No 1 (1964)' in GJ Stigler (ed), *The Organization of Industry* (Chicago: University of Chicago

a much less frequent phenomenon in concentrated markets than the republican antitrust tradition was inclined to believe.

The Chicago School also drew upon Ronald Coase's work on the theory of the firm and insights from transaction cost theory[56] to show that many horizontal and vertical agreements that were scorned as anticompetitive by republican antitrust actually allowed firms to reduce transaction costs and organise their production in a more effective way.[57] To Chicagoans, most types of horizontal and vertical agreements merely constituted efficient ways to internalise externalities and arrange the production or distribution of goods more effectively by expanding the function of the firm by means of contract.[58] Drawing on transaction cost economics, the Chicago School also dispelled the republican concern that vertical agreements would amount to an undue exercise of domination on the part of producers over their retailers. The Chicago scholars fiercely disputed the republican assumption that relationships of subordination are incompatible with liberty, even if they are the result of a voluntarily concluded contract. Instead, they saw vertical restraints in an entirely new light. Vertical restraints were increasingly considered as a legitimate exercise of contractual liberty, which enabled firms to overcome collective action and transaction cost problems. From this perspective, vertical restraints merely constituted a tool for firms to protect their negative liberty and property rights against expropriation by competing 'free riders'.[59]

By successfully challenging the central assumption of the S–C–P paradigm that market concentration inevitably leads to anticompetitive outcomes, the Chicago School also took aim at the continuous expansion of the notion of anticompetitive mergers by republican antitrust during the Warren Court era.[60] Chicago scholars argued that by championing a sweeping interpretation of the incipiency doctrine and by seeking to preserve an industry composed of many small players, the Warren Court had transformed the Clayton Act into a de facto prohibition of almost any merger.[61] For Chicagoans, concerns about concentration and the preservation of smaller competitors were ill-suited to form the foundations of a rational merger policy that would be capable of telling apart anticompetitive and innocuous mergers. Any horizontal merger necessarily contributes to an increase in economic

Press 1968) 39; Posner, 'Oligopoly and the Antitrust Laws' (n 54) 1569–75; Posner, *Antitrust Law* (n 13) 60–69.

56 RH Coase, 'The Nature of the Firm' (1937) 4(16) *Economica* 386; RH Coase, 'The Problem of Social Cost' (1960) 3 *Journal of Law & Economics* 1, 16–18.

57 LG Telser, 'Why Should Manufacturers Want Fair Trade?' (1960) 3 *Journal of Law and Economics* 86; FH Easterbrook, 'The Limits of Antitrust' (1984) 63(1) *Texas Law Review* 1, 4, 6, 13.

58 RH Bork, 'The Rule of Reason and the Per Se Concept: Price Fixing and Market Division' (1966) 75(3) *The Yale Law Journal* 775, 837.

59 For a critical discussion, see Fox and Sullivan, 'Antitrust-Retrospective and Prospective' (n 28) 945–46, 976, 983–84.

60 Posner, *Antitrust Law* (n 13) 118.

61 Bork, *The Antitrust Paradox* (n 16) 205; Posner, *Antitrust Law* (n 13) 122–23.

concentration. If they allow the parties to achieve greater efficiencies, then mergers also inevitably pose a threat to the survival of smaller businesses.[62]

The republican hostility towards industry concentration through merger was increasingly challenged by the growing consensus amongst antitrust scholars of all shades that, most of the time, mergers tend to generate important efficiencies.[63] Mergers were thus increasingly simply perceived as an alternative, often swifter, pathway to internal growth that allows firms to achieve an optimal size and efficient scale.[64] Only in exceptional circumstances would mergers result in lower output and higher prices, and thus harm total or consumer welfare. Anticompetitive harm is only plausible if the merger between two firms creates either a merged entity that is large enough to unilaterally raise prices and restrict output (merger to monopoly)[65] or the merger facilitates so-called tacit collusion.[66] The Chicago School thus largely dismissed a merger policy that was grounded in a structural or process-based understanding of competition because it resulted in an unwieldy and overly broad definition of anticompetitive mergers. Instead, the Chicago School developed the concepts of unilateral and coordinated effects as two clearly articulated behavioural theories of harm, which identify anticompetitive mergers purely on the basis of how they affect prices, output, and consumer welfare.[67]

6.3.3 *The Importance of Efficiencies*

The Chicago School also attributed the failure of the republican antitrust tradition to consistently and clearly distinguish anticompetitive harm from legitimate forms of competition to its reluctance to properly consider efficiencies. On this account, the Chicago scholars underscored the need to give appropriate weight to the potential pro-competitive efficiencies that are generated by impugned firm conduct and mergers to determine whether they entail, in the aggregate, harm to competition.[68] However, they took the view that efficiencies are extremely difficult, if not impossible, to quantify. Attempts to balance the pro- and anticompetitive effects of firm

62 Bork, *The Antitrust Paradox* (n 16) 200, 203, 206, 216.

63 Bork and Bowman (n 12); Bork, *The Antitrust Paradox* (n 16) 198.

64 DF Turner, 'Conglomerate Mergers and Section 7 of the Clayton Act' (1965) 78(7) *Harvard Law Review* 1313, 1317; Bork, *The Antitrust Paradox* (n 16) 199; Posner, *Antitrust Law* (n 13) 119.

65 GJ Stigler, 'Monopoly and Oligopoly by Merger: Reprinted from Papers and Proceedings, American Economic Review, Vol. XL, No. 2. (1950)' in GJ Stigler (ed), *The Organization of Industry* (Chicago: University of Chicago Press 1968) 95, 96–103; Bork, *The Antitrust Paradox* (n 16) 199, 200, 206, 210, 219–20.

66 Stigler, 'Monopoly and Oligopoly by Merger' (n 65) 103–06; GJ Stigler, 'Mergers and Preventive Antitrust Policy: Reprinted from University of Pennsylvania Law Review, Vol. 104, No 2 (1955)' in GJ Stigler (ed), *The Organization of Industry* (Chicago: University of Chicago Press 1968) 296, 299–303; Posner, 'Oligopoly and the Antitrust Laws' (n 54) 1598–605.

67 Bork, *The Antitrust Paradox* (n 16) 221–22; Stigler, 'Mergers and Preventive Antitrust Policy' (n 66) 300–03; Posner, 'Oligopoly and the Antitrust Laws' (n 54) 1601–05.

68 Bork, *The Antitrust Paradox* (n 16) 199, 221.

conduct and mergers would therefore confront courts with unsurmountable difficulties. Consequently, the Chicago School harboured doubts about the merits of an explicit efficiency defence for prima facie anticompetitive conduct or mergers that would involve such an intricate balancing exercise.[69]

Instead of advocating the balancing of welfare effects in individual cases, the Chicago School suggested that the welfare trade-off between pro- and anticompetitive effects should directly be translated into the design of competition rules. Competition law should be redesigned around presumptive filters and safe-harbours that automatically screen out competitively neutral or pro-competitive conduct.[70] These presumptive filters not only constitute an estimate of the likelihood and size of anticompetitive effects but also of the likelihood and size of efficiencies generated by firm conduct and mergers. To prevent the efficiency losses resulting from these presumptive filters from becoming too high, the Chicago scholars suggested that their prohibitive scope should be drawn narrowly and, in the case of doubt, should err on the side of non-intervention. Accordingly, the Chicago School envisaged the redesign of antitrust law following the maxim that the more permissive the antitrust laws, the less will antitrust policy deprive society of efficiencies.[71]

In challenging the economic predispositions of the S–C–P paradigm, the Chicago School articulated a powerful economic critique of the republican antitrust tradition and its concern about market concentration. Not only did the Chicago School show that market concentration may well be the result of fierce competition and efficiencies but it also inferred from this observation that anticompetitive conduct is far less important and frequent than usually implied by the overly expansive concepts of anticompetitive harm that were employed by the republican antitrust tradition. The Chicago School thus succeeded in discrediting the interventionist republican antitrust approach and its obsession with industry concentration as an economically flawed and irrational policy. Given that it accepted sacrifices of efficiencies to preserve a deconcentrated market structure, republican antitrust simply inflicted excessive welfare losses on society and was utterly 'anticonsumer'.[72] On this basis, the Chicago School championed a radical departure from the structuralist approach of republican antitrust and its replacement with the economically sound and parsimonious framework of welfare analysis, which was capable of generating unambiguous definitions of the concept of restrictions of or harm to competition. Rebuilding antitrust law on the new foundations of welfare economics appeared to be the only way towards a rational antitrust policy that preserves and promotes efficiency and consumer welfare.

69 Ibid. 219–21; Posner, 'Oligopoly and the Antitrust Laws' (n 54) 1604–05; Posner, *Antitrust Law* (n 13) 133–35.

70 Easterbrook, 'The Limits of Antitrust' (n 57) 17–38.

71 Posner, 'Oligopoly and the Antitrust Laws' (n 54) 1605; Posner, *Antitrust Law* (n 13) 134.

72 Bork, *The Antitrust Paradox* (n 16) 86.

6.4 THE CONSUMER WELFARE STANDARD AS A FRAMEWORK TO OPERATIONALISE A NEGATIVE CONCEPTION OF ECONOMIC LIBERTY

The standard account of the ascent of the Chicago School antitrust revolution mostly focuses on the economic line of attack (as discussed in the previous section), through which the Chicago School shook up the economic foundations of the republican antitrust tradition. The conventional scholarly literature explains the rise of the Chicago School by the fact that it supplemented, for good or for bad, the multi-dimensional goals of republican antitrust with the single goal of welfare maximisation. In effect, by elevating welfare economics to the central normative benchmark and methodology of antitrust analysis, the Chicago School claimed to purify antitrust law from the ideological ballast of non-economic social and political goals.[73] Commentators further entrenched this narrative by explaining the disappearance of the goal of liberty and the idea of a competition–democracy nexus from modern antitrust law by the fact that the Chicago School reduced the normative content of competition law to applied economics.[74]

This account, however, disregards that the implications of the Chicago School's campaign for a consumer welfare standard ran much deeper than merely reconciling antitrust law with modern economics. Antitrust scholarship largely ignores that the consumer welfare standard served the Chicago School as an effective rhetorical and analytical device to frame a concise and versatile theory of negative economic liberty through which it successfully assailed the value of republican liberty as the normative bedrock of antitrust law. Under the guise of modern welfare economics, the Chicago scholars completed what the proponents of the laissez-faire approach had failed to achieve during the late-nineteenth and early-twentieth centuries. The consumer welfare standard enabled the Chicago School to articulate and operationalise a novel conception of economic liberty as the normative foundation of a laissez-faire antitrust approach whose primary goal consists of insulating negative entrepreneurial liberty and property rights from state interference.[75] One only has to scratch the surface of the Chicago antitrust programme to see how welfare economics and the goal of welfare maximisation provided some allure of scientific

[73] RJ Peritz, *Competition Policy in America: History, Rhetoric, Law* (New York: Oxford University Press 2000) 238–39; Fox, 'Modernization of Antitrust' (n 2) 1155.

[74] Posner, 'The Chicago School of Antitrust Analysis' (n 2) 933–34; Pitofsky (n 2) 1051; Fox and Sullivan, 'Antitrust-Retrospective and Prospective' (n 28) 956, 956–60; EM Fox, 'The Battle for the Soul of Antitrust' (1987) 75(3) *California Law Review* 917, 918; L Khan, 'Amazon's Antitrust Paradox' (2017) 126 *Yale Law Journal* 710, 718–22; JJ Flynn, 'Antitrust Policy and the Concept of a Competitive Process' (1990) 35(4) *New York Law School Law Review* 893, 893–95; T Wu, *The Curse of Bigness: Antitrust in the New Gilded Age* (New York: Columbia Global Reports 2018) 83–92.

[75] For a similar argument, see Peritz, 'A Counter-History of Antitrust Law' (n 35) 299–311; Fox, 'Consumer Beware Chicago' (n 3) 558; Fox, 'Modernization of Antitrust' (n 2) 1156–57.

objectivity[76] to an inherently political attempt to realign antitrust policy with the ideal of negative liberty as non-interference.

6.4.1 *The Republican Paradox*

The Chicago School's economic critique had successfully shown that the concern about economic liberty, industry concentration, and market structure that underpin the republican approach obfuscated the very notion of restriction of competition. Any agreement, unilateral conduct, or merger restricts the economic freedom of some market participants and affects market structure. Consequently, equating the notion of 'restriction of competition' with that of a reduction in economic liberty or rivalry results in a situation where, at least theoretically, any business conduct may run afoul of competition law.[77] The Chicago School thus put the finger on the omission of the republican approach to advance a logically consistent and sound yardstick to decide when competition law intervention is warranted.

This failure of the republican approach to pin down a limiting principle for competition law enforcement is the immediate result of the thick concept of republican liberty. In a world where not only actual or likely interference but also the mere exposure to or dependence on a powerful agent capable of interfering with someone's actions qualify as preventing conditions (y) of liberty, any theoretically possible interference, be it ever so remote, can be viewed as an impairment of freedom that requires remedial state action. This means that virtually every social relationship may suddenly appear to be tainted by domination, and liberty becomes impossible.[78]

The broad definition of preventing conditions (y) combined with the modally robust character of republican liberty that is concerned about interference with individual actions (z), not only in the actual or nearby likely but across all (relevant) possible worlds, is the principal reason why the republican antitrust approach increasingly ran into difficulties. As the republican version of liberty requires that an individual's preferences are decisive and prevail across a potentially unrestricted number of possible domains, there may simply not exist any aggregate social choice function that could simultaneously satisfy the weak Pareto efficiency[79]

[76] Fox, 'Modernization of Antitrust' (n 2) 1155; Peritz, *Competition Policy in America* (n 73) 238–39.

[77] See, for instance, Bork, *The Antitrust Paradox* (n 16) 134–38. For a similar critique of the formative EU competition law, see BE Hawk, 'System Failure: Vertical Restraints and EC Competition Law' (1995) 32(4) *Common Market Law Review* 973, 977–78.

[78] I Carter and R Shnayderman, 'The Impossibility of "Freedom as Independence"' (2019) 17(2) *Political Studies Review* 136.

[79] The weak Pareto principle requires that unanimous individual preference rankings are reflected in social decisions; that is, if all individuals prefer option *a* to *b*, then society also prefers *a* to *b*. A Sen, 'Liberty and Social Choice' (1983) 80(1) *The Journal of Philosophy* 5, 5, 7.

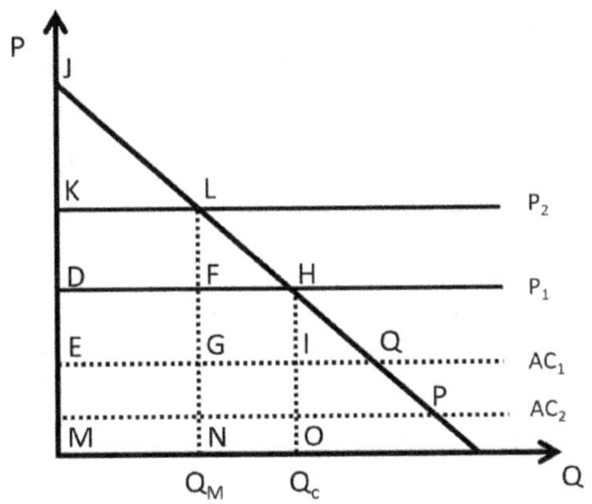

FIGURE 6.1 Scenarios of competition law intervention

principle and the demanding minimum requirements of the robust republican version of liberty.[80]

In concrete terms, this 'republican paradox' implies that the robust version of republican liberty leads to numerous frictions and conflicts between individual spheres of freedom. These frictions are the result of what is often referred to as the problem of the non-compossibility[81] of individual liberties and rights. This non-compossibility of liberties arises when individuals seek to simultaneously exercise their rights or liberties in relation to the same type of action and the exercise of the liberty by one individual obstructs that of the other.[82] For example, consider the sale of a product or service to the same group of consumers. The successful attempt to sell the product by one firm may actually prevent another player from doing the same.

The frictions that underpin the republican paradox and its tension with Pareto efficiency become palpable if we consider the republican approach through the lens of welfare economics. The stylised scenarios that are depicted in Figure 6.1 and Table 6.1 illustrate how the republican approach fails to provide a clear standard to determine when monopoly conduct – in the form of dominant firm conduct, horizontal or vertical agreements, or mergers – results in a restriction of and harm to competition.

Scenario 1 describes a situation where the Monopolist Firm A and its Competitors B are equally efficient because they have the same average costs ($AC_1 = AC_A = AC_B$;

80 For a seminal discussion of this 'liberal/republican paradox', see A Sen, 'The Impossibility of a Paretian Liberal' (1970) 78(1) *Journal of Political Economy* 152, 153–54; C List, 'The Impossibility of a Paretian Republican?: Some Comments on Pettit and Sen' (2004) 20(1) *Economics and Philosophy* 65, 74–75.

81 H Steiner, 'The Structure of a Set of Compossible Rights' (1977) 74(12) *The Journal of Philosophy* 767.

82 Ibid. 767–68.

TABLE 6.1 *Scenarios of competition law intervention*

	Scenario 1 As-efficient competitor surplus transfer		Scenario 2 Less efficient competitor surplus transfer		Scenario 3 Monopoly outcome with as-efficient competitors		Scenario 4 Monopoly outcome with less efficient competitors	
	t_1	t_2	t_1	t_2	t_1	t_2	t_1	t_2
Price (P)	$P_1 = P_A = P_B$	$P_1 = P_A$	$P_1 = P_A = P_B$	$P_1 = P_A$	$P_1 = P_A = P_B$	$P_2 = P_A$	$P_1 = P_A = P_B$	$P_2 = P_A$
Quantity of output (Q)	$Q_c = Q_A + Q_B$	$Q_c = Q_A$	$Q_c = Q_A + Q_B$	$Q_c = Q_A$	$Q_C = Q_A + Q_B$	$Q_M = Q_A$	$Q_c = Q_A + Q_B$	$Q_M = Q_A$
Average costs (AC)	$AC_1 = AC_A = AC_B$	$AC_1 = AC_A = AC_B$	$AC_1 = AC_A = AC_B$	$AC_1 = AC_B$ $AC_2 = AC_A$	$AC_1 = AC_A = AC_B$	$AC_1 = AC_A = AC_B$	$AC_1 = AC_A = AC_B$	$AC_1 = AC_B$ $AC_2 = AC_A$
Surplus Monopolist (A)	DFEG	DFEG+FHGI	DFEG	DFEG+EGMN+ FHGI+GINO	DFEG	DFEG+KLDF	DFEG	DFEG+ KLDF+ EGMN
Surplus consumers (C)	JDH	JDH	JDH	JDH	JDH	JKL	JDH	JKL
Surplus competitors (B)	FHGI		FHGI		FHGI		FHGI	
Consumer welfare loss						KLDF+LFH		KLDF+ LFH
Competitor surplus loss		FHGI		FHGI		FHGI		FHGI
Deadweight loss						FHGI+LFH		FHGI+ LFH
Welfare gains				EGMN+GINO				EGMN

in t_1 $Q_M = Q_A$ and $Q_B = Q_C - Q_M$). Monopolist A engages in conduct that excludes its Competitors B from the market. After the foreclosure of B, Firm A does not reduce output or raise prices above the level that had prevailed under competition (in t_2 $P_1 = P_A$; $Q_c = Q_A$). Firm A appropriates the surplus of its Competitors B (FHGI). While smaller competitors are harmed as their producer rents are redistributed to the monopolist, consumer (JDH) and total (DFEG + FHGI + JDH) welfare remain unchanged.

In Scenario 2, Competitors B are again driven out of the market by perpetrator Firm A. However, in this instance, Firm A becomes more efficient than its competitors because it operates on lower AC (in t_2 $AC_1 = AC_B$; $AC_2 = AC_A$). The foreclosure does not result in higher prices because Monopolist A replaces the production by B and increases its output to the competitive level Q_c. Competitors B are again harmed, as their surplus (FHGI) is appropriated by Monopolist A, but Consumers C do not suffer any welfare losses. Consequently, total welfare increases because Firm A takes over the production of smaller Competitors B ($Q_C - Q_M$) and generates productive efficiencies (EGMN + GINO). These productive efficiencies may benefit consumers in the long run; for instance, if they allow A to reduce future prices below the competitive level (say points Q or P where demand intersects AC_1 or even AC_2).

Scenario 3 comes closest to the economics textbook example of monopoly. Perpetrator Firm A and Competitors B are equally efficient ($AC_1 = AC_A = AC_B$). After foreclosing Competitors B from the market, A reduces output and raises prices. Perpetrator Firm A's monopoly conduct results in a reduction in consumer surplus (KLDF + LFH) and deadweight loss in total welfare (FHGI + LFH). Some consumer surplus (KLDF) is redistributed to Monopolist A. Competitors B and some Consumers C who can no longer afford the product are prevented from entering into mutually beneficial transactions (FHGI + LFH).

Scenario 4 is almost identical to Scenario 3, apart from the fact that Competitors B are less efficient than Monopolist A ($AC_1 = AC_B$; $AC_2 = AC_A$). The removal of the competitive constraint that was exercised by Competitors B allows A to reduce output and increase prices. Consumer welfare (KLDF + LFH) and a deadweight loss of total welfare (FHGI + LFH) ensue. However, there are potential countervailing total welfare gains because Monopolist A's conduct brings about productive efficiencies (EGMN). Depending on the relative size of Monopolist A's output (Q_M) compared to the share of the output of its Competitors B ($Q_C - Q_M$), these efficiencies may counteract or even outweigh the consumer and total welfare losses. This will benefit Consumers C in the long run if they enable A to reduce prices below the level that had prevailed under the previous competitive equilibrium.

The problem with the republican approach is that it failed to articulate a clear limiting principle to determine when harm to competitors and the ensuing loss or appropriation of the producer surplus of competitors (FHGI) by a monopolist amounts to a restriction of or harm to competition and when it is legitimate. The republican approach sought to preserve the content- and context-independent decisiveness not only of the preferences of consumers but also of smaller competitors. It thereby ensured the modally robust protection of competitors' economic liberties and maintained a polycentric market structure as an institution of antipower. Hence, republican antitrust advocated an enforcement of competition law that does not shy away from protecting competitors in the name of protecting competition as a deconcentrated market structure. As a consequence, under a republican approach, antitrust intervention would not only be legitimate in Scenario 3, where monopoly conduct results in a clear-cut reduction in consumer and total welfare. On the contrary, the republican antitrust tradition would also counsel antitrust intervention in Scenario 4, even though the monopolist is more efficient than its competitors. Given its concern about preserving a polycentric market structure and protecting the preference-decisiveness of competitors, republican antitrust would, at least in some instances, even intervene in Scenarios 1 and 2. In both scenarios, the republican antitrust tradition would support competition law intervention, although they solely involve a redistribution of producer rents (FHGI) between Competitors B and Monopolist A. In neither scenario are Consumers C and society at large worse off. In Scenario 2, Consumers and society at large would be even better off because the production by Competitors B is taken over by the more efficient Monopolist A.

The republican antitrust approach thus stood for an interpretation of competition law that ended up protecting the economic liberty, and hence the producer surplus and rents, of smaller competitors against stronger players, even when their displacement and departure from the market would not reduce total or consumer welfare. In some instances, the republican approach went as far as condoning antitrust intervention to protect the surplus of small competitors, even though a more centralised organisation of the production or distribution of goods or services might have turned out to be more efficient and would have enhanced consumer welfare. Consequently, the republican antitrust tradition failed to clearly articulate when firm conduct that harmed competitors amounted to an undue restriction of or harm to competition. Nor did it openly confront potential tensions between protecting the producer rents of smaller competitors, efficiency, and consumer welfare. The indeterminacy of the republican approach led to logically inconsistent outcomes. After all, the elimination of less efficient competitors and the appropriation of their surplus by other market players is the very essence of competitive rivalry and is a crucial driver of economic welfare.

Republican antitrust often brushed over this tension between the preservation of producer surplus and consumer welfare, assuming that the preferences and interests of competitors and consumers would be aligned for most of the time. It thus approached most cases as if they were to fall under Scenario 3 or 4, where equally or less efficient Competitors B impose an important constraint on the Monopolist

A that prevents A from raising prices, and where the overall welfare effects of their exclusion depend on the size of the productive efficiencies that the monopoly conduct brings about (only Scenario 4). Consequently, the republican antitrust tradition turned a blind eye to the manifold instances – Scenarios 1 and 2 – where there might be important conflicts between the interests of competitors and consumers in the event that consumer and competitor preference orderings are misaligned. All too often, republican antitrust failed to acknowledge that liberty in its robust republican sense can only be protected by relaxing the weak Pareto principle: in other words, republican liberty can only be preserved if we accept Pareto-inefficient outcomes.[83] This tension between guaranteeing economic liberty through a polycentric market structure, efficiency, and consumer welfare found little, if any, mention in the republican antitrust tradition. Instead, these frictions were obfuscated under the thick conception of economic liberty as non-domination. As a consequence of its broad and demanding understanding of economic liberty, the republican approach failed to provide a clear standard to determine when (i) firm conduct unduly interferes with the economic freedom of other market participants (boundary issue 1) and (ii) when such interference was sufficiently serious to warrant state intervention (boundary issue 2).

6.4.2 *Boundary Issue 1: Is There a Clash between Spheres of Economic Liberty?*

Against the backdrop of this failure of the republican antitrust tradition, the Chicago School proposed the consumer welfare standard as a versatile framework to decide how tensions between different spheres of liberties and rights should be resolved and balanced. However, what is often ignored by antitrust scholars is that the consumer welfare approach did not simply replace the republican commitment to liberty as non-domination and equal status with the allegedly depoliticised, purely economic, and value-neutral concept of welfare.[84] On the contrary, the consumer welfare standard itself encodes a specific, narrowly defined notion of negative liberty.

The consumer welfare standard enabled the Chicago School to overcome the major failure of republican antitrust to address the boundary issue of when business conduct gives rise to permissible and impermissible interference. The consumer welfare standard clearly and narrowly delineates those (from the vantage point of the Chicago School) rare instances in which businesses' unbridled exercise of negative economic liberty unduly interferes with the economic freedom of other market

[83] C List, 'Social Choice Theory' https://plato.stanford.edu.

[84] AD Melamed and N Petit, 'The Misguided Assault on the Consumer Welfare Standard in the Age of Platform Markets' (2019) 54(4) *Review of Industrial Organization* 741, 747.

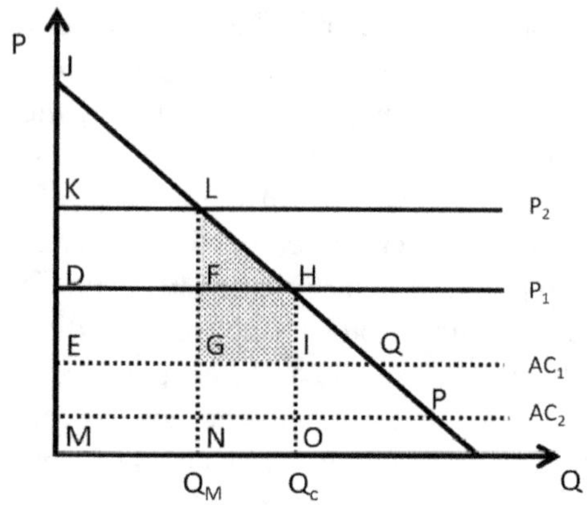

FIGURE 6.2 The Chicagoan consumer (a.k.a. total) welfare standard

participants so that antitrust intervention may be indicated.[85] In other words, the consumer welfare standard unequivocally defines the preventing conditions (y) of economic liberty by clearly identifying which type of conduct qualifies as undue interference with the economic liberty of other market participants.

While the republican approach failed to put forward a clear limiting principle as to when the exercise of entrepreneurial liberty unduly encroached upon the economic liberty of other market participants, the Chicagoan consumer welfare standard made it clear that any form of business conduct constitutes a perfectly legitimate manifestation of economic liberty as long as it is welfare-enhancing. Only if the exercise of contractual freedom and property rights by firms interferes with the economic liberty of other market participants in a welfare-decreasing manner and deprives them of the possibility to enter into mutually beneficial transactions without offering any compensation could it be considered a preventing condition of economic liberty.[86]

Figures 6.2 and 6.3, coupled with Table 6.2, illustrate how the consumer welfare approach allows for a clear determination of instances where firm conduct amounts to an undue restriction of economic liberty. The original version of the Chicagoan total welfare standard, which was disingenuously dubbed the 'consumer welfare standard' by Bork, construed the category of conduct that counts as preventing conditions very narrowly. It postulates that business conduct can only be considered anticompetitive if it entails a deadweight loss (LFH + FHGI in Figure 6.2) due to a restriction of output.[87] To be considered as giving rise to undue interference with the economic liberty of other market participants, the conduct of perpetrator Firm

[85] Peritz, 'A Counter-History of Antitrust Law' (n 35) 299–311; Fox, 'Consumer Beware Chicago' (n 3) 558.

[86] GJ Stigler, 'Wealth, and Possibly Liberty' (1978) 7(2) *The Journal of Legal Studies* 213, 217.

[87] Bork, *The Antitrust Paradox* (n 16) 110–13; Posner, *Antitrust Law* (n 13) 23–24.

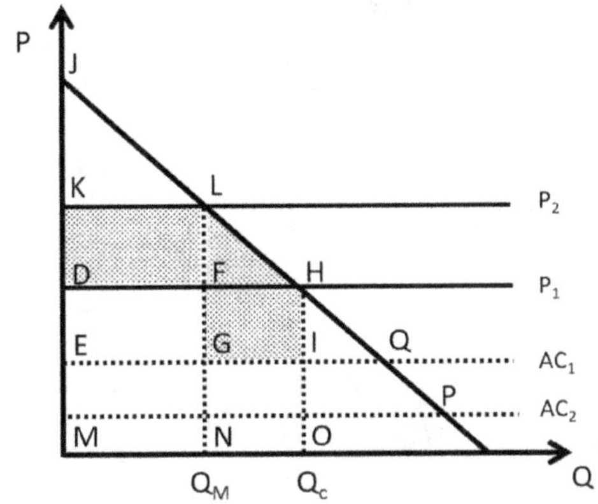

FIGURE 6.3 The genuine consumer welfare standard

A must restrict output and thus deflect some of Consumers C to second-best, less preferred substitutes.[88]

Not only does the total welfare standard precisely delineate when Monopolist A unduly interferes with the negative liberty of Consumers C but it also enables factfinders to decide when perpetrator Firm A impinges on the liberty of residual Competitors B. Under the total welfare standard, the fact that perpetrator Firm A's conduct excludes residual Competitors B from the market and reduces or appropriates their surplus only amounts to undue interference with the negative liberty of Competitors B if it entails a decrease in output, and thus a deadweight loss. In other words, perpetrator Firm A only invades the negative liberty of the residual Competitors B if its conduct prevents B from entering mutually beneficial economic transactions with consumers, which cannot be offered by perpetrator Firm A. However, this is only the case if the business conduct is likely to foreclose an equally or more efficient competitor (Scenario 3).[89] The total welfare standard thus only categorises business conduct as a preventing condition (y) that entails an undue interference with the economic liberty of other market participants if it reduces wealth, and hence the ability of market participants to enter mutually beneficial transactions.

The definition of preventing conditions of economic liberty under a genuine consumer welfare (i.e., consumer surplus) standard, which is favoured by post-Chicago scholarship,[90] differs only slightly from that under the Chicagoan total welfare standard. The consumer welfare standard merely broadens the category of conduct that qualifies as preventing conditions causing an illegitimate interference

88 Posner, *Antitrust Law* (n 13) 23–24.

89 Ibid. 194–97; RA Posner, 'Exclusionary Practices and the Antitrust Laws' (1974) 41(3) *The University of Chicago Law Review* 506.

90 See, for instance, RH Lande, 'Wealth Transfers as the Original and Primary Concern of Antitrust: The Efficiency Interpretation Challenged' (1982) 34(1) *Hastings Law Journal* 65.

TABLE 6.2 *Scenarios of competition law intervention*

	Scenario 1 As-efficient competitor surplus transfer		Scenario 2 Less efficient competitor surplus transfer		Scenario 3 Monopoly outcome with as-efficient competitors		Scenario 4 Monopoly outcome with less efficient competitors	
	t_1	t_2	t_1	t_2	t_1	t_2	t_1	t_2
Price (P)	$P_1 = P_A = P_B$	$P_1 = P_A$	$P_1 = P_A = P_B$	$P_1 = P_A$	$P_1 = P_A = P_B$	$P_2 = P_A$	$P_1 = P_A = P_B$	$P_2 = P_A$
Quantity of output (Q)	$Q_c = Q_A + Q_B$	$Q_c = Q_A$	$Q_c = Q_A + Q_B$	$Q_c = Q_A$	$Q_C = Q_A + Q_B$	$Q_M = Q_A$	$Q_c = Q_A + Q_B$	$Q_M = Q_A$
Average cost (AC)	$AC_1 = AC_A = AC_B$	$AC_1 = AC_A = AC_B$	$AC_1 = AC_A = AC_B$	$AC_1 = AC_B$ $AC_2 = AC_A$	$AC_1 = AC_A = AC_B$	$AC_1 = AC_A = AC_B$	$AC_1 = AC_A = AC_B$	$AC_1 = AC_B$ $AC_2 = AC_A$
Surplus Monopolist (A)	DFEG	DFEG+FHGI	DFEG	DFEG+EGMN+ FHGI+GINO	DFEG	DFEG+KLDF	DFEG	DFEG+ KLDF+ EGMN
Surplus consumers (C)	JDH	JDH	JDH	JDH	JDH	JKL	JDH	JKL
Surplus competitors (B)	FHGI		FHGI		FHGI		FHGI	
Consumer welfare loss						KLDF+LFH		KLDF+ LFH
Competitor surplus loss		FHGI		FHGI		FHGI		FHGI
Deadweight loss						FHGI+LFH		FHGI+ LFH
Welfare gains				EGMN+GINO				EGMN

with the negative liberty of other market participants. Under the consumer welfare standard, business conduct by perpetrator Firm A amounts to impermissible coercion not only if it deprives Consumers C of the ability to enter into mutually-beneficial voluntary transactions (deadweight loss LFH + FHGI in Figure 6.3) but also if it adversely affects the terms or conditions of those transactions or bargains to the benefit of perpetrator Firm A and at the expense of Consumers C. This is the case if perpetrator Firm A's conduct leads to higher prices (or lower quality, etc.), thus entailing a wealth transfer (KLDF in Figure 6.3) from Consumers C to Firm A.

The adoption of a consumer welfare standard also slightly changes the conditions under which conduct by perpetrator Firm A is to be considered as unduly interfering with the negative liberty of residual Competitors B. This is no longer only the case in the event that the exclusion of B leads to a deadweight loss because consumers are deprived of entering into mutually beneficial transactions with Competitors B that cannot be offered by perpetrator Firm A. Rather, under the consumer welfare approach, the liberty of Competitors B is also abrogated if consumers are deprived of the possibility to enter into market transactions with Competitors B that are at least as mutually beneficial as those offered by perpetrator Firm A, and therefore suffer a reduction of consumer surplus due to higher prices (or lower quality, etc.).

Table 6.3 summarises how the total and consumer welfare standards pinpoint when conduct by a perpetrator firm (e.g., a monopolist, a group of firms, or a merger) results in the restriction of negative economic liberty. Under both standards, this is the case if the conduct results in welfare-reducing interference. The only difference between the two lies in the welfare reduction that both standards consider relevant as anticompetitive harm. As the consumer welfare standard accounts for consumer surplus reduction as an additional source of relevant harm, it treats a theoretically broader range (LFH + FHGI + KLDF) of situations as harmful welfare-reducing interference than the total welfare standard (LFH + FHGI). Thus, the consumer welfare standard potentially encompasses a broader range of conduct as preventing conditions of the negative economic liberty of consumers or competitors. Yet, the theoretical subtleties of how the total and consumer welfare standard identify undue interference are unlikely to make a material difference in practice. This explains why post-Chicago scholars and antitrust enforcers widely followed the strategy that was proposed by the Chicago School to infer adverse effects on consumer surplus from the exclusion of an equally or more efficient competitor.[91] In endorsing the as-efficient competitor principle, the consumer welfare standard precludes any antitrust intervention in Scenario 4, although it is conceivable that even less efficient competitors offer a product or service at a lower price than an

[91] P Areeda and DF Turner, 'Predatory Pricing and Related Practices under Section 2 of the Sherman Act' (1975) 88(4) *Harvard Law Review* 697; WJ Baumol, 'Predation and the Logic of the Average Variable Cost Test' (1996) 39(1) *Journal of Law & Economics* 49.

TABLE 6.3 *Total and consumer welfare standards and preventing conditions of negative liberty*

	Total welfare standard	Consumer welfare standard
Obstruction of liberty of Consumers C	Interference of perpetrator Firm A • reduces the volume of mutually beneficial transactions • that consumers could enter in the absence of A's conduct	Interference of perpetrator Firm A • reduces the volume and/or deteriorates the conditions of mutually beneficial transactions • that consumers could enter in the absence of A's conduct
Elements of obstructive conduct	• Output restriction • Deadweight loss (LFH + FHGI)	• Output restriction • Deadweight loss (LFH + FHGI) • Price increase • Wealth transfer from consumers to the perpetrator firm (KLDF)
Obstruction of liberty of Competitors B	Interference of perpetrator Firm A • prevents Competitors B from entering mutually beneficial transactions with consumers • that would be available in the absence of A's conduct • and cannot be offered by A	Interference of perpetrator Firm A • prevents Competitors B from entering mutually beneficial transactions with consumers • that would be available in the absence of A's conduct • and either cannot be offered by A • or can only be offered at less advantageous conditions
Elements of obstructive conduct	• Foreclosure of an equally/more efficient competitor • Reduction in output • Deadweight loss (LFH + FHGI)	• Foreclosure of an equally/more efficient competitor • Reduction in output/increases in prices • Deadweight loss (LFH + FHGI) • Wealth transfer from consumers to the perpetrator firm (KLDF)

incumbent monopolist in the absence of competition, and thereby maximise consumer welfare.[92]

Both iterations of the consumer welfare standard (i.e., total welfare and genuine consumer welfare standard) offer a conception of economic liberty that effectively addresses the indeterminacy of the republican approach. Unlike the republican approach, the consumer welfare standard relies on welfare-decreasing interference as a clear benchmark to determine when the economic liberty of market participants is obstructed. Both versions of the consumer welfare approach thus clarified the meaning of the concept of restriction of competition to unambiguously tell

[92] JF Brodley and GA Hay, 'Predatory Pricing: Competing Economic Theories and the Evolution of Legal Standards' (1980–1981) 66(4) *Cornell Law Review* 738, 743–45.

anticompetitive apart from legitimate firm conduct. The consumer welfare standard departed from the sweeping scope of the republican antitrust tradition that had condoned antitrust intervention in a broad range of situations (i.e., Scenarios 1, 2, and 4) where firm conduct harmed competitors without necessarily reducing consumer or total welfare. In contrast, the consumer welfare standard indicates that the economic liberty of market participants is only unduly obstructed in Scenario 3 where firm conduct interferes with other market participants in a way that reduces consumer or total welfare.

This link between the consumer welfare standard and negative liberty also features prominently in the scholarly writings of members of the Chicago School. Chicago scholars asserted that the principle of wealth maximisation offers a strong normative justification for economic liberty, property rights, and their (re)assignment through free and competitive markets.[93] Wealth or welfare was thought to be nothing else than the aggregate sum of all voluntary mutually beneficial market transactions by which market participants express their (dollar-backed) preferences for the sale and acquisition of a particular good, service, property right, etc. Through the maximisation of welfare or wealth, the competitive market system enhances the negative liberty of market players through two channels. By maximising allocative efficiency, competition enables market participants to realise a maximum of mutually beneficial transactions.[94] Meanwhile, competition also contributes to the maximisation of the market participants' welfare and liberty by increasing productive efficiency. Competitive rivalry pushes individual firms to develop the most effective way of producing and selling products that appeal most to society's wants.[95] In compelling firms to be productively efficient, competitive markets ensure that individual players can only pursue their self-interest and maximise their wealth by engaging in activities that benefit others.[96] Hence, in a competitive market system, any form of interference with the sphere of autonomy or liberty of other market participants is constrained by the need to engage in a voluntary contractual transaction with the other individual; or in other words, by one's willingness to pay the other market participant in compensation for this interference.[97] In short, the competitive market system enhances the negative liberty of market participants because it enables them to enter mutually beneficial voluntary transactions free of coercion[98] and broadens the range of options market

[93] RA Posner, 'Utilitarianism, Economics, and Legal Theory' (1979) 8(1) *The Journal of Legal Studies* 103, 127; RA Posner, 'Wealth Maximization Revisited' (1985) 2(1) *Notre Dame Journal of Law, Ethics and Public Policy* 85, 96, 99–101. Stigler went as far as equalling wealth with liberty, arguing that the larger the sum of earnings and spending an individual could dispose of, the wider becomes their range of options and choices, see Stigler, 'Wealth, and Possibly Liberty' (n 86) 213–14.

[94] Bork, *The Antitrust Paradox* (n 16) 91, 101.

[95] Ibid. 91, 104–06.

[96] Posner, 'Utilitarianism, Economics, and Legal Theory' (n 93) 132.

[97] Posner, 'Wealth Maximization Revisited' (n 93) 99–101.

[98] Stigler, 'Wealth, and Possibly Liberty' (n 86) 212.

participants can choose from.[99] In linking the goal of welfare maximisation with negative liberty and individual rights,[100] the Chicago School harnessed the consumer welfare standard as a new tool to determine the normative foundation, content, and boundaries of economic liberty. Unlike the republican approach, the wealth maximisation principle and consumer welfare standard were able to provide an unequivocal answer to the question of which type of firm conduct unduly interferes with the economic freedom of other market participants in such a way that it can legitimately be said to constitute a preventing condition (y) of economic liberty.

6.4.3 *Boundary Issue 2: How to Manage Clashes between Spheres of Negative Liberty?*

The role of the consumer welfare standard in operationalising negative economic liberty is not limited to the fact that it offers a conceptually clear answer to the question of when impugned business conduct amounts to an undue restriction of the negative liberty of other market participants. The consumer welfare standard also offers a workable framework for balancing the rights and liberties of the relevant stakeholders (e.g., consumers, competitors, perpetrator firm(s)) to decide when such a prima facie liberty-reducing interference actually warrants state intervention. It thus provides a clear framework to deal with the problem of the non-compossibility of economic liberty by offering guidance on how frictions between spheres of liberty should be resolved (boundary issue 2).

The welfare standard thus also addresses the second shortcoming of republican antitrust. We have seen in the previous chapters that the proponents of a republican understanding of liberty recognise the possibility of non-arbitrary interference by public decision-makers who are subject to democratic and constitutional control.[101] For this reason, republican antitrust did not view every form of state interference with the economic activities of market participants as abrogating their liberty. On the contrary, assuming that antitrust laws are non-arbitrary qua their adoption and enforcement through processes which comply with democratic and rule-of-law principles, the republican antitrust tradition could easily make the case that competition rules enhance liberty by reducing the overall level of domination in society – even if they interfere with and restrict choices or discretion of some economic agents.

99 Ibid. 214–16.

100 Posner, 'Utilitarianism, Economics, and Legal Theory' (n 93) 135, 140. Posner argues that the principle of wealth maximisation draws on both utilitarian and Kantian ethics; see RA Posner, 'Norms and Values in the Economic Approach to Law' in AN Hatzis and N Mercuro (eds), *Law and Economics: Philosophical Issues and Fundamental Questions* (London: Routledge 2015) 1, 10.

101 See, for instance, P Pettit, 'Freedom in the Market' (2006) 5(2) *Politics, Philosophy & Economics* 131, 145–46.

The assumption that non-arbitrary and, ergo, non-dominating interference by public instances does not automatically frustrate the liberty of market participants is both an inherent strength but also a shortcoming of the republican understanding of liberty. On the one hand, it provides a much stronger normative justification and more policy space for a society to create institutions that enhance a more resilient form of liberty than negative liberty does. On the other hand, the proposition that state interference, if taking a non-arbitrary form, does not reduce liberty has been criticised as a 'moralized'[102] conception of liberty that easily degenerates into paternalism.[103] In the absence of a clear boundary principle to define when state intervention amounts to coercion and a reduction of liberty, the republican idea of non-arbitrary state interference may transform into a slippery slope that pushes antitrust towards an over-regulatory policy that stymies free enterprise instead of promoting it.

The Chicago School disputed this welcoming attitude of republican antitrust towards state intervention. In keeping with the tradition of negative liberty,[104] it perceived antitrust laws (in the same way as any other form of state intervention) as an interference with the liberty of market participants, and hence as coercion.[105] On the Chicagoan account, antitrust law interferes with the choices of perpetrator Firm A to prevent or remedy invasions of the negative liberty of Consumers C and/or residual Competitors B. Accordingly, competition law intervention inevitably reduces the negative liberty of the perpetrator Firm A. Chicago scholars therefore assumed that the application of antitrust rules calls for a balancing of the rights and interests of the perpetrator Firm A and Consumers C and/or Competitors B.

It is noteworthy that the way in which the Chicagoan welfare standard structures this balance of rights is largely in accordance with how Jeremy Bentham and other proponents of negative liberty during the eighteenth and nineteenth centuries

[102] For a comprehensive discussion of this critique, see C List and L Valentini, 'Freedom as Independence' (2016) 126(4) *Ethics* 1043, 1058–65.

[103] Philip Pettit seeks to fence off this charge of paternalism by arguing that for state interference not to invade liberty, it must always account for the interests of the people whose choices are interfered with. Otherwise, it cannot be considered non-arbitrary. At first sight, this reads like a very strong limiting principle. Yet Pettit further concedes that the individual's (long-term) interests do not necessarily coincide with their immediate wishes. If we transpose this reasoning to competition policy, then republicans might argue that state interference is ultimately even in the interest of the perpetrator firm that is found to have violated competition law rules because the latter also benefits – at least in the long-run – from the preservation of a competitive market. Although it is theoretically appealing, it remains doubtful that antitrust defendants would be persuaded by this argument. P Pettit, *On the People's Terms: A Republican Theory and Model of Democracy* (Cambridge: Cambridge University Press 2012) 58–59.

[104] P Pettit, 'Freedom as Antipower' (1996) 106(3) *Ethics* 576, 596; P Pettit, *Republicanism: A Theory of Freedom and Government* (Oxford: Oxford University Press 1997) 37–38, 42–44.

[105] RH Coase, 'The Federal Communications Commission' (1959) 2 *Journal of Law and Economics* 1, 14, 18, 27–29; Posner, 'Utilitarianism, Economics, and Legal Theory' (n 93) 130; Bork, *The Antitrust Paradox* (n 16) 133.

deemed it appropriate to resolve such clashes of rights.[106] The Chicagoan welfare standard indicates that antitrust intervention to remedy the undue reduction of negative liberty of Consumers C or residual Competitors B caused by interfering conduct on the part of perpetrator Firm A is only permissible as long as the resulting increase in liberty of Consumers C or Competitors B more than compensates for the reduction of the liberty of Monopolist A as a consequence of state interference. Thus, the welfare standard encapsulates the proposition that state interference is only legitimate if the reduction of negative liberty of perpetrating firms as a consequence of remedial state coercion is more than offset by the gains in liberty of other market players by reason of the fact that anticompetitive harm is averted or remedied.

A central appeal of the Chicagoan consumer welfare standard is that the wealth maximisation principle provides a handy device that allows competition authorities or courts to compare and balance the otherwise incommensurable values of the liberty or rights of all relevant stakeholders. The Chicagoan wealth maximisation principle offers a common cardinal unit[107] to measure the offsetting effects of (state) interference with the liberty of a perpetrator Firm A, Consumers C, and Competitors B. It suggests that state intervention is only legitimate if the gains of total wealth as a consequence of the increase in liberty of Consumers C or Competitors B outweigh any potential reduction in wealth due to the state interference with the liberty of the perpetrator Firm A. In other words, state intervention and coercion to remedy the interference with the liberty of B or C is only permissible if it maximises wealth more than the unrestrained exercise of negative liberty by the perpetrator Firm A does.[108] The wealth maximisation principle thus offers a clear limiting principle for antitrust policy. It indicates that antitrust intervention is only legitimate if it maximises the net expected liberty, measured in net expected welfare, in society.[109]

The Chicago School implemented this balancing principle by using the Williamsonian trade-off model between productive and allocative efficiency, which is depicted in Figures 6.4 and 6.5. The potential trade-off between productive efficiency and allocative efficiency provided the Chicago School with a framework to balance the costs and benefits of the reduction of liberty of perpetrator Firm A and Consumers C or Competitors B. The Chicago School postulated that antitrust intervention is only warranted if the reduction in allocative efficiency, and hence the liberty of Consumers C or Competitors B to enter into mutually beneficial transactions (LFH + FHGI) as the consequence of interfering conduct by

[106] Pettit, 'Freedom as Antipower' (n 104) 596, 598–99, 601; Pettit *Republicanism* (n 104) 44, 46.

[107] For the need of such a common cardinal unit to carry out meaningful balancing, see H Hovenkamp, 'Antitrust Balancing' (2016) 12(2) *New York University Journal of Law and Business* 369, 373.

[108] Posner, 'Utilitarianism, Economics, and Legal Theory' (n 93) 130.

[109] See for a similar formulation Pettit, 'Freedom in the Market' (n 101) 145.

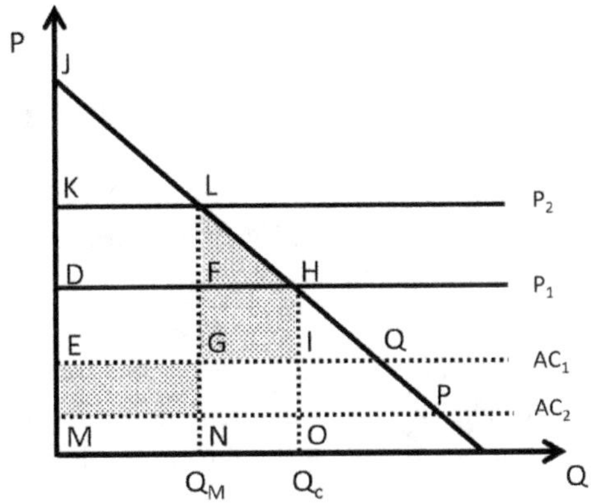

FIGURE 6.4 Balancing of rights under the total welfare standard

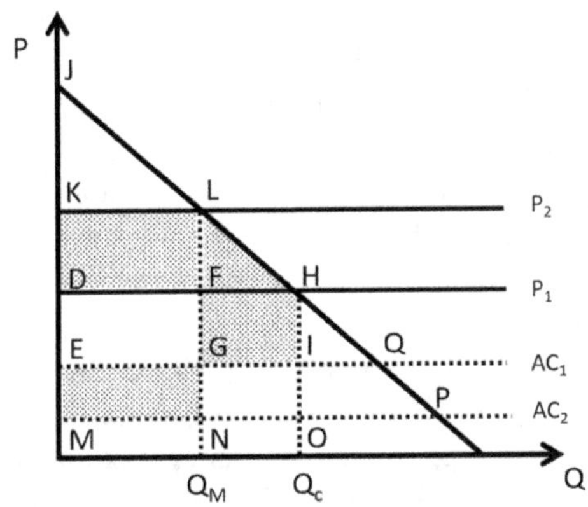

FIGURE 6.5 Balancing of rights under the consumer welfare standard

perpetrator Firm A, is not outweighed by gains in the form of productive efficiency generated (EGMN) through the exercise of the negative liberty by perpetrator Firm A, which might increase the total volume of mutually beneficial transactions (Figure 6.4).[110]

While total and consumer welfare standards follow the same balancing logic, their different views on what amounts to a preventing condition of liberty affect the outcomes of this balance of rights. Under the total welfare standard (Figure 6.4), the gains in productive efficiency (EGMN) that a perpetrator firm derives from the exercise of its negative liberty must only be large enough to theoretically compensate consumers for the reduction in allocative efficiency resulting from the loss of mutually beneficial transactions (the deadweight loss LFH + FHGI) caused by the

[110] Bork, *The Antitrust Paradox* (n 16) 107–10; Posner, *Antitrust Law* (n 13) 23, 29; Williamson (n 31).

impugned conduct. This balancing of rights relies on Kaldor–Hicks efficiency as a decision rule, which merely requires that the perpetrator firm be theoretically capable of compensating other market players for their losses in liberty, without the need for any actual compensation.[111]

Under the consumer welfare standard (Figure 6.5), the balancing exercise differs from that envisaged by the Chicagoan total welfare standard in two respects. First, the productive efficiencies must outweigh not only the deadweight loss (LFH + FHGI) but also any wealth transfer from consumers to the perpetrator firm (KLDF). This is the immediate consequence of the fact that proponents of a consumer welfare standard perceive not only the deadweight loss but also the wealth transfer resulting from anticompetitive conduct as undue interference, and hence as a source of unfreedom. As a result, the gains in productive efficiency that a perpetrator firm derives from the unrestricted exercise of its negative commercial liberty must be larger than under the total welfare standard for them to outweigh any losses in negative liberty, measured as wealth, on the part of consumers or competitors. Second, under the consumer welfare standard, it is not sufficient that the gains in productive efficiency allow the perpetrator firm to theoretically compensate consumers or competitors for the reduction in liberty suffered. Rather, the perpetrator firm must actually compensate consumers to make sure that consumers as a class are not worse off as a result of the exercise of its negative liberty. Therefore, the consumer welfare standard requires that the interfering business conduct generate Pareto-efficient, instead of Kaldor–Hicks or theoretically Pareto-efficient, outcomes. The consumer welfare standard thus establishes a lower threshold for state intervention (or conversely, a stricter standard for rebutting the prima facie finding of undue interference based on gains in productive efficiency) than the total welfare standard does. However, balancing under the post-Chicago consumer welfare standard remains fully within the perimeters of the framework set out by the Chicago School to balance the rights and liberties of various market participants.

The balancing under both the total and the consumer welfare standard has in common that neither requires any direct (theoretical/actual) compensation of competitors. The interests of competitors (measured in producer surplus) do not enter the equation of this balancing exercise. Competitor interests are only entering the picture indirectly as long as they enhance total or consumer welfare more than the gains in productive efficiency brought about by the perpetrator firm's interfering conduct. Hence, the consideration of the rights and interests of competitors is subordinate to their contribution to the consumers' or society's wealth.

By seeking to align competition law with the consumer welfare standard, proponents of the More Economic Approach proposed to overcome the republican paradox

[111] Posner, 'Wealth Maximization Revisited' (n 93) 102–03; Posner, 'Norms and Values in the Economic Approach to Law' (n 100) 11; Coase, 'The Federal Communications Commission' (n 105) 26–29; Coase, 'The Problem of Social Cost' (n 56) 10.

by reverting to Kaldor–Hicks (total welfare) or Pareto efficiency (consumer welfare standard) as a decision rule to balance and solve clashes between conflicting liberties of market participants. The balance of rights under the total and consumer welfare standard solves competing liberty claims in favour of the party that will contribute most to the maximisation of preference satisfaction, and thereby (at least theoretically) compensates parties whose liberty has been reduced. Competition law may only legitimately step in if the unrestricted exercise of negative entrepreneurial liberty fails to bring about such (theoretically) Pareto-efficient outcomes.

6.4.4 *The Chicagoan Error–Cost Framework*

While relying on the Williamsonian trade-off model as a framework to reconceptualise the balancing of rights for antitrust policy, the Chicago scholars insisted that in most cases no such balancing of pro- and anticompetitive effects is necessary to decide whether antitrust intervention is justified. In most instances, the effects of business conduct on productive and allocative efficiency pull in the same direction. Accordingly, most cases involve clear-cut welfare-enhancing conduct, maximising both allocative and productive efficiencies. Only in exceptionally rare cases has business conduct a clear-cut detrimental net effect on welfare so that state interference is legitimate to remedy the reduction in the liberty of other market participants.[112]

On this account, Chicago scholars asserted that antitrust law should encode the welfarist balance of rights in the design of antitrust standards and decisional filters, rather than engaging in a case-by-case balancing of pro- and anticompetitive effects.[113] The design of antitrust law should simply follow the premise that most business conduct tends to be pro-competitive or competitively neutral.[114] Chicago scholars therefore called for a radical departure from the interventionist penchant of republican antitrust. For most business conduct, apart from hard-core cartels and horizontal mergers to monopoly,[115] the scope of antitrust law should be scaled back lest it unduly interfere with the negative liberty of businesses.

Assuming that the population of welfare-enhancing clearly exceeds that of welfare-reducing business conduct, the Chicago School further asserted that antitrust enforcers and courts would only be confronted with a small number of hard cases falling within the grey area where state intervention would require a difficult balancing exercise between the conflicting claims about negative liberty. In these tight cases, the assumption that most business conduct on balance tends to be pro-

[112] Bork, *The Antitrust Paradox* (n 16) 108–09, 122–29, 133, 148–54 (predatory pricing), 303–07 (exclusive dealing), 380–88 (tying); Easterbrook, 'The Limits of Antitrust' (n 57) 10–11, 15.

[113] Bork, *The Antitrust Paradox* (n 16) 128–29, 219–22; Posner, *Antitrust Law* (n 13) 132–33; Easterbrook, 'The Limits of Antitrust' (n 57) 14–39.

[114] Bork, *The Antitrust Paradox* (n 16) 122–28, 133.

[115] FH Easterbrook, 'Workable Antitrust' (1986) 84(8) *Michigan Law Review* 1696, 1701.

TABLE 6.4 *Outcomes of antitrust intervention and stylised pay-offs*

	*H*1 is true	*H*o is true
Intervention	True positives $(1-\beta)G$	False positives αL
Non-intervention	False negatives βG	True negatives $(1-\alpha)L$

competitive or competitively neutral should operate as a tie breaker.[116] Accordingly, antitrust policy should 'play safe' and in the case of doubt opt for non-intervention.[117]

The Chicago School thus proposed a new design principle for antitrust law that formalises a skewed balancing of rights in favour of negative entrepreneurial liberty of alleged perpetrator firms. Chicago scholars operationalised this slanted balancing of rights by advocating an error–cost framework[118] that radically departed from the prophylactic and precautionary approach of republican antitrust. In line with decision theory, the Chicago School acknowledged that decision-making under uncertainty is always prone to error. Instead of trying to get every decision right, competition law enforcers and courts should seek to minimise the costs of false positives (type I errors) and negatives (type II errors) which are notated as L (costs of type I errors) and G (costs of type II errors), respectively, in Table 6.4.

Instead of attributing equal weight to the minimisation of the costs stemming from both types of errors, the Chicago School posited that the welfare costs of erroneous over-enforcement (L) (false positives) always tend to exceed the error costs resulting from under-enforcement (G) (false negatives) of antitrust law (i.e., $L > G$).[119] Along with the general costs of the administration of the legal system (including litigation), the Chicago School warned that erroneous antitrust intervention generates two forms of cost. On the one hand, the erroneous decision itself creates costs as it mistakenly prohibits efficient business conduct. On the other hand, false positives also create welfare costs through deterrence because other or future market players will also be dissuaded from engaging in efficient, welfare-enhancing conduct.[120] Therefore, the welfare costs of false positives tend to be generally high because even small gains in productive efficiencies implemented by all firms in an industry are sufficient to outweigh substantial price increases by the perpetrator firm.[121]

At the same time, the Chicago School also entrenched the view that the costs (G) of false negatives (type II errors) tend to be low relative to the costs (L) of false positives (type I errors). This proposition rested on two assumptions. The first relates

[116] Bork, *The Antitrust Paradox* (n 16) 133.

[117] Easterbrook, 'The Limits of Antitrust' (n 57) 15.

[118] The error-cost analysis has been pioneered by Chicago scholars; see I Ehrlich and RA Posner, 'An Economic Analysis of Legal Rulemaking' (1974) 3(1) *The Journal of Legal Studies* 257.

[119] Easterbrook, 'The Limits of Antitrust' (n 57) 3, 15–16.

[120] Ibid. 15.

[121] Ibid. 16.

to the share of overall output affected by type I and II errors. Chicago scholars suggested that erroneously acquitted anticompetitive conduct only leads to a restriction of output or price increases on the units sold by the firms indulging in the conduct. In contrast, mistaken condemnation of a pro-competitive business practice may prohibit or deter all firms from applying an efficient production technique to all units of the industry output. The second assumption relates to the propensity of market- and state-based institutional settings to self-correct errors. Chicagoans held the belief that the anticompetitive harm (e.g., price increases) resulting from false negatives would only be of temporary nature, as market entry would defeat any undetected monopoly harm resulting from false negatives (i.e., erroneously acquitted truly anticompetitive conduct) in the medium term. In contrast, potential efficiencies foregone by reason of mistaken inferences about the anticompetitive nature of specific conduct will be forever lost.[122] For judicial and legislative processes are unlikely to self-correct judicial errors taking the form of false condemnations.[123]

The Chicagoan School thus turned the assumptions of the precautionary error–cost framework that characterised the republican antitrust tradition upside down. While the republican antitrust tradition held the belief that the costs of type II errors by far exceed those of type I errors ($\beta G > \alpha L$), the Chicago School's error–cost framework suggested that the opposite is the case ($\beta G < \alpha L$). On the one hand, this reconfiguration of the error–cost framework was the outcome of diverging economic assumptions about the occurrence of anticompetitive harm. The structuralist approach of republican antitrust assumed the population of potentially anticompetitive conduct to be much larger than the Chicagoan consumer welfare standard. On the other hand, the redrawing of the error–cost framework is also the consequence of contrasting political views about the scope and nature of economic liberty. The thick and modally robust notion of economic liberty as non-domination cultivated by the republican antitrust approach seeks to prevent anticompetitive harm across all relevant possible worlds. Moreover, it assumes that antitrust harm is not confined to the economic sphere but has negative externalities on a democratic society and polity. At the same time, the republican notion of liberty suggested that the costs of non-arbitrary state interference are low. The republican antitrust tradition thus endorses a precautionary error–cost framework that sees preventing anticompetitive harm as a priority. In contrast, the narrow negative conception of economic liberty as the absence of welfare-reducing interference underpinning the consumer welfare standard assumed that antitrust policy only needs to be worried about harm in the actual or nearby likely world. By focusing exclusively on welfare maximisation as the goal of antitrust, the Chicago School's consumer welfare

[122] Ibid. 15–16.

[123] Bork, *The Antitrust Paradox* (n 16) 143–44; Easterbrook, 'The Limits of Antitrust' (n 57) 15; A Devlin and M Jacobs, 'Antitrust Error' (2010) 52(2) *William and Mary Law Review* 75, 84–85.

approach also discounted potential externalities of anticompetitive harm beyond the economic sphere. Furthermore, in considering any form of state intervention as liberty-reducing coercion, the Chicagoan negative conception of economic liberty assumed the costs of state intervention to be much higher than the republican approach.

Table 6.5 summarises the diverging predispositions of the republican precautionary and the Chicagoan laissez-faire error–cost framework. The republican precautionary error–cost framework rested on the assumption that the potential harm of a broad range of business conduct exceeds potential benefits. Therefore, the accuracy benefits of antitrust intervention outweigh the costs of over-enforcement ($(1-\beta)G > \alpha L$). In contrast, the laissez-faire error–cost framework operated on the premise that most business conduct is on balance beneficial or competitively neutral, and that the costs of state intervention therefore outweigh its accuracy benefits ($(1-\beta)G < \alpha L$).[124] Whereas the precautionary error–cost framework counselled an interventionist policy that seeks to minimise the type II error rate β, the laissez-faire error–cost framework of the Chicago School advocated a diametrically opposed approach towards antitrust intervention that seeks to minimise the type I error rate α. The Chicagoan laissez-faire error–cost framework thus entrenched the notion that the real problem of antitrust enforcement lies not in the risk that some form of anticompetitive conduct goes undetected but that efficient and aggressive competitive conduct is erroneously classified as anticompetitive.[125] In case of doubt, antitrust law should therefore err on the side of type II errors and the negative liberty of powerful firms.[126]

The assumption that state intervention in most cases tends to be more expensive than 'doing nothing',[127] and therefore that type II errors are preferable to type I errors, provided the Chicago School with a powerful economic argument in support of shielding the negative entrepreneurial liberty of alleged perpetrator firms against antitrust intervention. Indeed, the Chicago School error–cost framework puts some economic gloss on the assumption that most of the time the loss in commercial liberty suffered by powerful businesses as a consequence of antitrust intervention is not outweighed by any gains in liberty (measured as welfare) of other market participants, in particular consumers, that would justify such state interference in the first place.[128] The Chicagoan consumer welfare standard and error–cost framework thus envelop a balance of rights and design of competition rules that are geared towards preserving the negative liberty of businesses against state intervention.

[124] For the notion of 'accuracy benefits', see H First and S Weber Waller, 'Antitrust's Democracy Deficit' (2013) 81(5) *Fordham Law Review* 2543, 2570–72.

[125] Bork, *The Antitrust Paradox* (n 16) 157.

[126] Easterbrook, 'The Limits of Antitrust' (n 57) 16.

[127] Coase, 'The Problem of Social Cost' (n 56) 18.

[128] Bork, *The Antitrust Paradox* (n 16) 134–35, 143–44, 157, 196.

TABLE 6.5 *The precautionary and laissez-faire error–cost framework*

Variable	Republican antitrust	Laissez-faire antitrust
Gains of competition law intervention (G)	High Economic predispositions • Broad category of anticompetitive harm • Markets are unlikely to self-correct erroneous non-intervention Political predispositions • Type of preventing conditions: G includes not only isolated incidences of interference in the actual, but domination across various possible worlds • Location of harm: not only economic, but also political sphere	Low Economic predispositions • Narrow category of anticompetitive harm • Markets are likely to self-correct erroneous non-intervention Political predispositions • Type of preventing conditions: G includes only isolated incidences of welfare-decreasing interference in the actual or nearby likely world • Location of harm: only economic sphere
Losses of competition law intervention (*L*)	Low Economic predispositions • Lost efficiencies can be replicated through independent conduct or organic growth Political predispositions • Type of preventing conditions: non-arbitrary state interference does not lead to a reduction of liberty	High Economic predispositions • Lost efficiencies are forever lost Political predispositions • Type of preventing conditions: state interference always reduces liberty
Conclusions	• Costs of type II errors exceed the costs of type I errors ($\beta G > \alpha L$) • Accuracy benefits of antitrust enforcement exceed the costs of false positives ($(1-\beta)G) > \alpha L$) • Accuracy benefits of antitrust enforcement exceed the accuracy benefits of non-enforcement ($((1-\beta)G > (1-\alpha))L$)	• Costs of type I errors exceed the costs of type II errors ($\alpha L > \beta G$) • Accuracy benefits of antitrust enforcement fall short of the costs of false positives ($((1-\beta)G < \alpha L$) • Accuracy benefits of antitrust enforcement fall short of the accuracy benefits of non-enforcement ($((1-\beta)G < (1-\alpha)L$)
Type II error rate β	• Should be minimised	• Less of a concern
Type I error rate α	• Less of a concern	• Should be minimised

6.5 THE CHANGING GEOMETRY OF ECONOMIC LIBERTY AND THE RISE OF LAISSEZ-FAIRE ANTITRUST

With the consumer welfare standard and the Chicagoan error–cost framework, the Chicago School proposed a blueprint for an antitrust policy that was clearly skewed in favour of the protection of negative entrepreneurial liberty of businesses, and against state intervention to protect the liberty of consumers and competitors. Far from being grounded in robust economic theory or empirical findings, this preference for non-intervention was derived from the assumption or ideological 'belief'[129] that most business conduct being the outcome of entrepreneurial liberty is beneficial. At the same time, the Chicago School affirmed that the opposite is true for state intervention. It asserted that state interference or coercion is most of the time more costly and harmful than private interference with other market participants' liberty.[130]

6.5.1 *Economic Liberty as Negative Entrepreneurial Liberty*

The previous sections showed how the Chicago antitrust revolution successfully brought antitrust law in line with a laissez-faire understanding of negative liberty as entrepreneurial liberty. This laissez-faire approach dispelled the republican concern that the economic liberty of competitors and consumers must be protected against the domination of powerful firms. Instead, it claimed that it is the entrepreneurial liberty or the 'freedom of action of large business firms'[131] that has to be protected against any state intervention.[132] Accordingly, the Chicago School primarily perceived economic liberty as the unrestricted right of businesses to engage in welfare maximising behaviour and mutually beneficial transactions. 'Free enterprise' in the Chicagoan vocabulary stands in the first place for freedom from state interference, while it remains relatively indifferent towards interference with economic liberty by private players.[133] No one was more candid about this ideological bias of the Chicagoan framework in favour of negative entrepreneurial liberty than Robert Bork. He posited that in the case of doubt 'the general preference for freedom should bar legal coercion'[134] and the 'firm should be better left alone'.[135]

[129] Coase, 'The Problem of Social Cost' (n 56) 18–19.
[130] Bork, *The Antitrust Paradox* (n 16) 133; Coase, 'The Federal Communications Commission' (n 105) 18; Coase, 'The Problem of Social Cost' (n 56) 17–18.
[131] Posner, *Antitrust Law* (n 13) 26; Bork, 'The Goals of Antitrust Policy' (n 15) 252–53.
[132] Posner, 'Utilitarianism, Economics, and Legal Theory' (n 93) 127–30; Coase, 'The Federal Communications Commission' (n 105) 17–19.
[133] Posner, 'Utilitarianism, Economics, and Legal Theory" (n 93) 123, 127–34; Fox, 'Consumer Beware Chicago' (n 3) 1715.
[134] Bork, *The Antitrust Paradox* (n 16) 133.
[135] Ibid. 196.

By adopting the value of welfare maximisation as the unique goal of competition law, the Chicago School substituted republican liberty with a narrower notion of negative economic liberty as non-interference as the ultimate normative foundation of antitrust. The concern about potential domination and arbitrary interference by big business or by certain categories of business practices no longer had a place within this new vision of competition law. Instead, the Chicago School only perceived monopoly or specific firm conduct as objectionable if they lead to actual or likely interference with the liberty of other market participants in a way that entails welfare losses and reduces available opportunities to enter into mutually beneficial transactions.[136]

6.5.2 *Narrow Categories of Preventing Conditions, Relevant Actions, and Agents*

This move towards the laissez-faire approach radically sized down the scope of economic liberty protected by competition law. The Chicagoan welfare standard addressed the shortcomings of the broad definition of preventing conditions (y) by the republican concept of liberty by simply narrowing the type of acts (hindrances) that qualify as obstruction of liberty to welfare-reducing interference. In contrast, domination resulting from the mere capacity of powerful firms to arbitrarily interfere with other competitors or consumers no longer qualifies as an encroachment on liberty. In the absence of welfare-reducing conduct, economic power and firm size are no longer objectionable. On the contrary, they are thought to reflect the economic success of the firm in satisfying consumer wants, and thereby enabling a maximum of mutually beneficial voluntary transactions.[137]

Not only did the consumer welfare standard shrink the breadth of preventing conditions (y) against which competition law could protect economic liberty but it also restricted the range of actions (z) that can be considered to be unduly restricted to preference-satisfying actions in the actual or nearby likely world. The rise of the consumer welfare standard brought about the rescoping of the 'relevant domain' of worlds[138] across which economic liberty ought to be protected. The Chicagoan consumer welfare standard radically broke with the republican antitrust tradition. It no longer sought to guarantee a modally robust form of economic liberty that ensured the preference-decisiveness of market players across all relevant possible worlds ($\Box$) in a way that if individual i prefers a over b (aP_ib) society also prefers a over b (aPb), or vice versa, so that $\Box((aP_ib \rightarrow aPb) \wedge (bP_ia \rightarrow bPa))$ holds. Instead, in its extreme form, the consumer welfare standard

[136] Ibid. 101.
[137] Ibid. 104–06, 192.
[138] List, 'The Impossibility of a Paretian Republican?' (n 80) 70.

reduces the type of economic liberty protected under competition law to the non-frustration of actual preferences so that only $aP_ib \rightarrow aPb$ is guaranteed. It thereby endorses the extremely narrow, Hobbesian understanding of negative liberty that only views interference with the currently preferred option in the actual world as a source of unfreedom. This narrow, actualist approach towards economic liberty is only concerned about interference that closes (total welfare), or seriously undermines the access conditions to (consumer welfare), the preferred door. But it does not guarantee, in keeping with the more demanding, Berlinian version of negative liberty, the content-independent decisiveness of market participants' preferences so that $(aP_ib \rightarrow aPb) \wedge (bP_ia \rightarrow bPa)$ by considering the blocking of alternative doors in nearby likely counterfactual worlds as obstruction of liberty. Nor is it wary of the presence of powerful gatekeepers who may, whenever they see fit, close the currently preferred or alternative doors in a relevant range of possible other worlds (republican liberty).

In conditioning the protection of competitors on their performance in satisfying consumer preferences, the consumer welfare standard also de facto shrinks the type of agents (x) whose liberty ought to be guaranteed by competition law. The republican approach broadly assumed that the preferences of competitors and consumers were largely aligned. As a result, the range of agents whose equal liberty the republican approach assumed to protect encompassed consumers and competitors alike. In contrast, the total and consumer welfare standards only protect the decisiveness of competitors' preferences so long as they are actually aligned with consumer preferences. It thus limits the economic liberty afforded by competition law to consumers and as-efficient competitors; that is, those competitors whose products consumers prefer, or are at least indifferent to, relative to the products offered by the perpetrator firm. With the endorsement of the consumer welfare approach and its operationalisation through the as-efficient competitor principle, the Chicagoan and post-Chicagoan proponents of the consumer welfare standard disavowed the republican commitment to an egalitarian understanding of economic liberty and the preservation of broad-based economic opportunity amongst multiple market agents.

The Chicagoan consumer welfare standard thus remodelled the geometry of economic liberty to be protected by antitrust law. To escape the republican paradox resulting from the thick and demanding republican conception of economic liberty, the Chicago School put forward a thinned-out negative conception of economic liberty as the absence of welfare-decreasing interference. Table 6.6 shows how the consumer welfare standard implied the rescoping of the three core variables of economic liberty. Not only did the consumer welfare standard shrink the set of circumstances that qualify as preventing conditions (y) of liberty but it also narrowed the relevant domain of worlds and category of agents for which liberty ought to be guaranteed by retrenching the range of actions (z) and agents (x).

TABLE 6.6 *The rescoping of economic liberty*

	Republican antitrust	Laissez-faire antitrust
Preventing conditions (y)	Domination, i.e., exposure to someone else's ability to interfere arbitrarily	Welfare-decreasing interference
Range of actions (z)	All relevant possible worlds $\square((aP_ib \rightarrow aPb) \wedge (bP_ia \rightarrow bPa))$	Actual world $(aP_ib \rightarrow aPb)$ or nearby likely world $((aP_ib \rightarrow aPb) \wedge (bP_ia \rightarrow bPa))$
Type of agents (x)	Consumers and competitors, regardless of efficiency	Consumers and as-efficient competitors

6.5.3 *The Road to Laissez-Faire Antitrust*

The previous discussion shows that despite its claim to scientific objectivity,[139] the Chicago School's attempt to rebuild antitrust law on purely economic foundations turned out to be a profoundly ideological endeavour. The methodology of modern welfare economics served the Chicago School at the same time as a smokescreen to disguise a laissez-faire approach towards antitrust law and as a handy device to make operational its central goal of preserving the negative entrepreneurial liberty of businesses against state coercion.[140] The economic framework of the consumer welfare standard lent theoretical and normative support to the transformation of antitrust law into a 'minimal law'[141] and the curtailing of state interference with the negative liberty of businesses. The Chicago scholars themselves underscored that the principle of wealth maximisation endowed negative contractual liberty and property rights with a higher level of protection against state interference than did any deontological justification of economic liberty, which would require regular state intervention to remedy undue interference with the rights of market participants.[142] While the Chicago School accused the republican approach of being biased towards the protection of a privileged and idle class of small and independent businessmen, the Chicagoan playbook for laissez-faire antitrust policy was in itself tweaked in favour of big business and to the detriment of small market players.[143] This pro-business attitude was, at least in part, grounded in the empirically unsupported assumption that firm size is always positively correlated with efficiency and that large firms are therefore more efficient than smaller competitors.[144]

139 Posner, 'The Chicago School of Antitrust Analysis' (n 2) 928.

140 Fox, 'Modernization of Antitrust' (n 2) 1155.

141 Fox and Sullivan, 'Antitrust-Retrospective and Prospective' (n 28) 958.

142 Posner, 'Utilitarianism, Economics, and Legal Theory' (n 93) 123–27.

143 Peritz, 'A Counter-History of Antitrust Law' (n 35) 304–05; Flynn (n 74) 903–05.

144 Peritz, 'A Counter-History of Antitrust Law' (n 35) 309–11.

The central tenets of the Chicago School consumer welfare programme have become, albeit with some adjustments, the predominant framework for antitrust policy and law on both sides of the Atlantic.[145] This does not mean that some of the teachings and most extreme positions of the Chicago School were not met with opposition and criticism. Nevertheless, most of this critique came from inside the consumer welfare model that was set out by the Chicago School.[146] Post-Chicago antitrust paradigms fully endorsed the central proposition of the Chicago School that consumer welfare constitutes the adequate normative benchmark to determine the legality of business conduct.[147] Far from seeking to reverse the Chicago revolution, post-Chicago scholarship, for the most part, aimed to refine and improve the Chicago policy framework.[148]

The major innovation of post-Chicago School antitrust scholarship was that it complemented the Chicago School's static analysis of business conduct through the lens of neoclassical price theory with a more dynamic and game-theoretic perspective that accounts for the strategic behaviour of businesses.[149] Consequently, post-Chicago antitrust identified a broader category of business conduct as having the potential to entail anticompetitive, welfare-reducing effects than did the Chicago School.[150] Yet, by endorsing the Chicagoan welfare model to ascertain when business conduct restricts competition, post-Chicago antitrust remains firmly rooted in the logic of negative liberty. It also continues to operate within the framework that the Chicago School has set out to resolve clashes between spheres of economic liberty.[151] Indeed, post-Chicago scholarship remained attached to the Chicagoan insight of potential trade-offs between allocative and productive efficiency, which militates against any outright condemnation of business conduct but rather counselled a casuistic analysis and balancing of its welfare effects. Until recently, the Chicagoan laissez-faire error–cost framework also remained the predominant prism through which antitrust scholars and policy-makers framed the boundaries of competition enforcement under uncertainty.[152]

The ascendancy of the consumer welfare framework has not been exclusively limited to the United States. Over the last three decades, there has also been a

[145] See, for instance, the Supreme Court's endorsement of the Chicago consumer welfare standard in *Reiter v Sonotone Corp.* 442 U.S. 330 (1979) 343.

[146] Hovenkamp, 'Antitrust Policy after Chicago' (n 1) 256.

[147] Krattenmaker and Salop, 'Anticompetitive Exclusion' (n 52) 228.

[148] Ibid. 223.

[149] Hovenkamp, 'Antitrust Policy after Chicago' (n 1) 256–83; SC Salop and DT Scheffman, 'Cost-Raising Strategies' (1987) 36(1) *The Journal of Industrial Economics* 19; JB Baker, 'Recent Developments in Economics That Challenge Chicago School Views' (1989) 58(2) *Antitrust Law Journal* 645.

[150] WE Kovacic, 'The Intellectual DNA of Modern U.S. Competition Law for Dominant Firm Conduct: The Chicago/Harvard Double Helix' (2007) 1(1) *Columbia Business Law Review* 1, 22–23.

[151] Ibid. 34–35.

[152] Devlin and Jacobs (n 123) 82–100.

growing consensus amongst antitrust experts[153] and policy-makers[154] in Europe that consumer welfare constitutes a central, if not unique, goal of EU competition law. Following the endorsement of a More Economic Approach in the early-2000s, EU competition law has undergone several waves of modernisation that sought to align the interpretation and application of EU competition rules with a consumer welfare standard. This shift of EU competition law towards the More Economic Approach has indeed been portrayed and welcomed by many commentators as an attempt to emulate the insights of the Chicago and post-Chicago antitrust policy.[155] Against the backdrop of the convergence of competition law on both sides of the Atlantic towards the consumer welfare standard, Herbert Hovenkamp observed that '[f]ew people dispute that antitrust's core mission is protecting consumers' right to the low prices, innovation, and diverse production that competition promises.'[156] It is therefore no exaggeration to say that the goal of consumer welfare, and with it the narrow Chicagoan version of negative economic liberty, has become the hegemonic credo of modern antitrust law over the last few decades.

6.6 CONCLUSION

This chapter has described how the rise of Chicago School thinking and the consumer welfare standard set in motion the decline of republican liberty as non-domination and the idea of a competition–democracy nexus as the normative foundation of competition law on both sides of the Atlantic. However, unlike conventional antitrust scholarship, it shows that the displacement of republican antitrust is not exclusively the result of the Chicago School's successful attempt to align competition law with the exclusive goal of welfare maximisation and to eradicate all social and political goals. The decline of republican antitrust is not as much the triumph of economics over politics or ideology as the triumph of laissez-faire over republican liberalism.

This chapter has highlighted that the Chicago School devised the consumer welfare standard as a response to the shortcomings of the S–C–P paradigm and the structural approach through which republican antitrust had operationalised the goal

[153] AJ Padilla and C Ahlborn, 'From Fairness to Welfare: Implications for the Assessment of Unilateral Conduct under EC Competition Law' in C-D Ehlermann and M Marquis (eds), *European Competition Law Annual 2007: A Reformed Approach to Article 82 EC* (Oxford: Hart 2008) 55, 2–3; European Commission, 'Report by the Economic Advisory Group on Competition Policy (EAGCP) – An Economic Approach to Article 82' (2005) 3.

[154] N Kroes, 'European Competition Policy – Delivering Better Markets and Better Choice' (SPEECH/05/512 2005).

[155] AC Witt, 'From Airtours to Ryanair: Is the More Economic Approach to EU Merger Law Really about More Economics?' (2012) 49(1) *Common Market Law Review* 217, 244. For a comprehensive discussion A Witt, *The More Economic Approach to EU Antitrust Law* (Oxford: Hart 2016).

[156] H Hovenkamp, *The Antitrust Enterprise: Principle and Execution* (Cambridge, MA: Harvard University Press 2005) 1.

of preserving republican liberty. Meanwhile, the consumer welfare standard itself enwrapped a parsimonious and thin conception of economic liberty that laid down an avenue of escape from the republican paradox. The consumer welfare standard and the error–cost framework advanced by the Chicago School set out the blueprint for a new form of laissez-faire antitrust approach whose primary preoccupation is to shield entrepreneurial liberty from state interference. The rise of the consumer welfare standard hollowed out the thick concept of republican economic liberty by narrowing its broad understanding of preventing conditions, range of actions, and agents. Consequently, the consumer welfare standard replaced republican liberty with a narrow conception of economic liberty understood as the absence of welfare-decreasing interference.

7

The Operationalisation of Laissez-Faire Antitrust and the Decline of Republican Liberty

7.1 INTRODUCTION

The previous chapter has traced how the ascent of the Chicago School antitrust paradigm set in motion the decline of republican antitrust and the idea of a competition–democracy nexus. It describes how the Chicago School, under the guise of the consumer welfare standard and error-cost analysis, displaced the republican concern about republican liberty with a framework that aligned modern antitrust law with the goal of negative entrepreneurial liberty. The Chicago School revolution thus succeeded in substituting a narrow, negative conception of economic liberty as non-interference for the thick conception of republican liberty, understood as non-domination, as the normative foundation of antitrust law.

This chapter focuses on how this shift from republican to laissez-faire antitrust manifested itself in US antitrust and EU competition law. It shows that the ascent of the More Economic Approach that was coined by the Chicago School initiated a fundamental reconfiguration of modern antitrust law along four dimensions. The rise of laissez-faire antitrust entailed a profound transformation of the policy objective of competition law. With the growing influence of Chicago School-inspired antitrust thinking, both US and EU competition law increasingly abandoned the goal of preserving a polycentric market structure to the benefit of consumer welfare as the central policy objective of antitrust law. The triumph of the More Economic Approach also reshaped what we have identified as the major policy instruments through which the republican antitrust tradition had operationalised the concern about republican liberty as non-domination: namely, the role of presumptions, the standard of harm, and the understanding of the costs and benefits of antitrust law. Alongside the readjustment of the overarching policy objective, the recalibration of these three policy parameters constituted the major vector of the transformation of republican into laissez-faire antitrust.

In analysing the remodelling of antitrust law along these four dimensions, this chapter seeks to enhance our understanding of how modern antitrust law operationalises negative economic liberty and how the shift from republican to laissez-faire antitrust has affected the concrete interpretation and application of US and EU competition law. Only by understanding how this transition reconfigured the concrete application of competition law on both sides of the Atlantic can we fully grasp how the rise of the consumer welfare standard displaced republican liberty as non-domination by a thinned-out understanding of negative liberty as non-interference and led to the disappearance of the idea of a competition–democracy nexus.

This chapter discusses the recalibration of each of these policy parameters in turn. Section 7.2 analyses how US antitrust and EU competition law embraced the consumer welfare standard, and hence a normative commitment to negative economic liberty, as the overarching policy goal of modern competition law. Section 7.3 traces the decline of rule-like presumptions and their replacement with legal standards as a second channel through which US and EU competition law operationalised their normative commitment to negative liberty. Sections 7.4 and 7.5 shed light on how the reconfiguration of the standard of harm and error-cost framework contributed to the transition from a republican to a laissez-faire approach. Finally, Section 7.6 concludes this chapter.

7.2 FROM STRUCTURALISM TO THE CONSUMER WELFARE STANDARD

The ascendancy of the Chicago School thinking and the ensuing transition of republican to laissez-faire antitrust on both sides of the Atlantic occurred in several steps. The first way in which the rise of laissez-faire antitrust manifested itself is the reinterpretation of the policy objective of competition law. Over the last four decades, US antitrust law and EU competition law alike have moved, albeit at different speeds, towards a consumer welfare standard.

7.2.1 *The Endorsement of a Consumer Welfare Standard in US Antitrust Law*

The rise of the consumer welfare standard was pioneered in the United States. From the late-1970s onwards, the concern about the concentration of economic power and liberty as non-domination gave way to the view that Congress had enacted the Sherman Act as a 'consumer welfare prescription'.[1] The Supreme Court thus subscribed to the Chicagoan view that allocative efficiency[2] and consumer welfare

[1] *Reiter v Sonotone Corp.* 442 U.S. 330 (1979) 343.

[2] *Cont'l T.V. v GTE Sylvania*, 433 U.S. 36 (1977) Justice White concurring, 69.

constitute the 'fundamental goal[s] of antitrust law'.[3] In *GTE Sylvania*, the Supreme Court clarified that it would henceforth rely on a 'purely economic approach'[4] in interpreting § 1 of the Sherman Act. Accordingly, the essential task of antitrust analysis of agreements under § 1 of the Sherman Act was to distinguish 'between restraints with anticompetitive effect that are harmful to the consumer and restraints stimulating competition that are in the consumer's best interest'.[5]

The Supreme Court also increasingly restricted the prohibitive scope of antitrust law towards unilateral firm behaviour to conduct that excludes rival firms 'on some basis other than efficiency'.[6] Under this consumer welfare approach, the legality of single-firm conduct with § 2 of the Sherman Act has to be examined on the sole basis of its welfare effects. An essential element of the finding of unlawful monopolisation is that the impugned conduct has an actual or likely anticompetitive effect by foreclosing competitors by means other than superior efficiency and gives rise to consumer harm in the form of higher prices or lower output.[7]

US merger control was also remodelled on the basis of the consumer welfare standard. The adoption of the 1982 Merger Guidelines by the US Department of Justice under the direction of William Baxter, who was importantly influenced by the Chicago School thinking,[8] obliterated the structuralist thrust of the Warren Court case law and the 1968 Guidelines. Merger policy was no longer directed against the creation of situations of excessive concentration of economic power. Instead, the 1982 Guidelines limited the task of merger policy to the prevention of the exercise of market power. Accordingly, the government would only enjoin mergers that further the ability of the merging or non-merging firms 'profitably to maintain prices above competitive levels for a significant period of time'.[9] Under the auspices of the consumer welfare standard, the purpose of merger control was henceforth the prevention of mergers leading to a misallocation of resources and a wealth transfer from consumers to producers.[10]

The consumer welfare standard thus experienced a rapid ascent in US antitrust law. Within a decade, consumer welfare was elevated to the exclusive goal of US

3 *National Collegiate Athletic Ass'n v Board of Regents* 468 U.S. 85 (1984) 107, see also 100, 113, 114–16; *Cont'l T.V. v GTE Sylvania* (n 2) 53 fn. 21; *Broadcast Music, Inc. v Columbia Broadcasting System, Inc.* 441 U.S. 1 (1979) 20; *FTC v Indiana Federation of Dentists* 476 U.S. 447 (1986) 459.

4 *Cont'l T.V. v GTE Sylvania* (n 2) Justice White concurring, 69.

5 *Leegin Creative Leather Prods. v PSKS, Inc.* 551 U.S. 877 (2007) 886; *Ohio v American Express Co.* 585 U.S. ___ (2018) 9.

6 *Aspen Skiing Co. v Aspen Highlands Skiing Corp.* 472 U.S. 585 (1985) 605. The majority here explicitly quoted RH Bork, *The Antitrust Paradox: A Policy at War with Itself* [1978] (New York: Maxwell Macmillan 1993) 138.

7 *United States v Microsoft Corporation* 253 F.3d 34 (D.C. Cir.2001) 50–51, 58–59.

8 C Shapiro, 'The 2010 Horizontal Merger Guidelines: From Hedgehog to Fox in Forty Years' (2010) 77(1) *Antitrust Law Journal* 49, 53 fn. 15.

9 Antitrust Division of the US Department of Justice, 1982 Merger Guidelines, 2.

10 Ibid.

antitrust law. At the end of the 1970s, very little remained of the republican antitrust tradition in the interpretation and enforcement of antitrust by the judiciary and US agencies.[11] Concerns about liberty as non-domination, excessive concentration of economic power, and democracy had been eclipsed by the exclusive goal of consumer welfare.

7.2.2 *The Endorsement of a Consumer Welfare Standard in EU Competition Law*

Over the course of the 1980s and 1990s, the Chicago consensus on the consumer welfare standard also found growing support amongst practitioners and academics in Europe.[12] Its recognition as the ultimate goal of EU competition law took however much longer and was, at least initially, less sweeping than in the United States. Nevertheless, with the growing support for a More Economic Approach towards competition law in Europe, the Chicagoan consumer welfare framework gained growing influence on the thinking and case law of the EU Commission and Courts during the late-2000s and early-2010s.[13]

As part of the modernisation of EU competition law under the banner of the More Economic Approach, in the late-1990s and early-2000s the EU Commission published a number of Guidelines that disavowed the structural impetus and focus on economic liberty of the formative case law. Instead, the Commission's Guidelines endorsed the consumer welfare standard as the relevant normative benchmark against which the legality of business conduct under EU competition law ought to be assessed.[14]

For years, the EU Courts remained reluctant to unconditionally endorse consumer welfare as the ultimate goal of EU competition law.[15] However, towards the beginning of the 2000s, the first signs of a departure from a republican approach

[11] See for an outlier case, *Ariz. v Maricopa County Medical Soc.* 457 U.S. 332 (1982).

[12] V Korah, 'From Legal Form toward Economic Efficiency – Article 85 (1) of the EEC Treaty in Contrast to U.S. Antitrust' (1990) 35(4) *Antitrust Bulletin* 1009; European Commission, 'Report by the Economic Advisory Group on Competition Policy (EAGCP) – An Economic Approach to Article 82' (2005).

[13] N Kroes, 'European Competition Policy – Delivering Better Markets and Better Choice' (SPEECH/05/512 2005).

[14] See, for instance, European Commission, Guidelines on the Application of Article 81(3) of the Treaty, [2004] OJ C 101/97 paras. 5, 13, 24; European Commission, Guidance on the Commission's Enforcement Priorities in Applying Article 82 of the EC Treaty to Abusive Exclusionary Conduct by Dominant Undertakings, [2009] OJ C 45/7 paras. 5–6; European Commission, Guidelines on the Assessment of Horizontal Mergers, [2004] OJ C 31/5 para. 8; European Commission, Guidelines on the Assessment of Non-horizontal Mergers, [2008] OJ C 265/6 para. 10.

[15] Case C-501/06 P *GlaxoSmithKline Services and Others v Commission and Others* ECLI:EU:C:2009:610 paras. 61–64.

started to appear. The EU judiciary increasingly took the view that not every restriction of economic liberty must necessarily result in a restriction of competition.[16] In recent case law, the Court began to rely on the consumer welfare standard as the appropriate framework to identify when impugned firm conduct unduly interferes with the negative liberty of other market participants, and thus amounts to an undue restriction of competition. This evolution is, for instance, borne out in recent cases which suggest that Article 101 TFEU is directed against those types of agreement that negatively affect outcome-oriented variables of competition because they lead 'to fall in production and price increases, resulting in poor allocation of resources to the detriment, in particular, of consumers'.[17]

EU merger control also increasingly inched away from the structuralist towards a consumer welfare approach.[18] Following the introduction of the new Significant Impediment to Effective Competition (SIEC) test in the revised EU Merger Regulation (EUMR),[19] the 2004 Horizontal Merger Guidelines made it plain that the Commission would henceforth assess the competitive effects of mergers on the basis of the consumer welfare standard.[20] In a similar vein as the 1982 Merger Guidelines in the United States, the Horizontal Merger Guidelines and case law disavowed a structuralist approach, which is directed against industry concentration and the creation or strengthening of a dominant position as such. Instead, the EU Commission and Courts pointed out that the EUMR only outlaws those mergers that deprive consumers of the benefits of effective competition by significantly increasing the market power of firms,[21] thus enabling 'one or more firms to profitably increase prices' or deteriorate other parameters of competition.[22]

There are also signs of an incremental shift towards the consumer welfare standard in the Article 102 TFEU case law. From around 2010 onwards, the interpretation of Article 102 TFEU has gradually moved away from the structural approach of the republican era that perceived the existence of a dominant position

[16] European Commission, Guidelines on the Application of Article 81(3) of the Treaty (n 14) para. 24, fn. 31. See in this regard also Case T-112/99 *Métropole télévision (M6) and Others v Commission* ECLI:EU:T:2001:215 para. 76; Case C-309/99 *Wouters and others v Algemene Raad van de Nederlandse Orde van Advocaten* ECLI:EU:C:2002:98 para. 97.

[17] Case C-67/13 P *Groupement des cartes bancaires v Commission* ECLI:EU:C:2014:2204 para. 51; Case C-345/14 *Maxima Latvija* ECLI:EU:C:2015:784 para. 19.

[18] Case T-399/16 *CK Telecoms UK Investments v Commission* ECLI:EU:T:2020:217 para. 93. This judgment was recently annulled and remanded on appeal in Case C-376/20 P *Commission v CK Telecoms UK Investments* ECLI:EU:C:2023:561.

[19] Council Regulation (EC) No 139/2004 on the Control of Concentrations between Undertakings, [2004] OJ L 24/1 Article 2 (3).

[20] European Commission, Guidelines on the Assessment of Horizontal Mergers (n 14) para. 8. See also Case T-87/05 *EDP v Commission* ECLI:EU:T:2005:333 paras. 45, 49–50.

[21] European Commission, Guidelines on the Assessment of Horizontal Mergers (n 14) para. 8; Case T-342/07 *Ryanair v Commission* ECLI:EU:T:2010:280 paras. 224; Case T-399/16 *CK Telecoms UK Investments v Commission* (n 18) para. 360.

[22] European Commission, Guidelines on the Assessment of Horizontal Mergers (n 14) para. 8; Case T-399/16 *CK Telecoms UK Investments v Commission* (n 18) para. 90.

itself as a source of domination and has sought to preserve deconcentrated market structures as an institution of antipower. Instead, the EU judiciary has been adamant that 'it is in no way the purpose of Article 102 TFEU to prevent an undertaking from acquiring, on its own merits, the dominant position on a market.'[23] More recent case law also insists that it is the mission of EU competition law to protect competition and 'not competitors'.[24] Accordingly, it is not the role of EU competition law, and notably Article 102 TFEU, to 'ensure that competitors less efficient than the undertaking with the dominant position should remain on the market.'[25] On the contrary, 'competition on the merits may, by definition, lead to the departure from the market or the marginalisation of competitors that are less efficient and so less attractive to consumers.'[26] In highlighting that EU competition law does not intervene against dominant firm conduct that forecloses less efficient firms, the Court coined the as-efficient competitor principle as the central benchmark to make a determination of when dominant firm conduct unduly excludes competitors.[27] The increasing importance of the as-efficient competitor principle and test in recent case law brings the notion of restriction of competition under Article 102 TFEU fully in line with the consumer welfare standard. The gravitation of EU competition law towards a consumer welfare standard recently culminated in *Servizio Elettrico Nazionale* where the Court of Justice elevated consumer welfare to the paramount goal of Article 102 TFEU.[28] In its ultimate consequence, *Servizio Elettrico Nazionale* suggests that consumer welfare, in the event of a conflict, trumps the protection of a competitive market structure.[29] This marks a radical shift from the formative case law, which explicitly rejected a consequentialist reading of Article 102 in favour of a constitutive or even deontological interpretation because it considered the preservation of a competitive market structure as a goal in itself.[30] *Servizio Elettrico Nazionale* is, to this date, the most far-reaching commitment of the EU judiciary to the consumer welfare standard.

23 Case C-413/14 P *Intel v Commission* ECLI:EU:C:2017:632 para. 133.
24 Case T-399/16 *CK Telecoms UK Investments v Commission* (n 18) para. 362.
25 Case C-209/10 *Post Danmark A/S v Konkurrencerådet* ECLI:EU:C:2012:172 para. 21.
26 Ibid. para. 23; Case C-413/14 P *Intel v Commission* (n 23) para. 134.
27 See, for instance, Case C-52/09 *TeliaSonera Sverige* ECLI:EU:C:2011:83 paras. 24–25; Case C-209/10 *Post Danmark A/S v Konkurrencerådet* (n 25) paras. 21, 25; Case C-413/14 P *Intel v Commission* (n 23) paras. 133–34, 136; Case C-377/20 *Servizio Elettrico Nazionale and Others* ECLI:EU:C:2022:379 paras. 46, 80–82; Case C-680/20 *Unilever Italia Mkt. Operations* ECLI:EU:C:2023:33 paras. 39, 47, 52, 55–62; Case T-235/18 *Qualcomm v Commission* ECLI:EU:T:2022:358 paras. 349–51, 354; Case T-604/18 *Google and Alphabet v Commission (Google Android)* ECLI:EU:T:2022:541 paras. 639–45.
28 Case C-377/20 *Servizio Elettrico Nazionale and Others* (n 27) para. 47. The Court fully endorsed here the Opinion of Advocate General Rantos in Case C-377/20 *Servizio Elettrico Nazionale and Others* ECLI:EU:C:2021:998 paras. 88–100.
29 Ibid. para. 100; Case C-377/20 *Servizio Elettrico Nazionale and Others* (n 27) para. 47.
30 Case 6/72 *Europemballage Corporation and Continental Can Company v Commission* ECLI:EU:C:1973:22 para. 26.

The concern about republican liberty, which informed the goal of preserving a polycentric market structure as the underpinning rationale of republican antitrust in the United States and the European Union, has constantly lost ground over the last decade. While there are remaining ambiguities about whether EU competition law embraces the consumer welfare standard to the same extent as US antitrust law,[31] the direction of travel is clear. US and EU competition law largely endorsed the Chicagoan consumer welfare approach as the appropriate framework to identify when impugned firm conduct unduly interferes with the negative liberty of other market participants, and thus engenders an adverse effect on the competitive market structure that warrants antitrust intervention. Consistent with the laissez-faire antitrust paradigm championed by the Chicago School, US and EU competition law progressively narrowed the concept of restriction of competition to conduct that interferes with the negative economic liberty of other market participants in a way that reduces the volume or adversely affects the terms of mutually beneficial transactions which would have been otherwise carried out in the market.

Not only have US antitrust and EU competition law espoused the consumer welfare standard as a framework to determine when impugned conduct amounts to a preventing condition of liberty but they have also largely aligned themselves with the laissez-faire balance of rights to determine when welfare-reducing interference should be addressed by competition law intervention. US antitrust law has recognised a rule of reason-like balancing of welfare effects under all three branches of competition law.[32] Along similar lines, EU competition law has become more receptive to the assessment and balancing of countervailing welfare effects and efficiencies under Article 101 (3) TFEU,[33] Article 102 TFEU,[34] and EU merger control.[35] Consequently, competition law on both sides of the Atlantic allows for a balancing of rights in line with the concept of negative liberty. Under this balancing of rights, antitrust intervention is only warranted if the loss in entrepreneurial liberty (measured in terms of foregone pro-competitive efficiencies) as a consequence of antitrust intervention is compensated by the gains in negative liberty of other market participants (measured

[31] See, for instance, Case C-307/18 *Generics (UK) and Others* ECLI:EU:C:2020:52 paras. 147–48, 156, 161.

[32] See, for instance, *Cont'l T.V. v GTE Sylvania* (n 2) 49; *Leegin Creative Leather Prods. v PSKS, Inc.* (n 5) 885; *Aspen Skiing Co. v Aspen Highlands Skiing Corp.* (n 6) 608; *United States v Baker Hughes, Inc.* 908 F. 2d 981 (D.C. Cir. 1990) 226–27.

[33] See, for instance, Case T-168/01 *GlaxoSmithKline Services v Commission* ECLI:EU:T:2006:265 paras. 247–308; European Commission, Guidelines on the Application of Article 81(3) of the Treaty (n 14) para. 11.

[34] Case C-209/10 *Post Danmark A/S v Konkurrencerådet* (n 25) paras. 41–42; European Commission, Guidance on the Commission's Enforcement Priorities in Applying Article 82 of the EC Treaty to Abusive Exclusionary Conduct by Dominant Undertakings (n 14) paras. 28–32.

[35] Council Regulation (EC) No 139/2004 on the Control of Concentrations between Undertakings (n 19) recital 29; European Commission, Guidelines on the Assessment of Horizontal Mergers (n 14) paras. 76–88.

in terms of losses in consumer welfare) as a result of the remedying intervention. In adopting the consumer welfare standard to identify undue interference with and resolve conflicting claims about economic liberty, US and EU competition law have aligned themselves with the negative understanding of economic liberty that underpins the Chicagoan laissez-faire antitrust approach.

7.3 A LAISSEZ-FAIRE UNDERSTANDING OF THE COSTS AND BENEFITS OF ANTITRUST INTERVENTION

A second channel through which the reconfiguration of modern competition law from a republican to a laissez-faire approach took place is the growing endorsement of the Chicagoan understanding of error costs. On both sides of the Atlantic, competition law enforcement has been increasingly brought in line with the Chicagoan proposition that under-enforcement (type II errors) is less costly than, and hence preferable to, over-enforcement (type I errors) of competition law. The Chicagoan error-cost framework has indeed become the source-code of modern antitrust law. The ascent of the Chicagoan error-cost framework constituted a significant force behind the displacement of republican by laissez-faire antitrust.

7.3.1 *The Chicagoan Error-Cost Framework and US Antitrust Law*

The Chicagoan proposition that the costs of type I errors tend to exceed those of type II errors has, over the course of the last four decades, morphed into a central axiom of US antitrust law. Out of fear that an overly rigid enforcement of competition rules would erroneously outlaw or deter welfare-enhancing conduct, US courts have progressively disavowed a broad application of per se rules. Instead, they have increasingly favoured the more flexible rule of reason standard.[36] Indeed, the US Supreme Court has repeatedly cautioned that too broad an application of per se rules under § 1 of the Sherman Act would suffocate entrepreneurial liberty under the burden of overly rigid rules.[37]

Concerns over the costs of false positives also rendered US enforcers and courts increasingly hesitant towards an expansion of antitrust liability, notably towards unilateral conduct by powerful firms.[38] The Supreme Court repeatedly stressed that the 'cost of false positives counsels against an undue expansion of § 2 liability'.[39] The allegedly

[36] *Cont'l T.V. v GTE Sylvania* (n 2) 54; *National Soc. of Professional Engineers v United States* 435 U.S. 679 (1978) 688; *Broadcast Music, Inc. v Columbia Broadcasting System, Inc.* (n 3) 8.

[37] *Cont'l T.V. v GTE Sylvania* (n 2) 50 fn. 16; *Leegin Creative Leather Prods. v PSKS, Inc.* (n 5) 895.

[38] See, for instance, *Matsushita Elec. Indus. Co. v Zenith Radio Corp.* 475 U.S. 574 (1986) 594; *Brooke Group v Brown & Williamson Tobacco Corp.* 509 U.S. 209 (1993) 223, 226; *Verizon Communications Inc. v Law Offices of Curtis Trinko* 540 US 398 (2004) 414.

[39] *Verizon Communications Inc. v Law Offices of Curtis Trinko* (n 38) 414.

irrecoverable welfare costs and chilling effects of over-enforcement were a central consideration in the rejection of the Supreme Court and lower courts to broaden the essential facilities doctrine,[40] or recognise § 2 liability for exclusionary above-cost pricing in the form of discriminatory price cuts,[41] margin squeeze,[42] or discounts.[43] Based on the Chicagoan error-cost framework, the US courts instead established a clear bright line presumption of legality for above-cost pricing conduct, which broadly shields the economic liberty of dominant firms from antitrust intervention.[44]

The Chicagoan error-cost framework was also the key driver of the decline in scope and weight of merger presumptions and their alignment with a rule of reason-like sliding-scale inquiry.[45] US courts and competition authorities have largely adjusted their inquiry to the aversion against type I errors and their allegedly adverse effect on negative entrepreneurial liberty. This is reflected in the 2010 Merger Guidelines. The contrast between their philosophy and that animating the 1968 Guidelines and Warren Court case law could not be starker. The 2010 Guidelines embody the proposition that US merger policy is no longer grounded in the incipiency doctrine that sought to nip excessive industry concentration in the bud. On the contrary, its primary concern is to limit antitrust intervention to those few transactions that clearly give rise to anticompetitive effects, 'while avoiding unnecessary interference with mergers that are either competitively beneficial or neutral'.[46]

The enforcement of US antitrust law has thus moved a far cry away from the republican concern about the domination emanating from the mere existence of concentrated economic power, which informed the precautionary error-cost framework of republican antitrust. On the contrary, the major concern underpinning the application of competition rules has become that antitrust law might unduly interfere with the negative liberty of firms, and thereby chill their incentives to compete and innovate. Nowhere does this emerge more clearly than in *Trinko*, which goes as far as suggesting that antitrust law should not be over-enforced lest it prevent firms from charging monopoly prices:

> The mere possession of monopoly power, and the concomitant charging of monopoly prices, is not only not unlawful; it is an important element of the free-market

[40] Ibid. 409.

[41] *Brooke Group v Brown & Williamson Tobacco Corp.* (n 38) 223.

[42] *Verizon Communications Inc. v Law Offices of Curtis Trinko* (n 38) 414; *Pacific Bell Telephone Co. dba AT&T California, et al. v linkLine Communications, Inc. et al.* 555 U.S. 438 (2009) 451–52.

[43] See, for instance, *Eisai, Inc. v Sanofi Aventis U.S. LLC* 821 F.3d 394 (3d Cir. 2015) 408–09; *Cascade Health Solutions v PeaceHealth* 502 F.3d 895 (9th Cir. 2007) 910.

[44] *Barry Wright Corp. v ITT Grinnell Corp.* 724 F.2d 227 (1st Cir. 1983) 235; *Brooke Group v Brown & Williamson Tobacco Corp.* (n 38) 223; *ZF Meritor, LLC v Eaton Corp.* 696 F.3d 254 (3d Cir. 2012) 273–75.

[45] *United States v Baker Hughes, Inc.* (n 32) 984, 991–92.

[46] Antitrust Division of the US Department of Justice/Federal Trade Commission, 2010 Merger Guidelines 2.

system. The opportunity to charge monopoly prices – at least for a short period – is what attracts "business acumen" in the first place; it induces risk taking that produces innovation and economic growth. To safeguard the incentive to innovate, the possession of monopoly power will not be found unlawful unless it is accompanied by an element of anticompetitive conduct.[47]

7.3.2 *The Chicagoan Error-Cost Framework and EU Competition Law*

The proposition that the Chicagoan error-cost framework also had inroads into EU competition law may, at first sight, be surprising. Recent studies have suggested that competition law is more strictly enforced in the EU than in the United States.[48] However, although this claim is not necessarily supported by empirical or statistical evidence, there are a number of reasons to believe that the enforcement of EU competition law has not experienced the same decline as antitrust enforcement in the United States. Unlike their US counterparts, the Commission and EU Courts have continued to expand the scope of Article 102 TFEU to new forms of price, and in particular non-price abuses. The rise of the More Economic Approach notwithstanding, the EU Commission and EU Courts have applied Article 102 TFEU to numerous novel forms of abuses, such as margin squeeze,[49] patent hold-ups,[50] the abuse of administrative procedures,[51] strategies by originator drug producers to suppress generic entry,[52] and most recently self-preferencing.[53] Therefore, the European Commission's enforcement activity towards single-firm conduct has clearly outperformed that of its US counterparts.

These differences notwithstanding, the enforcement activity and the case law of the European Commission and the Court also exhibit a growing sensitivity towards the costs of over-enforcement. The Commission, and to a growing extent the Court of Justice, showed themselves to be increasingly receptive to the criticism that the form-based approach of the formative era had led to a large number of type I errors.[54] Indeed, the Commission and the EU judiciary adopted a number of steps to address

47 *Verizon Communications Inc. v Law Offices of Curtis Trinko* (n 38) 407.

48 See, for instance, G Gutiérrez and T Philippon, 'How EU Markets Became More Competitive Than US Markets: A Study of Institutional Drift' (2018). NBER Working Paper No 24700.

49 Case C-280/08 P *Deutsche Telekom v Commission* ECLI:EU:C:2010:603 paras. 157–84; Case C-52/09 *TeliaSonera Sverige* (n 27) paras. 31–33, 72–73, 87–98.

50 Case C-170/13 *Huawei Technologies* ECLI:EU:C:2015:477.

51 Case C-457/10 P *AstraZeneca AB and AstraZeneca plc v European Commission* ECLI:EU:C:2012:770 paras. 98–99.

52 Case C-307/18 *Generics (UK) and Others* (n 31) paras. 140–71.

53 Case No COMP/AT.39740 *Google Search (Shopping)*, C(2017) 4444 final see in particular paras. 334–40, 644–52.

54 AJ Padilla and C Ahlborn, 'From Fairness to Welfare: Implications for the Assessment of Unilateral Conduct under EC Competition Law' in C-D Ehlermann and M Marquis (eds), *European Competition Law Annual 2007: A Reformed Approach to Article 82 EC* (Oxford: Hart 2008) 55, 77–83; European Commission (n 12) 2, 4, 7, 14–15.

this criticism by enhancing the precision of competition law analysis with a view to reducing type I errors. Under Article 101 (1) TFEU, the Court recently expanded the range of factors or evidentiary filters that a competition authority or court must account for before it can conclusively categorise an agreement as a by-object restriction.[55] These filters serve as an additional safety valve[56] that allows the fact finder to double-check and, if necessary, correct the accuracy of the characterisation of an agreement as a by-object restriction.[57] In heightening the level of scrutiny for finding a by-object restriction, the Court sought to reduce the risk of erroneous inferences of illegality. The introduction of these additional evidentiary filters reshaped the by-object category in a way that in case of doubt errs in favour of the defendant, and hence leans towards under-enforcement (type II errors).[58]

Concerns about the over-enforcement of Article 102 TFEU to single-firm conduct have also been on the rise with the shift towards a More Economic Approach. One example of the increasing bearing of the Chicagoan error-cost framework on the application of Article 102 TFEU is the growing importance of the as-efficient competitor principle. This principle was primarily operationalised through the more frequent use of an incremental price-cost test (i.e., the so-called as-efficient competitor test) and the introduction of a clear safe-harbour for above-cost pricing. Even though economic theory suggests that above-cost price-cutting may lead to anticompetitive foreclosure and losses in consumer welfare,[59] the Commission and the EU Courts increasingly rely on a deliberately under-inclusive incremental price-cost test to decide when single-firm conduct leads to an abuse of dominance.[60] The adoption of the price-cost test is geared towards reducing type I errors to a minimum. It consequently insulates the negative commercial liberty of dominant firms from antitrust scrutiny and provides dominant firms with clear legal certainty as to the lawfulness of their conduct.[61] In the same way as the US courts, the Commission and, albeit to a lesser extent, EU Courts, appear to assume that the benefits of

55 Opinion of Advocate General Wahl in Case C-67/13 P *Groupement des cartes bancaires v Commission* ECLI:EU:C:2014:1958 paras. 36, 54.

56 Case C-67/13 P *Groupement des cartes bancaires v Commission* (n 17) paras. 78–79.

57 In this sense, Opinion of Advocate General Bobek in Case C-228/18 *Budapest Bank and Others* ECLI:EU:C:2019:678 paras. 43, 45.

58 This is so, even though as Advocate General Wahl observed, the competition authority could still address anticompetitive effects of an agreement under the by-effects analysis, see Opinion of Advocate General Wahl in Case C-67/13 P *Groupement des cartes bancaires v Commission* (n 55) para. 62.

59 JF Brodley and GA Hay, 'Predatory Pricing: Competing Economic Theories and the Evolution of Legal Standards' (1980–1981) 66(4) *Cornell Law Review* 738, 744–46; AS Edlin, 'Stopping Above Cost Predatory Pricing' (2002) 111(4) *Yale Law Journal* 941, 955–78.

60 Case C-280/08 P *Deutsche Telekom v Commission* (n 49) paras. 83–85, 177, 202–03; Case C-52/09 *TeliaSonera Sverige* (n 27) paras. 24–25; Case C-209/10 *Post Danmark A/S v Konkurrencerådet* (n 25) para. 38.

61 Case C-280/08 P *Deutsche Telekom v Commission* (n 49) para. 202.

scrutinising above-cost price cuts by dominant firms are outweighed by the costs of potential type I errors.[62]

More recent pronouncements by the EU judicature also suggest that the tide might further turn towards a more laissez-faire approach under Article 102 TFEU.[63] The growing sway of the laissez-faire error-cost framework on the interpretation of Article 102 TFEU has perhaps been most clearly articulated by Advocate General Wahl, who now acts as a judge at the Court of Justice of the European Union. In a recent opinion, Wahl uncritically endorsed the US Supreme Court's orbiter in *Trinko* that the possession of monopoly power constitutes an 'important element of the free market system', and added that high prices 'fulfil an important function in the competitive process'.[64]

The Chicagoan error-cost framework has also gained considerable influence on EU merger policy. With the rise of the More Economic Approach, the European Commission and the EU judiciary increasingly aligned EU merger control with an error-cost framework that in the case of doubt errs on the side of clearing the merger. In several cases, such as *Tetra Laval*, members of the EU judiciary warned that too robust a merger enforcement and the ensuing erroneous blocking of mergers would lead to irreparable welfare losses.[65] At the same time, it was argued that type II errors could be easily corrected by market forces and ex-post antitrust intervention under Article 102 TFEU. Therefore, more recent case law has sought to reconcile EU merger policy with an error-cost framework that in the case of doubt tips the balance in favour of type II errors.[66] Not only does such a one-sided error-cost framework reduce welfare losses resulting from the erroneous prohibition of mergers but it was

[62] J Temple Lang and R O'Donoghue, 'Defining Legitimate Competition: How to Clarify Pricing Abuses under Article 82' (2002) 26(1) *Fordham International Law Journal* 83, 127, 130.

[63] Case C-413/14 P *Intel v Commission* (n 23) paras. 133–41; Case C-525/16 *Meo–Serviços de Comunicações e Multimédia* ECLI:EU:C:2018:270 paras. 26–28, 31; G Monti, 'Abuse of a Dominant Position: A Post-Intel Calm?' [2019] *CPI Antitrust Chronicle* 1, 3.

[64] Opinion of Advocate General Wahl in Case C-177/16 *Biedrība "Autortiesību un komunicēšanās konsultāciju aģentūra–Latvijas Autoru apvienība" Konkurences padome (AKKA)* ECLI:EU:C:2017:286 para. 117.

[65] Opinion of Advocate General Tizzano in Case C-12/03 P *Commission v Tetra Laval* ECLI:EU:C:2004:318 para. 81; B Vesterdorf, 'Standard of Proof in Merger Cases: Reflections in the Light of Recent Case Law of the Community Courts' (2005) 1(1) *European Competition Journal* 3, 28–29; T Reeves and N Dodoo, 'Standards of Proof and Standards of Judicial Review in European Commission Merger Law: Fordham Law School Centennial Issue' (2006) 29(5) *Fordham International Law Journal* 1034, 1046–47.

[66] The recognition of an 'efficiency credit' in horizontal mergers by the General Court is the most recent example for this concern about type I errors in merger control. Case T-399/16 *CK Telecoms UK Investments v Commission* (n 18) paras. 270–82, most notably 277–79. The recognition of an 'efficiency credit' was, however, rejected by the Court of Justice on appeal in Case C-376/20 P *Commission v CK Telecoms UK Investments* (n 18) paras. 237–47.See also Opinion of Advocate General Kokott in Case C-376/20 *Commission v CK Telecoms UK Investments* ECLI:EU:C:2022:817 paras. 150–58.

TABLE 7.1 *Outcomes of antitrust intervention and stylised pay-offs*

	*H*1 is true	*H*o is true
Intervention	True positives $(1-\beta)G$	False positives αL
Non-intervention	False negatives βG	True negatives $(1-\alpha)L$

also perceived as a necessary step to ensure that EU merger policy preserves the negative commercial liberty and property rights of the merging parties.[67]

US antitrust and EU competition law have thus largely abandoned the precautionary error-cost framework that characterised the republican antitrust approach in favour of the Chicagoan take on competition law errors. The republican precautionary error-cost framework consistently assumed that antitrust intervention generates important accuracy benefits (G) that outweigh its costs (*L*) ($G > L$ in Table 7.1). Republican antitrust thus operated on the assumption that the accuracy benefits of antitrust enforcement (i.e., the gains of true positives $(1-\beta)G$) exceed the costs of false positives ($(1-\beta)G > \alpha L$). This is why the republican antitrust sought to minimise the type II error rate β. In contrast, modern antitrust law on both sides of the Atlantic shares the Chicagoan proposition that erroneous intervention is often more costly than false acquittals. From this perspective, the accuracy benefits of antitrust enforcement fall short of the costs of false positives ($(1-\beta)G < \alpha L$). Consequently, the modern error-cost framework increasingly operates on the twofold assumption that firm conduct less frequently results in anticompetitive harm than benefits, whereas the opposite is the case for state intervention. As a result, competition rules on both sides of the Atlantic are increasingly designed and enforced in a way that minimises the type I error rate α. The error-cost framework in the United States and, albeit to a lesser extent, in EU competition law is consistently slanted towards non-intervention and the entrepreneurial liberty of antitrust defendants.

7.4 THE UNDOING OF PRESUMPTIONS

The combined effect of the adoption of a consumer welfare approach and the endorsement of the Chicagoan laissez-faire error-cost framework had immediate repercussions on the modus operandi of modern antitrust analysis. Competition law on both sides of the Atlantic increasingly departed from the deductive mode of analysis of the republican antitrust tradition that heavily relied on presumptions to draw legal inferences from the specific form of impugned conduct. The extensive

[67] D Bailey, 'Standard of Proof in EC Merger Proceedings: A Common Law Perspective' (2003) 40(4) *Common Market Law Review* 845, 875–76; Vesterdorf (n 65) 28; Reeves and Dodoo (n 65) 1040–46.

use and broad scope of presumptions of illegality were increasingly viewed as a significant source of type I errors and a paradigmatic example of the lack of economic sophistication and accuracy of republican antitrust. Most importantly, the use of overly broad presumptions of illegality led to what was perceived as an excessive level of state interference with the negative entrepreneurial liberty of businesses. The proponents of a laissez-faire antitrust, therefore, advocated the adoption of the more versatile rule of reason standard, which requires an inductive analysis of case-specific evidence to determine the actual or likely effects of business conduct on consumer welfare.[68] With the growing influence of the More Economic Approach on competition law enforcement on both sides of the Atlantic, rule of reason-like legal standards became the prevailing modus operandi through which modern antitrust implements the consumer welfare standard and the concomitant normative commitment to a negative conception of economic liberty.

7.4.1 *The Shrinking Scope of Presumptions in US Antitrust Law*

The incremental undoing of presumptions of anticompetitiveness was set in motion by the US Supreme Court in the late-1970s. With the ascent of the consumer welfare standard, the US Supreme Court increasingly disavowed and cut back the scope of presumptions of anticompetitiveness.[69] From the late-1970s onwards, the Supreme Court increasingly concurred with the Chicagoan precept that per se rules under § 1 of the Sherman Act should be limited to a 'small group of restraints',[70] such as horizontal price fixing and market sharing agreements, which are highly likely to diminish output without generating any redeeming efficiencies.[71] Existing per se rules against vertical territorial restraints,[72] maximum[73] and minimum resale

[68] RH Bork, 'The Rule of Reason and the Per Se Concept: Price Fixing and Market Division' (1966) 75(3) *The Yale Law Journal* 775, 832–40; V Korah, 'The Rise and Fall of Provisional Validity: The Need for a Rule of Reason in EEC Antitrust' (1981) 3(2) *Northwestern Journal of International Law & Business* 320, 354; I Forrester and C Norall, 'The Laicization of Community Law; Self-Help and the Rule of Reason: How Competition Law Is and Could Be Applied' (1984) 21(1) *Common Market Law Review* 11.

[69] *Cont'l T.V. v GTE Sylvania* (n 2) 46–47, 54, 58; *Leegin Creative Leather Prods. v PSKS, Inc.* (n 5) 887–88; *Eastman Kodak Co. v Image Tech. Servs.* 504 U.S. 451 (1992) 466–67; *Ohio v American Express Co.* (n 5) 10–11.

[70] *Ohio v American Express Co.* (n 5) 8.

[71] *White Motor Co. v United States* 372 U.S. 253 (1963) 263; *Broadcast Music, Inc. v Columbia Broadcasting System, Inc.* (n 3) 26; *Leegin Creative Leather Prods. v PSKS, Inc.* (n 5) 886. *National Collegiate Athletic Ass'n v Board of Regents* (n 3) 100, 107; FH Easterbrook, 'Workable Antitrust' (1986) 84(8) *Michigan Law Review* 1696, 1701.

[72] *Cont'l T.V. v GTE Sylvania* (n 2) 57–58 overruling *United States v Arnold, Schwinn & Co.* 388 U.S. 365 (1967).

[73] *State Oil Co. v Khan* 522 U.S. 3 (1997) 15–20 overruling *Albrecht v Globe-Democrat Publishing Co.* 390 U.S. 145 (1968).

price[74] maintenance, and information exchange (in oligopolistic markets)[75] were progressively overruled.

While narrowing the scope of presumptions of illegality, US courts increasingly relied on a casuistic, rule of reason-based analysis of case-specific evidence to ascertain the actual or likely effects of impugned conduct.[76] The rule of reason-based analysis has gradually been enthroned as the default mode of assessment to determine the legality of vertical and horizontal agreements.[77] However, the US courts did not simply replace the per se rule with an unstructured rule of reason analysis that would require the balancing of pro-and anticompetitive effects in each and every case.[78] Instead, the US courts, over time, devised the rule of reason as a 'three-step, burden-shifting framework' to identify the competitive 'net effect' of a restraint.[79] Each step of this burden-shifting rule of reason reallocates the burden of proof between the parties. In the first step, the antitrust plaintiff has to put forth a prima facie showing that the agreement at issue restricts competition by demonstrating that it has an actual or likely substantial anticompetitive effect.[80] If the antitrust plaintiff discharges its burden of proving a prima facie anticompetitive restraint, then in the second step the burden shifts to the defendant who has to rebut the finding of unreasonableness by advancing a pro-competitive justification for the restraint.[81] If the defendant carries the burden by showing pro-competitive effects, then the burden once more shifts to the plaintiff who has to make the case that the pro-competitive efficiencies can be obtained through less restrictive means or that 'on balance' the pro-competitive efficiencies do not outweigh the anticompetitive effects of the agreement.[82]

A similar retreat of presumptions of illegality can also be discerned in the realm of unilateral conduct. This process was already initiated before the Chicago School revolution gained full traction. The *Grinnell* case,[83] which was decided at the height

74 *Leegin Creative Leather Prods. v PSKS, Inc.* (n 5) 900–07 overruling *Dr. Miles Medical Co. v John D. Park & Sons Co.* 220 U.S. 373 (1911).

75 *United States v United States Gypsum Co.* 438 U.S. 422 (1978) 440–41 overruling *United States v Container Corp.* 393 U.S. 333 (1969) 337–38.

76 *Cont'l T.V. v GTE Sylvania* (n 2) 49–51, 54–55; *Leegin Creative Leather Prods. v PSKS, Inc.* (n 5) 895; *National Soc. of Professional Engineers v United States* (n 36) 691–92.

77 *Cont'l T.V. v GTE Sylvania* (n 2) 49; *Ariz. v Maricopa County Medical Soc.* (n 11) 343; *Leegin Creative Leather Prods. v PSKS, Inc.* (n 5) 885.

78 *Chicago Board of Trade v United States* 246 US 231 (1918).

79 *California Dental Assn. v FTC* 526 U.S. 756 (1999) Justice Breyer dissenting, 782, 793; *Ohio v American Express Co.* (n 5) 9, Justice Breyer dissenting, 2–3, 8; H Hovenkamp, 'The Rule of Reason' (2018) 70(1) *Florida Law Review* 81, 102–18.

80 *FTC v Indiana Federation of Dentists* (n 3) 461–62; *National Collegiate Athletic Ass'n v Board of Regents* (n 3) 110; *California Dental Assn. v FTC* (n 79) 783; *Ohio v American Express Co.* (n 5) 9.

81 *FTC v Indiana Federation of Dentists* (n 3) 459–60; *California Dental Assn. v FTC* (n 79) 787–88; *Ohio v American Express Co.* (n 5) 9.

82 *Ohio v American Express Co.* (n 5) 10 and Justice Breyer dissenting, 3.

83 *United States v Grinnell Corp.* 284 U.S. 563 (1966).

of the Warren Court era in 1966, fashioned the basic conduct test that until today governs the application of the prohibition of monopolisation under § 2 of the Sherman Act. This two-pronged test posits that

> the offense of monopoly under the Sherman Act has two elements: (1) the possession of monopoly power in the relevant market and (2) the willful acquisition or maintenance of that power as distinguished from growth or development as a consequence of a superior product, business acumen, or historic accident.[84]

Although *Grinnell* does not contain an explicit reference to a conduct element, the US judiciary subsequently interpreted the second prong of the *Grinnell* test as conditioning § 2 liability on the finding of some exclusionary conduct in addition to the possession of monopoly power. Drawing on *Grinnell*,[85] the US Supreme Court[86] and lower courts[87] started to unequivocally rule out the application of any form of situational structuralism under § 2 of the Sherman Act that would trigger a presumption of illegality for monopolistic firms holding unreasonable market power in the absence of exclusionary conduct. The US courts incrementally reinstated in full force the principle announced in *US Steel*[88] that size as such is not unlawful under § 2; or, in other words, the 'possessing of monopoly power is not itself an antitrust violation.'[89] Instead, the US courts began to harness the *Grinnell* test as a scaffolding for a rule of reason analysis that determines the legality of unilateral conduct under § 2 of the Sherman Act on the basis of its impact on consumer welfare. Akin to the modernised structured rule of reason under § 1 of the Sherman Act, this rule of reason framework operates as a three-step burden-shifting mechanism.[90] By gradually developing a rule of reason approach towards monopolistic firms, the US courts realigned the § 2 analysis with *Standard Oil*, which had established the rule of reason as the overarching adjudicative principle to assess the legality of business conduct not only under § 1 but also under § 2 of the Sherman Act.[91]

As a result of this shift towards a burden-shifting rule of reason approach, presumptions of illegality against unilateral conduct have largely disappeared in

84 Ibid. 570–71.

85 Ibid.

86 *Aspen Skiing Co. v Aspen Highlands Skiing Corp.* (n 6) 596 fn. 19; *Eastman Kodak Co. v Image Tech. Servs.* (n 69) 481; *United States v Microsoft Corporation* (n 7) 58; *Verizon Communications Inc. v Law Offices of Curtis Trinko* (n 38) 407; *Pacific Bell Telephone Co. dba AT&T California, et al. v linkLine Communications, Inc. et al.* (n 42) 7.

87 See, for instance, *Cal. Computer Prod. v Int'l Business Machines* 613 F.2d 727 (9th Cir. 1979) 735–36 and fn. 9; *MCI Communications Corp. v American Tel. & Tel. Co.* 708 F.2d 1081 (7th Cir. 1983) 1106–11. See, however, *Berkey Photo, Inc. v Eastman Kodak Co.* F.2d 263 (2d Cir. 1979) 274–75; cf. 281.

88 *United States v U.S. Steel Corp.* 251 U.S. 417 (1920) 451.

89 *United States v Microsoft Corporation* (n 7) 51, 58.

90 Ibid. 50–51, 58–59.

91 Ibid. 59.

US antitrust law. The US courts reacted to the Chicago School's 'single monopoly profit'[92] critique and its refinement by post-Chicago analysis[93] by abandoning structural presumptions against exclusive dealing agreements that foreclose a high market share[94] and by curtailing the per se rule against tying arrangements.[95] Several Justices in *Jefferson Parish*,[96] lower courts,[97] and commentators[98] even went one step further and pushed for full alignment of the antitrust treatment of tie-ins with the rule of reason assessment of exclusive dealing agreements. A similar erosion of presumptions of illegality also reshaped the approach of US courts towards pricing conduct by dominant firms. In *Matsushita* (1986)[99] and *Brooke Group* (1993),[100] the Supreme Court jettisoned the republican view, which was most prominently embodied in the *Utah Pie* case, that aggressive non-linear pricing strategies by large companies are tainted with the inherent tendency to undermine a polycentric market structure and foreclose competitors.[101] Instead, the Court endorsed the position that aggressive pricing by large firms is most of the time pro-competitive, which was shared by Chicago and Harvard scholars alike.[102] In *Brooke Group* and subsequent cases,[103] the Court established the incremental price-cost[104] or so-called

92 A Director and EH Levi, 'Law and the Future: Trade Regulation' (1956) 51(2) *Northwestern University Law Review* 281, 288–96; WS Bowman, Jr. 'Tying Arrangements and the Leverage Problem' (1957) 67(1) *Yale Law Journal* 19, 19, 21, 23–24, 27–29.

93 See, for instance, M Whinston, 'Tying, Foreclosure, and Exclusion' (1990) 80(4) *American Economic Review* 837, 838.

94 See, for instance, *Tampa Electric Co. v Nashville Coal Co.* 365 U.S. 320 (1961); *Roland Machinery Company v Dresser Industries Inc.* 749 F. 2d 380 (7th Cir. 1984) 395; *Omega Environmental, Inc. v Gilbarco, Inc.* 127 F. 3d 1157 (9th Cir. 1997) 1162–63; *United States v Microsoft Corporation* (n 7).

95 *Jefferson Parish Hosp. Dist. No 2 v Hyde* 466 U.S. 2 (1984) 11, 16–18, 21; *Eastman Kodak Co. v Image Tech. Servs.* (n 69) 462; *Illinois Tool Works Inc. v Independent Ink, Inc.* 547 U.S. 28 (2006) 37; *U.S. Steel Corp v Fortner Enterprises (Fortner II)* 429 U.S. 610 (1977) 620–22.

96 *Jefferson Parish Hosp. Dist. No 2 v Hyde* (n 95) Justice O'Connor concurring, with whom the Chief Justice Powell, and Justice Rehnquist joined, 35–44.

97 *United States v Microsoft Corporation* (n 7) 59, 84, 90–93.

98 See, for instance, C Ahlborn, DS Evans, and AJ Padilla, 'The Antitrust Economics of Tying: A Farewell to per se Illegality' (2004) 49(1–2) *Antitrust Bulletin* 287, 290, 330–39; KN Hylton and M Salinger, 'Tying Law and Policy: A Decision-Theoretic Approach' (2001) 69(2) *Antitrust Law Journal* 469, 502, 506–07, 525–26.

99 *Matsushita Elec. Indus. Co. v Zenith Radio Corp.* (n 38) 589, 595.

100 *Brooke Group v Brown & Williamson Tobacco Corp.* (n 38) 223, 226.

101 *Utah Pie Co. v Continental Baking Co.* 386 U.S. 685 (1967).

102 Bork, *The Antitrust Paradox* (n 6) 145, 149, 151–54; RA Posner, 'The Chicago School of Antitrust Analysis' (1979) 127(4) *University of Pennsylvania Law Review* 925, 940; P Areeda and DF Turner, 'Predatory Pricing and Related Practices under Section 2 of the Sherman Act' (1975) 88 (4) *Harvard Law Review* 697, 697–98.

103 *Weyerhaeuser Co. v Ross-Simmons Hardwood Lumber Co.* 549 U.S. 312 (2007) 325; *Verizon Communications Inc. v Law Offices of Curtis Trinko* (n 38) 414; *Pacific Bell Telephone Co. dba AT&T California, et al. v linkLine Communications, Inc. et al.* (n 42) 11.

104 *Brooke Group v Brown & Williamson Tobacco Corp.* (n 38) 223; Areeda and Turner (n 102) 698–99, 711, 717–18.

as-efficient competitor test as 'a specific application of the "rule of reason" to exclusionary pricing conduct.'[105] The Court thus made it clear that only unilateral (pricing) conduct that actually or likely interferes with an equally efficient competitor whose foreclosure entails consumer harm in the form of price increases would be considered an obstacle to the economic liberty of other market participants running afoul of antitrust rules.

The US courts not only retrenched the scope of presumptions of anticompetitiveness but also alleviated the evidentiary weight of the remaining presumptions. This is what happened most notably with the structural presumption established in *Philadelphia National Bank*. While the Supreme Court never formally overruled the presumption, in *General Dynamics* and subsequent cases[106] it made it clear that the fact that a merger results in a significant increase in economic concentration alone was no longer sufficient to block a merger. Rather, the Supreme Court recognised the need to consider additional evidence in the form of structural, behavioural, or performance factors which suggest that the merger is likely to harm competition.[107] In *Baker Hughes*[108] and *Heinz*[109] lower courts repudiated the structural approach of the Warren Court era, which had treated relatively small increases in concentration as conclusive evidence for the anticompetitive effects of mergers.[110] This erosion of the structural presumption and shift towards a rule of reason analysis was also driven by the 1982 and subsequent Merger Guidelines published by the Department of Justice. These Guidelines attributed increasingly less weight to market share and concentration thresholds, while shifting the focus on the analysis of anticompetitive unilateral and coordinated effects.[111] The scope of the presumption of illegality under US merger policy has thus been radically cut back. While the republican approach of the Warren Court era had relied on the structuralist presumption to block numerous mergers in relatively unconcentrated mergers,[112] under the 2010 Merger Guidelines a presumption of illegality is only operative in a tiny minority of mergers in highly concentrated markets.[113]

105 *ZF Meritor, LLC v Eaton Corp.* (n 44) 273.

106 *United States v General Dynamics* 415 U.S. 486 (1974) 500; *U.S. v Citizens & Southern National Bank* 422 U.S. 86 (1975); *United States v Marine Bancorporation* 418 U.S. 602 (1974).

107 LA Sullivan, *Antitrust* (St. Paul: West Publishing 1977) 600–01.

108 *United States v Baker Hughes, Inc.* (n 32).

109 *FTC v H.J. Heinz Co.* 246 F.3d 708 (D.C. Cir. 2001).

110 SP Sullivan, 'What Structural Presumption: Reuniting Evidence and Economics on the Role of Market Concentration in Horizontal Merger Analysis' (2016) 42(2) *Journal of Corporation Law* 403, 416–20.

111 Shapiro, 'The 2010 Horizontal Merger Guidelines' (n 8) 53.

112 Antitrust Division of the US Department of Justice, 1968 Merger Guidelines para. 5.

113 Antitrust Division of the US Department of Justice/Federal Trade Commission, 2010 Merger Guidelines (n 46) 18–20.

7.4.2 *The Shrinking Scope of Presumptions in EU Competition Law*

Although the roll-back of presumptions of illegality is less far-reaching than in US antitrust law, the importance of presumptions in EU competition law has also decreased significantly notably since 2014. Recent case law exhibits a clear decline in the scope and weight of presumptions of anticompetitiveness. In *Cartes Bancaires* and subsequent cases, the Court introduced the principle that the presumption of illegality under the by-object category must be applied restrictively.[114] It stressed that the category of by-object restrictions ought to be applied only to agreements whose adverse effects on consumer welfare are so likely that any assessment of their actual effects becomes redundant.[115] This implies that the rule of reason-like effects-based analysis emerges as the default mode of analysis under Article 101 (1) TFEU.[116] In contrast, the application of presumptions of anticompetitiveness under the by-object category is increasingly considered to be the exception.

The shrinking of the scope of presumptions under Article 101 (1) TFEU remains less significant than that under § 1 of the Sherman Act. The EU Commission and EU Courts, for instance, cleave to the strict treatment of vertical minimum resale price maintenance,[117] vertical territorial restrictions on passive sales,[118] and information exchange related to prices and output[119] as by-object restrictions. Yet, agreements that had been previously considered qua their form output restricting[120] or price fixing agreements[121] amounting to a restriction of competition by-object are increasingly subject to a more casuistic by-effects analysis, notably when they are adopted in the context of multi-sided markets. The scope of the by-object presumption under Article 101 (1) TFEU is hence increasingly limited to plain-vanilla output-reducing or price fixing cartels whose adverse effect on consumer welfare is obvious.[122]

[114] Case C-67/13 P *Groupement des cartes bancaires v Commission* (n 17) para. 58. See also Case C-345/14 *Maxima Latvija* (n 17) para. 18; Opinion of Advocate General Bobek in Case C-228/18 *Budapest Bank and Others* (n 57) para. 40.

[115] Case C-67/13 P *Groupement des cartes bancaires v Commission* (n 17) paras. 51, 57.

[116] European Commission, Guidelines on the Application of Article 81(3) of the Treaty (n 14) para. 24, see also paras. 17–18; European Commission, Communication from the Commission on the Application of the Community Competition Rules to Vertical Restraints – Follow-up to the Green Paper on Vertical Restraints, [1998] OJ C 365/3 3–4.

[117] Case No COMP/AT.40428 *Guess* C(2018) 8455 final.

[118] Case C-230/16 *Coty Germany* ECLI:EU:C:2017:941.

[119] Case C-286/13 P *Dole Food and Dole Fresh Fruit Europe v Commission* ECLI:EU:C:2015:184 para. 122.

[120] Case C-67/13 P *Groupement des cartes bancaires v Commission* (n 17). The agreement in *Cartes Bancaires* was indeed considered similar to that in Case C-209/07 *Beef Industry Development and Barry Brothers* by the General Court. Case T-491/07 *Groupement des cartes bancaires v Commission* ECLI:EU:T:2012:633 paras. 197–99.

[121] Case C-228/18 *Budapest Bank and Others* ECLI:EU:C:2020:265.

[122] Case C-67/13 P *Groupement des cartes bancaires v Commission* (n 17) para. 51.

The decline of legal presumptions and the slow conversion towards an effects-based rule of reason approach have also made inroads into the application of Article 102 TFEU to unilateral conduct by dominant firms. The European Commission and recently also the European Courts[123] have started operationalising the consumer welfare standard by abandoning the form-based in favour of an effects-based analysis of unilateral conduct.[124] As form-based presumptions of illegality are increasingly disavowed, the Article 102 case law also edges towards an increasingly casuistic analysis. This becomes most apparent in the recent *Google Shopping* ruling, where the EU General Court ruled out the existence of any presumption of anticompetitiveness under Article 102 TFEU. It observed that the distinction between by-object and by-effect restrictions of competition, which structures the analysis of coordinated conduct under Article 101 (1) TFEU, does not exist under Article 102 TFEU.[125] Instead, the Court explained that under Article 102, the Commission is always required to ascertain the anticompetitive effects of the impugned conduct by considering 'all the relevant circumstances'.[126]

With the rise of the More Economic Approach, existing legal presumptions against exclusive dealing,[127] exclusivity rebates,[128] and tie-ins[129] have given way to a more detailed analysis of their foreclosure effects.[130] A similar trend is discernible with respect to predatory pricing. Although it stopped short of recognising a recoupment test,[131] the European Commission no longer relies exclusively on a

[123] Case C-413/14 P *Intel v Commission* (n 23) paras. 137–40.

[124] European Commission (n 12) 3–4, 7, 15; R O'Donoghue and AJ Padilla, *The Law and Economics of Article 82 EC* (Oxford: Hart 2006) 16–18.

[125] Case T-612/17 *Google and Alphabet v Commission (Google Shopping)* ECLI:EU:T:2021:763 paras. 435–36. See, however, Case C-307/18 *Generics (UK) and Others* (n 31) para. 155.

[126] Case T-612/17 *Google and Alphabet v Commission (Google Shopping)* (n 125) paras. 437–41; Case C-377/20 *Servizio Elettrico Nazionale and Others* (n 27) paras. 50–52, 69; Opinion of Advocate General Rantos in Case C-680/20 *Unilever Italia Mkt. Operations* ECLI:EU:C:2022:586 paras. 63, 71–79; Case C-680/20 *Unilever Italia Mkt. Operations* (n 27) paras. 40, 54, 62.

[127] Case 85/76 *Hoffmann-La Roche v Commission* ECLI:EU:C:1979:36 para. 89; Case C-413/14 P *Intel v Commission* (n 23) para. 137;

[128] Case 85/76 *Hoffmann-La Roche v Commission* (n 127) para. 89; Case C-413/14 P *Intel v Commission* (n 23) para. 137; Case C-680/20 *Unilever Italia Mkt. Operations* (n 27) paras. 46–54.

[129] Case No COMP/37.792 *Microsoft*, C (2004) 900 final para. 841; Case T-201/04 *Microsoft Corp v Commission* ECLI:EU:T:2007:289 paras. 857, 868.

[130] EU Commission, Guidance on the Commission's Enforcement Priorities in Applying Article 82 of the EC Treaty to Abusive Exclusionary Conduct by Dominant Undertakings (n 14) paras. 20, 34–36, 46, 48–49, 52, 53; Case T-65/98 *Van den Bergh Foods Ltd v Commission of the European Communities* ECLI:EU:T:2003:281 para. 160; Case T-201/04 *Microsoft Corp v Commission* (n 129) paras. 857, 868; Case T-604/18 *Google and Alphabet v Commission (Google Android)* (n 27) paras. 286–93; Opinion of Advocate General Rantos in Case C-680/20 *Unilever Italia Mkt. Operations* (n 27) paras. 71–79.

[131] The Court, indeed, rejected a recoupment requirement for the finding of predatory pricing in breach of Article 102 TFEU Case C-202/07 P *France Télécom v Commission* ECLI:EU:C:2009:214 paras. 110, 113.

presumption against below-AVC pricing to support the finding of abusive predatory pricing.[132] Instead, it looks into additional evidence to sustain a credible predation and recoupment story in line with post-Chicago models of predation strategies.[133] Most prominently, in *Intel* and progeny the EU Courts fundamentally narrowed the *Hoffmann-La Roche* presumption against loyalty rebates and exclusivity clauses to those types of loyalty rebates and exclusivity clauses that are capable of foreclosing equally efficient competitors.[134]

In recent years, the EU Commission and judiciary have also ruled out the existence of any structural presumption under the EU merger control regime. This demise of structural presumptions in EU merger policy was carried forward with the reform of European merger control that resulted in the replacement of the dominance test by the new SIEC test in Article 2 (3) of the revised Merger Regulation 139/2004.[135] Under the old dominance test of Regulation 4064/89 EC,[136] the finding that a merger leads to the creation or strengthening of a dominant position was sufficient to create a presumption of a SIEC, and hence of illegality.[137] By contrast, the establishment of the SIEC test cast doubt on this presumption. It instead aligned EU merger policy with a rule of reason-type analysis, which warrants an inquiry into the actual or likely anticompetitive effects of a merger to support the finding of a SIEC.[138]

The implicit abandoning of structural presumptions with the adoption of the SIEC test was also reflected in the Commission's 2004 Horizontal Merger Guidelines and case law by the EU judiciary. Both made it clear that high concentration levels, market shares, or the finding of a dominant position[139] alone would no

[132] Ibid. para. 109.

[133] European Commission, Guidance on the Commission's Enforcement Priorities in Applying Article 82 of the EC Treaty to Abusive Exclusionary Conduct by Dominant Undertakings (n 14) paras. 68, 20; European Commission (n 12) 18–19, 20–21. For a recent example for such a strategic analysis of predatory pricing Case No COMP/AT.39711 *Qualcomm (predation)*, C (2019) 5361 final paras. 398–440.

[134] Case C-413/14 P *Intel v Commission* (n 23) paras. 133–44; Case T-604/18 *Google and Alphabet v Commission (Google Android)* (n 27) paras. 639–46, 651; Case T-286/09 RENV *Intel Corporation v Commission* ECLI:EU:T:2022:19 paras. 124–26, 134, 144–45; Case T-235/18 *Qualcomm v Commission* (n 27) paras. 349–56; Case C-680/20 *Unilever Italia Mkt. Operations* ECLI:EU:C:2023:33 (n 27) paras. 47, 52, 55–62.

[135] Council Regulation (EC) No 139/2004 on the Control of Concentrations between Undertakings (n 19).

[136] Council Regulation (EEC) No 4064/89 on the Control of Concentrations between Undertakings, [1989] OJ L 395/1 Article 2 (3).

[137] G Monti, *EC Competition Law* (Cambridge: Cambridge University Press 2007) 249–50.

[138] V Verouden, C Bengtsson, and S Albaek, 'The Draft EU Notice on Horizontal Mergers: A Further Step toward Convergence' (2004) 49(1–2) *Antitrust Bulletin* 243, 243, 247; A Lindsay and A Berridge, *The EU Merger Regulation: Substantive Issues* (London: Sweet & Maxwell 2012) 43.

[139] European Commission, Guidelines on the Assessment of Horizontal Mergers (n 14) paras. 4, 21; Case T-282/06 *Sun Chemical Group* ECLI:EU:T:2007:203 paras. 138, 140, 142; Case T-405/08 *Spar Österreichische Warenhandels v Commission* ECLI:EU:T:2013:306 paras. 64–69; Case T-79/12 *Cisco v Commission* ECLI:EU:T:2013:635 paras. 69, 74.

longer suffice to challenge a merger. Instead, the Commission was henceforth required to examine the anticompetitive effects of mergers on the basis of clearly articulated theories of harm, namely coordinated,[140] non-coordinated (unilateral)[141] or foreclosure[142] effects. Recent case law has also clearly rejected any presumption of illegality of mergers under the EUMR.[143] The most emblematic example of the growing hostility of the EU judiciary towards structural presumptions is the recent *CK Telecoms* ruling by the General Court. The General Court annulled the European Commission's decision to block a merger that would have reduced the number of mobile telecommunication operators in the UK market from four to three out of fear that the Commission had implicitly relied on an undue presumption against four-to-three mergers in oligopolistic markets.[144]

The pivot of US antitrust and EU competition law from a republican towards a laissez-faire approach has narrowed the set of conduct that is made unavailable through presumptions of anticompetitiveness. Table 7.2 captures the narrowing of the scope of presumptions of illegality. The flipside of this shrinking of the scope of legal presumptions is that it went hand-in-hand with the trimming down of the right sets that shield market participants against potentially dominating conduct. As a result, the extent to which competition law on both sides of the Atlantic provides a modally robust prohibition of certain types of dominating conduct has been seriously curtailed.

This reduction in the size of the right sets is the immediate consequence of the narrowing of the concept of preventing conditions (y) following the transition from a republican to a negative conception of economic liberty that was triggered by the rise of the consumer welfare standard and laissez-faire antitrust. By narrowing the type of harm that a decision-maker may permissibly infer under presumptions of illegality to (consumer) welfare reduction, the laissez-faire approach limited the type of conduct to which presumptions of illegality might apply. Consequently, only a small fraction of the conduct that, due to its adverse effect on market structure, appeared to be inherently anticompetitive under the republican tradition and the S-C-P paradigm continued to be subject to anticompetitive presumptions under the laissez-faire approach because it had obvious welfare-reducing effects. Other conduct and market situations that the republican antitrust tradition perceived as a source of domination because of their adverse effect on a polycentric market

[140] European Commission, Guidelines on the Assessment of Horizontal Mergers (n 14) 39–57.

[141] Ibid. paras. 24–38.

[142] European Commission, Guidelines on the Assessment of Non-horizontal Mergers (n 14).

[143] Case T-79/12 *Cisco v Commission* (n 139) para. 48; Case C-413/06 P *Bertelsmann and Sony Corporation of America v Impala* ECLI:EU:C:2008:392 para. 48.

[144] Case T-399/16 *CK Telecoms UK Investments v Commission* (n 18) paras. 174, 249. This ruling was, however, recently annulled in Case C-376/20 *Commission v CK Telecoms UK Investments* (n 18).

structure are no longer deemed problematic from the perspective of the consumer welfare approach. The thinning out of the concept of economic liberty and its preventing conditions (y) brought about by laissez-faire antitrust law is thus directly reflected in a thinning out of the scope of legal presumptions and right sets of market

TABLE 7.2 *The evolution of presumptions of anticompetitiveness*

Republican approach – US antitrust law	Laissez-faire approach – US antitrust law
Coordinated conduct	Coordinated conduct
• Horizontal price fixing agreements (*Trenton Potteries; Socony-Vacuum*) • Market sharing agreements (*Timken Roller*) • Collective boycotts (*Fashion Originators' Guild*) • Vertical maximum (*Albrecht v Globe-Democrat Publishing* overruled by *State Oil Co. v Khan*) and minimum (*Dr Miles* overruled by *Leegin*) resale price maintenance • Exclusive territorial restrictions (*Arnold, Schwinn* overruled by *GTE Sylvania*) • Information exchange on prices in oligopolistic markets (*Container Corp.* overruled by *Gypsum Co.*)	• Horizontal price fixing agreements qualified in *BMI* and NCAA • Market sharing agreements qualified in *BMI* • Collective boycotts qualified in *Northwest Wholesale Stationers*
Dominant firm conduct/monopoly power	Dominant firm conduct/monopoly power
• Unreasonable monopoly power (*Alcoa, American Tobacco*) • Tying (*Int'l Salt*) • Exclusive dealing (*United States v United Shoe Mach. Co.* (1918); *Standard Oil* (1949). Weakened in *Tampa Electric Co. v Nashville Coal Co.*) • Territorial price discrimination (*Utah Pie Co. v Continental Baking Co.* overruled by *Brooke Group v Brown & Williamson Tobacco Corp.*).	• Tying qualified in *Microsoft*
Mergers	Mergers
• Mergers leading to an excessive level of concentration (*Philadelphia National Bank*)	• Mergers leading to an excessive level of concentration qualified in *Baker Hughes* and *Heinz*

(*continued*)

TABLE 7.2 (*continued*)

Republican Approach – EU Competition Law	Laissez-faire Approach – EU Competition Law
Coordinated conduct	Coordinated conduct
• Horizontal price fixing agreements (*BNIC v Clair*) • Market sharing (*BNIC v Aubert*) and output-reducing (*Suiker Unie; BIDS*) agreements • Collective boycotts (*IAZ*) • Vertical minimum resale price maintenance (*VVR v Sociale Dienst*) • Exclusive territorial restrictions (*Consten and Grundig*) • Information exchange on prices (*T-Mobile Netherlands*)	• Horizontal price fixing agreements qualified in *Budapest Bank* • Market sharing and output-reducing agreements qualified in *Cartes Bancaires* and *Generics* • Collective boycotts • Vertical minimum resale price maintenance • Exclusive territorial restrictions • Information exchange on prices
Dominant firm conduct	Dominant firm conduct
• Exclusive dealing and loyalty rebates (*Suiker Unie; Hoffmann-La Roche*) • Tying (*Hilti*) • Below average variable cost pricing (*Akzo*)	• Exclusive dealing and loyalty rebates qualified in *Intel* and *Unilever* • Tying qualified in *Microsoft* • Below average variable cost pricing qualified in *Servizio Elettrico Nazionale* and *Unilever*
Mergers	Mergers
• Mergers creating a single (*Air France v Commission*) or collective (*France and Société commerciale des potasses et de l'azote and Entreprise minière et chimique v Commission*) dominant position	

participants. The latter find themselves protected with respect to fewer types of potentially dominating conduct.

7.4.3 *The Reconceptualisation and the Decreasing Weight of Remaining Presumptions*

The rise of the consumer welfare standard and the Chicagoan error-cost framework not only precipitated the shrinking of the scope of the presumptions of illegality, but the shift from a republican towards a laissez-faire approach was also marked by a change in the rationale underpinning the remaining presumptions of illegality. Instead of fully jettisoning legal presumptions to the benefit of a freewheeling rule of reason approach, laissez-faire antitrust sought to maintain at least some presumptions of illegality to ensure the administrability and procedural economy of antitrust law. However, competition authorities and courts on both sides of the Atlantic started to provide a new welfarist and decision-theoretic rationalisation of presumptions of anticompetitiveness that algins their rationale with a narrow and probabilistic notion of negative economic liberty as non-interference.

With the ascent of the laissez-faire antitrust approach, presumptions of illegality were no longer grounded in the concern about domination. They ceased to constitute a generalisation of the magnitude of potential harm that specific types of coordinated and unilateral business conduct and mergers may generate across various relevant possible worlds by undermining a competitive market structure. Consequently, presumptions in modern antitrust law no longer take the form of $\frac{P(H|w_1)\ P(w_1) + \cdots + P(H|w_k)\ P(w_k)}{P(B|w_1)\ P(w_1) + \cdots + P(B|w_k)\ P(w_k)}$, where $w_1, \ldots, w_k$ describe all worlds accessible from the actual world, $P(w_1), \ldots, P(w_k)$ denote the respective probabilities of occurrence of these worlds, and $P(H\,|\,w_{1\ldots k})$ and $P(B\,|\,w_{1\ldots k})$ denote the respective conditional probabilities of the impugned conduct being harmful or beneficial in a given world $w_{1\ldots k}$.[145]

Legal presumptions no longer revolve around republican liberty as non-domination as their underlying rationale. Nor do they any longer establish a per se or prima facie rule against certain types of conduct or levels of power concentration based on the mere reason that they put private parties in a situation where they can arbitrarily interfere with the sphere of autonomy of other market participants. On the contrary, competition authorities and courts on both sides of the Atlantic increasingly perceive legal presumptions as simple probability estimates of the likelihood of certain conduct causing consumer harm in the actual $(P(H\,|\,w_1)\ P(w_1))$ or nearby likely $(P(H\,|\,w_1)\ P(w_1) + P(H\,|\,w_2)\ P(w_2))$ worlds. The remaining presumptions thus operate as generalisations of the likely adverse effect of certain types of conduct on consumer welfare,[146] and hence their likelihood of leading to welfare-decreasing interference with the economic liberty of other market players in the actual or nearby likely world. From this perspective, legal presumptions are increasingly conceptualised as simple Bayesian priors $\frac{P(H)}{P(B)}$ that incorporate an estimate of the odds ratio of the probability of conduct resulting in consumer harm $P(H)$ relative to it resulting in benefits $P(B)$ or being competitively neutral in the actual or nearby likely world. This probabilistic understanding of presumptions assumes that for certain types of agreements, an 'inquiry into the effect upon

145 This formalisation of republican presumptions draws on C List and L Valentini, 'Freedom as Independence' (2016) 126(4) *Ethics* 1043, 1054, fn. 23; P Pettit, *On the People's Terms: A Republican Theory and Model of Democracy* (Cambridge: Cambridge University Press 2012) 67–68. For a critical discussion of this approach and its limitation to capture the 'non-probabilistic' concept of republican liberty, see List and Valentini (n 145), 1058 and fn. 24.

146 *Cont'l T.V. v GTE Sylvania* (n 2) 50 fn. 16; *Ariz. v Maricopa County Medical Soc.* (n 11) 343; European Commission, Guidelines on the Application of Article 81(3) of the Treaty (n 14) para. 21; Opinion of Advocate General Wahl in Case C-67/13 P *Groupement des cartes bancaires v Commission* (n 55) paras. 26–30.

competition and economic justification would be similarly irrelevant' because judicial experience and economic analysis show that they lack any pro-competitive justification, and therefore are with an overwhelming likelihood anticompetitive.[147]

Consistent with this probabilistic reconceptualisation, presumptions of anticompetitive harm are henceforth increasingly treated as nothing more than a shortcut to a rule of reason inquiry into the likely welfare effects of specific types of conduct[148] or mergers.[149] Only those types of conduct that could be predicted with confidence to entail a high likelihood of welfare-reducing interference with the negative liberty of other market participants can trigger a presumption of illegality. This alignment of presumptions of illegality with a probabilistic and welfarist rationale has resulted in a reduction in their evidentiary weight, and the frequent blending of presumptions of illegality and legal standards into a sliding-scale rule of reason or effects-based analysis.

This shift towards a sliding-scale approach has been set in motion by the US Supreme Court, which began to blur the lines between the per se rule and rule of reason approach in the late-1970s and early-1980s. Over the years, the US courts have reverted to the original formulation of the rule of reason in *Standard Oil* which posited that the legality of all types of agreements and unilateral conduct with § 1 and § 2 of the Sherman Act must be assessed based on the standard of reason.[150] The Supreme Court's reformed approach to the per se rule and rule of reason divide reinstated the rule of reason standard as the overarching adjudicative principle of antitrust analysis under § 1 and § 2 of the Sherman Act.[151] As a result, the per se rule itself became just one expression of the rule of reason as the meta-principle of the interpretation of the Sherman Act.[152] Observing that the obviousness of

[147] *Broadcast Music, Inc. v Columbia Broadcasting System, Inc.* (n 3) 9–10; *National Collegiate Athletic Ass'n v Board of Regents* (n 3) 100 fn. 21; *Leegin Creative Leather Prods. v PSKS, Inc.* (n 5) 866; Case C-67/13 P *Groupement des cartes bancaires v Commission* (n 17) para. 51.

[148] *National Soc. of Professional Engineers v United States* (n 36) 692; *Broadcast Music, Inc. v Columbia Broadcasting System, Inc.* (n 3) 8, 9; *Ariz. v Maricopa County Medical Soc.* (n 11) 344; FH Easterbrook, 'The Limits of Antitrust' (1984) 63(1) *Texas Law Review* 1, 9–10, 15–16; Opinion of Advocate General Wahl in Case C-67/13 P *Groupement des cartes bancaires v Commission* (n 55) para. 31; Case C-67/13 P *Groupement des cartes bancaires v Commission* (n 17) paras. 51, 57.

[149] RA Posner, *Antitrust Law* (Chicago: University of Chicago Press 2001) 131–32; Antitrust Division of the US Department of Justice, 1982 Merger Guidelines (n 9) 14, 18; Antitrust Division of the US Department of Justice/Federal Trade Commission, 2010 Merger Guidelines (n 46) 3; European Commission, Guidelines on the Assessment of Horizontal Mergers (n 14) paras. 18, 27.

[150] *Standard Oil Co. of New Jersey v United States* 221 U.S. 1 (1911) 60–61.

[151] *National Soc. Of Professional Engineers v United States* (n 36) 690; *National Collegiate Athletic Ass'n v Board of Regents* (n 3) 103; *FTC v Indiana Federation of Dentists* (n 3) 458. This test is largely identical with the test set out in *Standard Oil Co. of New Jersey v United States* (n 150) 58.

[152] MS Popofsky, 'Defining Exclusionary Conduct: Section 2, The Rule of Reason, and the Unifying Principle Underlying Antitrust Rules' (2005) 73(2) *Antitrust Law Journal* 435, 454, 457.

anticompetitive effects, and hence the restrictive character of various types of conduct, is often a question of degree, the US courts increasingly recognised that their assessment may warrant different levels of analytical depth and might give rise to presumptions of varying strength.[153] The Supreme Court noted that there is no longer a 'categorical line' between the per se and rule of reason categories.[154] In some instances, the per se rule could only be established after some form of economic analysis of the likely competitive effects of the agreement at stake, focusing on the parties' market power, incentives, and ability to restrict competition.[155] In other instances, 'no elaborate industry analysis is required to demonstrate' the anticompetitive effects of particular conduct under the rule of reason assessment.[156] Instead, the unreasonableness of an agreement can be established 'in the twinkling of an eye' on the basis of a truncated rule of reason analysis.[157] Rather than relying on the classical per se rule and rule of reason dichotomy, US courts increasingly endorsed the argument coined by the Chicago School that the rule of reason analysis should be structured around a number of filters that organise a stepwise burden-shifting analysis of the reasonableness of an agreement.[158]

The transformation of substantive presumptions of illegality into procedural burden-shifting devices has substantially reduced their evidentiary weight; or, in other words, enhanced their rebuttability. This weakening of the weight of remaining presumptions has been compounded by the lowering of the evidential burden for the parties to rebut them. For instance, in the context of merger control, the US courts no longer require parties to make a 'clear showing'[159] that the merger, although leading to a substantial increase in concentration, will not entail anticompetitive harm. Since *Baker Hughes*, parties simply have to 'show' that the structural presumption does not accurately predict the competitive effects of the merger.[160] Under § 1 of the Sherman Act, the per se rule can no longer be considered as a strictly irrebuttable presumption. Rather, if firms put forth

[153] *National Collegiate Athletic Ass'n v Board of Regents* (n 3) 104, fn. 26; *California Dental Assn. v FTC* (n 79) 779.

[154] *California Dental Assn. v FTC* (n 79) 780–81.

[155] Ibid. 779; *Jefferson Parish Hosp. Dist. No 2 v Hyde* (n 95) 11–12; *Northwest Wholesale Stationers, Inc. v Pacific Stationery & Printing Co.* 472 U.S. 284 (1985) 294–98.

[156] *National Soc. of Professional Engineers v United States* (n 36) 692–93; *FTC v Indiana Federation of Dentists* (n 3) 459; *California Dental Assn. v FTC* (n 79) 770; *FTC v Actavis et al.* 570 U.S. 136 (2013) 20.

[157] *National Collegiate Athletic Ass'n v Board of Regents* (n 3) 109–10, fn. 39; *California Dental Assn. v FTC* (n 79) 769–71, 779–80; *FTC v Actavis et al.* (n 156) 20.

[158] Bork, *The Antitrust Paradox* (n 6) 125–29, 294–95; Easterbrook, 'The Limits of Antitrust' (n 148) 11–13, 19–23.

[159] *United States v Philadelphia National Bank* 374 U.S. 321 (1963) 363.

[160] *United States v Baker Hughes, Inc.* (n 32) 984, 991; SC Salop, 'The Evolution and Vitality of Merger Presumptions: A Decision-Theoretic Approach' (2015) 80(2) *Antitrust Law Journal* 269, 275; H Hovenkamp and C Shapiro, 'Horizontal Mergers, Market Structure, and Burdens of Proof' (2018) 127(7) *The Yale Law Journal* 1996, 2010–11.

undermining or countervailing evidence at the characterisation stage, then agreements that would otherwise qualify as per se infringements will be subject to a (sliding-scale) rule of reason analysis.[161] Similarly, the US courts also weakened the weight of the remaining presumptions, for instance against tying, when assessing unilateral exclusionary conduct.[162] The assessment of unilateral conduct under US antitrust law, and notably § 2 of the Sherman Act, has thus been largely aligned with a structured rule of reason analysis.[163]

A similar decrease in the weight of presumptions of illegality is currently underway in Europe. As in the United States, this dwindling weight of presumptions results from a shift towards a sliding-scale approach under Article 101 TFEU, Article 102 TFEU, and EU merger control. *Cartes Bancaires* and subsequent cases increased the options for defendants to rebut the finding of by-object restrictions by broadening the criteria that enforcers and courts have to account for at the characterisation stage before they can legitimately classify an agreement as a restriction of competition by object or effect.[164] Consequently, defendants are no longer limited to rebutting the by-object presumption by proffering offsetting evidence under Article 101 (3) TFEU or undermining evidence under the ancillary restraints doctrine.[165] Instead, the Court recently recognised that parties could overturn the presumption of anticompetitiveness against agreements that qua their form would qualify as a by-object restriction by advancing undermining evidence at the characterisation stage to show that, in the case at hand, they do not result in the inferred anticompetitive effects.[166] The Court also expanded the channels through which parties could advance offsetting evidence at the characterisation stage, showing that a prima facie by-object restriction would generate efficiencies capable of attenuating or muting its anticompetitive effect.[167] It thus departed from previous case law,[168] which required parties to demonstrate that their agreement met the demanding four-pronged test under Article 101 (3) to successfully rebut the by-object presumption on efficiency grounds.

[161] *Broadcast Music, Inc. v Columbia Broadcasting System, Inc.* (n 3); *National Collegiate Athletic Ass'n v Board of Regents* (n 3); *PolyGram Holding, Inc. v FTC* 416 F.3d 29 (D.C. Cir. 2005) 34–37.

[162] *United States v Microsoft Corporation* (n 7) 90–95.

[163] Popofsky (n 152).

[164] Case C-67/13 P *Groupement des cartes bancaires v Commission* (n 17) para. 53; Opinion of Advocate General Bobek in Case C-228/18 *Budapest Bank and Others* (n 57) para. 51; Case C-307/18 *Generics (UK) and Others* (n 31) paras. 67–68.

[165] Case 42/84 *Remia v Commission* ECLI:EU:C:1985:327 paras. 19–20; Opinion of Advocate General Kokott in Case C-307/18 *Generics (UK) and Others* ECLI:EU:C:2020:28 paras. 153–56.

[166] Case C-228/18 *Budapest Bank and Others* (n 121) paras. 81–83; Opinion of Advocate General Wahl in Case C-67/13 P *Groupement des cartes bancaires v Commission* (n 55) paras. 43–44.

[167] Case C-307/18 *Generics (UK) and Others* (n 31) paras. 103–08; Opinion of Advocate General Kokott in Case C-307/18 *Generics (UK) and Others* (n 165) paras. 147–80; Case C-211/22 *Super Bock Bebidas* ECLI:EU:C:2023:529 para. 36.

[168] Case C-209/07 *Beef Industry Development and Barry Brothers (BIDS)* (n 120) para. 21.

Similarly, the EU Commission and Courts also departed from a de facto presumption against mergers giving rise to large market shares. Although high market shares and concentration ratios continue to play a role as a factor indicating the anticompetitive potential of a merger, the Courts and Commission made it clear that they have adopted a sliding-scale approach towards market shares, whereby the finding of anticompetitiveness becomes more likely the higher the market shares are.[169]

This dilution of the weight of remaining presumptions also occurred under Article 102 TFEU. The Court recognised in *Intel* that defendants could rebut the presumption of illegality against loyalty rebates by advancing undermining evidence showing that, in the case at hand, they are not capable of foreclosing an as-efficient competitor.[170] The most blatant sign of weakening of the presumption against loyalty rebates under Article 102 TFEU can be found in *Google Android*. Had the Court of Justice previously consistently held that a dominant firm entering exclusivity agreements or granting loyalty rebates 'abuses' its dominant position,[171] the General Court in *Google Android* made it plain that loyalty rebates and exclusivity agreements are only indicative of the possibility that the dominant firm 'may be abusing its dominant position'.[172] At the same time, *Google Android* substantially lowered the evidentiary burden for defendants to reverse the presumption of illegality against loyalty rebates. It seems to suggest that defendants can simply raise doubts about the Commission's analysis of their foreclosure effects without being necessarily required to support these doubts with specific evidence.[173] Recent case law also clarifies that the ability of defendant dominant firms to rebut remaining presumptions under Article 102 by advancing undermining evidence is not confined to loyalty rebates.[174] Instead, it seems to apply across all types of conduct, and hence also the remaining presumptions against exclusive dealing clauses, tying and below-AVC pricing.[175]

The dwindling weight of presumptions under Article 102 TFEU is not only the result of the broadening of the category of undermining evidence that dominant firms can put forward to undermine presumptions of illegality. More recently, the Court of Justice appeared to recognise, alongside the well-established category of objective justification, a novel option for dominant firms to advance offsetting

[169] The EU Courts have adopted a sliding-scale approach towards market shares and concentration in merger control Case T-282/06 *Sun Chemical Group* (n 139) para. 148.

[170] Case C-413/14 P *Intel v Commission* (n 23) paras. 137–39.

[171] Case 85/76 *Hoffmann-La Roche v Commission* (n 127) para. 89; Case C-413/14 P *Intel v Commission* (n 23) para. 138.

[172] Case T-604/18 *Google and Alphabet v Commission (Google Android)* (n 27) para. 651.

[173] Ibid. paras. 789, 794–96.

[174] Case C-377/20 *Servizio Elettrico Nazionale and Others* (n 27) paras. 51–52.

[175] To this effect, Opinion of Advocate General Rantos in Case C-680/20 *Unilever Italia Mkt. Operations* (n 126) paras. 70–79; Case C-680/20 *Unilever Italia Mkt. Operations* (n 27) paras. 46–52.

evidence to demonstrate that the impugned practice generates efficiencies that outweigh its harm. As a consequence, dominant firms seem to be no longer bound by the strict evidentiary criteria of the objective justification to advance efficiency claims.[176] On the contrary, mirroring recent Article 101 TFEU case law,[177] the Court held that defendants could plead efficiencies as offsetting evidence at the characterisation stage of the conduct.[178] However, this frontloading of the assessment of pro-competitive effects comes with no clear evidentiary criteria attached.

The combined effect of the probabilistic reinterpretation, the curtailing of the scope, and the alleviation of the weight of presumptions of anticompetitiveness in EU competition law is three-fold. First, it raised the evidentiary burden for enforcers and private antitrust plaintiffs to activate presumptions of illegality by introducing a number of 'reality check[s]'[179] that have to be met before a presumption can be relied on.

Second, it increasingly collapsed the previous categories of by-object and by-effect restrictions of competition under Article 101 and 102 TFEU[180] into a sliding-scale rule of reason analysis that requires competition enforcers and courts to consider a considerable amount of case-specific evidence which had previously fallen within the domain of the by-effects analysis before they could legitimately characterise the impugned conduct as a presumably unlawful (by-object) restriction of competition.[181] Even though the Court's interpretation of the by-object category under Article 101 TFEU had always presupposed some consideration of the economic context of the agreement at issue,[182] the recent case law substantially raised the level of scrutiny of case-specific evidence a competition authority or court would have to carry out before it could rely on the presumption of illegality associated with the finding of a by-object restriction.[183] Since *Cartes Bancaires*, the baseline analysis necessary to establish a presumption of illegality under the by-object category clearly requires, along with a form-based analysis of the agreement, a more-or-less cursory

[176] Case C-377/20 *Servizio Elettrico Nazionale and Others* (n 27) para. 47.

[177] Case C-307/18 *Generics (UK) and Others* (n 31) paras. 103–08.

[178] Case C-377/20 *Servizio Elettrico Nazionale and Others* (n 27) para. 48; Case C-680/20 *Unilever Italia Mkt. Operations* (n 27) paras. 49–50, 53–54.

[179] Opinion of Advocate General Bobek in Case C-228/18 *Budapest Bank and Others* (n 57) paras. 43, 45; Opinion of Advocate General Wahl in Case C-67/13 P *Groupement Cartes Bancaires v Commission* (n 55) paras. 43–44.

[180] For the proposition that the by-object category also existed under Article 102 TFEU, see PI Colomo and A Lamadrid de Pablo, 'On the Notion of Restriction of Competition: What We Know and What We Do Not Know We Know' in D Gerard, M Merola, and B Meyring (eds), *The Notion of Restriction of Competition: Revisiting the Foundations of Antitrust Enforcement in Europe* (Brussles: Bruylant 2017) 333, 346.

[181] Opinion of Advocate General Bobek in Case C-228/18 *Budapest Bank and Others* (n 57) para. 47; See as a recent example, Case C-211/22 *Super Bock Bebidas* ECLI:EU:C:2023:529 paras. 34–37, 42–43.

[182] Case 56/65 *Société Technique Minière v Maschinenbau Ulm* ECLI:EU:C:1966:38 p. 250.

[183] Case C-67/13 P *Groupement des cartes bancaires v Commission* (n 17) para. 53; Case C-211/22 *Super Bock Bebidas* ECLI:EU:C:2023:529 paras. 34–37, 42–43; Case C-413/14 P *Intel v Commission* (n 23) para. 139.

analysis of the economic and legal context.[184] This analysis of the economic and legal context can only be truncated in cases of particularly serious restrictions of competition.[185] The Court thus called into doubt what was hitherto perceived as a 'fundamental difference'[186] between the concepts of by-object and by-effect restrictions of competition. Similarly, under Article 102 TFEU the EU Courts have introduced a number of filters that a competition authority needs to consider to demonstrate the anticompetitive nature of what was previously considered a by-object restriction of competition. These filters become operative in the event that the defendants put forward evidence that calls into question the capability of the impugned conduct of foreclosing competition.[187]

Third, recent case law has considerably alleviated the evidentiary burden for defendants to rebut remaining presumptions of anticompetitiveness.[188] As a result, legal presumptions increasingly operate as a mere procedural burden-shifting tool, whose weight moves along a spectrum and is adjusted to the case-specific likelihood of anticompetitive effects.

The role of presumptions in modern antitrust law thus fundamentally differs from the deductive approach of republican antitrust which was formalised in Chapter 5 Section 2.3.3 as follows: $\alpha \frac{P(H|w_1)\,P(w_1) + \cdots + P(H|w_k)\,P(w_k)}{P(B|w_1)\,P(w_1) + \cdots + P(B|w_k)\,P(w_k)} \times \beta \frac{P(e|H)}{P(e|B)} = \frac{P(H|e)}{P(B|e)}$. The deductive approach of the republican antitrust tradition attributed significant weight to rule-based presumptions relative to the analysis of case-specific evidence. This has fundamentally changed with the rise of the consumer welfare standard, which went hand-in-hand with the ascent of a more inductive mode of antitrust analysis. Modern antitrust law not only reconceptualised legal presumptions $\frac{P(H|w_1)\,P(w_1) + \cdots + P(H|w_k)\,P(w_k)}{P(B|w_1)\,P(w_1) + \cdots + P(B|w_k)\,P(w_k)}$ as a simple Bayesian probability estimate $\frac{P(H)}{P(B)}$ but it also refashioned the mode of antitrust analysis $\alpha \frac{P(H)}{P(B)} \times \beta \frac{P(e|H)}{P(e|B)} = \frac{P(H|e)}{P(B|e)}$ in such a way that presumptions are attributed considerably less weight (α) than the analysis of case-specific evidence (β). Whereas the republican antitrust approach relied on a deductive mode of analysis, whereby $\alpha > \beta$, laissez-faire antitrust is grounded in an inductive and casuistic mode of analysis, whereby $\alpha < \beta$.

[184] Accordingly, a recent opinion has suggested that the finding of the by-object category involves a two-step test Opinion of Advocate General Bobek in Case C-228/18 *Budapest Bank and Others* (n 57) paras. 41–45.

[185] Case C-469/15 P *FSL and Others v Commission* ECLI:EU:C:2017:308 para. 107; Case C-373/14 P *Toshiba Corporation v Commission* ECLI:EU:C:2016:26 para. 29; Opinion of Advocate General Bobek in Case C-228/18 *Budapest Bank and Others* (n 57) para. 47.

[186] Opinion of Advocate General Kokott in Case C-226/11 *Expedia* ECLI:EU:C:2012:544 para. 54. Cf. Opinion of Advocate General Bobek in Case C-228/18 *Budapest Bank and Others* (n 57) para. 24.

[187] Case C-413/14 P *Intel v Commission* (n 23) para. 139; Case T-286/09 RENV *Intel Corporation v Commission* (n 134) para. 125.

[188] Case C-67/13 P *Groupement des cartes bancaires v Commission* (n 17) paras. 70–79; Case T-604/18 *Google and Alphabet v Commission (Google Android)* (n 27) paras. 789, 794–96.

With the rise of the consumer welfare standard, the weight α of presumptions of illegality in all three fields of US and EU competition law has dwindled and given way to a sliding-scale effects-based or rule of reason analysis.[189] Under this sliding-scale approach, modern antitrust analysis operates along a continuum that assigns the burden of proof and weighs the strength of presumptions in accordance with the specific facts of the case. Presumptions nowadays primarily function as procedural and burden-shifting devices. They allocate and fine-tune the weight of the evidentiary burden and the requisite level of scrutiny. Hence, the remaining presumptions of illegality no longer constitute rigid substantive inferences about the harm specific conduct may cause across various relevant possible worlds $\frac{P(H|w_1)\ P\ (w_1) + \cdots + P(H|w_k)\ P\ (w_k)}{P(B|w_1)\ P\ (w_1) + \cdots + P(B|w_k)\ P\ (w_k)}$. Instead, their weight depends on the likelihood of anticompetitive effects of a given type of conduct $\frac{P(H)}{P(B)}$ and the quality of case-specific evidence supporting such an inference $\frac{P(e|H)}{P(e|B)}$. Rather than creating rigid rules against certain types of agreements, unilateral conduct, or mergers, presumptions of illegality nowadays operate as multipliers that adjust the weight of the prima facie case with the likelihood of anticompetitive effects, and thus tip the scales either in favour of the plaintiff or the defendant. Depending on the specific facts of the case, these presumptions supporting the prima facie case can be more or less easily rebutted by the defendants. Ultimately, this shift towards a sliding-scale approach seeks to maintain the advantages in terms of administrability and procedural economy that legal presumptions offer without subjecting the negative liberty of firms to the straitjacket of legal rules. The sliding-scale approach maximises the negative liberty of firms by optimising the precision of presumptions of illegality as administrative filters.[190] It does so by calibrating their weight to the degree of likelihood with which certain conduct interferes with competitors in a way that reduces consumer welfare.[191]

This decline of presumptions of anticompetitiveness has moved modern competition law further afield from a republican approach that guarantees a modally robust protection of economic liberty by making certain types of conduct that enable private players to engage in potential domination unavailable, or at least prohibitively costly. By reinterpreting the presumptions in probabilistic terms as estimates of the likelihood of anticompetitive effects, US and EU enforcers and courts aligned them with the narrow notion of negative liberty that considers only welfare-reducing actual or likely interference as a source of unfreedom. The protection of economic

[189] Case C-228/18 *Budapest Bank and Others* (n 121) para. 54.

[190] *Leegin Creative Leather Prods. v PSKS, Inc.* (n 5) 898; *FTC v Actavis et al.* (n 156) 21; *California Dental Assn. v FTC* (n 79) Justice Breyer, dissenting, 794.

[191] SC Salop, 'An Enquiry Meet for the Case: Decision Theory, Presumptions, and Evidentiary Burdens in Formulating Antitrust Legal Standards' (2017) https://scholarship.law.georgetown.edu.

liberty afforded by remaining presumptions not only covers a narrower set of rights but its protection has also become less robust because it is deprived of its rule-like modal character and becomes more contingent upon changing circumstances. Instead of securing liberty by non-probabilistic, modally robust presumptions that carry weight across all relevant possible worlds, the sliding-scale approach operates through a blend of probabilistic presumptions and the analysis of case-specific evidence.

Owing to its probabilistic rationale, the sliding-scale approach is only concerned about the impact of impugned business conduct on the market participants' range of actions (z) within the actual or a highly probable alternative world. US and EU competition law can no longer be thought of as attaching a necessity operator O to legal commands, which is to be read as '*it is obligatory that*'. Consequently, the remaining presumptions under laissez-faire antitrust constitute no longer moral desiderata that establish modally robust prohibitions of certain types of conduct across all permissible worlds, so that *O¬{price fixing cartels, loyalty rebates, tying, mergers in concentrated markets}* where ¬ stands for '*not*'. Instead, the sliding-scale approach of blending presumptions and standards can be conceptualised as attaching the possibility operator *P* to presumptions in the same way as to legal standards, which is to be read as '*it is permissible that*'. Under the sliding-scale approach, the remaining presumptions simply indicate that it is possible that specific types of conduct may be unlawful in some, but not all, relevant permissible worlds *P¬{price fixing cartels, loyalty rebates, tying, mergers in concentrated markets}*. The only difference between both legal commands is that remaining presumptions have a greater probability of holding true across a greater number of alternative worlds than do legal standards.

Legal presumptions in modern antitrust law thus no longer ensure that the market participants benefit from modally robust right sets taking the form □¬*{price fixing cartels, loyalty rebates, tying, mergers in concentrated markets}*, where □ is to be read as '*it is necessary that*'. Instead, most of the right sets guaranteed by modern antitrust law take the form ◇¬*{price fixing cartels, loyalty rebates, tying, mergers in concentrated markets}*, where ◇ is to be read as '*it is possible that*'. While the modally robust right sets secured by rule-like presumptions under republican antitrust operated as 'trump cards' that protected market participants against potential arbitrary interference across all relevant possible worlds, modern antitrust law on both sides of the Atlantic at best guarantees probabilistic rights[192] that give market participants a certain chance to avail themselves of their market liberties in court.

As a result, the robustness of the economic liberty protected by modern competition law has been substantially tuned down. The remaining legal presumptions ceased to secure a modally robust content- and context-independent decisiveness of

[192] For such a probabilistic conception of rights, see K Dowding and M van Hees, 'The Construction of Rights' (2003) 97(2) *American Political Science Review* 281.

the preferences of market participants. Accordingly, presumptions of illegality no longer ensure for all (relevant) possible worlds (□) that if individual i prefers a over b (aP_ib), then society also prefers a over b (aPb); and, conversely, where individual i prefers b over a (aP_ib), then society will give b preference over a, so that $\Box((aP_ib \rightarrow aPb) \wedge (bP_ia \rightarrow bPa))$, where □ is to be read as '*it is necessary that*', →is to be read as '*if* ... *then*' and ∧ as '*and*'. Instead, at best the remaining presumptions guarantee a Berlinian form of negative liberty $(aP_ib' \rightarrow aPb) \wedge (bP_ia \rightarrow bPa)$ by securing the preference-decisiveness of market participants in the actual and nearby likely world. In some instances, it is even conceivable that the remaining presumptions only embody a Hobbesian form of negative liberty $(aP_ib \rightarrow aPb)$, which only maintains a content- and context-dependent form of economic liberty in the present world.

7.4.4 *New Presumptions of Legality*

A fourth development in the role of presumptions in modern antitrust law further accentuated the move towards a laissez-faire approach. Not only did US and EU enforcers, and courts, curtail existing presumptions of anticompetitiveness but they also crafted new presumptions of *pro*-competitiveness of certain business conduct. Under the auspices of the Chicago and post-Chicago paradigms, US and EU competition law have both adopted a presumption of legality towards most types of vertical agreements[193] and mergers[194] in the absence of market power on the part of the parties. The most prominent example of the growing reliance of laissez-faire antitrust on presumptions of legality is, however, the alignment of § 2 of the Sherman Act and Article 102 TFEU with the as-efficient competitor principle.

Over the course of the last few decades, US[195] and EU[196] enforcers and courts alike have firmly established the principle that § 2 of the Sherman Act and Article

[193] *Leegin Creative Leather Prods. v PSKS, Inc.* (n 5) 898, 900; Bork, *The Antitrust Paradox* (n 6) 264–66; Easterbrook, 'The Limits of Antitrust' (n 148) 9; *Ohio v American Express Co.* (n 5) 10 fn. 7; Case C-32/11 *Allianz Hungária Biztosító and Others* ECLI:EU:C:2013:160 para. 43; R Whish, 'Regulation 2790/99: The Commission's "new style" Block Exemption for Vertical Agreements' (2000) 37(4) *Common Market Law Review* 887, 908.

[194] Antitrust Division of the US Department of Justice, 1982 Merger Guidelines (n 9) 14–19; European Commission, Guidelines on the Assessment of Horizontal Mergers (n 14) paras. 18–21; European Commission, Guidelines on the Assessment of Non-horizontal Mergers (n 14) para. 11. See also Case T-399/16 *CK Telecoms UK Investments v Commission* (n 18) paras. 277–79.

[195] For price conduct *Brooke Group v Brown & Williamson Tobacco Corp.* (n 38) 223; *Weyerhaeuser Co. v Ross-Simmons Hardwood Lumber Co.* (n 103) 325. For non-price conduct, see for instance *Omega Environmental, Inc. v Gilbarco, Inc.* (n 94) 1162–63; *McWane, Inc. v FTC* 783 F.3d 814 (11th Cir. 2015) 835, 837–38.

[196] For price conduct Case C-62/86 *AKZO v Commission* ECLI:EU:C:1991:286 para. 71; Case C-209/10 *Post Danmark A/S v Konkurrencerådet* (n 25) paras. 25, 38. For non-price conduct, see Case T-65/98 *Van den Bergh Foods Ltd v Commission of the European Communities* (n 130) para. 160; Case C-680/20 *Unilever Italia Mkt. Operations* (n 27) paras. 39, 47, 52, 55–62. See

102 TFEU only prohibit dominant firms from engaging in pricing and non-pricing conduct that forecloses equally efficient competitors. At the same time, widespread consensus emerged that conduct that is not capable of foreclosing an equally efficient competitor (e.g., above-cost pricing by dominant firms) should as a matter of principle be shielded from antitrust liability.[197]

The presumption of legality for pricing and non-pricing conduct that is not capable of foreclosing equally efficient competitors has been operationalised through the widespread use of the so-called as-efficient competitor test. Initially developed by Chicago[198] and Harvard[199] scholars, the as-efficient competitor test has become the litmus test to decide when unilateral conduct of a dominant firm unduly interferes with the negative liberty of competitors. The Chicago and Harvard scholars coined the consensus view that impugned exclusionary conduct should only raise antitrust concerns and trigger state intervention when it forecloses a competitor that is as efficient as the dominant firm, and thereby deprives consumers of welfare-enhancing transactions. Depending on whether it is applied to pricing or non-price conduct, this as-efficient competitor test can usually take two forms. Pricing conduct is only assumed to foreclose an equally efficient competitor if the defendant sets its price below a reasonable measure of its variable or incremental costs. Only in this case is it safe to assume that the impugned conduct forecloses an equally efficient competitor that has the same cost structure and productive efficiency as the defendant.[200] If applied to non-price conduct, the as-efficient competitor test requires the factfinder to determine whether the impugned conduct forecloses a large enough fraction of demand (i.e., the so-called foreclosure rate) to hinder competitors from achieving minimum efficient or viable scale (MES/MVS test).[201] If the foreclosure rate is sufficiently large to deprive competitors of important sales, then it can be assumed that even an equally efficient competitor would not be able to withstand the dominant firm's conduct and that the conduct is likely to lead to market power effects.

also, European Commission, Guidance on the Commission's Enforcement Priorities in Applying Article 82 of the EC Treaty to Abusive Exclusionary Conduct by Dominant Undertakings (n 14) paras. 20, 23–27, 34, 36, 41–44.

[197] *Pacific Bell Telephone Co. dba AT&T California, et al. v linkLine Communications, Inc. et al.* (n 42) 11; Case C-209/10 *Post Danmark A/S v Konkurrencerådet* (n 25) paras. 25, 38.

[198] Posner, 'The Chicago School of Antitrust Analysis' (n 102).

[199] Areeda and Turner (n 102).

[200] Ibid. 711. For a similar approach, see Posner, *Antitrust Law* (n 149) 215; Posner, 'The Chicago School of Antitrust Analysis' (n 102) 940.

[201] TG Krattenmaker and SC Salop, 'Anticompetitive Exclusion: Raising Rivals' Costs to Achieve Power over Price' (1986) 96(3) *The Yale Law Journal* 209, 234–38; DA Crane and G Miralles, 'Toward a Unified Theory of Exclusionary Vertical Restraints' (2010) 84(3) *Southern California Law Review* 605, 607–09, 639–41. For an alternative replicability test as as-efficient competitor test for non-price conduct, see Case C-377/20 *Servizio Elettrico Nazionale and Others* (n 27) paras. 78–79.

The as-efficient competitor test – both in its price- and non-price rendition – constitutes a successful attempt to translate the logic of the Chicagoan welfare standard as the ultimate benchmark to decide when unilateral firm conduct unduly interferes with the economic liberty of other competitors into concrete competition law analysis. It also imposes an effective limiting principle on state intervention in so far as it confines antitrust intervention to the (as the Chicago School argued) very rare instances where the exclusion of competitors is not caused by their lack of efficiency but the abuse of market power by the alleged perpetrator firm. In contrast, the as-efficient competitor test removes market exclusion of less efficient competitors from the realm of antitrust intervention because the market exit of inefficient firms is considered to be the natural or even desired outcome of welfare-enhancing price competition.[202] The as-efficient competitor test thus also identifies a relevant criterion of merit to decide whose economic liberty and equality of opportunity is worth protection under antitrust law.

Not only has the widespread adoption of the as-efficient competitor test aligned antitrust law with the logic of negative economic liberty but it also entrenched a standard that constitutes a highly permissive and under-inclusive approach towards exclusionary conduct by dominant players.[203] The reasons for the under-inclusiveness of the as-efficient competitor test are manifold and well-documented. For example, the as-efficient competitor test is primarily static[204] in nature and disregards the strategic deterrence effect of aggressive pricing.[205] It also pays little attention to the need for fixed cost recovery in capital-intensive and innovation-driven markets[206] and ignores size,[207] bidding,[208] and other incumbency advantages.[209] The as-efficient competitor test further disregards the asymmetric incentives of a dominant firm to sacrifice profits relative to smaller competitors or potential entrants.[210] As the as-efficient competitor test (in both its rendition as incremental price-cost and MES/MVS tests) relies on a total foreclosure standard, it fails to

[202] Areeda and Turner (n 102) 711; Posner, *Antitrust Law* (n 149) 215.

[203] This has already been recognised by the 'masterminds' of the as-efficient competitor test, Areeda and Turner (n 102) 716.

[204] Ibid.

[205] See, for instance, P Bolton, JF Brodley, and MH Riordan, 'Predatory Pricing: Strategic Theory and Legal Policy' (2000) 88(8) *Georgetown Law Journal* 2239, 2247–50, 2299–321.

[206] H Hovenkamp, 'The Areeda-Turner Test for Exclusionary Pricing: A Critical Journal' (2015) 46 (3) *Review of Industrial Organization* 209, 214.

[207] For instance, the ability to grant rebates across a large customer base; see WK Tom, DA Balto, and NW Averitt, 'Anticompetitive Aspects of Market-Share Discounts and Other Incentives to Exclusive Dealing' (2000) 67(3) *Antitrust Law Journal* 615, 615, 623–24, 627–29.

[208] SC Salop, 'The Raising Rivals' Cost Foreclosure Paradigm, Conditional Pricing Practices and the Flawed Incremental Price-Cost Test' (2017) 81(2) *Antitrust Law Journal* 371, 379, 400.

[209] Edlin (n 59) 944, 956–60.

[210] Krattenmaker and Salop, 'Anticompetitive Exclusion' (n 201) 269–70, fn. 190; E Hovenkamp and SC Salop, 'Asymmetric Stakes in Antitrust Litigation' (2020). USC Legal Studies Research Papers Series No 20-12 (2020). 1.

address situations where exclusionary price or non-price conduct may raise rivals' costs and stifle competition, even if it only brings about a partial foreclosure of competitors.[211]

The most important shortcoming of the as-efficient competitor principle – and its operationalisation through price-cost and non-cost-based tests – is that in many instances they fail to protect consumer welfare. The assumption underpinning the as-efficient competitor principle that consumer welfare and allocative efficiency will not be harmed by conduct that does not foreclose equally efficient competitors does not always hold true. Indeed, it omits to account for the fact that even less efficient competitors can effectively constrain the ability of a dominant player to raise prices. In the presence of high entry barriers or incumbency benefits, even the foreclosure of a less efficient competitor may lead to higher prices if it allows the dominant incumbent to restore or entrench its monopoly position. Therefore, the foreclosure of a less efficient competitor may result in a loss in consumer welfare that exceeds the savings flowing from the lower production costs of the monopolist.[212] The as-efficient competitor test thus disregards that less efficient competitors may impose important constraints upon the dominant firm's power to raise prices.[213]

Despite its under-inclusiveness, the as-efficient competitor principle has become the predilect legal and economic yardstick to determine when unilateral conduct brings about undue exclusion. On the contrary, the under-inclusiveness of the as-efficient competitor principle is one of the sources of its success. Scholars and courts alike have embraced the as-efficient competitor principle – notably in its iteration as incremental price-cost test – precisely because it errs in the case of doubt in favour of the alleged perpetrator firm[214] and makes it very difficult,[215] if not impossible, for plaintiffs to prove anticompetitive pricing conduct. This under-inclusiveness is fully aligned with the premise of the laissez-faire approach that the costs of state interference with the economic liberty of dominant firms are generally high.[216] Not only does the as-efficient competitor test allow judges to easily tell apart situations where unilateral firm conduct is a legitimate exercise of entrepreneurial liberty from instances in which it unduly interferes with the negative liberty of other market participants,[217] but it also constitutes an effective tool to operationalise the laissez-faire error-cost framework that was coined by the Chicago School, which assumes

[211] Salop, 'The Raising Rivals' Cost Foreclosure Paradigm, Conditional Pricing Practices' (n 208) 410–11; Case T-286/09 *Intel v Commission* ECLI:EU:T:2014:547 paras. 149–50.

[212] Brodley and Hay (n 59) 745.

[213] Salop, 'The Raising Rivals' Cost Foreclosure Paradigm, Conditional Pricing Practices' (n 208) 414–15. This has been recognised by the Court of Justice in Case C-23/14 *Post Danmark II* ECLI:EU:C:2015:651 paras. 59–60.

[214] Areeda and Turner (n 102) 707–09.

[215] *Brooke Group v Brown & Williamson Tobacco Corp.* (n 38) 226.

[216] Bork, *The Antitrust Paradox* (n 6) 157; Posner, *Antitrust Law* (n 149) 214.

[217] Areeda and Turner (n 102) 704–11.

that antitrust intervention against aggressive unilateral conduct by dominant incumbents is rarely, if at all, warranted.[218] By giving effect to the assumption that antitrust law should intervene as little as possible against aggressive unilateral conduct, the as-efficient competitor principle and test effectively shield a large range of unilateral conduct, for instance any above-cost pricing of defendant firms, from antitrust scrutiny, and thereby largely insulate negative entrepreneurial liberty from state intervention.

Modern antitrust law thus increasingly relies on presumptions of legality that shield a broad category of coordinated, unilateral conduct, and mergers from the scope of competition law intervention. These newly crafted presumptions of pro-competitiveness align US and EU competition law even further with the Chicagoan error-cost framework that errs in the case of doubt on the side of type II errors, non-intervention, and hence negative entrepreneurial liberty. The combined effect of the weakening of presumptions of anticompetitiveness and the creation of presumptions of legality is that the rights granting market participants protection against arbitrary private interference have been transformed into probabilistic 'lottery tickets',[219] while the rights protecting the entrepreneurial liberties of antitrust defendants against public interference have obtained the status of 'trump cards'. As a result, the range of actions (z) across which economic liberty of market participants is protected against private interference has been considerably curtailed. Moreover, by making the protection of economic liberties dependent on market participants being as efficient as the dominant firm, the rise of the as-efficient competitor principle and its operationalisation through presumptions of legality have further narrowed the range of agents (x) whose economic liberty is protected by modern antitrust law in the way that it was first contemplated by the Chicago School.[220] The endorsement of the as-efficient competitor principle and the under-inclusive as-efficient competitor test by US and EU Courts and enforcers thus also marks a fundamental rupture with the inclusive notion of the competitive process and the goal of protecting broad-based economic opportunities of the republican antitrust tradition.

7.5 A PROBABILISTIC STANDARD OF HARM

Another policy lever that has been essential to the move of modern US and EU competition law away from a republican towards a laissez-faire approach is the reconfiguration of the standard of harm. During the republican era, competition

[218] For price-conduct, see Bork, *The Antitrust Paradox* (n 6) 44, 149, 153–54. For non-price conduct Bowman (n 92) 21; Bork, *The Antitrust Paradox* (n 6) 156–58, 309, 375–80.

[219] For the notion of probabilistic rights as 'lottery tickets', see MA Lemley and C Shapiro, 'Probabilistic Patents' (2005) 19(2) *Journal of Economic Perspectives* 75, 80.

[220] For further discussion, see Chapter 6, Section 5.2.

law in the United States and in the European Union[221] primarily relied on a possibilist capability standard of harm that required plaintiffs to merely show that the impugned conduct had the potential or was capable of causing anticompetitive harm in a range of relevant possible worlds for it to be found in breach of competition rules. This 'capability standard'[222] became a central target of the critique of the proponents of the More Economic Approach. They contended that it was at odds with a serious assessment of the concrete welfare effects of business conduct, and therefore entailed too many false positives. On this account, the proponents of a More Economic Approach towards competition law called for a probabilistic standard of harm that requires competition authorities and courts to show that impugned conduct would result in actual or, at least, likely anticompetitive effects.[223]

7.5.1 *The Rise of the Probabilistic Standard of Harm*

The rise of the probabilistic standard of harm was foreshadowed by a reconceptualisation of the analysis of decision-making under uncertainty by Chicago economists. The Chicago School economists Leonard J. Savage and Milton Friedman[224] challenged the seminal distinction between 'risk' and 'uncertainty' that had been coined by Frank Knight[225] and John Maynard Keynes.[226] Knight and Keynes viewed risk as 'measurable uncertainty' that can be captured by assigning probabilities to specific events or outcomes. Risk fundamentally differs from (non-measurable) uncertainty to which no probabilistic value can be attributed. This dichotomy was overthrown by Savage and Friedman, who entrenched the nowadays prevailing view that individual decision-makers are able to attribute subjective or expected utilities to any type of uncertainty about future events.

This probabilistic turn in the analysis of decision-making under uncertainty shaped probabilistic approaches towards evidence[227] and the interpretation of the civil preponderance of evidence standard of proof under rule 401 of the US Federal

[221] Case C-8/08 *T-Mobile Netherlands BV and Others* ECLI:EU:C:2009:343 para. 31; Case C-32/11 *Allianz Hungária Biztosító and Others* (n 193) para. 38; Case 85/76 *Hoffmann-La Roche v Commission* (n 127) paras. 90, 127; Case T-201/04 *Microsoft Corp v Commission* (n 129) paras. 857, 868.

[222] Colomo and Lamadrid de Pablo (n 180) 361–63.

[223] Temple Lang and O'Donoghue (n 62) 110; J Kallaugher and B Sher, 'Rebates Revisited: Anticompetitive Effects and Exclusionary Abuse under Article 82' (2004) 25(5) *European Competition Law Review* 263, 263; Bork, *The Antitrust Paradox* (n 6) 122, 144, 156–57; Posner, *Antitrust Law* (n 149) 195, 214, 252–53.

[224] M Friedman and LJ Savage, 'The Expected-Utility Hypothesis and the Measurability of Utility' (1952) 60(6) *Journal of Political Economy* 463, 467.

[225] F Knight, *Risk, Uncertainty and Profit* (Boston: Houghton Mifflin 1921) 19–20.

[226] JM Keynes, *A Treatise on Probability* (London: Macmillan 1921) Chapter 3.

[227] MO Finkelstein and WB Fairley, 'A Bayesian Approach to Identification Evidence' (1970) 83 (3) *Harvard Law Review* 489; LH Tribe, 'Trial by Mathematics: Precision and Ritual in the Legal Process' (1970) 84(6) *Harvard Law Review* 1329, 1347.

Rules on Evidence, which entered into force in 1975.[228] Chicago law and economics scholars also embraced the probabilistic 'more likely than not' or 'preponderance of evidence' standard as being consistent with Bayesian decision theory and a More Economic Approach.[229] The subjective conception of probabilities also influenced the understanding of the appropriate evidentiary standard for finding anticompetitive conduct in antitrust law.[230] Today, the conventional antitrust literature tends to assume that any type of uncertainty about future events can be expressed and assessed by factfinders as subjective probability estimates or discounted expected utilities.[231] Accordingly, antitrust enforcement is warranted if, in the eyes of the fact finder, a given conduct or merger is at least on balance more likely than not to give rise to antitrust harm.[232]

7.5.2 *The Probabilistic Standard of Harm in US Antitrust Law*

This probabilistic turn towards the standard of harm materialised itself in the antitrust case law and enforcement on both sides of the Atlantic. From the late-1970s onwards, the US Supreme Court adopted a 'demanding standard'[233] for finding per se violations. Under this standard of harm, the finding of a per se violation is only warranted[234] if it is possible to 'predict with confidence' that the agreement at hand would be found in 'all or almost all instances' to breach § 1 of the Sherman Act under a rule of reason analysis[235] and is 'very likely without "redeeming virtue"'.[236] This probabilistic interpretation of the per se rule assumes

[228] 28 U.S. Code, Federal Rules of Evidence (Effective 1 July 1975, as amended to 1 December 2020).

[229] RA Posner, 'An Economic Approach to Legal Procedure and Judicial Administration' (1973) 2(2) *The Journal of Legal Studies* 399, 407–08; RA Posner, *Economic Analysis of Law* [1972] (Boston: Little, Brown & Comp 1977) 432–33.

[230] For such a probabilistic formulation of the standard of proof under US and EU competition law, see CF Beckner and SC Salop, 'Decision Theory and Antitrust Rules' (1999) 67(1) *Antitrust Law Journal* 41, 61; Salop, 'An Enquiry Meet for the Case' (n 191) 6; Salop, 'The Evolution and Vitality of Merger Presumptions' (n 160) 283; D Bailey, 'Presumptions in EU Competition Law' (2010) 31(9) *European Competition Law Review* 362, 363; C Ritter, 'Presumptions in EU Competition Law' (2018) 6(2) *Journal of Antitrust Enforcement* 189, 211.

[231] ML Katz and HA Shelanski, 'Merger Analysis and the Treatment of Uncertainty: Should We Expect Better?' (2007) 74(3) *Antitrust Law Journal* 537.

[232] Ibid. 548.

[233] *Cont'l T.V. v GTE Sylvania* (n 2) 50, 57; *Leegin Creative Leather Prods. v PSKS, Inc.* (n 5) 895.

[234] *National Soc. of Professional Engineers v United States* (n 36) 692; *Broadcast Music, Inc. v Columbia Broadcasting System, Inc.* (n 3) 8, 9; *Ariz. v Maricopa County Medical Soc.* (n 11) 344.

[235] *Ariz. v Maricopa County Medical Soc.* (n 11) 344, 351; *White Motor Co. v United States* (n 71) Justice Brennan dissenting, 265–66; *Leegin Creative Leather Prods. v PSKS, Inc.* (n 5) 386–87.

[236] *Broadcast Music, Inc. v Columbia Broadcasting System, Inc.* (n 3) 9; *National Soc. of Professional Engineers v United States* (n 36) 692; *Ariz. v Maricopa County Medical Soc.* (n 11) 351.

that the underpinning presumption of illegality encodes a generalisation about the 'probability of anticompetitive consequences' and their 'severity'.[237]

With respect to § 2 of the Sherman Act, the US Supreme Court also increasingly advanced the view that antitrust law only interferes with dominant firms' unilateral conduct if it entails actual or likely foreclosure and welfare effects.[238] Under this probabilistic standard of harm, unilateral conduct is only 'unlawful if it threatens actual monopolization'.[239] This suggests that the § 2 Sherman Act case law has moved towards a probabilistic, if not actualist, standard of harm. The mere possibility of potential harm, which informed the republican hostility against monopoly and specific single-firm conduct, has clearly become insufficient to warrant antitrust intervention.

US merger control also fully converged in a probabilistic understanding of the standard of harm. US enforcers and courts moved a considerable distance from the sweeping application of the incipiency doctrine during the Warren Court era, under which it was sufficient to show some form of potential harm for a merger to be considered in breach of § 7 of the Clayton Act. The Department of Justice and FTC have increasingly adopted a standard of harm that requires them to ascertain the likelihood of anticompetitive effects to decide whether or not to block a merger.[240] Critical observers even claim that this endorsement of a probabilistic standard of harm goes as far as requiring the government to prove anticompetitive effects 'to a near certainty' before they can block a merger under § 7 of the Clayton Act.[241]

7.5.3 *The Probabilistic Standard of Harm in EU Competition Law*

EU competition law is also about to move, albeit to a lesser extent than its US counterpart, away from the possibilist capability standard towards a probabilistic standard of harm. In respect to Article 101 TFEU, the European Commission committed itself as part of the modernisation process to a balance of probabilities standard of harm that would require it to show that the agreement at issue was likely

[237] *Cont'l T.V. v GTE Sylvania* (n 2) 50, fn. 16. See also the Court referring to 'high probability' and 'great likelihood': in *National Collegiate Athletic Ass'n v Board of Regents* (n 3) 100, 103.

[238] See, for instance, *Jefferson Parish Hosp. Dist. No 2 v Hyde* (n 95) 16. For the requirement of likely consumer harm in the form of recoupment *Brooke Group v Brown & Williamson Tobacco Corp.* (n 38) 223, 225–26.

[239] See, for instance, *Copperweld Corp. et al. v Independence Tube Corp.* 467 U.S. 752 (1984) 767; *Cargill, Inc. v Monfort of Colorado, Inc.* 479 U.S. 104 (1986) 122 fn. 17; *Verizon Communications Inc. v Law Offices of Curtis Trinko* (n 38) 414.

[240] Antitrust Division of the US Department of Justice, 1982 Merger Guidelines (n 9) 12–13; Antitrust Division of the US Department of Justice/Federal Trade Commission, 2010 Merger Guidelines (n 46) 2.

[241] For this criticism, see S. 1812 – Consolidation Prevention and Competition Promotion Act, 115th Congress (2017–19), 4.

(i.e., more likely than not) to result in anticompetitive effects.[242] The Court partially endorsed this probabilistic standard of harm, holding that by-object restrictions must be likely to cause anticompetitive effects.[243] Although the Court refrained from requiring the Commission to demonstrate that a by-object restriction resulted in actual anticompetitive effects,[244] the reference to likely effects stands in stark contrast with previous case law, which suggested that it is sufficient for the Commission to establish that an agreement is liable to give rise to potential anticompetitive effects for the agreement to qualify as a by-object restriction.[245] The standard of harm for by-effect restrictions is also currently heavily contested. Pursuant to early case law, the Commission was only required to demonstrate potential anticompetitive effects to support the finding of a by-effect restriction.[246] Yet, in *Servier* the General Court recently observed that for agreements that had already been implemented to qualify as by-effect restrictions, the Commission was obligated to show actual,[247] or at least likely,[248] anticompetitive effects.[249]

Under Article 102 TFEU, the question about the requisite standard of harm is also anything but settled. As part of the modernisation of EU competition law, the Commission adopted a probabilistic standard of harm whereby it would need to show that impugned conduct results in actual or likely anticompetitive effects.[250] However, in some cases the Commission and the Court seemed to have recently reaffirmed the capability standard.[251] In contrast, in other instances the EU judiciary embraced a balance of probabilities standard for some forms of unilateral conduct, such as specific pricing conduct[252] and loyalty-enhancing rebates.[253] More recently,

[242] European Commission, Guidelines on the Application of Article 81(3) of the Treaty (n 14) paras. 17–18, 22–24; European Commission, Guidelines on the applicability of Article 101 of the Treaty on the Functioning of the European Union to horizontal co-operation agreements, [2011] OJ C 11/01 para. 26.

[243] Case C-67/13 P *Groupement des cartes bancaires v Commission* (n 17) para. 51.

[244] Case C-228/18 *Budapest Bank and Others* (n 121) paras. 81–83.

[245] Case C-8/08 *T-Mobile Netherlands BV and Others* (n 221) paras. 29–32.

[246] Case C-238/05 *Asnef-Equifax* ECLI:EU:C:2006:734 para. 34; Case C-7/95 P *Deere v Commission* ECLI:EU:C:1998:256 paras. 59–61; Joined Cases 142 and 156/84 *BAT and Reynolds v Commission* ECLI:EU:C:1987:490 paras. 37, 39, 54, 57–58.

[247] Case T-691/14 *Servier and Others v Commission* ECLI:EU:T:2018:922 paras. 1120–28.

[248] Ibid. para. 1178.

[249] See, however, Opinion of Advocate General Kokott in Case C-176/19 P *Commission v Servier and Others* ECLI:EU:C:2022:576 paras. 288–13.

[250] European Commission, Guidance on the Commission's Enforcement Priorities in Applying Article 82 of the EC Treaty to Abusive Exclusionary Conduct by Dominant Undertakings (n 14) paras. 19–20.

[251] Case C-413/14 P *Intel v Commission* (n 23) paras. 138, 140; Case T-612/17 *Google and Alphabet v Commission (Google Shopping)* (n 125) paras. 436–38, 442–43, 459.

[252] Case C-209/10 *Post Danmark A/S v Konkurrencerådet* (n 25) para. 44; Case C-52/09 *TeliaSonera Sverige* (n 27) para. 67.

[253] Opinion of Advocate General Kokott in Case C-23/14 *Post Danmark II* ECLI:EU:C:2015:343 para. 82; Case C-23/14 *Post Danmark II* (n 213) para. 72. See also for a reference to 'likely' effects

one can also discern a tendency by the Commission and the Courts to ascertain the potential and actual effects of unilateral conduct.[254] The Article 102 case law thus seems to currently oscillate between a possibilist, probabilistic, and actualist conception of the standard of harm.

The area of EU competition law where the probabilistic standard of harm is most firmly established is EU merger control. With the adoption of the Horizontal[255] and Non-horizontal[256] Merger Guidelines in the aftermath of the introduction of the new SIEC test in the 2004 EUMR, the Commission made it clear that it would establish the anticompetitive nature of mergers based on a balance of probabilities standard by showing that the merger is more likely than not to result in anticompetitive effects. It thereby aligned its decisional practice with the prevailing standard of harm in phase 2 merger proceedings in other jurisdictions, such as the United Kingdom[257] and the United States.[258] The balance of probabilities standard was subsequently also endorsed by the EU Courts as the requisite standard under the EUMR.[259] In the recent *CK Telecoms* ruling, the General Court even went one step further in holding that merger control is, at least in certain cases, governed by a standard of proof stricter than the balance of probabilities standard.[260] While stopping short of requiring the Commission to show that a merger will lead to anticompetitive effects beyond any reasonable doubt, the General Court held that the Commission is obligated to demonstrate that the merger will with a 'strong probability' result in a SIEC.[261] This envisaged tightening of the standard of proof in EU merger control in *CK*

that need to be established beyond the 'existence of doubt', Case C-680/20 *Unilever Italia Mkt. Operations* (n 27) paras. 42–43.

[254] Case No COMP/AT.40099 *Google Android*, C(2018) 4761 final paras. 835–51, 854; Case T-604/18 *Google and Alphabet v Commission (Google Android)* (n 27) paras. 286–99; Case No COMP/AT.39740 *Google Search (Shopping)* (n 53) paras. 383 388, 402, 405, 446; Case T-612/17 *Google and Alphabet v Commission (Google Shopping)* (n 125) para. 445; Case C-377/20 *Servizio Elettrico Nazionale and Others* (n 27) paras. 50–58.

[255] European Commission, Guidelines on the Assessment of Horizontal Mergers (n 14) paras. 2–4, 8.

[256] EU Commission, Guidelines on the Assessment of Non-horizontal Mergers (n 14) para. 10.

[257] UK Office of Fair Trading and Competition Commission, Merger Assessment Guidelines 2010 2010, CC2/OFT1254 para. 2.2.

[258] Beckner and Salop, 'Decision Theory and Antitrust Rules' (n 230) 61–62.

[259] Case C-413/06 P *Bertelsmann and Sony Corporation of America v Impala* (n 143) para. 47; Case C-12/03 P *Commission v Tetra Laval* ECLI:EU:C:2005:87 para. 43; Case C-265/17 P *Commission v United Parcel Service* ECLI:EU:C:2019:23 para. 32; Opinion of Advocate General Kokott in Case C-413/06 P *Bertelsmann und Sony Corporation of America/Impala* ECLI:EU:C:2007:790 paras. 208–11.

[260] Case T-399/16 *CK Telecoms UK Investments v Commission* (n 18) para. 118.

[261] Case T-399/16 *CK Telecoms UK Investments v Commission* (n 18) para. 118. This stricter 'strong probability' standard was, however, recently annulled on appeal by the Court of Justice which seemed to reaffirm that all mergers reviewed by the Commission are subject to a balance of probabilities standard. Case C-376/20 P *Commission v CK Telecoms UK Investments* (n 18) paras. 69–88, notably 84 and 86.

Telecoms is not an outlier but responds to mounting calls for the adoption of a 'very probable' standard amongst members of the EU judiciary and commentators.[262]

7.5.4 *Implications of the Probabilistic Standard of Harm*

Over the last few decades, the possibilist standard of harm of the republican antitrust tradition has on both sides of the Atlantic increasingly given way to a probabilistic standard of harm. Because it requires the showing of actual or likely interference and anticompetitive effects for antitrust intervention to be warranted, this probabilistic standard of harm tallies with the probabilistic logic of negative liberty that only considers conduct which is actually or likely interfering with the sphere of autonomy of another individual to be a source of unfreedom.

The probabilistic standard of harm of modern antitrust law fundamentally differs from the possibilist balance of harm standard of republican antitrust which compelled antitrust intervention as long as the odds ratio of posterior probabilities of conduct being harmful exceeded the cost-benefit-ratio of antitrust intervention: $\frac{P(H|e)}{P(B|e)} > \frac{L}{G}$. This possibilist standard enabled antitrust intervention against conduct or situations that would give rise to a large magnitude of potential harm, and hence high accuracy benefits (G) of antitrust intervention, even though that harm was unlikely to eventuate in the actual or nearby likely world. As long as the potential gains of antitrust intervention outweigh its costs $G > L$ (e.g., because it remedies or prevents harm of a significant order of magnitude), then the possibilist standard of harm justified antitrust intervention to prevent merely potential harm in one relevant possible world, although it was less likely to materialise than not. In contrast, the probabilistic standard of harm of laissez-faire antitrust only condones antitrust intervention if the posterior probability of H given evidence e slightly exceeds 50 per cent that is $P(H|e) > 0.5$. Antitrust intervention is only warranted where the posterior probability of conduct being harmful $P(H|e)$ is greater than the posterior probability of the conduct given evidence e being beneficial $P(B|e)$. In other words, the posterior odds ratio of the conduct being harmful given evidence e must be greater than 1; that is, $\frac{P(H|e)}{P(B|e)} > \frac{0.5}{0.5}$ or 1.[263]

[262] For instance, Advocate General Tizzano suggested that even though the Commission cannot be required to show with 'absolute certainty' (i.e., beyond reasonable doubt) that the merger gives rise to anticompetitive effects, the Commission must demonstrate that such anticompetitive effects are 'very probable'; see Opinion of Advocate General Tizzano in Case C-12/03 P *Commission v Tetra Laval* (n 65) para. 74.

[263] Salop, 'An Enquiry Meet for the Case' (n 191) 14 fn. 40.

The link between this probabilistic standard of harm and a negative conception of economic liberty is two-fold. The balance of probabilities standard encodes the implicit default assumption of the Chicago School error-cost framework that firm conduct is on balance marginally pro-competitive or competitively neutral with ties going to the defendant.[264] This more exacting probabilistic conception of the standard of harm builds an implicit safe-harbour threshold or marginal presumption of pro-competitiveness into the evidentiary requirements. In the case of doubt, this safe-harbour threshold tilts the balance in favour of the defendant, and hence negative entrepreneurial liberty.[265] As antitrust plaintiffs have to show that the alleged anticompetitive effects of business conduct are more likely than not (i.e., will materialise with a probability of more than 50 per cent), the shift towards a probabilistic approach has introduced the default assumption that the impugned conduct of the antitrust defendant is 'marginally pro-competitive'.[266] Under the balance of probabilities standard, this margin of doubt operates as a tie-breaker that, in the rare cases of inconclusive evidence (*non liquet*), tips the scales in favour of the defendant and hence of entrepreneurial liberty.[267] The probabilistic standard of harm thus operationalises the commitment of laissez-faire antitrust to shelter the negative entrepreneurial liberty of businesses to the largest extent possible from state interference.

At the same time, this probabilistic standard of harm is fully in line with the probabilistic logic of negative liberty. The possibilist standard of harm of republican antitrust enabled antitrust intervention against conduct that may entail high-impact but low-probability harm across a range of relevant possible worlds $(P(H|w_1)\,P(w_1) + \cdots + P(H|w_k)\,P(w_k))$. It thus allowed intervention in instances where it was possible for powerful players to frustrate the preferences of individual market agents by arbitrarily interfering with their choices (i.e., $\Diamond(aP_ib \wedge \neg aPb) \vee (bP_ia \wedge \neg bPa)$), without that possibility reaching a probability of 50 per cent so that it is more likely than the alternative outcome. In contrast, the probabilistic standard of harm only allows for antitrust intervention when conduct is proven to result in interference in the actual $(aP_ib \wedge \neg aPb)$ or nearby likely world $(bP_ia \wedge \neg bPa)$ with a likelihood in excess of 50 per cent. Therefore, the probabilistic standard of harm moves modern antitrust law further away from the modally robust conception of republican liberty which ensures that $\Box((aP_ib \rightarrow aPb) \wedge (bP_ia \rightarrow bPa))$ holds true across all relevant possible worlds. Instead, the probabilistic standard of harm – in the same way as the reconceptualisation of presumptions of unlawfulness – further aligns modern antitrust law with a Berlinian $(aP_ib \rightarrow aPb) \wedge (bP_ia \rightarrow bPa)$ or Hobbesian $(aP_ib \rightarrow aPb)$ conception of economic liberty by securing the preference-decisiveness of market participants in the

[264] Ibid. 6, 14 fn. 40.

[265] Ibid. 7.

[266] Ibid. 7.

[267] Opinion of Advocate General Kokott in Case C-413/06 P *Bertelsmann und Sony Corporation of America/ Impala* (n 259) para. 223.

actual and nearby likely world (Berlinian) minimising $P(H \mid w_1)\, P(w_1) + P(H \mid w_2)\, P(w_2)$ or only in the actual world (Hobbesian) minimising $P(H \mid w_1)\, P(w_1)$.

7.6 CONCLUSION

This chapter has further traced the decline of the republican antitrust tradition, which was grounded in the ideal of republican liberty, and has described how it was dislocated by laissez-faire antitrust law that rests on a negative understanding of liberty. It has analysed how the rise of Chicago School inspired antitrust thinking has refashioned US antitrust law since the 1970s and EU competition law since the 2000s. This chapter shows that with the rise of the Chicago-inspired More Economic Approach, the republican tradition in US antitrust law and EU competition law gave way to a narrow understanding of negative liberty that only regards welfare-decreasing interference as a source of unfreedom. This reconfiguration of modern US and EU competition law took effect via four channels: (i) the transformation of the notion of competition from a polycentric market structure operating as an institution of antipower to a welfarist understanding of competition grounded in the consumer welfare standard; (ii) the endorsement of a laissez-faire error-cost framework; (iii) the probabilistic reinterpretation, shrinking of the scope and dilution of the weight of presumptions of anticompetitiveness; and (iv) the alignment of the standard of harm with the probabilistic logic of negative liberty. While the way in which this transformation materialised in the United States and European Union certainly differs in degree, one can discern an overall trend towards a laissez-faire approach along these four variables in both competition law systems. The recalibration of US and EU competition law along these four policy levers brought into being a laissez-faire antitrust approach that, under the guise of welfarism, seeks to protect above all the entrepreneurial liberty of powerful businesses.

The more economic turn in modern antitrust law and the ensuing rise of laissez-faire antitrust, this and the previous chapter have shown, are in the first place an attempt to overcome the 'republican paradox'[268] by radically re-scoping the economic liberty guaranteed by competition law. Until the 1970s in the case of the United States and the 2000s in the case of the European Union, competition law (i) protected a thick and robust notion of republican economic liberty that was guaranteed to a broad range of agents (x); (ii) tackled a wide range of preventing conditions (y), which included not only actual or likely interference but also focused on domination (i.e., the ability of firms to engage in dominating interference); and (iii) secured economic agents a modal set of actions (z) across all (relevant) possible worlds.

[268] As a reminder, this is the impossibility of securing a social aggregation function that is capable of ensuring the content- and context-independent decisiveness of the preference of at least two individuals and satisfies the weak Pareto principle, see C List, 'The Impossibility of a Paretian Republican?: Some Comments on Pettit and Sen' (2004) 20(1) *Economics and Philosophy* 65, 75.

TABLE 7.3 *The recalibration of economic liberty and its operationalisation under laissez-faire antitrust*

<table>
<tr><th></th><th>Variables operationalising a republican conception of economic liberty</th><th>Variables operationalising a negative conception of economic liberty</th></tr>
<tr><td>Type of agents (x)</td><td>• Broad
• Structuralism
• Rule-like presumptions as trump cards for weaker market participants</td><td>• Narrow
• Consumer welfare standard and its operationalisation by the as-efficient competitor principle and test</td></tr>
<tr><td>Type of preventing conditions (y)</td><td>• Broad (not only interference but domination)
• Structuralism
• Modal character of rule-like presumptions
• Possibilist standard of harm $\frac{P(H|e)}{P(B|e)} > \frac{L}{G}$
• Precautionary error-cost framework ($(1-\beta)\,G > \alpha L$)</td><td>• Narrow (only welfare-decreasing interference)
• Consumer welfare standard
• Narrow probabilistic presumptions and legal standards
• Probabilistic standard of harm $\frac{P(H|e)}{P(B|e)} > \frac{0.5}{0.5}$
• Laissez-faire error-cost framework ($(1-\beta)\,G < \alpha L$)</td></tr>
<tr><td>Range of restricted actions (z)</td><td>• Broad (all relevant possible worlds)
• Rule-like presumptions guaranteeing modally robust right sets $O((aP_ib \rightarrow aPb) \wedge (bP_ia \rightarrow bPa))$ so that $\Box((aP_ib \rightarrow aPb) \wedge (bP_ia \rightarrow bPa))$
• Possibilist standard of harm $\frac{P(H|e)}{P(B|e)} > \frac{L}{G}$
• Precautionary error-cost framework ($(1-\beta)\,G > \alpha L$)</td><td>• Narrow (actual and nearby likely world)
• Narrow probabilistic presumptions and legal standards guaranteeing probabilistic right sets $P((aP_ib \rightarrow aPb) \wedge (bP_ia \rightarrow bPa))$ so that $\Diamond((aP_ib \rightarrow aPb) \wedge (bP_ia \rightarrow bPa))$
• Probabilistic standard of harm $\frac{P(H|e)}{P(B|e)} > \frac{0.5}{0.5}$
• Laissez-faire error-cost framework ($(1-\beta)\,G < \alpha L$)</td></tr>
</table>

The rise of the laissez-faire approach has thinned out the form of economic liberty that is guaranteed by competition law along these three variables (see Table 7.3). First, in endorsing the consumer welfare standard, laissez-faire antitrust excluded less efficient competitors from the range of agents (x) whose economic liberty is deemed worthy of protection. It consequently considerably reduced the degree to which modern competition law protects broad-based economic opportunities and the inclusiveness of markets. Second, the rise of the consumer welfare standard and recalibration of legal presumptions excluded domination resulting from the mere capacity of powerful single or collective players to arbitrarily interfere with other market participants from what counts as preventing conditions of economic liberty (y).

Under the laissez-faire approach, competition law no longer shields market participants against domination but only against actual or likely welfare-reducing interference. The rise of the consumer welfare standard and the shrinking of the breadth of presumptions of anticompetitiveness considerably reduced the right sets of economic agents and notably competitors afforded by competition law by narrowing the range of conduct that is presumed to qualify as a preventing condition (y) of liberty, and therefore made unavailable or, at least, prohibitively costly. Third, the probabilistic reinterpretation of presumptions and the standard of harm also reduced the degree to which market participants' remaining, albeit curtailed, right sets remain stable across different relevant possible worlds.[269] Laissez-faire antitrust law no longer secures market participants' range of actions (z) content- and context-independently across all (relevant) possible worlds $\square((aP_ib \rightarrow aPb) \wedge (bP_ia \rightarrow bPa))$,[270] in the way that the broad rule-like presumptions and the possibilist standard of harm of the republican approach did. Instead, the laissez-faire approach remodelled presumptions of anticompetitiveness and the standard of harm in such a way that competition law only guarantees the non-frustration of preferred options in the actual $(aP_ib \rightarrow aPb)$ or nearby likely worlds $(aP_ib \rightarrow aPb) \wedge (bP_ia \rightarrow bPa)$. In brief, the response of modern antitrust law to the republican paradox was to reduce the inclusiveness (agents (x)), scope (preventing conditions (y)), and robustness (restricted actions (z)) of economic liberty and to accord it with the purely negative understanding of liberty.[271] This alignment of modern competition law with a thinned-out understanding of negative economic liberty has been further compounded by the rise of a laissez-faire error-cost framework that in the first place seeks to insulate the entrepreneurial liberty of large businesses from antitrust scrutiny and state interference.

The recalibration of these policy variables demonstrates how the decline of the concern about republican liberty, and with it the idea of a link between competition and democracy, is ultimately the result of the fear that too broad an application of antitrust law will unduly undermine the negative entrepreneurial liberty, contractual freedom, and property rights of businesses. Laissez-faire antitrust pursued the primary goal of unleashing corporate behemoths with a view to harnessing entrepreneurial liberty as a catalyst for economic growth and welfare. However, this shift from republican to laissez-faire antitrust came at a certain cost. The decline of presumptions of illegality and the displacement of rule-like presumptions by legal standards provides firms with greater leeway to exercise private government and to arbitrarily interfere with other market participants. The shift from a republican to laissez-faire antitrust has curtailed not only the prohibitive but also the protective

[269] C List, 'Republican Freedom and the Rule of Law' (2006) 5(2) *Politics, Philosophy & Economics* 201, 216–17.

[270] Pettit, *On the People's Terms* (n 145) 67–69.

[271] List, 'Republican Freedom and the Rule of Law' (n 269) 217.

scope of antitrust law. The form-based operationalisation of the concern about republican liberty as non-domination through rule-like presumptions provided a 'probabilistically unweighted'[272] protection of market participants against potential harm that may result from certain forms of business conduct by making this conduct more costly or unavailable. With the rise of laissez-faire antitrust, this thick and modally robust form of economic liberty of market participants has been hollowed out, and has become more contingent and less resilient. Laissez-faire antitrust law no longer makes specific business conduct unavailable because of its tendency to serve as a resource of domination. Rather, as a consequence of the shift towards a rule of reason-like effects-based analysis, antitrust law only ensures a probabilistic protection of the economic liberty of market participants. Consequently, economic liberty has become dependent on the contingencies and accuracy of an increasingly complex analysis in predicting the probabilities of anticompetitive effects of a particular business conduct. On top of that, the laissez-faire error-cost framework has skewed the balance of rights of modern antitrust law in favour of big business and to the detriment of powerless market participants.

The presumptive gains in welfare that were brought about by a shift towards a More Economic Approach in line with the concept of negative liberty came at the cost of the thinning out of the concept of economic liberty as non-domination and equal and independent status of all market participants. Arguably, it has led to an increase in the level of domination because market participants have become increasingly dependent on and exposed to the individual or collective exercise of private government by corporate behemoths. The ascent of the laissez-faire approach has led to the strengthening of the negative entrepreneurial liberty of powerful businesses, while concerns about the liberty as non-domination and equality of opportunity of smaller competitors have become largely irrelevant. The days in which US and EU antitrust law were geared towards the prevention of domination resulting from instances of concentrated economic power in the hands of a few with a view to ensuring competition as domination-free economic order and counterpart of a republican polity appear to be gone for good, in the same way as the fear about private government by corporate behemoths.

The abandoning of republican liberty as the central normative commitment of competition law has not only made the protection of economic liberty more precarious and less robust but it has also severed the relationship between economic liberty and a republican society and democracy. It is indeed this very shift from republican to laissez-faire antitrust that explains why the idea of a competition–democracy nexus has become largely irrelevant in US and EU competition law. As the conception of negative liberty that is guaranteed by modernised US and EU competition law can thrive under any type of government that follows a minimum

[272] P Pettit, 'Freedom in the Market' (2006) 5(2) *Politics, Philosophy & Economics* 131, 137–38.

degree of rule of law and constitutional principles, the idea of the interdependence between the economic, social and political order that lay at the heart of the US and European antitrust republicanism has become obsolete. Having given up its commitment to the preservation of a republican form of economic liberty as non-domination to the benefit of a thinned-out version of negative liberty, modern competition law no longer ensures the economic preconditions of a republican society and democracy of free and equals.

PART IV

The Revival of the Competition–Democracy Nexus

8

Main Findings and Avenues towards a Competition–Democracy Nexus 4.0

8.1 INTRODUCTION

This study started with a short, albeit complex puzzle: How can we explain the idea that competition and competition law promote democracy? And more specifically, what is the relationship between competition and democracy that informs the concept of a competition–democracy nexus in US antitrust law and EU competition law?

This chapter recapitulates how this book answers these questions by unpacking the idea of a competition–democracy nexus as a fundamental normative prior of competition law. Against the backdrop of the narration of the rise and fall of republican liberty as the coupling of the competition–democracy nexus, this chapter also looks ahead. It interrogates the implications of the republican conception of economic liberty for the current competition policy debate. It asks whether and how the republican antitrust tradition could inform a reform of competition law to strengthen the competition–democracy nexus in light of the challenges that rising levels of industry concentration and the ascent to power of digital platforms currently pose to our societies.[1]

Growing concerns over not only the economic but also societal and political implications of concentrated corporate power have given rise to calls for a more proactive and rigorous enforcement of competition rules on both sides of the Atlantic.[2] The consumer welfare standard orthodoxy, according to which competition law should confine itself to guaranteeing that markets offer consumers access to services and goods at the best possible price and quality level, has to battle

[1] D Autor and others, 'The Fall of the Labor Share and the Rise of Superstar Firms' (2020) 135(2) *The Quarterly Journal of Economics* 645.

[2] L Khan, 'Amazon's Antitrust Paradox' (2017) 126(3) *Yale Law Journal* 710; A Gerbrandy, 'Rethinking Competition Law within the European Economic Constitution' (2019) 57(1) *JCMS: Journal of Common Market Studies* 127.

increasingly stiff headwinds. At the same time, the proposition that competition law should attribute greater weight to societal and political considerations is gaining momentum and informs current policy initiatives to regulate digital platforms.[3]

In light of this re-emergence of political concerns over concentrated economic power and the renaissance of the idea of a competition–democracy nexus, this chapter asks what lessons we can draw from the republican antitrust tradition to address broader economic and societal challenges arising from the unprecedented concentration of economic power in the hands of a few digital and industrial behemoths. In particular, is it possible to reinvigorate the republican antitrust tradition to forge a competition–democracy nexus 4.0? And, what are the costs and inherent tensions of such a policy?

The remainder of this concluding chapter is organised as follows. Section 8.2 pulls the different strands of the analysis of the previous chapters together by tracing the rise and fall of republican liberty as the missing link between competition and democracy. Section 8.3 argues that a return to a more structuralist republican antitrust tradition that promotes a thicker republican conception of economic liberty as the foundation of a competition–democracy nexus 4.0 does not inevitably run counter consumer interests and welfare. Section 8.4 explores some of the avenues to operationalise the competition–democracy nexus 4.0, while minimising efficiency losses. Section 8.5 concludes by identifying the management of the republican paradox as the *real* antitrust paradox.

8.2 PULLING THE THREADS TOGETHER: THE RISE AND FALL OF REPUBLICAN LIBERTY AS THE CONNECTING PIECE OF THE COMPETITION–DEMOCRACY NEXUS

For a long time, the idea that the preservation of competition and the control of concentrated economic power through competition law contributes to the

[3] H.R.3816–American Choice and Innovation Online Act ('ACIO Act') 2021, 117th Congress (2021–2022); H.R.3825–Ending Platform Monopolies Act ('EPM Act') 2021, 117th Congress (2021–2022); H.R.3826–Platform Competition and Opportunity Act ('PCO Act') 2021 117th Congress (2021–2022); H.R.3849–Access Act ('Access Act') 2021, 117th Congress (2021–2022); Executive Order on Promoting Competition in the American Economy 9 July 2021, Executive Order 14036; Regulation (EU) 2022/1925 on Contestable and Fair Markets in the Digital Sector (Digital Markets Act), [2022] OJ L 265/1; A New Pro-competition Regime for Digital Markets, Advice of the Digital Markets Taskforce; Digital Markets, Competition and Consumers Bill, Bill 350 2022-23 (as amended in Public Bill Committee). See also for the recent recognition that competition law can 'contribute to achieving objectives that go beyond consumer welfare, such as plurality in a democratic society'. European Commission, Amendments to the Communication from the Commission Guidance on the Commission's enforcement priorities in applying Article 82 of the EC Treaty to abusive exclusionary conduct by dominant undertakings. C(2023) 1923 final, para. 1; Case T-604/18 *Google and Alphabet v Commission (Google Android)* ECLI:EU:T:2022:541, para. 1028.

protection of democracy has been a recurrent theme, if not even a foundational myth, of both US antitrust and EU competition law. Yet, our current and predominantly economic understanding of competition and competition law does little to enhance our understanding of this relationship between competitive markets and democracy. The present antitrust scholarship has as yet failed to put forth a coherent theory that elucidates this idea of a competition–democracy nexus.

8.2.1 *An Intellectual History of the Idea of a Competition–Democracy Nexus*

This study addresses this research gap by providing a clear, short, and coherent answer to the question as to what exactly the relationship between competition and democracy consists of. To shed light on the idea of a competition–democracy nexus, this book first traced its trajectory across more than four centuries of economic, political, and legal thought. It has shown how the idea of a competition–democracy nexus first took shape in the political thought and common law of sixteenth-century England. Various political, economic, and legal thinkers, such as Thomas More, Sir Edward Coke, the English Levellers, Montesquieu, James Steuart, and Adam Smith, were amongst the first to argue that competitive markets were drivers of a freer, more equal, and republican form of economy and society. Against the backdrop of the power struggle between the English Parliament and Crown, and the transition from a feudal to a market society, these early proponents of competitive markets coined the first version of a competition–democracy nexus 1.0.

The idea that competitive markets are conducive and concentrated economic power detrimental to democracy gained new momentum in the years preceding the adoption of the US Sherman Act. This iteration of a competition–democracy 2.0 featured prominently in the legislative debates leading to the Sherman Act, the progressive antitrust movement spearheaded by Louis Brandeis and Woodrow Wilson, as well as the limitist and Harvard School antitrust paradigms. Until the 1970s, the proposition of a competition–democracy nexus constituted a recurrent theme in US antitrust policy and discourse.

In the early-twentieth century, a third version of the competition–democracy nexus 3.0 emerged in Europe. Against the backdrop of the infamous role of German cartels and conglomerates in the downfall of the Weimar Republic and the rise of the German National Socialist regime, the Ordoliberal School in Germany championed the idea of a link between competition and democracy, which had a lasting imprint on European and national competition law in post-War Europe.

8.2.2 *Republican Liberty as the Conceptual Fabric of the Competition–Democracy Nexus*

Having traced the intellectual history of the idea of a competition–democracy, this book then ventured to explain the two assumptions underpinning the idea of a competition–democracy nexus: first, the concentration of economic power poses a threat to democracy; and second, the protection of competitive markets is a prerequisite for a liberal democratic order. Drawing upon the history of political thought, this book has shown that the idea of a competition–democracy nexus rests on the republican concept of liberty as non-domination. Unlike our predominant understanding of negative liberty, this republican concept of liberty, which can be traced back to the ancient Roman Republic, already perceives the mere exposure to domination and subordination rather than only interference as an obstruction of liberty. While the concept of negative liberty postulates that an individual enjoys freedom as long as no other person interferes with their choices and actions, the republican understanding of liberty assumes that an individual remains unfree even if they do not face actual or likely interference. The republican tradition does not associate unfreedom with interference but with a master–slave relationship. It stands for the proposition that individuals cannot be said to be free as long as they are exposed to asymmetric power relationships that make them dependent on the goodwill of another, more powerful person, who can arbitrarily interfere with their actions and choices whenever they see fit. Republican liberty can only be attained by emancipating individuals from the dependence on and subordination to the arbitrary will of the more powerful. Therefore, liberty, in its republican sense, does not limit itself to requiring the absence of interference. To be said to be free, individuals must not be subjugated to the arbitrary will of someone else. They must enjoy the independent status of free and equal citizens.

This republican conception of liberty allows us to explain two features that underpin the various iterations of the idea of a competition–democracy nexus. Republican liberty helps us to understand why various proponents of a competition–democracy nexus in early modern Europe, the United States, and the Ordoliberal movement were opposed to the existence of concentrated economic power as such and perceived it as a threat to democracy. This proposition that concentrated economic power constitutes in itself an abrogation of liberty is far from obvious. From the predominant perspective of negative liberty, the existence of economic power should only raise concerns if dominant firms abuse their power and interfere with the choices and actions of other market participants. In contrast, republican liberty can explain why concentrated economic power is viewed as a source of unfreedom. Indeed, from the vantage point of republican liberty, it is already the existence of this concentrated power and the ensuing capacity of potent firms to interfere with other market participants at whim, which constitute an obstruction of liberty.

In contrast to our primarily negative understanding of liberty as non-interference, the concept of republican liberty as non-domination also explains why this state of unfreedom that results from the existence of concentrated economic power is considered a problem for democracy. On a mainstream liberal account, the link between freedom and democracy is indeed anything but obvious. The attainment of negative liberty does not necessarily presuppose a democratic form of government, while the opposite is true for republican liberty. Unlike negative liberty, the republican concept of liberty is directly linked with a specific type of government, namely a republican democracy. Republican thinkers have emphasised that a republican democracy can only thrive if it is grounded in a society of free and equals. It hence presupposes the absence of domination, for instance, in the form of concentrated economic power. Consequently, republican democracy requires checks on and separation of power not only in the political but also in the social and economic spheres.

At the heart of various iterations of the idea of a competition–democracy nexus lay the assumption that competition enhances republican liberty by operating as an institution of antipower that imposes checks on and disperses concentrated economic power. By ensuring the domination-free self-coordination of economic agents, competition also plays an essential role in promoting the independent status and equality of opportunity of all market participants. Across the history of thought in competition law, the goal of a competition–democracy nexus was thus associated with the values of economic liberty as non-domination and its egalitarian dimension of equality of status and opportunity.

8.2.3 *The Operationalisation of the Competition–Democracy Nexus*

Aside from elucidating how the specific republican conception of economic liberty formed the conceptual basis of the idea of a competition–democracy nexus, this book has also shed light on how the competition–democracy nexus has been operationalised through concrete competition policy. It has discussed different ways in which various proponents of the idea of a competition–democracy nexus, such as early common lawyers, and the Harvard and Ordoliberal Schools sought to give effect to the idea of a competition–democracy nexus by securing a polycentric competitive market structure as an institution of antipower.

This book also traces how the various forms of structuralism envisaged by these schools of thought informed the interpretation and application of US antitrust law until the 1970s and EU competition law until the 2000s by competition authorities and courts. It identifies four principal policy levers, listed in Table 8.1, through which the republican antitrust tradition in the United States and the European Union translated the idea of a competition–democracy nexus into the concrete application of competition rules. The book shows that the republican antitrust paradigm pursued as an overarching policy goal (i) the protection of competition as a polycentric market structure that operates as an institution of antipower by keeping economic power in check and eroding concentrated power in the long term. By relying on situational and/or conduct-based structuralism, the republican antitrust tradition on both sides of the Atlantic sought not only to address instances of actual or likely interference by powerful individual or coalitions of market players but to minimise the level of domination flowing from the very existence of concentrated economic power.

TABLE 8.1 *The transition from republican to laissez-faire antitrust*

	Republican antitrust	Laissez-faire antitrust
Goals	• Preserving a polycentric market structure as an institution of antipower	• Consumer welfare
Legal commands	• $\alpha \frac{P(H\|w_1)\ P(w_1) + \cdots + P(H\|w_k)\ P(w_k)}{P(B\|w_1)\ P(w_1) + \cdots + P(B\|w_k)\ P(w_k)} \times \beta \frac{P(e\|H)}{P(e\|B)} = \frac{P(H\|e)}{P(B\|e)}$ where $\alpha > \beta$ • Broad rule-like presumptions guaranteeing modally robust right sets $O((aP_ib \rightarrow aPb) \wedge (bP_ia \rightarrow bPa))$ so that $\Box((aP_ib \rightarrow aPb) \wedge (bP_ia \rightarrow bPa))$ • Minimisation of $P(H\|w_1)\ P(w_1) + \cdots + P(H\|w_k)\ P(w_k)$	• $\alpha \frac{P(H)}{P(B)} \times \beta \frac{P(e\|H)}{P(e\|B)} = \frac{P(H\|e)}{P(B\|e)}$ where $\beta > \alpha$ • Narrow probabilistic presumptions and legal standards guaranteeing probabilistic right sets $P((aP_ib \rightarrow aPb) \wedge (bP_ia \rightarrow bPa))$ so that $\Diamond((cP_ib \rightarrow aPb) \wedge (bP_ia \rightarrow bPa))$ • Minimisation of $P(H\|w_1)\ P(w_1)$ or $P(H\|w_1)\ P(w_1) + P(H\|w_2)\ P(w_2)$
Standard of harm	• Possibilist standard of harm $\frac{P(H\|e)}{P(B\|e)} > \frac{L}{G}$ • Minimisation of $P(H\|w_1)\ P(w_1) + \cdots + P(H\|w_k)\ P(w_k)$	• Probabilistic standard of harm $\frac{P(H\|e)}{P(B\|e)} > \frac{0.5}{0.5}$ • Minimisation of $P(H\|w_1)\ P(w_1)$ or $P(H\|w_1)\ P(w_1) + P(H\|w_2)\ P(w_2)$
Error–cost framework	• Precautionary error–cost framework $((1 - \beta)\ G > \alpha L)$	• Laissez-faire error–cost framework $((1 - \beta)\ G < \alpha L)$

The republican antitrust tradition on both sides of the Atlantic was also characterised by a distinctive form of (ii) legal commands. Republican antitrust operated on a deductive mode of decision-making $\left(\alpha\frac{P(H|w_1)\,P(w_1)+\cdots+P(H|w_k)\,P(w_k)}{P(B|w_1)\,P(w_1)+\cdots+P(B|w_k)\,P(w_k)}\times\beta\frac{P(e|H)}{P(e|B)}=\frac{P(H|e)}{P(B|e)}\right)$ that heavily relied on broadly construed rule-like presumptions $\left(\frac{P(H|w_1)\,P(w_1)+\cdots+P(H|w_k)\,P(w_k)}{P(B|w_1)\,P(w_1)+\cdots+P(B|w_k)\,P(w_k)}\right)$ while attributing relatively limited weight $(\alpha>\beta)$ to the analysis of case-specific evidence $\left(\frac{P(e|H)}{P(e|B)}\right)$. The recourse to modally robust rule-like presumptions $\left(\frac{P(H|w_1)\,P(w_1)+\cdots+P(H|w_k)\,P(w_k)}{P(B|w_1)\,P(w_1)+\cdots+P(B|w_k)\,P(w_k)}\right)$ enabled the republican antitrust tradition to minimise not only arbitrary interference by powerful market players in the actual $(P(H|w_1)\,P(w_1))$ or nearby likely world $(P(H|w_1)\,P(w_1)+P(H|w_2)\,P(w_2))$ but to reduce domination by minimising arbitrary interference across all relevant possible worlds $(P(H|w_1)\,P(w_1)+\cdots+P(H|w_k)\,P(w_k))$. Owing to their rule-like character, the broadly construed presumptions guaranteed modally robust right sets $O((aP_ib\rightarrow aPb)\wedge(bP_ia\rightarrow bPa))$ for market participants that secured their content- and context-independent preference decisiveness across all relevant possible worlds $(\Box((aP_ib\rightarrow aPb)\wedge(bP_ia\rightarrow bPa)))$ by making dominating business conduct unavailable or prohibitively costly to powerful economic agents. The broad application of modally robust rule-like presumptions thus rendered the republican competition law tradition on both sides of the Atlantic conducive to the realisation of a non-probabilistic republican conception of economic liberty that is not only wary of actual or likely interference but perceives the very existence of concentrated economic power and the ensuing possibility of arbitrary interference as a source of unfreedom.

The republican antitrust approach on both sides of the Atlantic was also associated with (iii) a possibilist standard of harm that accounted not only for the plausibility but also for the magnitude of anticompetitive harm $\left(\frac{P(H|e)}{P(B|e)}>\frac{L}{G}\right)$. This possibilist balance of harm standard allowed for antitrust intervention against dominating conduct that had the potential or capability of causing significant harm to competition and market participants across a range of relevant possible worlds, even if this harm was not the most likely outcome. In a similar way to the reliance on rule-like presumptions, this possibilist standard of harm enabled US antitrust and EU competition law to give effect to the non-probabilistic, modally robust conception of economic liberty. By mandating antitrust intervention not only against actual or likely but potential arbitrary interference, this possibilist standard of harm was conducive towards the protection of market participants' preference-decisiveness in a content- and context-independent manner $(\Box((aP_ib\rightarrow aPb)\wedge(bP_ia\rightarrow bPa)))$ by minimising the probabilities of interference in a modally robust way across all relevant possible worlds ($P(H|w_1)\ P(w_1) + \cdots + P(H|w_k)\ P(w_k)$) regardless of the friendly or unfriendly disposition of powerful market players towards them.

Lastly, by virtue of its reliance on broadly designed presumptions and a relatively unexacting standard of harm, the republican antitrust tradition on both sides of the Atlantic followed (iv) a precautionary error–cost framework that in the case of doubt tips the scales towards state intervention. This precautionary error–cost framework assumed that the accuracy benefits of antitrust intervention tend to outweigh the costs arising from over-enforcement ($(1-\beta)\ G) > \alpha L$). This skewed perception of the costs and benefits of antitrust intervention was predicated on the economic assumption that markets are unlikely to self-correct anticompetitive conduct, while foregone efficiencies owing to erroneous state intervention will be readily recovered by the competitive process. The precautionary error–cost framework also rested on the political belief that the harm caused by arbitrary private interference with the economic liberty of market participants outweighs the losses of economic liberty caused by state intervention. From a republican perspective, the harm resulting from arbitrary private interference is not limited to the economic sphere but also has adverse societal and political repercussions, while non-arbitrary state interference does not automatically obstruct economic liberty. This precautionary error–cost framework thus gave shape to a preventative competition policy that sought in the first place to shield the economic liberty of market participants against potential arbitrary interference by powerful players, even if this precautionary antitrust intervention entailed considerable efficiency and welfare losses.

These four (i-iv) elements of the republican antitrust tradition made US antitrust law until the 1970s and EU competition law until the 2000s hospitable to the specific modalities of the republican conception of economic liberty listed in Table 8.2. They enabled competition law on both sides of the Atlantic to secure market participants against a broad category of preventing conditions (y), which includes not only interference but also domination as an obstacle to liberty. At the same time, they also made competition law amenable to an egalitarian understanding of economic liberty as broad-based economic opportunities for a wide range of agents (x). Moreover, these parameters guaranteed a modally robust protection of economic liberty for a wide set of actions (z), covering not only the actual or nearby likely but all relevant possible worlds. The republican antitrust approach in US antitrust and EU competition law thus promoted a conception of economic liberty as non-domination that was inextricably intertwined with the ideal of a society of free and equals and republican democracy.

8.2.4 *The Decline of the Competition–Democracy Nexus*

This book does not confine itself to an account of the importance of the ideal of republican liberty for and its operationalisation through US antitrust and EU competition law. It also illustrates how this concern about liberty as non-domination

TABLE 8.2 *The thinning out of economic liberty*

	Republican antitrust	Laissez-faire antitrust
Type of agents (x)	• Broad (consumers and competitors regardless of their efficiency)	• Narrow (consumers and as-efficient competitors)
Type of preventing conditions (y)	• Domination	• Welfare-decreasing interference
Range of restricted actions (z)	• Preference-decisiveness across all (relevant) possible friendly and unfriendly worlds $\square((aP_ib \rightarrow aPb) \wedge (bP_ia \rightarrow bPa))$ (minimisation of $P(H \mid w_1)\, P(w_1) + \cdots + P(H \mid w_k)\, P(w_k)$)	• Preference-decisiveness in the actual world $(aP_ib \rightarrow aPb)$ (minimisation of $P(H \mid w_1)\, P(w_1)$) or nearby likely world $((aP_ib \rightarrow aPb) \wedge (bP_ia \rightarrow bPa))$ (minimisation of $P(H \mid w_1)\, P(w_1) + P(H \mid w_2)\, P(w_2)$)

and with it the concept of a competition–democracy nexus faded away. The decline of republican antitrust and the idea of a competition–democracy nexus was triggered by the ascent of the Chicago School-inspired More Economic Approach in the United States and in Europe. This study unveils that the Chicago School successfully assaulted republican antitrust through two channels. First, by calling attention to the theoretical and methodological weaknesses of the underlying assumptions of the Structure–Conduct–Performance paradigm, the Chicago School deprived the republican approach of the economic arguments that supported the hostile approach against concentrated economic power. Second, the Chicago School put forth the consumer welfare standard as a versatile and principled framework that enabled antitrust policy to operationalise the concept of negative liberty. Instead of relying on diffuse fears about the presence of domination and concentrated power, which underpins the republican concept of liberty, the consumer welfare standard succeeds in clearly delimiting when economic liberty of other market participants is unduly obstructed. Under the consumer welfare standard, this is only the case if the conduct actually or likely interferes with competitors in a way that reduces consumer welfare. This study shows that the ultimate goal of the Chicago School's support of the consumer welfare standard was the preservation of entrepreneurial liberty against state coercion. With the ascent of the Chicago School and the consumer welfare standard, laissez-faire antitrust, which is primarily grounded in negative liberty, gradually superseded republican antitrust and its ideal of liberty as non-domination.

This book further highlights how the concept of negative liberty as the underpinning rationale of the consumer welfare standard has revolutionised the interpretation and application of antitrust law in the United States and the European Union. The shift from the republican to a laissez-faire antitrust approach also operated along the four policy levers listed in Table 8.1. First, US antitrust and EU competition law ceased to pursue (i) the overarching goal of preserving competition as a polycentric market structure. Instead, modern competition law on both sides of the Atlantic has largely aligned itself with the consumer welfare standard that protects consumers and as-efficient competitors only against welfare-reducing interference. Domination flowing from the very existence of concentrated economic power is no longer considered a source of unfreedom or concern that ought to be addressed by modern competition law.

Second, the transition from republican to laissez-faire antitrust reconfigured the (ii) type of legal commands and modus operandi of modern US antitrust and EU competition law. Following the rise of laissez-faire antitrust, the deductive mode of decision-making of republican antitrust gave way to an inductive approach $\left(\alpha \frac{P(H)}{P(B)} \times \beta \frac{P(e|H)}{P(e|B)} = \frac{P(H|e)}{P(B|e)}\right)$ that attributes greater consideration ($\beta > \alpha$) to the analysis of case-specific evidence. Consequently, the broadly construed rule-like presumptions were progressively narrowed and partly replaced by rule of reason-like standards. Remaining presumptions were stripped of their rule-like modally robust character. Instead, they were reconceptualised as simple probability estimates of anticompetitive harm $\left(\frac{P(H)}{P(B)}\right)$ that can, depending on the case at hand, be blended through a sliding-scale approach with a more casuistic analysis of case-specific evidence $\left(\frac{P(e|H)}{P(e|B)}\right)$. As a result, instead of securing a modally robust non-probabilistic protection of market participants against domination, the modus operandi and design of legal commands of modern competition law merely guarantee probabilistic right sets $P((aP_ib \rightarrow aPb) \wedge (bP_ia \rightarrow bPa))$ that only secure a contingent possibility that market participants' preferences remain decisive in the actual or nearby likely world: $\Diamond((aP_ib \rightarrow aPb) \wedge (bP_ia \rightarrow bPa))$. In line with the probabilistic conception of negative economic liberty, laissez-faire antitrust shields market participants only against interference in the actual $(P(H|w_1)\ P(w_1))$ or nearby likely world $(P(H|w_1)\ P(w_1) + P(H|w_2)\ P(w_2))$.

Third, modern competition law also departed from (iii) the possibilist standard of harm that accounted for the magnitude of potential anticompetitive harm. With the rise of the laissez-faire antitrust approach, modern competition law on both sides of the Atlantic increasingly endorsed a probabilistic standard of harm that focuses exclusively on the likelihood of business conduct resulting in anticompetitive effects. Consistent with the probabilistic negative conception of liberty as non-interference, this probabilistic standard of harm limits legitimate competition law intervention to conduct that is shown to be more likely than not to result in antitrust harm $\left(\frac{P(H|e)}{P(B|e)} > \frac{0.5}{0.5}\right)$. This recalibration of legal presumptions and the standard of harm hollowed out the modally robust republican conception of economic liberty that characterised the republican antitrust tradition. Under the laissez-faire antitrust approach, modern competition law only protects market participants against antitrust harm in the actual $(P(H \mid w_1)\ P(w_1))$ or nearby likely world $(P(H \mid w_1)\ P(w_1) + P(H \mid w_2)\ P(w_2))$. As a result, the thinned-out negative conception of economic liberty underpinning the laissez-faire approach protects market participants' preference-decisiveness across a narrowly defined domain of the actual $((aP_ib \rightarrow aPb))$ or nearby likely world $((aP_ib \rightarrow aPb) \wedge (bP_ia \rightarrow bPa))$. By contrast, the modal constraints and domination resulting from the mere possibility of arbitrary interference by powerful market participants fall increasingly outside the protective scope of modern competition law.

Lastly, the transition from a republican towards a laissez-faire approach also brought an end to the (iv) precautionary error–cost framework of the republican antitrust tradition in US antitrust and EU competition law. With the rise of the laissez-faire approach, modern competition law increasingly endorsed an error–cost framework that postulated that the costs of erroneous antitrust intervention outweigh the accuracy benefits of competition law intervention $((1-\beta)G) < \alpha L)$. Accordingly, this updated understanding of the costs and benefits of antitrust enforcement counsels competition authorities and courts to err on the side of non-intervention (type II errors). It thereby entrenches a laissez-faire approach that seeks in the first place to protect the negative entrepreneurial liberty of businesses against state interference.

This move from a republican towards a laissez-faire approach has thinned out the type of economic liberty that is protected by US antitrust law and EU competition law along the three dimensions listed in Table 8.2: it has narrowed the inclusiveness of economic liberty by reducing the range of agents (x) whose economic liberty is secured under competition law; it has curtailed the scope of economic liberty by shrinking the range of preventing conditions (y) that competition law seeks to address; and it has lowered the robustness of economic liberty by limiting the range of actions (z) that are guaranteed in a modally robust manner across all relevant possible worlds. The negative conception of economic liberty thus entirely displaced the republican ideal of liberty as non-domination as the ultimate normative foundation of US and EU competition law and replaced it with a narrow negative notion of economic liberty as the absence of welfare-decreasing interference.

The endorsement of the consumer welfare standard by US and EU competition law gradually obliterated the role of republican liberty as the underpinning link of the competition–democracy nexus. By jettisoning the ideal of republican liberty as non-domination and replacing it with a narrow, negative understanding of liberty as non-interference, the proponents of laissez-faire antitrust severed this link between competition and democracy. Unlike republican liberty, negative liberty is not tightly associated with a specific form of government. Negative liberty can, under certain circumstances, also thrive under an authoritarian regime. Nor does negative liberty depend on the absence of concentrated power, the elimination of subordination, and the equality of status, which the republican tradition perceived as economic corollaries of republican democracy. On the contrary, modern antitrust law is grounded in a concept of negative liberty that remains agnostic about concentrated economic power, dependence, or subordination, as long as they do not involve involuntary, welfare-reducing interference with other market participants. Within the framework of modern antitrust law, economic power is only relevant if it is exercised in the form of market power; that is if it entails output restrictions or price increases. Consequently, the dominating effects of the mere existence of concentrated economic power and the adverse effect of economic power beyond the strict perimeters of the market, for instance, on democracy, fall outside the realm of modern competition law analysis.

8.3 TOWARDS A COMPETITION–DEMOCRACY NEXUS 4.0

This account of the hollowing out of the republican approach and the decline of the competition–democracy nexus raises the question of whether the transition of US antitrust and EU competition law towards a laissez-faire approach is reversible; and if so, then whether a recalibration towards a more republican approach is desirable. This question has gained new momentum in light of growing concerns over the unprecedented concentration of economic power in the hands of a few powerful online platforms and rising levels of industry concentration, which have prompted calls for a radical rethink of competition law and the abandoning of the consumer welfare standard.[4]

The rise to power of digital platforms has indeed slowed down, if not brought to a partial halt, the incremental transition of US antitrust and EU competition law to a laissez-faire approach as envisaged by the proponents of the More Economic Approach. Over the last few years, the European Commission has handed down bold decisions against powerful online platforms and appears to reconsider some of the fundamental premises of the More Economic Approach.[5] Currently,

[4] Khan, 'Amazon's Antitrust Paradox' (n 2); T Wu, 'After Consumer Welfare, Now What? The "Protection of Competition" Standard in Practice' [2018]) *Competition Policy International* 1; M Steinbaum and M E Stucke, 'The Effective Competition Standard: A New Standard for Antitrust' (2020) 87(2) *The University of Chicago Law Review* 595; T Wu, *The Curse of Bigness: Antitrust in the New Gilded Age* (New York: Columbia Global Reports 2018); Antitrust Division of the US Department of Justice, Assistant Attorney General Jonathan Kanter Delivers Remarks at New York City Bar Association's Milton Handler Lecture (2022).

[5] For some prominent examples of the European Commission's enforcement activity in digital markets, see Case No COMP/AT.39740 *Google Search (Shopping)*, C(2017) 4444 final; Case No COMP/AT.40099 *Google Android*, C(2018) 4761 final; Case No COMP/AT.40411 *Google Search (AdSense)*, C(2019) 2173 final; European Commission, Press Release IP/21/2061 – Antitrust: Commission Sends Statement of Objections to Apple on App Store Rules for Music Streaming Providers (2021); European Commission, Press Release IP/20/2077 – Antitrust: Commission Sends Statement of Objections to Amazon for the Use of Non-public Independent Seller Data and Opens Second Investigation into its E-commerce Business

competition authorities across Europe are rushing towards new enforcement instruments to tackle the economic power of online platforms and preserve competition in digital markets.[6] At the same time, however, the EU judiciary appears to be digging in its heels and to cling to the consumer welfare standard and laissez-faire agenda of the More Economic Approach.[7] Calls for a more robust enforcement of competition law, notably in digital markets, have also gained momentum in the United States. Several bills to rein in the power of digital platforms and promote competition in digital markets have recently been introduced in both houses of the US Congress and the antitrust agencies are veering towards stricter enforcement standards to address growing concerns about industry concentration.[8] Following the appointment of Lina Khan,[9] Jonathan Kanter,[10] and Tim Wu[11] by the Biden administration, three prominent contemporary proponents of the idea of a competition–democracy nexus and outspoken critics of industrial size have been placed in key positions within the US Federal Trade Commission, the Antitrust Division of the Department of Justice, and the Council of Economic Advisers to the US President. With the adoption of the Presidential

Practices (2020). For the ongoing review process of the More Economic Approach, notably towards dominant firm conduct under Art. 102 TFEU, see EU Commission, Amendments to the Communication from the Commission Guidance on the Commission's enforcement priorities in applying Article 82 of the EC Treaty to abusive exclusionary conduct by dominant undertakings (n 3).

6 Regulation (EU) 2022/1925 on Contestable and Fair Markets in the Digital Sector (Digital Markets Act) (n 3); A New Pro-competition Regime for Digital Markets (n 3); Digital Markets, Competition and Consumers Bill (n 3); Zehntes Gesetz zur Änderung des Gesetzes gegen Wettbewerbsbeschränkungen (die 10. GWB-Novelle), BGBl. I, 2021 S. 2; Referentenentwurf des Bundesministeriums für Wirtschaft und Klimaschutz: Entwurf eines Gesetzes zur Verbesserung der Wettbewerbsstrukturen und zur Abschöpfung von Vorteilen aus Wettbewerbsverstößen (Wettbewerbsdurchsetzungsgesetz / die 11. GWB-Novelle) 15 September 2022; Gesetzentwurf der Bundesregierung, Entwurf eines Gesetzes zur Änderung des Gesetzes gegen Wettbewerbsbeschränkungen und anderer Gesetze 16 May 2023. Drucksache 20/6824.

7 See, for instance, Case T-399/16 *CK Telecoms UK Investments v Commission* ECLI:EU:T:2020:217; Case T-286/09 RENV *Intel Corporation v Commission* ECLI:EU:T:2022:19; Case C-377/20 *Servizio Elettrico Nazionale and Others* ECLI:EU:C:2022:379; Case T-235/18 *Qualcomm v Commission* ECLI:EU:T:2022:358. See, however, Case T-604/18 *Google and Alphabet v Commission (Google Android)* (n 3) para. 1028; Case C-376/20 P *Commission v CK Telecoms UK Investments* ECLI:EU:C:2023:561.

8 See, for instance, H.R.3849–Access Act ('Access Act') (n 3); H.R.3826–Platform Competition and Opportunity Act ('PCO Act') (n 3); H.R.3825–Ending Platform Monopolies Act ('EPM Act') (n 3); H.R.3816–American Choice and Innovation Online Act ('ACIO Act') (n 3); H.R.3460–State Antitrust Enforcement Venue Act, 117th Congress (2021–2022); S. 1811–Merger Enforcement Improvement Act, 115th Congress (2017–2019); S. 1812–Consolidation Prevention and Competition Promotion Act, 115th (2017–2019); Antitrust Division of the US Department of Justice/Federal Trade Commission, Draft 2023 Merger Guidelines.

9 Khan, 'Amazon's Antitrust Paradox' (n 2).

10 Antitrust Division of the US Department of Justice (n 4).

11 Wu, 'After Consumer Welfare, Now What?' (n 4) 4–7.

Order on Promoting Competition in America,[12] the Biden administration also made more proactive antitrust enforcement a key priority of its political agenda.

In light of the challenges of the digital revolution and rising concentration levels, US antitrust law, EU competition law, and other competition regimes across the world currently find themselves at a crossroads. Competition policymakers face a stark choice: either to complete competition law's alignment with the laissez-faire approach grounded in the consumer welfare standard or to recalibrate the enforcement of competition rules so that they can rise to the new challenges posed by the increasing concentration of corporate power. As the shift towards laissez-faire antitrust appears to reach its inflection point, the remainder of this chapter will explore whether competition law could revert to or at least incorporate some elements of the republican tradition by recalibrating the parameters listed in Table 8.1. with a view to addressing these novel challenges and revitalising the competition–democracy nexus. It sketches some avenues towards a renewed version of republican antitrust – in the following called competition–democracy nexus 4.0 – while also highlighting challenges and obstacles.

8.3.1 *Taking Industry Concentration Seriously*

A move towards a more republican approach and the reinvigoration of the competition–democracy nexus would require competition law to take concentrated economic power seriously again. To this end, competition law would need to resist a purely outcome-oriented approach that protects a competitive market structure only as long as it maximises consumer welfare. Rather, antitrust policy would have to account for the impact of economic concentration and firm conduct not only on consumer welfare but also on the market structure and the procedural virtues of competition in terms of economic liberty, equality of opportunity, and the independent status of the market participants. This would require nothing less than a reframing of the prevailing understanding of competition. Instead of the purely outcome-oriented understanding of competition as a generator of economic welfare, antitrust policy would once again have to be anchored in a Smithian understanding of competition as a polycentric market structure and institution of antipower that ensures the input-oriented legitimacy of markets by guaranteeing economic liberty and equality of opportunity. A renaissance of the republican antitrust tradition and the idea of a competition–democracy nexus would involve the reversal towards a more structuralist approach that seeks to tackle economic concentration with a view to maximising non-domination.

[12] Executive Order on Promoting Competition in the American Economy (n 3).

The consumer welfare standard has recently come under increasing strain as antitrust experts and academics have advanced proposals for alternative policy standards that give greater consideration to concerns over economic concentration and the preservation of a competitive market structure. A growing number of commentators have called for the readjustment or even the replacement of the consumer welfare standard with a 'protection of competition',[13] 'process of competition',[14] or 'effective competition'[15] standard. The consumer welfare standard is faulted for its exclusive focus on the outcomes of competition in terms of low prices for consumers, which allegedly fails to account for the fact that powerful firms, such as online platforms, can harm competition without necessarily charging higher prices to consumers. The opponents of a consumer welfare approach argue that the adoption of an alternative standard focusing on the protection of the competitive process would instead allow competition law to address concerns about conduct that adversely affects competitors and competition without necessarily leading to higher prices for consumers. A stronger focus on the procedural dimension of competition would thus realign antitrust law with its political ideals of preserving economic liberty and equality of opportunity. These proposals account for the fact that our societies like competition not only because it leads to better outcomes for consumers but also because it has certain desirable procedural characteristics that safeguard economic liberty, fairness, and equality.

Various iterations of the process of competition standard may provide an alternative to the predominant laissez-faire approach that under the consumer welfare standard protects an extremely narrow conception of economic liberty of market participants against welfare-decreasing interference in the actual or nearby likely world. A competition policy that seeks to guarantee competition as a polycentric process and market structure would enhance a thicker republican conception of economic liberty by ensuring that markets operate as institutions of antipower. To secure republican liberty as non-domination, competition law would thus have to address the position of power of potent economic agents who act as 'gatekeepers' and are able to interfere with market participants and close their options whenever they see fit, both in the actual or relevant possible worlds. Reorienting competition law towards a more structural approach that seeks to preserve a polycentric market structure and to secure the ability of residual competitors to effectively constrain and in the medium- to long-term erode instances of concentrated economic power may foster republican liberty and revive the ideal of a competition–democracy nexus.

[13] Khan, 'Amazon's Antitrust Paradox' (n 2) 737–46; L Khan, 'The New Brandeis Movement: America's Antimonopoly Debate' (2018) 9(3) *Journal for European Competition Law & Practice* 131, 132; Wu, *The Curse of Bigness* (n 4); Wu , 'After Consumer Welfare, Now What?' (n 4).

[14] Wu 'After Consumer Welfare, Now What?' (n 4) 7. T Wu, 'The "Protection of the Competitive Process" Standard' (2018). Columbia Public Law Research Paper No 14-612 4.

[15] Steinbaum and Stucke (n 4).

The recent initiatives and proposals by the EU legislator,[16] the UK Government,[17] the German legislator,[18] and US law makers[19] aimed at curtailing the gatekeeper power of vertically integrated digital platforms and securing the contestability of digital markets clearly move in this direction. They aim to preserve or even inject a polycentric market structure into digital markets. To this end, they envisage the imposition of a range of different rules and obligations on digital platforms that protect the economic liberty and opportunities of competing business users, regardless of their efficiency. In the ultimate consequence, the new platform regulations even contemplate the fragmentation of powerful incumbents to enhance a polycentric market structure. The extent to which this change in approach in the regulation of competition in digital markets will have spill over effects on 'regular' competition law analysis and enforcement remains to be seen. There are various ways in which the new platform regulations might constitute the blueprint for the transition towards a more republican approach in the enforcement of competition law across industries. For example, one way of aligning regular competition law with a more structural, republican approach would consist of discarding the notoriously under-inclusive[20] as-efficient competitor test as the relevant benchmark to decide when dominant firm conduct unduly forecloses competitors. This would allow competition law to enhance the contestability of concentrated markets and at the same time secure broad-based opportunities to compete.[21]

Despite these recent initiatives to regulate competition in digital markets, it remains largely unclear how the proponents of alternatives to the consumer welfare standard would imagine a competition policy that, for instance, implements the competitive process standard to function. Little has so far been said as to what is precisely meant by the 'competitive process'. Some commentators seem to advocate a structuralist

[16] Regulation (EU) 2022/1925 on Contestable and Fair Markets in the Digital Sector (Digital Markets Act) (n 3) Articles 1 (1) and (2); 2(1) and (3), recitals 3–6, 10.

[17] A New Pro-competition Regime for Digital Markets (n 3) notably, part 4 and Annex B–D; Digital Markets, Competition and Consumers Bill (n 3) ss 19–21.

[18] Zehntes Gesetz zur Änderung des Gesetzes gegen Wettbewerbsbeschränkungen (die 10. GWB-Novelle) (n 6) most notably § 19a.

[19] H.R.3849–Access Act ('Access Act') (n 3); H.R.3826–Platform Competition and Opportunity Act ('PCO Act') (n 3); H.R.3825–Ending Platform Monopolies Act ('EPM Act') (n 3); H.R.3816–American Choice and Innovation Online Act ('ACIO Act') (n 3); H.R.3460–State Antitrust Enforcement Venue Act (n 8); Merger Enforcement Improvement Act (n 8); Consolidation Prevention and Competition Promotion Act (n 8).

[20] SC Salop, 'The Raising Rivals' Cost Foreclosure Paradigm, Conditional Pricing Practices and the Flawed Incremental Price-Cost Test' (2017) 81(2) *Antitrust Law Journal* 371, 385–87; Case T-286/09 *Intel v Commission* ECLI:EU:T:2014:547 para. 150.

[21] For a recent partial departure from the 'as-efficient competitor' test, see Case T-612/17 *Google and Alphabet v Commission (Google Shopping)* ECLI:EU:T:2021:763 paras. 538–41. See also European Commission, Annex to the Communication from the Commission: Amendments to the Communication from the Commission Guidance on the Commission's enforcement priorities in applying Article 82 of the EC Treaty to abusive exclusionary conduct by dominant undertakings. C(2023) 1923 final Annex paras. 2–3.

standard under the labels of the 'process of competition' or 'effective competition' standards, which focuses on the impact of business conduct on market structure.[22] A competitive process standard would thus clearly depart from the truism of modern antitrust that competition law protects 'competition, not competitors'.[23] Protecting a competitive market, at least to some extent, implies the protection of competitors. Consequently, it draws on the long-standing insight that competition, at least in the medium to long term, 'requires the existence of competitors, in the plural'.[24]

A major shortcoming of an alternative competitive process standard is its indeterminacy. Unlike the consumer welfare standard, the competitive process standard fails to provide a similarly clear benchmark to decide which of the four scenarios described in Table 8.3 and discussed in detail in Chapter 6 would warrant antitrust intervention and which would not. As long as the protection of a competitive market structure presupposes the protection of competitors, the competitive process standard would compel competition law to protect the surplus and rents of competitors (FHGI in Table 8.3 assuming that in t_1 $Q_A = Q_M$ and $Q_B = Q_C - Q_M$). It is conceivable that the competitive process standard will entail antitrust intervention in Scenarios 1, 2, or 4, yet without providing a clear limiting principle as to when such intervention is necessary and when not; whereas the consumer welfare orthodoxy clearly limits antitrust intervention to Scenario 3. Adopting a competitive process standard may therefore undermine the administrability and consistency of competition policy. It also bears the risk of repeating previous aberrations of republican antitrust, for instance, during the Warren Court era, when competition law was used to protect inefficient local businesses and prevent mergers whose impact on concentration was marginal. For this reason, proponents of the consumer welfare standard warn that shifting towards a more structuralist approach under a competitive process standard would inescapably result in welfare losses and harm consumers.[25] Advocates of the antitrust status quo posit that the preservation of competitor surplus (FHGI) undermines consumer surplus whenever Competitors B are not as efficient as the perpetrator monopoly Firm A.

Yet, this proposition advanced by the advocates of the consumer welfare standard that competitor and consumer interests always tend to pull in opposite directions does not always hold true. There are at least three arguments that can be made to suggest that a competition policy that preserves a competitive and contestable

[22] Steinbaum and Stucke (n 4) 602; Wu, 'The "Protection of the Competitive Process" Standard' (n 14) 4.

[23] *Brooke Group v Brown & Williamson Tobacco Corp.* 509 U.S. 209 (1993) 224; *Brown Shoe Co. Inc. v United States* 370 U.S. 294 (1962) 320; Case T-399/16 *CK Telecoms UK Investments v Commission* (n 7) para. 362.

[24] C Kaysen and DF Turner, *Antitrust Policy: An Economic and Legal Analysis* (Cambridge, MA: Harvard University Press 1959) 7.

[25] To cite just one example, see AD Melamed and N Petit, 'The Misguided Assault on the Consumer Welfare Standard in the Age of Platform Markets' (2019) 54(4) *Review of Industrial Organization* 741, 747.

TABLE 8.3 *Scenarios of antitrust intervention*

	Scenario 1 As-efficient competitor surplus transfer		Scenario 2 Less efficient competitor surplus transfer		Scenario 3 Monopoly outcome with as-efficient competitors		Scenario 4 Monopoly outcome with less efficient competitors	
	t_1	t_2	t_1	t_2	t_1	t_2	t_1	t_2
Price (P)	$P_1 = P_A = P_B$	$P_1 = P_A$	$P_1 = P_A = P_B$	$P_1 = P_A$	$P_1 = P_A = P_B$	$P_2 = P_A$	$P_1 = P_A = P_B$	$P_2 = P_A$
Quantity of output (Q)	$Q_c = Q_A + Q_B$	$Q_c = Q_A$	$Q_c = Q_A + Q_B$	$Q_c = Q_A$	$Q_C = Q_A + Q_B$	$Q_M = Q_A$	$Q_c = Q_A + Q_B$	$Q_M = Q_A$
Average cost (AC)	$AC_1 = AC_A = AC_B$	$AC_1 = AC_A = AC_B$	$AC_1 = AC_A = AC_B$	$AC_1 = AC_B$ $AC_2 = AC_A$	$AC_1 = AC_A = AC_B$	$AC_1 = AC_A = AC_B$	$AC_1 = AC_A = AC_B$	$AC_1 = AC_B$ $AC_2 = AC_A$
Surplus Monopolist (A)	DFEG	DFEG + FHGI	DFEG	DFEG + EGMN + FHGI + GINO	DFEG	DFEG + KLDF	DFEG	DFEG + KLDF + EGMN
Surplus consumers (C)	JDH	JDH	JDH	JDH	JDH	JKL	JDH	JKL
Surplus competitors (B)	FHGI		FHGI		FHGI		FHGI	
Consumer welfare loss						KLDF + LFH		KLDF + LFH
Competitor surplus loss		FHGI		FHGI		FHGI		FHGI
Deadweight loss						FHGI + LFH		FHGI + LFH
Welfare gains				EGMN + GINO				EGMN

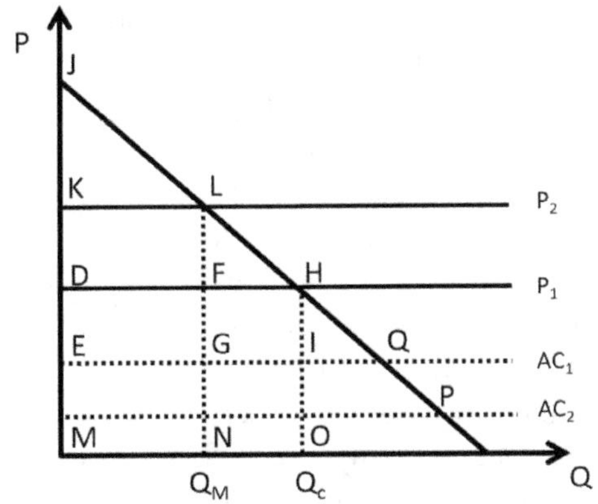

FIGURE 8.1 Scenarios of antitrust intervention

market structure by protecting competitor surplus may also further consumer welfare. This is the case if the competitor surplus (FHGI) generates a distinct benefit for consumers that is not credited by orthodox welfare economics.

8.3.2 *Static Efficiencies*

Welfare economics itself highlights that the protection of a polycentric market structure and the surplus of competitors may, under certain circumstances, enhance consumer welfare. There are indeed instances, such as in Scenario 4 in Figure 8.1 and Table 8.3, where competition law may maximise consumer welfare by preserving a competitive market structure and the surplus of residual Competitors B (FHGI), even though these competitors are less efficient than the dominant incumbent A. Economic analysis suggests that in the presence of high entry barriers, even the foreclosure of less efficient competitors (B) may lead to higher prices and lower output ($P_2 = P_A$, $Q_M = Q_A$ in t_2) if it allows the dominant incumbent (A) to restore or entrench its monopoly position. Consequently, the foreclosure of less efficient competitors may result in a loss in consumer welfare (KLDF + LFH) that exceeds the putative welfare gains flowing from the lower production costs of the more efficient monopolist (EGMN).[26] Maintaining a competitive market structure composed of even less efficient players thus does not necessarily harm but may actually protect consumer welfare. This is because the mere presence of even less efficient competitors may impose important constraints upon the dominant firm's ability to raise prices.[27]

26 JF Brodley and GA Hay, 'Predatory Pricing: Competing Economic Theories and the Evolution of Legal Standards' (1980–1981) 66(4) *Cornell Law Review* 738, 744–46.

27 For the proposition that less-efficient competitors may impose important constraints on the market power of monopolistic firms and thus benefit consumers Salop, 'The Raising Rivals'

The example given in Scenario 4 shows that the assumption underpinning the as-efficient competitor principle and test as the normative yardstick of laissez-faire antitrust according to which consumer welfare and allocative efficiency will not be harmed by conduct that does not foreclose equally efficient competitors does not always hold true. The as-efficient competitor principle fails to account for the fact that even less efficient competitors can effectively constrain the ability of a dominant player to exercise power.[28] Advocates of the consumer welfare orthodoxy who criticise the competitive process standard because it protects less efficient competitors and leads to inconsistent outcomes disregard that protecting the surplus of even less efficient competitors may be essential to preserve consumer welfare. A consumer welfare approach, properly so called, would indicate a departure from the as-efficient competitor principle and support competition law interventions in situations such as those described in Scenario 4. Protecting a polycentric market structure and less efficient competitors may not necessarily be at odds with but may even be required by a consumer welfare standard. This suggests that there are a number of important overlaps and synergies between a republican approach that seeks to guarantee a competitive market structure and a consumer welfare standard. Even from a static efficiency perspective, a reversal to a more republican approach does not inevitably lead to consumer welfare and efficiency losses.

8.3.3 *Preference for Flexibility*

A second situation where the preservation of competitor surplus may enhance consumer welfare is when a polycentric market structure generates 'option value'. Economic and social choice theory has shown that consumers and society may have a 'preference for flexibility'[29] and often derive important benefits from keeping their options open. The option value literature[30] suggests that it may indeed be welfare maximising and rational for economic agents not only to choose the currently preferred option but also to maintain their ability to choose alternative options in the future, although they are not preferred at the time of the decision-making. This is notably the case if (i) the commitment to a specific option *a* is irreversible because

Cost Foreclosure Paradigm' (n 20) 414–15. This has been recognised by the Court of Justice in Case C-23/14 *Post Danmark II* ECLI:EU:C:2015:651 paras. 59–60.

28 Brodley and Hay (n 26) 745.

29 DM Kreps, 'A Representation Theorem for "Preference for Flexibility"' (1979) 47(3) *Econometrica* 565.

30 BA Weisbrod, 'Collective-Consumption Services of Individual-Consumption Goods' (1964) 78 (3) *The Quarterly Journal of Economics* 471; KJ Arrow and AC Fisher, 'Environmental Preservation, Uncertainty, and Irreversibility' (1974) 88(2) *The Quarterly Journal of Economics* 312; CJ Cicchetti and AM Freeman, 'Option Demand and Consumer Surplus: Further Comment' (1971) 85(3) *The Quarterly Journal of Economics* 528; A Sen, 'Markets and Freedoms: Achievements and Limitations of the Market Mechanism in Promoting Individual Freedoms' (1993) 45(4) *Oxford Economic Papers* 519, 523.

the alternative option *b* will no longer be available within a reasonable time frame or because switching to option *b* will be too costly and (ii) if there is uncertainty or insufficient information about future preferences, future supply conditions, or the future consequences of choosing option *a* (or not choosing *b*). In this situation, economic agents and/or society gain an additional benefit from keeping their options open by postponing their commitment to a specific option until they have gained more information about the implications of choosing options *a* or *b*.[31]

The option value literature highlights that a polycentric market structure that keeps various competing options – for instance, a portfolio of alternative solutions to a technological problem – available operates like an insurance policy that diversifies risks and bolsters society's capacity to swiftly adapt to future environmental and technological changes.[32] Polycentric markets thereby produce a distinct benefit that is not fully captured by the consumer welfare standard as it is commonly understood.[33] The key insight of the option value literature is that consumers and society may gain from not (irreversibly) committing to a single option until market processes generate more detailed information about the consequences and values of alternative options. In other words, option value theory suggests that in the presence of irreversibility, uncertainty, or increasing value of future information, it may be in the interest of consumers and society to preserve a polycentric market structure where there are different competing alternatives available, even if one of the alternatives is currently preferred.[34] This is in particular the case because polycentric markets themselves play a crucial role in generating relevant information regarding these options endogenously.[35]

This suggests that antitrust intervention may even be warranted in Scenarios 1 and 2, as described in Table 8.3 and Figure 8.1, where a monopolist forecloses as-efficient (Scenario 1) or less efficient (Scenario 2) competitors from the market without (immediately) raising prices or reducing output. Even if consumers were to prefer

[31] Arrow and Fisher (n 30) 314–18.

[32] M Polanyi, *The Logic of Liberty* (London: Routledge 1951) 117–22, 171–75; E Ostrom, 'Why Do We Need to Protect Institutional Diversity?' (2012) 11(1) *European Political Science* 128, 129; K Carlisle and RL Gruby, 'Polycentric Systems of Governance: A Theoretical Model for the Commons' (2017) 47(4) *Policy Studies Journal* 927.

[33] Some authors indeed refer to the option value as some form of 'risk aversion premium' Cicchetti and Freeman (n 30) 536. See in this sense also W Kerber, 'Competition, Innovation and Maintaining Diversity through Competition Law' in R Podszun, W Kerber, and J Drexl (eds), *Competition Policy and the Economic Approach: Foundations and Limitations* (Cheltenham: Edward Elgar 2011) 173, 178, 184.

[34] For the relationship between option value and the value of future information C Henry, 'Option Values in the Economics of Irreplaceable Assets' (1974) 41(5) *The Review of Economic Studies* 89, 90; BS Bernanke, 'Irreversibility, Uncertainty, and Cyclical Investment' (1983) 98(1) *The Quarterly Journal of Economics* 85, 86; W Hanemann, 'Information and the Concept of Option Value' (1989) 16(1) *Journal of Environmental Economics and Management* 23, 29, 35–36.

[35] The option value is indeed high when information can only be obtained endogenously by observing a specific environment for a period of time. Hanemann (n 34) 35–36.

perpetrator Firm A's product over the products offered by Competitors B, or were indifferent between them at the time when the foreclosure takes place, the elimination of Bs' products as future options may generate a loss in consumer welfare that is distinct from price increases.

Economic literature on option value theory and the virtues of polycentric systems thus offers valid and well-established arguments in support of preserving a diversity of competing options in the market place.[36] Securing option value militates for an antitrust policy that guarantees a thicker protection of economic liberty going beyond a content-dependent, Hobbesian form of negative liberty according to which individuals are free as long as they are not hindered in choosing their preferred option ($aP_ib \rightarrow aPb$). The fact that individuals confronted with uncertainty may have a rational preference for future flexibility[37] offers a strong economic justification for a commitment to a content-independent protection of liberty that keeps not only the preferred but all doors open.[38] Accordingly, it may be rational for antitrust policy not only to minimise the probability of hindrance of option *a*, when *a* is the preferred option between *a* and *b*, but also to secure preference-decisiveness in the instance of sudden changes of consumer preferences whereby *b* becomes the preferred option ($(aP_ib \rightarrow aPb) \wedge (bP_ia \rightarrow bPa)$).[39] This preference for future flexibility also makes a strong economic case to go beyond the protection of thick negative economic liberty and to endorse a competition policy grounded in republican liberty that protects content- and context-independent preference-decisiveness across all (relevant) possible worlds ($\Box((aP_ib \rightarrow aPb) \wedge (bP_ia \rightarrow bPa))$). In fact, the liberty to choose between options *a* and *b* in the future becomes illusionary if powerful gatekeepers have the capacity to easily interfere with these choices whenever they see fit. For instance, this would be the case if powerful digital platforms 'turn rogue' and harness network effects to tip[40] markets in their favour, and thereby lock-in the choice of option *a* irreversibly while making option *b* unavailable. Therefore, a robust and resilient protection of technological option value calls for a republican antitrust approach that secures a modal protection of the availability of options *a* and *b* across a range of worlds where circumstances are friendly and unfriendly.[41] In basic terms, this would mean that competition law should no longer only protect

36 J Farrell, 'Complexity, Diversity, and Antitrust' (2006) 51(1) *The Antitrust Bulletin* 165; Kerber (n 33).

37 TC Koopmans, 'On Flexibility of Future Preference' (1962). Cowles Foundation Discussion Paper 150; Kreps (n 29).

38 Sen, 'Markets and Freedoms' (n 30) 523, 530; PK Pattnaik and Y Xu, 'On Ranking Opportunity Sets in Terms of Freedom of Choice' (1990) 56(3/4) *Recherches économiques de Louvain/ Louvain Economic Review* 383.

39 P Pettit, *On the People's Terms: A Republican Theory and Model of Democracy* (Cambridge: Cambridge University Press 2012) 34–35.

40 For the origin of the concept of tipping markets, see ML Katz and C Shapiro, 'Systems Competition and Network Effects' (1994) 8(2) *Journal of Economic Perspectives* 93, 105–06.

41 Pettit, *On the People's Terms* (n 39) 67–69.

market participants' liberty to open the door that they actually or likely prefer but it would have to ensure that they could open other doors without hindrance by powerful players in a number of (relevant) possible counterfactual worlds.

The option value of maintaining the stable availability of different options across different possible worlds is particularly high in digital and other new technology markets where the future consequences of a specific technology on consumers, public health, environmental sustainability, or – as the events on Capitol hill of Epiphany 2021 have shown in the case of digital platforms – democracy remain often unknown. Not only does the modal preservation of option value and technological flexibility[42] permit consumers to easily switch to alternative technological solutions if the currently preferred technology turns out to have unsustainable effects but it also reduces the costs for democratically elected legislators to regulate or, indeed, outlaw certain technological solutions, as technological alternatives are readily available.

8.3.4 *Dynamic Efficiencies*

This option value argument also implicitly alludes to a third way in which the protection of a polycentric market structure, and thereby the preservation of republican economic liberty, may go hand-in-hand with greater consumer welfare. The option value literature not only underscores the costs of an irreversible reduction of alternative choices but it also highlights the role of markets in generating valuable information about the value of competing options endogenously.[43] Modern welfare economics, in which the consumer welfare standard is anchored, all too easily assumes that firms possess all the relevant knowledge to decide which type of innovation will serve society and consumer preferences. As a result, the consumer welfare standard attributes little importance to the role of polycentric markets in generating knowledge by facilitating parallel experimentation and learning.[44] Indeed, to use Hayek's famous formula, polycentric markets operate as a 'discovery procedure' that allows society to gain information about otherwise unknown facts.[45] Economic and social science literature[46] therefore emphasises the propensity of

[42] Kerber (n 33) 179.

[43] See the literature cited in note 34.

[44] Hayek raised this central methodological criticism of neoclassical price theory; see FA Hayek *Individualism and Economic Order* (Chicago: University of Chicago Press 1948) 92–94; FA Hayek, 'The Use of Knowledge in Society' (1945) 35(3) *American Economic Review* 519, 319–20, 330.

[45] FA Hayek, 'Competition as Discovery Procedure' translated by Marcellus S. Snow (2002) 5(3) *The Quarterly Journal of Austrian Economics* 9.

[46] Ibid; Hayek, The Use of Knowledge in Society' (n 44); Polanyi (n 32); V Ostrom, 'Polycentricity: The Structural Basis of Self-Governing Systems' in F Sabetti and P Dragos Aligica (eds), *Choice, Rules and Collective Action: The Ostroms on the Study of Institutions and Governance* (Colchester: ECPR Press 2014) 45; RR Nelson, 'Uncertainty, Learning, and the Economics of Parallel Research and Development Efforts' (1961) 43(4) *The Review of Economics and Statistics* 351.

polycentric markets to facilitate broad-based parallel experimentation and learning by multiple, independent decision-making centres as a central force of economic innovation and progress. Along similar lines, the work of Daron Acemoglu and James A. Robinson documents the historical importance of inclusive economic institutions characterised by broad-based economic opportunities for economic progress and innovation across global economic history.[47]

Different strands in economic research thus suggest that there is an added value in having a polycentric market structure in which equal competitive opportunities are spread amongst many players who embark on a diversity of innovation paths and engage in parallel experimentation.[48] Even if only the technological solution of one firm eventually turned out to be the most efficient or valuable, there is an added value in protecting the 'paths not taken'.[49] Without multiple players experimenting in parallel, society would not have gained the necessary knowledge and information to decide which technological solution is the most effective one. Keeping markets open for parallel experimentation is hence tantamount to keeping the future open for new knowledge being generated endogenously by the competitive process.

Most importantly, the work of Acemoglu and Robinson suggests that it is not sufficient to protect the economic opportunities of market participants against actual or likely interference to ensure that they have the incentives to experiment independently. Instead, they suggest that the mere presence of a powerful agent – be it a despotic state or dominant private player – may stymie the incentives of other market players to engage in parallel experimentation. This is because the ability of the powerful agent to appropriate the investments in and gains of innovation by smaller market participants may deter the latter from investing in innovation in the first place.[50] Acemoglu and Robinson add an interesting economic dimension to the insight of the republican paradigm that the very presence of domination may have a psychological effect on weaker parties that pushes them towards ingratiating behaviour.[51] It also shows that the mere presence of concentrated economic power and its psychological impact on the incentives of other market participants may have an economic cost that is not captured by the static consumer welfare standard.

[47] D Acemoglu and JA Robinson, *Why Nations Fail: The Origins of Power, Prosperity, and Poverty* (London: Profile Books 2013) 76–77, 208, 319–34.

[48] See, for instance, WM Cohen and S Klepper, 'The Tradeoff between Firm Size and Diversity in the Pursuit of Technological Progress' (1992) 4(1) *Small Business Economics* 1.

[49] I Letina, 'The Road Not Taken: Competition and the R&D Portfolio' (2016) 47(2) *The RAND Journal of Economics* 433.

[50] D Acemoglu and JA Robinson, *The Narrow Corridor* (London: Viking-Penguin 2019) 113–14, 125, 132, 142–44. For a model exploring how a monopolistic incumbent can pre-empt innovation efforts of potential entrants RJ Gilbert and DMG Newbery, 'Preemptive Patenting and the Persistence of Monopoly' (1982) 72(3) *The American Economic Review* 514, 515–20, 524.

[51] P Pettit, *Republicanism: A Theory of Freedom and Government* (Oxford: Clarendon Press; Oxford University Press 1997) 24–25.

By promoting a more deconcentrated market structure and securing a modally robust and resilient protection of economic liberty against arbitrary interference, not only in the present but across a range of relevant possible worlds, a more republican approach to competition law may importantly enhance the incentives of smaller competitors to innovate and further long-term consumer welfare. Conduct that allows a monopolist to foreclose competitors and appropriate their surplus (FHGI) may harm consumer welfare, even if it does not lead to immediate price increases (Scenarios 1 and 2) and/or the affected competitors are not as efficient as the dominant firm (Scenarios 2 and 4). This would be the case if this surplus (FHGI) enables competitors to invest in parallel experimentation and innovation. From the perspective of dynamic competition, even competition law intervention in Scenarios 1, 2, and 4 might be warranted if dominant firm conduct undermines broad-based decentralised learning and innovation.

This dynamic efficiency argument in support of a more republican approach markedly differs from the predominant Schumpeterian[52] take on the relationship between market structure and innovation, which regularly celebrates monopoly power as a driver of economic progress.[53] Instead of focusing on the incentives of large incumbents to innovate, this republican dynamic efficiency argument turns our attention to the incentives of smaller competitors to invest in innovation. Unlike the Schumpeterian paradigm, the republican account offers a more inclusive vision of innovation in which not only the opportunity to innovate but also the gains of innovation are shared more evenly amongst multiple players instead of being concentrated amongst a handful of large firms.

In conclusion, contrary to what proponents of laissez-faire antitrust conventionally claim, the replacement of the consumer welfare standard by a competitive process standard that promotes a structuralist, republican approach to competition law must not necessarily run counter to the goal of (consumer) welfare maximisation. However, while this insight may persuade some sceptics, it also carries a discomforting message. It implies that competition policy by emulating Pareto-efficient outcomes or revealed consumer preferences may not necessarily maximise consumer welfare. One can indeed conceive of a situation where consumers genuinely prefer a relatively deconcentrated market structure – for instance, because it ensures option value or reduces domination and thereby protects a democratic society and polity – but behave in a way that actually contributes to greater concentration when they engage in market transactions. This would, for instance, be the case if consumers with a genuine preference for a deconcentrated market structure 'free ride'

[52] JA Schumpeter, *Capitalism, Socialism and Democracy* [1942] (New York: Harper & Row 1962) 82–88 and entire chapter 7.

[53] *Verizon Communications Inc v Law Offices of Curtis Trinko* 540 US 398 (2004) 414; *FTC v Qualcomm Inc.* 969 F. 3d 974 (9th Cir. 2020) 990.

by buying the cheaper product from large producers in the hope that others continue to buy from a smaller, less efficient producer.[54]

From this perspective, the preservation of a relatively deconcentrated and polycentric market structure may constitute a positive externality or public good, which is actually valued by consumers but is not internalised in the market price that they (are willing to) pay because its benefits, for instance, in the form of greater option value, are difficult to appropriate.[55] This sheds a different light on the role of the structural approach of the republican antitrust tradition. Instead of emulating the functioning of efficient markets, it approaches excessive concentration as a market failure that results from the unrestrained interaction of market forces. From this perspective, competition law operates on a similar logic as environmental regulation – while environmental regulation seeks to avert a situation where the unrestricted interplay of market forces results in an excessive level of pollution, competition law would seek to keep the level of economic concentration to a sustainable level.[56]

8.4 THE OPERATIONALISATION OF A COMPETITION–DEMOCRACY NEXUS 4.0

This observation raises the question of how competition law could achieve a 'sustainable' level of concentration that is conducive to and compatible with a republican democracy. The answer to this question is anything but obvious, most notably because the republican antitrust tradition lacks a clear and administrable benchmark that, akin to the consumer welfare standard, conclusively indicates at what point the concentration of economic power becomes excessive. Unlike the consumer welfare standard, a republican competition law approach struggles to provide a clear-cut limiting principle that indicates when competition law intervention in Scenarios 1 to 4 is warranted.

The synopsis of the various strands of the republican antitrust tradition in the United States and Europe in this book shows that such a limiting principle is, however, not a prerequisite to put into effect the idea of a competition–democracy nexus. There is not one unique but a number of different strategies to operationalise

[54] H Hovenkamp, 'Antitrust Policy after Chicago' (1985) 84(2) *Michigan Law Review* 213, 242–44. The Chicago scholars have clearly excluded these values from their definition of wealth maximisation, by defining wealth narrowly as everything to which consumers attach value backed by dollars. RA Posner, 'Utilitarianism, Economics, and Legal Theory' (1979) 8(1) *The Journal of Legal Studies* 103, 120.

[55] Free riding is one reason why markets often fail to generate option value, which explains its public-good character, see Weisbrod (n 30) 473–76; Cicchetti and Freeman (n 30) 537–38.

[56] The assumption being that concentrated economic power or its consequences are, like environmental pollution, costly to reverse; see Arrow and Fisher (n 30) 319. For a similar argument describing excessive levels of concentration as a market failure, see F Böhm, *Freiheit und Ordnung in der Marktwirtschaft* [1971] (Baden-Baden: Nomos 1980) 215–16.

the ideal of republican liberty by keeping the level of economic concentration to a sustainable level. Most importantly, maintaining a sustainable level of concentration does not necessarily presuppose a direct regulation of concentration through situational structuralism, as it was contemplated by US courts, as well as the Harvard and the early Ordoliberal Schools. This situational structuralism is fraught with difficulties. It is virtually impossible objectively to determine ex ante the exact level above which industry concentration is no longer sustainable. The implementation of situational structuralism through the breakup of large firms will also inevitably sacrifice substantial efficiencies.[57] The conduct-based structuralism envisaged by the Ordoliberals Böhm and Mestmäcker, and implemented by the formative EU case law, however, shows that the level of industry concentration can also be regulated indirectly by securing a sufficient degree of market contestability. The various strategies and elements of situational and conduct-based structuralism differ in the degree to which they proactively seek to promote republican liberty by regulating the level of concentration through positive action, and hence their degree of intrusiveness and welfare costs.

8.4.1 *A Recalibration of the Error–Cost Framework*

The least intrusive way to realign contemporary competition law with a more republican approach is the recalibration of the conventional laissez-faire error–cost framework that, in its current form, is slanted towards non-intervention. Such a recalibration would give greater weight to the costs of type II errors; or, in other words, the foregone 'accuracy benefits' of antitrust intervention against truly anticompetitive conduct.[58] Not least, option value theory provides a number of valid arguments as to why it is rational to err in certain circumstances on the side of antitrust intervention (type I errors). This is notably the case in markets characterised by considerable uncertainty about the future value of different alternative options and/or the risk that some of these options are eliminated irreversibly because, for instance, a dominant firm benefits from substantial network effects and engages in conduct that may tip the market in its favour on a lasting basis.[59] In the face of uncertainty and irreversibility, what has been criticised as 'precautionary antitrust'[60] by some may actually constitute an economically sensible policy.[61]

57 For an insightful discussion, see RA Posner, *Antitrust Law* (Chicago: University of Chicago Press 2001) 111–17.

58 H First and S Weber Waller, 'Antitrust's Democracy Deficit' (2013) 81(5) *Fordham Law Review* 2543, 2570–72; JB Baker, 'Taking the Error Out of "Error Cost" Analysis: What's Wrong with Antitrust's Right' (2015) 80(1) *Antitrust Law Journal* 1.

59 Arrow and Fisher (n 30) 319.

60 A Portuese, 'Precautionary Antitrust: A Precautionary Tale in European Competition Policy' in K Mathis and A Tor (eds), *Law and Economics of Regulation* (Cham: Springer International Publishing 2021) 203.

61 Farrell (n 36) 170.

A more precautionary error–cost framework would, in the case of doubt, counsel that antitrust law should err on the side of intervention to preserve the contestability of market power, notably in markets where the harm resulting from erroneous non-intervention is particularly high. Erring on the side of contestability would not only ensure the openness of innovation paths and future technological option value but it would also lead, in the medium to long term, to a reduction in industry concentration if new or residual competitors erode the market power of the dominant incumbent.

8.4.2 A *Recalibration of the Standard of Harm*

A second, slightly bolder avenue to incorporate elements of the republican approach into contemporary competition law would consist of reconsidering the transition towards a purely probabilistic standard of harm. This proposal may also turn out to be less controversial than it at first sight appears. Indeed, the decision-theoretic literature shows that to minimise decision errors, competition authorities and courts should consider not only the likelihood but also the magnitude of harm of impugned conduct. For instance, when certain unilateral conduct or mergers have the potential to result in harm of a sizeable order of magnitude, then it may be economically reasonable to prohibit them, even if the harm is unlikely to materialise. In the presence of high-impact but low-probability harm, decision theory suggests that antitrust law should rely on a 'balance of harm' standard that is less demanding than the balance of probabilities standard and should intervene, even though the probability of harm lies below 50 per cent.[62] Such a possibilist standard of harm would be particularly indicated in situations where harm is irreversible[63] or where (non-measurable) uncertainty does not allow the assignment of specific probabilities to counterfactual events.[64] Lowering the standard of harm would, for instance, be appropriate in markets that are characterised by high barriers of entry, substantial network effects, or considerable uncertainty about future innovation.

8.4.3 A *Greater Role of Differentiated Rule-Like Presumptions*

Reinforcing the role of rule-like presumptions constitutes a third avenue through which competition law could implement a more republican approach. The

62 CF Beckner and SC Salop, 'Decision Theory and Antitrust Rules' (1999) 67(1) *Antitrust Law Journal* 41, 61–62; L Kaplow, 'Efficiencies in Merger Analysis' (2021) 83(3) *Antitrust Law Journal* 557, 46–47.

63 Arrow and Fisher (n 30) 319.

64 For the distinction between risk as 'measurable uncertainty' that can be captured by assigning probabilities to specific events or outcomes and (non-measurable) uncertainty, in the strict sense, to which no probability can be attributed, see F Knight, *Risk, Uncertainty and Profit* (Boston: Houghton Mifflin 1921) 20.

transition towards a possibilist standard of harm and a greater role of rule-like presumptions would dissociate competition law from the probabilistic logic that typifies the negative concept of liberty and would enable it to secure a more modally robust form of republican liberty.[65] Rule-like presumptions may thereby also prove to be an effective tool to indirectly erode excessive concentration as they make conduct that tends to reduce market contestability unavailable.

Giving greater weight to and expanding the scope of presumptions must not necessarily result in the revival of 'old-school' formalism. Economic literature and the EU's experience, for instance, in the area of vertical restraints,[66] suggest that rule-like presumptions can be fine-tuned and updated in light of new economic insights to reduce excessive welfare losses.[67] For instance, rule-like presumptions can be tailored to markets that are characterised by insufficient contestability. Rule-like presumptions can also be adjusted with respect to the type of market participants they protect and the duration of this protection. It is conceivable to design rule-like presumptions in a way that shields both equally and less efficient competitors from exclusionary conduct for a certain period of time with a view to protecting nascent competitors and entrants. Once that period has lapsed, the presumptions could be made conditional on an efficiency requirement. A more bespoke differentiation of rule-like presumptions allows for a more granular approach that may enhance consumer welfare to a greater extent than the hard-and-fast application of the under-inclusive as-efficient competitor principle and test. At the same time, in defining the range of agents whose economic liberty is guaranteed robust protection by competition law more broadly, the finetuning of rule-like presumptions would also ensure a greater inclusiveness of the competitive process than laissez-faire antitrust does under the as-efficient competitor principle.

8.4.4 *The Blending of Conduct-Based and Situational Structuralism*

Embracing optimally differentiated presumptions as a way to revive the republican antitrust tradition does not preclude the occasional recourse to situational structuralism. The use of more heavy-handed regulatory or structural deconcentration interventions may be an effective or even necessary tool to enhance contestability,

[65] P Pettit, 'Freedom and Probability: A Comment on Goodin and Jackson' (2008) 36(2) *Philosophy & Public Affairs* 206, 218–19; C List, 'Republican Freedom and the Rule of Law' (2006) 5(2) *Politics, Philosophy & Economics* 201, 216.

[66] Commission Regulation (EC) No 2790/1999 on the Application of Article 81(3) of the Treaty to Categories of Vertical Agreements and Concerted Practices, [1999] OJ L 336/21.

[67] A Christiansen and W Kerber, 'Competition Policy with Optimally Differentiated Rules Instead of per se Rules vs. Rule of Reason' (2006) 2(2) *Journal of Competition Law and Economics* 215, 220–29.

notably in those markets that are characterised by consistently high levels of concentration and barriers to entry. The various strands of structuralism envisaged by the Harvard and Ordoliberal Schools suggest that situational and conduct-based structuralism can be blended into a multi-layered competition policy, where antitrust intervention is escalated as a function of the degree of domination or entrenched concentration prevailing in a given market. Arguably, the proposed EU Digital Markets Act, the UK New Pro-Competition regime for digital markets, and various US bills to regulate digital platforms contemplate such a multi-layered approach that combines a number of differentiated and modal rule-like presumptions[68] with more heavy-handed enforcement tools[69] that are directly geared towards increasing the contestability of concentrated market structures.[70]

At least on a conceptual level, there is no reason why the greater role of rule-like presumptions and direct interventions against excessive economic concentration should necessarily be limited to the digital sphere and not be used against conduct by non-digital firms that have similar adverse effects on competition,[71] and/or in other industries characterised by limited contestability and the importance of technological option value.[72] Digital markets are not the only markets that exhibit high levels of industry concentration. There are a large number of other sectors, for instance, container shipping[73] and the agrochemical industry,[74] that are highly concentrated oligopolistic markets and play a crucial role in our daily lives because they shape our nutrition and operate as the backbone of the international supply chains of the goods we consume. Instead of merely focusing on digital markets, a consistent republican approach would call for a holistic and coherent approach towards high concentration levels across industries.

68 Regulation (EU) 2022/1925 on Contestable and Fair Markets in the Digital Sector (Digital Markets Act) (n 3) Articles 5–7; A New Pro-competition Regime for Digital Markets (n 3) paras. 4.33–44; Digital Markets, Competition and Consumers Bill (n 3) ss. 19–21.

69 Regulation (EU) 2022/1925 on Contestable and Fair Markets in the Digital Sector (Digital Markets Act) (n 3) Articles 12, 19; A New Pro-competition Regime for Digital Markets (n 3) paras. 4.60–81; Digital Markets, Competition and Consumers Bill (n 3) ss. 45–50; H.R.3825–Ending Platform Monopolies Act ('EPM Act') (n 3) s. 2 (a); H.R.3816–American Choice and Innovation Online Act ('ACIO Act') (n 3) s. 2 (f) (2) (D).

70 E Deutscher, 'Reshaping Digital Competition: The New Platform Regulations and the Future of Modern Antitrust' (2022) 67(2) *Antitrust Bulletin* 302, 310–12, 331.

71 Ibid. 331.

72 For instance, the European Commission considered the creation of a 'New Competition Tool' that would enable it to address structural competition issues across digital and non-digital industries, see Inception Impact Assessment–New Competition Tool ('NCT'), Document Ares (2020)2877634, 3.

73 O Merk and A Teodoro, 'Alternative Approaches to Measuring Concentration in Liner Shipping' (2022) 24(4) *Maritime Economics & Logistics* 723.

74 I Lianos and D Katalevsky, 'Merger Activity in the Factors of Production Segments of the Food Value Chain: A Critical Assessment of the Bayer/Monsanto Merger' (2017). Policy Paper Series 1/2017.

8.5 MANAGING THE REPUBLICAN PARADOX

This book shows that competition law has a number of levers that it could use to adjust to and reinvigorate the republican tradition, and thereby promote a republican form of economic liberty that is compatible with a republican ideal of a society and polity of free and equals. Adopting a more precautionary error–cost framework, recalibrating the standard of harm, expanding the use of rule-like presumptions, discarding the as-efficient competitor test, and having recourse to tailored structural interventions are only a few of the conceivable pathways through which a reinvigorated republican antitrust approach could promote a competition–democracy nexus 4.0. These different levers play a complementary role and may be blended with one another. The more that the variables considered above are recalibrated, the more radical will be the departure from the predominant laissez-faire antitrust paradigm and the more consequential will be the shift towards a republican approach.

While protecting a polycentric market structure and protecting consumer welfare do not always have to be at loggerheads, their relationship is not without tension. A transition towards republican antitrust will inevitably entail costs. A major failure of the earlier republican antitrust tradition was to simply obfuscate this tension and ignore the republican paradox, which describes the fact that republican liberty cannot be maximised across all domains without sacrificing (Pareto) efficiency.[75] Any attempt to move competition law towards a more republican approach would need to acknowledge this trade-off head-on by explicitly devising strategies and mechanisms to manage, if not to escape, the republican paradox. This trade-off between protecting republican liberty and efficiency losses will depend on the specific choice and combination of the above instruments, which will ultimately determine how much welfare and efficiency are sacrificed in the pursuit of a more resilient form of economic liberty.

This trade-off between efficiency and republican liberty will operate along three dimensions: (i) the scope of the liberty protected in terms of preventing conditions (y), (ii) the robustness of this protection in terms of the range of actions (z), and (iii) the range of agents (x) whose liberty is protected.[76] The republican paradox may be attenuated by compromising on the robustness of the protection of republican liberty. Instead of endorsing a possibilist and probabilistically unweighted protection of liberty across a range of relevant possible worlds, republicans could at least in part accept a more probabilistic and hence less robust protection of liberty. This would involve a narrowing of the relevant alternative possible worlds across which competition law maximises non-interference, for instance, by calibrating the lowering of the standard of harm to specific markets where the costs of type II errors are

75 C List, 'The Impossibility of a Paretian Republican?: Some Comments on Pettit and Sen' (2004) 20(1) *Economics and Philosophy* 65, 73–75.

76 List, 'Republican Freedom and the Rule of Law' (n 65) 217–18.

particularly high or ensuring the rebuttability of presumptions of anticompetitiveness. Another way to alleviate the republican paradox is to restrict the domain, or more generally speaking the range of preference or right sets, for which a robust, modal protection of liberty ought to be guaranteed, for instance, by limiting the scope of rule-like presumptions to a relatively narrow set of conduct that is considered to be a preventing condition of economic liberty. A third way to address the republican paradox consists of limiting the type of economic agents whose liberty ought to be protected by only discarding the as-efficient competitor test in a limited set of markets or for a limited period of time.[77] Thus, robust protection of liberty may only be possible for a restricted domain of preference or right sets, or a limited category of agents. Consequently, a shift towards a more republican approach with a view to reinvigorating the competition–democracy nexus would require competition law to strike a balance between the scope (preventing conditions (y)), robustness (actions (z)), and inclusiveness (agents (x)) of (republican) economic liberty of market participants and efficiency.

Such a recalibration of antitrust law towards a republican approach and a competition–democracy nexus will come at a certain cost and will entail many challenges. The mission of competition law would no longer be to merely emulate and restore efficient markets. Rather, it would have to operate along similar lines as environmental regulation and even intervene in otherwise efficient markets to maintain a socially and politically sustainable level of economic concentration. This reinterpretation of the role of competition law as 'anti-concentration law' would demand a general agreement about the fact that even otherwise efficient markets fail to 'price in' all of the economic, societal, and political costs of excessively concentrated markets. It would also require some consensus about when economic power and concentration reach a level that gives rise to domination. Some of the major challenges that lie ahead include developing new metrics of economic power and its contestability.

Even though a republican approach does not have to automatically clash with consumer welfare and efficiency, it is impossible to secure republican liberty across an unlimited domain of relevant worlds without sacrificing Pareto efficiency. This republican paradox is at the origin of what Robert Bork lucidly pinpointed as the antitrust paradox:[78] On the one hand, competition law seeks to enhance rivalry between firms; while on the other hand, once the successful winner of the rivalrous competitive contest grows too powerful, competition law goes after it in order to preserve the economic liberty of consumers and competitors. To Bork, the two propositions could not be squared. As long as the paradox was not eliminated,

[77] List, 'The Impossibility of a Paretian Republican?' (n 75) 75–77; A Sen, 'The Impossibility of a Paretian Liberal' (1970) 78(1) *Journal of Political Economy* 152, 153.

[78] RH Bork, *The Antitrust Paradox: A Policy at War with Itself* [1978] (New York: Maxwell Macmillan 1993).

competition law was condemned to be at war with itself. To escape the republican paradox, Bork and fellow Chicago scholars successfully introduced (theoretical) Pareto efficiency as the basic decision rule for antitrust law. The consumer welfare standard redefined economic liberty so narrowly that it coincided with economic efficiency. Although the proposed solution of aligning competition law with the single goal of wealth maximisation was certainly an elegant and appealing way to avoid tensions between conflicting values, it did not resolve the paradox itself other than defining it away. The tensions between economic liberty and efficiency remained. However, in embracing the consumer welfare standard, laissez-faire antitrust internalised the Chicagoan proposition that value conflicts no longer had a place in competition law.

Ongoing controversies about the implications of growing levels of economic concentration and the market power of digital platforms show that these value conflicts between economic liberty and efficiency have anything but disappeared. On the contrary, they are once again on full display. The way in which Bork and the antitrust orthodoxy resolved the republican antitrust paradox no longer appears to provide a satisfactory answer. In a similar way to the republican antitrust tradition, laissez-faire antitrust ended up in obfuscating the republican paradox by couching value judgments in the economic language of the consumer welfare standard and error–cost framework.

Bork was correct in pinpointing the antitrust paradox as the central challenge for competition law and policy. However, Bork and his fellow architects of laissez-faire antitrust erred in perceiving it as an existential threat to competition law that can and ought to be simply eradicated. They failed to recognise that the protection of republican liberty often involves the loss of some efficiencies and that this is not a problem as such – in our liberal democracies, we accept such sacrifices every day.[79] Rather than denying its existence or relevance, the essential challenge and task of competition law are to manage the republican paradox by clearly articulating trade-offs between liberty and efficiency, and by wrestling with the question of how they can be balanced and the tensions minimised. Managing the republican antitrust paradox instead of obfuscating it is anything but easy. It may render competition law less consistent and messier. It may also entail the sacrifice of considerable efficiencies. But less consistency and efficiency may be the cost of reinvigorating the symbiosis between competitive markets and republican democracy.

[79] List, 'The Impossibility of a Paretian Republican?' (n 75) 78.

Bibliography

TABLE OF CASES

English Common Law Cases (Alphabetical Order)

The Blacksmith's Case [1587] 74 ER 643.
Colgate v Bacheler [1569] 78 ER 1097.
Darcy v Allein ('The Case of Monopolies') [1602] 77 ER 1260.
Davenant v Hurdis [1599] 72 ER 769.
Dyer's Case (1414) 2 Hen V, fol 5, pl 26.
Gloucester Grammar School's Case (1410) YB 11 Hen IV, fo pl 201, 23.
Ipswich Tailors' Case [1614] 77 ER 1218.
Mitchel v Reynolds [1711] 24 ER 347.
Mogul Steamship Co Ltd v McGregor, Gow & Co [1892] AC 25.

Supreme Court of the United States (Alphabetical Order)

Addyston Pipe & Steel Co. v United States 175 US 211 (1899).
Albrecht v Globe-Democrat Publishing Co. 390 US 145 (1968).
American Tobacco Co. v United States 328 US 781 (1946).
Appalachian Coals, Inc. v United States 288 US 344 (1933).
Ariz. v Maricopa County Medical Soc. 457 US 332 (1982).
Aspen Skiing Co. v Aspen Highlands Skiing Corp. 472 US 585 (1985).
Broadcast Music, Inc. v Columbia Broadcasting System, Inc. 441 U.S. 1 (1979).
Brooke Group v Brown & Williamson Tobacco Corp. 509 U.S. 209 (1993).
Brown Shoe Co. Inc. v United States 370 U.S. 294 (1962).
California Dental Assn. v FTC 526 U.S. 756 (1999).
Cargill, Inc. v Monfort of Colorado, Inc. 479 U.S. 104 (1986).
Chicago Board of Trade v United States 246 U.S. 231 (1918).
Cont'l T.V. v GTE Sylvania 433 U.S. 36 (1978).
Copperweld Corp. et al. v Independence Tube Corp. 467 U.S. 752 (1984).
Dr. Miles Medical Co. v John D. Park & Sons Co. 220 U.S. 373 (1911).
Eastern Railroad Presidents Conference v Noerr Motor Freight, Inc. 365 U.S. 127, 135 (1961).
Eastern States Lumber Ass'n v United States 234 U.S. 600 (1914).

Eastman Kodak Co. v Image Tech. Servs. 504 U.S. 451 (1992).
Fashion Originators' Guild, Inc. v FTC 312 U.S. 457 (1941).
FTC v Actavis et al. 570 U.S. 136 (2013).
Fortner Enterprises v U.S. Steel (Fortner I) 394 U.S. 495 (1969).
FTC v Anheuser-Busch, Inc. 363 U.S. 536 (1960).
FTC v Indiana Federation of Dentists 476 U.S. 447 (1986).
FTC v Procter & Gamble 386 U.S. 568 (1967).
Henry v Dick Co. 224 U.S. 1 (1911).
Illinois Tool Works Inc. v Independent Ink, Inc. 547 U.S. 28 (2006).
Int'l Salt Co. v United States 332 U.S. 392 (1947).
Jefferson Parish Hosp. Dist. No. 2 v Hyde 466 U.S. 2 (1984).
Kiefer-Stewart Co. v Seagram & Sons 340 U.S. 211 (1951).
Klor's, Inc. v Broadway-Hale Stores, Inc. 359 U.S. 207 (1959).
Leegin Creative Leather Prods. v PSKS, Inc. 551 U.S. 877 (2007).
Matsushita Elec. Indus. Co. v Zenith Radio Corp. 475 U.S. 574 (1986).
Montague & Co. v Lowry 193 U.S. 38 (1904).
Moore v Mead's Fine Bread Co. 348 U.S. 115 (1954).
Motion Picture Co. v Universal Film Co. 243 U.S. 502 (1917).
National Collegiate Athletic Ass'n v Board of Regents 468 U.S. 85 (1984).
National Cotton Oil Co. v Texas 197 U.S. 115 (1905).
National Soc. of Professional Engineers v United States 435 U.S. 679 (1978).
Northern Pacific RY. Co. v United States 356 U.S. 1 (1958).
Northern Securities Co. v United States 193 U.S. 197 (1904).
Northwest Wholesale Stationers, Inc. v Pacific Stationery & Printing Co. 472 U.S. 284 (1985).
Ohio v American Express Co. 585 U.S. ___ (2018).
Pacific Bell Telephone Co. dba AT&T California, et al. v linkLine Communications, Inc. et al. 555 U.S. 438 (2009).
Radiant Burners, Inc. v Peoples Gas Light & Coke Co. 364 U.S. 656 (1960).
Reiter v Sonotone Corp. 442 U.S. 330 (1979).
Schine Theatres v United States 334 U.S. 110 (1948).
Silver v New York Stock Exchange, 373 U.S. 341 (1963).
Standard Fashion Company v Magrane-Houston Company 346 U.S. 258 (1921).
Standard Oil Co. of New Jersey v United States 221 U.S. 1 (1911).
Standard Oil Co. v United States 337 U.S. 293 (1949).
State Oil Co. v Khan 522 U.S. 3 (1997).
Tampa Electric Co. v Nashville Coal Co. 365 U.S. 320 (1961).
Times-Picayune Pub. Co. v United States 345 U.S. 594 (1953).
Timken Roller Bearing Co. v United States 341 U.S. 593 (1951).
U.S. Steel Corp v Fortner Enterprises (Fortner II) 429 U.S. 610 (1977).
U.S. v Citizens & Southern National Bank 422 U.S. 86 (1975).
United Mine Workers v Pennington 381 U.S. 657 (1965).
United Shoe Mach. Co. v United States 258 U.S. 451 (1922).
United States v American Tobacco 221 U.S. 106 (1911).
United States v Arnold, Schwinn & Co. 388 U.S. 365 (1967).
United States v Colgate & Co. 250 U.S. 300 (1919).
United States v Columbia Steel Co. 334 U.S. 495 (1948).
United States v Container Corp. 393 U.S. 333 (1969).
United States v Continental Can Co. 378 U.S. 441 (1964).
United States v E. C. Knight Co. 156 U.S. 1 (1895).

United States v General Dynamics 415 U.S. 486 (1974).
United States v Griffith 334 U.S. 100 (1948).
United States v Grinnell Corp. 284 U.S. 563 (1966).
United States v Int. Harvester Co. 274 U.S. 693 (1927).
United States v Joint Traffic Ass'n 171 U.S. 505 (1898).
United States v Marine Bancorporation 418 U.S. 602 (1974).
United States v Pabst Brewing Co. 384 U.S. 546 (1966).
United States v Paramount Pictures 334 U.S. 131 (1948).
United States v Philadelphia National Bank 374 U.S. 321 (1963).
United States v Sealy, Inc. 388 U.S. 350 (1967).
United States v Socony-Vacuum Oil Co. 310 U.S. 150 (1940).
United States v Swift & Co. 286 U.S. 106 (1932).
United States v Topco Assocs. Inc. 405 U.S. 596 (1972).
United States v Trans-Missouri Freight Asso. 166 U.S. 290 (1897).
United States v Trenton Potteries Co. 273 U.S. 392 (1927).
United States v United Shoe Mach. Co. 247 U.S. 32 (1918).
United States v United States Gypsum Co. 438 U.S. 422 (1978).
United States v U.S. Steel Corp. 251 U.S. 417 (1920).
United States v Von's Grocery Co. 384 U.S. 270 (1966).
Utah Pie Co. v Continental Baking Co. 386 U.S. 685 (1967).
Verizon Communications Inc v Law Offices of Curtis Trinko 540 U.S. 398 (2004).
Weyerhaeuser Co. v Ross-Simmons Hardwood Lumber Co. 549 U.S. 312 (2007).
White Motor Co. v United States 372 U.S. 253 (1963).

United States Court of Appeals and District Courts (Order by Circuit)

United States Court of Appeals for the First Circuit *Barry Wright Corp. v ITT Grinnell Corp.* 724 F.2d 227 (1st Cir. 1983).
United States Court of Appeals for the Second Circuit *United States v Alcoa* 148 F.2d 416 (2d Cir. 1945).
United States Court of Appeals for the Second Circuit *Berkey Photo, Inc. v Eastman Kodak Co.* F.2d 263 (2d Cir. 1979).
United States Court of Appeals for the Third Circuit *ZF Meritor, LLC v Eaton Corp.* 696 F.3d 254 (3d Cir. 2012).
United States Court of Appeals for the Third Circuit *Eisai, Inc. v Sanofi Aventis U.S. LLC* 821 F.3d 394 (3d Cir. 2015).
United States Court of Appeals for the Seventh Circuit *MCI Communications Corp. v American Tel. & Tel. Co.* 708 F.2d 1081 (7th Cir. 1983).
United States Court of Appeals for the Seventh Circuit *Roland Machinery Company v Dresser Industries Inc.* 749 F. 2d 380 (7th Cir. 1984).
United States Court of Appeals for the Ninth Circuit *Cal. Computer Prod. v Int'l Business Machines* 613 F.2d 727 (9th Cir. 1979).
United States Court of Appeals for the Ninth Circuit *Omega Environmental, Inc. v Gilbarco, Inc.* 127 F. 3d 1157 (9th Cir. 1997).
United States Court of Appeals for the Ninth Circuit *Cascade Health Solutions v PeaceHealth* 502 F.3d 895 (9th Cir. 2007).
United States Court of Appeals for the Ninth Circuit *FTC v Qualcomm Inc.* 969 F. 3d 974 (9th Cir. 2020).

United States Court of Appeals for the Eleventh Circuit *McWane, Inc. v FTC* 783 F.3d 814 (11th Cir. 2015).
United States Court of Appeals for the District of Columbia Circuit *United States v Baker Hughes, Inc.* 908 F. 2d 981 (D.C. Cir. 1990).
United States Court of Appeals for the District of Columbia *FTC v H.J. Heinz Co.* 246 F.3d 708 (D.C. Cir. 2001).
United States Court of Appeals for the District of Columbia *United States v Microsoft Corporation* 253 F.3d 34 (D.C. Cir. 2001).
United States Court of Appeals for the District of Columbia *PolyGram Holding, Inc. v FTC* 416 F.3d 29 (D.C. Cir. 2005).

Other United States Courts

Supreme Court of Michigan *Richardson v Buhl et al.* 43 N.W. 1102, 77 Mich. 632.
United States District Court for the District of Massachusetts *United States v United Shoe Machinery Corp.* 110 F. Supp. 295 (D. Mass. 1953).

Court of Justice of the European Union (Chronological Order)

Case 56/64 *Consten and Grundig v Commission of the EEC* ECLI:EU:C:1966:41.
Case 56/65 *Société Technique Minière v Maschinenbau Ulm* ECLI:EU:C:1966:38.
Case 41/69 *Chemiefarma v Commission* ECLI:EU:C:1970:71.
Case 40/70 *Sirena v Eda* ECLI:EU:C:1971:18
Case 6/72 *Europemballage Corporation and Continental Can Company v Commission* ECLI:EU:C:1973:22.
Case 40/73 *Suiker Unie and Others v Commission* ECLI:EU:C:1975:174.
Case 27/76 *United Brands v Commission* ECLI:EU:C:1978:22.
Case 85/76 *Hoffmann-La Roche v Commission* ECLI:EU:C:1979:36.
Case 19/77 *Miller v Commission* ECLI:EU:C:1978:19.
Case 77/77 *B.P. v Commission* ECLI:EU:C:1978:141.
Case 32/78 *BMW Belgium v Commission* ECLI:EU:C:1979:191.
Case 172/80 *Züchner v Bayerische Vereinsbank* ECLI:EU:C:1981:178.
Case 322/81 *Michelin v Commission* ECLI:EU:C:1983:313.
Case 86/82 *Hasselblad v Commission* ECLI:EU:C:1984:65.
Case 96/82 *IAZ v Commission* ECLI:EU:C:1983:310.
Case 107/82 *AEG v Commission* ECLI:EU:C:1983:293.
Case 123/83 *BNIC v Clair* ECLI:EU:C:1985:33.
Case 243/83 *Binon v AMP* ECLI:EU:C:1985:284.
Case 42/84 *Remia v Commission* ECLI:EU:C:1985:327.
Joined Cases 142 and 156/84 *BAT and Reynolds v Commission* ECLI:EU:C:1987:490.
Case 311/85 *VVR v Sociale Dienst van de Plaatselijke en Gewestelijke Overheidsdiensten* ECLI:EU:C:1987:418.
Case C-62/86 *AKZO v Commission* ECLI:EU:C:1991:286.
Case 66/86 *Ahmed Saeed Flugreisen and Others v Zentrale zur Bekämpfung unlauteren Wettbewerbs* ECLI:EU:C:1989:140.
Case 136/86 *BNIC v Aubert.* ECLI:EU:C:1987:524.
Case 27/87 *Erauw-Jacquery v La Hesbignonne* ECLI:EU:C:1988:183.
Case C-18/88 *RTT v GB-Inno-BM* ECLI:EU:C:1991:474.
Case C-202/88 *France v Commission* ECLI:EU:C:1991:120.

Case C-199/92 P *Hüls v Commission* ECLI:EU:C:1999:358.
Case C-235/92 P *Montecatini v Commission* ECLI:EU:C:1999:362.
Case C-266/93 *Bundeskartellamt v Volkswagen and VAG Leasing* ECLI:EU:C:1995:345.
Case C-399/93 *Oude Luttikhuis and Others v Verenigde Coöperatieve Melkindustrie Coberco* ECLI:EU:C:1995:434.
Case C-68/94 *France and Société commerciale des potasses et de l'azote and Entreprise minière et chimique v Commission* ECLI:EU:C:1998:148.
Case C-333/94 P *Tetra Pak v Commission* ECLI:EU:C:1996:436.
Case C-7/95 P *Deere v Commission* ECLI:EU:C:1998:256.
Case C-306/96 *Javico v Yves Saint Laurent Parfums* ECLI:EU:C:1998:173.
Case C-395/96 P *Compagnie Maritime Belge Transports and Others v Commission* ECLI:EU:C:2000:132.
Case C-7/97 *Bronner v Mediaprint* ECLI:EU:C:1998:569.
Case C-9/99 *Échirolles Distribution* ECLI:EU:C:2000:532.
Case C-238/99 P *Limburgse Vinyl Maatschappij and Others v Commission* ECLI:EU:C:2002:582.
Case C-309/99 *Wouters and others v Algemene Raad van de Nederlandse Orde van Advocaten* ECLI:EU:C:2002:98.
Case C-12/03 P *Commission v Tetra Laval* ECLI:EU:C:2005:87.
Case C-327/03 *ISIS Multimedia and Firma 02* ECLI:EU:C:2005:622.
Case C-189/02 P *Dansk Rørindustri and Others v Commission* ECLI:EU:C:2005:408.
Case C-95/04 P *British Airways plc v Commission of the European Communities* ECLI:EU:C:2007:166.
Case C-238/05 *Asnef-Equifax* ECLI:EU:C:2006:734.
Case C-413/06 P *Bertelsmann and Sony Corporation of America v Impala* ECLI:EU:C:2008:392.
Case C-501/06 P *GlaxoSmithKline Services and Others v Commission and Others* ECLI:EU:C:2009:610.
Case C-49/07 *MOTOE* ECLI:EU:C:2008:376.
Case C-202/07 P *France Télécom v Commission* ECLI:EU:C:2009:214.
Case C-209/07 *Beef Industry Development and Barry Brothers (BIDS)* ECLI:EU:C:2008:643.
Case C-8/08 *T-Mobile Netherlands BV and Others* ECLI:EU:C:2009:343.
Case C-280/08 P *Deutsche Telekom v Commission* ECLI:EU:C:2010:603.
Case C-52/09 *TeliaSonera Sverige* ECLI:EU:C:2011:83.
Case C-439/09 *Pierre Fabre Dermo-Cosmétique* ECLI:EU:C:2011:649.
Case C-209/10 *Post Danmark A/S v Konkurrencerådet* ECLI:EU:C:2012:172.
Case C-457/10 P *AstraZeneca AB and AstraZeneca plc v European Commission* ECLI:EU:C:2012:770.
Case C-32/11 *Allianz Hungária Biztosító and Others* ECLI:EU:C:2013:160.
Case C-226/11 *Expedia* ECLI:EU:C:2012:795.
Case C-68/12 *Slovenská sporiteľňa* ECLI:EU:C:2013:71.
Case C-67/13 P *Groupement des cartes bancaires v Commission* ECLI:EU:C:2014:2204.
Case C-170/13 *Huawei Technologies* ECLI:EU:C:2015:477.
Case C-286/13 P *Dole Food and Dole Fresh Fruit Europe v Commission* ECLI:EU:C:2015:184.
Case C-23/14 *Post Danmark II* ECLI:EU:C:2015:651.
Case C-345/14 *Maxima Latvija* ECLI:EU:C:2015:784.
Case C-373/14 P *Toshiba Corporation v Commission* ECLI:EU:C:2016:26.
Case C-413/14 P *Intel v Commission* ECLI:EU:C:2017:632.
Case C-469/15 P *FSL and Others v Commission* ECLI:EU:C:2017:308.

Case C-230/16 *Coty Germany* ECLI:EU:C:2017:941.
Case C-525/16 *Meo–Serviços de Comunicações e Multimédia* ECLI:EU:C:2018:270.
Case C-265/17 P *Commission v United Parcel Service* ECLI:EU:C:2019:23.
Case C-228/18 *Budapest Bank and Others* ECLI:EU:C:2020:265.
Case C-307/18 *Generics (UK) and Others* ECLI:EU:C:2020:52.
Case C-377/20 *Servizio Elettrico Nazionale and Others* ECLI:EU:C:2022:379.
Case C-680/20 *Unilever Italia Mkt. Operations* ECLI:EU:C:2023:33.
Case C-376/20 P *Commission v CK Telecoms UK Investments* ECLI:EU:C:2023:561.
Case C-211/22 *Super Bock Bebidas* ECLI:EU:C:2023:529.

Opinions of Advocate Generals of the Court of Justice of the European Union (Chronological Order)

Opinion of Advocate General Roemer in Case 56/64 *Consten and Grundig v Commission of the EEC* ECLI:EU:C:1966:19.
Opinion of Advocate General Fennelly in Case C-395/96 P *Compagnie Maritime Belge Transports and Others v Commission* ECLI:EU:C:1998:518.
Opinion of Advocate General Alber in Case C-9/99 *Échirolles Distribution* ECLI:EU:C:2000:299.
Opinion of Advocate General Tizzano in Case C-12/03 P *Commission v Tetra Laval* ECLI:EU:C:2004:318.
Opinion of Advocate General Kokott in Case C-413/06 P *Bertelsmann und Sony Corporation of America/ Impala* ECLI:EU:C:2007:790.
Opinion of Advocate General Kokott in Case C-8/08 *T-Mobile Netherlands BV and Others* ECLI:EU:C:2009:110.
Opinion of Advocate General Kokott in Case C-226/11 *Expedia* ECLI:EU:C:2012:544.
Opinion of Advocate General Wahl in Case C-67/13 P *Groupement des cartes bancaires v Commission* ECLI:EU:C:2014:1958.
Opinion of Advocate General Kokott in Case C-23/14 *Post Danmark II* ECLI:EU:C:2015:343.
Opinion of Advocate General Wahl in Case C-177/16 *Biedrība "Autortiesību un komunicēšanās konsultāciju aģentūra–Latvijas Autoru apvienība" Konkurences padome (AKKA)* ECLI:EU:C:2017:286.
Opinion of Advocate General Bobek in Case C-228/18 *Budapest Bank and Others* ECLI:EU:C:2019:678.
Opinion of Advocate General Kokott in Case C-307/18 *Generics (UK) and Others* ECLI:EU:C:2020:28.
Opinion of Advocate General Kokott in Case C-176/19 P *Commission v Servier and Others* ECLI:EU:C:2022:576.
Opinion of Advocate General Kokott in Case C-376/20 *Commission v CK Telecoms UK Investments* ECLI:EU:C:2022:817.
Opinion of Advocate General Rantos in Case C-377/20 *Servizio Elettrico Nazionale and Others* ECLI:EU:C:2021:998.
Opinion of Advocate General Rantos in Case C-680/20 *Unilever Italia Mkt. Operations* ECLI:EU:C:2022:586.

General Court of the European Union (Chronological Order)

Case T-14/89 *Montedipe v Commission* ECLI:EU:T:1992:36.
Case T-30/89 *Hilti v Commission* ECLI:EU:T:1991:70.

Case T-65/89 *BPB Industries and British Gypsum v Commission* ECLI:EU:T:1993:31.
Case T-83/91 *Tetra Pak v Commission (Tetra Pak II)* ECLI:EU:T:1994:246.
Case T-2/93 *Air France v Commission* ECLI:EU:T:1994:55.
Case T-17/93 *Matra Hachette v Commission* ECLI:EU:T:1994:89.
Case T-290/94 *Kaysersberg v Commission* ECLI:EU:T:1997:186.
Case T-221/95 *Endemol v Commission* ECLI:EU:T:1999:85.
Case T-102/96 *Gencor v Commission* ECLI:EU:T:1999:65.
Case T-228/97 *Irish Sugar v Commission* ECLI:EU:T:1999:246.
Case T-65/98 *Van den Bergh Foods Ltd v Commission of the European Communities.* ECLI: EU:T:2003:281.
Case T-112/99 *Métropole télévision (M6) and Others v Commission* ECLI:EU:T:2001:215.
Case T-310/00 *MCI, Inc. v Commission* ECLI:EU:T:2004:275.
Case T-168/01 *GlaxoSmithKline Services v Commission* ECLI:EU:T:2006:265.
Case T-203/01 *Michelin v Commission (Michelin II)* ECLI:EU:T:2003:250.
Case T-201/04 *Microsoft Corp v Commission* ECLI:EU:T:2007:289.
Case T-87/05 *EDP v Commission* ECLI:EU:T:2005:333.
Case T-432/05 *EMC Development v Commission* ECLI:EU:T:2010:189.
Case T-282/06 *Sun Chemical Group* ECLI:EU:T:2007:203.
Case T-342/07 *Ryanair v Commission* ECLI:EU:T:2010:280.
Case T-491/07 *Groupement des cartes bancaires v Commission* ECLI:EU:T:2012:633.
Case T-405/08 *Spar Österreichische Warenhandels v Commission* ECLI:EU:T:2013:306.
Case T-286/09 *Intel v Commission* ECLI:EU:T:2014:547.
Case T-286/09 RENV *Intel Corporation v Commission* ECLI:EU:T:2022:19.
Case T-79/12 *Cisco v Commission* ECLI:EU:T:2013:635.
Case T-691/14 *Servier and Others v Commission* ECLI:EU:T:2018:922.
Case T-399/16 *CK Telecoms UK Investments v Commission* ECLI:EU:T:2020:217.
Case T-612/17 *Google and Alphabet v Commission (Google Shopping)* ECLI:EU:T:2021:763.
Case T-235/18 *Qualcomm v Commission* ECLI:EU:T:2022:358.
Case T-604/18 *Google and Alphabet v Commission (Google Android)* ECLI:EU:T:2022:541.

European Commission Decisions (Chronological Order)

Case No IV/M.053 *Aerospatiale-Alenia/de Havilland*, [1991] OJ L 334/42.
Case No IV/31043 *Tetra Pak II*, [1992] OJ L 72/1.
Case No IV/M.190 *Nestlé/Perrier*, [1992] OJ L 356/1.
Case No IV/M.308 *Kali-Salz/MdK/Treuhand*, [1994] OJ L 186/38.
Case No IV/M.619 *Gencor/Lonrho*, [1997] OJ L 11/30.
Case No IV/M.784 *Kesko/Tuko*, [1997] OJ L 110/53.
Case No IV/M.1221 *Rewe/Meinl*, [1999] OJ L 274/1.
Case No IV/36.748 *Reims II*, [1999] OJ L 275/17.
Case No COMP/M.2220 *General Electric/Honeywell*, C(2001) 1746 final.
Case No COMP/M.1741 *MCI WorldCom/Sprint*, [2003] OJ L 300/1.
Case No COMP/M.2337 *Nestlé/Ralston Purina*, Document No 301 M2337.
Case No COMP/37.792 *Microsoft*, C (2004) 900 final.
Case No COMP/AT.39740 *Google Search (Shopping)*, C(2017) 4444 final.
Case No COMP/AT.40099 *Google Android*, C(2018) 4761 final.
Case No COMP/AT.40428 *Guess*, C(2018) 8455 final.
Case No COMP/AT.40411 *Google Search (AdSense)*, C(2019) 2173 final.
Case No COMP/AT.39711 *Qualcomm (predation)*, C(2019) 5361 final.

LEGISLATION AND ENFORCEMENT GUIDELINES

English Common Law

Statute of Monopolies 1623 Act, 1623 c. 3.

German Competition Law (Chronological Order)

Deutscher Bundestag, Gesetz gegen Wettbewerbsbeschränkungen, BGBl. I, 1957, 1081.

Bundesrepublik Deutschland, Zehntes Gesetz zur Änderung des Gesetzes gegen Wettbewerbsbeschränkungen (die 10. GWB-Novelle), BGBl. I, 2021 S. 2.

Bundesministerium für Wirtschaft und Klimaschutz, Referentenentwurf des Bundesministeriums für Wirtschaft und Klimaschutz: Entwurf eines Gesetzes zur Verbesserung der Wettbewerbsstrukturen und zur Abschöpfung von Vorteilen aus Wettbewerbsverstößen (Wettbewerbsdurchsetzungsgesetz/ die 11. GWB-Novelle).

Deutscher Bundestag, Gesetzentwurf der Bundesregierung Entwurf eines Gesetzes zur Änderung des Gesetzes gegen Wettbewerbsbeschränkungen und anderer Gesetze. Drucksache 20/6824.

United States Legislation

Congress of the United States, 15 U.S. Code Chapter 1 §§ 1–11.

Congress of the United States, 15 U.S. Code Chapter 1 § 12–14.

Congress of the United States, 15 U.S. Code Chapter 1 § 13.

Congress of the United States, 15 U.S. Code Chapter 1 § 18.

Congress of the United States, 28 U.S. Code, Federal Rules of Evidence.

The White House of the United States, Executive Order on Promoting Competition in the American Economy, Executive Order 14036.

United States Enforcement Guidelines

Antitrust Division of the US Department of Justice, 1968 Merger Guidelines.

Antitrust Division of the US Department of Justice, 1982 Merger Guidelines.

Antitrust Division of the US Department of Justice/Federal Trade Commission, 2010 Merger Guidelines.

Antitrust Division of the US Department of Justice/Federal Trade Commission, Draft 2023 Merger Guidelines.

European Union Primary Legislation (Chronological Order)

European Coal and Steel Community, Treaty Establishing the European Coal and Steel Community.

European Economic Community, Treaty Establishing the European Economic Community.

Treaty on the Functioning of the EU the following reference: European Union, Consolidated version of the Treaty on European Union, [2012] OJ C 326/13.

European Union, Consolidated version of the Treaty on the Functioning of the European Union, [2012] OJ C 326/47.

European Union Secondary Legislation (Chronological Order)

Council of the European Economic Community, EEC Council Regulation 17/62 implementing Articles 85 and 86 of the Treaty, [1962] OJ L 13/204.

Council of the European Union, Council Regulation (EEC) No 4064/89 on the Control of Concentrations between Undertakings, [1989] OJ L 395/1.

European Commission, Commission Regulation (EC) No 2790/1999 on the Application of Article 81(3) of the Treaty to Categories of Vertical Agreements and Concerted Practices, [1999] OJ L 336/21.

Council of the European Union, Council Regulation (EC) No 1/2003 on the implementation of the rules on competition laid down in Articles 81 and 82 of the Treaty, [2003] OJ L 1/1.

Council of the European Union, Council Regulation (EC) No 139/2004 on the Control of Concentrations between Undertakings, [2004] OJ L 24/1.

European Union, Regulation (EU) 2022/1925 on Contestable and Fair Markets in the Digital Sector (Digital Markets Act), [2022] OJ L 265/1.

European Commission Guidelines (Chronological Order)

European Commission, Notice on Exclusive Dealing Contracts with Commercial Agents, [1962] OJ 139/2921.

European Commission, Communication from the Commission on the Application of the Community Competition Rules to Vertical Restraints – Follow-up to the Green Paper on Vertical Restraints, [1998] OJ C 365/3.

European Commission, Commission Guidelines on the Assessment of Horizontal Mergers, [2004] OJ C 31/5.

European Commission, Guidelines on the Application of Article 81(3) of the Treaty, [2004] OJ C 101/97.

European Commission, Guidelines on the Assessment of Non-horizontal Mergers, [2008] OJ C 265/6.

European Commission, Guidance on the Commission's Enforcement Priorities in Applying Article 82 of the EC Treaty to Abusive Exclusionary Conduct by Dominant Undertakings, [2009] OJ C 45/7, Guidance Paper.

European Commission, Guidelines on the applicability of Article 101 of the Treaty on the Functioning of the European Union to horizontal co-operation agreements, [2011] OJ C 11/01.

European Commission, Amendments to the Communication from the Commission Guidance on the Commission's enforcement priorities in applying Article 82 of the EC Treaty to abusive exclusionary conduct by dominant undertakings. C(2023) 1923 final.

European Commission, Annex to the Communication from the Commission: Amendments to the Communication from the Commission Guidance on the Commission's enforcement priorities in applying Article 82 of the EC Treaty to abusive exclusionary conduct by dominant undertakings. C(2023) 1923 final Annex.

OTHER POLICY DOCUMENTS AND HISTORICAL SOURCES

United States Antitrust Bills (Chronological Order)

Congress of the United States, S. 1167–Industrial Reorganization Act, 93rd Congress (1973–1974).

Congress of the United States, S. 1811–Merger Enforcement Improvement Act, 115th Congress (2017–2019).
Congress of the United States, S. 1812–Consolidation Prevention and Competition Promotion Act, 115th Congress (2017–2019).
Congress of the United States, H.R.3460–State Antitrust Enforcement Venue Act, 117th Congress (2021–2022).
Congress of the United States, H.R.3816–American Choice and Innovation Online Act ('ACIO Act'), 117th Congress (2021–2022).
Congress of the United States, H.R.3825–Ending Platform Monopolies Act ('EPM Act'), 117th Congress (2021–2022).
Congress of the United States, H.R.3826–Platform Competition and Opportunity Act ('PCO Act'), 117th Congress (2021–2022).
Congress of the United States, H.R.3849–Access Act ('Access Act'), 117th Congress (2021–2022).

United States Legislative History (Chronological Order)

Congress of the United States, 19 Cong. Rec. 6041 (1888).
Congress of the United States, 19 Cong. Rec. 8519 (1888).
Congress of the United States, 19 Cong. Rec. 8559 (1890).
Congress of the United States, 20 Cong. Rec. 1457 (1890).
Congress of the United States, 20 Cong. Rec. 1765 (1890).
Congress of the United States, 20 Cong. Rec. 2455 (1890).
Congress of the United States, 19 Cong. Rec. 7512 (1890).
Congress of the United States, Senate Report no. 698, to accompany H.R. 15,657, 63rd Congress (1913–1915).

Other United States Sources (Alphabetical Order)

Assistant Attorney General Jonathan Kanter Delivers Remarks at New York City Bar Association's Milton Handler Lecture (2022).
The Attorney General's National Committee to Study the Antitrust Laws, 1955 *Report* (Washington: Superintendent of Documents, U.S. Government Printing Office 1955).
Business Advisory Council, 'Effective Competition: Report to the Secretary of Commerce by His Business Advisory Council with a Letter of Comment from the Secretary of Commerce' (1952).
CNN, 'Trump Speaks in Pennsylvania; Examining Proposed Actions in First 100 Days of Trump Administration: Unofficial Transcript' (22 October 2016).
Roosevelt, FD, 'Message to Congress on Curbing Monopolies [1938]' www.presidency.ucsb.edu.
Roosevelt, T, 'New Nationalism Speech [1910]' https://teachingamericanhistory.org (15 September 2019).
Temporary National Economic Committee, 'Relative Efficiency of Large, Medium-Sized, and Small Business' (1941). TNEC Monograph 13.
Warren, E, 'Break Up Big Tech' (24 April 2020).

Historical Sources on European and German Competition Law (Alphabetical Order)

'Accord relatif à la cessation des fonctions de l'Autorité Internationale de la Ruhr (27 mai 1952)' www.cvce.eu (25 June 2021).

'Agreement for an International Authority for the Ruhr (London, 28 April 1949)' www.cvce.eu.

Alliierte Hohen Kommission (Allied High Commission), Gesetz N°27 hinsichtlich der Umgestaltung des deutschen Kohlenbergbaues und der deutschen Stahl- und Eisenindustrie (16. Mai 1950).

The Berlin Conference of the Three Heads of Government of the U.S.S.R. U.S.A. and U.K. Potsdam Agreement–Protocol of the Proceedings, August I, 1945.

Bureau A, 'Rapport d'Albert Bureau sur la déconcentration de la sidérurgie allemande (28 juin 1951)' www.cvce.eu.

Council of Europe, Report by the Heads of Delegations to the Foreign Ministers, SG 7 A (56) (4).

Der Bundesminister für Wirtschaft, 'Dokument 111: Vorschlag der Kommission zu einer ersten Durchführungsverordnung zu den Artikeln 85 und 86 des EWG-Vertrages, 31.05.1961: Protokoll einer Wirtschaftsausschußsitzung, die Fragen zum Vorschlag der Kommission zu einer 1. Durchführungsverordnung behandelt. Neben den allgemeinen Bedenken, insbesondere gegenüber einer vorgesehenen Anzeigepflicht, wird die Möglichkeit einer von deutscher Seite angestrengten Normenkontrollklage behandelt' in T Hoeren and R Schulze (eds), *Dokumente zum europäischen Recht: Band 3: Kartellrecht (bis 1957)* (Berlin: Springer 2000), 457.

European Coal and Steel Community, 'Second General Report on the Activities of the Community' (1954).

European Parliament, Resolution on the 12th Report of the Commission of the European Communities on Competition Policy.

European Parliament, Resolution on the Eighteenth Report of the Commission of the European Communities on Competition Policy.

Gesetz 75 der amerikanischen und britischen Militärregierungen zur Umgestaltung des Deutschen Kohlenbergbaues und der Deutschen Eisen- und Stahlindustrie sowie Durchführungsbestimmungen, Bundesarchiv, BArch B 109/619.

Legislative Reference Service of the Library of Congress, 'Fascism in Action: A Documented Study and Analysis of Fascism in Europe Prepared at the Instance and under the Direction of Representative Wright Patman of Texas by Legislative Reference Service of the Library of Congress under the Direction of Ernest S. Griffith' (1947).

Leroy-Beaulieu P, 'Note de Paul Leroy-Beaulieu sur le transfert du pouvoir de déconcentration de l'Autorité internationale de la Ruhr à la Haute Autorité (11 novembre 1950)' www.cvce.eu.

Monnet J, 'Lettre de Jean Monnet à Robert Schuman (Paris, 22 janvier 1951)' www.cvce.eu.

Monnet J, 'Lettre de Jean Monnet à Robert Schuman (Paris, 1er juillet 1952)' www.cvce.eu.

'Note on the Relationship between the International Authority for the Ruhr and the European Coal and Steel Community (7 November 1950): Anonymous French Note on the Coexistence of the International Authority for the Ruhr and the High Authority of the European Coal and Steel Community (ECSC)' www.cvce.eu.

Schuman R, 'The Schuman Declaration – 9 May 1950' https://europa.eu.

Spaak, P-H, 'Rapport des chefs de délégation aux Ministres des Affaires Étrangères = Report of the Heads of Delegation to the Ministers of Foreign Affairs' (21 April 1956) http://aei.pitt.edu.

Verordnung Nr 78 Verbot der übermäßigen Konzentration deutscher Wirtschaftskraft–Ordinance No. 78 Prohibition of Excessive Concentration of German Economic Power, Brit. VoBl. 1947, 412.

Verwaltung des Vereinigten Wirtschaftsgebietes, Gesetz über Leitsätze für die Bewirtschaftung und Preispolitik nach der Geldreform vom 24. Juni 1948–Ordinance

No 37 Concerning Guiding Principles for Economic Control and Price Policy after Currency Reform, VfWMBl. 1948 II S. 91; Brit. VoBl. 1949, 77.
Weimarer Republik (Reichsregierung), Kartellverordnung, Verordnung gegen Missbrauch wirtschaftlicher Machtstellungen, RGBl I, 1067.

Other European Commission Policy Documents (Alphabetical Order)

'Vth Report on Competition Policy' (1975).
'VIIth Report on Competition Policy' (1977).
'IXth Report on Competition Policy' (1979).
'XIIth Report on Competition Policy' (1982).
'XVth Report on Competition Policy' (1985).
Kroes N, 'European Competition Policy – Delivering Better Markets and Better Choice' (SPEECH/05/512 2005).
'La Communauté économique européenne et notre régime économique et social. Discours de M. Hans von der Groeben, membre de la Commission de la Communauté économique européenne. Munich, 29 novembre 1962' (1962).
'Le problème de la concentration dans le marché commun: The problem of concentration in the Common Market.' (1966). Information Memo P-1/66.
Inception Impact Assessment–New Competition Tool ('NCT'), Document Ares(2020) 2877634.
Press Release IP/20/2077–Antitrust: Commission Sends Statement of Objections to Amazon for the Use of Non-public Independent Seller Data and Opens Second Investigation into its E-commerce Business Practices (2020).
Press Release IP/21/2061–Antitrust: Commission Sends Statement of Objections to Apple on App Store Rules for Music Streaming Providers (2021).
Proposal for a Regulation (EEC) of the Council on the Control of Concentrations between Undertakings, COM (73) 1210 Final.
'Report by the Economic Advisory Group on Competition Policy (EAGCP) – An Economic Approach to Article 82' (2005).
Vestager, M, 'Keynote of EVP Vestager at the European Competition Law Tuesdays: A Principles Based Approach to Competition Policy' (25 October 2022). SPEECH/22/ 6393.
Vestager, M, 'Remarks by Executive Vice-President Vestager for the Political Agreement on the Digital Markets Act' (25 March 2022) SPEECH/22/2042.

Other Sources

Aktionskreis Freiburger Schule, 'Die Freiburger Ordoliberale Schule' www.freiburger-schule .de.
Competition and Markets Authority (CMA), Merger Assessment Guidelines, CMA 129.
Competition and Markets Authority, A New Pro-competition Regime for Digital Markets, Advice of the Digital Markets Taskforce.
OECD, 'Market Concentration: Issues Paper by the Secretariat' (2018). DAF/COMP/WD (2018)46.
Office of Fair Trading and Competition Commission, Merger Assessment Guidelines 2010, CC2/OFT1254.
UK Government, Digital Markets, Competition and Consumers Bill, Bill 350 2022-23 (as amended in Public Bill Committee).

SECONDARY LITERATURE

Abraham, D, *The Collapse of the Weimar Republic: Political Economy and Crisis* (New York: Holmes & Meier 1986).

Acemoglu, D and Robinson, JA, *The Narrow Corridor* (London: Viking Penguin 2019).

Why Nations Fail: The Origins of Power, Prosperity, and Poverty (London: Profile Books 2013).

Adams, W, 'The Aluminium Case: Legal Victory – Economic Defeat' (1951) 41(5) *The American Economic Review* 915–22.

'Dissolution, Divorcement, Divestiture: The Pyrrhic Victories of Antitrust' (1951) 27(1) *Indiana Law Journal*, 1–37.

'The Rule of Reason: Workable Competition or Workable Monopoly' (1954) 63(3) *Yale Law Journal*, 348–71.

The Structure of American Industry (London: Macmillan 1971).

Adelman, MA, 'Effective Competition and the Antitrust Laws' (1948) 61(8) *Harvard Law Review*, 1289–350.

Ahlborn, C, Evans, DS, and Padilla, AJ, 'The Antitrust Economics of Tying: A Farewell to per se Illegality' (2004) 49(1–2) *Antitrust Bulletin*, 287–341.

Akman, P, 'Searching for the Long-Lost Soul of Article 82 EC' (CCP Working Paper 2007).

Amato, G, *Antitrust and the Bounds of Power: The Dilemma of Liberal Democracy in the History of the Market* (Oxford: Hart 1997).

Anderson, E, 'Liberty, Equality and Private Government' in M Matheson (ed), *The Tanner Lectures on Human Values* (Cambridge: Cambridge University Press 2016), 63–122.

Areeda, P and Turner, DF, 'Predatory Pricing and Related Practices under Section 2 of the Sherman Act' (1975) 88(4) *Harvard Law Review*, 697–733.

Arnold, T, 'Fair Fights and Foul: Chapter XIV – The Sherman Act as Charter of Economic Freedom' (1965) 10(5–6) *Antitrust Bulletin*, 655–66.

Arnold, TW, 'The Bottlenecks of Business [1940]' in DA Crane and H Hovenkamp (eds), *The Making of Competition Policy: Legal and Economic Sources* (New York: Oxford University Press 2013), 206–20.

Arrow, KJ and Fisher, AC, 'Environmental Preservation, Uncertainty, and Irreversibility' (1974) 88(2) *The Quarterly Journal of Economics*, 312–19.

Autor, D and others, 'The Fall of the Labor Share and the Rise of Superstar Firms' (2020) 135 (2) *The Quarterly Journal of Economics*, 645–709.

Bailey, D, 'Presumptions in EU Competition Law' (2010) 31(9) *European Competition Law Review*, 362–69.

'Standard of Proof in EC Merger Proceedings: A Common Law Perspective' (2003) 40(4) *Common Market Law Review*, 845–88.

Bain, JS, *Barriers to New Competition* (Cambridge, MA: Harvard University Press 1956).

Industrial Organization (New York: John Wiley & Sons 1959).

'Industrial Organization: Chapter 10 – The Relation of Market Structure to Market Performance' in DA Crane and H Hovenkamp (eds), *The Making of Competition Policy: Legal and Economic Sources* (New York: Oxford University Press 2013), 320–37.

'Relation of Profit Rate to Industry Concentration: American Manufacturing, 1936–1940' (1951) 65(3) *The Quarterly Journal of Economics*, 292–324.

'Workable Competition in Oligopoly: Theoretical Considerations and Some Empirical Evidence' (1950) 40(2) *American Economic Review*, 35–47.

Bajgar, M and others, 'Industry Concentration in Europe and North America' (OECD Productivity Working Papers 18 2019).

Baker, JB, *The Antitrust Paradigm: Restoring a Competitive Economy* (Cambridge, MA: Harvard University Press 2019).

'Recent Developments in Economics That Challenge Chicago School Views' (1989) 58(2) *Antitrust Law Journal*, 645–55.

'Taking the Error Out of "Error Cost" Analysis: What's Wrong with Antitrust's Right' (2015) 80(1) *Antitrust Law Journal*, 1–38.

Balderston, T, *Economics and Politics in the Weimar Republic* (Cambridge: Cambridge University Press 2002).

Baumol, WJ, 'Predation and the Logic of the Average Variable Cost Test' (1996) 39(1) *Journal of Law & Economics*, 49–72.

Beckner, CF and Salop, SC, 'Decision Theory and Antitrust Rules' (1999) 67(1) *Antitrust Law Journal*, 41–76.

Behrens, P, 'The Ordoliberal Concept of "Abuse" of a Dominant Position and Its Impact on Article 102 TFEU' (Discussion Paper No 7/15, 2015).

Bentham, J, 'Anarchical Fallacies' in J Bowring (ed), *The Works of Jeremy Bentham* (Edinburgh: William Tait 1843).

Theory of Legislation (London: Trübner 1873).

Berle, AA and Means, GC, *The Modern Corporation and Private Property* (Piscataway: Transaction Publishers 1932).

Berlin, I, 'Two Concepts of Liberty' in H Hardy (ed), *Liberty: Incorporating Four Essays on Liberty* (Oxford: Oxford University Press 2002), 166–217.

Bernanke, BS, 'Irreversibility, Uncertainty, and Cyclical Investment' (1983) 98(1) *The Quarterly Journal of Economics* 85–106.

Bernatt, M, *Populism and Antitrust: The Illiberal Influence of Populist Government on the Competition Law System* (Cambridge: Cambridge University Press 2022).

Böhm, F (ed), *Wettbewerb und Monopolkampf: Eine Untersuchung zur Frage des wirtschaftlichen Kampfrechts und zur Frage der rechtlichen Struktur der geltenden Wirtschaftsordnung* [1933] (Baden-Baden: Nomos 2010).

'Das Problem der privaten Macht. Ein Beitrag zur Monopolfrage [1928]' in N Goldschmidt (ed), *Grundtexte zur Freiburger Tradition der Ordnungsökonomik* (Tübingen: Mohr Siebeck 2008), 49–67.

'Democracy and Economic Power in Cartel and Monopoly in Modern Law [1961]' in DA Crane and H Hovenkamp (eds), *The Making of Competition Policy: Legal and Economic Sources* (New York: Oxford University Press 2013), 264–81.

'Die Bedeutung der Wirtschaftsordnung für die politische Verfassung: Kritische Betrachtungen zu dem Aufsatz von Ministerialrat Dr. Adolf ARNDT über das "Problem der Wirtschaftsdemokratie in den Verfassungsentwürfen"' (1946) 1(6) *Süddeutsche Juristen-Zeitung*, 141–49.

Freiheit und Ordnung in der Marktwirtschaft [1971] (Baden-Baden: Nomos 1980).

'Freiheit und Ordnung in der Marktwirtschaft [1971]' in N Goldschmidt (ed), *Grundtexte zur Freiburger Tradition der Ordnungsökonomik* (Tübingen: Mohr Siebeck 2008), 299–312.

'Kartellauflösung und Konzernentflechtung: Spezialistenaufgabe oder Schicksalsfrage?' (1947) 2(9) *Süddeutsche Juristen-Zeitung*, 495–506.

'Rule of Law in a Market Economy [1966]' in AT Peacock and H Willgerodt (eds), *Germany's Social Market Economy: Origins and Evolution* (Houndmill: Macmillan 1989), 46–67.

Böhm, F, Eucken, W, and Großmann-Doerth, H, 'Unsere Aufgabe (The Ordoliberal Manifesto) [1936]' in N Goldschmidt (ed), *Grundtexte zur Freiburger Tradition der Ordnungsökonomik* (Tübingen: Mohr Siebeck 2008), 27–37.

Bok, DC, 'Section 7 of the Clayton Act and the Merging of Law and Economics' (1960) 74(2) *Harvard Law Review*, 226–355.

Bolton, P, Brodley, JF, and Riordan, MH, 'Predatory Pricing: Strategic Theory and Legal Policy' (2000) 88(8) *Georgetown Law Journal*, 2239–330.

Bork, RH, *The Antitrust Paradox: A Policy at War with Itself* [1978] (New York: Maxwell Macmillan 1993).

'The Goals of Antitrust Policy' (1967) 57(2) *The American Economic Review*, 242–53.

'Legislative Intent and the Policy of the Sherman Act' (1966) 9(1) *Journal of Law & Economics*, 7–49.

'The Rule of Reason and the Per Se Concept: Price Fixing and Market Division' (1966) 75 (3) *The Yale Law Journal*, 775–847.

Bork, RH and Bowman, WS Jr., 'The Crisis in Antitrust' (1965) 65(3) *Columbia Law Journal*, 363–73.

Boucoyannis, D, 'The Equalizing Hand: Why Adam Smith Thought the Market Should Produce Wealth without Steep Inequality' (2013) 11(4) *Perspectives on Politics*, 1051–70.

Bowman, WS Jr., 'Tying Arrangements and the Leverage Problem' (1957) 67(1) *Yale Law Journal*, 19–36.

Brady, RA, *The Spirit and Structure of German Fascism* (New York: Citadel Press 1971 [1937]).

Brandeis, L, 'Shall We Abandon the Policy of Competition?: Reprinted from The Curse of Bigness [1934]' in DA Crane and H Hovenkamp (eds), *The Making of Competition Policy: Legal and Economic Sources* (New York: Oxford University Press 2013), 185–89.

Brandeis, LD, *Other People's Money: And How the Bankers Use It* (New York: Frederick A. Stokes Company 1914).

Brietzke, PH, 'The Constitutionalization of Antitrust: Jefferson, Madison, Hamilton, and Thomas C. Arthur' (1987) 22(2) *Valparaiso University Law Review*, 275–330.

Brodley, JF and Hay, GA, 'Predatory Pricing: Competing Economic Theories and the Evolution of Legal Standards' (1980–1981) 66(4) *Cornell Law Review*, 738–803.

Buchanan, JM, 'Social Choice, Democracy, and Free Markets' (1954) 62(2) *Journal of Political Economy*, 114–23.

Burtis, MM, Gelbach, JB, and Kobayashi, BH, 'Error Costs, Legal Standards of Proof, and Statistical Significance' (2017) 25(1) *Supreme Court Economic Review*, 1–57.

Calabresi, SG and Leibowitz, LC, 'Monopolies and the Constitution: A History of Crony Capitalism' (2015) 36(3) *Harvard Journal of Law & Public Policy*, 983–1098.

Caldwell, B and Montes, L, 'Friedrich Hayek and His Visits to Chile' (2015) 28(3) *The Review of Austrian Economics*, 261–309.

Carlisle, K and Gruby, RL, 'Polycentric Systems of Governance: A Theoretical Model for the Commons' (2017) 47(4) *Policy Studies Journal*, 927–52.

Carter, I, 'Liberty' in R Bellamy and A Mason (eds), *Political Concepts* (Manchester: Manchester University Press 2003), 4–15.

A Measure of Freedom (New York: Oxford University Press 1999).

Carter, I and Shnayderman, R, 'The Impossibility of "Freedom as Independence"'(2019) 17(2) *Political Studies Review*, 136–46.

Chamberlin, E, *Theory of Monopolistic Competition* (Cambridge, MA: Harvard University Press 1933).

Chappell, VC (ed), *Hobbes and Bramhall: On Liberty and Necessity* (Cambridge: Cambridge University Press 1999).

Christiansen, A and Kerber, W, 'Competition Policy with Optimally Differentiated Rules Instead of per se Rules vs. Rule of Reason' (2006) 2(2) *Journal of Competition Law and Economics*, 215–44.
Churchill, EF, 'Monopolies' (1925) 41(3) *Law Quarterly Review*, 275–96.
Cicchetti, CJ and Freeman, AM, 'Option Demand and Consumer Surplus: Further Comment' (1971) 85(3) *The Quarterly Journal of Economics*, 528–39.
Cicero, MT, *On the Commonwealth and on the Laws* (Cambridge: Cambridge University Press 1999).
Clark, JM, 'Toward a Concept of Workable Competition' (1940) 30(2) *The American Economic Review*, 241–56.
Coase, RH, 'The Federal Communications Commission' (1959) 2 *Journal of Law and Economics*, 1–40.
'The Nature of the Firm' (1937) 4(16) *Economica*, 386–405.
'The Problem of Social Cost' (1960) 3 *Journal of Law & Economics*, 1–44.
Cohen, WM and Klepper, S, 'The Tradeoff between Firm Size and Diversity in the Pursuit of Technological Progress' (1992) 4(1) *Small Business Economics*, 1–14.
Coke, E, *Institutes of the Laws of England* [1628].
The Third Part of the Institutes of the Laws of England: Concerning High Treason, and other Please of the Crown and Criminall Causes (London: By M. Flesher for W. Lee and D. Pakeman 1644).
Collins, WD, 'Trusts and the Origins of Antitrust' (2013) 81(5) *Fordham Law Review*, 2279–348.
Collinson, P, 'The Monarchical Republic of Queen Elizabeth I' (1987) 69(2) *Bulletin of the John Rylands Library*, 394–424.
Colomo, PI and Lamadrid de Pablo, A, 'On the Notion of Restriction of Competition: What We Know and What We Do Not Know We Know' in D Gerard, M Merola, and B Meyring (eds), *The Notion of Restriction of Competition: Revisiting the Foundations of Antitrust Enforcement in Europe* (Brussles: Bruylant 2017), 333–74.
Constant, B, *Political Writings* (Cambridge: Cambridge University Press 1988).
Cowgill, B, Prat, A, and Valletti, T, 'Political Power and Market Power' (2021). CEPR Press Discussion Paper No 17178.
Crane, DA, 'Antitrust and Democracy: A Case Study from German Fascism' (2018). University of Michigan Law & Econ Research Paper No 18-009 https://papers.ssrn.com.
'Fascism and Monopoly' (2020) 118(7) *Michigan Law Review*, 1315–70.
'Rules versus Standards in Antitrust Adjudication' (2007) 64(1) *Washington and Lee Law Review*, 49–110.
'Structuralism: Introduction' in DA Crane and H Hovenkamp (eds), *The Making of Competition Policy: Legal and Economic Sources* (New York: Oxford University Press 2013), 318–20.
Crane, DA and Miralles, G, 'Toward a Unified Theory of Exclusionary Vertical Restraints' (2010) 84(3) *Southern California Law Review*, 605–60.
Dahl, RA, *Democracy and Its Critics* (New Haven: Yale University Press 1989).
A Preface to Democratic Theory (Chicago: Chicago University Press 1956).
Dellis, K and Sondermann, D, 'Lobbying in Europe: New Firm-level Evidence' (2017). ECB Working Paper Series No 2071/June 2017.
Demsetz, H, 'Two Systems of Belief about Monopoly' in HJ Goldschmid, HM Mann, and JF Weston (eds), *Industrial Concentration: The New Learning* (Boston: Little Brown 1974), 164–83.

Deutscher E 'Causation and Counterfactual Analysis in Abuse of Dominance Cases: Lessons from the General Court's Qualcomm ruling' (2023) 19(3) *European Competition Journal* 481–521.

'Reshaping Digital Competition: The New Platform Regulations and the Future of Modern Antitrust' (2022) 67(2) *Antitrust Bulletin*, 302–40.

Deutscher, E and Makris, S, 'Exploring the Ordoliberal Paradigm: The Competition-Democracy Nexus' (2016) 11(2) *Competition Law Review*, 181–214.

Devlin, A and Jacobs, M, 'Antitrust Error' (2010) 52(1) *William and Mary Law Review*, 75–132.

Di Lorenzo, TJ, 'The Origins of Antitrust: An Interest-Group Perspective' (1985) 5(1) *International Review of Law and Economics*, 73–90.

Diarmuid, J, *Hell's Cartel* (London: Bloomsbury 2008).

Director, A and Levi, EH, 'Law and the Future: Trade Regulation' (1956) 51(2) *Northwestern University Law Review*, 281–96.

Douglass, R, 'Montesquieu and Modern Republicanism' (2012) 60(3) *Political Studies*, 703–19.

Dowding, K and van Hees, M, 'The Construction of Rights' (2003) 97(2) *American Political Science Review*, 281–92.

Easterbrook, FH, 'The Limits of Antitrust' (1984) 63(1) *Texas Law Review*, 1–40.

'Workable Antitrust' (1986) 84(8) *Michigan Law Review*, 1696–713.

Editors, 'The Industrial Reorganization Act: An Antitrust Proposal to Restructure the American Economy' (1973) 73(3) *Columbia Law Review*, 635–76.

'Section 3 of the Clayton Act – "Law Unto Itself"' (1954) 22(1) *University of Chicago Law Review*, 233–44.

Edlin, AS, 'Stopping Above Cost Predatory Pricing' (2002) 111(4) *Yale Law Journal*, 941–91.

Ehrlich, I and Posner, RA, 'An Economic Analysis of Legal Rulemaking' (1974) 3(1) *The Journal of Legal Studies*, 257–86.

Elkins, S and McKitrick, E, *The Age of Federalism* (Oxford: Oxford University Press 1993).

Erhard, L, *Wohlstand für alle* [1957] (Köln: Anaconda 2009).

Eucken, W, 'Das Problem der wirtschaftlichen Macht' in W Eucken and W Oswalt (eds), *Wirtschaftsmacht und Wirtschaftsordnung: Londoner Vorträge zur Wirtschaftspolitik und zwei Beiträge zur Antimonopolpolitik* (Münster: Lit 2001), 9–22.

Grundsätze der Wirtschaftspolitik (Tübingen: Mohr Siebeck 2004).

Eucken, W and Hutchison, TW, 'On the Theory of the Centrally Administered Economy: An Analysis of the German Experiment. Part I' (1948) 15(58) *Economica*, 79–100.

'On the Theory of the Centrally Administered Economy: An Analysis of the German Experiment. Part II' (1948) 15(59) *Economica*, 173–93.

Eucken, W and Meyer, FW, 'The Economic Situation in Germany' (1948) 260(1) *Annals of the American Academy of Political and Social Science*, 53–62.

Evans, W, Froeb, LM, and Werden, GJ, 'Endogeneity in the Concentration-Price Relationship: Causes, Consequences, and Cures' (1993) XLI(4) *The Journal of Industrial Economics*, 432–38.

Ewards, CD, 'An Appraisal of the Antitrust Laws' (1946) 36(2) *The American Economic Review*, 172–89.

'Can the Antitrust Laws Preserve Competition?' (1940) 30(1) *The American Economic Review*, 164–79.

Farrell, J, 'Complexity, Diversity, and Antitrust' (2006) 51(1) *The Antitrust Bulletin*, 165–73.

Fèvre, R, A *Political Economy of Power: Ordoliberalism in Context, 1932–1950* (New York: Oxford University Press 2022).

Finkelstein, MO and Fairley, WB, 'A Bayesian Approach to Identification Evidence' (1970) 83 (3) *Harvard Law Review*, 489–517.

First, H and Weber Waller, S, 'Antitrust's Democracy Deficit' (2013) 81(5) *Fordham Law Review*, 2543–74.

Fleischacker, S, 'Adam Smith on Equality' in CJ Berry, MP Paganelli, and C Smith (eds), *The Oxford Handbook of Adam Smith* (Oxford: Oxford University Press 2013), 485–500.

Flynn, JJ, 'Antitrust Policy and the Concept of a Competitive Process' (1990) 35(4) *New York Law School Law Review*, 893–916.

Forrester, I and Norall, C, 'The Laicization of Community Law; Self-Help and the Rule of Reason: How Competition Law Is and Could Be Applied' (1984) 21(1) *Common Market Law Review*, 11–51.

Foucault, M, *Naissance de la biopolitique: Cours au Collège de France, 1978–1979* (Paris: Gallimard; Seuil 2004).

Fox, EM, 'Antitrust and Democracy: How Markets Protect Democracy, Democracy Protects Markets, and Illiberal Politics Threatens to Hijack Both' (2019) 46(4) *Legal Issues of Economic Integration*, 317–28.

'The Battle for the Soul of Antitrust' (1987) 75(3) *California Law Review*, 917–23.

'Consumer Beware Chicago' (1986) 84(8) *Michigan Law Review*, 1714–20.

'Modernization of Antitrust: A New Equilibrium' (1980) 66(6) *Cornell Law Review*, 1140–92.

'The Politics of Law and Economics in Judicial Decision Making: Antitrust as a Window' (1986) 61(4) *New York University Law Review*, 554–88.

'The Symbiosis of Democracy and Markets: OECD – Directorate for Financial and Enterprise Affairs Competition Committee – Global Competition Forum – Competition and Democracy' (2017) www.oecd.org.

Fox, EM and Sullivan, LA, 'Antitrust-Retrospective and Prospective: Where Are We Coming From? Where Are We Going?' (1987) 62(5) *New York University Law Review*, 936–88.

Freyer, TA, *Antitrust and Global Capitalism, 1930–2004* (Cambridge, New York: Cambridge University Press 2006).

Friedman, M, *Capitalism and Freedom* (Chicago: University of Chicago Press 1962).

Friedman, M and Savage, LJ, 'The Expected-Utility Hypothesis and the Measurability of Utility' (1952) 60(6) *Journal of Political Economy*, 463–74.

Furman, J and Orszag, P, 'Slower Productivity and Higher Inequality: Are They Related?' (2018). Working Paper 18-4.

Gaertner, W, Pattanaik, PK, and Suzumura, K, 'Individual Rights Revisited' (1992) 59(234) *Economica*, 161–77.

Gerber, DJ, 'Constitutionalizing the Economy: German Neo-liberalism, Competition Law and the "New" Europe' (1994) 42(1) *American Journal of Comparative Law*, 25–84.

'Heinrich Kronstein and the Development of United States Antitrust Law' in Lutter et al (eds), *Der Einfluss deutscher Emigranten auf die Rechtsentwicklung in den USA und in Deutschland* (Tübingen: Mohr Siebeck 1993), 155–69.

Law and Competition in Twentieth Century Europe: Protecting Prometheus (Oxford, New York: Clarendon Press; Oxford University Press 1998).

Gerbrandy, A, 'Rethinking Competition Law within the European Economic Constitution' (2019) 57(1) *JCMS: Journal of Common Market Studies*, 127–42.

Gilbert, RJ and Newbery, DMG, 'Preemptive Patenting and the Persistence of Monopoly' (1982) 72(3) *The American Economic Review*, 514–26.

Gillens, M and Page, BI, 'Testing Theories of American Politics: Elites, Interest Groups, and Average Citizens' (2014) 12(3) *Perspectives on Politics*, 564–81.

Gillingham, J, 'Zur Vorgeschichte Der Montan-Union: Westeuropas Kohle Und Stahl in Depression Und Krieg' (1986) 34(3) *Vierteljahrshefte für Zeitgeschichte*, 381–405.

Gill-Pedro, E, 'Freedom to Conduct Business in EU Law: Freedom from Interference or Freedom from Domination?' (2017) 9(2) *European Journal of Legal Studies*, 103–34.

Goebel, T, 'The Political Economy of American Populism from Jackson to the New Deal' (1997) 11(1) *Studies in American Political Development*, 109–48.

Goodin, RE and Jackson, F, 'Freedom from Fear' (2007) 35(3) *Philosophy & Public Affairs*, 249–65.

Groeben, H von der 'Competition Policy as Part of Economic Policy in the Common Market' (1965) 10(5–6) *Antitrust Bulletin*, 911–32.

'Competition Policy in the Common Market and in the Atlantic Partnership' (1965) 10(1) *Antitrust Bulletin*, 125–54.

'Competition in the Common Market.' Speech by Hans von der Groeben, Member of the Commission of the European Economic Community, during the debate on the draft regulation pursuant to Articles 85 and 86 of the EEC Treaty in the European Parliament. Strasbourg, 19 October 1961. Includes French version.

'Competition Policy in the Common Market' (1965).

'Policy on Competition in the EEC: Supplement to Bulletin of the European Economic Community No 7–8' (1961).

Grundmann, S, 'The Concept of the Private Law Society: After 50 Years of European and European Business Law' (2008) 16(4) *European Review of Private Law*, 553–81.

Gutiérrez, G and Philippon, T, 'How EU Markets Became More Competitive Than US Markets: A Study of Institutional Drift' (2018). NBER Working Paper No 24700.

Gyselen, L, 'Rebates: Competition on the Merits or Exclusionary Practice?' in C-D Ehlermann and I Atanasiu (eds), *European Competition Law Annual 2003: What Is an Abuse of a Dominant Position?* (Oxford: Hart 2003), 287–324.

'Vertical Restraints in the Distribution Process: Strength and Weakness of the Free-Rider Rationale under EEC Competition Law' (1984) 21(4) *Common Market Law Review*, 647–68.

Hamilton, A, Madison, J, and John, J, *The Federalist Papers* (Oxford: Oxford University Press 2008).

Hanemann, W, 'Information and the Concept of Option Value' (1989) 16(1) *Journal of Environmental Economics and Management*, 23–37.

Hansen, HC, 'Robinson-Patman Law: A Review and Analysis' (1983) 51(6) *Fordham Law Review*, 1113–218.

Hawk, BE, 'System Failure: Vertical Restraints and EC Competition Law' (1995) 32(4) *Common Market Law Review*, 973–89.

Hayek, FA von (ed), *Individualism and Economic Order* (Chicago: University of Chicago Press 1948).

'Competition as Discovery Procedure – Translated by Marcellus S. Snow' (2002) 5(3) *The Quarterly Journal of Austrian Economics*, 9–23.

The Constitution of Liberty [1960] (Chicago: University of Chicago Press 2011).

The Road to Serfdom (London: Routledge 2001).

'The Use of Knowledge in Society' (1945) 35(3) *American Economic Review*, 519–30.

Heffner, RD (ed), *A Documentary History of the United States* (New York: Penguin 2013).

Henry, C, 'Option Values in the Economics of Irreplaceable Assets' (1974) 41(5) *The Review of Economic Studies*, 89–104.

Hill, C, *The World Turned Upside Down: Radical Ideas during the English Revolution* [1972] (London: Penguin 2020).

Hirschman, AO, *The Passions and the Interests: Political Arguments for Capitalism before Its Triumph* (Princeton: Princeton University Press 1977).

Hobbes, T, *Leviathan: Or the Matter, Form & Power of a Common-Wealth Eclasticall and Civill* [1651] (London: Penguin Classics 1985).

Hofstadter, R, *The American Political Tradition and the Men Who Made It* (New York: Vintage Books 1948).

'What Happened to the Antitrust Movement' in DA Crane and H Hovenkamp (eds), *The Making of Competition Policy: Legal and Economic Sources* (New York: Oxford University Press 2013), 223–51.

Hovenkamp, E and Salop, SC, 'Asymmetric Stakes in Antitrust Litigation'. USC Legal Studies Research Papers Series No 20-12 (2020).

Hovenkamp, H, 'Antitrust Balancing' (2016) 12(2) *New York University Journal of Law and Business*, 369–84.

The Antitrust Enterprise: Principle and Execution (Cambridge, MA: Harvard University Press 2005).

'Antitrust Policy after Chicago' (1985) 84(2) *Michigan Law Review*, 213–84.

'The Areeda-Turner Test for Exclusionary Pricing: A Critical Journal' (2015) 46(3) *Review of Industrial Organization*, 209–28.

'The Neal Report and the Crisis in Antitrust' (2009). Penn Law Faculty Scholarship 1794.

'The Rule of Reason' (2018) 70(1) *Florida Law Review*, 81–167.

Hovenkamp, H and Shapiro, C, 'Horizontal Mergers, Market Structure, and Burdens of Proof' (2018) 127(7) *The Yale Law Journal*, 1996–2025.

Howse, R, 'Montesquieu on Commerce, Conquest, War and Peace' (2006) 31(3) *Brooklyn Journal of International Law*, 693–708.

Hurwitz, JD and Kovacic, WE, 'Judicial Analysis of Predation: The Emerging Trends' (1982) 35(1) *Vanderbilt Law Review*, 63–156.

Hüttenberger, P, 'Wirtschaftsordnung und Interessenpolitik in der Kartellgesetzgebung der Bundesrepublik 1949–1957' (1976) 24(3) *Vierteljahrshefte für Zeitgeschichte*, 287–307.

Hylton, KN and Salinger, M, 'Tying Law and Policy: A Decision-Theoretic Approach' (2001) 69(2) *Antitrust Law Journal*, 469–526.

Jefferson, T, *Political Writings* (Cambridge: Cambridge University Press 2004).

Joliet, R, *Monopolization and Abuse of Dominant Position: A Comparative Study of the American and European Approaches to the Control of Economic Power* (La Haye/Liège: Martinus Nijhoff 1970).

Jones, A and Kovacic, WE, 'Identifying Anticompetitive Agreements in the United States and the European Union: Developing a Coherent Antitrust Analytical Framework' (2017) 62 (2) *The Antitrust Bulletin*, 254–93.

Kalintiri, A, 'Analytical Shortcuts in EU Competition Enforcement: Proxies, Premises, and Presumptions' (2020) 16(3) *Journal of Competition Law & Economics*, 392–433.

Evidence Standards in EU Competition Enforcement: The EU Approach (Oxford: Hart 2019).

Kallaugher, J and Sher, B, 'Rebates Revisited: Anti-Competitive Effects and Exclusionary Abuse under Article 82' (2004) 25(5) *European Competition Law Review*, 263–85.

Kalyvas, A and Katznelson, I, *Liberal Beginnings: Making a Republic for the Moderns* (Cambridge: Cambridge University Press 2008).

Kaplow, L, 'Efficiencies in Merger Analysis' (2021) 83(3) *Antitrust Law Journal*, 557–619.

'Likelihood Ratio Tests and Legal Decision Rules' (2014) 16(1) *American Law and Economics Review*, 1–39.

'Rules versus Standards: An Economic Analysis' (1992) 42(3) *Duke Law Journal*, 557–629.

Katz, ML and Shapiro, C, 'Systems Competition and Network Effects' (1994) 8(2) *Journal of Economic Perspectives*, 93–115.

Katz, ML and Shelanski, HA, 'Merger Analysis and the Treatment of Uncertainty: Should We Expect Better?' (2007) 74(3) *Antitrust Law Journal*, 537–74.

Kauper, TE, 'The Influence of Conservative Economic Analysis on the Development of the Law of Antitrust' in R Pitofsky (ed), *How the Chicago School Overshot the Mark: The Effect of Conservative Economic Analysis on U.S. Antitrust* (Oxford: Oxford University Press 2008), 40–50.

Kaysen, C and Turner, DF, *Antitrust Policy: An Economic and Legal Analysis* (Cambridge, MA: Harvard University Press 1959).

Kerber, W, 'Competition, Innovation and Maintaining Diversity through Competition Law' in R Podszun, W Kerber, and J Drexl (eds), *Competition Policy and the Economic Approach: Foundations and Limitations* (Cheltenham: Edward Elgar 2011), 173–201.

Keynes, JM, *A Treatise on Probability* (London: Macmillan 1921).

Khan, L, 'Amazon's Antitrust Paradox' (2017) 126(3) *Yale Law Journal*, 710–805.

Khan, L, 'The New Brandeis Movement: America's Antimonopoly Debate' (2018) 9(3) *Journal for European Competition Law & Practice*, 131–32.

Klobuchar, A, *Antitrust: Taking on Monopoly Power from the Gilded Age to the Digital Age* (New York: Alfred A. Knopf 2021).

Knight, F, *Risk, Uncertainty and Profit* (Boston: Houghton Mifflin 1921).

Knortz, H, *Wirtschaftsgeschichte der Weimarer Republik: Eine Einführung in Ökonomie und Gesellschaft der ersten Deutschen Republik* (Göttingen: Vandenhoeck & Ruprecht 2010).

Koltay, G, Lorincz, S and Valletti, T, 'Concentration and Competition: Evidence From Europe and Implications For Policy' (2023) 19(3) *Journal of Competition Law & Economics*, 466.

Koopmans, TC, 'On Flexibility of Future Preference' (1962). Cowles Foundation Discussion Paper 150.

Korah, V, 'From Legal Form toward Economic Efficiency – Article 85 (1) of the EEC Treaty in Contrast to U.S. Antitrust' (1990) 35(4) *Antitrust Bulletin*, 1009–36.

'The Rise and Fall of Provisional Validity: The Need for a Rule of Reason in EEC Antitrust' (1981) 3(2) *Northwestern Journal of International Law & Business*, 320–57.

Kovacic, WE, 'The Intellectual DNA of Modern U.S. Competition Law for Dominant Firm Conduct: The Chicago/Harvard Double Helix' (2007) 1(1) *Columbia Business Law Review*, 1–80.

Kramer, MH, *The Quality of Freedom* (Oxford: Oxford University Press 2003).

Krattenmaker, TG and Salop, SC, 'Anticompetitive Exclusion: Raising Rivals' Costs to Achieve Power over Price' (1986) 96(3) *The Yale Law Journal*, 209–93.

Kreps, DM, 'A Representation Theorem for "Preference for Flexibility"' (1979) 47(3) *Econometrica*, 565–77.

La Castillo de Torre, F and Gippini Fournier, E, *Evidence, Proof and Judicial Review in EU Competition Law* (Cheltenham: Edward Elgar 2017).

Lande, RH, 'Wealth Transfers as the Original and Primary Concern of Antitrust: The Efficiency Interpretation Challenged' (1982) 34(1) *Hastings Law Journal*, 65–152.

Larouche, P and Schinkel, MP, 'Continental Drift in the Treatment of Dominant Firms: Article 102 TFEU in Contrast to § 2 Sherman Act' (TILEC Discussion Paper No 2013-02, Tilburg 2013).

Lemley, MA and Shapiro, C, 'Probabilistic Patents' (2005) 19(2) *Journal of Economic Perspectives*, 75–98.

Letina, I, 'The Road Not Taken: Competition and the R&D Portfolio' (2016) 47(2) *The RAND Journal of Economics*, 433–60.

Letwin, W, *Law and Economic Policy in America: The Evolution of the Sherman Antitrust Act* [1959] (Chicago: Chicago University Press 1981).

Leucht, B, 'Expertise and the Creation of a Constitutional Order for Core Europe: Transatlantic Policy Networks in the Schuman Plan Negotiations' in W Kaiser, B Leucht, and M Gehler (eds), *Transnational Networks in Regional Integration: Governing Europe 1945–83* (New York: Palgrave Macmillan 2010), 18–37.

'Transatlantic Policy Networks in the Creation of the First European Anti-trust Law: Mediating between American Anti-trust and German Ordo-liberalism' in W Kaiser, B Leucht, and M Rasmussen (eds), *The History of the European Union: Origins of a Trans- and Supranational Polity 1950–72* (New York: Routledge 2009), 56–73.

Leucht, B and Marquis, M, 'American Influences on EEC Competition Law: Two Paths, How Much Dependence?' in KK Patel and H Schweitzer (eds), *The Historical Foundations of EU Competition Law* (Oxford: Oxford University Press 2013), 125–61.

Leucht, B and Seidel, K, 'Du Traité de Paris au règlement 17/1962: Ruptures et continuités dans la politique européenne de concurrence, 1950–1962' (2008) 27(1) *Histoire, économie & société*, 35–46.

Levi, EH, 'The Antitrust Laws and Monopoly' (1947) 14(2) *University of Chicago Law Review*, 153–83.

Lianos, I and Katalevsky, D, 'Merger Activity in the Factors of Production Segments of the Food Value Chain: A Critical Assessment of the Bayer/Monsanto merger' (2017). Policy Paper Series 1/2017.

Lilburne, J, 'England's New Chains Discovered [1649]' in A Sharp (ed), *The English Levellers* (Cambridge: Cambridge University Press 2004), 140–57.

'Postscript to the Freeman's Freedom Vindicated [1646]' in A Sharp (ed), *The English Levellers* (Cambridge: Cambridge University Press 2004), 31–32.

and others, 'The Petition of 11 September 1648 [1648]' in A Sharp (ed), *The English Levellers* (Cambridge: Cambridge University Press 2004), 131–39.

Lindeboom, J, 'Formalism in Competition Law' (2022) 18(4) *Journal of Competition Law and Economics*, 832–80.

Lindsay, A and Berridge, A, *The EU Merger Regulation: Substantive Issues* (London: Sweet & Maxwell 2012).

List, C, 'The Impossibility of a Paretian Republican? Some Comments on Pettit and Sen' (2004) 20(1) *Economics and Philosophy*, 65–87.

'Republican Freedom and the Rule of Law' (2006) 5(2) *Politics, Philosophy & Economics*, 201–20.

'Social Choice Theory' https://plato.stanford.edu.

List, C and Pettit, P, *Group Agency: The Possibility, Design, and Status of Corporate Agents* (Oxford: Oxford University Press 2013).

List, C and Valentini, L, 'Freedom as Independence' (2016) 126(4) *Ethics*, 1043–74.

Llorens Albors, A, 'The Role of Objective Justification and Efficiencies in the Application of Article 82 EC' (2007) 44(6) *Common Market Law Review*, 1727–61.

Loecker, J de, Eeckhout, J, and Unger, G, 'The Rise of Market Power and the Macroeconomic Implications' (2020) 135(2) *The Quarterly Journal of Economics*, 561–644.

Lynn, BC, *Liberty from All Masters: The New American Autocracy vs. the Will of the People* (New York: St. Martin's Press 2020).

Ma, T-C, 'Antitrust and Democracy: Perspectives from Efficiency and Equity' (2016) 12(2) *Journal of Competition Law & Economics*, 233–61.

MacCallum, GC, 'Negative and Positive Freedom' (1967) 76(3) *The Philosophical Review*, 312–34.

Machiavelli, N, *Discourses on Livy* (Chicago: University of Chicago Press 1998).
Maier-Rigaud, F, 'On the Normative Foundations of Competition Law: Efficiency, Political Freedom and the Freedom to Compete' in D Zimmer (ed), *The Goals of Competition Law* (Cheltenham: Elgar 2012), 132–68.
Marshall, A, *Principles of Economics: An Introductory Volume* (London: Macmillan 1920).
Martin, AW and Schum, DA, 'Quantifying Burdens of Proof: A Likelihood Ratio Approach' (1987) 27(4) *Jurimetrics*, 383–402.
Mason, ES, 'The Current Status of the Monopoly Problem in the United States' (1949) 62(8) *Harvard Law Review*, 1265–85.
Economic Concentration and the Monopoly Problem (Cambridge, MA: Harvard University Press 1959).
'Monopoly in Law and Economics' (1937) 47(1) *The Yale Law Journal*, 34–49.
'Schumpeter on Monopoly and the Large Firm' (1951) 33(2) *The Review of Economics and Statistics*, 139–44.
May, J, 'Antitrust in the Formative Era: Political and Economic Theory in Constitutional and Antitrust Analysis, 1880–1918' (1989) 50(2) *Ohio State Law Journal*, 257–396.
McCormick, JP, 'Machiavellian Democracy: Controlling Elites with Ferocious Populism' (2001) 95(2) *American Political Science Review*, 297–313.
Meadowcroft, J and William, R, 'Hayek, Friedman, and Buchanan: On Public Life, Chile, and the Relationship between Liberty and Democracy' (2014) 26(3) *Review of Political Economy*, 358–67.
Meese, AJ, 'Liberty and Antitrust in the Formative Era' (1999) 79(1) *Boston University Law Review*, 1–92.
Melamed, AD and Petit, N, 'The Misguided Assault on the Consumer Welfare Standard in the Age of Platform Markets' (2019) 54(4) *Review of Industrial Organization*, 741–74.
Merk, O and Teodoro, A, 'Alternative Approaches to Measuring Concentration in Liner Shipping' (2022) 24(4) *Maritime Economics & Logistics*, 723–46.
Mestmäcker, E-J (ed), *Wirtschaft und Verfassung in der Europäischen Union* (Baden-Baden: Nomos 2003).
'Competition Policy and Antitrust: Some Comparative Observations' (1980) 136(3) *Zeitschrift für die gesamte Staatswissenschaft/ Journal of Institutional and Theoretical Economics*, 387–407.
'Die Beurteilung von Unternehmenszusammenschlüssen nach Artikel 86 des Vertrages über die Europäische Wirtschaftsgemeinschaft [1965]' in E-J Mestmäcker (ed), *Wirtschaft und Verfassung in der Europäischen Union* (Baden-Baden: Nomos 2003), 597–623.
'The Development of German and European Competition Law with Special Reference to the EU Commission's Article 82 Guidance of 2008' in LF Pace (ed), *European Competition Law: The Impact of the Commission's Guidance on Article 102* (Cheltenham: Edward Elgar 2011), 25–62.
'Wirtschaftsordnung und Staatsverfassung' in F Böhm, E-J Mestmäcker, and H Sauermann (eds), *Wirtschaftsordnung und Staatsverfassung: Festschrift f. Franz Böhm z. 80. Geburtstag* (Tübingen: Mohr Siebeck 1975), 383–420.
Mestmäcker, E-J and Schweitzer, H, *Europäisches Wettbewerbsrecht* (München: Beck 2014).
Miksch, L, 'Die Wirtschaftspolitik des Als-Ob' (1948) 105(2) *Zeitschrift für die gesamte Staatswissenschaft*, 310–38.
'Versuch eines liberalen Programms [1949]' in N Goldschmidt (ed), *Grundtexte zur Freiburger Tradition der Ordnungsökonomik* (Tübingen: Mohr Siebeck 2008), 163–70.
Wettbewerb als Aufgabe: Grundsätze einer Wettbewerbsordnung (Godersberg: Verlag Helmut Küpper 1947).

Mill, JS, *On Liberty, Utilitarianism and Other Essays* [1859] (Oxford: Oxford University Press 2015).
Miller, ST, 'The Case of the Monopolies: Some of Its Results and Suggestions' (1907) 6(1) *Michigan Law Review*, 1–24.
Montesquieu, Charles-Louis de Secondat, *De l'esprit des lois* [1748] (Paris: Garnier-Flammarion 1979).
Monti, G, 'Abuse of a Dominant Position: A Post-Intel Calm?' [2019] *CPI Antitrust Chronicle*, 1.
'The Concept of Dominance in Article 82' (2006) 2 (sup1) *European Competition Journal*, 31–52.
EC Competition Law (Cambridge: Cambridge University Press 2007).
'The Scope of Collective Dominance under Articles 82 EC' (2001) 38(1) *Common Market Law Review*, 131–57.
More, T, *The Utopia: In Latin from the Edition of March 1518, and in English from the First Edition of Ralph Robynson's Translation in 1551 with Additional Translations, Introduction and Notes by J.H. Lupton* [1516] (Oxford: Clarendon Press 1895).
Utopia: Translated, Edited and Introduced by Dominic Baker-Smith [1516] (London: Penguin Classics 2012).
Möschel, W, 'Competition Policy from an Ordo Point of View' in AT Peacock, H Willgerodt, and D Johnson (eds), *German Neo-liberals and the Social Market Economy* (London: Macmillan 1989), 142–59.
Müller, P, 'Sovereignty Trade-Offs between Politics and the Economy: The Deconcentration of IG Farben after 1945' (2022) 55(1) *Central European History*, 53–69.
Müller-Armack, A, 'The Social Market Economy as an Economic and Social Order' (1978) 36 (3) *Review of Social Economy*, 325–31.
Nachbar, TB, 'Monopoly, Mercantilism, and the Politics of Regulation' (2005) 91(5) *Virginia Law Review*, 1313–80.
Neal, PC and others, 'Report of the White House Task Force on Antitrust Policy' (1968–1969) 2(2) *Antitrust Law & Economics Review*, 11–52.
Nelson, RR, 'Uncertainty, Learning, and the Economics of Parallel Research and Development Efforts' (1961) 43(4) *The Review of Economics and Statistics*, 351–64.
Neumann, F, *Behemoth: The Structure and Practice of National Socialism, 1933–1944* [1942] (New York: Octagon 1963).
Nic Shuibhne, N, 'The Resilience of EU Market Citizenship' (2010) 47(6) *Common Market Law Review, Issue*, 1597–628.
O'Donoghue, R and Padilla, AJ, *The Law and Economics of Article 82 EC* (Oxford: Hart 2006).
Olson, M, *The Logic of Collective Action: Public Goods and the Theory of Groups* [1965] (Harvard: Harvard University Press 1971).
Ophüls, CF, 'Das Wirtschaftsrecht des Schumanplans' (1951) 4(10) *Neue Juristische Wochenschrift*, 381–84.
Oppenheim, CS, 'Federal Antitrust Legislation: Guideposts to a Revised National Antitrust Policy' (1952) 50(8) *Michigan Law Review*, 1139–244.
Orbach, BY, 'The Antitrust Consumer Welfare Paradox' (2011) 7(1) *Journal of Competition Law and Economics*, 133–64.
Ostrom, E, 'Why Do We Need to Protect Institutional Diversity?' (2012) 11(1) *European Political Science*, 128–47.
Ostrom, V, 'Polycentricity: The Structural Basis of Self-Governing Systems' in F Sabetti and P Dragos Aligica (eds), *Choice, Rules and Collective Action: The Ostroms on the Study of Institutions and Governance* (Colchester: ECPR Press 2014), 45–60.

Overton, R, 'An Arrow against all Tyrants [1646]' in A Sharp (ed), *The English Levellers* (Cambridge: Cambridge University Press 2004), 54–72.

Overton, R and Walwyn, W, 'A Remonstrance of Many Thousand Citizens [1646]' in A Sharp (ed), *The English Levellers* (Cambridge: Cambridge University Press 2004), 33–53.

Padilla, AJ and Ahlborn, C, 'From Fairness to Welfare: Implications for the Assessment of Unilateral Conduct under EC Competition Law' in C-D Ehlermann and M Marquis (eds), *European Competition Law Annual 2007: A Reformed Approach to Article 82 EC* (Oxford: Hart 2008), 55–101.

Paine, T, *Political Writings* (Cambridge: Cambridge University Press 2000).

Park, JW, 'The Utopian Economics of Sir Thomas More' (1971) 30(3) *The American Journal of Economics and Sociology*, 275–88.

Patel, KK and Schweitzer, H, 'Introduction' in KK Patel and H Schweitzer (eds), *The Historical Foundations of EU Competition Law* (Oxford: Oxford University Press 2013), 1–18.

Pattnaik, PK and Xu, Y, 'On Ranking Opportunity Sets in Terms of Freedom of Choice' (1990) 56(3/4) *Recherches économiques de Louvain/Louvain Economic Review*, 383–90.

Peltzman, S, 'Toward a More General Theory of Regulation' (1976) 19(2) *The Journal of Law and Economics*, 211–40.

Peritz, RJ, *Competition Policy in America: History, Rhetoric, Law* (New York: Oxford University Press 2000).

'A Counter-History of Antitrust Law' (1990) 39(2) *Duke Law Journal*, 263–320.

Petersen, N, 'Antitrust Law and the Promotion of Democracy and Economic Growth' (2013) 9 (3) *Journal of Competition Law & Economics*, 593–636.

Petit, N, 'Competition Cases Involving Platforms – Lessons from Europe: Comment on Federal Trade Commission ("FTC") Hearing #3 on Competition and Consumer Protection in the 21st Century' (2018).

Pettit, P, 'Capability and Freedom: A Defence of Sen' (2001) 17(1) *Economics and Philosophy*, 1–20.

'Freedom as Antipower' (1996) 106(3) *Ethics*, 576–604.

'Freedom in the Market' (2006) 5(2) *Politics, Philosophy & Economics*, 131–49.

'Freedom and Probability: A Comment on Goodin and Jackson' (2008) 36(2) *Philosophy & Public Affairs*, 206–20.

'The Instability of Freedom as Noninterference: The Case of Isaiah Berlin' (2011) 121(4) *Ethics*, 693–716.

On the People's Terms: A Republican Theory and Model of Democracy (Cambridge: Cambridge University Press 2012).

Republicanism: A Theory of Freedom and Government (Oxford: Oxford University Press 1997).

'Republican Freedom: Three Axioms, Four Theorems' in C Laborde and J Maynor (eds), *Republicanism and Political Theory* (Malden : Blackwell 2008), 102–30.

Philippon, T, *The Great Reversal: How America Gave Up on Free Markets* (Cambridge, MA: Harvard University Press 2019).

Pitkin, HF, 'Are Freedom and Liberty Twins?' (1988) 16(4) *Political Theory*, 523–52.

Pitofsky, R, 'The Political Content of Antitrust' (1979) 127(4) *University of Pennsylvania Law Review*, 1051–75.

Pocock, JGA and Whatmore, R, *The Machiavellian Moment: Florentine Political Thought and the Atlantic Republican Tradition* [1975] (Princeton: Princeton University Press 2016).

Polanyi, M, *The Logic of Liberty* (London: Routledge 1951).

Popofsky, MS, 'Defining Exclusionary Conduct: Section 2, The Rule of Reason, and the Unifying Principle Underlying Antitrust Rules' (2005) 73(2) *Antitrust Law Journal*, 435–82.

Portuese, A, 'Precautionary Antitrust: A Precautionary Tale in European Competition Policy' in K Mathis and A Tor (eds), *Law and Economics of Regulation* (Cham: Springer International Publishing 2021), 203–32.

Posner, RA, *Antitrust Law* (Chicago: University of Chicago Press 2001).

'The Chicago School of Antitrust Analysis' (1979) 127(4) *University of Pennsylvania Law Review*, 925–48.

Economic Analysis of Law [1972] (Boston: Little, Brown & Comp 1977).

'An Economic Approach to Legal Procedure and Judicial Administration' (1973) 2(2) *The Journal of Legal Studies*, 399–458.

'Exclusionary Practices and the Antitrust Laws' (1974) 41(3) *The University of Chicago Law Review*, 506–35.

'Information and Antitrust: Reflections on the Gypsum and Engineers Decisions' (1979) 67 (5) *Georgetown Law Journal*, 1187–204.

'Norms and Values in the Economic Approach to Law' in AN Hatzis and N Mercuro (eds), *Law and Economics: Philosophical Issues and Fundamental Questions* (London: Routledge 2015), 1–15.

'Oligopoly and the Antitrust Laws: A Suggested Approach' (1968–1969) 21 *Stanford Law Review*, 1562–604.

'Utilitarianism, Economics, and Legal Theory' (1979) 8(1) *The Journal of Legal Studies*, 103–40.

'Wealth Maximization Revisited' (1985) 2(1) *Notre Dame Journal of Law, Ethics and Public Policy*, 85–105.

Quinn, TK, *Giant Business: Threat to Democracy: The Autobiography of an Insider* (New York: NY Exposition Press 1953).

Rahman, KS, 'Domination, Democracy, and Constitutional Political Economy in the New Gilded Age: Towards a Fourth Wave of Legal Realism?' (2016) 94(7) *Texas Law Review*, 1329–60.

Raymond, FI, *The Limitist* (New York: W.W. Norton & Co 1947).

Reeves, T and Dodoo, N, 'Standards of Proof and Standards of Judicial Review in European Commission Merger Law: Fordham Law School Centennial Issue' (2006) 29(5) *Fordham International Law Journal*, 1034–67.

Ritter, C, 'Presumptions in EU Competition Law' (2018) 6(2) *Journal of Antitrust Enforcement*, 189–212.

Robinson, J, *The Economics of Imperfect Competition* (London: Macmillan 1933).

Röller, L-H and De la Mano, M, 'The Impact of the New Substantive Test in European Merger Control' (2006) 2(1) *European Competition Journal*, 9–28.

Roosevelt, T, 'The Trusts, the People, and the Square Deal' in DA Crane and H Hovenkamp (eds), *The Making of Competition Policy: Legal and Economic Sources* (New York: Oxford University Press 2013), 107–17.

Röpke, W, *Jenseits von Angebot und Nachfrage* [1958] (Düsseldorf: Verl.-Anst. Handwerk 2009).

Rosanvallon, P, *Le libéralisme économique: Histoire de l'idée de marché* (Paris: Seuil 1989).

Rostow, EV, 'Monopoly under the Sherman Act: Power or Purpose' (1949) 43(6) *Illinois Law Review*, 745–93.

'The New Sherman Act: A Positive Instrument of Progress' (1947) 14(4) *The University of Chicago Law Review*, 567–600.

Rothschild, E, 'Adam Smith and Conservative Economics' (1992) 45(1) *The Economic History Review*, 74–96.

Rousseau, J-J, *Du contrat social* [1767] (Paris: Flammarion 2001).

Rubinfeld, DL, 'On the Foundations of Antitrust Law and Economics' in R Pitofsky (ed), *How the Chicago School Overshot the Mark: The Effect of Conservative Economic Analysis on U.S. Antitrust* (Oxford: Oxford University Press 2008), 51–58.

Sacks, DH, 'Commonwealth Discourse and Economic Thought: The Morality of Exchange' in S Doran and N Jones (eds), *The Elizabethan World* (London: Routledge 2014), 389–410.

'Parliament, Liberty, and the Commonweal' in JH Hexter (ed), *Parliament and Liberty from the Reign of Elizabeth to the English Civil War* (Stanford: Stanford University Press 1992), 85–121.

Salop, SC, 'An Enquiry Meet for the Case: Decision Theory, Presumptions, and Evidentiary Burdens in Formulating Antitrust Legal Standards' https://scholarship.law.georgetown.edu (2017).

'The Evolution and Vitality of Merger Presumptions: A Decision-Theoretic Approach' (2015) 80(2) *Antitrust Law Journal*, 269–306.

'The Raising Rivals' Cost Foreclosure Paradigm, Conditional Pricing Practices and the Flawed Incremental Price-Cost Test' (2017) 81(2) *Antitrust Law Journal*, 371–422.

Salop, SC and Scheffman, DT, 'Cost-Raising Strategies' (1987) 36(1) *The Journal of Industrial Economics*, 19–34.

Scherer, FM and Ross, D, *Industrial Market Structure and Economic Performance* (Boston: Houghton Mifflin 1990).

Schumpeter, JA, *Capitalism, Socialism and Democracy* [1942] (New York: Harper & Row 1962).

Schwartz, E, 'Politics as Usual: The History of European Community Merger Control' (1993) 18(2) *Yale Journal of International Law*, 607–62.

Schwartz, LB, 'Institutional Size and Individual Liberty: Authoritarian Aspects of Bigness' (1960) 55(1) *Northwestern University Law Review*, 4–24.

'"Justice" and Other Non-economic Goals of Antitrust' (1979) 127(4) *University of Pennsylvania Law Review*, 1076–81.

Schweitzer, H, 'Das Wettbewerbsrecht und das Problem privater Macht' in F Möslein (ed), *Private Macht* (Tübingen: Mohr Siebeck 2016), 447–73.

'The History, Interpretation and Underlying Principles of Section 2 Sherman Act and Article 82 EC' in C-D Ehlermann and M Marquis (eds), *European Competition Law Annual 2007: A Reformed Approach to Article 82 EC* (Oxford: Hart 2008), 119–64.

Scott, SP, 'The Enactments of Justinian – The Code–Book IV' in SP Scott (ed), *The Civil Law: Including The Twelve Tables, The Institutes of Gaius, The Rules of Ulpian, The Opinions of Paulus, The Enactments of Justinian, and The Constitutions of Leo: Translated from the Original Latin, Edited, and Compared with All Accessible Systems of Jurisprudence Ancient and Modern. By S. P. SCOTT, A. M.* (Cincinatti: The Central Trust Company 1932).

Seaborne Davies, D, 'Further Light on the Case of Monopolies' (1932) 48(3) *Law Quarterly Review*, 394–414.

Seidel, K, 'DG IV and the Origins of a Supranational Competition Policy: Establishing an Economic Constitution for Europe' in W Kaiser, B Leucht, and M Rasmussen (eds), *The History of the European Union: Origins of a Trans- and Supranational Polity 1950–1972* (New York: Routledge 2009), 131–47.

Sen, A, *Development as Freedom* [1999] (New York: Anchor Books 2013).

'The Impossibility of a Paretian Liberal' (1970) 78(1) *Journal of Political Economy*, 152–57.
'Liberty and Social Choice' (1983) 80(1) *The Journal of Philosophy*, 5–28.
'Markets and Freedoms: Achievements and Limitations of the Market Mechanism in Promoting Individual Freedoms' (1993) 45(4) *Oxford Economic Papers*, 519–41.
Shapiro, C, 'The 2010 Horizontal Merger Guidelines: From Hedgehog to Fox in Forty Years' (2010) 77(1) *Antitrust Law Journal*, 49–107.
Shapiro, I, *The State of Democratic Theory* (Oxford: Oxford University Press 2004).
Simons, HC, *Economic Policy for a Free Society* (Chicago: Chicago University Press 1948).
Skinner, Q, *Liberty before Liberalism* (Cambridge: Cambridge University Press 1998).
'Rethinking Political Liberty' (2006) 61(1) *History Workshop Journal*, 156–70.
'A Third Concept of Liberty: Isaiah Berlin Lecture' in The British Academy (ed), *Proceedings of the British Academy: 2001 Lectures*. Volume 117 (Oxford: Oxford University Press; British Academy 2002), 237–68.
Smith, A, *An Inquiry into the Nature and Causes of the Wealth of Nations* [1776] (Oxford: Oxford University Press 1976).
The Theory of Moral Sentiments [1759] (New York: Penguin 2009).
Smith, F, 'Why Not Abolish Antitrust?' (1983) 7(1) *Regulation*, 23–28.
Spector, C, 'Commerce' in C Volpilhac-Auger (ed), *Dictionnaire Montesquieu* (2013) https://dictionnaire-montesquieu.ens-lyon.fr.
Spoerer, M and Steg, J, *Neue Deutsche Wirtschaftsgeschichte* (München 2013).
Steinbaum, M and Stucke, ME, 'The Effective Competition Standard: A New Standard for Antitrust' (2020) 87(2) *The University of Chicago Law Review*, 595–623.
Steiner, H, 'The Structure of a Set of Compossible Rights' (1977) 74(12) *The Journal of Philosophy*, 767–75.
Steuart, J, *An Inquiry into the Principles of Political Oeconomy: Being An Essay on the Science of Domestic Policy in Free Nations* (London: A. Millar and T. Cadell 1768).
Stevens, WHS, 'The Clayton Act' (1915) 5(1) *The American Economic Review*, 38–54.
Stigler, GJ, 'Barriers to Entry, Economies of Scale, and Firm Size' in GJ Stigler (ed), *The Organization of Industry* (Chicago: University of Chicago Press 1968), 67–70.
'Imperfections in the Capital Market: Reprinted from *Journal of Political Economy*, Vol. LXXV, No. 3, June 1967' in GJ Stigler (ed), *The Organization of Industry* (Chicago: University of Chicago Press 1968), 113–24.
'Mergers and Preventive Antitrust Policy' Reprinted from *University of Pennsylvania Law Review*, Vol. 104, No 2 (1955)' in GJ Stigler (ed), *The Organization of Industry* (Chicago: University of Chicago Press 1968), 296–305.
'Monopoly and Oligopoly by Merger' Reprinted from Papers and Proceedings, *American Economic Review*, Vol. XL, No. 2. (1950)' in GJ Stigler (ed), *The Organization of Industry* (Chicago: University of Chicago Press 1968), 95–107.
'Smith's Travels on the Ship of State' (1971) 3(2) *History of Political Economy*, 265–77.
'The Theory of Economic Regulation' (1971) 2(1) *The Bell Journal of Economics and Management Science*, 3–21.
'A Theory of Oligopoly: Reprinted from Journal of Political Economy Vol. LXXII, No 1 (1964)' in GJ Stigler (ed), *The Organization of Industry* (Chicago: University of Chicago Press 1968), 39–65.
'Wealth, and Possibly Liberty' (1978) 7(2) *The Journal of Legal Studies*, 213–17.
Stoller, M, *Goliath: The 100-Year War between Monopoly Power and Democracy* (New York: Simon & Schuster 2019).
Stucke, ME, 'Reconsidering Antitrust's Goals' (2012) 53(2) *Boston College Law Review*, 551–629.

Sullivan, LA, *Antitrust* (St. Paul: West Publishing 1977).

Sullivan, SP, 'What Structural Presumption: Reuniting Evidence and Economics on the Role of Market Concentration in Horizontal Merger Analysis' (2016) 42(2) *Journal of Corporation Law*, 403–44.

Suttle, O, 'The Puzzle of Competitive Fairness' (2022) 21(2) *Politics, Philosophy & Economics*, 190–227.

Tarbell, IM, *The History of the Standard Oil Company* (New York: McClure, Phillips & Co 1904).

Taylor, RS, 'Market Freedom as Antipower' (2013) 107(3) *American Political Science Review*, 593–602.

Teachout, Z and Khan, L, 'Market Structure and Political Law: A Taxonomy of Power' (2014) 9(2) *Duke Journal of Constitutional Law & Public Policy*, 37–74.

Telser, LG, 'Why Should Manufacturers Want Fair Trade' (1960) 3 *Journal of Law and Economics*, 86–105.

Temple Lang, J and O'Donoghue, R, 'Defining Legitimate Competition: How to Clarify Pricing Abuses under Article 82' (2002) 26(1) *Fordham International Law Journal*, 83–162.

Thorelli, HB, *The Federal Antitrust Policy: Origination of an American Tradition* (Baltimore: Johns Hopkins Press 1955).

Tinbergen, J, *On the Theory of Economic Policy* (Amsterdam: North-Holland Publishing Company 1952).

Titus Livius (Livy), *The History of Rome: Translated from the Original with Notes and Illustrations by George Baker, A.M.* (New York: Peter A. Mesier et al. 1823).

Tom, WK, Balto, DA, and Averitt, NW, 'Anticompetitive Aspects of Market-Share Discounts and Other Incentives to Exclusive Dealing' (2000) 67(3) *Antitrust Law Journal*, 615–40.

Tooze, A, 'The German National Economy in an Era of Crisis and War, 1917–1945' in HW Smith (ed), *The Oxford Handbook of Modern German History* (Oxford, New York: Oxford University Press 2011), 400–22.

Townshend, H, *Historical Collections; or, An Exact Account of the Last Four Parliaments of Q. Elizabeth of Famous Memory* (London: Printed for T. Basset, W. Crooke, and W. Cademan 1680).

Tribe, LH, 'Trial by Mathematics: Precision and Ritual in the Legal Process' (1970) 84(6) *Harvard Law Review*, 1329–93.

Turner, DF, 'Conglomerate Mergers and Section 7 of the Clayton Act' (1965) 78(7) *Harvard Law Review*, 1313–95.

'The Definition of Agreement under the Sherman Act: Conscious Parallelism and Refusals to Deal' (1962) 75(4) *Harvard Law Review*, 655.

'The Scope of Antitrust and Other Economic Regulatory Policies' (1969) 82(6) *Harvard Law Review*, 1207–44.

'The Validity of Tying Arrangements under the Antitrust Laws' (1958) 72(1) *Harvard Law Review*, 50–75.

Vande Walle, S, 'Competition and Competition Law in Japan: Between Scepticism and Embrace' in MW Dowdle, J Gillespie, and Maher Imelda (eds), *Asian Capitalism and the Regulation of Competition: Towards a Regulatory Geography of Global Competition Law* (Cambridge: Cambridge University Press 2013), 123–43.

Verouden, V, Bengtsson, C, and Albaek, S, 'The Draft EU Notice on Horizontal Mergers: A Further Step toward Convergence' (2004) 49(1–2) *Antitrust Bulletin*, 243–85.

Vesterdorf, B, 'Standard of Proof in Merger Cases: Reflections in the Light of Recent Case Law of the Community Courts' (2005) 1(1) *European Competition Journal*, 3–33.

Viner, J, 'Adam Smith and Laissez Faire' (1927) 35(2) *Journal of Political Economy*, 198–232.

Wagner, DO, 'Coke and the Rise of Economic Liberalism' (1935) 6(1) *The Economic History Review*, 30–44.
Walras, L, *Elements of Pure Economics: Or, the Theory of Social Wealth* (Fairfield: A.M. Kelley 1977, 1954).
Walwyn, W, 'Gold Tried in the Fire [1647]' in A Sharp (ed), *The English Levellers* (Cambridge: Cambridge University Press 2004), 73–91.
Watson, A (ed), *The Digest of Justinian: Volume I* (Philadelphia: University of Pennsylvania Press 1985).
Weber Waller, S, 'The Antitrust Legacy of Thurman Arnold' (2004) 78(3) *St. John's Law Review*, 569–614.
'Antitrust and Democracy' (2019) 46(4) *Florida State University Law Review*, 806–60.
Weisbrod, BA, 'Collective-Consumption Services of Individual-Consumption Goods' (1964) 78(3) *The Quarterly Journal of Economics*, 471–77.
Wells, WC, *Antitrust and the Formation of the Postwar World* (New York: Columbia University Press 2002).
Whinston, M, 'Tying, Foreclosure, and Exclusion' (1990) 80(4) *American Economic Review*, 837–59.
Whish, R, 'Regulation 2790/99: The Commission's "new style" Block Exemption for Vertical Agreements' (2000) 37(4) *Common Market Law Review*, 887–924.
Whish, R and Sufrin, B, 'Article 85 and the Rule of Reason' (1987) 7(1) *Yearbook of European Law*, 1–38.
Wigger, A, 'Debunking the Myth of the Ordoliberal Influence on Post-war European Integration' in C Joerges and J Hien (eds), *Ordoliberalism: Law and the Rule of Economics* (Oxford: Hart 2018), 161–78.
Williamson, OE, 'Economies as an Antitrust Defense: The Welfare Tradeoffs' (1968) 58(1) *The American Economic Review*, 18–36.
Wilson, W, *The New Freedom* (Leipzig: Tauchnitz 1913).
'The Tariff and the Trusts' in DA Crane and H Hovenkamp (eds), *The Making of Competition Policy: Legal and Economic Sources* (New York: Oxford University Press 2013), 119–24.
Witt, A, *The More Economic Approach to EU Antitrust Law* (Oxford: Hart 2016).
Witt, AC, 'From Airtours to Ryanair: Is the More Economic Approach to EU Merger Law Really about More Economics?' (2012) 49(1) *Common Market Law Review*, 217–46.
Wootton, D, 'Leveller Democracy and the Puritan Revolution' in JH Burns and M Goldie (eds), *The Cambridge History of Political Thought 1450–1700* (Cambridge: Cambridge University Press 2008), 412–42.
Wu, T, 'After Consumer Welfare, Now What? The "Protection of Competition" Standard in Practice' [2018]) *Competition Policy International*, 1–12.
The Curse of Bigness: Antitrust in the New Gilded Age (New York: Columbia Global Reports 2018).
'The "Protection of the Competitive Process" Standard' (2018). Columbia Public Law Research Paper No 14-612.
Zingales, L, 'Towards a Political Theory of the Firm' (2017) 31(3) *Journal of Economic Perspectives*, 113–30.

Table of Names

Table of Cases US

Table of Cases EU

COURT OF JUSTICE OF THE EUROPEAN UNION

OPINIONS OF ADVOCATE GENERALS

GENERAL COURT OF THE EUROPEAN UNION

EUROPEAN COMMISSION

Table of Legislation

US LEGISLATION AND POLICY DOCUMENTS

EUROPEAN, UK AND GERMAN LEGISLATION AND POLICY DOCUMENTS

Index

For EU product safety concerns, contact us at Calle de José Abascal, 56–1°,
28003 Madrid, Spain or eugpsr@cambridge.org.

www.ingramcontent.com/pod-product-compliance
Lightning Source LLC
LaVergne TN
LVHW011659200926
848484LV00004B/1002
* 9 7 8 1 3 1 6 5 1 3 6 7 5 *